FANSHEN

A Documentary of Revolution in a Chinese Village

William Hinton

93-1235

 VINTAGE BOOKS *A Division of*
Random House, New York

For

CARMELITA
whose life began with and remains part of New China
and
JOANNE, MICHAEL, ALYSSA, and CATHERINE
for whom a better world is long overdue

Acknowledgments

Without the co-operation of the Communist Party and the People's Government of Lucheng County and the help of President Fan Wenlan of Northern University, the interpreters Ch'i Yun and Hsieh Hung, the Long Bow work team and above all the peasants of Long Bow the material for this book could never have been collected.

Without the hard driving legal virtuosity of Milton H. Friedman and generous financial aid from Carmelita Hinton, Corliss Lamont and hundreds of other friends and well wishers this same material could never have been pried loose from the U. S. Customs and later from Senator Eastland's Committee on Internal Security.

After I regained possession of my notes, aid from Carmelita Hinton and the Louis M. Rabinowitz Foundation of New York made possible the endless hours of sifting, corollating and revising that later drafts of the manuscript required. I am especially indebted to Susan Warren, Far Eastern expert and free lance writer, for protracted consultation and editing and to Nell Salm of the Monthly Review staff for editorial innovations and the detailed, laborious preparation of the final draft. The making of this book has been, at every stage, a collective effort, and this is as it should be.

I also owe thanks to Angus Cameron for encouragement and advice generously given over many years and to Ida Pruitt and Adele and Allyn Rickett for moral support and critical readings of the manuscript. I am especially grateful to my wife, Joanne, for the patience and good humor with which she has forgone job security, a decent home, recreation and vacations while all our surplus energy and funds poured into the making of this book.

Fanshen

Every revolution creates new words. The Chinese Revolution created a whole new vocabulary. A most important word in this vocabulary was fanshen. *Literally, it means "to turn the body," or "to turn over." To China's hundreds of millions of landless and land-poor peasants it meant to stand up, to throw off the landlord yoke, to gain land, stock, implements, and houses. But it meant much more than this. It meant to throw off superstition and study science, to abolish "word blindness" and learn to read, to cease considering women as chattels and establish equality between the sexes, to do away with appointed village magistrates and replace them with elected councils. It meant to enter a new world. That is why this book is called* Fanshen. *It is the story of how the peasants of Long Bow Village built a new world.*

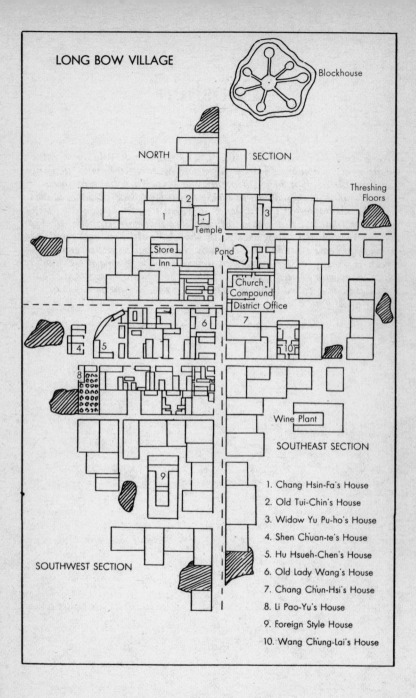

LONG BOW VILLAGE

Blockhouse

NORTH   SECTION

Threshing
Floors

2

1   3

Temple

Store   Pond
Inn
                Church
                Compound
                District Office

6   7

4 5   10

8

Wine Plant

SOUTHEAST SECTION

9

1. Chang Hsin-Fa's House

2. Old Tui-Chin's House

3. Widow Yu Pu-ho's House

4. Shen Ch'uan-te's House

5. Hu Hsueh-Chen's House

6. Old Lady Wang's House

7. Chang Ch'un-Hsi's House

SOUTHWEST SECTION

8. Li Pao-Yu's House

9. Foreign Style House

10. Wang Ch'ung-Lai's House

Preface

THIS BOOK is based on extensive notes gathered in the village of Long Bow, Lucheng County, Shansi Province, China, during the spring and summer of 1948.* At that time, local land reform, which had already been in progress for two years, was under investigation by a work team dispatched jointly by the People's Government and the Communist Party Committee of Lucheng County. I was attached to this work team as an observer.

The main focus of the book is on the conditions which the members of the work team found and the actions which they subsequently led the people of the village to take. But since it would be impossible to understand these conditions or these actions without a review of the revolutionary upheaval that led up to them, and since this upheaval in turn could hardly be understood without some knowledge of the traditional society which brought on and was itself transformed by revolution, a large section of the book (Parts I and II) is devoted to a history of the village.

This history was not easily assembled. The past was reviewed for me by a multitude of people whose memories of what had happened differed somewhat and whose stories contained both contradictions and gaps. Where contradictions could not be resolved or gaps filled in through careful checking and cross-checking, I have had to adopt such interpretations and solutions as seemed most consistent with other known facts. If the history that has thus emerged is not accurate in every detail, its main content and spirit nevertheless portray the truth about Long Bow.

What I have tried to do in the book as a whole is to reveal, through the microcosm of Long Bow Village, something of the essence of the great anti-imperialist, anti-feudal revolution which transformed China in the first half of the twentieth century and unleashed political and social forces so tremendous that they continue to shake not only China but the world.

---

* The Chinese name for this village is *Changchuang*. *Chang* is a common Chinese surname. It is also a word that means to extend, publish, open or boast. In written Chinese the character for *chang* is made up of 11 brush strokes. The first three comprise the radical *kung* which means bow—the hunter's bow. The last eight comprise the phonetic *chang* or *ch'ang* which means long. It is from these separate elements of the written word rather than from the meaning of the spoken word that I have extracted the designation "Long Bow."

The question naturally arises as to whether Long Bow can be considered a microcosm typical enough to reveal the essence of the Chinese Revolution. Was Long Bow's development universal or unique? The answer can only be that it was something of both.

Throughout rural China the social forces in conflict, the basic problems, the goals and the final outcome of the Revolution were the same. In Long Bow the same classes stood in opposition to each other as stood opposed nationally. United action of all laboring people was as vital to revolutionary victory in Long Bow as it was in the country as a whole. The petty-producer mentality of Long Bow's peasants did not differ in quality from that which characterized the peasants country-wide, and the tendency toward extremism, which in Long Bow grew to alarming proportions, had to be checked wherever peasants moved to divide the land.

At the same time, certain external circumstances, certain internal characteristics, and the specific course of events which shaped Long Bow were unique. For one thing, the village had a sizeable Catholic minority in a country where only one or two million people out of 600 million were Catholics. For another, it contained many families without ancestral roots or ancestral graves in the region. This meant a weak clan structure in a country where clans have traditionally played a very important role. Furthermore, on the edge of an area that was surrounded but never conquered by the Japanese, Long Bow was one of the few villages which the Japanese invaders occupied and fortified.

As a consequence, Long Bow had a very different history from that of the average North China community lying within the wide net of Japanese encirclement during the years 1937–1945. At the same time, its history was very different from that of the great majority of Chinese villages which had never been cut off by Japanese armies and were wrested from Kuomintang rather than Japanese control by the revolutionary armies after 1949.

As an occupied village, Long Bow did not benefit at all from that long period of united resistance, democratic rule, and moderate reform which laid the groundwork for basic changes throughout the Communist-led Base Areas of North China once the Japanese War was over. Nor did Long Bow benefit from that extended period of internal peace that enabled communities in South, Central, and West China to carry out land reform calmly, step by step, in orderly fashion after the Civil War was over. Freed from Japanese control at a turning point in history, 1945, Long Bow leaped perforce from reactionary bastion to revolutionary storm center in the course of a few days. All the changes that subsequently occurred were not only compressed into a relatively short space of time; they were also warped by the intense pressures of all-out Civil War as wave after wave of Nationalist attacks swept across the highlands of Southeast Shansi. Long Bow was not the only village in China to be transformed under forced draft, but such villages were the exception, not the rule.

In Long Bow the sudden destruction of the power and privileges of the gentry led to rapid social advances, to the release of unprecedented popular energy, to burgeoning enthusiasm, optimism, and popular confidence. It also led to excesses and tragedies. At least a dozen people were beaten to death by angry crowds; some hardworking small holders were wrongly dispossessed; revolutionary leaders at times rode roughshod over their followers. When the land reform team to which I was attached came to the village in 1948, its main job turned out to be righting the wrongs of the immediate past.

Before these wrongs could be righted they had to be exposed. The work team, the village officers, and the majority of the population concentrated for an extended period on what was wrong with past policies and the conduct of individual leaders. They did this, not because the wrongs of the situation outweighed the rights—on the contrary, quite the reverse was true—but because the wrongs constituted a serious obstacle to further progress, an illness that if not cured could become lethal. This book, by reflecting this concentration, gives crimes, mistakes, detours and discouragement more weight than they deserve in any over-all evaluation of Long Bow's development. It thus tips the scale even further toward the exceptional and away from the typical.

When it comes to telling the story of the Chinese Revolution, however, all of these exceptional factors, far from creating obstacles, present very definite advantages. Because contradictions arose in especially acute form in Long Bow and problems tended to etch themselves in very sharp relief, I felt able to observe the revolutionary process more fully and to understand it more deeply than I would have been able to do under more average circumstances and in more average surroundings. But the reader should keep in mind that not many villages in China followed such a tortuous path to liberation or experienced so much pain on the way.

Everyone in the revolutionary ranks learned from the kind of mistakes made in Long Bow at the height of the Civil War and when, in 1949, land reform workers went out from the Taihang Mountains by the tens of thousands to lead the Revolution in South and West China, they were far wiser men and women than they had been when they challenged the local gentry for control of the future at the end of the Japanese War.

The revolutionary process as it unfolded in China included advances and retreats, swings to the Right and swings to the Left, daily, hourly, minute-by-minute accretions and sudden, qualitative changes of state. Above all, the process went deep. It remade not only the material life of the people, but also their consciousness. It was this latter aspect that constituted the special strength of the Revolution and ensured, insofar as anything could, that the changes which it wrought would be both profound and lasting.

Because I have tried to delineate not only dramatic leaps in the life of the people, but also that slow accumulation of small changes without which no leaps could have occurred, I have written a book of considerable length. Along the way I borrowed from the literary arsenal of the novelist, the journalist, the social scientist, and the historian. What I have produced, finally, seems to me to resemble, in spirit and in content, a documentary film. I call it, then, a documentary of revolution in a Chinese village.

In the last analysis, what made such a documentary possible was the involvement of hundreds of people in its creation. Collectively the people of Long Bow, the members of the work team, and the two interpreters who helped me, delved into the past of the community and revealed it in its dynamic, many-faceted complexity.* Hence, the reader will find here, not one man's analysis of a small community in transition, but the community's own self-examination, its own estimate of what happened during the most crucial years of its existence. That examination was characterized by honesty, thoroughness, and depth, because on it would be based not only understanding but action, not only theory but practice—practice that must vitally affect the lives of millions.

The relevance of Long Bow's history to the present day can hardly be overemphasized. The story revolves around the land question. Without understanding the land question one cannot understand the Revolution in China, and without understanding the Revolution in China one cannot understand today's world.

But the impact of the land question on world affairs is not a function of China's specific gravity alone. Who shall own the land? Who shall rule the countryside? These are primary questions in the revolution that is sweeping the whole of Asia, Africa, and Latin America.

---

* The language spoken in Southern Shansi is not pure Mandarin but a dialect. In addition to pronouncing most words in their own local way, Shansi peasants use many words that do not appear in any Chinese dictionary. Even interpreters well versed in Chinese dialects often find themselves at a loss to decipher the details of conversations between peasants. Thus, though I had a working knowledge of Chinese, it would have been impossible for me to follow the meetings without help.

That revolution, far from dying away, is intensifying. Sooner or later, all those countries where agricultural production is a main source of wealth—and the relation between owners and producers a main source of social conflict—will undergo great transformations. An understanding of the issues involved and the solution already applied by one great nation is therefore important. In countries that stand on the verge of land revolution, people are eager to study such lessons. In countries like our own, whose leaders have the capacity to hasten or delay—though not forever to prevent—such transformations in other lands, people *ought* to study them.

Because of these facts, I believe that this book is at least as timely today as it would have been had it come out 18 years ago when I first gathered the raw notes for it in Long Bow Village. What happened in China yesterday may well happen in Brazil, Nigeria, or India tomorrow.

Land reform is on the agenda of mankind.

William Hinton

Fleetwood, Pa.
May, 1966

Contents

Maps and Tables

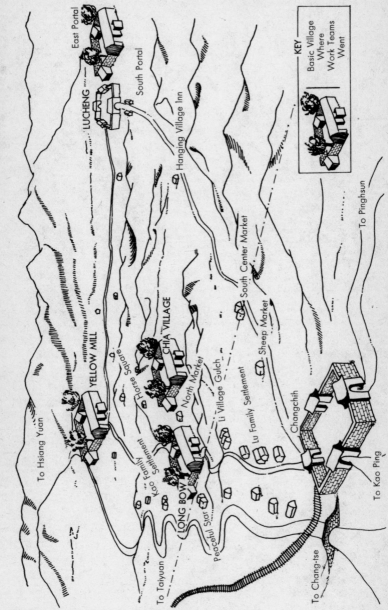

CHANGCHIH LUCHENG AREA

East Portal

LUCHENG

South Portal

Hanging Village Inn

YELLOW MILL

Horse Square

CHIA VILLAGE

North Market

Kao Family
Settlement

LONG BOW

Li Village Gulch

Peaceful Star

South Center Market

Sheep Market

Lu Family Settlement

Changchih

To Pinghsun

To Kao Ping

To Chang-tse

To Taiyuan

To Hsiang Yuan

KEY
Basic Village
Where
Work Teams
Went

West and away the wheels of darkness roll,
  Day's beamy banner up the east is borne,
Spectres and fears, the nightmare and her foal,
  Drown in the golden deluge of the morn.

A. E. Housman

Prologue

China is a vast country. "When night falls in the east, the west is still lit up; when darkness covers the south, the north remains bright." Hence, one need not worry about whether there is room to move around.

Mao Tse-tung

ALL THROUGH the spring season the earth's canted axis swings ever closer into line with the sun. Each day more heat is concentrated on the crust of the northern hemisphere until, with the arrival of the summer solstice, the full force of the solar fire is turned on the seas and mountains, the deserts and the plains of the temperate zone. This heat bakes the rocks until they flake, sets forest and tundra steaming, vaporizes the surface of the lakes and oceans. In the vast turbulence of the atmosphere thus created, gigantic mushrooms of hot air push skyward from the heart of continents and suck inland beneath them the cool, rain-laden sea winds that break the spring drought.

So vast is the continent of Asia, so immense the winter-stilled and frozen wastes of Mongolia, Sinkiang, Kazakhstan, and Tibet, so chilled the deserts of the Gobi and Takla Makan that the solstice has come and gone, the arctic pole has already turned from the sun, and the days have already begun to grow shorter before the accumulated heat of Central Asian sand and rock can reverse the seasons and bring on the monsoon.

This ancient lag, this ever-recurring cosmic overlap of heat and cold, cold and heat, brings a violence to the climate of all North China that is incalculable in its effect. From February to June cold winds blow from Mongolia outward toward the sea, gripping all the land from the Yangtze to the Amur in drought. Then, after weeks of hot and pregnant calm, the skies reverse themselves. Fierce torrential rains sweep in from the Pacific, flash floods carve up the earthen hills of Shansi and Shensi, swell the rivers with mud-clogged water, and inundate the flat plains bordering the sea.

These plains are, in fact, a creation of this cycle. But for the silt flung into the rivers and deposited over the millenniums on the ocean floor, the Yellow Sea would still lap the Taihang Mountains on Shansi's border and Shantung's hills would still be, as they were in ancient times, an island range.

3

The great coastal plain of China, mother to a tenth part of the human race, is thus herself the child of a monsoon which never ceases to harass the world it has created. The very winds, upon which all rains and hence all life depend, periodically threaten the very existence of that life. Drought and flood, flood and drought, alternating in perpetual procession, yearly call the Chinese people to battle against the waters that sustain them.

The year 1947 was no exception. If anything, the rains that summer came earlier and fell more heavily than usual. Even before the end of June the drought-cracked fields of Hopei and the sun-baked soil of Shansi's mountain valleys had lost their structure completely and dissolved into mud. Carts bogged to the axles. Mules, their sweating flanks stained red from the earth thrown up by their churning hooves, strained in the harness, lurched forward and fell back panting. Along a million once solid tracks connecting village to village, field to field, in a network that covered the countryside like a filigree of lace, the battle between the carters and the husbandmen spread with ever-increasing intensity. At each mudhole the carters tried to detour onto the more solid, crop-firmed soil of the fields themselves. But the peasants, determined to defend their developing harvests, countered with deep pits dug beside the road to keep the carts in line. As the season wore on these pits grew into a system of interconnected moats and trenches until the countryside took on the appearance of a plain prepared for war. This contest, as old as the wheel itself, never slackened as long as the rains continued to fall. Nor could there be, by nature of the combat, any final victory or defeat but only an infinite series of minor catastrophes—here a cart overturned in a water-filled trap, there a field of green corn mangled in the mud.

And while this persistent battle between man and man intensified, a larger struggle between man and nature unfolded week by week. With each succeeding rain the hollows and the low spots of the land filled up with water. The muddy overflow spilled onto the crops. Small gullies that ten months of the year lay dry and dusty suddenly bulged with flowing water. Whole villages were threatened. Between and around all this the rivers, the Yungting, the Ying, the Chin, the Hutou and the Wei, rose and swelled and rose some more to menace whole counties. Meanwhile to the south, from the gap in the mountains called San Men, the great Yellow River itself, "China's Sorrow," lapped at the top of its dykes, and spread fear throughout three provinces.

Throughout the Liberated Areas of the north country the battle of the rivers was joined.* Along threatened dykes vast armies of men, women, and children toiled day and night, carrying earth in wicker baskets, firming it down with rope-flung tamping stones, and fixing in place the rock-laden mats that could halt a breakthrough. At night one could follow the course of the waters by observing the fires set at intervals by flood watchers who huddled in mat shelters to keep out of the weather. They constantly filled and lit their pipes in order to stay awake, and every hour measured the height of the dark waters that glided so silently, so menacingly past their emergency stations.

As with the battle of the fields, there was in this struggle neither ultimate victory nor final defeat, but only an endless series of tactical gains and losses—here a dyke that held, a whole county saved, there a river run riot, a million people left homeless and hungry.

But even this battle, gigantic and far-flung as it was, was dwarfed that year by yet another conflict, a Civil War almost as cosmic in scale as the monsoon itself. From the borders of Siberia to the mouth of the Red River in the South China Sea, armies Red and White marched and counter-marched, encircled and counter-encircled, besieged and broke siege in turn until over vast areas of countryside every nursing child, every worried mother, every grandfather filling his pipe by the village gate, every young man with a hoe on his shoulder and every young woman with a needle in her hand had experienced this war.

Top-level squires and rural bullies fled for safety to Peking, Tientsin, Mukden, Shanghai, and even New York. Second-ranking gentlemen ran to such provincial towns as Taiyuan, Tsinan, Paoting, and Kaifeng. Those of third rank took refuge behind the thick fortress walls of county seats such as Anyang, Yungnien, Kalgan, and Tatung. Lesser fry, lacking the means to get away, threw themselves on the mercy of the newly-empowered Peasants' Associations and Village Congresses, and lived for the day when the Home Return Corps, organized in the cities by their fleeing brethren, would sally forth to wreak vengeance. These brethren in turn, fully controlling the coastal cities and still able to deploy the manpower of vast areas in South and West China, placed their hopes for victory on supply lines that reached out across the wide Pacific into the streets and workshops of

---

* Liberated Areas was the name originally given to those extensive tracts of countryside that were liberated from Japanese control by the Eighth Route Army and its supporting militia during the years 1937–1945. Since liberation usually began in mountainous regions straddling the lines between provinces, these areas were also called Border Regions. During the Civil War they expanded greatly.

America, where hundreds of thousands toiled to make the weapons
with which Chinese might slaughter Chinese.

In this, the Armageddon of Chinese feudalism, the terrible many-
layered war of the land revolution, no weapon was overlooked. The
very floods of the monsoon became swords in the hands of opposing
armies, and silt-swollen rivers were unleashed by both sides in an
effort to annihilate the enemy or split his forces asunder.

At Yungnien, a black-walled fortress city halfway between Peking
and the Yellow River, a Kuomintang warlord named Yang entrenched
himself with flour, wine, and women for a three-year siege. Communist-led militia, driven back when they tried to storm the battlements
by frontal assault, raised a dyke around the town and turned the
waters of the Wei River upon it. Just before the rising flood burst
open the city's massive gates, bombers, summoned by radio from
Peking, blasted the dyke and loosed a torrent that spread havoc
through three counties.

Farther north, in Central Hopei, American-equipped troops under
General Fu T'so-yi drove south out of Tientsin in the middle of the
rainy season and cut the dykes of the Grand Canal just as the crest
of the flood rolled down. Five counties west of the canal were inun-
dated, hundreds of people drowned, tens of thousands lost their
homes and harvests. By this action General Fu's armies won a respite
of several weeks from partisan attacks in the famed Peking-Tientsin-
Paoting triangle, an area the Japanese, in eight long years, had never
been able to pacify.

Devastating as these hydraulic thrusts proved to be, they were mere
hose-play compared to the return of that fearsome dragon, the Yellow
River, to the course from which it had been blasted ten years before
in a vain attempt to stop Japan's headlong drive southward. The re-
diversion was carried out in March, 1947, by the Kuomintang Army
with the aid of United Nations Relief and Rehabilitation Administration technicians, funds, and supplies, and on orders from Generalissimo Chiang Kai-shek himself.

The river, rushing back into its pre-war bed, cut the Liberated
Area of Shantung in half, placed half a mile of water between the
Shansi-based revolutionary armies of one-eyed General Liu Po-ch'eng
in the West and the Shantung-based revolutionary armies of General
Ch'en Yi in the East. The artificial flood disrupted the economy of a
whole region. Some 500 villages that had housed 100,000 people
for more than a decade were submerged within a few days. The high
water that followed the summer rains threatened a plain inhabited
by five million. When the peasants, by the hundreds of thousands,
gathered to repair the long abandoned dykes, Generalissimo Chiang

sent bombers to blast the renovated earthworks and fighter planes to strafe the dyke workers.*

Thus did the war grow in ferocity and ruthlessness. As both sides girded for increasingly decisive battle the possibility of compromise receded swiftly into the background. Each day brought new evidence that 1947 would be a year of decision in China's modern history.

****

In 1947 the Chinese Communist Party, confident of the strength of the 100 million people in the guerrilla Base Areas of the North, moved from the defensive to the offensive in the war against the Kuomintang. Its military forces, completely encircled on land and without a single plane in the air, confounded friend and foe alike by suddenly thrusting three complete armies southward into the Nationalist rear. In the Center, General Liu's men drove all the way from the north bank of the Yellow River to the Tapieh Mountains on the banks of the Yangtze overlooking Nanking. In the East, General Ch'en Yi filed down into North Kiangsu and Anhwei to outflank the strategic railway town of Kaifeng. In the West, General Chen Keng forded the Yellow River and swept to the Hupeh border, thus isolating Loyang. By re-establishing three important guerrilla bases in East, Central, and West China these three armies turned the war inside out, converted encirclement into counter-encirclement and disrupted Chiang's plan to strangle the Revolution in its war-devastated North China redoubt.

The military offensive of 1947 was accompanied by an equally important political offensive. The heart of this second offensive was the Draft Agrarian Law, formulated in the fall of 1947 and announced to the world on December 28 of that year. With sentences as abrupt as the strokes of a fodder-chopping knife, the new law proclaimed the death of landlordism:

Article I—The agrarian system of feudal and semi-feudal exploitation is abolished. The agrarian system of "land-to-the-tiller" is to be realized.

Article II—Landownership rights of all landlords are abolished.

Article III—Landownership rights of all ancestral shrines, temples, monasteries, schools, institutions, and organizations are abolished.

Article IV—All debts incurred in the countryside prior to the reform of the agrarian system are cancelled.

* The bombing of these dykes was described to me by Phillip Thomford of Pennsylvania, an agricultural officer of UNRRA, who witnessed it. It was also documented by the Chinese Liberated Areas Relief Administration in the report of their work issued in Shanghai in 1948.

With these provisions of the law the revolutionaries of China once again threw down the gauntlet to Chiang Kai-shek and his American backers. They now demanded, not some modified relationship between the classes such as had served to unite the nation against Japan, not a settling of accounts with profiteers and collaborators such as had stirred the Liberated Areas after Japan's surrender, but the abolition of the rural class system itself, complete, unequivocal, universal. From the Amur to Hainan, from Shanghai to Chengtu, the land must be distributed to those who worked it. The manner of the distribution was set forth in Articles VI and VIII:

Article VI—. . . . All land of landlords in the village, all public land, shall be taken over by the village peasants' associations, and together with the other village lands, in accordance with the total population of the village, irrespective of male or female, young or old, shall be unifiedly and equally distributed; with regard to the quantity of land, surplus shall be taken to relieve dearth, and with regard to the quality of land, fertile land shall be taken to supplement infertile, so that all the people of the village shall obtain land equally; and it shall be the individual property of each person.

Article VIII—Village peasants' associations shall take over the land-lords' animals, agricultural implements, houses, grain and other properties, shall further expropriate the surplus animals, agricultural implements, houses, grain and other properties of rich peasants, and these shall be distributed to peasants lacking these properties, and to other poor people, and furthermore an equal portion shall be distributed to the landlords. The property distributed to each person shall be his personal property, thus enabling all village people to obtain proper materials for production and for livelihood.

This new Draft Agrarian Law was destined to play as important a role in China's Civil War of 1946–1950 as the Emancipation Proclamation played in the American Civil War of 1861–1865. Lincoln's Emancipation Proclamation confiscated without compensation $3 billion worth of property in slaves; put an end to the possibility of compromise between the industrial North and the slave-holding South in the military contest then raging; made the slave system itself, rather than regional autonomy, the nub of the conflict; cleared the way for the recruitment of hundreds of thousands of emancipated black men into the Union Army; and spread the war into every corner of Confederate territory with devastating effect.

Mao's Draft Agrarian Law confiscated without compensation $20 billion worth of property in land; put an end to all possible compromise between the Communist Party and the Kuomintang; made country-wide overthrow of the landlords and the compradores, rather than the defense of the Liberated Areas, the main aim of the war;

facilitated the capitulation and recruitment of huge blocks of Chiang's soldiers into the People's Liberation Army; inspired peasant unrest in the far corners of China; and gave impetus to demonstrations of workers, students, merchants, and professional people in urban centers throughout the Kuomintang rear.

Nor was the impact of the new Draft Law confined, as one might suppose, to territories as yet unconquered by the Revolution. Inside the old Liberated Areas, where land reform in one form or another had begun the day the Japanese surrendered, the Draft Law inaugurated a new stage in the continuing struggle. Its provisions served as a yardstick by which to measure the achievements of three years (1945–1947) of more moderate reforms in an area as large as France and Germany combined. Had the land been equally divided? Had the political power of the gentry been broken? Had the poor peasants and hired laborers taken control of village affairs? If not, why not?

The new Draft Law also served as a yardstick by which to measure the political position of every revolutionary, of every Communist Party member, of every government functionary, every leader of a mass organization, and every individual teacher, peasant, student, peddler, worker, soldier, tradesman, or intellectual who opted for progress and a new, democratic China. On which side do you stand? Do you stand with the poor peasants and hired laborers, the most oppressed and exploited people in the nation, or do you stand with the landlords, the rich peasants, and the feudal exploiters? Do you intend to carry the Revolution through to its end by creating a new system of land tenure or do you intend to stand in the way, to act as a brake, to stop things halfway?

With the promulgation of the new Draft Law, a "thunder and lightning, drum and cymbal" attack was launched on the remnants of traditional exploitation and on the residues of landlord and rich-peasant thinking in the revolutionary ranks throughout the Liberated Areas of North China.

In honor of the campaign, red flags, which had entirely disappeared during the years of the Japanese War, suddenly blossomed over streets, courtyards, and village gates. The Chinese sun on a blue field, symbol of the Anti-Japanese United Front, vanished from the badges that adorned many caps and lapels, and in its place the red star and hammer and sickle emblem reminiscent of the Red Army of the 1930's reappeared. Down from the compound walls came the six-feet-high slogans of moderation and defense, and up in their place went the flaming words of the offensive: "Equally Divide the Land" and "Drive to Nanking; Capture Chiang Alive!"

The Lunar New Year—traditionally an occasion for week-long feasting, relaxation and Chinese opera—was transformed that winter, into a mass demonstration of support for the Chinese Communist Party, the Draft Agrarian Law, and the leadership of Mao Tse-tung.

****

In Changchih City, the main urban center of the South Shansi Highlands, local residents and peasants from the surrounding villages turned out by the thousands to celebrate 1948. The city was decorated from one end to the other. In front of every shop a bright red flag, replete with gold hammer and sickle, proudly waved. Across the streets and alleys on all but invisible strings fluttered countless pennants of colored paper. Each bore a slogan supporting the new land law or denouncing Chiang Kai-shek and his bandit gang. From a distance these pennants looked like red and blue confetti dancing in the sun. Along three of the four main streets—north, south, and west—stages·large enough for full-scale theatrical performances were set up on heavy timbers and hung with red silk.

Peasants, pouring through the recently-levelled gates of the walled town, jammed the roadways with their animals and vehicles. From the valleys came mule carts with iron-shod wooden wheels four feet in diameter. From the mountain heights came ridiculous little donkey-drawn vehicles with platforms three feet across and wheels the size of cooking pots. On the wooden framework of these carts, large and small, sat mothers, grandmothers, and children of all ages, dressed in bright silks and many-colored cottons.

Among the attractions which drew them to the town was the *yangko* dancing. A small parade preceded the performance of each *yangko* team. In the lead came young men with red banners bearing the name of the club, block committee, or Peasants' Association which they represented. Behind them came the musicians with their drums, cymbals, gongs, and pipes. Next came the acting group and then a long column of dancers.

When the group arrived at a likely spot—any place where large numbers of people stood around waiting for something to happen— the dancers started to form a big circle doing the *yangko* rock (three steps forward, one step back) the body swaying in time to the music, the arms swinging gracefully. The girls all carried wide scarves of silk that were tied to their waists with large red bows. They held the two free ends in their hands so that the silk waved and fluttered with each movement of the arms. Like shimmering butterflies they wove figure eights and clover leaves and other intricate patterns and finally formed a circle inside of which the actors assembled to perform the plays and skits which they themselves had written.

The most popular theme of these many plays was land reform. The two points which most of them hammered home were the need to depend on the poor-and-hired peasants and the importance of uniting with the middle peasants. Many groups portrayed a villainous landlord who tried to sabotage all land division, a rich peasant who schemed with him, a middle peasant who worried lest the new land law be used against him, and a village political worker who sold out the poor for favors from the rich. But a hired laborer with the help of a Communist Party member always won the confidence of the people in the end. The landlord and his running dog cowered in disgrace, the poor peasant danced a merry jig with the middle peasant, while the boys and girls of the dancing brigade burst into joyous song and began their *yangko* all over again.

Other skits had to do with the national and international scene. Chiang Kai-shek came in for much buffeting about, as did the Soongs, the K'ungs and the Ch'ens—China's three other ruling families. These men were represented in typical fashion—Soong always with a Western-style hat, Ch'en in a black landlord's gown, Chiang in preposterous military regalia, and K'ung, the banker, always clutching a large briefcase stuffed with money.

Adding to the merriment and confusion of sound were other groups performing stick dances. The participants carried bamboo rods about three feet long that were decorated at each end with bells and tassels. To a very fast beat these sticks were struck against different parts of the body and with each blow the bells jingled. When 20 or 30 people did this in perfect unison, the rhythmic effect stirred the feet of every bystander.

The streets overflowed with *yangko* and stick dancers, each orchestra trying to play louder than the last, each group of dancers striving to step out more vigorously than the one in front of it, each actor attempting to outdo in gesture and voice the others in the cast. Add to this the thousands upon thousands of country people milling about; the peddlers vending hot mutton soup, candy, peanuts, and pears; the hundreds of carts going and coming; the red banners and the colored paper spinning and twirling in the air. It was a scene of immense vigor and public rejoicing such as that ancient county town had rarely if ever witnessed.

And, as if all this were not enough, the three great stages on the three main streets presented a continuous succession of plays, each to an enormous changing crowd. Farther on, at the fairgrounds on the east side of the town, a commercial circus displayed the talents of trained monkeys and trick riders, while, from the platform of an abandoned temple, a traditional opera troupe sang to an audience of thousands.

For two days and nights the festivities continued without letup.

****

I observed the tumultuous New Year activity in Changchih as a member of the faculty of Northern University, the educational and cultural center of the Shansi-Hopei-Honan-Shantung Border Region. I had come to China one year earlier as a tractor technician with the United Nations Relief and Rehabilitation Administration (UNRRA), and had been sent to the Communist-led area of South Hopei to supervise a project there. When UNRRA closed down all over the world in the fall of 1947, the tractors under my care were put in storage for lack of gasoline, and I accepted an invitation from Northern University to teach English in South Shansi.

The University was a guerrilla institution which moved according to the dictates of war. It was housed at that time in a huge expropriated mission compound at Kao Settlement, a village in the Fifth District of Lucheng County, ten miles north of Changchih. I had no sooner settled down to teach there than half the faculty and students of the institution departed to join the land reform movement, an exodus that occurred a few days after the New Year celebrations. Hundreds of volunteers from the University joined an equal number of local county and subcounty (district) cadres* to make up work teams that were assigned to key villages throughout the region. In groups of 10 or 12 these cadres went out to survey the true condition of the peasant population and carry the land reform through to completion.

The excitement generated by the departure of so many of its students and staff members electrified the whole University. Young men and women in blue ran back and forth tying up belongings, roll-

---

* The Chinese word for cadre is *kanpu*, which means "backbone personnel." It has no satisfactory English equivalent, even though it is commonly translated by the French word "cadre." Since "cadre," as ordinarily used in English, means a group of trained persons, it is not exactly suitable for referring to individual members of such a group. Yet the Chinese word is used both for the group and for the individual.

In this book the word "cadre" is used to designate any person who plays a full- or part-time leading role in any area of political activity whether it be the government, the Communist Party, or the Peasants' Association. It is also used to describe technical personnel in industry, agriculture, education, etc., who are employed by the government.

ing their quilts into tight bundles, fastening shoulder straps to impro-
vised bedrolls, singing snatches of song and talking excitedly to one
another. Many who had not been chosen to go stood around with
wistful expressions, revealing how much they too would have liked to
be on their way to the countryside.

When, at last, all the volunteers were ready, they assembled in
the street with their bundles on their backs and a bright red flag
flying over them. The President of the University, the famous historian Fan Wen-lan, lean, slightly stooped, peering with failing eyes
through thick glasses, gave them a gentle, scholarly farewell talk.
Then, to the accompaniment of rolling drums and clashing cymbals,
the adventurous brigade strode off. At the first crossroad it split into
two columns, one marching east, the other south. Last farewells were
said and handshakes quickly concluded. One student grabbed the
staff of the red flag and waved it high in the air. Others put their
caps on their walking sticks and whirled them triumphantly overhead.

The swiftly-moving volunteers gradually merged into the landscape,
leaving only two streaks of wind-whipped dust hanging over the paths
they had taken. In the wide, bright sky, clouds like puffs of cotton
sped southward on the wind. The mountains in the distance were
white with the year's last snow. At least it seemed to be the last,
for the breath of spring in the air that day made one forget winter.
Soon the peasants would be out plowing, and before the time to
plant arrived, ten million ragged, landless families would join that vast
army of those who already owned their own good earth.

Standing in the road, watching the dust kicked up by the students'
departure gradually settle, I was overcome with longing to join the
great adventure. My job at the University was to teach English, but
how could the teaching of English compare with the remolding of
the world through land reform?

I walked directly from the edge of the village to President Fan's
office on the second floor of the enormous Kao Settlement monastery.
The President was in. Quietly, with sympathetic attention, he listened
to my plea.

"Here is one of history's great moments," I said. "I want to see and
take part in it more than I have ever wanted to do anything in my life.
Can't I join one of the teams, at least as an observer, and learn at
first hand what the land reform is all about?"

President Fan could not give me an immediate answer. He had to
consult with the subregional and county authorities. Three days later
he called me in and said that I could go to one of the nearby villages
where a land reform work team was already stationed, on condition
that I continue to teach a few English classes each week. He assigned

a young woman instructor, Ch'i Yun, to accompany me and to act as my interpreter.

The village nearest to Kao Settlement that had been chosen as a base for the work of a land reform team was a community named Long Bow. It lay approximately one mile to the south. I had already walked through it several times, had even had a bowl of hot soup at the village inn there on one occasion, but had heretofore paid very little attention to the place. It was, outwardly at least, no different from a thousand other hamlets that dotted the valleys of South Shansi. As a matter of fact, I was a little disappointed that the land reform which I was to observe was to take place right at the doorstep of the University. It would be more adventurous to walk to some distant place, to work in some isolated valley that I had not yet seen. But I had no alternative. Since both Ch'i Yun and I had to teach, we either had to choose the nearest village or not go at all.

On the morning of March 6, 1948, the two of us finally set off for the first time on the road to Long Bow and began the long process of getting to know its people, their history, their progress, their mistakes and their complex current problems.

PART I

Sowing the Wind

O masters, lords and rulers in all lands,
How will the future reckon with this Man?
How answer his brute question in that hour
When whirlwinds of rebellion shake all shores?
How will it be with kingdoms and with kings—
With those who shaped him to the thing he is—
When this dumb Terror shall rise to judge the world,
After the silence of the centuries?

From Edwin Markham's
"The Man with the Hoe"

1

Long Bow Village

Times and seasons, what things are you,
Bringing to my life ceaseless change?
I will lodge forever in this hollow
Where springs and autumns unheeded pass.

Tao Yun

LONG BOW VILLAGE lies in the southeast quarter of Shansi Province on the high plateau country that butts against the back of the Taihang Mountains. It is 400 miles southwest of Peking and 100 miles from the gap in the mountains directly to the south, through which the Yellow River flows out onto the North China plain.

The South Shansi plateau, known as the Shangtang (associated with heaven) because of its elevation, is itself creased with barren mountains, but between the ranges are wide valleys containing considerable areas of fertile soil. In the heart of one of these valleys lies the old county town of Changchih. The road running north from Changchih proceeds on the level for seven miles, through and past numerous mud villages, and then climbs gently over a long hill. Just beyond the hill, where the land levels out again, is the village of Long Bow.*

The land revolution in Long Bow began with the retreat and surrender of the Japanese Army and its Chinese puppet forces in 1945. For how many centuries prior to that year this village had endured in this place almost without change I do not know. Certainly for hundreds of years, any tired traveler who paused to rest at the crest of the hill and looked out over the flat to the north saw substantially the same sight—a complex of adobe walls under a canopy of trees set in the middle of a large expanse of fields. These fields

* Since the county line runs along the southern edge of the hill, Long Bow is not in Changchih County but in the County of Lucheng, the next walled town to the north. The counties of China have traditionally been divided into several districts, or *ch'u,* for administrative purposes. The southwestern district of Lucheng County was called the Fifth District. If Long Bow had any distinction at all it was as the seat of the Fifth District administration.

were barren, brown and desolate in winter, while in summer they
were green, yellow and clothed with diverse crops.

To look down on this valley in January was to look upon a world
of frozen immobility. Through most of each day not even a wisp of
smoke could be seen curling up from the squat mud chimneys that
poked above the gently sloping roofs marking the settlement; the rich,
who kept their fires burning day and night, burned a coal and earth
mixture that gave off no smoke, and the poor, who burned roots,
straw, and wild dry grasses, lit their fires only at meal time, and
then only long enough to boil a few handfuls of millet.

In the depths of winter the temperature often went below zero.
Rich and poor alike stayed indoors. Only on the main north-south
road could any sign of human activity be seen. This was the route
taken by the carters who hauled freight out of the mountains regardless of weather. In the stillness of the cold mountain air the crashing
of their iron-shod wheels against the frozen ruts could be heard at a
great distance. From the top of the hill it sounded like the rumbling
of distant drums or the busy pounding of some tireless carpenter
knocking together a hollow barrel.

With the coming of warm weather this all but lifeless scene was
transformed. From the first cock-crow in the semi-darkness before
dawn until the red sun went down behind the western mountains at
night, peasants by the hundreds came and went on the land, plowing,
hauling manure, planting, harvesting. There were always so many
people in the fields that they could talk to one another as they
worked without leaving their own plots.

From the hill this scene took on the likeness of some slow-motion
ritual dance of man and nature that completely obscured the painful,
backbreaking labor that was in progress. The stage never seemed to
be crowded. Yet everywhere the eye rested something was sure to
move—here a donkey strained at the plow; there a man, stripped to
the waist, raked together corn stubble; nearby a barefoot boy spread
night soil, three women on their knees thinned millet, a child, naked
as the day he entered this world, played with some sticks in a ditch.
Over the traveler's head the warm, motionless air hummed and
whistled as a flight of swallows swooped low. Birds, people, oxen,
sheep, children, dogs—it was like one of Breughel's marvelously
crowded paintings—and always in the background, the heavily
laden carts moved in both directions, their iron thunder muffled now
by the long-thawed resilience of the loess-like soil.

If the traveler, rested at last, walked on down the hill, he found that
the village street was but the continuation of the long gully that had
brought him from the heights. During the heavy July rains the run-off

from all the higher ground to the south rushed down the gully, poured along the village street and emptied into the village pond, a large natural basin conveniently located at the center of the community. In this way the supply of soft water for washing clothes was periodically replenished, and in the shade of the willows by the water's edge a few women and girls could always be found scrubbing away on the flat rocks that served as washboards.

Both sides of this gully-like main street were lined with mud walls six to eight feet high, broken here and there by covered gateways that led into the courtyards of the people. Beside each gate was the family privy, hopefully placed at the edge of the public road in anticipation of a contribution to the domestic store of fertilizer from any traveler who might be in need of relief.

Running off at right angles from the main road were several smaller lanes, also lined with walls set at intervals with courtyard gates. From these lanes, still smaller alleys ran off in turn to other entrances so that the whole village was rather like a maze, regular in outline, yet haphazardly filled in with lanes, alleys, walls enclosing courtyards, and low mud houses built against these walls.

Over the centuries, in spite of much new construction, the village persisted in presenting a crumbled look. Built of adobe from the earth underfoot, any neglected wall, any unattended roof soon returned, under the hammering of summer rains, to the soil from whence it came. Always there were walls that had collapsed, gates that had fallen down, roofs that had buckled. In places one could wander into courtyards directly from the street through great gaps in the adobe, and people continually found new shortcuts and created new paths along which to move from house to house. Only the rich could afford to keep their walls standing sharp and clean, capped with the lime and straw mixture that alone could withstand a few seasons of weather. Some of the gentry even built with fired brick. Such houses stood through many generations, while the peasants' huts washed out, were rebuilt, and washed out again and again.

Beside the village pond, whose banks served as a social center as well as a laundry for the women, was an open space large enough to park many carts and still leave the main road free. Day and night there were always carts in this square, for while the most heavily-traveled route skirted the village to the east, many a driver, on reaching Long Bow, was hungry enough, tired enough, or lonely enough to direct his animals into the village street and pull up in the square in search of refreshment, rest, and companionship. All three were offered by the village inn which served hot water to all comers and to the hungry steamed bread, noodles, or unleavened pancakes chopped up in order to be fried or boiled together with whatever vegetables were in season. Owned at different times by various prosperous gentry and run by one or another of their agents or dependents, this inn was nothing more than an adobe hut with a canopy of reed matting built out over the street in front to shelter a table or two. Behind the hut a long shed contained a platform for the carters to sleep on and, at the far end, a set of feed troughs from which their animals could dine on chopped straw and kaoliang stalks.

Beside the inn was a little store that had also changed hands many times. It was a down-at-the-heels adobe structure with a squeaking door and tattered paper on the windows. Out front, sheltered from the sun by a reed mat similar to that which adorned the inn, the storekeeper could usually be found sipping hot water from a cracked teapot as he concentrated on a game of Chinese chess. Inside he sold tobacco, soap, towels, needles, wine, bean oil, salt, sugar, biscuits, a little cloth, and other assorted articles necessary to daily life that could not be made at home. There was no hurry about such sales. Customers, as often as not, joined the storekeeper in a game of chess before going inside to make their purchases.

Soldiers could usually be seen loitering about the store and inn. In earlier times they were the troops of the Imperial Garrison commanded by Manchu officers. In 1911 these were replaced by the conscripts of Yen Hsi-shan, warlord governor of Shansi, who were ousted in turn by the Japanese in 1938. These soldiers, regardless of their allegiance, were quartered on the people, lived a dissolute and corrupt life, and took whatever they wanted for their pleasure, including the wives and daughters of the poor peasants. Their officers, wined and dined by the gentry, pursued the same pleasures in more genteel surroundings and by more subtle means. In this they had the tacit consent of their hosts, who found in the troops a guarantee of their personal safety and the continued smooth collection of land rents.

Just to the north of the store and also on the edge of the square was a solid brick and timber Buddhist temple, whose upturned roof corners might well remind the traveler of the propped-up flap of a Mongolian tent. This temple was built by the Shen clan and was managed through the years by leading gentry of that name. There the people came to burn incense and offer prayers for good fortune, abundant crops, and many children. At several other points in and around the village there were small mud temples or shrines adorned with the clay likenesses of various minor gods—the god of agriculture, the god of fertility, and the god of health. At these temples also the people burned incense, murmured prayers, and left the offerings of steamed bread and sweet cakes that enabled many a poor beggar to survive. In the southern part of the village, a second clan temple sat in the center of a large courtyard. It was surrounded by numerous outbuildings, all of which, along with the temple itself, had long been abandoned to rats, dogs, and mischievous children.

The only other points of interest in Long Bow outside the village homes themselves were the distilleries and hole-in-the-wall craft establishments manned by peasants skilled at different trades. The number of distilleries varied over the years, depending on the prosperity of the landlord families that owned and ran them, but all of them made the same thing—a hard white liquor called *paikar* that was distilled from fermented sorghum or corn. The craft shops included a blacksmith's forge, a drug dispensary that carried in stock a few hundred of the many thousand drugs and herbs sold by Chinese apothecaries, a number of carpentry shops that made everything from wooden shovels to cartwheels, and several weaving establishments with looms capable of turning out rough cloth about two feet in width. No matter what these craftsmen did, in the summer they also worked on the land. It took every able-bodied person in the village to plant, hoe, and harvest the crops—every able-bodied person, that is, save the landlords, who, with their inch-long fingernails and ankle-length gowns, never dreamed of soiling their hands with labor of any sort.

The population of the village varied drastically in size. A poor crop year could easily cut the number of residents in half, a part of the poor dying in the huts where they lived and the rest fleeing to other regions in a desperate gamble for survival. By and large, however, the thousand acres of land that encircled the village could support between 200 and 300 families and no sooner did famine on the Shangtang plateau cut down the number of Long Bow people and drive them to other places than famine in other parts of North China drove new people to the plateau to settle in their place.

The erratic nature of the weather was thus responsible for a very heterogeneous population. There are many villages in China where the majority of the inhabitants have the same surname, consider themselves to be of one family and are in fact related by common descent from the original settlers. Not so in Long Bow. The various families living there often bore as many as 40 different surnames. Even though the village itself was called Changchuang or Chang Settlement by its inhabitants, often only a small minority of families bore that name. They were at times outnumbered two to one by the Wangs, and even the Kuos surpassed them in households more than once. Other names common in the village were Shen, Li, and Shih, to mention but a few.

Counting noses among the 200-odd families one could ordinarily
tally up about a thousand persons altogether. This meant that on the
average there was one acre of land for every man, woman, and child.*
The crops from this one acre, in a good year, were ample for the
support of a single person, considering the very low standard of living
that prevailed. But the poor who rented land or worked out as hired
laborers got less than half the crops they tilled, while the rich got the
surplus from many acres. That is why some were able to build
enormous underground tombs marked for eternity, or so they thought,
with stone tortoises bearing obelisks inscribed with the family name,
while others when they died were thrown into a hole in the ground
with only a reed mat wrapped around them and a few shovelfuls
of earth to mark the place.

Graves large and small dotted the land around Long Bow. As if
this were not enough obstruction to tillage, the fields were divided
into countless narrow strips and plots, each one owned by a different
family. Even on the level there were few fields larger than half an
acre, while on the hill, where the land was terraced, there were strips
only a few yards wide that ran in great S curves around the slopes,
and small triangles at the top end of gullies that contained but a few
square yards of ground. Land was so valuable in the Shangtang that
the peasants found it necessary to build stone walls as high as 15
feet to hold back a few feet of earth and make it level. Where the
hills were too steep to terrace, they ploughed anyway and cropped
the ground for a year or two until the soil washed away completely.
In the mountains to the east of Long Bow Village men plowed hills
so steep that an extra person was needed to stand on the slope above
and keep tension on a rope tied around the ox lest he slip and roll
away.

Although on level ground roads and paths led out through the
fields, no hill fields could be reached with a cart, and farm implements had to be light enough for one man to carry. The plows, harrows, seeders, and other equipment used were all light enough to be
picked up with one hand and were made entirely of wood except for
the point of the plow itself. All of these implements, although in use
for centuries, were still only supplementary to the main tool, the hoe,
handed down almost unchanged since prehistoric times. The hoe used
in Long Bow was a great iron blade weighing several pounds and
fastened to the end of a stick as large as a man's wrist. This tool,
which was designed to turn soil and sod, was also used for the delicate
work of thinning millet and weeding corn. By hard work a man

* The acres mentioned here and throughout the text of the book are
English acres, each being equivalent to six Chinese *mou*.

could hoe one sixth of an acre a day. Since all the peasants aspired
to hoe their crops at least three times, a great part of every growing
season was spent in hoeing.

The crops grew only on what was put into the soil each year;
hence manure was the foundation of the whole economy. The chief
source of supply was the family privy, and this became, in a sense,
the center of the household. Long Bow privies were built in the
form of a deep cistern, topped with timber, or stone, and provided
with a single narrow slot at ground level for both deposition and ex-
traction. Here night soil in liquid form accumulated all winter. Legendary in the region were the landlords so stingy that they would
not allow their hired men to defecate in the fields but made them walk
all the way back to the ancestral home to deposit their precious
burden. Other landlords would not hire local people on a long-term
basis because local people were wont to use their own privies while
a man from outside used that of his employer.

Animal manure, together with any straw, stalks, or other waste
matter, was composted in the yard. So highly was it valued that old
people and children constantly combed the roads and cart tracks for
droppings which they scooped up and carried home in baskets. This
need to conserve every kind of waste and return it to the land was
responsible for the tidy appearance of the streets and courtyards
even though the walls were crumbling and the roofs falling in. Nothing, absolutely nothing, was left lying around. Even the dust of the
street was swept up and thrown on the compost heap or into the
privy, for village dust was more fertile, by far, than the soil in the
fields.

The clothes that people wore and the food that they ate were all
products of the village land. Even the gentry, who possessed for
festive occasions silks and satins imported from the South, donned
for everyday wear the same homespun cottons that served to clothe
their servants and their tenants.. Though styles did evolve over the
centuries, the basic workday clothing changed little. In summer
everyone wore thin jackets and pants of natural cotton bleached
white or dyed blue or black with indigo. Long Bow women liked to
wear white jackets and black pants, but this was by no means
universal.

In cold weather everyone wore clothes padded with cotton. These
made people look twice as big as they really were and provided
warmth in two ways, first by the insulation of the thick layer of
cotton and second by the lice which made themselves at home in the
seams. Since the padded clothes could not be washed without taking
the lining out— a major operation—it was almost impossible to get

rid of lice from day to day. Their constant biting and the interminable scratching that accompanied it generated a fair amount of heat. On any warm day in winter a large number of people could always be found sitting in various sunlit corners with their padded jackets across their knees. There they hunted the lice, picked them out, and crushed them expertly between their thumbnails.

Children under five were exposed from below in all weather because their padded clothes were not sewn together at the crotch. The slit, which ran upward from just above the knees to a point a little below the tip of the backbone, was very convenient when nature called but was drafty in winter. It must be said, however, that the children didn't seem to mind at all and ran about in the bitterest weather just as if they were all sewn in like their elders.

Shangtang shoes were also made of cotton cloth but, because the soles consisted of many layers sewn through and through with hemp thread, they were as tough as any leather and lasted from four to six months even with hard wear on the mountain roads. Only the women had no need for such heavy shoes. Their feet were bound, the toes bent under, and the bones stunted so that they formed a crushed stump not more than two or three inches in length. Women walked as if on stilts. They could not run at all. Yet widowed women among the poor often had to work in the fields from dawn until dark. Foot binding came to an end almost everywhere in the period between the two world wars but even in 1945 young girls with crippled feet could still be found in the mountain counties of Shansi.

The food eaten in Long Bow was very simple. Since maize was the major crop everyone ate corn dumplings, called *keta,* in the morning, and corn meal mush, or noodles made of corn at noon. At night they ate millet porridge with a few noodles in it. After the wheat harvest in July everyone ate noodles for several days, but this was considered quite a luxury and only the most fortunate carried the custom on into August. These same families were the only ones who ate three meals a day throughout the year. Most people cut down to two meals, or even one when winter set in. Thus undernourished they moved about as little as possible and tried to conserve their strength until spring.

In addition to the cereal grains people ate salt turnip all year round, cabbage when they had it, and other vegetables such as eggplant, scallions, chives, and wild herbs in season. But these were simply garnishment to the main dish which was always corn, millet, or wheat. The big problem facing the peasants over the years was not to obtain some variety in their diet, but to find anything to eat at all. They often had to piece out their meager harvest of grain with bran, chaff, wild herbs from the hills or even the leaves from the trees or tree bark as the *ch'un huang* (spring hunger) set in. Each day that one survived was a day to be thankful for and so, throughout the region, in fat years and in lean, the common greeting came to be not "Hello" or "How are you?" but a simple, heartfelt "Have you eaten?"

2

Can the Sun Rise in the West?

Dirty frogs want to feed on crane,
Poor scum hope for great happenings in vain.
Look at yourself in some ditch water, do!
What great deeds can be done by the likes of you?
Can snow fall in mid-July?
Can the sun rise in the western sky?

Landlord Ts'ui
From the opera
Wang Kuei and Li Hsiang-hsiang

LONG BOW VILLAGE shared in the turbulent history of feudal China.* Over the centuries the Empire was many times invaded and twice conquered from without. From within the body politic was rocked by violent rebellion no less than 18 times. Province-wide and county-wide revolts were too numerous to record. But neither conquest nor rebellion altered the basic contours of society. The invaders were pastoral nomads who grafted themselves onto the apex of the country's power structure without modifying its base. The rebels were most of them peasants. Even though these peasants several times brought dynasties low they proved historically unable to establish any alternative to the emperor-ruled, landlord-tenant system. After each upheaval life returned once again to the old way.

Even the century of mounting crisis and change that began for China with the British-imposed Opium War of 1840 failed to shatter, though it certainly weakened, the hold of the gentry over China's

---

* Many scholars use the word feudal to describe only the vassal-lord, serf-and-manor system characteristic of medieval Europe. In this book the word is used in a broader sense to describe a society in which a ruling class, basing its power on the private ownership of and control over land, lived off a share of the produce extracted from that land by a class of laboring people. The latter, though neither slaves nor serfs, were still so closely bound to the land which they cultivated as to make them little better than serfs of the landed proprietors. It was a society, furthermore, in which these two classes constituted the main social forces and determined the contours of development.

26

good earth and the peasants who tilled it. As late as 1945 many
gentry in the interior still could not conceive of basic change as
possible. Families might rise and fall, rebel armies advance or retreat, new gods challenge old, machine textiles replace handwoven
goods, steam and electricity replace man and mule in distant ports,
but in the quiet countryside landlords continued to don long gowns,
collect exorbitant rents, pay off the soldiery, manicure their fingernails, and eat white flour made from wheat. Tenants continued to
wear dirt-stained trousers, sweat in the fields, render up the major
part of what they raised in taxes and rent, and shiver through the
winter on coarse millet, chaff, and bran. When anyone mentioned
change, the gentry asked confidently: "Can the sun rise in the west?"

This confidence of the gentry was based on the stability of the
land system and the culture it engendered—a system and a culture
that had survived and often flourished since before the time of Christ.
Under this system, which in one decade abruptly disappeared forever
from mainland China, a typical community was made up of a small
number of landlords and rich peasants and a large number of hired
laborers, poor peasants and middle peasants.* The landlords and rich
peasants, who made up less than 10 percent of the rural population,
owned from 70 to 80 percent of the land, most of the draft animals
and the bulk of the carts and implements. The hired laborers, the
poor peasants, and the middle peasants, who made up more than 90
percent of the population, held less than 30 percent of the land, only
a few draft animals,, and a scattering of implements and carts—a condition which placed them perennially at the mercy of the more well-
to-do and condemned them to a life of veritable serfdom.

If one takes the percentages above as a yardstick one finds that
the people of Long Bow were more fortunate than the average, for
the concentration of land ownership there, in the early 1940's, was not
nearly as high as was general in other parts of China, or even in other

* "Those who possess a great deal of land, who do not themselves labor
but depend entirely on exploiting the peasants through rent and usury, sus-
taining themselves without toiling—*these are the landlords*. Those who own
large amounts of land, plow animals and farm implements, who themselves
take part in labor although at the same time they exploit the hired labor of
peasants—*these are the rich peasants*. Those who have land, plow animals,
and farm implements, who labor themselves and do not exploit others, or do so
only slightly—*these are the middle peasants*. Those who have only a small
amount of land, farm implements and plow animals, who labor on their own
land but at the same time have to sell a part of their labor power—*these
are the poor peasants*. Those who have no land, plow animals, or farm implements and who must sell their labor power—*these are the hired laborers*."
(From Jen Pi-shih, *Several Problems Regarding Land Reform*, 1948. Not
published in English.)

parts of the Shangtang region. On the eve of the land revolution the landlords and the rich peasants together made up about seven percent of the population and owned directly 164 acres, or 18 percent of the land. Through religious and clan associations they controlled another 114 acres bringing the total land under their control to 278 acres, or 31 percent. They also owned 18 oxen, mules, and donkeys, or about 33 percent of the draft animals. These were low figures compared to many other Chinese communities.

If the landlords and rich peasants held less than was usual, the middle peasants held much more. They made up 40 percent of the population, held 45 percent of the land and 66 percent of the draft animals. Even so, they were not the largest group in the village. The poor peasants outnumbered all others with 47 percent of the population. They held only 24 percent of the land. Six percent of the people were hired laborers. The two most exploited groups thus made up more than half of the population, owned less than a quarter of the land, and only five percent of the draft animals.

Very interesting and significant was the factor of family size. The landlords and the rich peasants averaged more than five persons per household, the middle peasants fewer than five, the poor peasants between three and three and a half, and the hired laborers about three. There was thus a direct correlation between the size of the family and its basic economic security measured in terms of productive property. Although the birth rate in all established families was approximately the same, those with land, tools, and stock were able to maintain larger families and prosper. Those without land or with very small holdings were often unable even to marry. If they did marry they were unable to hold their families together, lost more children to disease and famine, had to sell children, or even sell wives, and thus had households about half the size.

If the land holdings of the prerevolutionary period were calculated on the basis of the number of families, rather than per capita, the concentration of wealth in the hands of the landlords and rich peasants was more marked. On that basis—a very realistic one for China, where the traditional emphasis has always been on the family rather than on the individual—the landlords and rich peasants, with only five percent of the families, controlled 31 percent of the land; the middle peasants, with less than a third of the families, held 45 percent of the land; and the poor peasants and hired laborers together, with 62 percent of the families, held only 24 percent of the land. Even on this basis the concentration of land ownership in Long Bow was not high; the landlords and rich peasants were relatively poor; and the middle peasant group was unusually large, a factor which was to have considerable influence on the whole future of the community.

One reason for the comparative dispersion of land ownership was the poor quality of the land. Whereas in many parts of China it took only half an acre or less to support one person, in the southern districts of Lucheng County it took about one acre. Irrigation easily could have doubled yields, but without large-scale engineering projects no general irrigation was possible, even on the flat that surrounded the village. In addition, a good part of the land—at least one third—was on the hill and therefore impossible to irrigate. The whole region, located at the very end of Shansi's fertile central valley only a few miles from high, often rocky mountains, was extremely high and cold and hence a peripheral area agriculturally. In general, in every country in the world the highest concentration of landholding is to be found in the richest, most fertile valleys, and the lowest concentration in the poorest mountain regions where the surplus possible from one man's labor is least, and hence the rate of exploitation is the lowest. The mountainous regions of Southeastern Shansi were no exception to this rule.

The land held by the landlords and rich peasants, while ample, was not enough in itself to make them the dominant group in the village. It served primarily as a solid foundation for other forms of open and concealed exploitation which taken together raised a handful of families far above the rest of the inhabitants economically and hence politically and socially as well. Usurious interest rates on loans, profits from commercial and industrial ventures, the spoils of public office, and graft or commissions from the management of temple, church, and clan affairs—when added to the revenues from land ownership and land management—gave these families an influence in gross disproportion to their numbers or to the acreage which they held.

Long Bow's richest family, the seven-member household of the landlord Sheng Ching-ho tapped every one of these income sources. Sheng Ching-ho was a healthy, able-bodied man, but he never engaged in any form of manual labor. He did not have to. His income was many times that of the most prosperous middle-peasant family. He cultivated long fingernails, wore a long gown that made manual work impossible and considered it beneath his dignity even to lift his bag onto his cart when he went on a trip.

The heart of Ching-ho's "empire" consisted of 23 acres of fertile land—the largest holding in the village if one excludes the land of the "Carry-On Society" of the Catholic Church.* To work these acres he hired two year-round laborers plus extra hands at harvest time. In livestock, the second most important category of rural wealth, he

* For a description of this society and its operations, see Chapter 5.

owned two draft animals, a flock of sheep, and several hogs. He employed two boys full time to look after the sheep. His industrial enterprise was a small distillery where *paikar* was made from kaoliang grain. The wine cost about 20 cents a catty to make and sold for about 30 cents a catty.* When in full production this distillery turned out over 100 catties a day. In this plant Ching-ho employed two men for about seven months every year. The distiller's grains left over from the process were fed to fattening hogs.

The income from these enterprises was fairly large and since the family lived very frugally, Sheng Ching-ho had a yearly surplus. Some of this surplus he converted into silver coin which he buried in the back part of his courtyard. Another part he invested in a distillery owned by another landlord, Fan Pu-tzu. The rest he loaned out to peasants in desperate need and, by charging exorbitant interest rates (up to 50 percent a month), often doubled or tripled his principal in one season. Those who were unable to pay lost their land to him. If they had no land, they lost their livestock, their carts, their implements. This loan business was actually run by his wife, a woman with a very sharp business head who kept careful track of every copper coin.

With his wife in command of the loans, Ching-ho himself had plenty of time for such equally lucrative operations as managing the affairs of the Pei Lao Shih or North Temple Society, a charitable organization set up to help support the village school, lend money to members in distress, give insurance-type benefits, and placate the gods. This was a Buddhist religious group to which many peasants contributed money and grain. The society owned about five acres of land which Ching-ho managed. He also ran the group's annual fair and hired the traveling players who staged the opera without which no fair could be called a success. Since Ching-ho was in charge of all the funds, it was a simple matter for him to deduct a suitable commission. It was also a simple matter for him to arrange the accounts in such a way that the amount written down as the cost of the entertainment was always greatly in excess of the sum actually spent. He pocketed the difference. Once every 40 years the North Temple Society sponsored an especially grand fair. On such occasions much more money was spent and Ching-ho's share, when this fete finally fell to him, was proportionately greater. He himself confessed that he made more than 500 silver dollars on this one big fair alone.**

As a fertility and good luck offering to the gods, each member

---

* A catty is equal to half a kilogram or 1.1 English pounds.
** The silver dollars mentioned in this book are worth about 50 cents in U.S. currency.

of the North Temple Society had to pay annually a certain amount of grain per acre. All this grain went to Ching-ho's home and eventually found its way to his distillery. No accounting for this wealth was ever made to the people.

Concerning the manager of a similar temple society in South China, the well-known sociologist, Fei Hsiao-tung, has this to say:

He is theoretically selected by common consent; in practice, the position is held in rotation by influential men of the village by their common consent. The invariable practice of ignoring the poor in questions of administration is justified by the statement that their poverty disqualified them, since they could not reimburse the public coffers were they to make mistakes. It is impossible to say how much profit accrues to the treasurer, for, since the only concern of the people is that the traditional functions be performed, there is no system of auditing or making public his accounts.*

By no means a man to place all his eggs in one basket, Ching-ho also headed the *K'ung Tzu Tao* (Confucian Association) of the whole Fifth District. The Confucians of 30 villages were under his leadership. In Long Bow the overwhelming majority of the people belonged to the Confucian Association. Periodically Ching-ho held a banquet for its members and collected contributions to pay for the food and the entertainment. The contributions were usually greater than the cost of the banquet, and Ching-ho kept the difference. Since the Confucians of the whole district contributed, the income was large.

This Association undertook another service to members from which the income was also considerable. This was spirit talking. For a sum of money or grain one could talk, with the aid of a medium, to a parent long dead. This was called *yuan kuang*—the distant view. For an equivalent sum one could talk to one who had just died. This was called *hui yin*—the return impression. Payments for both types of messages were paid to Ching-ho, who managed the whole procedure. The ability to arrange these conversations with the dead gave him awesome power over that wide cross section of the people who believed in this occult practice.

To round out his career Sheng Ching-ho was active in politics. He served for many years as village head under the administration of Shansi's Governor, Yen Hsi-shan. This office carried with it no salary but it put the incumbent in a position to receive all kinds of emoluments —gifts and invitations to feasts on holidays, favors in return for the arbitration of disputes between families, graft in the collection of taxes and the assembling of materials for public works, commissions on

* Fei Hsiao-tung and Chang Chih-i, *Earthbound China,* Chicago: University of Chicago Press, 1947, p. 55.

the handling of public funds of all kinds. By far the largest source
of Ching-ho's administrative "take" came from the cut he took of
all taxes. If the county magistrate demanded two bushels of grain
per family, he demanded five and kept three. He accepted no excuse
for failure to pay. People had to deliver their tax grains even if
they had to sell their children to do it. In fairness to Ching-ho it
must be added that of the three bushels he held back, only a portion
went into his own granary. He had to split the taxes many ways with
subordinate officials, soldiers, etc.

Since Long Bow was the district seat and a garrison town, in addition to the frequent tax collections, the population had to bear the
burden of feeding soldiers and officers who walked in and demanded
meals. If anyone offered them coarse food such as millet, they threw
it in the privy. They wanted good things to eat. They often went to
the village inn, ate their fill and made the people pay, but they never
bothered Ching-ho in such petty ways. They depended on him for
tax gathering, public administration, and the adjustment of community
disputes. It was Ching-ho himself who invited officers to his home,
entertained them lavishly, fed them wheat dumplings, and gave them
the finest tobacco to smoke. He, of course, paid for all this with
public funds.

As village head Sheng Ching-ho was also a member of the Kuomintang Party. Although, out of prudence, he resigned from village office
just before the Japanese conquerors arrived, he kept up his Kuomintang membership throughout the occupation and the subsequent surrender in 1945.

The power which Ching-ho wielded by means of these various
connections was enormous in terms of village life. He used it to
acquire wealth and more wealth. He was especially vigorous in taking
over other people's land and houses. Han-sheng was an old man who
owned half an acre of very good land just to the east of the village.
In a crisis he once borrowed $13 from Sheng Ching-ho. Three years
later the principal plus interest amounted to a very large sum. Though
Han-sheng paid off some of it, he couldn't pay it all. Ching-ho then
seized the half acre and the summer harvest that had just been reaped
on it. Because he did not want the millet he plowed it under and
planted wheat in the fall. Han-sheng was left with nothing.

The middle peasant Shih Szu-har borrowed $125 from the North
Temple Society managed by Ching-ho. Two years later, when Szu-har
was unable to pay, he lost his land—all six acres, his eleven-section
house, his donkey, and his cart.* The whole family, including several

* A section of a Chinese house is from six to nine feet wide and may
or may not be marked off by a partition. It is determined by the distance
between the main rafters which hold up the roof.

very young children, were driven outside to live in the open. Luckily Szu-har had both loyal friends and skill as a carpenter. He found shelter and work and was able to save his family from starvation.

At the time when Ching-ho took possession of Szu-har's land it had just been planted. The young millet shoots were pushing through the soil and they had been hoed once. Ching-ho put the land up for sale but the price he asked was so high that no one could afford to buy it. Though weeds smothered the young millet, Ching-ho would not allow Szu-har to go on the field and the crop was lost.

A poor peasant named Shen borrowed $4 from Ching-ho in order to buy medicine for his sick wife. As a guarantee for the loan he indentured his son Fa-liang to Ching-ho for seven years. At the end of seven years, because of illness, deductions for broken tools, and outright cheating on the part of Ching-ho, Fa-liang owed many times the original debt and had to tear down part of his house and sell the roof timbers to win his freedom.

The landless and the land poor were not the only victims of Sheng Ching-ho. A prosperous rich peasant, P'ei Ho-yi, owned 13 acres and a fine house of 20 sections. This house adjoined Ching-ho's and the landlord wanted very much to add it to his own. In order to do so he first had to bankrupt Ho-yi. He encouraged Ho-yi to smoke opium, and when Ho-yi could no longer afford to buy opium, he loaned him the money with which to keep the supply coming. When Ho-yi's debt had grown to alarming proportions, Ching-ho decided to form a revolving loan society by means of which, in the course of several years, Ho-yi could pay off his debt. Quite a few peasants were drawn into this scheme. Each contributed three or four silver dollars to a fund which each in turn could use interest free for a year. Ho-yi was made secretary of the society and got the first year's pot. Since he was floating in an opium trance most of the time, Ho-yi easily lost track of the exact standing of the shares and, when Ching-ho suddenly announced that $50 was missing, he had no way to refute it. Ching-ho came forward with a solution. He took Ho-yi's house and three acres of his land in return for paying off the other partners. To settle the rest of the debt to Ching-ho, Ho-yi had to sell what remained of his land. Completely bankrupt, he and his family were driven into the street and forced to leave Long Bow.

Next to Sheng Ching-ho the most important landlord in Long Bow Village was the Catholic, Fan Pu-tzu. He owned 14 acres of land, a flock of sheep, several hogs, a distillery—larger than the one run by Ching-ho—and a liquor store in Horse Square, one mile to the north. He employed two full-time laborers, two shepherds, three distillery workers, two clerks, and seasonal help when needed. His household was notorious for the bad treatment meted out to laborers and servants. He paid one youthful worker in the distillery $7 a year, called him off the straw in the cowshed at three o'clock in the morning and set him to grinding grain. At noon, when the whole family took a nap, this boy was not allowed to rest but had to carry water. In the afternoon the family ate an extra meal of noodles, but the laborers got only the two regular meals of coarse millet and corn dumplings.

Among the rich peasants—men who themselves labored on the land but earned more through exploitation than they did by their own labor—Kuo Fu-wang and his brother Ch'ung-wang were the best known. In fact, they were considered to be the meanest employers in the whole village. The brothers owned 22 acres that yielded each year close to eight tons of grain, two draft animals, and all such necessary farm tools and equipment as carts, plows, harrows, and seeders. Part of their land they worked themselves with the help of hired labor. The rest they rented out to tenants.

During the famine years of 1942–1943, Ch'ung-wang had no mercy on his tenants. The Miao brothers had been paying rent to him for many years, but in 1942 they did not harvest enough of a crop to live on. Ch'ung-wang insisted on payment in full. They offered him some of their own land. He refused it. In order to settle up with him they were then forced to borrow grain from others. After paying the rent they had nothing to eat. Both of them died of starvation before spring. P'ei Mang-wen's mother, another of Ch'ung-wang's debtors, also died after paying him back $1.50. A third peasant, Ho-p'ang, lost crop, clothes, and household furniture to Ch'ung-wang.

At the height of the famine, with the people dying of starvation on every side, Ch'ung-wang collected all the grain he could and held it for speculative prices in an underground vault that served as the family tomb. He held it so long that much of it rotted.

Kuo Ch'ung-wang also evaded taxes for more than 20 years on three acres of land that were not registered with the county. His official deeds called for three acres less than he actually owned and the evasion of taxes on this land threw an extra burden on the middle peasants who had to bear the brunt of all grain levies. This type of tax evasion was common among those gentry with wealth or influence enough to bribe or otherwise pressure the makers of deeds and the collectors of taxes.* The acres so held were called "black lands."

---

* The word gentry is used here to describe landlords, rich peasants, and persons who made a career of serving them and their interests (such as bailiffs, public officials, village scholars) whose standard of living was comparable to that of the wealthy and came from the same source—the exploitation of the peasants.

The wealth accumulated by Kuo Ch'ung-wang, Fan Pu-tzu, Sheng Ching-ho and the other gentry through usury, land rent, and the exploitation of hired labor could not easily be converted into capital—that is, it could not easily be invested where it would yield a profit and reproduce itself with certainty.

The returns from money-lending were large, but the risks were also great. There was no limit to the number of poor peasants in desperate need of grain and funds, but few could offer anything by way of security. All the possessions of many a family could not realize $5 on the market. Children could be seized in lieu of property, but in a bad crop year teen-aged girls sold for less than a hundredweight of grain, and they had to be fed.

A profit could be turned by making liquor but there was a limit to the amount of grain available for mash and a very restricted market. People were willing enough to drink liquor, but they had nothing with which to pay for it.

There were no savings banks; there was little commerce and less industry. The only thing left to invest in was land. Land was safe, but the returns were small when compared with those from usury because scarcity drove land prices ever upward.* The amount of good land on the market in Long Bow and the surrounding villages was never large while prospective buyers were numerous. Improving the land was out of the question. Irrigation would have doubled yields but the water table was too low for the donkey-powered bucket pumps so common on the plains of Hopei a hundred miles to the east. In order to bring water, a canal several miles long was required—a project that was beyond the power of any one landlord or even of the whole village. For such a project county-wide cooperation and support was necessary, but the bureaucrats of the *Yamen* (county government) were not interested. So the land remained dry while the waters that drained from the ranges to the East flowed untapped to the North China plain.

Money could have been spent on indigenous fertilizers, better seed, and improved implements, but there was no guarantee of any immediate return. A dry year could make fertilizer useless. Should the yield by chance go up, taxes claimed the increase. Under such conditions no one developed fertilizers, seeds, or implements. The landlord's surplus grain was converted instead into coinage and buried in the ground.

* J. Loessing Buck in his *Chinese Farm Economy* estimated that the interest on capital invested in land averaged only 8.4 percent annually. Usurious loans yielded 30 percent a month and more. See R. H. Tawney, *Land and Labour in China,* London: George Allen and Unwin, Ltd., 1932, p. 67.

The loans that were made to the peasants went mainly to cover emergency expenses such as funerals, illnesses, weddings, and the food consumed during the "spring hunger," rather than for productive improvements such as wells, plows, or stock. Once the money was spent, neither the borrower nor the economy had anything to show for it.

Money spent on land likewise added nothing to the productive forces. It only gave the purchaser the right to demand whatever share of the tenant's meager crop current social relations allowed. It in no way increased that crop.

Hoarding the remainder of the surplus only deepened and perpetuated the stagnation. A community in desperate need of development could not use the only capital at hand. While a fortune in gold and silver lay in secret caches underground, peasants for whom an ox or a plow might mean prosperity were condemned to starvation; at least half the population sat idle five months of the year because they lacked the resources for handicraft production, for small local industries, even for the mules and carts with which to do transport work once the crops were harvested in the fall. The iron ore in the hill south of Long Bow and the coal in the mountain north of Lucheng were never mined for lack of funds, while thousands of people in the villages between roughed it through the winter like cattle, doing nothing, and eating as little as possible in order to make their grain last until spring.

Unused resources, wasted manpower, declining production—these were the fruits of a system that in the long run could only bring disaster on its victims and beneficiaries alike.

3

Eating Bitterness

In spring seeds are sown and for each grain planted
Many are harvested; no land is left uncultivated,
Yet still do many peasants die of hunger.
Working with their hoes under the hottest sun,
Their sweat drips down and mingles with the earth.
Who will understand that the food we eat
Has been paid for with such bitter toil?

Li Shen

THE GENTRY of Long Bow—the landlords, the rich peasants, the clan elders, the overseers of temple property and the managers of religious societies—would not have been considered well off in any Western land. Their lives were luxurious only in contrast to the absolute poverty and near starvation of the great mass of the people. They did not live in palaces. They enjoyed none of the conveniences of modern life. In most cases, the only difference between their homes and those of the rest of the population was in the construction materials used. The prosperous built with brick, the poor with adobe. Both materials came from the earth underfoot and the interior plan and conveniences of a brick home differed little from those of a house built of adobe.

What made the lives of the gentry so enviable to the working peasants was the security they enjoyed from hunger and cold. They at least had a roof over their heads. They had warm clothes to wear. They had some silk finery for feast days, wedding celebrations, and funerals. They had quilts to sleep under. They even had fuel for their stoves and for their *k'angs*.* They had a little variety in their diet. They could eat wheat often and even meat once in a while. The

---

* A *k'ang* is a raised platform made of mud bricks that usually takes up one whole side of a room in a Chinese house. It is so constructed that the flue from the cooking fire runs under it and warms it. In the winter the women live and work on the *k'ang* during the day. The whole family sleeps on it at night. When the *k'ang* is in a room where no cooking is done, a fire for the purpose of warming the *k'ang* can be built under it.

true landlords among them did no manual labor either in the field or in the home. Hired laborers or tenants tilled the fields, servant girls and domestic slaves cooked the meals, sewed, washed and swept up.* The menfolk of these families busied themselves with managerial affairs, money lending, and religious and clan functions. They amused themselves with women, opium smoking, and gambling.

Education was another great advantage which the gentry enjoyed. They often hired special tutors to live in the home and had set up a village school for their progeny. When their young people grew older, they were sent on to middle school (high school) at the county seat, and even to college in Taiyuan or Peking. As college graduates they had a chance to move into the higher bureaucracy, the officer corps of the army, or one of the larger commercial or banking establishments in the provincial capital.

This world of security, relative comfort, influence, position, and leisure was maintained amidst a sea of the most dismal and frightening poverty and hunger—a poverty and hunger which at all times threatened to engulf any family which relaxed its vigilance, took pity on its poor neighbors, failed to extract the last copper of rent and interest, or ceased for an instant the incessant accumulation of grain and money. Those who did not go up went down, and those who went down often went to their deaths or at least to the dissolution and dispersal of their families.

The extremes to which never-ending vigilance had to be carried was demonstrated most clearly when the crops began to ripen. Then every family, whether landlord, middle peasant, or tenant, had to maintain guards in the fields day and night. Toothless old grandmothers and children in split pants hardly big enough to carry a stick stood eternal watch against thieves. To protect these pitiful sentries from the sun at noon and the dew before dawn little shelters of kaoliang stalks or mud bricks mushroomed suddenly on every plot and strip. For weeks at a time almost half the population of every community lodged overnight in the fields, each family keeping an eye on all the rest. Thus both prosperous and poor peasants were forced to expend their often exhausted energies on a guard duty that was sheer waste from the point of view of society, but that meant the difference between life and death to every cropper. Any strip left unwatched was almost sure to be looted by some half-starved family trying to stay alive just a few more days until its own poor crops matured.

---

* Poor peasant children, especially girls, were bought and raised as slaves. At 13 to 15 years of age, they were sold as brides. Young girls were also hired as servants.

To have no crops at all was the worst fate that any peasant could imagine; yet six percent of the population was in exactly such straits. Here is the story told to me by Shen Fa-liang, the boy indentured to Sheng Ching-ho for seven years in order to pay off his father's $4 debt:

When I first went to work for Sheng Ching-ho I was only 14. All the same I had to do chores around the house. I was too small to carry full buckets, but I had to carry water from the well. I filled the buckets half full and brought them in that way. All the years I worked for Ching-ho I never had a full stomach. I was hungry all the time. Every day he ate solid enough food but he gave me only a little soup with millet in it. You could count the grains that were floating around in the water. Twice I got sick—worn out with work. And I was always cold. I never had food or clothes enough to keep warm. When I got sick I couldn't work. Then the landlord was very angry. He got two men to carry me home so that he wouldn't have to feed me while I was sick. And he made my father pay for the laborer that took my place. My sickness cost him nothing. My own family had to bear the entire burden.

No matter how hard I worked I couldn't begin to pay off that debt. By the time I had been there several years we owed him $15 instead of $4. I told him, "It's no use working for you. No matter what I do the debts get bigger. I want to leave." But he wouldn't let me. The contract said seven years, and he held us to it. By that time I had grown up. I could do a man's work. He finally promised to pay me $10 a year instead of $8. I said I wouldn't ask for more money and he said he wouldn't jump the interest on the debt. But even so, it was no use. Whenever I broke anything he made me pay a high price for it. Once there was a long drought. The soil was very hard. He pushed us to finish the hoeing quickly. In my hurry I cracked the handle of the hoe. When he saw it, he was very angry. He knocked several dollars off my year's wages—enough to buy two new handles—even though that one could still be used. In fact, I did use the hoe for a long time after that. At the end of the year I didn't get enough wages to buy a pair of pants.

Any small mistake and he blew up. I had to carry water through the gate. There was a threshold there and a sharp turn. If I spilled some water on the ground, he cursed me for messing up the courtyard. Once I tore the horse's collar. He cursed me and my ancestors.. I didn't dare answer back. I think that was worse than the food and the filthy quarters—not being able to talk back. In those days the landlords' word was law. They had their way. When it was really hot and they said it was not, we dared not say it was hot; when it really was cold and they said it wasn't, we dared not say it was cold. Whatever happened we had to listen to them. You could never finish telling of the abuse the landlords gave us.

At the end of each year Ching-ho subtracted all the things he claimed I broke, the time I was sick, and such things. What was left was never enough to pay off the interest on the money, so he kept everything. I got no wage at all. When the seven years were up, I had to tear down two sections of my house, sell the wood and the bricks, and only then was I able to pay Ching-ho off.

Then I went to work for Wang Lai-hsun. I took it for granted that perhaps some other family treated people better but I soon found out that all the crows in the world are black. Lai-hsun's household was no better. In the famine year I had to sell the rest of my house to live at all. I sold it to Sheng Ching-ho, but the money came too late to save my wife. She was so sick with hunger that she died a few days later. The money did no good at all. I used some of it to bury her. We bought millet with the rest of it. But the millet wasn't enough to live on, and we had to go out in the hills to dig herbs—wild herbs. Before the year was up all we had left to eat was herbs and weeds and the leaves off the trees.

Even so, the worst days of my life were when I was a child. I often had nothing to eat. In the winter I had no padded clothes to wear. One suit of padded clothes had to last for many years. It was patched over and over again. It wore so thin that it was no better than a summer jacket. How then could I pass the winter? I can't imagine how we got through. I can't even remember. When we didn't have any millet, we drank hot water. If we had any money we bought coal, but most of the time we had none.

What was the happiest day of my life? I haven't passed any happy days. But if you want to compare, the days since Liberation have been good.

Another story that demonstrates with painful clarity what had to be endured by families of landless peasants is that of Wang Ch'ung-lai's wife. Wang Ch'ung-lai was the brother by adoption of Wang Lai-hsun, the second-largest landholder in Long Bow. Lai-hsun inherited the Wang family land and wealth but never prospered because he was a hopeless drug addict. In fact, neither he nor his brother, Ch'ung-lai, were true sons of old man Wang. Both were bought as children by the landlord and raised in his home as sons because he had no progeny. When the old man died, his shrewd wife did not fancy dividing the property between two heirs, neither of whom had a legitimate claim. One son was enough to carry out the duties of ancestor worship and produce a new generation. She therefore treated one boy, Lai-hsun, as a son, and the other, Ch'ung-lai, as a servant and hired laborer.

To ensure help in the house the old lady bought Ch'ung-lai a wife. The girl was nine years old at the time, cost the family nine strings of cash, and lived in the home as a servant for six years before she was actually wed to Ch'ung-lai.*

"Being a child wife I was often beaten and cursed by everyone in the family," she said when telling her life story years later.

At the beginning, since I was only nine, I took care of some sheep and pigs. Every day I went out on the hill to watch the sheep, and when I came back I fed the pigs. At that time Lai-hsun's first wife was alive and

* A string of cash was made up of copper coins, each with a hole in the center so that it could be strung on a string. There were 100 coins to a string. Nine strings could buy one silver dollar.

she cooked for the family. The first wife was not so bad, and besides I was out all day. Still, I was beaten by the old lady. It was for no reason except that she thought I didn't work hard.

I was married at 15. After that it was worse, much worse. That was because Lai-hsun married again and the second wife was most terrible. She never beat me herself; she just complained to the old lady and let her beat me. I was beaten too many times to remember. I was beaten almost every day so it is hard to remember anything special about it.

They ate *mien* (noodles). I cooked for them but I was not allowed to eat even the leftover noodles. Ch'ung-lai and I ate millet, broth made of screenings, and ground corn.

At that time I thought to myself, "Because I have no parents and these people are so terrible, there is no way out for me." I often wandered beside the well, but no one wants to jump into the well, so finally I thought it was better to lead a beggar's life than to kill oneself by one's own hand, so my hope was to go out and work for others.

One day the mother-in-law broke my arm. The water in the pot was boiling. I asked her what I should cook and how much millet was in the pot. She did not answer. So I asked her again. Then she got angry and beat me. She said I annoyed her and was too stupid. That was the way it usually was. But that time she took up an iron poker and broke my arm with it. My arm hurt so I lay on the *k'ang* for a fortnight and couldn't work or even move.

Then Lai-hsun took a knife and threatened us. He said that unless we left he would kill us both. I wanted to go away and find work somewhere else but Ch'ung-lai was afraid. He feared death from hunger, for once we left the family we would never get a thing. But in the end we were driven out anyway; they drove us out barehanded.

Ch'ung-lai went to Taiyuan to pull a rickshaw. He sent back money when he could. I myself cooked for a landlord in Fu-t'sun. Life there was better than at home. Anyway I got enough to eat, and when I asked them what to cook they answered me. Sometimes they even gave me old clothes or rags to wear, and I earned about $1 a month.

After six years we saved enough to buy an acre of land. Then came the famine year. Ch'ung-lai had to come home from Taiyuan but he was sick. From the land we got two bags of grain. After paying the tax there was nothing left. Hunger made Ch'ung-lai sicker. By that time I had two children, a boy and a girl. We three went out to beg. Sometimes we had to go very far away and couldn't get back at night. So often we slept in temples and often we couldn't find a temple to stay in and had to sleep outdoors. Once I asked the children, "Are you frightened?" They said, "We are not afraid as long as we can find something to eat."

But because it was a famine year it was very hard to find food. We had to sell the land. We got six bushels of millet and lived a whole year on it. We added whatever we could find to go with it. But it was hard to find anything. There weren't even any leaves left on the trees.

We went back to Long Bow to beg from Wang Lai-hsun. His whole family still ate well. We knelt down before them and begged for something to eat. We asked pity for the children. "We do not ask things from you. We know there is no hope for us, but we wish you would have some pity on the children for they are your own grandson and granddaughter."

But they took sticks and beat the children. We stayed there past noon but could not even get a bowl of water from them. So we took the children to other villages and got something. Strangers treated us better than our own relatives.

After the famine year there was a good summer harvest but then we had no land. Ch'ung-lai went to work as a hired laborer, and I cooked out for others as before. We had to leave the children at home alone. Every few days I returned home and gave them a little millet or corn. They themselves went out to beg. At the end of the year I saw that every family had prepared noodles and other good things to eat. I asked the mistress to give me a little corn to take to the children so that they too could pass the New Year. But she only cursed and drove me out.

So I had no job and returned home with a little corn flour that I bought with my wages. When the chidren saw me they wept. We three wept the whole day. My children said to me, "We will beg together and die together rather than live apart." So we went out to beg again.

After the summer harvest we all went out to glean wheat in the fields. One day I looked up. There was a wolf. He just stood and stared at me. I was frightened. I dared not move. I stared right back at him. My daughter saw the wolf and ran, but the wolf chased her and caught her. I couldn't move. I only stood there and watched the wolf open his great mouth and bite my daughter. My son cried, "See how big the mouth is and the terrible red tongue!"

At this moment a cart passed on the road. The men in the cart jumped out and began to beat the wolf. Still I stood frozen to the spot. The men drove the wolf away. They called me. My daughter was still alive. When I went up to her, I saw that the wolf had bitten a big piece of flesh from her leg and slashed her cheeks but her eyes were clear and stared at me. I clasped her to my breast and tried to carry her home, but after a little while she died. Still I held her dead body. Then I fainted and the carters put me in the cart with the boy. They left her little body in the field and carried me home. When I recovered consciousness, I was in a stupor. Every day I just sat behind closed doors and said, "The wolf is coming! The wolf is coming!" The neighbors pitied me and sent a little food.

These life stories reflect but a small fraction of the chronic social tragedy that permeated the community and the society at large. The extreme hardship borne by Shen Fa-liang and Wang Ch'ung-lai and his wife did not surpass in degree the sufferings endured by many other poor peasants in Long Bow, in the neighboring villages, and in thousands of similar villages scattered throughout China. The following are only a few incidents culled at random from the life stories of peasants with whom I talked.

• There were three famine years in a row. The whole family went out to beg things to eat. In Chinchang City conditions were very bad. Many mothers threw newborn children into the river. Many children wandered about on the streets and couldn't find their parents. We had to sell our eldest daughter. She was then already 14. Better to move than to die, we thought. We sold what few things we had. We took our patched quilt on a carrying pole and set out for Changchih with the little boy in the basket on the other end. He cried all the way from hunger. We rested before a gate. Because the boy wept so bitterly a woman came out. We stayed there three days. On the fourth morning the woman said she wanted to buy the boy. We put him on the *k'ang*. He fell asleep. In the next room we were paid five silver dollars. Then they drove us out. They were afraid when the boy woke up he would cry for his mother. My heart was so bitter. To sell one's own child was such a painful thing. We wept all day on the road.

• I almost starved to death. One day I lay on the street. A cart came along. The driver yelled at me to move. I was too weak. I didn't care if he drove over me or not. He finally had to drive around me.

• During the famine we ate leaves and the remnants from vinegar making. We were so weak and hungry we couldn't walk. I went out to the hills to get leaves and there the people were fighting each other over the leaves on the trees. My little sister starved to death. My brother's wife couldn't bear the hunger and ran away and never came back. My cousin was forced to become a landlord's concubine.

• I and the children worked for others thinning millet. We got only half a quart of grain. For each meal we cooked only a fistful with some weeds in it. The children's stomachs were swollen and every bone in their bodies stuck through their skin. After a while the little boy couldn't get up. He just lay on the *k'ang* sick with dysentery and many, many worms, a whole basin full of worms crawled out from his behind. Even after he was dead the worms kept coming out. The little girl had no milk from me, for I had nothing to eat myself, so, of course, she died.

People could not speak of the past without weeping. Nor could one listen to their stories dry-eyed. Yet, as the details piled up, horror on horror, one's senses became dulled. The barbarity, the cruelty, the terror of the old life was so overwhelming that in time it ceased to shock. One began to take for granted that worms crawled from dying children, that women and children were bought and sold like cattle, that people were beaten to death, they they fought each other for the leaves on the trees. The impossible took on the aura of the commonplace.

The most terrible thing about the conditions of life in Long Bow in those days was not any single aspect of the all but universal misery; it was that there was no hope of change. The fearful tragedy played and replayed itself without end. Insofar as things did change, they changed for the worse as the crisis of China's social system deepened.

For the majority of the peasants who, like Shen Fa-liang and Ch'ung-lai's wife, were caught in the downward drift, conditions became more and more intolerable as time went on.*

Some of the decline can be attributed to the economic dislocations and social disorders generic to periods of dynastic decay. More important was the unprecedented intervention from abroad which began around 1840. One immediate consequence of intervention was a whole series of wars which sapped the country's reserves. These wars, defensive in nature as the Western powers invaded, became fratricidal as these same powers backed one warlord against another for spheres of influence, or their favorite of the moment against popular resistance. The trading and investment concessions accruing to the victors enabled foreigners to transfer substantial quantities of real wealth from the "underdeveloped East" to the advanced industrial West and Japan.

This bleeding away of sorely needed capital was aggravated by the simultaneous destruction of capital formation in important handicraft industries. Large-scale importation of cheap, machine-made goods undermined one sector of the economy after the other. This was especially true of the textile trades. Millions of weavers, unable to compete with the power-driven looms of Lancaster, Tokyo, and later Shanghai, lost their main means of livelihood and were thrown into the swelling stream of those bidding for the scarce and already depleted land.

The rising tide of landless and destitute people enabled landowners to stiffen the terms of tenancy, to raise rents and jack up interest rates. It enabled grain dealers to force harvest time prices lower and winter and spring prices higher. It enabled merchants to widen the gap between farm produce and industrial products. Not only the laborers and tenants but also the land-owning middle peasants felt the squeeze more and more. To maintain bare subsistence they had to increase working hours, get up earlier, finish later, and work harder on the job. Even then they could not make ends meet. They had to go ever more frequently to the money-lender and, once saddled with debt, found it impossible to break free. It was an exceptional family in Long Bow that did not owe the equivalent of several years' earnings.

People said, "The debts of the poor begin at birth. When a boy is a month old the family wishes to celebrate; but they have to borrow money in order to make dumplings and so, before the child can sit

* "There is even reason to believe that, with the increased pressure on the land caused by the growth of the population, the condition of the rural population, in some parts of China, may actually be worse than it was two centuries ago." (R. H. Tawney, *Land and Labour in China*, p. 71.)

up, he is already in debt to the landlord. As he grows the interest mounts until the burden is too great to bear."

Weighed down by high interest rates, harassed by heavy taxes, caught in the snares of a rigged market, many landowning peasants went bankrupt, sold out their holdings strip by strip, and ended up with the yoke of rent around their necks, or left for the city hoping to find some work in industry or transport that would keep them alive. Others became soldiers in the armies of the warlords or joined local bandit gangs.

"There are districts in which the position of the rural population is that of a man standing permanently up to the neck in water, so that even a ripple is sufficient to drown him," wrote R. H. Tawney in 1932.* The Fifth District of Lucheng County was such a district and Long Bow such a place.

* *Ibid.,* p. 77. See also Edgar Snow, *Red Star Over China,* New York: Modern Library, 1944, p. 83.

4

Three Pillars of Heaven

A man is poor,
Ever thinner, ever blacker,
Goes to borrow fifty coins,
Is asked a hundred in return,
Turns to go,
Knows he's taken for a thief;
> *A man is rich,*
> *Ever fatter, ever whiter,*
> *Goes to borrow fifty pieces,*
> *Has a hundred pressed upon him,*
> *Turns to go,*
> *Is urged to stay and drink.*

Shantung Chant

DROWNING MEN are prone to violence.

With so many of Long Bow's peasants on the verge of ruin, how did a handful of landlord and rich peasant families maintain their system of exploitation? How did they enforce the payment of rent and interest through years of famine and war? How did they protect their hoarded wealth from looting and seizure by their tenants and hired laborers who, after all, needed only to join together to bring the whole system down?

To answer this question one would have to examine the whole superstructure of China—political, military, religious, and cultural—and beyond that, the policies of the imperialist powers who propped that superstructure up with loans and arms, even while they attacked with modern industry and commerce the economic foundation upon which it rested.

There is no space here for such an exhaustive study. I can only try to describe in brief how a small group of gentry dominated Long Bow Village itself. The reader must keep in mind that at all times much greater power than could possibly be mustered locally hovered in the background in the shape of county, provincial, and national officials and the armed forces under their control. Helpless as they proved to be in defending the country against external attack, they were usually adequate to the task of crushing internal revolt and could always be called upon to protect the interests of those few families who stood to gain from the preservation of the old agrarian system.

That a few families ran the affairs of Long Bow Village was well known to the whole population. In the 1920's, the village even achieved a certain notoriety because of the "Eight Squires" who co-operated with a group of foreign priests in an effort to make converts to Catholicism. These eight were Yang, Li, Wang, Kao, Sheng, Liu, and the two Fans. By the early 1940's Kao and Liu were no longer influential, having been replaced by Shih, Ch'eng, and Kuo, but there were still eight or ten powerful families and they still dominated the village. By consulting together, by acting in unison when that counted most, and by the backing they gave to whomever they chose to openly manage affairs, this group maintained a virtual monopoly of power. This is not to imply that they were all equally active, that they acted without friction and jealousy among themselves, or that they ruled without allies among other strata of the population. Four families took the lead. These were Sheng, Fan, Shih, and Kuo. They had the backing of the other families of means and brought certain middle peasants and even poor peasants into the ruling circle to carry out routine tasks and to share, to some extent, in the spoils. As for the rest of the population, they occupied the position of the mighty stone tortoises who stood in front of the grave mounds of the gentry, bearing forever on their backs the stone obelisks which the wealthy loved to erect for their dead. The policy of the gentry toward them was to deceive, intimidate, divide and rule.

The rule exercised by this group of gentry rested on several pillars, not the least of which was tradition. Several thousand years of Confucian teachings had established a climate of opinion in which no one, or at best only a few persons in the whole village, questioned the system as such. Rich and poor alike looked on land ownership as the most important form of property, the foundation of family life, and the basis for the proper observance of ancestral rites, as well as the security of future generations. The more land the better. Everyone wanted to own land, bought additional land when he could, and if he succeeded in buying more than he could work, saw nothing wrong in renting it out. Success in this scramble for land was regarded as a reward for virtuous living and right thinking.

Viewed in this frame of reference the expropriation of a large part of the wealth of Long Bow by a few families—which was in essence a form of armed plunder—presented itself as a demonstration of moral law. And if this was too hard for the land-poor to swallow (the virtue of the gentry was often most conspicuous by its absence), they could always blame the fates. The rich were rich, so their tenants were taught to reason, because they were born under a lucky star; and the poor were poor because the heavens were out of joint when they emerged from the womb. This could be determined by an examination of the eight characters.* An even more potent variation on this theme was belief in geomancy, or the magical influence of burial grounds. The rich prospered, it was said, because their fathers were buried in auspicious places in relation to flanking hills, flowing water, and the prevailing winds. The poor were poor because their fathers were buried in the wrong places. Since the rich, with the help of professional geomancers could often pick their spot while the poor had to be content with whatever sorry ditch they were thrown into, this fate had an inevitability that was hard to beat.

The squires of Long Bow did not leave the propagation of such attitudes to chance. They actively supported all the various ways and means by which "right thinking" could be impressed upon the people. A village school for that small minority able to attend emphasized the study of *The Four Books* and *The Five Classics* of Confucius; operas at New Year's drove home the theme of the contrasting rewards of virtue and vice; a Confucian Association promoted ancestor worship and provided mediums who could converse with the spirits of the dead; a temple society kept Buddhism, with its passive acceptance of fate, alive. In later years the Catholic Church, with its centuries of experience in the defense of European feudalism and feudal remnants, became a most stalwart bulwark against social change.

At the same time Sheng Ching-ho and his peers in Long Bow were not so naive as to believe that the cultivation of "right thinking" alone was sufficient guarantee of their position and property. Sanctions more concrete than the teachings of the sages were needed to maintain the collection of rents and the settlement of debts in Long Bow. A more practical pillar on which the rule of the gentry rested was thus the village government with its power to tax, arrest, flog, fine, and ultimately to execute.

The structure of this government was not complicated. At its apex stood the village head or *ts'un chang*. He was assisted by several staff members: a village secretary who kept accounts, handled correspondence, and issued licenses and documents; a public affairs

---

* According to this method of fortune-telling, one's fate could be determined by a study of the two written ideographs standing for zodiacal signs which ruled respectively the year, month, day, and hour of one's birth.

officer who allocated labor service;* and a village constable who made arrests, administered punishments, and kept the local lockup. None of these positions carried any regular salary, but they placed a man in a position to make a silver dollar by one means or another.

In Long Bow, with its population of close to 1,000, intermediate levels of organization were also deemed necessary. There were three or four *lu chang* or neighborhood leaders and twenty odd *chia chang* or heads of ten family groups.

As a guarantee that the orders of these officials would be carried out, the village maintained a Peace Preservation Corps boasting several dozen rifles shouldered on a part-time basis by chronically underemployed young men who, for a little millet, a few personal favors, perhaps a fix of heroin, and a chance to bully, loot, and rape could be depended on to do the will of the gentry.

From the village head to the ten family leaders all of the officials were locally chosen, but they were by no means chosen by universal suffrage. As a matter of fact, insofar as I could determine, no general election had ever been held at any time for any position in the whole history of the village. The office of village head was simply assumed by one or another of the gentry after consultation with the rest, or was parcelled out, after similar consultation, to some person of lesser means who had earned their esteem. The same method was used in filling the rest of the posts. Once the personnel had been selected they were usually confirmed in office by the district head or the county magistrate who cared not one kaoliang stalk as to their fitness for the work, so long as the local gentry were satisfied with them.

To qualify as a village official one had to be fluent, unscrupulous, ingratiating when dealing with those of superior station and threatening when dealing with poorer and weaker persons. Above all one had to be willing to submit to the whims of the gentry and not feel humiliated when ordered to carry out some business for them.

The peasants had their own less than flattering title for such people. They called them *kou t'ui-tzu,* which means "leg of the dog."

It can be readily understood that such an administration did not serve people impartially. As far as the higher authorities were concerned, the main purpose of the village government was the collection of taxes, the supply of manpower for public works, and the conscription of soldiers. As long as the extremely heavy quotas in these three spheres were met, no one cared how they were distributed. The

---

* Labor service consisted of work on government transport, public projects such as roads and dykes, and gathering and transporting materials for these purposes. Finding food and lodging for dignitaries traveling on public business was also handled under "public affairs."

gentry saw to it that their own obligations were as light as possible. They avoided taxes whenever they could and made up the difference with extra levies on the rest of the population; they sent middle and poor peasants to move earth, build roads, and repair the fortress-like walls of important villages and towns, while they themselves stayed at home; they conscripted their tenants and laborers for the army, while their own sons went to school.

These evasions of public duty were all dividends that came with control over the village administration. More important in the long run was the leverage over the peasants which the power to distribute the quotas at lower levels gave to those in control. There were many ways in which an obstinate peasant could be taught to bow his head. He could be ordered to haul grain for some warlord in the middle of the planting season. His only son could be tied up and dragged off to the army. His deeds could be doctored to cheat him of land. Taxes could be piled on taxes until he went under. The Peace Preservation Corps could "accidentally" march through his crops. He could be entered in the special register reserved for criminals and thieves. He could be discriminated against in the arbitration of disputes.

There were always bitter quarrels among the peasants over the use of privies, the ownership of trees, the exact boundaries of fields, the possession of women, and many other matters. A peasant who was out of favor with the authorities could easily get the worst of any settlement. A minor case, picked at random from the life of Long Bow Village, will serve to show how this worked.

One day a fairly prosperous middle peasant and cloth peddler, Li Pao-yu, found out that his neighbor Hsiao-tseng often slept with his wife while he himself was away buying cloth. Since he was older and much less solidly put together than Hsiao-tseng, Pao-yu complained to the village office. An investigation proved the truth of the complaint. The village head thereupon ordered both the wife and her lover flogged. After the flogging the two were hung by the arms from the gable of the village office for eight hours. Then the village head fined them both several silver dollars. Since his wife had no money of her own, Pao-yu had to pay the fine. Even though Hsiao-tseng continued to consort with the woman, poor Pao-yu never complained again. He didn't want to part with more silver dollars.

To the extent that Pao-yu's wife was actually to blame, a certain rough justice was meted out in this case, but Pao-yu certainly felt that he had been cheated and so, almost invariably, did other peasants who went with complaints to the village office. Without influence one might as well appeal to a mud wall. And so, when disputes arose among the poor, they were usually settled by force. The strong won the day and the weak "ate bitterness." Just so long as the quarrel did not affect the revenue of the gentry, no one in authority cared how unjust the settlement was.

If one peasant could be discriminated against, another could be favored. As a reward for loyal service and good behavior a man could be given light labor service at convenient times. Lucrative contracts for the supply of materials (such as kaoliang stalks for flood control) could be thrown his way. His sons could be passed over as conscripts and left to help with the field work at home or recommended for good positions at the county seat. He could be assured of a sympathetic hearing in case he had a dispute with anyone else.

But even such a system of favors and penalties did not guarantee permanent control of village life. There was always the danger that the patient tortoise might upset the obelisk altogether. Physical force, naked and unadorned, was therefore the third important pedestal on which the power of the gentry in Long Bow rested. Violence was chronic at all levels of human relationship. Husbands beat their wives, mothers-in-law beat their daughters-in-law, peasants beat their children, landlords beat their tenants, and the Peace Preservation Corps beat anyone who got in the way. The only living creatures that could hope to avoid beatings, it seemed, were adult male gentry and draft animals—the donkeys, mules, horses, oxen, and cows that were the basis of Long Bow's agriculture.*

Violence reached its zenith in relations between landlord and tenant, creditor and debtor. The gentry literally held the power of life and death over the peasants and personally carried out whatever punitive measures they deemed necessary when their interests were damaged or threatened. If they caught a thief, he was dealt with on the spot. One famine year a Long Bow peasant child, only six years old, stole some leaves from a tree belonging to his father's employer. The landlord caught the boy, beat him black and blue with a stout stick, and docked his father $12. This amounted to the father's earnings for the entire year. He had to borrow money from a relative to get through the winter and was still paying off the debt a decade later.

In the village of Sand Bank, not far to the west of Long Bow, a poor peasant named Hou took a few ears of ripe corn from the field of a rich relative named Hou Yu-fu. Hou Yu-fu caught the culprit, dragged him into an open yard in the village, had him strung to a tree, and personally flogged him until he lost consciousness. Not long afterwards this man died of internal injuries.

Similar direct action was taken when rent fell in arrears or interest

* Unlike the peasants of Mexico, Spain, Italy, and Russia, the Chinese, at least in my experience, were very tender with their animals.

went unpaid. Then the landlord went in person to the home of his tenant and demanded the grain due him. If it was not forthcoming, he drove the peasant off the land or out of the house. If the peasant resisted, the landlord or one of his retainers beat him.

Should a peasant attempt to defend himself, affairs could easily take a very ugly turn. One Taihang peasant struck back at a landlord who raped his wife. He was hung by the hair of his head and beaten until his scalp separated from his skull. He fell to the ground and bled to death.

Only if the landlord found it impossible to cope with a peasant did he go to the village government for help. Then the constable, who carried a revolver, and a few stalwarts from the Peace Preservation Corps armed with rifles, soon straightened out the matter. Should the local forces prove inadequate the rifles of the whole district could easily be concentrated on one village and if this was not enough, the county magistrate had at his disposal a standing force of several score armed men in permanent garrison.

Little wonder that the peasants seldom resisted the demands of the gentry. They knew only too well what would happen to them if they struck back. In their own experience and in the history of the region there was no lack of precedents.

In most cases involving disputes with peasants, direct action by the gentry, backed up when necessary by the armed forces of the village government, was enough to preserve law and order. But this was not so when the gentry themselves fell out. Since the village head was only their servant, or at best their peer, the most he could do was mediate. He could not impose a solution. When mediation failed there was no recourse but to enter a lawsuit at the county court or *Yamen*. There cases were fought out with a full regalia of lawyers, briefs, counter-briefs, witnesses, and liberal handouts to all and sundry. Public morality being what it was, the family with the most resources, the best connections, and the least scruples usually won. The loser was often punished with a public flogging and, in addition, was required to throw a banquet for the entertainment of all involved, at which time the public apologies were offered that wound up the case.

So ruinous were court cases that most families avoided them like the plague. If they were unable to settle matters out of court, their quarrels could harden into feuds in the course of which each family in the dispute tried to damage the persons and property of the other. To repay an insult or avenge an injury, gangs were organized, beatings administered, crops fired, wells plugged, carts and implements broken, trees cut down, women and children kidnapped, and men murdered.

The impassive mud walls of Long Bow thus harbored a never-ending "war of all against all" which absorbed a great part of the energy of the people and tended to conceal that basic conflict, the struggle between the gentry and the peasants over the fruits of the land, which would eventually overwhelm everything else.

It was this background of corruption, favoritism, influence peddling, and violence that drove many a young peasant into the gangster-type secret societies such as the "Red Rifles" that were endemic in the region. It was this same background that made it possible for certain powerful gentry to organize their own private armed forces, oppress and rob people at will, loot and rape and murder without fear of reprisal, and, when successful, build themselves up into local warlords with power over whole districts, whole counties, and even provinces. Between raids and debaucheries their rifles were always available for the suppression of revolt and many an adventurer built a career and fortune looting and killing under the guise of hunting rebels and, in later years, Communists. Yang Hu-sheng, for many years the warlord of neighboring Shensi Province, and one of the men who kidnapped Chiang Kai-shek in Sian in 1936, started out as a soldier-bandit in command of a small armed detachment.

The gentry who operated gangs on a village or district level were known as *opa* or "local despots." In the 1940's Long Bow had its own local despot, Fan Tung-hsi (son of Fan Pu-tzu), but since his exploits more properly belong to the period of the Japanese War they will be dealt with in a later chapter.

When agrarian revolt flared in isolated parts of China after the suppression of the Great Revolution in 1927, neither the legitimate gangs of the village politicians nor the illegitimate gangs of the local despots were enough to suppress them. Then Chiang Kai-shek introduced additional forms of control into every village reached by his power—the *pao-chia* system of mutual responsibility, and the Kuomintang Party organization.

The *pao-chia* system was a variant of the traditional *lu* (neighborhood) and *chia* (10-family group) system already described. The ten families of the *chia* and the hundred families of the *pao* (the *lu* was an intermediate level) were held collectively responsible for the activities of each and every one of their members. Key individuals were expected to report their neighbors' every move, and everyone was punished when any member of the group was suspected of involvement in revolutionary activity. Mass executions were carried out under the slogan: "Better to kill one hundred innocent people than to allow one Communist to escape."

Shansi was one of the provinces where a reign of terror was instituted along these lines in the 1930's. Many peasants were seized and killed in Lucheng County and young men dared not leave home to look for work for fear of being picked up as agitators. Taking a defiant attitude or wearing a red scarf was enough to cause suspicion.

Since family and class loyalties tended to be far stronger than any loyalty to national or local government it is doubtful if the *pao-chia* system was very effective in rooting out subversion. A much better instrument for this purpose was the Kuomintang Party, which recruited as members young gentry such as Fan Tung-hsi and built with their aid a counter-revolutionary political force able to gather intelligence, expose suspects, and co-ordinate activities over a wide area. Around this hard core of diehard gentry were gathered teachers, students, officials, and persons of normal ambition in public life. For such people as these a Kuomintang membership card was obligatory.

In Long Bow most of the leading gentry and their "dog's legs" were Kuomintang members. They agitated in favor of that peculiar blend of nationalism, fascism and Confucianism immortalized by Chiang Kai-shek in his book, *China's Destiny*, maintained strict thought control over all village life, and mobilized the landlord class for a showdown with the rising peasant revolution.

The ruthless way in which the slightest defiance on the part of tenants and laborers was suppressed over the years created in the peasants a deep, almost instinctive, reluctance to mount an attack against the power of the gentry. Revolt after revolt had been crushed during 20 centuries of gentry rule. Those who raised their heads to lead them had either been bought off or had had their heads severed. Their followers had been cut to pieces, burned, flayed, or buried alive. Gentry in the Taihang proudly showed foreign visitors leather articles made from human skin. Such events and such mementos were a part of the cultural heritage of every peasant in China. Traditions of ruthless suppression were handed down in song and legend, and memorialized in the operas which were so popular everywhere.

It is no wonder, then, that only the most severe provocation could overcome the peasants' great reluctance to act, and set them in motion. But once in motion they tended to extremes of cruelty and violence. If they struck, they struck to kill, for common sense and millenniums of painful experience told them that if they did not, their enemies would inevitably return another day to kill them.

The extreme and often misdirected violence of peasant uprisings in China was an indication of certain basic weaknesses in the peasants as a political force, weaknesses which were cultivated anew in each generation by the very nature of the fragmented, small-holding, peddlers' economy in which they were all reared.

The first of these weaknesses was an all-pervading individualism engendered by the endless, personal struggle to acquire a little land and to beat out the other fellow in the market place. Peasants individually driven to bankruptcy viewed economic disaster not as a social but as a personal matter, to be solved in isolation by whatever means came to hand. This essentially divisive and selfish approach made co-operation between peasants on any level other than the family extremely difficult, greatly increased the leverage of the gentry's divide-and-rule tactics, and made inevitable the corruption of a certain percentage of peasant leaders who, when they found a way out themselves, abandoned their brothers.

A second crucial weakness was the lack of vision that arose directly out of small-scale production with its rudimentary division of labor and indirectly out of the cultural isolation which this type of economy, with its limited market, imposed on the community. Of the great waves of political, cultural, and scientific thought that broke on China's shores in the early twentieth century scarcely a ripple reached such inland villages as Long Bow. The peasants heard little provincial, less national, and almost no world news. Less than one person in ten could read. Completely absorbed in crop production, family life, and the desperate battle for daily survival, they were true victims of the "idiocy of village life."

As victims of village idiocy the peasants had little opportunity to learn of large-scale production and the potential abundance that it offered mankind. Their idea of the good society was one in which everyone had a plot of land, a roof overhead, clothes to wear, and wheat dumplings to eat. The equalitarianism they dreamed of was noble, but it was also utopian—there being no conceivable way in which every family could enjoy a prosperous life on a long-term basis as long as production was atomized by small private holdings and cursed with primitive technique. Even if all the means of production could be equally divided, what was to prevent the old process of differentiation which had originally produced landlord and tenant from producing them all over again?

Only a new set of social and productive relations could break through the vicious circle, release China's productive power, and open the road to a prosperous future. But of new sets of social relations, of other modes of production, the peasants knew nothing, could imagine nothing, and hence had no beacons to guide them in any search for liberation. They were in the position of a man trying to survey the sky while imprisoned at the bottom of a well.

The despair of men standing up to their necks in water coupled with the ignorance engendered by a "well-bottom" view of social relations led inevitably to impetuosity in action—a third great weakness of the peasants. Because they so desperately wanted a way out they deluded themselves about the difficulties involved. They thought in terms of short, drastic action to divide existing wealth rather than the "hundred-year great task" of releasing and creating new productive forces through a fundamental transformation of society. Therefore, when they did act, they were not prepared for two or three years, not to mention decades, of bitter struggle and were easily discouraged when revolt did not quickly bring any improvement in their situation. Armed uprisings almost always ended in a self-defeating, Robin-Hood-type banditry because the peasants did not see the need for, or were unwilling to undertake, the long hard mobilization of the whole laboring population that alone could transform society and bring about their liberation. A temporary, partial victory could elate these roving insurgents, but a minor defeat could plunge them into black despair, and even cause them to abandon the campaign altogether.

Mao Tse-tung, long before he became chairman of the Chinese Communist Party, catalogued the weaknesses exhibited by peasants as revolutionary soldiers. Among them were:

(1) The purely military viewpoint—a tendency to regard fighting as the only task of the army; avoidance of such political tasks as educating and organizing the mass of the people, arming them, and helping them to establish their own political power. Without this political work the whole fight lost its meaning and the revolutionary his reason for existence.

(2) Extreme democracy—aversion to discipline, each commander and each soldier going his own way in a carefree manner.

(3) Absolute equalitarianism—a demand that everyone be treated alike regardless of circumstances; opposition to extra rations for wounded soldiers, horses for officers who had to travel, lighter loads for older persons and the sick, etc.

(4) Subjectivism—holding opinions and voicing criticisms without a realistic examination of the facts and without regard for political principle; basing opinions on random talk and wishful thinking; focusing criticism on minor issues, petty defects, and personal quirks. All of these could only lead to mutual suspicion and unprincipled quarrelling between people.

(5) Individualism—vindictiveness, cliquism, the mercenary viewpoint; holding oneself responsible to individual leaders rather than to the revolution as a whole; hedonism—an urgent desire for personal comfort and pleasure, a longing to leave the hard life of struggle and find some softer spot.

(6) The idea of roving insurgents—military opportunism, avoidance of hard political organizing in favor of "hiring men and buying horses"; living off the land like any ordinary bandit.

(7) Adventurism—acting blindly regardless of conditions and the state of mind of one's forces; slack discipline on the one hand but corporal punishment and the execution of deserters on the other; attempting to enforce rather than to inspire loyalty to the cause.*

The gentry of Long Bow were well aware of these weaknesses of the peasants. They played on them to prevent any challenge to their rule before the Revolution began and counted on them to disrupt the Revolution once it got under way.

* Mao Tse-tung, *Selected Works*, New York: International Publishers, 1954, Vol. I, pp. 105–115.

5

The Teaching of the Lord of Heaven

What would you say if I sent bonzes and lamas to preach in your country?

Emperor Ch'ien Lung

In 1916 the outward calm of Long Bow Village was disrupted by unprecedented activity. Long lines of carts hauled grey bricks from kilns in many parts of the county and unloaded them in the village square. Local contractors hired masons from as far away as Wuan and Hantan, at the edge of the Hopei plain, to lay the brick. Slowly, in the very center of the community, a large Gothic-style church arose—the first architectural innovation in a thousand years. A tall, square tower that thrust above every other structure in the neighborhood topped the church and served as a landmark that could be seen for miles around. This tower would have made Long Bow unique had it not been for the fact that even taller, more ostentatious towers were constructed in other nearby villages at about the same time—at Kao Settlement, Horse Square, and South Temple, to name but a few.

These churches were built under the direction of Catholic missionaries from Europe who established a firm base in Lucheng County in the late nineteenth and early twentieth centuries and converted a significant minority of the peasants to their faith. No analysis of the dominant forces in Long Bow in the decades preceding the Revolution would be complete, therefore, without a description of the *T'ien Chu Chiao* or "Lord of Heaven Teaching" brought by these fathers. Though the Church did nothing to modify the land system or the landlord-tenant relationship based on it—on the contrary, it reinforced them by its teachings, and by becoming a landholder in its own right—it did serve as the opening wedge for Western influence. By disrupting and dividing the community, demanding special privileges for its converts, engendering cliques and counter-cliques, imposing humiliations on civil and religious leaders alike, it won for itself the bitter hatred of the majority outside the Church. Its influence, even after it disappeared as an organized force, was deep and lasting.

The first missionaries arrived in the Taihang Mountains in the de-

cade after 1840, following the defeat of China in the First Opium
War. They were Italian Franciscans. In the latter part of the nineteenth century these Italians were reinforced by French and Dutch
priests of the same order. From all that I could learn in Long Bow, it
was the Dutch who concentrated in the Shangtang region and built
the mission in Changchih to which the church in Long Bow was a
satellite.

The Franciscan fathers, once they gained admission to the region,
went vigorously to work; they bought land, built buildings, brought
in Catholic converts from other areas, and set up small Christian
communities. Through the Chinese Christians as intermediaries, rather
than through preaching or evangelism, they hoped to reach out to the
local people and eventually establish entire Catholic villages and even
Catholic counties.

With each defeat suffered by the Ch'ing Dynasty at the hands of
the Western powers, greater and greater concessions were granted
to the Catholic missionaries, all of whom, regardless of nationality,
were under French protection. The French government lost no opportunity to win special privileges and powers for foreign priests,
which enabled them to influence the population around them more
effectively and to gain converts.

The treaties forced on the Chinese government by the Second
Opium War (1856–1860)

placed not only missionaries, but Chinese Christians under the aegis of
foreign powers. This gave to the converts a certain assurance of protection
and stimulated the numerical growth of the church. The provision had,
however, implications and results which were, to say the least, unfortunate.
It tended to remove Chinese Christians from the jurisdiction of their
government and make of Christian communities *imperia in imperio,* widely
scattered enclaves under the defense of aliens.*

Missionaries usurped the powers of civil officials over their converts; and it was not surprising to find that

Catholic missionaries interfered from time to time in lawsuits in which
Christians were one of the parties. Sometimes a mere gesture from a
missionary—a visit or his card—was enough to obtain a decision in favor
of a convert, for the official did not wish to become embroiled with
foreigners who, through their consuls and ministers, could make trouble
for him with his superiors. It is not strange, then, that individuals and
families and even entire clans and villages professed conversion in the
hope of obtaining support against an adversary.**

* Kenneth Scott Latourette, *A History of Christian Missions in China,*
New York: Macmillan Co., 1929, p. 279.
** *Ibid.,* pp. 309–310.

Nor was it so strange that by the end of the nineteenth century "the confusion between the Christian religion and European politics had become inextricable. The missionaries profit from Europe's armed might and suffer from the hatred it arouses."*

In 1899, under French pressure, an imperial rescript was issued which granted to Catholic bishops—all of whom were foreigners— equal rank with regional viceroys and provincial governors, and to foreign priests equal rank with provincial treasurers, provincial judges, and county magistrates. This only confirmed and made official a practice which had been growing since 1860. Bishops had long flaunted official buttons, caused cannons to be fired when they arrived in town, had an umbrella (a Chinese sign of rank) carried ahead of them, and issued proclamations in forms similar to those used by officials.**

Such factors as these, at a time when the great powers were quite openly preparing to divide up China, led the peasant rebels of 1900 —the Boxers—into anti-foreign and anti-missionary action.

Shansi Province, under Governor Yu Hsien, was one of the storm centers of this revolt. In the Shangtang area Catholic churches were sacked, Catholic priests and their Christian converts killed, and Catholic property seized.

Due in part to the treachery of the Empress Dowager, who pretended to back the movement while at the same time encouraging foreign intervention to crush it, and in part to the spontaneous, poorly organized nature of the Boxers themselves, the rebellion failed.† A joint expedition of eight powers marched to Peking, sacked the city, and forced on the government a treaty which demanded, among other things, the execution of various leaders of the rebellion, 450 million silver dollars in indemnities and the death penalty for any Chinese who joined an anti-foreign society in the future.

Overnight the situation in the Shangtang was reversed. From almost complete rout, the Catholic missions came back stronger than ever. Over two million dollars of the indemnity money was turned over to the Franciscans in Changchih and they began to build churches, settle Catholic believers, and win converts on an increasingly large scale.

In the two decades that followed the Boxer Rebellion, 57 churches

---

* Chanoine Leclerq, *La Vie du Père Lebbe*, as quoted by Simone de Beauvoir, *The Long March*, Cleveland: The World Publishing Co., 1958, pp. 400–401.

** Reid, *Sources of Anti-Foreign Disturbances in China*, as quoted by Latourette, *A History of Christian Missions in China*, p. 55.

† For a Chinese interpretation of the role played by the Empress Dowager, see Hu Sheng, *Imperialism and Chinese Politics*, Peking: Foreign Languages Press, 1955, p. 141.

were built in Lucheng County alone—along with rectories, nunneries, seminaries, and orphanages. Enormous compounds of brick and stone rose from the ground. With this "renaissance" the church threatened to become the dominant community organization in the region. For many years people dared not openly oppose what the church initiated, carried on their Buddhist rites in secret, and lived in fear of exposure to the priests.

It was during this period that the huge church in Long Bow was built. Even before the structure itself was completed, a concerted drive for new membership was launched by the Dutch fathers. This drive, as it was described to me by villagers who remembered it, took many forms.

First, the Church brought in Catholic families from villages where larger Christian communities existed. Some of these families were recruited locally, and some came from as far away as the Hopei plain. These immigrants were settled on land belonging to the Church or its auxiliary organizations, or on land of local gentry who had been converted. Thus the nucleus of Catholics in Long Bow was greatly enlarged. Second, the Church used charity to attract new members. Reliable Catholics who had stood by the Church during the rebellion received four ounces of silver per person from the Boxer indemnity funds. Similar favors in the form of money and grain were handed out, especially in poor crop years, to those who would agree to enter the Church and study its doctrines. In this way many poor people in desperate need were drawn into the fold.

A third great source of recruits was the orphanage that was housed in an extensive complex of buildings adjoining the Church. Because the peasants lived from year to year on the verge of starvation and in bad years often died themselves, it was impossible for them to raise all their children. Boys, when they grew up, stayed home to help support their parents. Therefore every effort was made to save them. But girls, after 12 years of feeding, could only be sold for a few bags of grain, or given in marriage for the equivalent of a few dollars. Therefore in times of distress girl children were sometimes abandoned or even killed at birth. The orphanage in Long Bow was built specifically to care for such abandoned children. From picking up babies in the streets and fields, the custom developed of accepting babies directly from their parents, or even of paying modest sums for girl children in order to encourage their mothers to part with them. Once they become the property of the orphanage, the infants were farmed out to wet nurses, in some cases their own mothers, until old enough to eat millet. They were then reclaimed by the Church to be raised as Catholics.

At a very early age these girls were put to work cleaning, cooking, and sewing. Certain products of their labor were sold on the market to provide a source of income for the orphanage and the Church.

Having paid their way by long hours of toil—the older girls often worked up to 12 or even 14 hours a day—the young women were betrothed in their early teens to local peddlers, traders, peasants, or soldiers in return for a substantial remuneration. This not only helped the Church financially, but also insured new converts and a younger generation brought up as Catholics. For in order to obtain a wife from the orphanage the husband had to promise to become a Catholic, and any children resulting from the union were automatically pledged to the faith. Since the orphanage was the main source of unpromised brides, and since its prices were about one-third lower than the average in the region, many poor peasants who wanted to get married had little alternative but to buy a Catholic wife.

If the operation of the orphanage created ill will and distrust, the economic activities of the Church sharply aggravated this feeling. The institution through which the financial affairs of the Church in Long Bow were handled was called the *Chin Hsing Hui,* or "Carry-On Society." This was ostensibly a charitable organization set up after the 1911 revolution to help fellow Christians in distress. The Catholic peasants were taught that by contributing to it they would earn merit in the eyes of God and get to heaven faster after death. When members of the group died all the Catholics in the village prayed for their souls. Those who did not join got no such support in the after-life. Many poor peasants contributed a coin or half a coin to this venture. In the beginning the total capital was about three *ch'uan* (altogether about one-third of a silver dollar). By loaning this money out at high interest rates amounting to 30 percent a month, the Society made money, bought land, and acquired land through default on loans. By the late 1930's the Society owned 30 acres of land, collected rent from 25 tenant families, and extracted interest from another 32. It was the largest single landholder in the village.

Loans from the Society were given out with a written contract that was standard for the whole region and included many oppressive clauses not ordinarily stipulated by landlord-usurers. Article Six of this contract forced any debtor who was in default to pay the travel fees of the collectors who came to demand the money. The fee demanded was ten cents for every ten *li* (three miles) traveled, plus room and board if the trip involved an overnight journey. (Lest anyone wonder why there should be travel fees for collecting Long Bow loans, it should be explained that this was for loans made from the central office at the Cathedral in Changchih.) The seventh article called for an additional five percent per month interest on all defaulted debts, and this interest was compounded.

Of the 32 families in Long Bow who owed money to the Society in its last years, three were forced to sell all the land they had in order to clear their debts. Another three sold their houses. The Society occupied by force the land of another three. Other families sold sons, daughters, and draft animals to pay off their debts.

Since the Society, as a religious institution, paid no taxes on the land it owned, the tenants had to pay all levies demanded by the various government bodies in addition to the heavy rents. Rents to the Society varied over the years, but ran as high as a bushel of wheat for each *mou*—something like 50 percent of the crop. Catholics could rent land more cheaply than non-Catholics. They paid one eighth of a bushel less per *mou* per year. Tremendous pressure was exerted on all tenants and borrowers to become members of the Church.

For the wealthy landlords and rich peasants of the village the Society served as a sort of bank. They could put funds into it and draw 15 percent a month in interest. The advantage of this was that they could get their money out at any time instead of only after the harvest or at the approach of the new year as was the case when loans were made to individual peasants. Sheng Ching-ho, Fan Pu-tzu, and the other leading landlords all had sums invested in the Carry-On Society. It thus had the backing of the landlord group as a whole. The peasants, for their part, had a different name for it. They called it the "Peel and Pare Society." ("Peel and pare" is the literal translation of the word "exploit" in Chinese.)

Charity was the professed aim of the Society and charity it always practiced. For one thing, it gave ten bags of grain each year for the support of the church orphanage. This was by no means enough to keep the orphanage going, but as we have seen, it had other sources of income.

Various Catholic laymen managed the affairs of this profitable charitable society over the years. In the decade prior to 1945 the manager was a man named Wang Kuei-ching. He began life as a poor laborer, but from the day he took over the affairs of the Carry-On Society, with the backing of the leading gentry, he prospered mightily. The foreign fathers dealt with no outsider directly. Whenever they had any business to do they called in Wang Kuei-ching. All they knew about the village and the community they learned through him. Thus, Wang became a power to be reckoned with and a man to be feared. He himself tilled the best land owned by the Society. It was rumored that he got 50 percent of all interest on loans. Whether this was true or not he most certainly got a commission on all transactions that passed through his hands, and this included not only the business of the Carry-On Society but all the financial affairs of the

Church as well. He was the business manager for the whole institution, holding the key to the safe and letting the contracts for new construction. It was common knowledge that he kept eight percent of the wages of those who built the church buildings. But this was not enough for him. When the construction was over, he managed to carry home such valuable items as the steel cable used on the hoist.

Society Chairman Wang made use of his key position in the Church to extend his influence both inside the hierarchy and in the realm of politics. His eldest son, Wang En-pao, was early recruited into the Kuomintang Party and in the 1940's became its district secretary. A second son became a Catholic priest. A daughter became a nun.

In handling the financial affairs of the Society and the Church, Wang Kuei-ching was ruthless. Hu Hsueh-chen, a poor peasant woman, was allowed to borrow a hundredweight of grain from the Society in the spring, for which she had to pay 1.2 hundredweight in the fall. It was a dry year and her whole crop amounted to less than she borrowed. Society Chairman Wang seized everything that she had grown, including the poor beans she had planted between the rows of corn, and left her without any food at all. She had to go into the streets to beg soon after the harvest.

During the famine year this same woman went to Chairman Wang's door and asked for something to eat. "I am poorer than you," he said as he picked bits of his last meal from between his teeth with an ivory toothpick. "You had better get out of here." With that, he kicked her from his entry and closed the gate in her face.

Wang was as hard on his poor relatives as he was on everyone else who had too little to invest in his Society. A cousin named Hsiu Feng worked for many years in his household as a maid servant. He cheated her of her wages and gave her very little to eat. During the famine year she was forced to sell her own children and look for work as a wet nurse in another village. But Society Chairman Wang told everyone that he fed and cared for her over the years out of the kindness of his heart.

Wang knew all the traditional methods for cheating the peasants and was noted far and wide for the practice of them. When he loaned out millet it was full of dirt and chaff, but when, after the harvest, he came to collect the rent or interest due he asked for pure, clean millet. He winnowed and rewinnowed it until only the big, full kernels were left. The millet he loaned out he measured with a small bushel measure, but the millet he took in he measured with a large measure.

When Wang loaned out money he first subtracted a month's interest so that if one borrowed 30 dollars one actually received 20 dollars, but paid interest, after the first month, on 30. Emergency loans were more expensive. Wang charged as high as 10 percent per day compounded. He never loaned money to landless persons. He invariably demanded land as security, and when, because of the high interest rates, the poor borrower defaulted, the land changed hands as surely as autumn gave way to winter.

The Carry-On Society was not above using the special legal power and privilege possessed by the mission to add to its holdings. For decades half an acre of irrigated land adjacent to the Church had been tilled as public property and the proceeds used for education, charity, and other community needs. In 1925 the Society tried to buy this land for the Church and turn it into a vegetable garden. The people of the village refused to sell. Then Fan Ching-ch'eng, a land-lord and leader of the Catholic minority, began a campaign of slander against the non-Catholic majority. He persuaded a young co-religionist named Chang Kuo-chi to claim the land as his inheritance. One night Chang's father was found cutting a tree on the land. A crowd gathered to stop him. The Catholics turned out in force to protect him and a pitched battle ensued. Into the fray stepped Fan Ching-ch'eng as mediator. His solution, presented a few days later, was to sell the land to the Church.

This so angered the people that 900 of them walked all the way to the *Yamen* at Lucheng to protest and petition for the return of the land to the village. Under pressure from the mission and fearful of repercussions should the foreigners be angered, the county magistrate ordered soldiers to drive the petitioners away. Deserted by their own government they had nowhere to turn. The Church took the land without payment. As far as the mission was concerned, the incident was closed, but the people did not forget so easily.

Nor did peasants like Wang Ch'eng-yu forget the long years of abuse they suffered at the hands of the Church and its Carry-On Society. The story this land-poor peasant told me was certainly very one-sided, but I report it here as he remembered it. His memory was bitter.

Before the turn of the century Wang Ch'eng-yu's father rented land in Horse Square, one mile north of Long Bow. He was a Buddhist in a village that boasted a large Catholic mission and a Catholic majority. He may well have taken part in the attack on the Church that marked the Boxer uprising. In any case, when the Rebellion was crushed, he fled to avoid persecution at the hands of vengeful Catholics. Hunger finally drove him back to Horse Square. The priest ordered him arrested. He was strung up and beaten. He decided to move to Long Bow where the Church was not so powerful. But the priest in Long Bow called him in and said, "Wherever you go you must be a Christian, for if you do not join the Church you will be taken for a Boxer and you will suffer for it." In the end, without food, land, or house, he accepted relief from the Church and was listed thereafter on its roster of members. The relief during this period consisted of one silver dollar a month—a fair sum in those days.

This peasant had four sons. His brother had four daughters. He swapped with his brother—a son for a daughter. Both he and his wife became very fond of the baby girl but found it difficult to support four children. The church orphanage then stepped in with an offer of aid. The parents turned the girl over to the orphanage. The orphanage, in turn, left the little girl with her mother to be nursed, fed, and care for, and paid a small subsidy for her support. There was one condition that had to be met—the arrangement was valid only as long as the girl's parents faithfully followed the teachings of the Church.

Summer that year came in hot and dry. People brought large offerings to the Church and the priest said many masses to bring rain, but no rain fell. Then Wang Ch'eng-yu's father sought out the Buddhists. He wore a green willow branch on his cap and took part in the Buddhist rites that were supposed to bring rain. When the priest of the Church found out about this he cut off all relief from the family and took the girl back to the orphanage. Her mother wept bitterly and pleaded with the priest, but he said they had broken the agreement and could no longer be trusted with the girl. The mother believed that her daughter was mistreated in the orphanage, grieved a great deal over her loss, and died soon afterwards. Her sons were convinced that she died of grief.

When Wang Ch'eng-yu grew up, he managed to save a little money. With it he bought some land. This land was mortgaged to the Carry-On Society as security for a $35 loan that enabled him to marry. Crops were bad that year. In order to pay the $15 of interest on the loan, he had to sell his wife's wedding ornaments, all her clothes, and the winter's supply of grain. Hardship and grief finally drove his wife insane. The priest said many masses for her, but it did no good. All the neighbors said she was haunted by the spirit of a monkey. When Ch'eng-yu finally managed to save up a little money again, he gave it to the Buddhist group in return for rites which were supposed to drive the monkey spirit out of his wife. The rites were no more effective than the masses. The priest heard about the attempt and sent Society Chairman Wang to punish Ch'eng-yu for his breach of faith. "You have betrayed Christianity," said Chairman Wang. "By calling on the Buddhists you betray God himself."

Wang Ch'eng-yu was dragged into the churchyard and beaten. He thought, "My wife has been driven mad and now I am beaten by the Church. I don't want to live any longer." But since he didn't want to commit suicide either, he lived on to pay many a tithe to the Church.

Although the kind of fear and persecution which Ch'eng-yu suffered gradually simmered down as the memory of the Boxer Rebellion faded, the Church became so powerful that Buddhist leaders like Sheng Ching-ho, men who in their own right lorded it over the rest of the village, found it expedient to curry favor with it. This landlord and political boss cultivated good relations with the Catholic fathers, dined with them often, invested money in the Carry-On Society, and co-operated in many projects initiated by the Church.

All the power of the Church and all its efforts to convert Long Bow to Catholicism failed in the end. The Catholics remained a minority group, never numbering more than a quarter of the population. In 1940, after a hundred years of missionary work in the region and approximately 40 years in the village, there were altogether 64 Catholic families out of a total of 257. This was slightly more than a fifth of all the households.

It should not be concluded that these 64 families were all Catholics against their will, or that they remained in the Church simply out of expediency, because of pressure, favors, the right to rent church land, or to buy a wife from the orphanage. Regardless of how they originally entered the Christian fold, many became sincere believers and passed on to their children as devout a faith as any existing in the world. By its impressive ritual, by its forceful doctrine, by dispensing a certain amount of charity, by raising a loyal younger generation in its own orphanage, and by emphasizing its precarious minority position, the Church built up in its converts a cohesion, a unity of interest and purpose that deeply affected many of its members. It also set them apart from the rest of the community and thereby won them the scorn and often the hatred of the majority of their countrymen. Because Catholic privilege was built and maintained under the protection of foreign gunboats, because Catholic construction was paid for out of funds extracted from all the people by armed aggression, because Catholic converts were exempt from collections to support local religious rites and age-old customs, Catholicism had been known as "the agents' religion" for a long time. During the course of the next decade the Church in the Shangtang further consolidated this reputation and set the stage for its own demise.

Important as the Catholic Church became in its heyday, it was never more than one facet in that complex of social relations and natural conditions which fashioned the reality of the times for Long Bow. By the second quarter of the twentieth century these relations and conditions had reduced Southern Shansi to a nadir of rapacious exploitation, structural decay, chronic violence, and recurring famine which has few parallels in history; they had also rendered the region and the country of which it was a part all but incapable of effective defense against aggression from without, a circumstance that was duly noted by the warlords of Japan.

6

Invasion

And now lies burnt
Our eastern capital.
No use saying two
Can defend the pass against one hundred,
For everywhere there is wavering.
As for our northern defenses,
Built in the time of ancient kings,
Who dares ask if they have been maintained?

Tu Fu

SUDDENLY all the dogs in Long Bow began to bark.

The fierce cacophony startled the young mother Hu Hsueh-chen. She sat in the dilapidated shed where her husband had abandoned her and wondered where she could go that day to beg enough food for herself and her two children.

"Why do the dogs make such a row?" Hsueh-chen called out to her neighbor, Ch'ou-har's wife.

Through the doorless aperture that was the only entrance to her home, the answer came clearly back.

"The Japanese devils have come!"

Hsueh-chen ran to the courtyard gate to see if the alley was still free. If so, she would call her children and flee to the open fields until nightfall.

She was too late.

The Japanese column had already turned the corner. No sooner did she step into the street than a soldier looked up, broke ranks and started after her. Hsueh-chen fled inside her own hovel and ducked to the left. The soldier ran past her into the room. He knocked down her six-year-old son, stepped squarely on the little boy's hunger-swollen stomach, then plunged on into the back room hoping to catch his mother. Hu Hsueh-chen did not wait for him to come out. She ran to the next house and hid.

When the soldier, cursing his luck, left the courtyard, neighbors found Hsueh-chen's boy lying unconscious on the floor. He regained his senses, but on the next day fell ill with fever. Four days later he died. On his deathbed he cried out over and over again: "Mother, the devils are coming, the devils are coming!"

****

The all-out drive that brought the Japanese Army into the hamlet of Long Bow in the summer of 1938 began in July 1937 at Lukuo-chiao, just outside Peking. There a detachment of Chinese soldiers had the temerity to resist some Japanese on "maneuver" who demanded the right to search a village for a missing compatriot. This violation of the peace of "Greater East Asia" provided the pretext which Hiro-hito's legions had been waiting for. When Chiang Kai-shek refused to accept Japan's conditions for settlement of the dispute, the Japa-nese army confidently resumed the conquest of all China which it had begun in the Northeast in 1932.

Discounting the possibility of massive popular resistance, the Japanese generals determined on classic blitzkrieg tactics. With the overwhelming forces already gathered in East Hopei, where they had earlier wrung from Chiang the right to station troops, they quickly smashed the poorly-armed and too often traitorously-led armies that stood in their way and drove south and west down the main trunk railroads into the heart of the country.* For a year all went well. They occupied most of the Chinese cities well known in the West—Peking, Tientsin, Tsingtao, Shanghai, Nanking, Hankow, and Canton—and, with the exception of the Hankow-Canton line, most of the railroads and highways that connected these cities.

Japanese strategists took it for granted that control of the cities, the railways, the whole modern communications network, would bring them control of the countryside thus enmeshed and surrounded. This was a serious error. While their mechanized armies pushed on tri-umphantly into Central China, a resistance movement grew up be-hind them. This resistance soon confined the conqueror's effective control to the cities and the narrow railroad corridors between them. Before any further conquests could be made, before any real plums could be plucked from the conquest of the North, Japan had to wipe

---

* When in 1937 the Japanese invaders advanced southward to attack Shantung, Han Fu-ch'u, the Kuomintang warlord who ruled Shantung, re-treated all the way to Honan without fighting a battle. He was executed by Chiang Kai-shek for treason as was another general, Li Fu-ying. Liu Chih, a warlord commanding Chiang Kai-shek's personal troops in Honan, was re-sponsible for the defense of the Paoting area in Central Hopei. He also fled. For other instances, see Chalmers A. Johnson, *Peasant Nationalism and Com-munist Power*, Stanford: Stanford University Press, 1962.

out the guerrilla fighters in her rear. Large numbers of combat troops had therefore to be recalled from far-flung battlefronts to "pacify" rural areas already "conquered." Thus began a fierce and prolonged military struggle—the famous stalemate stage of China's "Protracted War" (1939-1944).

In this fierce contest, the Taihang Mountains inevitably became a most savagely contested region, for the Taihang Mountains dominate the North China plain, which in turn provides the main base, marshalling ground, and granary for any drive southward. As long as the Japanese were unable to clear the mountains, their hold was never secure in the lowlands, and all their efforts in other parts of the country, even in other parts of the world, were greatly hampered. Chinese armed groups from bases in the mountains went down into the flat country, crossed the Peking-Hankow railway and set up new bases in the swamps and lakes of Hochien and the roadless cotton lands of South Hopei. When hard pressed, the regular forces withdrew behind the Taihang's formidable ranges while the plains people carried on their resistance underground.*

It became a matter of life and death, therefore, for the Japanese to clear the mountains. The first major effort to do this consisted of a drive to cut the Taihang range in half. After taking Taiyuan, Warlord Governor Yen Hsi-shan's provincial capital in 1938, a part of the Japanese Army pushed through the mountains to Changchih and then drove eastward through Lucheng and Licheng toward Hantan on the plain. But even though a second column simultaneously marched westward into the mountains from Hantan by way of Wuan, the two forces were never able to link up. A guerrilla offensive destroyed one motorized column in a deep mountain gorge. Ambushes and man-made landslides slowed down the other column. Snipers took a continuous toll both of the marching troops and of the garrisons they left behind. In the end the drive bogged down. The remnants of both columns withdrew—in the East to Wuan, in the West to Lucheng. The latter small walled city thus became the last garrison point on the western flank of the Taihang Mountains to be held by the invaders.

Even though the Japanese Army garrisoned Lucheng and with

---

* In the flat country the "underground" was not simply a figure of speech. There actually were large areas where the peasants connected villages to each other with tunnels dug through the deep silt soil. When the enemy occupied one village, people escaped through these tunnels to the next. Dry wells, horses' troughs, sleeping platforms—every ruse and camouflage that a people fighting for its life could devise—were used to hide the exits. In 1948, when I walked on foot through this region, the remains of these tunnels were still very much in evidence. Many people I talked to had fought in them.

the help of a series of blockhouses, controlled the highway leading
out to the county town of Changchih, they did not control more
than a fraction of Lucheng county's rural villages. A guerrilla government operated throughout the highlands. Guerrilla troops and
their supporting militia moved at will through occupied territory,
and even into occupied villages at night. In order to protect the
Changchih-Lucheng highway, flanking villages such as Long Bow had
to be occupied and fortified. Long Bow itself thus became the last
permanently garrisoned outpost on the road to Yellow Mill, a mining
town at the base of the mountains. Outside the village one stepped
into no-man's land, and only a few miles away Chinese-controlled
guerrilla territory began. Long Bow was thus established as a fortified point on one side of a narrow finger of occupied territory thrust
across the flat from Changchih toward the higher ranges of the
Taihang.

Having failed in their efforts to cut the mountain bases in half,
the Japanese used their occupied salient as a jumping-off point for
punitive raids against the regions they were unable to conquer. Three
times they launched major "Kill All, Burn All, Loot All' campaigns.
Throughout whole counties dwellings were razed or burned, livestock slaughtered, implements smashed, wells plugged, and people
driven back and forth across the hills and plains like hunted herds.
Tens of thousands were killed outright; hundreds of thousands
starved. Only those who had buried their grain in advance and who
hid in secluded mountain gorges or caves until the enemy left survived. When on top of this man-made carnage, drought and flood
unleashed the silent killer famine, the suffering became indescribable.
Even the Japanese found it hard to live. They increased their pressure
on the occupied villages, wrung the last peck of grain from already
starving peasants, slaughtered the draft cattle for meat, and dismantled
houses for the fuel in the timbers of the roofs and doorways. In desperate need of garrison forces and fortifications, they press-ganged
the able-bodied into puppet units and labor gangs. If the guerrilla
areas suffered the flames of hell, the occupied areas suffered the tor-
tures of purgatory.

In these times of terrible trial, every person and every human
institution was put on the rack, and the quality of the metal from
which they were made was ruthlessly tested. Under this stress two
main political trends developed: resistance and collaboration.

7

Collaborators

Even the dung beetles are arrayed
With beautiful wings of gauze.
So think I in sadness when I see
Our officials decked out in such splendor.
With our country in imminent danger
Where shall we find refuge?

The Book of Odes

WHEN THE Japanese army drove into the rural districts of the hinterland, the most conspicuous men in every community were, of course, the leading gentry who headed the village administrations and ran the economic, social, and religious institutions. The Japanese took it for granted that these people would not resist, and for the most part they were not disappointed. After all, the leading gentry had the most property to lose in any annihilation campaign. They dared not mobilize and arm the peasantry for fear that these armies would someday turn against them. When the chips were down, when they were forced to choose between collaboration and, resistance, they often found that they had more in common with the invaders than they had with their own tenants. At least the Japanese officers shared their own respect for private property, the sanctity of land rents, and the importance of orthodox religious worship.*

The resulting collaboration, to be sure, was not always straightforward and direct. The people of the Taihang region had a saying about the occupation politics of landlords—*liang t'ou hsiao, chung chien ch'u* or "thin at the ends and wide in the middle."

As the Japanese moved in, the gentry retired from public life, not knowing how long the enemy would stay and therefore not wanting to identify too closely with them. During the middle period they

* In the first flush of victory in North China, the Japanese looted everything in sight and slaughtered peasant and landlord alike, thereby driving many landlords into the ranks of the resisters. But later on the Japanese found common ground with many gentry and worked with and through them to maintain traditional "law and order."

collaborated actively and openly, believing that the Japanese would
be around for a long time, if not forever. At the end, with Russia's
armies driving Hitler back to Berlin, with America winning victories
in the Pacific, and the popular forces in the mountains growing
stronger day by day, they retired behind the scenes again, aware
that a change was in the making. As soon as the Japanese surrendered, they came out of "retirement," reorganized village affairs, and
applied the name "Anti-Japanese Village Government" to their administrations in an effort to cash in on the fruits of victory.

The gentry of Long Bow were no exception to this rule. When
the Japanese troops were still beyond the hill, Sheng Ching-ho relinquished public control of the village office. The Catholic landlords, Fan Pu-tzu, Shih La-ming, and Wang Lai-hsun, then set up
a new administration using as a front man one Chou Mei-sheng, a
capable and clever middle peasant who was willing to play their
game and turn a tidy penny in the process. Chou Mei-sheng was appointed secretary to the village government and became notorious
as the chief of staff of the whole puppet regime, a position which
he held for seven long years. Mei-sheng, in turn, picked a poor
peasant, Shang Shih-t'ou, as village head and staffed his office with
two more poor peasants—Kuo Fu-kuei as head of the police, and
his brother Kuo Te-yu as head of public affairs. All these positions
continued to pay off handsomely with graft and loot. The gentry were
openly represented in this set-up only by Wang Lai-hsun, who served
as a street captain for four years, and Kuo Ch'ung-wang, the rich
peasant who worked closely with Chou Mei-sheng in the village
office. No serious decisions were taken, however, without consultation between the members of the ruling clique as before.

In Long Bow Village the duties of this government were the same
as those of any previous administration—to collect taxes, organize
labor service, conscript soldiers, and maintain "law and order." The
chief difference was that this time the demands were heavier and
the enforcement more brutal. Now when the village officials went
to collect grain, Japanese or puppet soldiers went with them. Entering each courtyard in turn they threw bags on the ground and demanded that the peasants fill them up. If they brought along two
bags, the family had to fill two; if they brought three bags, the
family had to fill three. The collections were not based on how much
land or how big a crop the family had harvested, but on how much
grain the enemy wanted to collect. Anyone who had no grain had to
run away before the collection began or face serious punishment.

Labor service, made many times heavier by the demands of war,
became a burden no less onerous than taxes. Whenever there was

work to be done—a road to be built, a fortification to be constructed, supplies to be transported—the word went out to the village office and the peasants were ordered to report for service no matter what urgent task they themselves were engaged in. The only ones who never went were the gentry and the village officialdom.

In 1943 a fort was built by conscript labor at the north end of Long Bow on the edge of no-man's land. Every able-bodied male in the village had to go and dig. One poor peasant, Wu-k'uei, was just at that time putting a new roof on his own hut. He did not want to stop while he had no roof overhead, so he hired a young boy to go in his place. For this he was arrested, beaten until an arm and a leg were broken, and left lying in the newly dug moat that surrounded the fort. A group of his neighbors had to beg for permission to carry him home.

The fortification was so large that Long Bow Village labor was not enough to complete it. People were ordered there from other villages as well, some from two, three, or even ten miles away. They had to get up before dawn in order to get there on time. They had to feed themselves. Anyone who worked slowly or made mistakes was beaten and thrown in the moat. Since the water was not deep, they did not risk drowning, but it was nevertheless a cruel punishment because the weather was cold. Victims had to climb out and go on working in a wind that froze their clothes and brought pneumonia and death to many.

The labor service demanded by the Japanese was not always so close to home that the conscripts could walk back and forth each day. When the enemy decided to build a railroad from Taiyuan to Changchih, young men were rounded up from many counties. From hundreds of villages each family had to send one person. Landlords, however, sent their hired laborers instead of their own sons. This was the first time any of these wage workers had ever been considered a part of the family.

The conscripts, quartered in huts behind barbed wire, were marched to the building site under guard, and made to work 14 or 16 hours a day. Every detail of their lives was regulated, even the length of time for passing water. The men soon learned to wet as large an area as possible, whenever they had to urinate, for a small spot on the ground was regarded as proof of malingering and could lead to a beating. If anyone slowed up the pace while at work, he was tortured in ways invented on the spot by the guards. One of these was to make two men stand face to face and strike each other. Anyone who didn't strike out with all his strength was promptly beaten by the guards.

Chinese guerrillas sometimes came near. Whenever the guards heard shots, they swept the whole countryside with machine gun fire. In their panic they killed more than one of the laborers who happened to get in the way. "In the evening when we returned to our huts we laughed and congratulated ourselves that we still lived," said one survivor as he told me of those days. "But every morning as we went to work before dawn we trembled for what might happen that day."

The wholesale terror of the labor gangs, calculated as it was to strike fear into the heart of every peasant, sowed hatred of the conqueror far and wide. The offhand brutalities—such as the wanton killing of Hu Hsueh-chen's little son—and the incidental havoc wrought by the occupation burned this hatred even deeper.

One such incidental cruelty accompanied the expropriation of the land on which the fort at Long Bow was built. It was confiscated from an old man named Wen Tui-chin, called Lao (old) Tui-Chin by everyone in the village. He had inherited part of his meager holdings from his father. Another part, on which stood a house of 12 sections, he had bought only two years earlier with the savings of a lifetime of labor in Sheng Ching-ho's distillery. In the enclosure around the house he had planted 30 trees.

One day in July 1942, Shang Shih-t'ou, the puppet village head, called Old Tui-chin in and told him his house had to be removed to make way for the fort. He gave him a week to tear down the structure or to sell it to someone who would. Before Tui-chin had time to do anything about the house, the labor gangs were ordered to begin work on the moat. He had to offer the structure to whoever would buy it at whatever price he was willing to pay. At that point—was it quite by coincidence?—three members of the puppet administration and the landlord Sheng Ching-ho suddenly stepped in, offered him 50 silver dollars per section, and tore down the house. But after they had hauled away the bricks and the timbers they paid him only half the price. They took his fruit trees for nothing. Old Tui-chin did not dare complain.

The site of the fort included his half-acre of crop land. On it he had planted millet that was already ripe for harvesting. He never had a chance to reap it. Puppet soldiers came in the evening, staked out the lines of the fort, and trampled his ripe grain into the mud. He begged them to wait until morning so that he could rescue his coming winter's food, but they asked him, "Can you guarantee our safety tonight?" Afraid of the Eighth Route Army, they wasted no time digging in. Old Tui-chin received not one coin of compensation for all the land and the grain that he lost. He had to flee to his nephew's home in South Temple to avoid starvation.

The village administration of Long Bow was more than usually effective as a recruiting office for the puppet armed forces. This was because several Long Bow men with long-standing ties to the dominant faction were among the commanders of the local puppet forces. Shih Jen-pao, a son of the landlord Shih La-ming, was an officer of the Fourth Column of the puppet garrison of Lucheng County. Shen Chi-mei, a middle peasant and erstwhile henchman of the "dog's leg" Chou Mei-sheng, commanded the puppet security police of the Fifth District. Ch'ing T'ien-hsing, also of Long Bow, assisted him. Between them they were able to impress about 50 young men into the puppet forces as rank-and-file soldiers and policemen. These forces were used not only to garrison Long Bow itself, but also to hold down several nearby communities.

The above-named puppet leaders did not enter the service of the enemy in the first days of the occupation. On the contrary, when the Japanese entered Shansi, they were officers of a Nationalist army detachment commanded by Fan Pu-tzu's son, Fan Tung-hsi. Fan Tung-hsi and Shih Jen-pao were brothers-in-law by parental arrangement. They were also schoolmates. Together they graduated from middle school in Taiyuan, won a reputation as intellectuals, and, what was more lucrative, commissions in the provincial armed forces under the over-all command of Governor Yen Hsi-shan. Since every ambitious officer who wanted to advance his career had to build around himself a loyal group of supporters, they naturally recruited Long Bow men as assistants.

When Yen's old-style provincial armies crumbled before the Japanese advance in 1937, many units remained more or less intact and retreated into the hinterland. The unit officered by Fan Tung-hsi and Shih Jen-pao found its way back to Lucheng County and made the Fifth District its main base.

As long as Yen himself kept fighting they carried on a resistance of sorts, but when Yen shifted his policy to one of limited collaboration with the Japanese in return for aid in fighting the guerrillas who were carrying through social reforms and successfully organizing and arming the people for all-out war, his erstwhile officers had to make a choice. They either joined the guerrillas and accepted their program, or they worked out a *modus vivendi* with the Japanese. Fan Tung-hsi chose the latter course. Being no match for the Japanese Army that moved into the valley behind him, he avoided battle, was allowed to hold certain hilly areas unmolested, and set himself up there as a petty tyrant. His unit gradually disintegrated into a band of armed marauders—living off the land, robbing, looting, killing, and raping in the best tradition of Chinese militarism.

When Fan Tung-hsi's troops needed grain, they descended on the villages in the valley and made collections in the name of the central government. In the famine year of 1942, when the puppet administration had already squeezed out all the grain that could be found in Long Bow and many people were already near death from hunger, Shih Jen-pao and Shen Chi-mei led over a hundred men into the village. Under cover of darkness they went from house to house, searched every courtyard and seized much grain that had until then been successfully hidden. They made off that night with many cartloads of corn and millet. Almost a third of the people later died of starvation.

When not looting villages, Fan Tung-hsi's men preyed on commerce. They considered merchants on the highway fair game. One day they attacked 13 freight-laden carts traveling the road from Lucheng to Changchih. They threw the carters into a mountain gully, killed them with stones, and made off with their goods and mules.

They also had their way with local women, courting all who took their fancy. Those whom they could not win over with gifts and favors they forced into submission with threats and beatings. If their men resisted they dispatched them without mercy. In mid-winter Fan Tung-hsi raped a young woman in Li Village Gulch, a settlement three miles south of Long Bow. The girl's fiance enlisted in the Japanese military police in order to get arms for revenge, but before he could carry out his plan he was ambushed in Long Bow, thrown into a dry well, and buried with rocks.

In Tung-hsi's command was a man named Mao Tan who secretly courted the leader's own favorite of the moment. Tung-hsi shot him in the back for his temerity.

Shih Jen-pao was equally ruthless. He seduced the wife of one village leader and later tracked the man himself into the mountains and killed him. He fired at, but missed, another man whose wife he had raped. He beat his own sister-in-law so brutally that everyone said he was responsible for her death.

Fan Tung-hsi, Shih Jen-pao, and their henchman Shen Chi-mei were particularly ruthless in dealing with their political enemies, the underground resistance forces that had progressive leanings. Many times they attacked small groups of guerrilla fighters when the latter were under the most severe pressure from the Japanese and least able to fight back. When they sacked a village for loot, their excuse always was that the place had been infiltrated by Communists.

By such acts as these the Long Bow trio won a well-deserved reputation as "local despots." Had the Sino-Japanese War been a conflict of the traditional type, Fan Tung-hsi might well have become a powerful warlord in his own right, but in this war new social forces, forged in the fires of national resistance, made a traditional warlord career difficult, if not impossible. Fan Tung-hsi himself was killed by a detachment of guerrilla troops that included Long Bow men. Soon thereafter the group he had commanded took the final step to complete betrayal by going over, lock, stock, and barrel to the Japanese. With this move they sealed their fate.

When the ex-soldiers turned bandit went over to the enemy, they were reorganized as part of the Fourth Column of the Lucheng County Garrison, with Shih Jen-pao as commander. Simultaneously, Shen Chi-mei was appointed head of the district security police. He specialized thereafter in hunting down resistance leaders; responsible for the death of many people, he grew to be one of the most hated men in the valley.

The defection at Lucheng was by no means an isolated incident. In the later years of the Anti-Japanese War, years that were characterized by a stalemate on the regular battlefronts, the surrender to the Japanese of whole units intact with their arms was arranged over and over again by high ranking Nationalist officers. "The number of Kuomintang commanders above the rank of major general who put their troops under Japanese command was 12 in 1941, 15 in 1942, and 42 in the peak year, 1943. By early 1944 more than 60 percent of the puppet armies, then numbering about 425,000, was composed of former Kuomintang elements."* In the Taihang Mountains General P'ang Ping-hsun, Commander of the 24th Group Army, went over with all his troops in May 1943, and was appointed Commander-in-Chief of the Shansi-Hopei, Honan-Shantung Communist Extermination Army as well as of the 24th Group Army of Peace and National Salvation.

These shocking defections, which increased as world-wide victory over fascism approached, were part of a planned "Trojan Horse" strategy conceived by Chiang Kai-shek's high command as the only means by which the Kuomintang could regain control of North China and the Yangtze Valley from the resistance forces when the war ended. Certain that victory would eventually be won by the hard fighting and sacrifices of the Allied Forces, particularly the Americans, Chiang and his clique turned their attention to the question of postwar control of China. With the approval of their own high command, unit after unit of the Nationalist Army went over to the enemy and took up garrison duty at strategic points where they would be in a position to take over control of all the occupied areas once the Japanese were finally brought to their knees by forces outside China.

---

* Israel Epstein, *The Unfinished Revolution in China*, Boston: Little Brown and Company, 1947, p. 317.

This was euphemistically called "national salvation by a curved path."

As far as Chiang's strategists were concerned, the Fourth Column was but a small pawn in this devil's chess match, but in Lucheng County the men of the Fourth Column made up a formidable force. With their knowledge of the terrain and their intimate ties with the local people, especially the gentry who ran the occupied villages, they made the occupation many times more oppressive and ruthless than it might otherwise have been.

The whole collaboration apparatus in Lucheng County and in Long Bow—the commanders of the Kuomintang irregulars-turned-puppet, the gentry who stood behind the puppet village government, and the middle and poor peasants who staffed it and did the dirty work—was made up of Catholics. From the time that the Japanese arrived until they were finally routed in August 1945, Long Bow Village had a solidly Catholic administration under the dictatorship of the Japanese.

This make-up of the village administration and the puppet forces was not unusual. There seemed to be a definite correlation between collaboration and Catholicism throughout the Taihang and in the Catholic strongholds of Central Hopei. This, after all, was only the continuation of a situation long prepared by the methods through which these Catholic missions spread their influence and established their position in the first place. From the very beginning, as we have seen, Catholicism had advanced in China under the protection of foreign powers. During the Japanese War the tone for collaboration was set by the highest Church authorities, the hierarchy of the Cathedral in Changchih, the largest town in the area, and the hierarchy in Hsingtai, the largest city on the plain at the foot of the mountains.

To cite but one example: A leading priest, Father Kuo Lo-ts'ai, on his return trip from America in 1938, stopped off in Japan and obtained a letter of introduction to the Japanese ambassador in China from the Ministry of Foreign Affairs. This letter carried instructions to all whom it might concern to give special care and attention to the bearer. It was apparently effective for, upon his arrival in China, Father Kuo received a universal travel permit from the Japanese military headquarters and was permitted to move freely all over North China. After the Japanese surrender, more than 100 travel blanks of the kind issued only to top Japanese military personnel and civilian administrators were found in his effects together with many snapshots of his venerable personage standing with leading Japanese officials and the chief puppet of the Hsingtai area, one Kao Te-ling.

One reason for the shift to a Catholic administration in small

centers such as Long Bow was the universal belief that the invaders
would respect the sanctity of the Church, if not from fear of God, then
at least from respect for the foreign powers that stood behind that
Christian institution. A measure of safety was thus seen in Church
membership and in good relations with the local priest and his en-
tourage. Events confirmed this presumption. As they moved into the
interior the Japanese troops did not, as a rule, enter churches. Therefore, on the eve of the arrival of the Japanese soldiers in Long Bow,
most of the wealthy of the village and many of the poor took their
valuable possessions to the Church for safekeeping. Many of them
asked for personal protection as well. The local priest, quick to sense
the full potential of the situation, coined the slogan, "protection for
those who are members; no protection for those who are not." To save
themselves and their property, quite a few families joined the Church
within a few days. Even so, the protection afforded the poor was
minimal. Landlords and rich peasants and their families occupied all
the available shelter, and most of the poor who crowded into the
open courtyard, whether they were Catholic or not, were finally turned
back into the street.

Those who remained did not get protection for nothing. While
landlords and officials found the facilities of the Church open to
them as a matter of course, it was understood that as a token of gratitude the poor would give 20 percent of all the property they brought
with them to God.

After Pearl Harbor, the Dutch fathers of the mission all left, or
were removed from the occupied regions. Then Father Sun, the
Chinese priest who took over in their place, tried once more to swing
the whole village into the Catholic fold. One day all the gentry of
the village were invited to a Western-style banquet in the rectory.
At the end of the feast the father called on his guests to help make
every peasant a Church member. He argued that since the Church
had given sanctuary when the Japanese came, they should show their
gratitude and faith in God by joining it themselves and recruiting
others. Members of the Carry-On Society then went from house to
house, smashed all the ancestral tablets and clay idols that they found,
threw their remains into the deep outdoor toilets, and hung up
pictures of the Virgin Mary. In one day every house in the village
took on the trappings of Catholicism. Those who protested were
scolded and told, "If the Japanese return in force you will not be
allowed into the Church, and if you are killed that is your fault. We
shall not care and we shall not come to your rescue." Many of the
pictures were later torn down without dire consequences, but the
people never forgot this attempt at religious coercion.

8

Seeds of Change

Taihang mountains, high, oh high!
One hundred times ten thousand men
Take up the cry.
Young men of the soil
Fear not shell or knife.
Each shot we fire
Takes an enemy life.

                              Song of the Taihang Militia

SHANG SHIH-T'OU, the figurehead of the puppet administration, did not sleep easily at night. In spite of the hundred-strong Japanese garrison so close at hand, in spite of the expanded Peace Preservation Corps pledged to support his regime, in spite of the efficient police work of his henchman Kuo Fu-kuei, he was afraid of the people. Someone in the village—he had no idea who—was in touch with the resistance forces in the mountains. Every so often Shang Shih-t'ou found a stone lying in his courtyard with a letter wrapped around it. The letter described everything he had done in the previous few weeks, warned of swift and terrible retribution unless he changed his ways, and advised him to go to a designated spot for a conference with a certain Commander Liu to discuss ways of helping his country and atoning for his treason.

Shang Shih-t'ou never went to the suggested rendezvous. He had no intention of risking his lucrative career as village head by contact with hairbrained patriots who were probably atheistic Communists. To be on the safe side, however, he never slept at home at night, nor did he ever sleep in the same place twice in a row. Should guerrilla fighters raid the village looking for him, they would have a hard time finding him. This plan worked well enough until his wife became suspicious. She refused to believe that he never came home at night because he was afraid of assassination. An aunt of hers had told her that Shang spent his nights gambling, drinking, and carousing. The aunt mentioned at least three mistresses that Shih-t'ou had been known to sleep with and hinted that there were several more in other villages. This information so infuriated Shih-t'ou's wife that she went to the village office and denounced him in public. She also denounced him to her pastor, Father Sun. She told everyone she met on the street that her husband never came home because he spent his nights with "broken shoes" (prostitutes).

There was, of course, some truth to these rumors. In order to silence his wife, Shang Shih-t'ou was forced to stay at home several nights in a row. On his own *k'ang* he slept hardly at all. He started at each sound. He rose and looked around several times each night. Each time he found nothing. The village lay absolutely still under the stars. Everyone, including the Japanese soldiers and their sentries, was asleep. On the third night, worn out with fear and taut nerves, he finally fell asleep in spite of himself.

He woke as he was dragged from his wife's side by several strong hands. When he tried to scream, a piece of cotton was jammed into his mouth. He fell to the floor, felt a gun barrel in his back, and dared not move while his assailants bound him tight. He heard a stifled scream as they also bound and gagged his wife. Then he was half dragged, half carried through the courtyard to the street. Someone ordered him to kneel down. He knelt. A single shot rang out in the stillness, followed by the muffled sound of cloth-shod feet running up the street. The footsteps gradually receded. But Shang Shih-t'ou did not hear them fade out. He was already dead.

The execution of Shang Shih-t'ou paralyzed the puppet regime for several weeks. All the leading officials knew that such a bold raid could never have been carried out without an underground organization in the village itself. Even in broad daylight they hardly dared step outside Japanese headquarters for many days thereafter. The arrogant Japanese feigned unshaken confidence, but belied it by doubling the men on guard duty and carrying out extra security checks at night.

The peasants, on the other hand, could hardly conceal their delight. Had it not been for the fact that the least sign of jubilation could bring arrests, beatings, perhaps even executions, they would have demonstrated in the streets. The landlords and their running dogs had shamed the whole village by taking the road of collaboration for whatever security, comfort, or profit this despicable path had to offer. Here now was dramatic proof that there were patriots in Long Bow who chose instead the path of resistance in spite of all the dangers and hardships that guerrilla war and underground activity made inevitable. The execution of Shang Shih-t'ou redeemed the village not only in the eyes of its own inhabitants, but before the whole county, and with this act the process of revolutionary transformation in Long Bow began.

****

It is one of the great ironies of history that the warlords of Japan, who insisted *ad nauseam* that they were "intervening" in China only to build prosperity in "Greater East Asia" and save the Chinese people from a fate worse than death—Communism—greatly hastened by that very intervention the triumph of the Communist-led Revolution.

The Japanese conquerors cleared the ground for revolution in many ways—by the extreme brutality of their tactics, which left not only the peasants but many gentry as well no choice but to fight; by driving the higher levels of the Kuomintang bureaucracy and army out of North China; by enticing the lower levels of this same bureaucracy and army into collaboration in the occupied zones, thereby compromising them permanently in the eyes of the people; and by leaving in the wake of their conquering armies extensive areas of countryside which they were unable to garrison. Into the political and military vacuum thus created, the Communist Party and the armed forces under its direction were able to move.* Within a very short period of time, they mobilized tens of millions of hard-pressed peasants for resistance, and that resistance, by reaching out to all strata of society, laid the groundwork for the social revolution to come.

Within a few days after the Japanese began their attack at Lukuochiao in 1937, detachments of seasoned troops from the Communist-led Workers' and Peasants' Red Army (known as the Eighth Route Army from the time of the United Front Agreement with Chiang Kai-shek in 1937) left Yenan in North Shansi, crossed the Yellow River, and took up positions in both the Taihang and the Wutai ranges of Eastern Shansi. These detachments, small as they were, did not cluster in one place but split into numerous armed working groups that filtered through the advancing enemy lines and spread out into the valleys, the plains, and the villages of every region to organize, train, and direct the great influx of peasant recruits that soon came seeking weapons and instructions. Each working group thus surrounded itself with detachments of peasant militia who lived at home, tilled their fields during the daytime and the summer season,

---

* For a description of how the Communist Party arose in China and how it came to be in a position to fill vacuums in North China, see Edgar Snow's *Red Star Over China*.

and fought during the night and the off season. From among the best fighters and leaders of the militia, recruits were drawn to replace those killed and wounded and to expand the growing regular forces.

The mushroom-like growth of the Eighth Route Army and its supporting militia was paralleled by the growth of the Chinese Communist Party which counted among its members most of the Army commanders and recruited steadily among the most active of the rank-and-file soldiers. But the Communist Party did not confine itself to military mobilization alone. When the veterans of the ten-year Civil War crossed the Yellow River, hundreds of civilian organizers came with them to do political work. Under the protection of the Eighth Route Army they too fanned out into the rural villages and organized the Peasants' Associations, the Women's Associations, the consumer co-operatives and the village councils that became the mass civilian base for a miltary effort that could not succeed without the support of the overwhelming majority of the population. The best, the most active leaders of these groups were recruited into the Communist Party to form local branches made up, in the main, of working peasants. Into the Party also were drawn many students, intellectuals, and professionals from the cities who crossed the battle lines by the thousands to join the resistance.

Wherever the Eighth Route Army and the Communist Party found a foothold the disintegration resulting from defeat, panic, and the flight of the old officialdom was stopped. Out of chaos order was gradually restored. Wherever possible the remnant armed forces of the Kuomintang were regrouped and brought under unified leadership. Most important of all, as a result of these measures the Japanese were driven from or denied access to the area unless they came in great strength, in which case the resistance forces temporarily retreated, only to flow back again when the Japanese wave receded.

From the first small pockets these resistance bases reached out to encompass whole counties. These counties in turn were linked into chains and systems to form extensive Liberated Areas, or Border Regions.

In the Liberated Areas new anti-Japanese resistance governments were set up by a coalition of parties and social forces that included patriotic Kuomintang elements and many outstanding individuals who belonged to no party. These governments were staffed by people from all walks of life, including landlords. Democratic elections were held to choose representative assemblies at the district, the county, and the regional level; and these assemblies, in turn, chose executive officers to carry out their will. Even though the Communist Party was the main organizer and leader of this movement, it limited its own members to one third of all elective and appointive posts.*

The leaders of the Liberated Areas governments, Communist and non-Communist alike, set as their task the full mobilization of the Chinese people's potential for resistance against Japan. This potential could only be realized if the peasants were given an alternative to the exploitation and oppression of the past. Without real improvement in the conditions of tenure, rates of interest, distribution of taxes, and the right to bear arms, and without a voice in the making of policy, the peasants could not be mobilized to fight effectively. Nevertheless, to advocate at that time a thorough revolution in social relations, the expropriation of the landlords, and a new system of land tenure would have led to disaster. For such a revolution could only mean civil war, could only drive the landlords wholesale into the arms of the Japanese and split the nation at a time when unity alone could save it. The Communist Party therefore abandoned the "Land to the Tiller" program which had prevailed in its old South China bases and joined with other parties and groups in a program of reforms designed to win the support of all factions and classes. The heart of this program was the "Double Reduction"—reduction of rents and reduction of interest rates.

The landlords were asked to reduce rents by at least 25 percent and to scale down interest rates on loans from 30 percent or even up to 100 percent a year to not more than 10 percent. These requests were based on a law passed by the Kuomintang government in 1933. The peasants, who by virtue of the arms in their possession, could have stopped payment of rent altogether and repudiated their debts, were asked to pay these reduced rents and interest charges and to produce as much as possible in support of the war. According to the principle, "He who can give labor should give labor and he who can give money should give money," a system of differential taxes was introduced exempting those with the lowest income from any taxes at all and scaling the rates upward for each income level to reach a maximum of 30 percent for the large landowners. These policies were effective in arousing the enthusiasm of the peasants and were accepted by the majority of the gentry in the interest of national salvation.

On the basis of such policies the Communist Party, the Eighth Route Army, and the Liberated Areas expanded year by year. By 1942, they became such a threat to Japanese control that the enemy concentrated most of its expeditionary force in an attempt to wipe

* See Michael Lindsay, *American Magazine,* March 31 and April 14, 1944.

out the North China bases. The annihilation drives of that year and the following year reduced the Liberated Areas and destroyed part of the Eighth Route Army, but not all of it. Japan was unable to keep up the pressure, and as soon as it was relaxed the process of growth began again. By 1945 the Taihang Region, which surrounded Long Bow Village, was but half of a larger entity known as the Shansi-Hopei-Honan Liberated Area, and this in turn was but one of eight Liberated Areas in North China. To these must be added the 11 smaller areas in Central and South China created by the New Fourth Army and the South China Anti-Japanese Brigade, making a grand total of 19 Liberated Areas containing approximately 100 million people, defended by a regular army of one million troops, a militia of more than two million, and a self-defense corps of ten million.*

****

The morale, the fighting experience, and the organizing ability which the Eighth Route Army and the Communist Party brought to Lucheng County in 1937 met an immediate response. Within a few days after the first detachments reached the area dozens of recruits showed up. At least two of them were from Long Bow Village— 19-year-old Shih Ts'ai-yuan, son of a prosperous middle peasant, and 18-year-old Chao Yin-kuei, a landless hired laborer.** In the short period that remained before the Japanese Army arrived, Communist political organizers joined local leaders of the "Dare to Die Corps" (a progressive resistance movement sponsored, during United Front days, by Yen Hsi-shan) in setting up an Anti-Japanese county government.

By the time the Japanese troops marched into the county seat, the walled town of Lucheng, units of the Eighth Route Army were already well established in the highlands and the new government had already mobilized a large number of villages for resistance. When the enemy moved in, the leading personnel of the administration

---

* The New Fourth Army, created out of units left behind when the main forces of the Workers' and Peasants' Red Army pulled out on the Long March to Yenan, filtered behind the Japanese lines on both sides of the Yangtze River and created Liberated Areas there along much the same lines as the Areas in the North. The South China Anti-Japanese Brigade, organized by Communists in Kwangtung, established bases on Hainan Island and in the mountains near Canton.

** Before the Japanese surrender in 1945, another four men followed these two so that Long Bow Village could boast altogether six Eighth Routers, a fair record for a village not only occupied but also fortified.

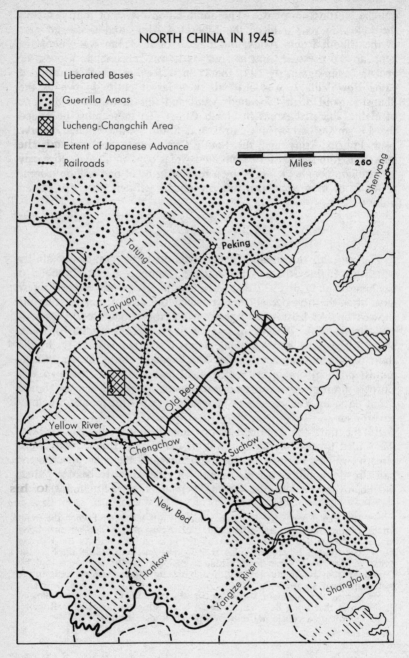

NORTH CHINA IN 1945

Liberated Bases

Guerrilla Areas

Lucheng-Changchih Area

Extent of Japanese Advance

Railroads

0   Miles   250

Shenyang

Tatung

Peking

Taiyuan

Old Bed

Yellow River

Chengchow   Suchow

New Bed

Hankow

Yangtze River   Shanghai

simply moved out into the countryside, set up offices in whatever village proved safest at the moment, and kept on working.

A district leader was appointed for each of the five districts of the county. Like the county government, the district offices were mobile and were popularly said to reside in the district leaders' dispatch cases as they walked from village to village.

Long Bow Village lay in the fifth and southernmost district, the most heavily garrisoned part of the county. There the enemy garrisons were a serious obstacle to organization, but while their rule was supreme during the daylight hours, the foreign soldiers and their puppets withdrew to their headquarters after dark, afraid of snipers and sudden ambush. It was then possible for other forces to come and go. By organizing at night the people of the Fifth District, like those of the other four, were able to build up a resistance government, and maintain a district leader, a secret Communist Party Committee, and a militia.

In certain occupied villages such as Little Gully, only three miles from Long Bow, the puppet village chairman was in touch with the resistance movement, worked under the direction of the Fifth District leader, and did what he could to support the war against Japan. He served the puppet government in name only. Through such men contacts were made with courageous peasants in other occupied villages, thus establishing and maintaining an underground network under the very noses of the Japanese.

Long Bow Village, with its seven-sided blockhouse, its garrison of 100 men and its Catholic-staffed puppet administration was the most dangerous spot of all in which to work; yet Long Bow too developed an active core of underground workers. The first of these was Chang T'ien-ming, the poor nephew of the village head of Little Gully. Though 20 years old and eligible, he was still a bachelor and lived alone.* His father, a Peking blacksmith, was dead. His mother had left home in a famine year and settled with her other son, a carpenter, in Hungtung, 40 miles to the west. Left behind in Long Bow, T'ien-ming cultivated the lone family acre, hired out to his landlord neighbors for seasonal work and did a little carpentry on the side. With nothing to keep him at home after sunset he often visited his uncle in Little Gully and there met the district leader, learned about the anti-Japanese work that was being done, and volunteered to do some himself.

At about the same time, another Long Bow peasant, the hired laborer Shen So-tzu, got in touch with the district leader through a

* Most Taihang young men were married before they were 18.

relative who headed the resistance government of Ku-yi, an unoccupied village five miles to the north. Shen So-tzu, in turn, enlisted
the help of his close friend Kung Lai-pao, a youth as destitute and
as eager to strike a blow for liberation as he was.

A fourth man was contacted by still another means. This was
Shih Fu-yuan, younger brother of Ts'ai-yuan who had enlisted in
the Eighth Route Army when its first brigade appeared. As a regular
soldier Ts'ai-yuan roamed far afield with his unit but he always returned to his Lucheng base, and when he had a chance, came home
to visit his father, his mother, his two brothers, and their wives and
children—altogether a family of ten. They shared a courtyard that
boasted 25 sections of housing, farmed eight acres of land, and were
considered to be one of the most prosperous laboring families in the
village. Since they had no connection with the dominant clique, their
prosperity made them the victim of every looting soldier and every
hungry official. The taxes they paid were endless in number and
suffocating in amount. The whole family hated the old regime and
doubly hated the puppet apparatus that succeeded it. Before he
returned to his unit Ts'ai-yuan told Fu-yuan how to reach him in
the mountains in case of need. Several times Fu-yuan made the trip,
and it was while visiting his brother at Eighth Route divisional headquarters that Fu-yuan met the district leader. A few talks with the
latter were enough to convince him that he should work actively
against the Japanese. Put in touch with Shen So-tzu, he soon joined
the other three who were already at work.

At first the underground group performed modest tasks, running
errands for the District Office, delivering messages and helping transport supplies; but in 1942, the year of the great famine and the most
terrible mopping-up campaigns, the Fifth District leader decided to
strengthen the work in Long Bow by organizing a regular underground administration. The group met and chose Shen So-tzu as
village head, Kung Lai-pao as vice-leader, Fu-yuan as public affairs
director, and T'ien-ming as director of public security, i.e., police
and counter-intelligence. This group of young men, all of them under
25, worked in the strictest secrecy. They told no one that a resistance
government had actually been organized. Only their most trusted
friends and relatives were mobilized to carry out the various tasks
which they set themselves or which the district set for them. Nevertheless they did too much not to attract attention, were eventually
betrayed, and did not all survive the war. What inspired them to
take such risks? Why did they remain in the village where they could
be seized and killed at any moment when they might with equal
honor have joined the regulars in the mountains and fought with

guns in hand? There at least a man had a chance to fight and run and live to fight another day.

I never discovered the answer to this question. The survivors of the Long Bow underground who afterwards told me of its exploits seemed to regard it as the most normal thing in the world for them to have done. People were needed for the work in the occupied villages. They lived there and did the work. If things got too hot they could always leave for the hills—if they could get away. If they needed help they could always call on the Eighth Route Army—if there was time.

There is no doubt that the enthusiasm of a resistance movement nation-wide in scope inspired them to acts which they would not otherwise have undertaken. That they passionately believed in the liberation of China and in the new society which they saw coming was proven by their deeds. But they were reticent about such things and much preferred action to talking of it afterward.

A most important aspect of their work was the collection of food and clothes for the Eighth Route Army. Once, after weeks of careful preparation, they collected 60 hundredweight of grain from sympathetic families and carted it all away in one night. They followed this up with repeated collections of clothing and shoes—articles made especially for the front by women of the village who sat sewing in the open street day after day. The strutting sentries in the pay of the Japanese never knew that the shoes put together within reach of their hands were destined for the feet of their enemies.

An equally important task was the collection of intelligence. This was T'ien-ming's specialty. He kept close watch on all the activities of the enemy troops and the puppet government. Every few days he met with an Eighth Route liaison man either at his uncle's home in Little Gully or on Great Ridge Mountain south of Long Bow Village. There he had a small plot of land that he could visit without suspicion. When he had something to report he made a little pile of stones, and one day later at an agreed time the army man always appeared.

T'ien-ming passed on to him whatever he or the others learned about troop movements, the numbers in the fort, how many horses they had, how much grain, whether they could be easily taken, who came to Long Bow from other places, what they did there, who were the important collaborators, and whether they could be won over.

He took back with him to the village news of the resistance in other places, reports of victories on far-flung battlefronts and of the extension of Liberated Areas to new regions, and news of the outside world where, according to the puppet press, all trends pointed toward victory for the "Greater East Asia Co-Prosperity Sphere." He also delivered the letters which the puppet village head, Shang Shih-t'ou, found lying in his courtyard. It was the hope of the Fifth District leader that Shang Shih-t'ou could be persuaded to co-operate with the Anti-Japanese government just as T'ien-ming's uncle was doing in Little Gully. But the letters, as we have seen, elicited no response.

When the Fifth District leader found that Shang Shih-t'ou could not be weaned from his treasonous course, he reported the matter to the county government. The Long Bow puppet leader was tried in absentia and sentenced to death. A detachment of Eighth Route soldiers was assigned to carry out the sentence. Several times they entered the village at night, but were unable to find where the condemned man slept.

T'ien-ming then thought of a way to bring him home, at least for a while. He personally got in touch with Shang Shih-t'ou's wife's aunt and encouraged her to spread the rumor about Shih-t'ou's nocturnal doings that led to his capture.

A tip from T'ien-ming also brought to an end the career of the marauding Kuomintang commander, Fan Tung-hsi. Not wishing to foment civil war, the Eighth Route commanders had left Fan Tung-hsi's forces more or less to themselves. They hoped eventually to persuade them to join the liberation struggle. But as time went on and Tung-hsi's crimes increased, the peasants of many communities demanded that something be done. One evening Tung-hsi brought ten men into Long Bow for a night of carousal. Word was quickly passed to the hills. The Eighth Route Army sent a squad on the double. In the early hours of the morning they surrounded the house where the men were staying. When Fan Tung-hsi refused to surrender, they fired the whole courtyard. Fan Tung-hsi and his ten colleagues burned to death. It was shortly after this that the rest of the detachment, under Shih Jen-pao, surrendered to the Japanese and were incorporated into the puppet Fourth Column.

In between collections of grain and clothing, the gathering of intelligence, the frequent trips to the hills, and the backbreaking work of making a living from Long Bow's hard soil, the young men of the underground took what time they could to study politics. The county leaders regarded them as the nucleus for the future transformation of the village and hoped to develop in them a revolutionary consciousness. In the Liberation Areas beyond the reach of the enemy this was done by daily study in every armed unit, every government office, and every mass organization. Regular schools were also set up where outstanding fighters and workers were sent to learn political theory. For underground workers such organized instruction was much more difficult. The best they could do was talk with the district leader whenever there was an opportunity and learn from him about the protracted war they were fighting, the united front of all classes that made it possible, and the New Democracy which Mao Tse-tung predicted once victory was won. The district leader also gave them the writings of Mao Tse-tung on these subjects. None of them was able to read well but they worked through them as best they could. In this way they made their first acquaintance with such basic concepts as classes, the importance of labor as the source of wealth, stages in the development of society, and the necessity of land reform as the key to China's future.

The development of the peasants' political consciousness did not proceed very far. The war intervened. In 1943 the village leader of Ku-yi, their main contact, was killed. So was the underground leader of the Fifth District. Such a strict blockade was set up north of Long Bow that it was all but impossible to get through to the Liberated Areas. For awhile the Long Bow underground lost touch with the county and district government altogether. To make matters worse, So-tzu and Lai-pao had no food to carry them through the winter and had to leave to look for work in Taiyuan. They took with them a few dollars that had been collected for the support of the resistance front. This left a bad impression with those villagers who had contributed it. When the two men returned in the spring they refunded the money, re-established contact with the district government and set to work once again, but this time underground activity was more dangerous than ever and the people were more afraid to act.

The enemy had not been idle. Kuo Te-yu, former head of public affairs, had replaced Shang Shih-t'ou as village head. He made exposure of the underground his main task. Afraid, like his predecessor, to sleep at home, he made a practice of lodging in the homes of those whom he suspected of resistance activity. He and his brother, Kuo Fu-kuei, the new head of the police, spent many a night on Fu-yuan's k'ang hoping to surprise and kill the Eighth Router Ts'ai-yuan, should he arrive from the hills for a visit. During the day they hauled one peasant after another into the village office for questioning and did not hesitate to beat half to death those who were slow in answering. Thus they spread a net to take advantage of any break that could lead them to their quarry. The Eighth Route Army, decimated by the "Three All" campaigns of the two previous years, was too hard pressed to intervene.

Under such conditions the slightest slip could lead to disaster. A cousin's illicit love affair in another village almost cost T'ien-ming his life. This cousin, who lived in Little Gully, got involved in an affair with a girl from Li Village Gulch, the first village to the south of Long Bow. He was wont to climb over her compound wall and stay all night, much to the distress of her family who spread a rumor that he was a member of the Eighth Route Army. They had no idea that this was really so, but said it for revenge.

Their revenge was not long in coming and must surely have satisfied the most macabre sense of injury. The troops in the fort in Long Bow, having heard the rumor, conducted a search for the young man and found him in T'ien-ming's home. Both he and T'ien-ming were arrested, taken to the fort, and tortured when they refused to talk. The next morning T'ien-ming's cousin was beheaded with a fodder-chopping knife. T'ien-ming would have suffered the same fate but for the fact that the soldiers had no real information about him. All the men in the village insisted that he was nothing but a hard-working peasant who meant no harm to anyone. They put their thumb-prints to a document guaranteeing his behavior. This, plus a sum of money realized through the sale of T'ien-ming's half-interest in a donkey, secured his release. Without the donkey it was difficult to see how he could survive the next crop season, but at least he walked the streets alive.

Shen So-tzu and Kung Lai-pao were not so lucky. A drug addict named Tseng Tung-hsi, who made a practice of smoking heroin with the commander of the puppet troops, somehow learned the details of the underground village government. He passed the information on. So-tzu, Lai-pao, and Fu-yuan were immediately arrested. Eighteen days of torture and near starvation failed to break them down. So-tzu was shot, Lai-pao cut to pieces with a samurai sword, and Fu-yuan finally released.

Fu-yuan was released because the puppet forces were afraid his brother Ts'ai-yuan would bring the Eighth Route Army back for revenge and because his family was in a position to pay a handsome ransom. The puppet commander Wen Ch'i-yung demanded and got $7,000 in puppet currency (probably worth about $70 in U. S. currency at that time), a large quantity of heroin, a guarantee of Fu-yuan's good behavior from the whole village and a promise from Fu-yuan that he would entice his brother into a village ambush within six months.

This condition almost drove Fu-yaun to suicide. "The demand that I betray my brother frightened me," he said years later. "I was determined to do no such thing. Every time I heard the puppet soldiers' boots pounding the wooden bridge as they crossed the moat, I thought they were coming for me. I ran to the well and sat beside it. I was determined that they should never take me alive again. Whenever our dog barked at night, people thought my brother had come. I killed the dog.

"When I got a little better and was able to walk I tried to leave for the mountains but the rest of the family would not let me go. Their thumb-prints were on the guarantee. They said that if I disappeared they would all be killed and the whole village punished. Finally I went to stay with some poor relatives in another village."

These tragic events occurred only a few weeks before the war ended. The two leaders of the Long Bow underground, too poor to buy their way out, died rather than betray their comrades. They thus saved the lives of half a dozen young men whom they had had time to organize and educate. On this half dozen devolved the task of Long Bow's reconstruction.

9

The Whirlwind

If the sharp sword be not in your hand,
How can you hope your friends will remain many?

The Liberator
Emperor Wu Ti

THE EMPEROR of Japan surrendered to the Allies on August 10, 1945.

Long Bow Village was liberated by the Eighth Route Army and the People's Militia of Lucheng County on August 14, 1945, after three days of fighting.

Why, if the war was over on August 10th, should there have been a bitter battle for Long Bow that lasted until the 14th? Research into this question throws considerable light on subsequent events in China.

The local resistance forces had to fight their way into Long Bow Village because, within a few hours after the Japanese surrender, Chang Kai-shek issued two orders which brought his "Trojan Horse" strategy to its infamous fruition. The first commanded the Eighth Route Army to stop where it was and to take no action against the Japanese or puppet troops which it confronted. The second directed the puppet troops, over 400,000 of whom garrisoned the North, to maintain "law and order," resist any advance on the part of the Eighth Route Army, and hold all occupied territory pending the arrival of representatives from Chungking. Within a very short time, leading puppet politicians and generals were appointed officials of the Nationalist administration and officers of the Nationalist Army. The Japanese were ordered to surrender to them and to them alone. General MacArthur, Supreme Commander for the Allied Powers, gave full American backing to this move by issuing a general order making Chiang Kai-shek's forces sole agent for receiving the surrender of the Japanese forces in China proper.*

* *United States Relations with China,* Washington, D. C.: Department of State, August, 1949, p. 312.

By this extraordinary maneuver, Chiang attempted, without firing a shot, to re-establish traditional gentry power throughout those vast areas of China where for eight long years of war the Communist-led Eighth Route Army, New Fourth Army, South China Anti-Japanese Brigade, with the aid of the People's Militia had held at bay 69 percent of the Japanese forces in China and 95 percent of the puppet troops.*

From the military point of view this was an audacious strategy. When viewed in terms of troop numbers, fire power, and the strategic location of forces, it looked like a sure formula for victory. At a minimum Chiang expected the puppet forces to hold their own until, by massive airlift and naval ferry, the Americans helped him shoehorn into the North the newly equipped and trained divisions which he had been holding in reserve in the hinterland. Then with his most modern armies in position, Chiang expected to liquidate the Liberated Areas in a matter of months.

Politically the maneuver was disastrous. The destiny of nations is rarely determined by manpower or fire power alone. Chiang and his American advisers reckoned, as usual, without the people of China. What to them seemed a brilliant coup appeared to the vast majority of the Chinese people a ghastly betrayal of everything for which they had fought and suffered. This was particularly true in the Liberated Areas where the population had borne the full fury of the Japanese assault and hated the puppet troops with a hatred more bitter than that which they nursed against the Japanese themseleves. When Commander-in-Chief Chu Teh ordered the Eighth Route Army and the New Fourth Army to take the offensive and force the surrender of the troops that faced them, millions of militia men and tens of millions of ordinary people gave them the most enthusiastic support. Within a few days several hundred thousand square miles of territory with a population of over 50 million people were liberated.**

Finding himself unable to stem the popular tide by the use of puppet troops turned patriot by decree, Chiang made a further desperate move. He ordered the Japanese Army back into battle. On August 23, 1945, Ho Ying-ch'in, Commander-in-Chief of the Nationalist Armies, directed Yasugi Okamura, Commander-in-Chief of

* For various estimates of the proportion of Japanese and puppet troops tied down by the Eighth Route Army see: Israel Epstein, *The Unfinished Revolution in China*, p. 317; Liao Kai-lung, *From Yenan to Peking* (Peking: Foreign Languages Press, 1954) p. 9; Mao Tse-tung, *Selected Works*, Vol. IV, p. 29; Edgar Snow, *Red Star Over China*, p. 500.

** By the time this campaign was concluded, over a third of China's population and a quarter of her territory were in Communist-led areas.

Japan's forces in China, to defend the positions they already held and to recover the territories recently lost to the Liberated Areas.*

Simultaneously, the American military, by no means confident of Chiang's strength, and fearful lest neither his "Trojan Horse" puppets nor the demoralized Japanese could hold out against the Communist-led offensive, dumped 50,000 marines into the port of Tientsin and deployed them rapidly north and west along the main trunk railroads. The marines paid special attention to the line to Mukden.

Fanning out along the railroads, ostensibly to help take over from the Japanese, American forces became involved in skirmishes with Eighth Route guerrillas whose survival depended on smashing the tracks. More than once American marines and ex-puppet Kuomintang forces conducted joint operations against the "red bandits" who were "disrupting communications."** No more damaging coalition of forces could possibly have been assembled in a planned and conscious effort to dissipate the "reservoir of goodwill" which American wartime policy had built up in China. The attack on the Liberated Areas brought China to the brink of all-out civil war, and made the United States an aggressor in the eyes of millions of Chinese.

Such were the events taking place on a national and world scale which made a battle for Long Bow Village necessary. The village was not surrendered to the popular forces that surrounded it. It had to be taken.

---

* Ho Ying-ch'in's order read as follows:

A. As illegally armed units are without warrant disarming Japanese troops, your command must take effective defensive measures pending the arrival of the Nationalist Army designated by Generalissimo Chiang and Commander-in-Chief Ho to accept your surrender.

B. As bandit units are attacking Kaifeng, Tientsin, Chengchow, and other cities—special attention must be paid to the above-mentioned facts and Japanese troops already designated must, in accordance with our memorandum No. 4, be swiftly concentrated in these cities, as well as other places, for effective defense. If these places fall into the hands of bandit units, your troops will be held responsible for their recovery. (See Liao Kai-lung, *From Yenan to Peking*, p. 10.)

** On July 29, 1946, U.S. troops in Tientsin, in coordination with Chiang Kai-shek units, assaulted the town of Anping, Hsiangho County, Hopei Province. On June 16, 1946, U.S. troops at Tangshan, Hopei Province, raided Sungchiaying and other places; in July they raided Sanho Village, Luanhsien County, and Hsihonan Village, Changli County, both near Tangshan. On March 1, 1947, U.S. troops made a military reconnaissance of positions at Hohsipao, in Northeast China. Of numerous attacks in Eastern Shantung the most widely known were one by U.S. warships on Langnuankou and Hsiali Island, Mouping County, on August 28, 1947, and one by U.S. forces in conjunction with Kuomintang troops on Wanglintao Village, north of Chino County on December 25, 1947. (See Mao Tse-tung, *Selected Works*, Vol. IV, p. 439.)

Even though the Japanese contingent of the garrison had been withdrawn sometime in July, the forces in the Long Bow blockhouse were still formidable. One hundred men of the puppet Fourth Column, well equipped with modern Japanese weapons, were entrenched there. Additional manpower was provided by several dozen new recruits who made up the *Ai Hsiang Tuan* or "Love the Village Corps," a creation of the Shansi provincial Kuomintang working through the puppet administration. The "Love the Village Corps" was a last-minute attempt to give collaborators and "running dogs" the status of "patriots" and provide some framework in occupied territory for the return of the Kuomintang to power. The Long Bow youths who joined this corps were young men who had collaborated in one way or another with the Japanese during the years of the occupation. They were the street captains, Self-Defense Corps rank and file, and minor village officials who had been conscripted or appointed, often against their will, to posts in the apparatus of oppression. Fearing revenge at the hands of the victorious Eighth Route Army, they asked for protection in the fort and many took an active part in its defense.

But all the remnant puppet forces and the last-minute irregulars organized by the Kuomintang were no match for the Eighth Route Army and its supporting militia. The seasoned anti-Japanese troops surrounded all the strong points that flanked the Changchih-Lucheng highway simultaneously and still had several hundred regulars to spare for the biggest blockhouse of them all, at Long Bow. They did not immediately storm its stake-lined moats and mud walls but moved quietly into position, probed the defenses, and exchanged scattered shots in order to play on the nerves of the defenders while their own "Trojan Horse" tactic had time to bear fruit. The Trojan Horse in this case was T'ien-ming. He had joined the "Love the Village Corps" and gone inside the fort to feel out sentiment, count the defenders, and estimate their weapons and ammunition. After three days on the inside, T'ien-ming came out with a report that food supplies were almost gone and morale close to zero. By that time the militiamen from all over the county had been brought up. The fields were alive with armed men. They clogged every strip of corn and tall kaoliang that served as cover in the open countryside and overflowed into the cotton and potato patches. Peasants in the village estimated their number at well over a thousand. When, in the dead of night, the bugle sounded the call to attack, militiamen and regulars swarmed over the walls from all sides. The battle was soon over. The Fourth Column surrendered unconditionally.

Like a string of Chinese firecrackers exploding on New Year's Day, the attacks followed one another down the valley. Dozens of occupied villages were liberated within a few hours. Leaving the militia to mop up the rear, the main attack units then moved southward to surround the walled city of Changchih where the Japanese troops still held out in force.

PART II

Sunrise in the West
The Year of Expropriation

There were two "Reigns of Terror" if we would but remember it and consider it; the one wrought murder in hot passion, the other in heartless cold blood; the one lasted mere months, the other lasted a thousand years; the one inflicted death upon a thousand persons, the other upon a hundred millions; but our shudders are all for the "horrors" of the minor terror, the momentary terror, so to speak; whereas, what is the horror of swift death by the axe compared with lifelong death from hunger, cold insult, cruelty, and heartbreak? What is swift death by lightning compared with slow death by fire at the stake? A city cemetery could contain the coffins filled by the brief Terror which we have all been so diligently taught to shiver and mourn over; but all France could hardly contain the coffins filled by the older and real Terror—that unspeakably bitter and awful Terror which none of us has been taught to see in its vastness or pity as it deserves.

Mark Twain

10

Which Road?

If you Americans, sated with bread and sleep, want to curse people and back Chiang Kai-shek, that's your business and I won't interfere. What we have now is millet plus rifles, what you have is bread plus cannon. If you like to back Chiang Kai-shek, back him as long as you want. But remember one thing. To whom does China belong? China definitely does not belong to Chiang Kai-shek; China belongs to the Chinese people. The day will surely come when you will find it impossible to back him any longer.

Mao Tse-tung, 1945

IN LONG BOW, the eight-year-long Anti-Japanese War had come to a sudden end. With the surrender of the Fourth Column not only the Japanese occupation but centuries of landlord rule were also terminated. The end of an era carried in its wake the end of a millennium. It happened so quickly that neither the new forces nor the old were able to grasp the profound significance of the change. It was to take at least three years before the shift wrought in the course of one night of battle could be consolidated by popular action, before a new pattern of life based on the equal ownership of the land could be created.

In China as a whole, a much longer period would be needed before the forces left in command of China's destiny by the destruction of Japan's overriding threat established a new balance. In August 1945, a resistance so prolonged that it had become a way of life suddenly gave way to reconstruction. But what kind of China would the Chinese people reconstruct? Would it be the China of the past, stagnant, all but helpless, its great potential strangled by the weight of domestic reaction and foreign intervention and investment, or would it be a new, vigorous, revolutionary China, a China fundamentally remade, a China that stood on her own feet?

Mao Tse-tung compared the victory won by the people of the Liberated Areas to the liberation of a peach tree heavy with fruit. Who should be allowed to pick the fruit? Those who had tended and watered the tree with their sweat and their blood, or those who had sat far away with folded arms?

103

Mao's answer was clear. Only those who had tended the tree had the right to pick the fruit.

Chiang's answer was also clear. The logic of his "Trojan Horse" surrender strategy left no room for doubt. He who from distant Chungking had preached and practiced victory through a curved road intended to pick the fruit himself. With some three million troops, with hundreds of thousands of puppet soldiers, with the Japanese Army itself under his command, with the support of a huge American military establishment, with a "great rear" encompassing some 300 million people ravaged very little by war at his disposal, and with the ultimate sanction of the *bomb* behind him, he felt strong enough to conquer the Liberated Areas and restore their traditional rulers.

What about the people, the 100 million who lived in the Anti-Japanese Bases in the plains and mountains of North, Northeast, and Central China, the myriad progressives who lived in the "great rear," all the people who had learned to look to the Communist Party for leadership? They wanted peace, they demanded peace, they were willing to make concessions for peace, but in the long run the question of peace or war was not entirely in their hands. Chiang, with American backing, meant to enforce his own peace terms. Did they have the strength to defend themselves? Did they dare? This was the crucial question that faced the Communists and all other revolutionary leaders at that fateful moment.

Many people, including many Communists in responsible positions, were afraid. They did not see how the war-ravaged guerrilla areas of the North could survive the kind of attack that Chiang Kai-shek was mounting. It had taken the resources of much of the world to defeat Japan. Could a fraction of the Chinese people hope to defeat a Kuomintang backed by the resources of the United States? And if they did indeed have some initial success, would the Americans not use the dread bomb which had ravaged Hiroshima and Nagasaki rather than lose influence over a continent? These leaders could hardly help reflecting on various forms of compromise, could hardly refrain from cautioning against actions which they thought might provoke a showdown.

Among the compromisers were many people of landlord or middle-class origin. They had come to the support of the Communist Party during the period of the National United Front. They were not prepared for the sharp break in this front that followed Japan's surrender. Without close ties or deep sympathy with the common people, they lacked faith in the ability and determination of workers and peasants to fight on and win.

Other equally sincere people of similar background were confused by the political climate. Talk of a negotiated settlement, talk of a coalition government, Marshall's peace mission, promises of a national assembly, all these generated illusions. People were so tired of war, so exhausted by eight years of horror, so desirous of a peaceful settlement that they could not believe anyone could contemplate the invasion of the Liberated Areas and demand the surrender of the heroic Anti-Japanese Bases as the price for peace. As the guns, tanks, planes, and ammunition left over from the war in the Pacific poured in to arm Chiang's many-millioned legions, they looked the other way, placed their hopes entirely on negotiations, and refused to face the prospect of open armed conflict.

In this situation Mao Tse-tung and the other leaders of the Chinese Communist Central Committee found it necessary to carry out a dual policy. On the one hand they made serious efforts to bring about a peaceful settlement. To this end they agreed to reduce the size of the Eighth Route Army and ordered abandoned eight Liberated Areas in South and Central China. On the other hand, they prepared the 100 million people under their administrative control for the attack on the Liberated Areas of North China which they expected Chiang Kai-shek to mount. A most critical part of this preparation consisted in refuting the capitulationist ideas outlined above. Mao undertook this task in good time. Patiently but firmly he insisted that the people of the Liberated Areas could defend themselves, and that the people of all China possessed sufficient strength to bring about fundamental changes in the country as a whole. The strength of Chiang and his Western backers, Mao said, was more apparent than real. Money they had, resources they had, arms they had, but the hearts of the people they could never win. In the long run people, not weapons, would be decisive. "The people," said Mao, "will destroy the bomb; the bomb will not destroy the people."

This strategic concept was summed up in the phrase, "Imperialism and all reactionaries are paper tigers." This was Mao's paraphrase, in August 1946, of Lenin's famous dictum that imperialism is a colossus with feet of clay. Imperialism and all reactionaries are paper tigers, said Mao, in the sense that they can be defeated by an aroused people. At the same time they are real tigers in the sense that they are capable of inflicting serious damage, terrible wounds. Therefore, said Mao, the Chinese people should slight the enemy strategically, but take full cognizance of him tactically. On the one hand they should dare to defend themselves, dare to struggle, dare to win. On the other hand, they should take the struggle seriously—i.e., devote full attention to each campaign and to each battle, seek out all possible allies and mobilize as much support from the people of the whole world as possible. Not to struggle was to surrender to Right opportunism. Not to take the struggle seriously, to ignore allies, to go it alone meant to surrender to Left sectarianism. First and foremost, however, was the decision to struggle, to dare to fight, to dare to win. Unless this basic decision was made, defeat was certain.

In Long Bow those who were for transforming the village gave full support to the Communist Party, to the Eighth Route Army, to the People's Militia that had liberated them, and to the program which these forces brought to the village. Those who were undecided, those who were afraid worried about the possibility of a "change of sky." They feared that the Communist Party, the Eighth Route Army, and the People's Militia would not be strong enough to hold what they had taken, that a counter-offensive from the nationalist areas, backed by the enormous strength of the United States might well succeed in bringing back the old sky, the old way of life, the old oppression. To go all out, to fight and struggle, or to hang back, to wait and see, to hold a finger in the wind—this was the big question that the people of the village, like the people of the Liberated Areas as a whole, debated in the days that followed the surrender of the Fourth Column.

For the young activists who had fought in the underground the answer had never been in doubt. They were for struggle.

11

Beat the Dog's Leg

*All actions labelled as "going too far" had a revolutionary significance.
To put it bluntly, it was necessary to bring about a brief reign of terror in
every rural area; otherwise one could never suppress the activities of the
counter-revolutionaries in the countryside or overthrow the authority of
the gentry. To right a wrong it is necessary to exceed the proper limits, and
wrong cannot be righted without the proper limits being exceeded.*

Mao Tse-tung, 1927

THE VICTORY celebrations that followed the surrender of the Fourth
Column lasted several days and nights. They had hardly subsided
when the peasants of Long Bow in their huts and hovels, on their
clay brick *k'angs,* and in their packed earth courtyards, on streets
and in alleys made muddy by the monsoon rains, and even in the
crop-laden fields far beyond the last adobe walls that marked the
settlement, heard a strange sound that many at first mistook for the
hoarse braying of a donkey. It came, so it seemed, from the heavens.
Looking upward all eyes were drawn to the highest point around them,
the square tower of the Catholic Church. There they saw, not some
skyborne donkey, but the figure of a young man silhouetted against
outer space and holding to his face a megaphone which he directed
first toward one quarter of the earth and then toward another, shouting all the while at the top of his voice:
"There will be a meeting—a meeting today—in the square after the
noon meal—an anti-traitor meeting—everybody out, everybody
out—there will be a meeting—today—."
Whichever way the young man turned his body, the people directly
in front of him heard the words distinctly, while those to the right
and the left and the rear heard only an unintelligible roaring, but
since, before he finished, he boxed the compass with his megaphone,
the people in each quarter of the village were alerted in turn.
A meeting! Not since the quarrel with the Church over the ownership of the vegetable garden 20 years before had there been a public
meeting in Long Bow. The call, coming just before noon, aroused the
whole population and set the village buzzing like a hornet's nest that

107

has been struck. It had always been a mealtime custom for both men and women to take their bowls of steaming millet or corn dumplings outdoors, there to gather in congenial groups for random talk and gossip. On this day the groups eating in the larger courtyards and in the streets were double or triple their normal size as every person able to walk and carry a bowl gathered outside to talk over the news. Old women leaning on sticks and canes hobbled out on their bound feet. Young mothers, holding their babies to their breasts with one hand and wielding chopsticks with the other, balanced their bowls on their knees and strained to hear what the neighbors had to say. Barefoot, half-naked boys and girls ran from group to group and alley to alley helping spread the rumors that flew in a matter of minutes from one end of the village to the other. Only the notorious traitors and their families made themselves conspicuous by their absence; but even they, consumed with curiosity and fear, sent relatives and friends to circulate among the people in order to pick up what incidental intelligence they could.

What puppet leader would be accused first? Would he be shot? How much property did he own? Who would get it? Had there been a victory at Changchih? Were the Japanese coming back under Yen Hsi-shan's command? Did the Eighth Route Army seize conscripts? These and a hundred other questions were on every tongue.

Long before the usual noon siesta had run its course the people began to gather in the square. Animated small knots grew and merged until the whole open area beside the village pond was filled with ragged, soiled, work-worn humanity. The predominant color of the gathering was dark blue merging into black for this was the hue of the cheap, machine-made cloth from which wives and mothers had cut the majority of their clothes. This dark background was leavened however with dashes of white or dirty gray for this was the color of the hand towels which both men and women wore on their heads. It was also the head-to-foot color displayed by those few peasants who could afford neither dye nor machine-made cloth. They wore bleached homespun. To this somber black and gray a brilliant flash of color was added here and there by the bright red tunic of an unmarried girl, or the dragon cap in blue, green, or yellow of some precious boy child held tightly in his mother's arms.

The men of the village naturally gathered toward the front of the crowd. They faced the inn. Before it a slight rise in the ground made a convenient platform for those who would lead the meeting. The women, reticent and shy, hung back in clusters of their own. Milling about in front of the men and shoving each other right up the slope to the door of the inn itself were scores of children, laughing, shouting, and pushing, each intent on finding a place in the very front row so that he or she would miss nothing. The men talked quietly among themselves and smoked; laboriously they took small pinches of shredded tobacco from the leather pouches that hung at their waists, pressed them into the pea-sized brass bowls of their long-stemmed pipes, and struck flint against steel to get a spark with which to light up. A pipe, once lit up, was passed from hand to hand so that from each effort four or five peasants had at least a taste of smoke before the tobacco burned itself out and the process had to be repeated.

While the men smoked and talked, many of the women busied themselves with work brought from home. The children had to have clothes to wear even if the sky should fall, and the days were too short to allow a single moment to go to waste. Some of them spun the small blocks of wood that twisted hemp into thread. Others used the thread already made to sew together the many layers of cloth that made up the soles of the shoes worn in the Taihang Mountains.

Tempted by the prospect of sales to such a large gathering, a few peddlers had even appeared, as if out of nowhere. They made their way among the people hawking dried thorn dates, roasted peanuts, and fresh-baked, unleavened cakes.

Mingled throughout the crowd but conspicuous only on its fringes were the militiamen, organized only a day or two earlier. A few had rifles. The rest carried red-tassled spears. Regardless of the weapon, each stood proud, erect, watchful. All were conscious of the sidelong glances of the young women, both married and unmarried, who, because they were rarely allowed to leave home at all, now looked about wide-eyed and curious.

The mood of the gathering was expectant, yet skeptical. The peasants were full of hatred for traitors, yet afraid of the revenge traitors might inflict. They were ready to believe in the Eighth Route Army and in the Liberated Areas' Government, but doubtful that either would act in the end. And if action were taken, who could foresee what the final result would be? After all, everyone knew that the puppet running dogs had powerful connections. Had not the priest himself wined and dined the Japanese? Had not Sheng Ching-ho, the richest man in Long Bow, backed up "Chief-of-Staff" Chou Mei-sheng?

All talk stopped abruptly as a man, hands bound behind his back, body twisted slightly, head lowered, walked slowly into the square from the south. He was urged on from behind by a heavy-set militiaman who carried his rifle as if it were a hoe. The bound man was Kuo Te-yu, who had replaced the executed Shang Shih-t'ou as puppet village head, a position he had held until three days before.

"So they're going to begin with the turtle's egg village head," said an old peasant at the edge of the crowd.

"It's the village head, rape his mother!" said another.

This word spread through the gathering.

Behind Te-yu and his awkward guard came several young peasants. They immediately took charge of the meeting. To the astonishment of all, one of these peasants was Chang T'ien-ming. Another was the underground district leader, Kuo Huang-kou or Yellow Dog Kuo (about whose exploits many had heard, but a man whom few had actually seen). A young cadre of local peasant origin still in his early twenties, Huang-kou had taken the steps that made this meeting possible. On that night in August 1945 when the Fourth Column surrendered, neither Yellow Dog Kuo nor anyone else in Long Bow had any conception of the scale of the revolutionary changes to come. One thing was clear, however; if the political and military vacuum left by the surrender of the garrison and the collapse of the puppet village government was not quickly filled by the resistance forces, the gentry would fill it themselves by reshuffling their old political machine and varnishing it with a resounding new title such as "Anti-Japanese Patriotic Government." Such maneuvers had already taken place in other areas. Determined that no such thing should happen in Long Bow, the young district leader moved to set up a new administration while the battle for the village still raged. Since the whole puppet organization, including the important civilian leaders, had fled to the fort for protection, the village itself was already free. Setting up his headquarters in the abandoned village office, Yellow Dog Kuo called together all those who had been active in the struggle against the Japanese and, in addition, a few poor peasants untainted by collaboration—the most oppressed, the most *lao shih* young leaders that he could find.* About a dozen men, all of them in their early twenties, met that evening. As the Eighth Route Army and the massed militia began their final assault on the fort, these 12 established a new "People's Government."

District leader Kuo asked T'ien-ming to assume the post of village chairman. T'ien-ming (who had just returned from his dangerous mission inside the fort) felt himself too handicapped by illiteracy for such a big job. He declined and asked to be allowed to continue the work he had done in the underground, that of public security officer. Kuo himself temporarily assumed the post of village chairman. Kuei-ts'ai, a life-long hired laborer who had arrived in Long Bow 20 years

---

* *Lao shih* literally translated means "honest," but in Chinese it means more than that; it means genuine, without guile, steady, hardworking, easily imposed upon perhaps, but formidable when aroused.

before suspended from his father's carrying pole, became vice-chairman. Chang San-ch'ing, a young man who had worked as a clerk in a drug shop in occupied Taiyuan and knew how to write and to figure on an abacus, became secretary for the group. Chang Chiang-tzu, a very brave and steadfast peasant, was appointed captain of the militia and head of military affairs. Shih Fu-yuan, who, next to T'ien-ming, had the longest underground record of them all, missed that first meeting. He was still staying with relatives in the faraway village where he had gone to avoid having to betray his brother, Ts'ai-yuan, to the puppet forces.

By the time the puppet garrison walked out of the fort as captives, the new People's Government had already taken full control of the village. The young men asked nobody's permission. They were not elected or appointed. They took power on the assumption that the underground work of their key leaders had earned them the right to administer the liberated village. A large majority of the people held them in high regard. With an armed force of militiamen hastily organized and the moral support of most of the peasants, no one was in a position to challenge their *de facto* rule. Recognition by the Fifth District Office and consequently by the People's Government of Lucheng County, now in its eighth year, made this rule *de jure* as well.

Under Yellow Dog Kuo's guidance, the group proceeded at once to tackle two great tasks: the mobilization of the whole community in support of the drive on Changchih and a settling of accounts with the personnel of the puppet administration. To accomplish the first task, grain was collected, loaded in carts, and dispatched to the front. A large group of men followed, armed with shovels and hoes. They went to do whatever labor the army found necessary. Even the militia were no sooner organized than a group was sent south to join in the battle. Most of them had no firearms; some had never even handled a rifle. But numbers were needed so they marched off with spirit enough to make up, at least in part, for the deficiencies of their equipment and training.

As for the puppet administration, none of the leading collaborators had run very far. Some of them were captured in the fort as they fought alongside the Fourth Column; others were picked up on the road to Changchih as they tried to escape and were escorted back to the village by the Fifth District militiamen. As soon as they found guarantors who pledged that they would not leave the village, they were set free to await trial.

The People's Government of Lucheng County, now permanently housed in the *Yamen* at the county seat, launched its first postwar campaign with two slogans—"Down with Traitors, Down with Kuomintang Agents, Down with Local Despots" and "Liquidate the Bloody Eight Years' Debt." These slogans were directed at the puppet officials, but since, in many cases, the actual officials were but fronts for the real rulers who operated behind the scenes, they also raised a third slogan—"Beat Down the Dog's Legs to Find his Head; Beat Down the Little Fellows to Find the Leaders."

At Yellow Dog Kuo's suggestion, T'ien-ming called all the active young cadres and militiamen of Long Bow together and announced to them the policy of the county government, which was to confront all enemy collaborators and their backers at public meetings, expose their crimes, and turn them over to the county authorities for punishment. He proposed that they start with Kuo Te-yu, the puppet village head. Having moved the group to anger with a description of Te-yu's crimes, T'ien-ming reviewed the painful life led by the poor peasants during the occupation and recalled how hard they had all worked, and how as soon as they harvested a little grain the puppet officials, backed by army bayonets, took what they wanted, turned over huge quantities to the Japanese devils, forced the peasants to haul it away, and flogged those who refused.

The young men agreed to conduct a public meeting of the whole population the very next day.

And so it was that Kuo Te-yu, running dog of the landlords, informer, torturer, grafter, and enemy stooge, found himself standing before a crowd of several hundred stolid peasants whom he had betrayed. His face was ashen, his tunic shabby and soiled. A stranger might well have taken him for a thief caught stealing melons, hardly for a village tyrant.

As the silent crowd contracted toward the spot where the accused man stood, T'ien-ming stepped forward.

"Comrades, countrymen," he began. Immediately his short, handsome figure became the center of attention. Was this dark, assured young man with the quick, piercing eyes the same T'ien-ming they had seen running barefoot and ragged in the streets only a few bitter years ago? Was this the reticent laborer they had all stood guarantor for? Who would have thought a few days earlier that he could speak before a crowd? Yet now his words came naturally, passionately: "This is our chance. Remember how we were oppressed. The traitors seized our property. They beat us and kicked us. Now the whole world is ours. The government and the Eighth Route Army stand behind us. Let us speak out the bitter memories of the past. Let us see that the blood debt is repaid."

He paused for a moment. The peasants were listening to every word but gave no sign as to how they felt.

"In the past we were despised. Who did not feel it every day? Only now can we hold our heads up and speak like men. Look, the village is ours." He swept his arm in a wide arc that took in the crowd clad in dark cloth all patched and faded, the crumbling compound walls that bounded the square, the pond green with slime, the sagging doors on the weathered brick church, the partly caved-in roof of the Buddhist temple, the rutted street leading out to the fields, and the fields themselves with their crops trampled in the rainy season mud as a result of the battle—a vista of neglect, collapse, and decay universal enough to discourage even the stoutest heart, the most optimistic spirit. "What is there to be afraid of? When we beat down the traitors, we can stand up. We can divide the fruits of their corruption and start a new life."

He spoke plainly. His language and his accent were well understood by the people among whom he had been raised, but no one moved and no one spoke.

"Come now, who has evidence against this man?"

Again there was silence.

Kuei-ts'ai, the new vice-chairman of the village, found it intolerable. He jumped up, struck Kuo Te-yu on the jaw with the flat of his hand. "Tell the meeting how much you stole," he demanded.

The blow jarred the ragged crowd. It was as if an electric spark had tensed every muscle. Not in living memory had any peasant ever struck an official. A gasp, involuntary and barely audible, came from the people and above it a clear sharp "Ah" from an old man's throat.

Te-yu, in a spasm of fear, could utter only a few incoherent sentences. This so angered Kuei-ts'ai that he struck him again.

"One bag of tax grain . . ." Only those who were standing very close could hear Te-yu's hoarse whisper.

"One bag! You took only one bag?" shouted Kuei-ts'ai.

"But it was not my fault. There were seven pecks . . ."

"Now you deny it. Not even one bag. It was not my fault . . ." Kuei-ts'ai strode back and forth in front of Te-yu and mimicked his words.

Kuei-ts'ai, like T'ien-ming, was short and husky, but he could not be called handsome. He had a heavy brow, and a high-bridged nose that made his eyes appear extraordinarily deep-set. Now his whole face was contorted with anger like the head of a war god on a New Year's poster.

"Don't lie to us," he shouted, shaking his fist in the cringing man's face. The cry was taken up by the rest of the militiamen who had moved in behind Te-yu: "Don't lie to us."

This frightened the village head still more. Words gagged in his throat. Further blows only made him cringe. He bowed his head low before the meeting but revealed nothing of the graft he had wallowed in.

The people in the square waited fascinated, as if watching a play. They did not realize that in order for the plot to unfold they themselves had to mount the stage and speak out what was on their minds. No one moved to carry forward what Kuei-ts'ai had begun.

T'ien-ming was upset. Without the participation of hundreds the record could never be set straight. He called a hasty conference of his fellow village officers. They decided to put off the meeting until the next day. In the interim they hoped to mobilize at least a dozen people who would speak out and lead the way.

When T'ien-ming announced the postponement a murmur went through the crowd, but it was difficult to say whether it was a murmur of approval or a murmur of disappointment. Kuo Te-yu was led away to the village lockup, a crowd of small boys following closely on his heels. Slowly the people in the square dispersed until only a small knot of cadres and militiamen remained in front of the inn. There they vigorously discussed the failure of the people to step forward, until their children came to call them home for supper.

That evening T'ien-ming and Kuei-ts'ai called together small groups of poor peasants from various parts of the village and sought to learn what it was that was really holding them back. They soon found that the root of the trouble was fear. The landlords and the Kuomintang Party organization of the district, headed by Wang En-pao, son of the Carry-On Society's chairman, Wang Kuei-ching, already had a fairly clear idea of what was coming and had taken vigorous steps to forestall and divert the attack. They spread rumors to the effect that Yen Hsi-shan, with the help of the Japanese Army, would soon be back. That this was no idle boast had been made clear by Yen's acts. The old warlord had no sooner re-entered his old capital, Tai-yuan, than he ordered General Roshiro Sumita, Commander of all the Japanese forces in Shansi, to re-occupy his imposing wartime headquarters and mastermind the campaign for the recovery of the Liberated Areas. General Sumita threw 40,000 men into the battle. Lest anyone have the nerve to act in the face of this offensive, the gentry also let it be known that lists were being drawn up of active revolutionaries who were to be dispatched by firing squads when Yen's troops returned. Along with these threats went a campaign to discredit the resistance movement; rumors were spread that women were nationalized in the Liberated Areas, ancestral graves violated, and all peasants forced to eat *ta kuo fan* or "food out of one big pot." The other side of this coin was the claim that collaboration had really been resistance, that by bending temporarily to Japan's will the puppets had worked for national salvation along a curved path. Was not the final surrender of the Japanese proof of this?

All this activity was not without effect. Many peasants who might have been eager to strike a blow against collaborators hesitated. They were afraid to act. They had little confidence that the Eighth Route Army, soldiers without boots, without helmets, and without heavy weapons could hold the region. Fighting was still heavy around Changchih, only ten miles away. Who could tell? Perhaps the "sky would change again" and the old regime would return with fire and sword. Was it not better to lie low and see how things turned out? The old reluctance to move against the power of the gentry, the fear of ultimate defeat and terrible reprisal that had been seared into the consciousness of so many generations lay like a cloud over their minds and hearts.

The mere collapse of the fort and the arrest of the puppet leaders were clearly not enough to bring the peasants of Long Bow into action. The mobilization of the population could spread only slowly and in concentric circles like the waves on the surface of a pond when a stone is thrown in. The stone in this case was the small group of *chi chi fen-tse* or "activists," as the cadres of the new administration and the core of its militia were called.

That evening they talked plain facts to the selected people in the small groups that they had called together. They discussed "change of sky." Could the Kuomintang troops or the Japanese ever come back? "Even if they do," T'ien-ming said, "we younger men can go off to the higher mountains with the Eighth Route Army, so why be afraid? If we don't move now, the chance will be lost." He reviewed again the evil record of the traitor clique, the death of So-tzu and Lai-pao, and the beatings suffered by himself, Fu-yuan, and countless others, the seized grain, the forced labor.

Emboldened by T'ien-ming's words, other peasants began to speak out. They recalled what Te-yu had done to them personally. Several vowed to speak up and accuse him in the morning. After the meetings broke up, the passage of time worked its own leaven. In many a hovel and tumble-down house talk continued well past midnight. Some people were so excited they did not sleep at all. As the village cocks began to crow they found themselves still discussing whether or not to act, and if so, how.

On the following day the meeting was livelier by far. It began with a sharp argument as to who would make the first accusation and T'ien-ming found it difficult to keep order. Before Te-yu had a chance to reply to any questions a crowd of young men, among whom were several militiamen, surged forward ready to beat him.

At this crucial moment the district leader, Yellow Dog Kuo, strode between the young men and their victim. He blocked the assault with his own body and then explained to the crowd that the puppet leader was but a "dog's leg"—a poor peasant who had been used. To kill him would gain them nothing. It was the manipulators behind him who had to be exposed.

"Let him tell what he knows," Kuo urged. "Let him expose the others."

Once again T'ien-ming demanded that the prisoner talk.

This time Te-yu finally found his tongue and spoke out so that the whole gathering could hear him, but he rambled so much in his explanation, and went into such detail making clear the extenuating circumstances of his every act that no coherent account of money and grain emerged. Furthermore his own statements and the memory of his accusers conflicted. The cadres decided to charge him with ten hundredweight of grain for good measure and set his case aside for the time being. They searched his home for the grain that same afternoon and swapped it in Lucheng for four rifles for the militia.

With this inconclusive action the local struggle was called off for a few days while the more important and notorious puppet leaders of the district were brought before large representative meetings. Shih Jen-pao, of the Fourth Column, had unfortunately escaped, but Wen Ch'i-yung, commander of the puppet garrison in Long Bow fort, Shen Chi-mei, head of the Fifth District police, and Ch'ing T'ien-hsing, his assistant, were brought face to face with 190 peasants from all over the district—more than ten from each village—who came together in Long Bow's square as delegates from their respective communities. These were the people who had suffered the most from puppet depredations, whose homes had been looted, whose sons and husbands had been killed, whose wives and daughters had been seduced or raped.

Hundreds of accusations were made that day against the leading traitors and all those who worked with them. A Long Bow woman told how her son, Chin-mao, had been killed. When she came to the part where the police threw him, gagged and bound, into a well, she broke down weeping and could not go on. Many in the crowd wept with her. Shen Ch'uan-te, also of Long Bow, charged the puppet regime with the death of his brother. "My brother was killed by the Eighth Route soldiers," he said, "but they killed him because he was carrying a message for the traitors. The traitors forced him to carry it. Why didn't they carry their own messages? They are the real killers."

Yellow Dog Kuo finally asked, "What is the origin of these murders? Who stood back of these puppets? How was it possible for their puny troops to have such power? Who served as their eyes and ears? Who informed on the peasants and exposed them to attack?"

Many then spoke out and said it was Shen Chi-mei and the landlords who backed him that lay at the root of the disaster that had befallen them. Before the meeting ended, Commander Wen and Police Officer Shen were condemned to death. They were taken to an empty field at the edge of the village and there, in sight of the fort they had done so much to build and to defend, they were shot. While the dead Shen Chi-mei lay still warm on the ground where he fell, a Long Bow militiaman, Yu-hsing, stripped a sweater off his corpse. Someone else took off his shoes. They left the body to his relatives to bury as they would.

Ch'ing T'ien-hsing, the third prisoner, was not sentenced that day. He was handed over to the County Court at Lucheng for investigation. He escaped from the lockup in the middle of the night but the militiamen from Long Bow who had taken him to Lucheng the day before, hunted him down, caught him in Horse Square, and killed him on the spot.

During the next few days the militia led thousands of people in a search for all the property that the soldiers of the Fourth Column had stolen. The loot had been placed in various village homes for safekeeping. Many families volunteered information that led to its discovery. Several hundred suits of clothes, several thousand feet of cloth, and many other valuable household articles were recovered and returned to their rightful owners. A large cache of this looted property was found in Landlord Wang Lai-hsun's home. The land, tools, stock, and household effects of the executed men were confiscated.

12

Find the Leaders

How was the question of Toryism dealt with by the Revolutionary fathers? Up to the time of Lexington, the main resort of the patriots was persuasion and exhortation, liberally spiced with extra-legal pressures ranging from boycott to physical assault. After Lexington, persuasion gave way to compulsion, which took five main forms. These were: (1) deprivation of all civil and some social rights; (2) confiscation of property; (3) exile; (4) confinement; (5) execution.

Herbert Aptheker

THE DEATH of the two most notorious puppet leaders of the Fifth District dispersed some of the fear that still hung over the village. Victories on the battlefront dissipated it further. The Eighth Route Army took Changchih early in September and drove the front back another 30 miles. The offensive launched by Yen Hsi-shan toward Hsiangyuan, Tungliu, and Lucheng later in the month was also smashed. With an army made up of some 38,000 Japanese, former puppet and regular Nationalist troops, Yen tried to subdue the Shang-tang plateau and seize the autumn harvest. But in October this whole force was surrounded, and 35,000 of the invaders were killed, wounded, or captured. The rest ran away.

Peasants who went to help the army with shovels and mattocks saw with their own eyes how shoeless fighters struck fear into the hearts of heavily armed troops who had nothing to fight for. The militiamen who joined the battle with spears even brought back some rifles as their share of the spoils.

In this triumphant atmosphere peasants who had attended the district-wide meeting in Long Bow and had seen the traitors shot went back to their villages in every part of the territory and sparked a fierce campaign against collaborators. Important leaders who had gone into hiding were found, arrested, and tried. Several men, as much hated by the people as Shen Chi-mei, were shot. In Liu Village a list of Kuomintang Party members was unearthed. This led to the arrest of many collaborators hiding out in parts of the district never occupied by the enemy. They had secretly gathered information th* enabled the puppet troops to ambush and kill resistance leaders and fighters.

As this mass anti-traitor campaign got under way the Fifth District leader, Yellow Dog Kuo, was transferred by the county government to the First District. An experienced organizer named Liang was sent to Long Bow to take his place. Liang had no desire to be both Fifth District Leader and village head of Long Bow as Kuo had been, so he looked around for someone to fill this latter post. By that time Shih Fu-yuan was back in the village and already deeply involved in the campaign against the puppets who had caused him such suffering. The new district leader picked Fu-yuan as head of Long Bow Village.

Under Fu-yuan's leadership the village office brought Kuo Te-yu, Kuo Fu-kuei, Li T'ung-jen and many other active collaborators before new village-wide meetings. Each time more people stepped forward to accuse than had dared to do so before. When the damages brought out by these accusations were totalled, all the property owned by the collaborators was not enough to repay their victims. It was not a question of graft alone. The collaborators had seized outright many valuable things and had avoided terms of labor service that added up to many months of labor. This last item was figured as grain now owed to those who had been forced to go in their stead.

From "dog's legs" such as Te-yu the movement spread out in both directions attacking, on the one hand, those who had only been street or block leaders, and on the other, those who had been the real pillars of the puppet regime, men such as Chou Mei-sheng, secretary and key organizer of the village administration throughout the occupation, and Father Sun, the priest of the Church, whose liaison with both the Japanese and the group of Catholic landlords who were the real power behind the puppet office, was notorious.

A special meeting was called to confront Chief-of-Staff Chou with his crimes. Particularly bitter were the complaints about salt. Throughout the occupation salt could not be bought or sold freely. It was handled as a government monopoly and was supposed to be rationed on a per capita basis. Chou Mei-sheng got the salt ration from the county office and then passed it out, not according to need, but according to political expediency. Relatives and friends got an extra share. Those who quarrelled with him got less or none. By controlling the salt, a necessity of life, he wielded tremendous power and rewarded or punished people according to his whim.

Chou Mei-sheng was also responsible for many tax abuses and for discrimination in the allocation of labor service. He dispensed forced labor as freely as he withheld salt, and to the same end—to punish his enemies and reward his friends. Those who resisted were beaten. Of those who went off to work, some never returned.

When the cadres figured out how much he had grafted it came to over 100 large bags of grain. To settle this debt to the people he had to give up all his land and houses, all his grain and property. They left him but one room to live in and grain enough to last only until winter.

In the course of this struggle no one came to Chou Mei-sheng's defense. As soon as the new cadres led the village against him, the landlords who had backed him disowned him without hesitation. To clear their own skirts they pretended that they had had nothing to do with him. But Father Sun was not so easily isolated. As the one remaining priest of the Church he was the leader of more than 200 people in the village. Most of them believed strongly in his teachings even if they disapproved of his pro-Japanese views and activities. Some backed both his politics and his religion. With their support Father Sun felt secure enough to openly denounce the Eighth Route Army, the liberation of the village from puppet and consequently from Kuomintang control, and the "Anti-Traitor Movement" itself.

When the Eighth Route Army soldiers entered the village and moved on down the valley he told everyone he met that misfortune had fallen upon the Church and the faithful. His sermons predicted a "change of sky." "The Eighth Route Army is nothing but a bandit rabble," he declared. "The Eighth Route soldiers do not believe in God. They oppose Catholicism, they tear down temples, they smash Buddhas. They don't even wear shoes. How can they long remain? Surely the troops of the Central Government will soon return."

When the village government punished collaborators by the confiscation of their land and property and distributed this wealth among the landless and the land poor he scathingly denounced the practice in his sermon. He said, "Man was created by God, food is given by God, everything in the world happens by God's will. We must obey God's orders. God determined that the poor should be poor. They should not aspire to be rich. Only those who can endure pain and suffering in this life can hope to enter heaven after death. The more patient you are, the more suffering you bear, the sooner you will enter heaven and see God."

When Shen Chi-mei, the traitor, was executed, Father Sun went out of his way to say mass for the salvation of his soul and soon thereafter announced that this man's spirit had entered heaven from purgatory.

These acts and statements invited retaliation. T'ien-ming, who was responsible for public security, ordered Father Sun arrested. All the cadres of the village office then began to mobilize the people against him. They went among the Catholics and found several who were already disillusioned with the religion and were eager to attack the Church. Among them was one potential leader, a former hired laborer named Kuo Cheng-k'uan. He had worked many years for the Catholic landlord Fan Pu-tzu, and later had hired out as a mule driver to the Cathedral in Changchih. All his life he had suffered nothing but abuse from the Church.

With Cheng-k'uan's help the cadres called the Catholics of the village together to discuss the case of Father Sun. Experience in other villages had already shown that a direct attack on the Catholic religion was not an effective tactic. While a few were ready to repudiate their faith, most believers were not. Whenever the teachings of the Church were attacked the majority of the faithful only rallied more strongly around the institution itself. For this reason the Long Bow cadres did not challenge Father Sun's theology, but concentrated their fire on his secular activities. District Leader Liang adopted a selective approach when he opened the meeting. "After all," he said, "no one knows about God. No one has seen him. Whether or not God exists, whether there is one God or whether there are many, is not the question before us here. The question before us is Father Sun, his collaboration with the Japanese, the heavy charges he made for giving protection to your property, the way he tried to force the whole village into the Church, his discrimination against the poor in all things."

This speech moved even some of the most faithful believers. They began to recall one instance after another of injustice at the hands of Father Sun. Within a few hours more than 60 grievances were registered against him.

The next day the whole population of the village was called together. When the cadres asked the people if they dared accuse the priest everyone kept silent at first. Then District Leader Liang spoke again. He reviewed Father Sun's record and this time stressed the exploitation he had practiced. "For every mass the Father read he spent but a few minutes, but for that few minutes he charged a whole quarter bushel of millet. He wouldn't take a quart, he had to have a quarter bushel."

At this point Sheng Kuei-t'ing, a former secretary of the Carry-On Society, a man who had managed the finances of the Church before the job fell to Wang Kuei-ching, stood up. " I will be the first to accuse," he said. "I know in detail how the whole system worked. I myself was peeled and pared," and he told all he knew about the income and the expenditures of the Father, the Church, and the

Carry-On Society. When he had finished, many others volunteered, saying to one another, "If you will speak out, I will follow. If you are not afraid of God, then neither am I."

As the meeting progressed Father Sun was brought from the lock-up and made to stand before the crowd. One after another his own parishioners accused him to his face.

"You preach suffering and hardship for the people," shouted Cheng-k'uan. "You say the poor should eat plain food and endure cold, never get angry and never do bad things. Then why should you eat meat and white flour every day? And if the taste doesn't suit you, you order the cook to make it over again. And every night you sleep with the nuns. It's suffering and virtue for others but for yourself, it's comfort and sin."

Father Sun did not deign to answer this. He stood before them defiantly and kept his mouth shut.

"And as for the mass," continued Cheng-k'uan. "If anyone gave you a lot of money, you said it for him very quickly. If anyone gave you a little money you did the mass after a while, but if anyone had no money at all, there was no mass at all either. Is your mass a service to the people or is it just a business to earn some money?"

This brought the peasant Hsiao-su to his feet. "You told us a lot of lies," he said, walking straight up to the priest and shaking his fist in his face. "You said that no one must bite the wafer you handed out. You said that if we bit it with our teeth blood would flow from it and we would be punished by God. But I didn't believe it. One morning I took the wafer to the privy behind the church and I broke it with my teeth and crumbled it up. I found nothing but wheat flour. Not a drop of blood flowed out of it. Your words are nothing but lies. All you do is deceive people."

"That's right, all you do is deceive," said Cheng-k'uan, joining Hsiao-su in front of the priest. "The Carry-On Society is supposed to help people, but the best land is farmed by the head of the Society and the landlord Fan Pu-tzu. When the Japanese came, we all asked for shelter in the Church. You found room for the landlords, but we poor Catholics could only wander about the yard until we were finally driven back onto the street. And of everything we brought to you for protection, you took 20 percent. Is that the way you help people?"

"Help people! Help people! They never help people," said Wang Ch'eng-yu. "I have been a Catholic all my life and all I ever got for it was beatings." The words poured from him in a torrent as he told how his little sister was taken into the orphanage and how he himself was beaten for joining the Buddhist rites. "When the Japanese came I was a match peddler," he sobbed. "I was afraid they would seize my stock. I brought 70 boxes of matches to the Church for safekeeping. Society Chairman Wang put them in a drawer, but three days later when I returned there were only three boxes left. When I asked him what became of the matches he said, 'Better ask the drawer.' When I asked him again, he beat me up."

By the time Ch'eng-yu had finished, other people were angry enough to speak out. A storm of accusations followed, many of them somewhat wide of the target, which was supposed to be the priest and his relations with the enemy. The fire tended to concentrate, instead, on the many-sided exploitation practiced by the Church and its leaders —a portent of the hurricane to come.

A non-Catholic, P'ei Shing-k'uan, said that he owed $50 to a church member. When he was unable to pay, Society Chairman Wang stepped in with an offer to mediate. He suggested that P'ei sell an acre and a half of land to the Church and then remain on it as a tenant. "I sold the land to the Church," said the unhappy P'ei, pointing a finger at Father Sun, "but my creditor got nothing. It went to the Church as a contribution to God. When I asked to rent the land, I was told that I myself must join the Church. I refused and to this day I have not been allowed on that land."

A Catholic, Yin Ch'in-ch'un, said, "Now I know that Catholic or not makes little difference. In the famine year I had nothing to eat. My children were sick. I was forced to sell four *mou*. The land was worth $50 for each *mou* but the Church demanded that I sell at $20. I was told I could have the crop, but when harvest time came round, I got nothing."

Altogether more than 100 grievances against the Church and the Carry-On Society were voiced that day. Before the meeting was over, Father Sun was attacked by several angry peasants and badly beaten up. That night, with the help of persons still loyal to him, he escaped to Horse Square, and from there fled to Hungtung, a city in the Nationalist-held area to the west.

Father Sun fled with nothing but the clothes on his back. He left behind a gun, many vestments, a desk full of personal papers, and five acres of land that included an irrigated vegetable garden, one of a handful in the whole village. Among his papers were found a letter of introduction from Japanese headquarters in North China and instructions issued by the puppet New People's Society for the improvement of the work of the rural Church.

Father Sun's personal property was added to the wealth confiscated from 26 other families that had been brought before the village on charges of collaboration. Altogether the People's Government took one hundred bags of grain from the accused as payment for grafted property and abuses of power made possible by their position as Japanese stooges.

All of this property was divided among the poorest people of the village according to the losses of each made public at the meetings. Those who took an active part and spoke out about the damages they had suffered got compensation. Those who did not speak out got less or nothing. In the course of these early distributions the leaders of the movement—Fu-yuan, T'ien-ming, Kuei-ts'ai, and the leading militiamen—took nothing, on the advice of District Leader Liang. They adopted this policy in order to demonstrate that the movement was for the benefit of all the people who had suffered from the occupation and not just for the leaders—a clean break with all the traditions of the past.

These early distributions did not go smoothly by any means. One of the main problems was fear. Many people who should have been compensated with property were still afraid to accept it. This was particularly true of the valuable and conspicuous things which could easily brand a person as a participant in the struggle. If the counter-revolution should gather enough strength to strike back, those who had property that originally belonged to collaborators would be the first to suffer. No lists would be necessary.

For several days two militiamen led one donkey all over the village begging household after household to accept it, but found no takers. A fine cart belonging to Wang Lai-hsun, the landlord who had been a puppet street captain, also stood for days without a claimant, even though it was the best cart in the whole village. It was worth at least 1,000 pounds of grain. The cadres, who had agreed not to accept anything themselves, had to knock on doors and persuade someone to be brave enough to take it. Finally a middle peasant named Chang-hsun, a man with a village-wide reputation for greed and stinginess, found the cart too tempting to resist. His ingrained shrewdness overcame whatever fear he had and, even though he already had one cart, he bought the cart that had belonged to Wang Lai-hsun for three hundredweight of grain—a real bargain. Later, when others began to lose their fear of a counter-attack, they complained that he had no right to buy a cart when many families had no cart at all. Then Chang-hsun offered to give the cart back to the village, but the cadres told him to keep it. To turn it back at such a time might lead some to think that he had lost confidence in the ability of the Eighth Route Army to hold the region.

****

The Anti-Traitor Movement in the whole Fifth District was brought to a close in December 1945. In the course of the struggle, important gains were made, but serious shortcomings also marred the record. The gains, as seen by a leading district cadre who made a report to the County Committee of the Communist Party, included the complete rout of the gentry-Kuomintang attempt to set up a regime based on the old political machine and the wartime collaborators. In the course of this rout, half the landlords and rich peasants in the district were attacked and punished with the confiscation of some or all of their property, thus cutting back considerably the holdings on which the old system was based. Many people were mobilized, organized, and educated by these events and learned to see some connection between collaboration and the dominant feudal class.

The shortcomings consisted of failure to draw the majority of the population into active participation—the cadres and militia did too much, the people as a whole too little—and lack of discrimination in the attack, little or no distinction having been made between collaborators on the basis of their class origin or motivation.

While some Communist leaders, at least on the county level, saw the Anti-Traitor Movement as an initial skirmish in an all-out war against the landlords as a class and tried to guide it in that direction, the majority of the active peasants saw it only as a movement of revenge for wartime injuries. They hated the traitors and wanted to strike them down once and for all. But the traitors, in Long Bow at any rate, were drawn from all classes. When the gentry withdrew from open participation in the village government, they found others to carry on for them. Hence there were middle peasants, poor peasants, and even hired laborers among the puppets. The members of the village police or Self-Defense Corps were all poor peasants, the block and street captains mostly middle peasants. Many of these people went along under economic pressure or were drafted into action under threat of violent reprisal. Some of them served the enemy only a few months, a few weeks, or even a few days. This latter group were known as the "one meal of wheat" traitors. By striking them all down as if they were equally to blame, the village cadres and the active peasants took shadow for substance, confused puppet with master, and punished the poor as heavily as they did the rich who were considered to be the real source and backbone of the collaboration. The poor were punished more heavily, in fact, for the main form of punishment was the confiscation of property, an effective and justifiable policy when applied to the gentry who had plenty of property to spare and had acquired most of it by exploitation past or present in the first place—but a disastrous policy when applied to poor working people who had very little to begin with, earned most of it by their own hard labor, and were reduced to beggary by the loss of it.* The collective nature of the punishment was also unjust. The whole family had to pay for the collaboration of one leading member.

Such a policy atomized the community, frightened many people, drove many middle peasants who were potential allies of the coming revolution toward, if not into, the arms of the opposition. In Long Bow Village alone, 16 middle peasant families and six poor peasant families were expropriated, in whole or in part, for collaboration. In the whole Fifth District the figure reached 181.

If the class question was obscured by the indiscriminate attacks of the Anti-Traitor Movement, the religious question was disastrously sharpened. Even though the charges centered on the activities rather than the religious beliefs of the collaborators, the fact that almost all of them were Catholics gave the movement a definite sectarian slant. This religious sectarianism reached a fever pitch with the escape of Father Sun. Since the Father himself was suspected of being a Kuomintang agent, all those suspected of aiding him were arrested, beaten in an effort to extract confessions, and accused of being agents also. The landlord Fan Pu-tzu's second son, Fan Ming-hsi, and two poor Catholic peasants, Hu-sheng and Hsien-pao, were held in the county jail for eight months while the incident was investigated. Hou Chin-ming, a third poor peasant, was charged with actually opening the door for the father. He was badly beaten and ran away to Hung-tung while he was still able to use his limbs. He left behind half an acre of land, three sections of house, and a young wife bought from the church orphanage a few years earlier.

The indiscriminate attack on all collaborators and the sectarian overtones that accompanied it gave the real agent, Wang En-pao, and his followers, a lever in their counter-campaign. As secretary of the Fifth District Kuomintang, Wang En-pao had organized a group of about 20 men, most of them landlords, in the various villages of the district. They attacked the new cadres for real abuses and spread rumors about imaginary ones. In Long Bow Kuei-ts'ai became a chief target. He was always in the lead when direct action was taken and had beaten many people. Wang Man-hsi, the man who tied up and led Kuo Te-yu into the first meeting, a 19-year-old of tremendous strength and enthusiasm, was another target. For the blows he meted out he was already admired by some and feared by others as the "King of the Devils."

---

* Inherited property was no less suspect than property bought with in-comes acquired through rent and interest since there would have been no property to inherit had not the previous generations "peeled and pared" the landless and the land poor of their day.

In Long Bow these verbal attacks produced no incidents, but in other places the landlord clique managed to incite certain people to action. One South Market militiaman named Ming Chun was found one morning hanging on the limb of a tree. A group of angry peasants strung him there after hearing rumors that he had taken valuable property to his own home and had forced his attentions on several women, all of them wives and daughters of collaborators. In Li Village Gulch, a strong Catholic center, the former district leader Yellow Dog Kuo, was thrown into a dry well and badly injured.

The hesitancy of some middle peasants, the anger of many Catholics, and the occasional counter-attacks that were the backlash of the sharp campaign could not halt or even delay the rising tide of struggle. A description of the reverse eddies should not be allowed to obscure the enormous enthusiasm which the punishment of the collaborators and the distribution of their property aroused in the great majority of the peasant families, whether or not they themselves had been active. When, in late December, the Eighth Route Army called for volunteers to strengthen the region against attack, Chang Chiang-tzu, the conscientious young head of the militia, led 25 men to the recruiting office at the county seat. Five were rejected for physical reasons, among them Chang Kuei-ts'ai, the vice-head of the village, who had syphilis, but 20 went on to join that army which alone could guarantee continued control of Long Bow by the landless and the land poor. This was the first example the people had ever seen of a government in power that asked for volunteers. Under the Kuomintang the young men had been led off to war with ropes tied around their necks. Now an expensive banquet was spread for the volunteers before they departed from the village, and each was given some spending money as a token of appreciation. They marched off with red carnations pinned to their jackets in a cacophony of beating drums, clashing cymbals, and the gay shouting of a crowd of small children who followed them all the way to Horse Square.

13

Dig Out the Rotten Root of Feudalism

In a very short time, in China's central, southern, and northern provinces, several hundred million peasants will rise like a tornado or tempest, a force so extraordinarily swift and violent that no power, however great, will be able to suppress it. They will break all the trammels that now bind them and rush forward along the road to liberation. They will send all imperialists, warlords, corrupt officials, local bullies, and bad gentry to their graves.*

Mao Tse-tung

OUT OF the confusion and near anarchy of the tempestuous Anti-Traitor Movement that followed the Japanese surrender came an assault on the land system itself. From chaotic revenge against collaborators, the young men of the resistance were led by the district Communist Party to a conscious planned attack on the landlords as a class. With this shift in emphasis, China's 20-year-old land revolution, temporarily suspended by the war, began again in earnest and rapidly gathered a momentum too great to be checked by any political party or leader.

The campaign in the Fifth District of Lucheng County started with a famous meeting in Li Village Gulch, the first settlement south of Long Bow on the road to Changchih. This meeting was held on January 16, 1946, in an effort to educate the young revolutionary cadres in the fundamentals of class relations and class consciousness so that they could, as they themselves said, "get at the root of calamity." All the young men who had just led the Anti-Traitor Movement to completion were brought together by the district leaders. The meeting lasted three days and three major issues were discussed: (1) Who depends upon whom for a living? (2) Why are the poor poor and the rich rich? (3) Should rent be paid to landlords?

---

* This quote is from a 1927 report written by Mao Tse-tung. The phenomenon which he predicted was delayed for two decades. Nevertheless it took place much as he had foreseen and, historically speaking, within a short time.

The participants had no trouble voicing grievances against individual landlords. They protested all kinds of feudal services, such as the forcing of tenants to pick up and deliver landlords' relatives, carry sedan chairs at weddings, give gifts at the New Year. They condemned the gentry for having taken the peasants' wives and daughters to their beds almost at will, made concubines of them, or simply raped them and left them. They also catalogued the ways in which the landlords cheated when loans were given out or rents paid: the use of the small measure for passing out grain, but the substitution of the big measure when grain was collected; the adulteration of grain given out, but the thorough cleaning and winnowing of grain taken in. They pointed out how the landlords took advantage of the illiteracy of the peasants by keeping dishonest records.

The cadres were all in favor of a reduction in rents and interest. They went further and demanded that past overcharges be paid back and that families who had avoided taxes, throwing all the burden on the poor and middle peasants, be charged with all the back taxes they had not paid over the years. But when it came to the land system itself, there was some confusion. Many thought that where the land belonged to the landlords, through legitimate purchase or inheritance, rents should be paid. "If the landlords did not let us rent the land we would starve," they said. Others disagreed sharply with this. "Can land be eaten? No. Land itself cannot produce food without labor and only those who labor have the right to eat. Why should one man have the right to say, 'This land is mine,' and then, without lifting a hoe himself, demand half of what is grown on it? Rent itself is exploitation."

But many still said, "When I worked for the landlord he fed me, and at the end of the year he paid me. That was the agreement. If he had cheated me of my pay or refused to feed me I could accuse him, but since he did feed and pay me there is nothing wrong."

Hour after hour the discussion went on in small groups and large meetings where the district leaders made reports and explained to the cadres the economic basis of the old society. They figured up how much grain the labor of one man could produce and then calculated how much food and wages a hired laborer received from the landlord for a year's work. From these figures it became clear, not only that there was exploitation, but that the exploitation was heavy. The atrocities committed by the traitors were open and vicious. Everybody could see them and oppose them. The open oppression of some landlords was equally cruel and vicious. Everyone could see that too and oppose it. But the *jan po hsueh,* the hidden exploitation, of the average landlord, the exploitation inherent in land rent itself had to be pointed out and exposed, for was it not the root of all the other evils?

When the meeting broke up on the third day the three main questions had been settled in the minds of most: (1) The landlords depended on the labor of the peasants for their very life. (2) The rich were rich because they "peeled and pared" the poor. (3) Rent should not be paid to the landlords.

With this conclusion the peasant leaders of Lucheng County jumped beyond the official policy of the Communist Party of China and the Liberated Areas Government as a whole. Official policy was still "double reduction"—reduce rents and reduce interest rates. This was the policy of the wartime united front against Japan. Chairman Mao Tse-tung had proposed that this should continue to be the policy in the immediate postwar period because, although fighting had begun and had even developed on a large scale in some areas, it had not yet escalated into all-out civil war. It was incumbent on the Communist Party to explore every possible avenue of compromise that might bring peace while still preserving the basic gains won by the people of China. During such a period of exploration, the continuation of "double reduction" was mandatory. To have called for land expropriation at this time would have been provocative.

The initial talks between the Communist Party and the Kuomintang seemed to make headway. With General Marshall, special representative of the United States, acting as intermediary, a truce was signed on January 13, 1946. The two parties agreed that all fighting should cease for a six-month period while the possibility of a political settlement through some form of coalition government was explored. Pending such a settlement, the policy of the Communist Party Central Committee in Yenan was to carry into effect all coalition agreements, including "double reduction," and hold the gentry to them. However, demands for land kept coming from below. The arming of the people for resistance had placed the peasants in a position to challenge the landlords and usurers in the countryside, and not even the tremendous prestige of the Communist Party or the critical situation of the country and the world could prevent this challenge from breaking out in one form or another and carrying with it many lower echelon cadres and Party Committees.

This increasingly explosive force was channeled for a time into forms of attack against the gentry that did not formally violate the provisions of "double reduction," yet nevertheless transferred land from the gentry to the peasants. Conventional grievances concerning lower rents and lower interest rates were made retroactive to cover the war years in villages where the occupation had given the landlords a free hand not only to continue the collection of rent and interest but to increase the rate of both. Now the peasants demanded not only the correction of abuses but also the repayment of overcharges and the restoration of lands and property seized in default of debts which were, by "double reduction" standards, illegal. In practice, when the grievances were totalled up, the charges almost always mounted up to more than most gentry families could pay, and everything they owned was expropriated for distribution. The peasants even matched the excesses of the 1930's by a policy of *sao ti ch'u men,* or "sweep the floor out the door," which meant to clean the family out of house and home and drive them from the area. They called this whole movement "settling accounts."

****

In Long Bow the young men returned from the district meeting full of enthusiasm. Chang San-ch'ing, the secretary of the village government, who was one of the participants, later said: "I was very happy when I returned from Li Village Gulch. Up until that time I had been just a little afraid. I carried a burden on my back. I figured that if all those who had worked for the Japanese were to be struggled against, then I too would become a victim, for I had worked for a Japanese drug company for more than one year. But at that meeting we were told that the Anti-Traitor Movement was over. We decided that we would now struggle against the landlords who had oppressed us for so long. Everyone who had been oppressed or exploited, who had borrowed money or rented land could now make accusations and get revenge. I was very happy. I was no longer the least bit afraid for I thought—I too have been oppressed. From childhood my family suffered under loans at high interest and I worked out as a hired laborer for so many years, and later, when I went out to work, I just served the master of the shop. So all my life I have been oppressed and exploited. Now my time has come."

The first task faced by this group when they returned to the village was to organize a local Peasants' Association. This was a voluntary organization of all working peasants recognized by the Liberated Areas Government of Shansi-Honan-Hopei-Shantung as the only legal organ for carrying out agrarian policy, conducting the struggle against the landlords, receiving confiscated property, and distributing it to the landless and land poor.

Farm laborers, poor peasants, middle peasants, rural handicraftsmen, and impoverished intellectuals such as schoolteachers, letter writers, and clerks sympathetic to the new land policies were all entitled to join when approved by the elected committee of the Association. All members had the right to speak, vote, elect, and be elected, and also the right to criticize and replace elected officers. They were obligated to abide by the rules of the Association, carry out its decisions, and pay dues. These dues amounted to one catty of millet a year.

Two cadres from the old Liberated Area in the Second District, where village Peasants' Associations had existed for a long time, came to help organize the local group in Long Bow. Thirty of the poorest peasants in the village were first called together. They included women whose sons had been killed in the fort, peasant families whose able-bodied members had been forced into rear service far from home, and long-term hired helpers who owned nothing but the clothes on their backs.

Some of these families had already received food and clothes as a result of the Anti-Traitor Movement. Fu-yuan and T'ien-ming explained to them that the preceding distributions were only the beginning, that such a small amount of goods could not solve any real problems, that they should tackle the land question itself. Fu-yuan posed to them the question of "who lives off whom?" He urged each member to tell his or her life story and to figure out for himself the root of the problem.

Once again Kuei-ts'ai led off. In order to move the others he told his own history. "In the past when I lived in Linhsien I stayed with my uncle," he said. "In order to get married my uncle borrowed 20 silver dollars. Within a year the interest plus the principal amounted to more than 300 dollars. We could not possibly repay this. The landlord seized all our lands and houses and I became a migrant wandering through the province looking for work."

This reminded poor peasant Shen T'ien-hsi of the loss of his home. "Once when we needed some money we decided to sell our house. We made a bargain with a man who offered a reasonable price, but Sheng Ching-ho, who lived next door, forced us to sell our house to him for almost nothing."

Then poor peasant Ta-hung's wife spoke up. "You had to sell your house, but my parents had to sell me. We lived in a prosperous valley but we owned no land. In the famine year we were starving and my parents sold me for a few bushels of grain. If we had had some land I could have found a husband and been properly married. Instead, I was sold like a donkey or a cow."

Story followed story. Many wept as they remembered the sale of children, the death of family members, the loss of property. The village cadres kept asking "What is the reason for this? Why did we all suffer so? Was it the 'eight ideographs' that determined our fate or was it the land system and the rents we had to pay? Why shouldn't we now take on the landlords and right the wrongs of the past?"

T'ien-ming finally challenged them to action. "Now, the only question is, do we dare begin? The Eighth Route Army and the Liberated Areas Government stand behind us. Already in many places the landlords have been beaten down. We have only to follow the example of others. We have only to act with our own hands. Then we can all *fanshen*."

"There are not enough of us," said one.

"Then we have to find more members. Each one here should go out and find others. All the poor are brothers together. If we unite no one can stand in our way."

Each of the 30 went home, visited with neighbor and friend, and each found two or three more peasants who could be approved by the whole group. Soon over 100 families had joined the Peasants' Association. Most of them were poor, but among them were scattered a few middle peasants. Kuo Cheng-k'uan, the poor Catholic who had led the attack on Father Sun, a man who had worked all his life as a laborer, and whose wife had died of starvation in the famine year, was elected chairman.

Another Catholic, Wang Yu-lai, was elected vice-chairman. He came originally from Lin County, high in the Taihang range. He had once been a member of the local Kuomintang army, had later taken up banditry as a way of life, and was said to have joined the "Red Rifle" secret society as a young man. He had always been poor. Throughout the ten years he had lived in Long Bow he had worked as a hired laborer. During the Anti-Traitor Movement, and especially in the struggle against Father Sun, Yu-lai and his 18-year-old son, Wen-te, were noted for their courage and energy.

Several days of intense activity followed the establishment of the new Association. Many active members neglected all their regular work in order to mobilize the majority of the people for the struggle to come. And so, toward the end of January, the campaign to "settle accounts" with the landlords finally began.

The committee of the Peasants' Association decided to tackle Kuo Ch'ung-wang first. He was not the richest man in the village but he was one of the meanest. His close association with the puppet Chief-of-Staff Chou Mei-sheng tarred him with the collaborationist brush. More important was the fact that while his tenants died of starvation during the famine year, he seized grain and hoarded it for speculation. The cadres, having learned from the failure of their first big meeting, held small group meetings ahead of time in order to gather opinions against Ch'ung-wang. Those with serious grievances were encouraged to make them known among their closest neighbors and were then mobilized to speak out at the village-wide meeting to come.

While the small meetings were in progress, the militia arrested Kuo Ch'ung-wang, searched his house and unearthed tons of grain. Much of it was rotten. On the day of the big meeting, the grain, which could have saved the lives of dozens of people, lay in the courtyard in a stinking mildewed heap. The people who crowded in to accuse walked over the grain and, as the courtyard filled up, some of them sat down on it. The smell and the sight of it reminded them of those who had died for want of a few catties and filled them with anger. Next to the grain stood two jars of salt water—salt that had been hoarded so long it had undergone hydrolysis. While the landless and the land poor went weeks without salt, Ch'ung-wang had let salt go to waste.

At this critical meeting, Fu-yuan, the village head, was the first to speak. Because he was a cousin of Ch'ung-wang, his words carried extra weight with the rest of the village. When a man was moved to accuse his own cousin, the provocation had to be serious.

"In the famine year," Fu-yuan began, talking directly to Ch'ung-wang, "my brother worked for your family. We were all hungry. We had nothing to eat. But you had no thought for us. Several times we tried to borrow grain from you. But it was all in vain. You watched us starve without pity."

Then Ho-pang, a militiaman, spoke up. His voice shook as he told how he had rented land from Ch'ung-wang. "One year I could not pay the rent. You took the whole harvest. You took my clothes. You took everything." He broke down sobbing as a dozen others jumped up shouting.

"What was in your mind?"

"You took everything. Miao-le and his brother died."

"Yes, what were your thoughts? You had no pity. Didn't you hound P'ei Mang-wen's mother to her death?"

"Speak."

"Yes, speak. Make him talk. Let's hear his answers!"

But Ch'ung-wang had no answers. He could not utter a word. When the peasants saw that he could not answer them they realized that they had him cornered, that they had already won a victory. Many who had been afraid to open their mouths found themselves shouting in anger without thought of the consequences.

The meeting lasted all day. In the evening, when the committee reckoned up all the charges against Ch'ung-wang, they found that he owed one hundred bags of grain. That night, under a full moon, the militia went to the fields with measuring rods and measured Ch'ung-wang's land. They found that he had three acres more than were listed in his deeds and that for 20 years he had evaded taxes on that land while others had paid and paid. When they added this to the other damages claimed against him they realized that all his lands, all his houses, his grain, his clothes, his stock, and everything else that he owned would not be enough to settle the debt. Yet when they looked in his storeroom they found not hundreds, but only a paltry six bags of grain that could be seized.

The next morning when the people met again to carry on the campaign against Ch'ung-wang excitement ran high. Women even went so far as to bring food with them so that they and their families could stay right through the day and not miss a single minute. Liang, the district leader, opened the attack. He said, "This is our only chance to settle the blood-and-sweat debt of the landlord. Even if you take all his property it will never be enough. Ask him where he has hidden his gold and silver. Make him give up his precious things."

"Yes, speak out. Where are the coins? Where have you buried the money?" came the shouts from the crowd. But Kuo refused to say anything beyond the fact that he had no silver and never had had any. Since nobody believed him, the militia were ordered into his house to make a search. They were joined by more than 60 peasant volunteers. They dug up the floors, ripped the mud bricks off the tops of the k'angs, tapped the walls. It was all in vain. They found nothing.

When the search proved fruitless, a few of the cadres took Ch'ung-wang aside. They told him that it was no use trying to hide his wealth. Since all his ordinary property was not enough to settle his account with the people, they would surely find his hidden wealth sooner or later. It would therefore be much safer and wiser for him to hand this over voluntarily than to face their wrath once they found it on their own. After several people had talked to him in the same vein Ch'ung-wang finally gave in. He told them where to dig. They found 50 silver dollars in an earthen crock.

When this money was brought before the people at the meeting, they became very angry. Here was proof that Ch'ung-wang had lied to them. Scores of people jumped up, ran forward, and began to beat him with whatever came to hand.

"Tell us where the rest is. You know that is not all," they shouted.

Someone struck him a blow in the face. Ch'ung-wang held his bleeding mouth and tried to speak.

"Don't hit me. I'll tell you. I'll tell you right away. There is another 80 dollars in the back room."

The meeting adjourned immediately while the militia and their enthusiastic helpers again went to search. They very soon found another cache of coins, but this only whetted their appetites and angered them still further. Ch'ung-wang was playing with them as a cat plays with a mouse in spite of the fact that he was their prisoner. First grain, then salt, now silver dollars—the bastard was richer than they thought! When they got back to the courtyard, they beat him again.

That day he gave up more than 200 silver dollars.

In the evening they let him go home but, unknown to him, set several militiamen to watch his house and listen in, if possible, on the conversations that went on inside it.

Landlord Sheng Ching-ho, the richest man in the village, sat at home all that day and listened to the angry shouts of the people as they accused Ch'ung-wang and swarmed over his house. After dark he crept out onto the street and stole to Ch'ung-wang's door hoping to learn something about what had happened. Perhaps some plan could be worked out to counter this new offensive. He knocked quietly on the wooden door that was the sole entrance to Ch'ung-wang's courtyard, but before anyone appeared to open it he was seized from behind by several militiamen and dragged off to the village lockup. It was then two days before the Chinese New Year. The wealthy families had planned all sorts of good things to eat and their wives and servants had been preparing and cooking for days. The leaders of the Peasants' Association decided not to let Ching-ho pass such a happy holiday. They set the attack on him for the next day, even though that meant they had no time to mobilize opinions against him. As it happened, a blunder on the part of Ching-ho's brother, Sheng Ching-chung, aroused the people more than several days of mobilization could possibly have done.

As soon as Sheng Ching-chung heard that his brother Ching-ho had been detained, he took a bag of wheat flour on his shoulder and went calling. He found the assistant village head, Kuei-ts'ai, at home talking with San-ch'ing, the village secretary. He set his bag of flour by the door, greeted them both warmly, and sat himself down to have a friendly chat. It did not take him long to get to the point. "I know your life is hard," he said. "Since we are people of one village please do not stand on ceremony but help yourselves to this flour and pass a happy New Year. Later on, if you should meet with any difficulties, you should know that my door is always open and I am always ready to help."

The two young cadres could hardly believe their eyes and ears. What did he take them for—rats who could be bought with a bag of flour? They drove him and his burden out of the house and went immediately to T'ien-ming. The next afternoon Kuei-ts'ai and San-ch'ing told a village-wide meeting how Ching-chung had tried to bribe them. Their story aroused a storm of protest and a flood of accusations.

"In the famine year he gave us nothing. He even drove beggars away from his door, but now suddenly he weeps for our hard life —now we are 'people of one village,'" said one.

"It is clear he only wants to buy off the leaders and undermine our ranks. We should never be taken in by such tricks," added another.

"This should be a lesson to all of us," said T'ien-ming. "Never trust a landlord; never protect a landlord. There is only one road and that is to struggle against them."

The cadres had been afraid that the people might hold back their accusations against Ching-ho, but Kuei-ts'ai's report broke the dam. There was no holding back. Over 100 grievances were registered at that one meeting. So vicious had been Ching-ho's practices and so widespread his influence that more than half of the families in the village had scores to settle with him.

What happened on the following day was told to me by Kuo Cheng-k'uan, Chairman of the Peasants' Association:

When the final struggle began Ching-ho was faced not only with those hundred accusations but with many many more. Old women who had never spoken in public before stood up to accuse him. Even Li Mao's wife—a woman so pitiable she hardly dared look anyone in the face—shook her fist before his nose and cried out, "Once I went to glean wheat on your land. But you cursed me and drove me away. Why did you curse and beat me? And why did you seize the wheat I had gleaned?" Altogether over 180 opinions were raised. Ching-ho had no answer to any of them. He stood there with his head bowed. We asked him whether the accusations were false or true. He said they were all true. When the committee of our Association met to figure up what he owed, it came to 400 bags of milled grain, not coarse millet.

That evening all the people went to Ching-ho's courtyard to help take over his property. It was very cold that night so we built bonfires and the flames shot up toward the stars. It was very beautiful. We went in to register his grain and altogether found but 200 bags of unmilled millet —only a quarter of what he owed us. Right then and there we decided to call another meeting. People all said he must have a lot of silver dollars— they thought of the wine plant, and the pigs he raised on the distillers' grains, and the North Temple Society and the Confucius Association.

We called him out of the house and asked him what he intended to do since the grain was not nearly enough. He said, "I have land and house."

"But all this is not enough," shouted the people. So then we began to beat him. Finally he said, "I have 40 silver dollars under the *k'ang*." We went in and dug it up. The money stirred up everyone. We beat him again. He told us where to find another hundred after that. But no one believed that this was the end of his hoard. We beat him again and several militiamen began to heat an iron bar in one of the fires. Then Ching-ho admitted that he had hid 110 silver dollars in militiaman Man-hsi's uncle's home. Man-hsi was very hot-headed. When he heard that his uncle had helped Sheng Ching-ho he got very angry. He ran home and began to beat his father's own brother. We stopped him. We told him, "Your uncle didn't know it was a crime." We asked the old man why he had hidden money for Ching-ho and he said, "No one ever told me anything. I didn't know there was anything wrong in it." You see, they were relatives and the money had been given to him for safekeeping years before. So Man-hsi finally cooled down. It was a good thing for he was angry enough to beat his uncle to death and he was strong enough to do it.

Altogether we got $500 from Ching-ho that night. By that time the sun was already rising in the eastern sky. We were all tired and hungry, especially the militiamen who had called the people to the meeting, kept guard on Ching-ho's house, and taken an active part in beating Ching-ho and digging for the money. So we decided to eat all the things that Ching-ho had prepared to pass the New Year—a whole crock of dumplings stuffed with pork and peppers and other delicacies. He even had shrimp.

All said, "In the past we never lived through a happy New Year because he always asked for his rent and interest then and cleaned our houses bare. This time we'll eat what we like," and everyone ate his fill and didn't even notice the cold.

That was one of the happiest days the people of Long Bow ever experienced. They were in such a mellow mood that they released Ching-ho on the guarantee of a relative, let him remain at home unguarded, and called off the struggle for the rest of the holiday season.

But Ching-ho did not wait around to see what would happen when action resumed. He ran away the very next day. So did Kuo Ch'ung-wang. He and his wife fled to another county where they found temporary employment as primary school teachers. Later they fled that school and disappeared altogether. Nobody in Long Bow heard of their whereabouts thereafter.

In Ch'ung-wang's absence, his brother and partner in business, Fu-wang, was brought before the Peasants' Association. He was beaten so severely that he died a few days later, but in spite of this violent treatment he gave no hint as to where any further wealth might be found.

14

Wang Lai-hsun Is Next

A revolution is not the same as inviting people to dinner, or writing an essay, or painting a picture, or doing fancy needlework; it cannot be anything so restrained and magnanimous. A revolution is an uprising, an act of violence whereby one class overthrows another.

Mao Tse-tung

WANG CH'UNG-LAI'S WIFE returned to Long Bow late in 1945. Driven out by the family that bought her as a child wife and forced into beggary, she and her husband had lived in another village for 20 years. When they heard that the landlords would be brought to account and old debts repaid, they hurried home only to be met by a stone wall of hostility from the local cadres. T'ien-ming, Fu-yuan, Kuei-ts'ai, and Cheng-k'uan had never heard of the couple. They were reluctant to let them join the struggle for they didn't want to share the "fruits" with outsiders. When Ch'ung-lai's wife went to the district office and protested, Fu-yuan was directed to call in Wang Lai-hsun's mother for questioning.

The old lady denied that Ch'ung-lai was her son. "I only borrowed him," she said. "He lived here half a year and then he ran away. I never ill-treated him."

"Then why did you buy a wife for him?" cried Ch'ung-lai's wife in anger. "And why, if he was not your adopted son, did I live in your family and suffer six years of beatings? Everyone in this village knows how C'h'ung-lai worked hard for more than ten years like a hired laborer in your family. Can you cover the sky with your hand?"

Fu-yuan believed her then, but since she and her husband were still strangers to most of the younger people, the Peasants' Association gave them no property. They were allowed to live in part of Lai-hsun's house and to farm one and one-half acres of Lai-hsun's land, but nothing was turned over to them as their own. Ch'ung-lai and his wife had waited a long time; they could wait some more. They moved into their borrowed quarters and looked forward to the day when the struggle against Lai-hsun would come. They did not have long to wait.

139

Wang Lai-hsun followed Kuo Fu-wang to the tribune. When he appeared before his tenants and laborers, Ch'ung-lai's wife was standing in the front row. She was the first to speak.

"How was it that you stayed at home while we were driven out?" she asked, stepping in front of the astounded landlord on her small bound feet.

"Because Ch'ung-lai had a grandfather. He had another place to live," said Lai-hsun looking at the ground. He did not have the courage to look her in the face.

"But you too had in-laws. You too had a place to go. Why did you drive us out and make beggars of us? During the famine year we came to beg from you, our own brother, but you gave us nothing. You drove us away with a stick and beat me and the children with an iron poker."

"I remember that day," said Lai-hsun.

"Why?" shouted Ch'ung-lai's wife, tears rolling down her dirt-stained face. "Why?"

"I was afraid if you returned you would ask to divide the property with me."

This answer aroused the whole meeting.

"Beat him, beat him," shouted the crowd.

Ch'ung-lai's wife then took a leather strap from around her wasting body and she and her son beat Lai-hsun with the strap and with their fists. They beat him for more time than it takes to eat a meal and as they beat him Ch'ung-lai's wife cried out, "I beat you in revenge for six years of beatings. In the past you never cared for us. Your eyes did not know us. Now my eyes do not know you either. Now it is my turn."

Lai-hsun cringed before them and whimpered as the blows fell on his back and neck, then he fainted, fell to the ground, and was carried to his home.

After that meeting, Ch'ung-lai and his family were given outright the ten sections of house and the acre and a half of land that had only been loaned to them up until that time.

Wang Lai-hsun's debt to the people added up to a very large sum but the militia found very little wealth in his home. In addition to the land and the houses he had only a few bags of grain. Even when beaten severely he insisted that he had not hidden silver or gold. He was a heroin addict, he said. He had spent all his money on heroin.

The peasants did not believe him, however, and, after getting nowhere by beating him, decided to carry the struggle to his wife. The meeting that day was held in the temple. When the people questioned Lai-hsun's wife, she said that she did have some coins but that she had given them to Ch'ung-lai's wife for safekeeping. This angered everyone. The militia ran to find Ch'ung-lai's wife. When they brought her to the temple they asked her, "Why did you hide money for that landlord?"

"I never did," said Ch'ung-lai's wife. "Who told you that?"

"She did," said the cadres, pointing to Lai-hsun's wife.

Ch'ung-lai's wife went livid with rage and rushed at the woman who had been her bitterest enemy for so long. But the cadres tore her from her victim and questioned her further. They didn't believe her story. They thought she had fooled them.

"Tell us where you have the money," they demanded.

When she answered, "How could I do such a thing? She is my enemy!" they started to beat her. Chin-chu, one of the poor peasants who had been a hired laborer for Lai-hsun, got out a pair of scissors and cut her flesh with them. Blood gushed out over her tunic.

But Ch'ung-lai's wife screamed and fought back. "She didn't even hide a needle in my home. She hates me because we moved back into the courtyard that she ruled for so long. She is accusing me to make trouble and you believe her!"

At last the young men decided that Ch'ung-lai's wife was telling the truth. They let her go. Wang Lai-hsun and his family were driven from the courtyard just as they themselves had driven out the other half of the family so long ago. Now it was their turn to go and live in abandoned temples and beg for food. But they could not stand such a life. After a few weeks they left Long Bow altogether. All their land, property, houses, clothes, tools, and furniture were confiscated. Only the old lady, Lai-hsun's and Ch'ung-lai's foster mother, remained in the village. She stayed in an abandoned hovel just off the main street. One day she came to Ch'ung-lai's home to beg a little food. The boy, her grandson by adoption, remembered her. He ran into the street and beat her with a stick, saying, "I'll give you some of your own medicine."

This old woman finally maimed herself badly trying to get warm in front of some burning straw. A gust of wind set her clothes on fire. Large areas of her skin were scorched. The pain was so great that she could no longer go out to beg. She died of starvation.

Thus were old scores settled one by one. The brutality of the old system echoed again and again in the convulsions of its demise.

* * * * * * * * * * *

As soon as the Peasants' Association finished "settling accounts" with Wang Lai-hsun, the other wealthy families were tackled one after the other. The landlords Li Tung-Sheng, Shih La-ming, Fan Pu-tzu, Hsu Cheng-p'eng, and Cheng Lin-so were all dispossessed within a few days.

Because Li Tung-sheng had two adopted sons who had joined the Eighth Route Army, he was at first treated leniently, allowed to retain some land, and left to live in his own home. But the hunt for buried treasure soon changed all this. When the peasants asked him where his silver was buried he refused to tell them anything. Angered by his defiance, they beat him severely. They did not mean to inflict mortal blows but he died nevertheless a few days later. His wife and child thereupon handed over $200. They were allowed to stay in their house.

Shih La-ming was beaten to death at a large public meeting by an aroused group of his accusers. His daughter-in-law died of starvation after she was driven out of the family home. Her husband, the puppet officer and local despot, Shih Jen-pao, was already far away serving once again in the army of Yen Hsi-shan.

Fan Pu-tzu died of illness after being driven from the village. His surviving son, Fan Ming-hsi, was beaten to death as a Kuomintang agent, and his 17-year-old grandson ran away. His two daughters-in-law remarried in the village.

Cheng Lin-so had a brother who was a battalion commander in the Kuomintang Army. The peasants took no chances with him. They drove him and his whole family out.

Hsu Cheng-p'eng, the Kuomintang general, was an absentee landlord and he never came back to the village to be tried. His sister and her husband lived in his enormous house and tilled half his land. A cousin paid rent and tilled the other half. The Peasants' Association took over all the land but took pity on the brother-in-law, who in fact had never been more than a hired laborer for Hsu. They gave him three acres. The cousin also received land of his own to till.

While the outright landlords reeled under this broad attack, other gentry whose status was not quite so clear also came under fire. Yang Kuei-sheng, a prosperous landlord's son who himself labored on the land, was driven from the village with his whole family. Wang Ch'ang-yi, professional livestock castrator and self-proclaimed veterinarian, whose savings had been invested in Long Bow land, was deprived of seven acres. Yu Ken-ch'eng, the owner of several large tracts, lost eight of nine acres. Only the widow, Yu Pu-ho, who owned eight acres, escaped expropriation.

In the heat of the campaign even relatively minor exploiters were not safe. Families that rented out small plots of land, hired some labor, or loaned out modest sums at high interest were called rich peasants and attacked as such. To the 16 families of moderate means who were wholly or partly dispossessed in the Anti-Traitor Movement another half-dozen were added. Among them were Wang Ch'un-le, who owned six acres and a mule; Kuo Chao-ch'eng, who owned eight acres and an ox; K'ang Chen-niu, who owned ten acres and a donkey; and the three Ts'ui brothers, sons of a landlord, who between them owned 20 acres.

While individuals who exploited others in some degree constituted the main target of the Peasants' Association, the various gentry-dominated institutions of the village were by no means forgotten. In these institutions the gentry had accumulated and effectively controlled more wealth than was privately possessed by all the landlords put together. All the assets of the North Temple Society, the Confucius Association, the village school, and several other religious, cultural, and clan organizations were liquidated. Over 30 acres of land were seized from such sources, not to mention grain, money, and buildings.

All this was but a warm-up for the main assault, the attack on the Catholic Church itself, for the Church was the primary center of wealth in the whole village and its financial arm, the Carry-On Society, was the largest single landholder. The campaign against the Church in Long Bow had begun, months before, with the arrest of Father Sun as a collaborator. Then it had died down, to flare up anew as the dispossession of the gentry aroused the population of the whole plateau region. The region-wide campaign reached its climax with a large mass meeting in Changchih where Catholics from 27 villages in three counties gathered to make accusations against their bishop, several foreign fathers, and the whole staff of the great South Cathedral that was the heart and nerve center of the Catholic faith in the Shangtang.

As a result of this huge meeting the property of the central institution was expropriated. Only the Cathedral itself and its immediate grounds were left to the Church. Everything else was distributed to the Catholics of the tri-county area, for it was well known that it was their contributions, voluntary and otherwise, that had made possible its accumulation. Lucheng County's share was taken to Horse Square and there divided up. Long Bow alone got about half a million Border Region dollars' worth of property (about $500). Fifty-two Catholic families of the village shared nine tons of grain, over 200 sets of fine clothes, and thousands of dollars among them. In cash alone, each person got $1,500 Border Region currency ($1.50 U.S.).

Taking the expropriation of the Cathedral at Changchih as precedent, the cadres of Long Bow and the leaders of its Peasants' Association moved against the local institution soon afterwards. From the Church, the orphanage, the orphanage hospital, and the Carry-On Society they confiscated more than 40 acres of land, four milk cows, large stores of wheat and corn, 100 new quilts, 15 sets of priestly vestments, many sets of new children's clothes, two bicycles, glassware, stocks of medicinal drugs, hundreds of candles, bronze crosses, bronze candelabras, 16 bronze lamps, and 2,000 silver dollars.

This time the property was not distributed to the Catholics alone but was pooled together with the property seized from the rest of the gentry for use by public organizations and for distribution to all the village poor.

As a final blow at Catholicism the leading lay leader of the Church, the manager of the Carry-On Society, Wang Kuei-ching, was attacked as a landlord. Judged by his landholdings alone, this man was only a middle peasant, but in the eyes of the peasants he deserved a landlord's fate as one of those people who "collected rent and managed landed property for the landlords and depended on the exploitation of the peasants by the landlord as his main means of livelihood."

When Wang Kuei-ching was brought before the village, feeling against him mounted to such a pitch that he was beaten to death then and there. The peasants might not have taken such drastic action had it not been for his two sons, Wang En-pao and Wang Hsiao-wen, both of whom had been exposed as leaders of the Kuomintang underground organization only a short while before, an exposure which revived all the open and latent suspicion of the Catholic community as a nest of agents and traitors.

The man who cracked the secret Kuomintang organization was a former clerk in the puppet administration of the county, one K'ang T'ien-hsing. K'ang wanted to become a teacher in one of the new village schools. The new county administration sent him to a special school where "old style intellectuals" received political instruction. There he began to question his past activities. He turned over a Kuomintang Party membership card to the school office and said that he had received it from Wang En-pao of Long Bow. The latter was immediately arrested. He admitted that he was the district secretary of the Kuomintang Party, that he was the leader of a group dedicated to the destruction of the Liberated Area, and that he was in contact with Yen Hsi-shan's organization in Taiyuan, the provincial capital. T'ien-ming, who was responsible for police work, ordered Wang En-pao held for further investigation. That night the militiaman sent to guard him fell asleep. In the morning Wang En-pao had disappeared. After a thorough search the militia found his body at the bottom of a well.

The Kuomintang leader's younger brother, Wang Hsiao-wen, accused the cadres of having killed En-pao. He publicly vowed to take revenge and was put under close surveillance by the militia. Hsiao-wen lived in a courtyard next to an old couple who could not see well. They were loyal supporters of the new government. One day they discovered some broken needles in a pan of millet that they planned to eat. They suspected their neighbor and warned T'ien-ming. After that the militia kept an even closer watch on Hsiao-wen. They found that he had struck up a friendship with several former Kuomintang officers who were quartered in the village as part of the student body of the Anti-Japanese Political and Military University, an institution housed at that time in the church compound. The officers were prisoners of war assigned to political training in anticipation that they could be won over to the side of the revolution. Within the confines of the village they came and went without supervision. Before Wang En-pao's arrest and suicide they often visited with him. Afterwards, they got in touch with his brother, Hsiao-wen.

One day one of these officers escaped. Hsiao-wen was arrested and sharply questioned. Before the meeting he confessed that he had carried on the work interrupted by his brother's death, that he had gathered information about the struggle in Long Bow—who had been attacked, who beaten, who killed, who were the leaders and who the active followers; that he had drawn up lists of names, given them to the captured officer, and helped him to escape. In this way he hoped to take revenge for the dispossession of the gentry and the death of his brother. This confession so aroused the people—and especially the militia—that Hsiao-wen was also beaten to death. They carried this anger with them into the struggle against his father, Wang Kuei-ching, and this is why he suffered the same fate.

Before the Liberation there had been 15 members in Society Chairman Wang's family. Now none were left. Two had been killed, one committed suicide, and the rest ran away. Thus did the peasants settle accounts with the leading Catholic family of the village and at the same time erase an important center of counter-revolutionary activity.

With the destruction of the Wang family the Church ceased to exist as an organized institution in Long Bow. Although scores of believers remained, many of them bitter and angry over the struggle against the Church, no services were held, no sacraments were administered, and no offerings were collected. The sanctuary itself was turned into a warehouse for government grain. The great tower, minus its bells, was used only as a platform for megaphone announcements of village meetings and news of the world. The rest of the extensive compound was borrowed by various government organizations as temporary headquarters. Among these were the Anti-Japanese Political and Military University and the Fifth District Office.

****

The campaign to "settle accounts," launched in January 1946, lasted about four weeks. The destruction of the feudal land system, well begun by the Anti-Traitor Movement, was almost completed in this one month of drastic action. As a result of these two movements together, 211 acres were seized from exploiters, large and small, and 55 acres from various institutions. This amounted to more than a quarter of the village's 931 acres. The situation was the same in regard to livestock, implements, stocks of grain, and housing. Twenty-six draft animals were taken from their owners. This was more than half of all the large farm animals in the community. Of a total of around 800 sections of housing, 400 were confiscated. Over 100 tons of stored grain were seized. Hundreds of silver dollars, much jewelry, many rooms full of furniture, dozens of implements and tools, and hundreds of sets of clothes of all descriptions were also taken.

It is difficult to make an estimate of the total value in U.S. dollars of all this property, movable and otherwise. Assuming the land to be worth $200 an acre, the stock $100 a head, the housing $40 a section, the grain $50 a ton, and other goods in proportion, everything added together could not have exceeded $100,000 in value. In terms of the capitalist West this was a ridiculously small figure. It was hardly enough to set up one large modern dairy farm in any fertile region of the United States in the late 1940's. But in terms of Long Bow Village, its prevailing standard of living and the productivity of its peasant labor, this was an enormous sum, representing approximately five years' average income for every man, woman, and child in the community.

The peasants called the expropriated property *tou cheng kuo shih* —the fruits of struggle. On these fruits they based their hopes for a new life.

15

The Fruits of Struggle

How can republican institutions, free schools, free churches, free social intercourse, exist in a mingled community of nabobs and serfs; of the owners of 20,000 acre manors with lordly palaces and the occupants of narrow huts inhabited by "low white trash"? If the South is ever to be made a safe republic let her land be cultivated by the toil of the owners or the free labor of intelligent citizens. . . . This country will be well rid of the proud, bloated, and defiant rebels . . . the foundations of their institutions must be broken up and relaid, or all our blood and treasure have been spent in vain.

Thaddeus Stevens at Lancaster, Pa., 1865

MARCH CAME IN cold and clear. The sun moved in brilliant splendor across a cloudless sky but cast so little heat upon the earth that it did not even begin to melt the light mantle of snow that had fallen in the night. The glistening snow miraculously transformed the dusty, crumbling, adobe village and turned it into a fairyland of black and white, as pure and clean as the day the world was born.

In the reflected brightness of the open street that ran past the gate of South Temple stood two militamen. As they shuffled their benumbed cloth-shod feet and blew on their frost-bitten fingers, an impatient crowd of peasants in tattered winter garments, frayed shoes, patched shawls, and worn-out quilts grew in size before them.

Behind the massive wooden gates of the temple yard a dozen other militiamen ran to and fro, called to each other, carried out goods, led livestock back and forth, placed furniture in rows, and dumped clothes in neat piles as if preparing for a fair. As a result of these efforts the ancient temple, with its heavy wooden columns and upturned tile roof was soon surrounded by what amounted to a veritable exhibition of domestic artifacts, agricultural implements, and animal husbandry. On the street side of the yard stood the restless livestock section, its prime exhibit a yellow bullock with manure-caked flanks. Beside him stood a black mule, brushed until it glistened and decorated with strands of red yarn woven into its mane and forelock. Underfoot, tied by one hind leg, was a black sow, her dry shapeless teats dragging in the snow. Beside her romped two fat piglets from her fall litter. Close by, in a woven bamboo basket crouched a dozen chickens, their feathers bright with all the colors of the rainbow. Six longhaired sheep baaed and milled about in a flimsy stockade of kaoliang stalks.

On the right, behind the livestock, the farm implements were lined up. They included a large two-wheeled cart with iron-rimmed wheels, a wooden plow with an iron-tipped point, a harrow made of woven wattles, four heavy mattock-like hoes, a dozen three-pronged wooden pitchforks made from tree limbs that branched three ways, wooden shovels, rakes, seeders, manure buckets, a winch rope and a winch for raising water from a well, and many other useful things too numerous to mention.

To the left stood the great crocks, jars, and tightly woven baskets that the gentry used for storing their grain. There were also reed mats that could be made into field shelters, storage bins, or sleeping covers for a k'ang.

In the very center of the yard, tastefully arranged, were several finely shaped yet sturdy hardwood chairs and stools. Behind them stood tables, dressers, sideboards, and carved chests of cherry and mahogany, the latter fitted with massive brass corner guards and locks. Here also were displayed three large mirrors, one a full-length glass free from a single blemish. On the tables and on boards laid across wooden horses sat dozens of household implements—a loom, several spinning wheels, reels for winding cotton yarn, round-bottomed iron pots, bamboo baskets for steaming bread, and a stout press for forcing specially treated corn meal through holes in a steel plate to form corn noodles. Here also were needles, shuttles, a strong bow for fluffing cotton, and a flour sifter made of very fine mesh copper screen that was worth its weight in gold.

Other makeshift tables, closer still to the temple steps, were laden with clothes of all shapes, sizes, colors, and styles, from crude homespun work cottons to silk gowns and satin caps, embroidered undergarments, embroidered slippers, silk handkerchiefs, and kerchiefs of lace. Three great fleece-lined gowns for men lay at one end of the central table and beside them several silk-padded undertunics highly prized for winter wear. Here also were babies' caps with silken dragons' jaws and ears sewn on, a silver rattle, several silver bracelets, some earrings and other jewelled ornaments, bolts of machine-made cloth, odd bits of cotton, dyed and undyed, sleeve protectors for women who cooked, two alarm clocks, a chest full of rags useful for making shoe soles, and a whole table full of shoes, new and old, large and small—from satin shoes for the exquisite bound feet of a bride to coarse cotton and hemp workshoes already half worn through in the sole. Another whole table was piled high with cotton and silk quilts of every bright color—flowered, striped, and plain.

Here on display was the whole domestic and agricultural wealth of several prosperous gentry families, all of which had been transformed by bitter struggle into "fruits" belonging to the people.

Every item had been carefully recorded by a committee of poor peasants whose members, at that very moment, sat conferring at a table on the raised platform of the temple. Before them were scrolls of paper many feet in length, rolled up for convenience on round wooden sticks. On these scrolls, in black grass characters, were written the name and value in millet of every article in the yard.* Several young peasants who knew how to write, even if it was only by means of a brand of phonetic shorthand that would have shocked a true scholar, were busy trimming their writing brushes and rubbing their ink tablets in water in preparation for recording the decisions of the crowd that now filled the street, growing noisier with each interval of delay.

Finally everything was ready. The militiamen on the outside threw open the gates. People poured through waving in their hands the papers that showed they had been chosen, because of extreme poverty or proved grievances, for the privilege of first choice. The militiamen turned back all those without a paper and, after about 50 people had gone in, shut the gates entirely.

The bustle that had characterized the preparations in the temple gave way to pandemonium as the excited peasants surged from table to table, from display to display. Large items such as the farm cart, the bullock, and the mule had already been allocated by the committee. The men of the households that were to share the animals gathered round to look them over, push, feel, examine, and discuss them. It seemed that they would never tire of leading the animals up and down, holding their mouths open to judge their age, patting their flanks, or just standing back to admire their shapes. These were the first livestock many of them had ever owned. Even if each individual share was one leg, they were proud that leg was so sound.

While these lucky few looked over the livestock and the cart, the rest of the men and women, with all the enthusiasm of a crowd of country people at a big city fair, made the rounds of the courtyard, turned piles of clothes inside out and upside down, tried on gowns for size, paraded with silk tunics held up in front of them, put on the one large wolfskin hat and gesticulated with it before the full-length

---

* Grass characters are ideographs written free-style by hand as contrasted to ideographs blocked out in square form and printed.

mirror. They spread out quilts, felt the texture of bolts of cloth, seated themselves in chairs, tested tables for steadiness, and all the while called to each other, joked, laughed, and carried on in the highest of spirits. Never since the world began had there been a day like this.

Each peasant had the right to choose one item. Before making a final decision all wanted plenty of time to look over the goods that were there, yet all hesitated to delay too long lest they lose their heart's desire to some more decisive soul. Before many minutes had passed first one and then several more had made up their minds. With their chosen articles in hand they walked up to the steps of the temple and showed the committee what they proposed to carry home.

"Are you sure that's what you want?" asked San-ch'ing, the most skillful writer in the whole village, of old Tui-chin the bachelor, who balanced on his shoulder a baked clay jar almost as large as himself.

"That's it," said the old man cockily. "I haven't anything at all for my grain. Never had that much grain before. This is just the thing."

After some searching through the lists San-ch'ing found the crock on the scroll where it was catalogued along with other storage items and entered Tui-chin's name alongside it.

"It's listed at 50 catties," he said, a note of doubt in his voice.

"That's all right with me," said old Tui-chin. "It's worth all of that."

Tui-chin was given a slip of paper listing the item and its price. This he handed to the militiaman as he went out the gate. As he trudged home he greeted all he met on the street with a broad grin. *"Fan shen le ma?"* (Have you turned the body?) asked several. *"Fan le i ke k'ung shen,"* (I've turned an empty body) replied Tui-chin, pointing to the huge jar and laughing heartily at his own pun. To "turn an empty body" meant to get nothing in the *fanshen* movement.

Others did not find what they wanted as easily as old Tui-chin. Or if they did they were not alone in their choice. Two old women decided at the same time on one flowered quilt. They fell to quarreling over it and ended up in a tug of war, each pulling the quilt to her with all her might while shouting oaths and insults at the other at the top of her voice. Cheng-k'uan, the Chairman of the Peasants' Association, who was supervising the clerks at the table, had to rush down and step between them.

"If you fight that way you'll tear the quilt in half and no one will have it," he admonished good-humoredly. "Now tell me, why do you both want that one?"

Both women started talking at once, but Cheng-k'uan, who knew them well, hardly needed to listen. He decided that the quilt should go to the one with the largest family. He advised the loser to pick out a different quilt. "After all," he said, "there are plenty more, even if this one is the best."

In less time than it took to cook a noon meal over a straw fire the courtyard began to empty out, and soon thereafter in every lane and alley peasants could be seen trudging homeward with their newly acquired possessions. As soon as the first group had cleared the gate the call went out for the second, the representatives of households just a little better off, who were to get second choice. Most of them had already been waiting their turn for a long time. When the gate was opened they rushed in as eagerly as their poorest neighbors had done earlier.

And so it went all morning and all afternoon until the snow in the temple yard had all been trampled into the dirt and the whole area took on once again an ancient, dilapidated look that matched the growing disarray of the much-handled goods on the tables and the ground. Before night fell the last peasants had made their selections and carried or carted them away. Still there were quite a few things left behind. The militiamen, who had been on duty since before dawn and now had to clean up, decided that each of them had earned the right to pick out something and, though it was not strictly legal, each man set aside a small article before carrying the remaining wealth back to the storehouse.

****

Such was a typical distribution in the course of the Settling Accounts Movement. The system described above was arrived at only after much trial and error, many meetings of the cadres and the officers of the Peasants' Association, and several county-wide conferences at which the experiences of many villagers were pooled. When the first confiscated property was distributed in Long Bow, it was handed out not according to need but according to the grievances expressed at the meetings. This was done under the slogan *shui tou, shui fen*— "he who struggles gets a share." This was logical at the time and based on a rough measure of justice. Those who had been robbed and cheated should have their property restored; those who had been exploited most heavily should get supplementary wages and benefits. Also, since many did not yet dare attack the gentry for fear of reprisal, those who dared accuse should be rewarded.

The actual distribution of property based on openly made accusations had a tremendous impact. People said, "Now we have proof that the Eighth Route Army really backs the poor. They take action and are not satisfied with empty talk. Yen's troops talked well but cared nothing for us. They only seized our property and dragged us off to the front." When they saw that active struggle actually paid off in land, houses, clothes, and grain, more people joined each succeeding movement. But even so, after several distributions it became clear that the more active peasants, the brave and the vocal, were getting more than their fair share of the "fruits," while many a poor family that had suffered as much if not more, and needed land and chattels as much if not more, went without. It thus became obvious that active participation alone could not be the only criterion. Distribution on the basis of need had to be introduced. To handle such distribution the Peasants' Association set up a special committee of 60. It was composed of the village cadres, the elected leaders of the Peasants' Association, and delegates elected by the working peasants of each village neighborhood. (There were three such neighborhoods —southwest, southeast, and north.)

Where land was concerned the task of fair distribution was not too difficult. Since the village as a whole possessed approximately an acre of land per capita, those families who had less than the average were given enough to make up the difference. Complications that arose by virtue of the fact that the plots varied in fertility and that all plots were not equally close to the peasants' homes were adjusted by painstaking calculation and juggling until most families were satisfied.

The redistribution of housing was handled in the same way. The village as a whole had less than a section of house per capita. Families without this average were given additional sections wherever possible. Here complicating factors were personal prejudice—some families would not share a courtyard with others whom they disliked —and the location of privies and wells. Privies were vital to every family's economy. They were also very expensive to construct. They were deep, stone-lined cisterns large enough to hold all the solid and liquid excrement of a large family for a whole year. From them came the night soil, in semi-liquid form, on which almost the entire yield of the land was based. Since there were not enough privies to go around, families had to share them. If the families were on good terms, the sharing went well. If not, endless quarrels ensued.

As for wells, no one expected that every family should own one, but it was important that no one should have to walk too far for water. Judicious allocation of housing sections solved this problem in the main.

Draft animals and carts were even scarcer than privies and wells. Since there were only 50 animals in the whole village and since no animals owned by working peasants could be expropriated, the available animals had to be shared. It was common to allocate one ox to as many as four families, each of which thus became the proud possessor of "a leg." This led to quarrels, but it also solved problems. At least those with one leg were better off than those who had none; for even when the draft animals were shared four, six and in some cases even ten ways, there were still not enough to go around. Carts were distributed in about the same proportion as the livestock.

The headaches encountered by the distribution committee in dividing land, houses, and stock were as nothing compared to those encountered in redistributing the miscellaneous property in a way to satisfy everyone. The village cadres and the delegates to the committee met for days on end to evaluate fairly all expropriated property in terms of millet, the standard grain, and to set up a system of grades which would properly classify all families on the basis of need. Various systems for making everything come out even were adopted, but in the end the most successful was a system that combined the direct adjustment of grievances with extra aid for the poorest and most needy.

The system worked as follows: The total value of all the goods available—grain plus household articles, tools, implements, and livestock—was first figured as a grain equivalent. Then every family was put in a "grade" based on need. Those families who had serious grievances against a landlord or rich peasant also had the value of the damage due them figured as a grain equivalent. If the family was already comparatively well off and therefore in a high "grade," its damages were then reduced by a certain percentage. For example, a grievance worth one hundredweight of millet might be cut back to 70 pounds if the family had most of the things needed for carrying on production. The grain left over after the serious grievances were accounted for was then allocated to all the rest of the families based on their "grade." As a result of all this figuring, each family was entitled to take home a certain amount of grain or its equivalent in other forms of property. When an article was chosen, its value was deducted from the total grain allowance for that family. The balance, if any, was paid in grain. Should the article chosen amount to more value than the grain allotted to them, the family had to pay the difference in money or grain according to the same scale.

This was a very complex system, but so too was the problem. Since the movement had a dual purpose, the rewards had to be based on a dual principle—repayment for past injuries and damages, and the *fanshen* or economic turnover of every family in the village. That it worked at all was due to a very definite measure of correlation between the grievances and the poverty of the families that made them. It was those who had suffered the most who made the most charges in the long run and at the same time needed the most to put them on a par with the rest of the village.

In order to insure that no one should take advantage of his or her newly won power, the village cadres and militiamen did not share in the first few distributions. "Wait until the people see that you are getting nothing and they themselves suggest that you should get a share," was the advice given to Fu-yuan and T'ien-ming by District Leader Liang. But although the cadres were patient and waited unselfishly, no one suggested that they also should benefit from the struggle. Many militiamen decided that it was better to be a common peasant than a leading "activist" and asked to be mustered out. This brought the matter to a head and it was decided that everyone should be put in a "grade" according to his economic position and that everyone—cadres, militia, and ordinary citizens—should share and share alike.

At the same time, in recognition of the special burden borne by the militiamen, a certain amount of property was turned over to the corps for the benefit of that organization as a whole. This property included several acres of wheat land that had belonged to the collaborator Wang Hsiao-nan. The militia harvested the wheat and used a portion of the harvest plus some millet from a later distribution to set up a little shop where cigarettes and other articles of daily use were sold. There the militiamen doing guard duty at night could gather for a cup of hot water and a chat. The little shop became a sort of militiamen's club.

The militia corps was the first but not the only organized body to receive "fruits" for common use. The Peasants' Association took over the Western Inn from the Fan family and invested several hundred-weight of expropriated grain as operating capital. Wang Yu-lai, vice-chairman of the Association, managed the inn and managed it so well that its capital increased several-fold in one year. From its profits came funds for the village school, oil for the lamps used at public meetings, and other incidental village expenses.

The Western Inn grew into the same sort of center for the cadres that the little shop had become for the militia. Cadres gathered there for meetings, for figuring up accounts, and for pleasure. As a result, many a free meal was eaten there in the course of the next two years, an incipient form of corruption that boded no good for the future.

The two confiscated distilleries also became public property. They were turned over to the Border Region Government liquor monopoly and operated thereafter as part of a wide network of publicly owned distilleries, the revenue of which helped in great measure to finance the cost of the Liberated Areas Government and the military effort necessary to defend it. Certain other "fruits of struggle" were turned over to the distilleries to help them maintain production. Other "fruits" were given to the consumer co-operative to put it on its feet. Most important among the latter were a cart and a mule which the co-op used to haul supplies.

****

By the middle of March, when all the "fruits" had been distributed, the landless and land-poor found themselves living in an entirely new world. Two hundred and forty-two acres of land had been allocated to the families in this group, thereby doubling the acreage in their possession. Their holdings had jumped from an average of .44 acres per capita, to an average of .83 acres per capita. This amount of land did not make them wealthy by any means, but it was sufficient to maintain a minimum standard of living. It meant that they had moved from the ragged edge of starvation into relative security. Peasants who formerly grew only half enough to live on and had to work out or rent land for the remainder of their subsistence suddenly became peasants who could raise enough to live on, on their own land.

What was true of land was also true of other means of production. Families who had not possessed adequate shelter, draft animals, implements, and seed grain became families who owned all these things in sufficent quantity to maintain life. This happened not to just a few individuals but to more than half the population of the village. A hundred and forty families with 517 members "turned over" economically in the course of this movement.

The impact of this shift on the outlook and morale of the landless and land poor was tremendous. For the first time in their lives they felt some measure of control over their destiny. They slept under their own roofs, walked on their own land, planted their own seed, looked forward to harvesting their own crops and, what was perhaps best of all, owed neither grain nor money to any man. They were completely free of debt.

Shen Fa-liang, the former hired laborer in Sheng Ching-ho's household, said, "Life is much better than before. Now I have land and house and work to do. There is grain in my house. I work very hard but I enjoy the results of my work because I carry all the results of my work back home and put it in my own jars. But in the past it was just the opposite. I labored very hard regardless of rain or shine, but all that work was for others, not for me. All the crops were very beautiful, but all the crops I had to carry to someone else's granary. I couldn't even see them any more, not to mention eating them. So in the past I worked for others. Now I work for myself and no longer suffer the painful life, the unhappy life of working for others."

Ch'ung-lai's wife felt the same way. "In the old days I worked as a servant; I was busy every night until midnight, and I had to get up before dawn. Now I am very busy too, but now I work for myself. This is happy labor. No one oppresses me and the money that I earn is my own. My condition now is good. I've got house, land to till, clothes to wear, and the right to speak. Who dared speak before? In the past when I served in other families, even when they didn't beat or curse me, still, if I committed some trifling error their eyebrows and their eyes met. It is hard to eat with another's bowl. To live in one's own house and eat out of one's own bowl is the happiest life."

Wu-k'uei's wife, a woman who had been forced to sell her son and who had been sold twice herself, summed up her feelings in one sentence:

"It seems as if I have moved from hell to heaven."

Such feelings, when multiplied by 500, made for an atmosphere of extraordinary elation that soon changed even the everyday vocabulary of the village. The peasants all began to call one another "comrade" after the custom of the Eighth Route Army, and in place of the age-old greeting, "Countryman, have you eaten?" many poor peasants asked one another, "Comrade, have you turned over?"* To that question a large number could already answer, "I have turned."

---

* The use of the word "comrade" as a general form of address was universal in all the Liberated Areas during the Civil War period. Copied after the custom of the Communist Party, which later spread to the Red Army, it eventually came into common usage throughout revolutionary society.

16

Half of China

How sad it is to be a woman!
Nothing on earth is held so cheap.
Boys stand leaning at the door
Like Gods fallen out of heaven.
Their hearts brave the Four Oceans,
The wind and dust of a thousand miles.
No one is glad when a girl is born:
By her the family sets no store.

Fu Hsuan

WHILE THE dramatic, violent, and often macabre scenes of the "settlement of accounts" and the exuberant, lively, often humorous incidents of the "distribution of the fruits" unfolded like the intricate plot of some day-long Chinese opera, another struggle began whose object was the liberation of women from the oppression of their husbands and from domestic seclusion.

A few poor peasant women in Long Bow, the wives of leading revolutionary cadres, early organized a Women's Association where brave wives and daughters-in-law, untrammeled by the presence of their menfolk, could voice their own bitterness against the traitors, encourage their poor sisters to do likewise, and thus eventually bring to the village-wide gatherings the strength of "half of China," as the more enlightened women, very much in earnest, liked to call themselves. By "speaking pains to recall pains," the women found that they had as many if not more grievances than the men and that once given a chance to speak in public they were as good at it as their fathers and husbands, as had been proven by Chin-mao's mother in that first district-wide anti-traitor meeting.

But the women found as they organized among themselves, attended meetings and entered into public life, that they met more and more opposition from the men, particularly from the men of their own households, most of whom regarded any activity by wives or daughters-in-law outside the home as "steps leading directly to adultery." Family heads, having paid sound grain for their women,

157

regarded them as their private property, expected them to work hard, bear children, serve their fathers, husbands, and mothers-in-law, and speak only when spoken to. In this atmosphere the activities of the Women's Association created a domestic crisis in many a family. Not only did the husbands object to their wives going out; the mothers-in-law and fathers-in-law objected even more strenuously. Many young wives who nevertheless insisted on going to meetings were badly beaten up when they got home.

Among those who were beaten was poor peasant Man-ts'ang's wife. When she came home from a Women's Association meeting, her husband beat her as a matter of course, shouting, "I'll teach you to stay home. I'll mend your rascal ways." But Man-ts'ang's wife surprised her lord and master. Instead of staying home thereafter as a dutiful chattel, she went the very next day to the secretary of the Women's Association, militiaman Ta-hung's wife, and registered a complaint against her husband. After a discussion with the members of the executive committee, the secretary called a meeting of the women of the whole village. At least a third, perhaps even half of them, showed up. In front of this unprecedented gathering of determined women a demand was made that Man-ts'ang explain his actions. Man-ts'ang, arrogant and unbowed, readily complied. He said that he beat his wife because she went to meetings and "the only reason women go to meetings is to gain a free hand for flirtation and seduction."

This remark aroused a furious protest from the women assembled before him. Words soon led to deeds. They rushed at him from all sides, knocked him down, kicked him, tore his clothes, scratched his face, pulled his hair and pummelled him until he could no longer breathe.

"Beat her, will you? Beat her, and slander us all, will you? Well, rape your mother. Maybe this will teach you."

"Stop, I'll never beat her again," gasped the panic-stricken husband who was on the verge of fainting under their blows.

They stopped, let him up, and sent him home with a warning—let him so much as lay a finger on his wife again and he would receive more of the same "cure."

From that day onward Man-ts'ang never dared beat his wife and from that day onward his wife became known to the whole village by her maiden name, Ch'eng Ai-lien, instead of simply by the title of Man-ts'ang's wife, as had been the custom since time began.

A few similar incidents, one of which resulted in an errant husband spending two days in the village lockup, soon taught the poor peasant men to be more circumspect in their treatment of their wives, even if it did not teach them to appreciate women in public life any more than they had before.

The institution of wife beating was, of course, not ended in a few weeks by such means. But having once shown their power the women did not have to beat every man in order to make progress on this question. Thereafter, a serious talk with a strong-armed husband was often enough to make him change his ways, at least for the time being.

Chou Cheng-fu was a bare poor peasant who got land and house for the first time in the distribution that followed the "settling of accounts." Land and house made possible the acquisition of a wife. Through a go-between he made a match with a puppet soldier's widow ten years his junior. Perhaps because of the difference in their ages, Cheng-fu proved to be a very jealous husband. He would not allow his wife out of his sight for even an instant. Over this issue they soon fell to quarrelling. To settle the matter, he beat her, and she, being a woman of some spirit, went to the Women's Association as Ch'eng Ai-lien had done before. Instead of retaliating against Chou Cheng-fu with sticks and kicks, the women sent a delegation to talk to him. They reminded him how hard it was for a poor peasant to get a wife at all. Once married he ought to treat his woman with great respect, be patient with her, and help her to overcome her mistakes, especially since she was younger than he. If he beat her she would only learn to hate him, their relations would steadily worsen, and in the end she might demand a divorce. In that case he would lose his wife completely. Since Chou Cheng-fu did not like the idea of a divorce he decided to be gentle with his wife thereafter. Later, when he went away to do rear service at the battlefront, he got a literate companion to write a letter thanking the Women's Association for their help. The letter was written in the formal style used by scholars of the old school: "After I left home I thought it over and realized that you were kind enough to try and help us. Now I know that it is only through mutual love and respect that husband and wife can live happily together and build a good life."

When asked if, as a result of these actions, women had yet won equality, one of the leaders of the Association said, "No, not yet. Things are a little better than before. Still, there are beating cases and most men still despise women's words and think women are no use. We have to struggle for a long time to win equality. When we have land of our own it will help a lot. In the past men always said, 'You depend on me for a living. You just stay home and eat the things I earn.' But after women get their share they can say, 'I got this grain from my own land and I can live without you by my own labor.' When it comes to labor on the land, women can work just as hard as men even if they are weaker. They can do everything except plowing. They can even hoe if they can't hoe so fast. But they cannot drive carts. Well, even this they can do, but some of the animals are pretty hard to handle."

It was not long before the Women's Association in some parts of the county set up plowing classes for women, and the fame of those who mastered agricultural labor spread far and wide. A widow in Shen Settlement startled everyone with her strength and skill. She could do everything a man could do and more. She could even push a loaded wheelbarrow on the highway and earn $12 a day, Border Region currency, transporting bricks. She was so skilled at planting that in the spring all the peasants in Shen Settlement wanted her, and no one else, to plant their millet.

In another village, only five miles from Long Bow, a woman was elected as village head.

Women such as these were rare, but as news of their exploits spread, others were greatly encouraged.

It would be very one-sided to imply that the only goal of the Women's Association was equality for women. Without the successful transformation of society, without the completion of land reform, without a victorious defense of the Liberated Areas against the probing attacks of the Nationalist armies, it was impossible to talk of liberation for women. Many women realized this as if by intuition, and they made the Women's Association an instrument for mobilizing the power of women behind the revolution in all its aspects —behind the "settling of accounts," behind the drive for production, and behind the defense effort. Through the Association, classes were organized for literacy and for the study of politics, cotton loans were made to stimulate spinning and weaving, the women were brought together to make uniforms and shoes for the soldiers, and wives and mothers were urged to encourage their husbands, sons, and brothers to enlist in the army.

All of these activities were intimately linked up with the struggle for equality, with the demand on the part of women that they should no longer be treated as chattels. If this demand alarmed the men, the all-out support which the women gave to over-all revolutionary goals disarmed them and won from them a grudging admiration. In their hearts they had to admit that they could not win without the help of "half of China."

17

Counter Measures

M en revolted in earlier ages too,
There's nothing rare about such an ado.
Strange things pass on earth, as in the sky;
How else can the Heavenly Dog eat the moon on high?
In it goes at one side, and out it pops again;
Brightly as ever the moon shines then.
It's always the good who come out on top,
The devil's disciples soon have to stop.

Landlord Ts'ui in
Wang Kuei and Li Hsiang-hsiang

THE REACTION of the gentry to the devastating blows of the Settling Accounts Movement was as drastic as those who remained
behind could make it. As far as the privileged classes were concerned, permanent expropriation was unthinkable. If the peasants
could enforce the confiscation of land and property or even "double
reduction," then life was not worth living. Therefore, even though
their sword—the local Peace Preservation Corps—had been broken,
and their shield—the provincial and central armies of the Kuomintang—had been cast out, the landlords, the rich peasants, and their
"dog's legs" inside the Liberated Areas desperately contested the
field. Those who ran away fled with the intention of returning to
take revenge, and those who remained used all the resources at
their command to disrupt the developing peasant power, neutralize as
many people as possible, isolate the active young cadres, and preserve whatever was left of their power and prosperity. They hoped,
at a minimum, to have something left to build on when the great
offensive, being prepared in Chungking with American support,
turned the tide of history, crushed the Liberated Areas, and put the
traditional rulers back in power. It never entered their heads that
this offensive too would be defeated in the long run.

As an elementary precaution the gentry concealed what valuable
property they could in the homes of poor relatives, friends, tenants,
and employees. Many peasant families who had little basic sympathy

for the wealthy were cajoled, bribed, tricked, or threatened into helping them. Hsu Cheng-p'eng, the landlord who was a Kuomintang general, sent his cousin, who was a tenant on his land, 220 silver dollars for safekeeping. The puppet Chief-of-Staff Chou Mei-sheng turned half an acre of his best soil over to a long-term hired laborer, Chang Fu-hsin. He also hid 80 silver dollars in a second laborer's house. The latter, Wang Chi-kao, covered the silver coins with copper ones and set the jar on a shelf. In each case, when the leaders of the Peasants' Association found out about the concealed property, the poor peasants involved were beaten and wholly or partly expropriated themselves.

General Hsu wrote a letter to his cousin asking about the silver dollars. When the letter was intercepted by the village office, it touched off an attack on the cousin himself. Chang Fu-hsin, the laborer, was arrested and beaten when the captain of the militia found him planting Chou Mei-sheng's half acre with his own seed. Wang Chi-kao went himself to the Peasants' Association Committee to report the jar full of coins but was beaten nevertheless for having concealed it.

Families such as these were labelled "air raid shelters" by the other peasants and were mercilessly punished. As a result, persons who, by fair means or foul, had been persuaded to become "air raid shelters" tended to be passive, even antagonistic to further struggle because they feared, with reason, that if they were exposed they would be as fiercely attacked as the gentry themselves. They thought, "The landlords have put their feudal tails in our homes. When the people come for their property the landlords may lose their tails, but we will lose our heads!"

The severe punishment meted out to those who were found out and the fear that this engendered among those already enmeshed suggested to the gentry a new tactic. They converted what began as a movement to hide property into a movement to divide the people. They hid property in others' homes in order to sow distrust and suspicion, in order to divert the attack from themselves and to set the peasants to fighting one another. They even went a step further and spread rumors that they had hidden property with others when in fact they had not. Since a negative is hard to prove, the victims of these rumors found it very difficult to clear their names. As had been demonstrated in the case of Ch'ung-lai's wife, one landlord's word that she had concealed money for Wang Lai-hsun led to a fearful beating and flesh-cutting torture. A false charge that could cause that much dissension was more valuable to the gentry than jars full of silver and gold.

Coquetry and seduction were also powerful weapons. The women of the gentry were often very beautiful. After all, landlords and rich peasants had long had their pick of the most beautiful girls in the countryside for wives and concubines. In addition to their natural graces, these women were taught to dress and pamper themselves. They knew how to charm men. While the wives of the poor labored endlessly in their huts and in the fields, gathered manure by the roadside, dug herbs in the hills, and were burned black by the sun, the landlords' wives bathed, dressed in elegant clothes, spent hours combing their fine black hair, treated their fair skin with powder and oil, and developed the social graces necessary for entertaining important guests.

As the Settling Accounts Movement gathered momentum, the poor laborers who led it suddenly found themselves the objects of solicitous attention from women who had formerly never so much as glanced at them, much less spoken to them.

In Long Bow there was a young hired laborer named Ch'un-hsi who worked for a landlord in the neighboring Kao Settlement. The family treated him as one of their cattle, lodging him in the stable with the ox and the sheep, and giving him nothing but millet and chaff to eat. During the famine year his own mother appeared at the gate one day to beg for something to eat. When he slipped into the kitchen and took a bowl of millet for her, he was thoroughly beaten for his pains. When his mother came back again he was so afraid of another thrashing that he drove her away.

After the liberation of the region, the landlord's daughter-in-law, who had formerly winced when he with his sheep dung odor went by, suddenly began to flirt with him. She cooked meat dumplings and other delicacies for his dinner, mended his torn clothes, and ultimately invited him to sleep in her quarters. All this was not for nothing, however. As soon as Ch'un-hsi's head was well turned, she persuaded him to hide clothes and other valuable things for her father-in-law. When the peasants of the village launched a sharp attack against the family, which owned over 70 acres and had financed one member through the university at Peking, Ch'un-hsi protected them in every way that he could. When this property finally was divided, the daughter-in-law went out to work as a nurse; only then—when the family could no longer afford to hire him—did Ch'un-hsi return to his mother's home in Long Bow. But he took no part in the struggle. He refused to accept any land, houses, or other property in the division then going on and persuaded his mother not to make any accusations because, he said, the Kuomintang would soon be back and punish them all.

This type of seduction was repeated many times with many variations. Even though a number of small exploiters were attacked in Long Bow, there was one rather wealthy family whose property was never seized. This was the family of the widow Yu Pu-ho. There were many reasons for her miraculous immunity but not the least of them was her very beautiful daughter, Pu-ch'ao. This girl had married a poor peasant from a distant village, a former puppet trooper who volunteered for service in the Eighth Route Army. After he left for the front she returned home to stay with her widowed mother. As a soldier's wife she was entitled to help from the peasants of Long Bow Village. She lost no time in getting acquainted with the village leaders. She carried on flirtations and liaisons with a number of them simultaneously and even bore a son. No one knew who the father was, but since the baby died within a few days his parentage never became an issue. Disarmed by her status as a poor peasant's wife and soldier's dependent, and personally fond of her, the cadres made no move to confiscate her mother's property.

A further twist to this motif was the man trap. The landlords used their daughters-in-law to entice the village cadres, encouraged them to sleep together, and then exposed the whole affair to the peasants in an attempt to discredit their leaders and destroy their prestige with the people. Carrying this one step further, they spread rumors about liaisons that did not in fact exist.

Simple bribery was another often attempted method. How Sheng Ching-ho came to Kuei-ts'ai and San-ch'ing with a bag of white flour has already been related. Other landlords did the same but on a more massive scale. They invited every cadre in the village into their homes to eat wheat, definitely a luxury meal, and thrust gifts of clothing, leather shoes, and watches at them. In Long Bow such invitations were not too successful, due in large part to the influence of T'ien-ming, but in Wang Village, in the same district, a large proportion of the young men newly catapulted into leadership compromised themselves in this way.

Here again, when the gentry were not successful in bribing leaders, they spread rumors to the effect that the leaders had been bribed, mentioned valuable things which they claimed had disappeared from their homes, and in every way tried to discredit the young cadres and cause friction between them and their followers.

In Long Bow a big issue was made of the altar lamps, cloth, and candles that were confiscated from the Church. Rumor had it that the altar lamps were made of solid silver—some said gold—worth hundreds, perhaps thousands of dollars. Once they left the Church they were seen no more, yet no equivalent sum of money or grain found its way into the wealth available for distribution. The truth of the matter was that the lamps were made of brass, not silver or gold. They brought only a modest sum in the Changchih market and the money had immediately been spent on ammunition and rifles for the militia. In regard to other items that rumor claimed "missing" there were also explanations. The cloth had been made into shirts and quilts which were presented free to every volunteer who enlisted in the army. The wax candles were burned by the militia in their temple lodgings since they had no other source of light. But in the absence of a clear accounting, rumors of misappropriation gained wide currency, and the reputation of the village cadres was tarnished accordingly.

The most sophisticated tactic used by the gentry was infiltration. Able young men posed as revolutionaries, won the confidence of local Party organizations and village governments, and then carried on their wrecking activities from the inside. Although such infiltration was common in the Taihang region, in Long Bow no member of any wealthy family attempted such a thing.

To the methods of disruption mentioned above must be added the power of the landlord's religious and superstitious authority. As has been pointed out, Confucianism and ancestor worship were deeply ingrained in the consciousness of the majority of the peasants. By claiming that their land and property came from their ancestors and therefore should remain inviolate, the owners caused many a peasant to hold back in the struggle. They also summoned fate to their side once more. "If you are poor, that is your fate. That is determined in heaven and no man can go against heaven," they declared; or, "If you are poor, that is because your father's tomb is poorly located. No one can defy the influence of air and water." In the face of adversity they preached patience. If one went bankrupt, one could only wait for one's luck to change, select a more suitable spot for one's own grave, and hope that the eight ideographs of earth and heaven would be in better conjunction when one's son was born. They also prophesied destruction from on high of all those who struggled against the existing order. They said the gods would punish all rebels for their temerity. "Can the sun rise in the west?" they cried once again, and pointed to the strikingly red sunsets in the summer of 1946 as a portent of the destruction of the Communist Party.

To lend weight to such ideas they used the spirit-talking technique for all it was worth. "The return visit" and the "distant view" turned out to be highly political. Those peasants who could be enticed into a seance together held up a tray that was sprinkled with a coating of sand. Then a medium, usually a young girl in an induced trance, held a chopstick suspended in her outstretched hand so it just touched the sand. As both the tray and the chopstick moved, lines were drawn in the sand which were immediately interpreted by the master of the seance as ideographs prophesying doom for those who raised their hands against the owners of property. "Chiang Kai-shek will return," was another common message.

This last idea was the most persistent theme of the landlords' propaganda activity. By spirit talking, by rumor, in conversation, and in public announcements, the gentry stressed over and over again the inevitable return of the Kuomintang and the swift punishment in store for all active participants in the Revolution. Weight was given to their words by the activity of the Home Return Corps, a semimilitary organization created to take over and hold any area won back from the Liberated Areas by the Nationalist offensives. This corps, composed of landlords' sons, their "dog's legs," hired thugs, and miscellaneous adventurers, instituted a white terror in the wake of the Central troops wherever they returned. They hunted down and killed not only active cadres but also their wives, children, and relatives, buried whole families alive, flayed people, and cut off their heads. The Home Return Corps also sent individuals deep into the Liberated Areas to carry out assassinations, poison wells, loot, kill, and spread panic. Assassinations, carried out at night, were common enough to acquire a name of their own, "black shots," and there was no person in the revolutionary ranks, no matter how brave, who did not feel a twinge of fear when stepping outdoors after dark or travelling at night on deserted paths between one village and another.

To co-ordinate and direct all the elements of this offensive, the gentry built and rebuilt the Kuomintang Party and tried to maintain underground branches in every village. It was through the Party organization that information was gathered about developments in the countryside, lists of active revolutionary leaders and their peasant supporters were drawn up, money distributed where it would do the most good, and the over-all strategy and tactics of the conflict planned and put into practice. This whole effort depended for ultimate success on victories on the field of battle. Such victories could only be won by a strong, well-trained, militant army. With all the manpower of South, Central, and West China to draw upon, with thousands of American officers to train the conscripts, with all the surplus weapons of the Pacific War as their basic armament, and with the arsenals of America pouring in new arms all the time, the gentry felt confident of the future. Should all these fail, America still had, did she not, a monopoly on the atomic bomb? If they could not hold China, then they could destroy her.

To meet this many-sided offensive of the gentry the peasants had one basic weapon—unity—a weapon which, in the past, they had never been able to forge. That the peasants were able to forge such a weapon after the Second World War and employ it in the face of landlord disruption, terror, and massive, foreign-supported military mobilization was due to one primary factor—the leadership of the Communist Party.

18

Founding the Village Communist Party Branch

The Communist Party of China is the organized vanguard of the Chinese working class and the highest form of its class organization. The Party represents the interests of the Chinese nation and the Chinese people. While at the present stage it works to create a system of new democracy in China, its ultimate aim is the realization of a system of communism in China.

Constitution of the Communist Party of China, 1945

ONE NIGHT in April, T'ien-ming, the former underground worker now in charge of public security, and Kuei-ts'ai, the vice-leader of the village, stood guard together on the road that led south out of Long Bow toward the walled town of Changchih. Under the soft light of a full moon they walked up and down in silence. Several times during the first hour T'ien-ming slowed down his pace and turned toward Kuei-ts'ai as if prepared to say something, but apparently he thought better of it and walked on as briskly as before. Finally, he did speak.

"Comrade," he said, looking Kuei-ts'ai straight in the eye. "In regard to the Eighth Route Army, what are your thoughts?"

Kuei-ts'ai was a little taken aback.

"What are my thoughts?" he exclaimed, hoisting his rifle onto his other shoulder. "What should my thoughts be? In the past I had nothing. I had an empty bowl. Now I have *fanshened*. Everything I have the Eighth Route Army gave to me. Wherever the Eighth Route Army goes I will follow."

"And the Communist Party?" asked T'ien-ming.

"The Communist Party?" said Kuei-ts'ai, drawing his heavy eyebrows together so that a crease ran up the middle of his forehead. "The Communist Party and the Eighth Route Army—it's all the same, isn't it?"

"No, not exactly," said T'ien-ming. "The Communist Party organized the Army. In the Army there are Communist Party members. The Communist Party directs the Army, but there are many soldiers in the Army who are not in the Communist Party. And it is the Communist Party, not the Eighth Route Army, that leads us in the battle against the landlords. It is the Communist Party that leads our *fanshen*."

"I understand," said Kuei-ts'ai, still not too clear as to just what the Communist Party was.

"If only we follow the Communist Party the working people will certainly win victory. We will overthrow the old capital holders and we will become masters in the house," said T'ien-ming starting to walk again, this time very slowly.*

"Where is the Party then?" asked Kuei-ts'ai. "I want to see it."

"It's far away but there are Party members in the Army and also in the countryside. I too would like to see the Party. Will you go with me to find it?"

"Yes," answered Kuei-ts'ai without a moment's hesitation. "Let's go as soon as possible."

After that, every time Kuei-ts'ai found T'ien-ming alone he asked him when they would start out, but T'ien-ming put him off several times. Finally T'ien-ming said, "Why are you so anxious? Don't you know that it is a long journey, and a very difficult and dangerous one?"

"Never mind how difficult or dangerous it is," said Kuei-ts'ai impatiently. "You say the Communist Party leads us to *fanshen*. There is no other way out for us except with the Communist Party, so let's go find it."

"Think it over some more," said T'ien-ming. "Are you willing to risk your life for the Party? In the future there will be many dangers, many hardships. You must be willing to sacrifice even your life, maybe even the safety of your family."

"I have already made up my mind," said Kuei-ts'ai. "Why do you keep talking about dangers, as if we weren't in danger already?"

"In that case, your journey is over," said T'ien-ming, smiling broadly. "The Party is right before your eyes. I am a member of the Communist Party."

Kuei-ts'ai was astonished but he was also angry.

"Why did you trick me?" he asked.

"Because the Communist Party is a secret organization. If the enemy should ever come back we would all be killed. No one is allowed to tell of his membership. Even if you are arrested and

---

* The phrase "capital holders," used by T'ien-ming to designate capitalists, came from some of the basic Marxist documents which he had studied. Among them was most probably the *Communist Manifesto,* in which the fundamental contradiction between workers and capitalists was explained. T'ien-ming was here thinking in general terms, not merely of Long Bow or Lucheng County.

beaten to death, you should never tell. You can say you belong to the Eighth Route Army but never that you belong to the Communist Party."

Thus did Kuei-ts'ai first come into contact with the Communist Party. He was formally enrolled as a member a few days later.

T'ien-ming, who recruited him, had only been a member for a few weeks himself. He was picked as the first Party recruit in Long Bow Village by District Leader Liang when it became obvious that without a Party branch in the village itself the work of the Revolution could not progress. The gentry had made it very clear that their strategy was to split the peasants, set them to quarrelling with one another, undermine their morale, frighten them into inaction, isolate them from their political allies, and undermine the leadership of the Communist Party. The strategy of the peasants therefore had to be to unite all working people, overcome differences in their ranks, instil confidence in ultimate victory, isolate the gentry, and undermine their political leadership—the Kuomintang.

Such a strategy required a far-sighted, politically conscious, guiding core of individuals with close ties to the masses of the people at every level. None of the existing organizations in Long Bow could satisfy these requirements.

The village government was essentially an administrative organ in the service of the *fanshened* peasants. The village functionaries had their hands full solving the daily problems of the people, and acting as a two-way liaison between the village and higher levels of government.

The People's Militia was the peasants' own armed force. On the local level, it was their chief guarantee that their will would be carried out, but the militia did not determine what that will was. It was the servant, not the leader, of the peasant community. The problem was to keep it that way, for there was a strong tendency for those with arms in their hands to become an independent political force and follow the road to banditry and militarism.

The Women's Association, organized to represent and mobilize "half of China," could not very well be the guiding force for the other half, the males.

The Peasants' Association was the militant popular organization of both men and women formed for the express purpose of carrying on the struggle against the gentry. But just because it was a popular organization open to all working people, it required a core of conscious, disciplined, dedicated people able to give guidance and unselfish service as leaders. There was no guarantee that such a core of leaders would be generated spontaneously by the struggle itself.

Nor was there any reason to think that if such a core did develop it could break through the limitations imposed on the average peasant consciousness by the small-scale, fragmented private economy of which it was a product.

With four important organizations in the village a further problem arose, the problem of co-ordination. How could the village government, the People's Militia, the Women's Association, and the Peasants' Association maintain a unified outlook? How could the contradictions that arose between them by virtue of their different functions be adjusted? Only a political party that drew its membership from among the leaders and active rank and file of all four of them could guide and co-ordinate the many-faceted revolutionary movement and solve the problems that faced the peasants in their drive to *fanshen*. This was exactly the role played by the Communist Party in every village in which a Party branch existed.

In the absence of such a Party organization in Long Bow, District Leader Liang, a Communist Party member of several years' standing, guided the work of the young cadres for many months. Since his headquarters were in the village, he was often on hand when they needed him. But Liang was only one person. His presence was demanded in a dozen places every day. As the responsible leader of a whole district he could not possibly keep in close touch with all the problems of any one village. Even if he could have done so, no individual, no matter how brilliant, could match a dedicated collective body in wisdom. As the peasant uprising in Long Bow developed momentum it became imperative to organize a Communist Party branch that could guide it from within.

As soon as District Leader Liang and Secretary Liu of the Fifth District Committee of the Communist Party of Lucheng County decided that the military situation was relatively stable and that a reliable group of vigorous young leaders had emerged in Long Bow, they moved to recruit them into the Party and set up a village branch. T'ien-ming, the most mature and experienced of the village cadres, was an obvious choice as the first member. As T'ien-ming related it later, this is how he himself was recruited:

I heard about the Communist Party when I was in Hungtung as a carpenter in 1940. At that time there were many underground workers not five *li* [one *li* = ⅓ mile] from the city. They often talked to us carpenters but I didn't understand the difference between the Communist Party and the *Palu* [the Eighth Route Army]. I thought they were the same thing. Once a cadre told me that they were not the same; that though the Eighth Route Army was under the leadership of the Communist Party, it was not the Communist Party itself. Though I didn't understand how this could be, I knew anyway that the Party was to serve the poor and overthrow the wealthy. When I returned to Long Bow and worked as an underground cadre I heard more.

After the Liberation, toward the end of the year, I once asked District Secretary Liu, "What is the Party and what is the connection between the Party and the Army, and can I join the Party?" He said, "You had better work hard and later we will talk about this again." So he observed how I worked and that I was very steadfast in the struggle. Then he called me aside one day and said, "A Communist Party member is not the same as an ordinary person. He must make up his mind to sacrifice his life for the working people and struggle against the owning classes." Then he told me something about the bright future of the proletariat and the Party. "If all the dispossessed unite together and work hard, the future belongs to us. But if you want to join the Party, you must remember that every Communist Party member must fight for the working people forever and never compromise."

In April 1946, I was finally accepted as a member in the Communist Party without any period of probation and after that I worked even harder, both in the struggle and in the work of supervising and educating the other cadres so that they would not falter, take graft, or ask for more than their share of the "fruits."

T'ien-ming's first big task after he joined the Party was to develop a local branch and bring in other members. The basic requirement for new members was that they be of poor peasant origin. In addition to that they must be active in the struggle against the landlords and have prestige with the people. T'ien-ming picked Kuei-ts'ai as his first recruit. Others whom he approached were not so easily mobilized. There was, for instance, the young hired laborer Hsin-fa, a man who had owned neither land nor house in the past. He was brought up by a stepfather and ill-treated at home for many years. When Long Bow was liberated he was working in another village and returned only after the struggle with the landlords had begun. He immediately joined the militia, was honest, hard-working, and well liked. The young cadres decided to make Hsin-fa educational director of the militia, but he was worried about his past record and did not think he was fit to be a leader.

What worried him was the fact that he had once illegally transported heroin for the landlord T'ang Hsu-wen, a man who, in addition to supervising his many tenants in another village, led a gang of bandits. This gang smuggled heroin through the Japanese lines, and Hsin-fa, who was nothing but a hired laborer, was ordered to transport it. The first time he made a smuggling trip he didn't know what was on his cart until he reached his destination. After that it was too late. He was already implicated and was forced by the gang to transport heroin many more times.

"Since I myself committed such crimes, how can I lead others?" asked Hsin-fa.

But T'ien-ming said, "Never mind, the main thing is to tell the truth about it and to try and understand the root of your mistakes. Even if you had killed someone there might be a reason for it, a reason that would explain it, and the Eighth Route Army will pardon those who speak frankly and are sincere with their comrades."

So Hsin-fa told the whole story of his smuggling and T'ien-ming said to him, "Think how dangerous it was for you. You carried the heroin but they got the money. If you had been caught by the puppet police it would have been your head that came off, not theirs. You risked your life and got nothing. You did not want to go. This was not a great error."

"That's true," said Hsin-fa, greatly relieved. "It was so dangerous that even now, whenever I think of it I break into a sweat. But now the *Palu* have brought me not only land and a house but they have also made me see clearly and relieved my mind of a great burden. I always thought that was a black mark against me, but now I understand that it is not my fault but that turtle's egg of a landlord."

After Hsin-fa accepted a position of leadership with the militia and had worked as a leader in education as well as in action, T'ienming decided to bring him into the Communist Party.

"What do you think of the Communist Party?" he asked Hsin-fa one day.

"The Communist Party is good. It has led us to turn over and I myself have turned over. What do you think?"

"I agree," said T'ien-ming, "and I want to go find the Communist Party. Will you go with me?"

"Well," said Hsin-fa, "I understand that the Communists are good but that word 'Party,' I don't like it. Now we all fight so hard against the Nationalist Party (Kuomintang) and everyone hates the Nationalist Party. Maybe afterward they will hate the Communist Party just as they hate the Nationalist Party now. If you want to go, go ahead, but I'm happy with my present position. Later, if I should be arrested by the Kuomintang, I can tell them that I am just a villager and though I worked for the Eighth Route Army I am not a member of the Communist Party."

This was honest talk. T'ien-ming respected Hsin-fa for speaking frankly but he still hoped to convince him that he should join the Party. He warned him never to mention their conversation to anyone and later sent Kuei-ts'ai to talk with him and test him out.

"I heard that T'ien-ming visited you and talked with you about joining the Party," said Kuei-ts'ai.

"No, T'ien-ming never said anything to me," Hsin-fa answered.

T'ien-ming sent three others to test him in the same manner but he told them nothing. They asked him if T'ien-ming was a member of the Communist Party but Hsin-fa answered, "I know nothing about it."

T'ien-ming decided that Hsin-fa could keep a secret and that he was very honest. If only he understood the Communist Party he would join. Having gone so far, he could not stop in the middle in any case. He sent other members to talk with Hsin-fa. They reviewed the past with him, asked him how he had *fanshened,* and if it was not true that the Communist Party had led him to his new life.

"Yes," said Hsin-fa. "I know the Communist Party is good and leads us to stand up, but I still don't think I want to go and find it."

Then T'ien-ming went again himself.

"I have already found the Communist Party," he announced.

Hsin-fa was amazed.

"You have found it! Where did you find it? Since you have found it I will go with you, as long as I am not the first."

"Think it through," said T'ien-ming. "Prepare some food and some money and when you are ready we will go."

"How much do you think I will need?" asked Hsin-fa eagerly.

"You'd better think it over thoroughly. We don't want to make any decisions that we will regret later," cautioned T'ien-ming.

But this time Hsin-fa was not to be denied. The very next day he appeared at T'ien-ming's door with food and money for a long journey.

"Don't be anxious," said T'ien-ming. "The Party is right here."

"Where?"

"I myself am a member," said T'ien-ming, looking closely at Hsin-fa to see if he would get angry as Kuei-ts'ai had done. But Hsin-fa was a much more easygoing man than Kuei-ts'ai. "Well," he said. "If you are a member, of course I want to join. Maybe there will be more like us. I'm not the first but neither am I the last." With that Hsin-fa too became a member of the Long Bow branch of the Communist Party of China.

****

As the Party branch grew, women were recruited into it as well as men. Within a year more than 30 peasants joined, of whom seven were women.

One of the first women to become a Communist in Long Bow was a former beggar, Hopei-born Hu Hsueh-chen, a stocky mother of great physical strength and stamina. Her square jaw, prominent nose, and swarthy skin gave her a masculine appearance which was heightened by her bobbed hair and the loose-hanging pantaloons typical of male attire which she wore. She was the first woman in the village to bob her hair and discard the tapered trousers which most women preferred.

For 28 years prior to the Liberation she had lived a life that could only be described as a nightmare. As a young girl her father almost sold her to settle a debt. She talked him out of it, only to be married against her will to a pauper. She was then 16. Harried by famine from Hopei to Shansi, she was forced into beggary when her husband became a gambling addict and sold everything in the house, including their only quilt, for gambling stakes. She watched her first three children die before her eyes. One was trampled to death by a Japanese soldier, the second died of parasites and distended belly in the famine year, while the third wasted away in her arms when her own breasts shrivelled from starvation. When the fourth, a girl, was born to her she finally drove her thieving, good-for-nothing husband out and managed to survive the last years of the Anti-Japanese War by begging, gleaning in the fields after the harvest, spinning cotton for others, and hunting herbs in the hills. Without a quilt for a cover she and her daughter slept in a pile of straw through sub-freezing winter weather and somehow survived.

Liberation and the Settling Accounts Movement were to Hu Hsueh-chen what water is to a parched desert. She won clothes and threw away her rags, she won a quilt and burned her pile of flea-infested straw, she won land and gave up begging, and she won a roof over her head and set up a home for her little daughter. Knowing that all these gains were the result of struggle and not gifts from heaven, she attended every meeting and supported those who were active, even though she herself was afraid to talk in public and afraid to step forward and beat the "bastard landlords" herself.

Then she met a remarkable revolutionary cadre who helped to make her *fanshen* complete. This man, the "doctor" in charge of the infirmary at the Anti-Japanese Political and Military College which made the village Church its temporary headquarters, was also from Hopei. His home village was only ten miles from the one where Hu Hsueh-chen was born. He was first attracted to her when he heard the familiar broad accents of his parents on her lips. He came to pay a call. They talked about old times and familiar places. Soon thereafter, through a third person, he asked for her hand in marriage. Hu Hsueh-chen hesitated. She asked for a conference in order to make known to him the whole story of her past. She told him she could not stand any more suffering or oppression at the hands of a man. He, in turn, told her of his own life, how he had been driven from home at the age of 14 by a stepmother who hated him, how he had gone to Peking to work in a shop and later, when the Japanese came, had escaped into the Western Hills and joined the Eighth Route Army as an orderly or "little devil" in the medical corps. All the medicine he knew he had learned in the field caring for the casualties of the "Kill All, Burn All, Loot All" campaigns. He persuaded Hu Hsueh-chen that he was a man of principles and standards far in advance of the peasants whom she had known all her life. Most important to her was the fact that, as a product of the revolutionary army and its Communist education, he believed in equality for women.

They were married in February, 1946, and Hu Hsueh-chen never regretted having taken this step. Far from opposing her taking an active part in village affairs, her husband encouraged it. He even cooked supper for himself and the little girl so that his wife could attend meetings—a practice unheard of in Long Bow. He talked with her for hours at a time explaining the whole Chinese Revolution, its past and present, and described for her the society called Communism that they would eventually build.

When the struggle against the gentry reached its height, Hu Hsueh-chen's new husband saw that she hesitated to lead, dared not speak in public, and dared not join in beating those under attack. He criticized her gently and asked if she wanted to save face for the landlords. "You must know that only after the destruction of the feudal system and the overthrow of the landlords can we poor peasants *fanshen*. From whence do the 'fruits' come? Only through struggle. You ought to work hard and lead the movement to help win *fanshen* for everyone."

She became more active then, overcame some of her fear and shyness, and was elected a group leader in the Women's Association. This made her husband very happy. He encouraged her to do even more, saying, "I have heard all about your hard life and suffering in the past, so now you should think—where did my *fanshen* come from?—my land, my house, my freedom to talk, my freedom to marry? Was it not because of the leadership of the Communist Party?"

A few weeks later the infirmary of the Military College was transferred to the village of Kao Settlement, about a mile to the northwest. Thereafter, the doctor came home only once a week. But when he came he always inquired how his wife's work was going, and, as before, offered to cook supper so that she could be more active. He said, "Now I work outside and you work at home. You serve the people in your way and I will serve them in mine. Later, when we have time,

I will teach you to read and write, just as the Army taught me, and in the future we can help each other a great deal."

In late 1946 the Anti-Japanese Political and Military College moved away altogether. As long as he was in the Army, Hu Hsueh-chen's husband had to move with it, but he regularly wrote letters asking after his wife's welfare and urging her to work hard. "When you run into trouble don't be gloomy," he advised. "For there can be no trouble to compare with the past." She took what he wrote to heart and became more active than ever in all the affairs of the village. When Militiaman Ta-hung nagged his wife into resigning as secretary of the Women's Association so that she would pay more attention to her home, Hu Hsueh-chen was elected to take her place.

Soon after she took up her new duties, Hsin-fa came and asked her which was better, the Communist Party or the Kuomintang Party.

"Everyone knows the answer to that," said Hu Hsueh-chen. "It was the Communist Party that liberated us from poverty and led us to *fanshen*. It was the Communist Party that liberated us from the Kuomintang. As for me, I got house and land while in the past I was nothing but a beggar. I could find no more than half a bowl of millet to eat every day and my children died of starvation. So how could I forget the Communist Party and the Eighth Routers?"

Later T'ien-ming himself came to talk with her. He asked her if anyone had spoken to her about the Party. She knew that the Party was supposed to be secret so she denied that anyone had come even though T'ien-ming asked her several times. A few days later he returned with an application blank and helped her to fill it out. While doing this he asked her if she would give her life for the Party and obey the discipline of the Party and its leaders. "If you should by chance be captured by the enemy could you keep silent even when threatened with death?"

To all this Hsueh-chen answered with a firm "I could," and so she too was enrolled into the Party to which her husband, unknown to her, had long belonged.

The other women recruited into the Communist Party at this time included two of Hu Hsueh-chen's assistants in the Women's Association, two wives of leading cadres who were brought into the branch by their husbands even though they were not active leaders among the women, and two rather remarkable young women, each of whom, though already married, had fallen in love with a cadre and Party member; they were recruited into the organization by their lovers. One of these was Village Head Fu-yuan's paramour, Shih Hsiu-mei. Her husband, a local carpenter, had left Long Bow several years before and had never returned. Ch'eng Ai-lien, whose husband, Man-ts'ang, had been beaten by the Women's Association, was the other. Man-ts'ang had since died from an illness and Ch'eng Ai-lien had married the poor peasant Chin-sui. She had driven a hard bargain with the latter, refusing to take his name and retaining under her own control all of Man-ts'ang's property. Mistress of her own fate at last, she came and went to suit herself and dispensed her favors as she pleased.

Of the 30-odd members of the Communist Party branch in Long Bow as it was finally constituted in that period, 80 percent were land-poor peasants or landless tenants and hired laborers and about 20 percent were land-owning peasants such as Fu-yuan. There were no members of rich peasant or landlord origin and there were no industrial workers.

19

Peasants or Workers?

Experience shows that after joining our Party on our terms, most of them (peasants and intellectuals) did seriously study and accept the Party's education in Marxism-Leninism and Mao Tse-tung's theory of the Chinese Revolution, observe Party discipline, and take part in the practical revolutionary struggles of the people. In the course of doing this they changed their original character and became Marxist-Leninist fighters of the proletariat. Many of them have even sacrificed their lives for the Party's cause, the cause of Communism in China.

Liu Shao-ch'i

"AT ALL TIMES and on all questions, a Communist Party member should take into account the interests of the Party as a whole, and place the Party's interests above his personal problems and interests," wrote Liu Shao-ch'i in 1943. He went on to say:

If a Party member has only the interests and aims of the Party and Communism in his ideology, if he has no personal aims and considerations independent of the Party's interests, and if he really is unbiased and unselfish, then he can show loyalty and ardent love for all his comrades, revolutionaries and working people, help them unconditionally, treat them with equality and never harm any one of them for the sake of his own interests.

He will worry long before the rest of the world begins to worry and he will rejoice only after the rest of the world has rejoiced. . . . Both in the Party and among the people he will be the first to suffer hardship and the last to enjoy himself. He never minds whether his conditions are better or worse than others, but he does mind as to whether he has done more revolutionary work than others or whether he has fought harder. . . . He is capable of possessing the greatest firmness and moral courage to resist corruption by riches or honors, to resist tendencies to vacillate in spite of poverty and lowly status and to refuse to yield in spite of threats of force. . . .

He is never afraid of truth. He courageously upholds truth, expounds truth to others and fights for truth. Even if it is temporarily to his disadvantage to do so, even if he will be subjected to various attacks for the sake of upholding truth, even if the opposition and rebuff of the great majority of people forces him into temporary isolation (glorious isolation) and even if on this account his life may be endangered he will still be able to stem the tide and uphold truth and will never resign himself to drifting with the tide. So far as he himself is concerned he has nothing to fear.

He takes care not to do wrong when he works independently and without supervision and when there is ample opportunity for him to do all kinds of wrong things. . . .

If for the sake of certain important aims of the Party and of the Revolution he is required to endure insults, shoulder heavy burdens and do work which he is reluctant to do, he will take up the most difficult and important work without the slightest hesitation and will not pass the buck.*

Such were the standards set for all Communists by the leaders of the Party. Communists were expected to give serious attention to these standards, not merely lip-service. If it could be said that few attained the level of selflessness and objectivity described, still hundreds of thousands strove to live up to these ideals and honored those individuals who most closely embodied them in real life.

Raw recruits from China's isolated countryside quite naturally fell short in many important ways. In examining the motives which brought these peasant recruits to the Party Liu Shao-ch'i found some who from the beginning wanted to "fight for the realization of Communism, for the great aim of emancipating the proletariat and mankind." But others had a variety of more personal, more selfish reasons for taking this important political step. As Liu Shao-ch'i wrote:

Some peasant comrades regarded as "Communism" the striking down of the local despots and the distribution of the land which we carried out in the past, and they did not understand genuine Communism as meaning anything more when they joined the Party. At the present time quite a few people have joined the Party chiefly because of the Communists' determined resistance to Japan and because of the anti-Japanese national united front. Certain other people have joined the Party as a way out because they could not find a way out in society—they had no trade, no job, no school to attend, or they wanted to escape from their families, or from forced marriages, etc. Some came because they looked up to the prestige of the Party, or because they recognized, though only in a vague way, that the Communist Party can save China, and finally there were even some individuals who came because they counted on the Communists for tax reduction, or because they hoped to become influential in the future, or because their relatives and friends brought them in, etc. It was very natural that such comrades should lack a clear and definite Communist outlook on life and world outlook, should fail to understand the greatness and difficulties of the Communist cause, and should be unable to take a firm proletarian stand.**

A more apt analysis of the motives of the Communist Party recruits in Long Bow could hardly be drawn up. "Striking down the local

* Liu Shao-ch'i, *How to Be a Good Communist,* New York, New Century Publishers, 1952, pp. 31–33.
** *Ibid.,* p. 37.

despots and the distribution of the land" were no doubt the main things that drew these young people to the Party, but other motives were also prominent. Some saw in Party membership a chance to become influential. Militiaman Wang Man-hsi said when his reasons for joining the Party were later questioned; "I thought to join the Party was glorious. If one joined the Party one could get position and power. I went to the District Secretary to fill out the form but really I knew nothing about the Party at that time. The Secretary explained the requirements—serve the masses, devote your life to their interests, never compromise with the enemy or submit to difficulties—but, after I joined I was proud. I thought I had found a screen to protect myself and I did every bad thing."*

Chao Ch'uan-e, an attractive young woman with a willowy figure, joined the Party primarily to protect her husband and her brother-in-law at a time when they were in danger of attack from the Peasants' Association. She was a daughter-in-law in a well-to-do household that owned land both in Long Bow and in the Western Mountains many miles away. Because the family hired at least one year-round laborer, its members were regarded at the time as rich peasants. To ward off the attack Chao Ch'uan-e sought out the young cadres of influence, carried on affairs with several of them, and was invited by them to join the Party. By the time she actually did so, there is no doubt that her motives had undergone a subtle change. She had unintentionally caught some of her suitors' enthusiasm for the Revolution. Her desire to protect her family remained basic in her decision to become a Communist, but it was tempered by the hope of something better for China and especially for China's women—a free choice in marriage, the right to own property, the right to be treated as a person and not simply as some man's chattel.

Among the Long Bow Communist Party members were also those who joined simply because their relatives and friends brought them in. This was certainly the main reason why militia captain Li Hung-er's wife, Wang Man-ying, militiaman Shen T'ien-hsi's wife, Chen Tung-erh, and militiaman Hsiao Wen-hsu's wife, Jen Ho-chueh, originally made application. Nevertheless, they all answered questions as satisfactorily as Hu Hsueh-chen and were potentially as good Communists as she.

The relative shortsightedness, subjectiveness, even opportunism of

* In judging Man-hsi's motives it should be kept in mind that at the time he joined the Communist Party there was absolutely no guarantee that the Revolution would be victorious. He did not hesitate to take a position in the front ranks at a time when the real opportunists were waiting quietly at home to see which way the tides of war would flow in the country as a whole. In other words, opportunism, like everything else, is relative, and a man who saw glory in being a Communist in China in 1946 chose a very hard road.

the Long Bow peasants' motives should not be exaggerated, however, for there were in the village a substantial number of young men who had had industrial experience and hence some knowledge of and sympathy for working class concepts of solidarity—the all-for-one, one-for-all basis of trade unionism. These men were semi-proletarian not only by virtue of being propertyless poor peasants who had worked much of their lives as hired laborers, but also by virtue of the fact that bankruptcy, famine, and war had forced them to leave home and seek employment in distant parts of the country where they became for a time either members of the industrial working force or employees closely associated with this group.

Ten of the early members of the Long Bow Party branch had, at one time or another, worked in industry, transport, or large-scale construction jobs far from home.

T'ien-ming's father was a bronzesmith who labored for wages in Peking. T'ien-ming himself had worked out as a carpenter in a rail-road center in Southwestern Shansi, and he first heard of the Communist Party from a fellow carpenter on the job. Hsin-fa, forced to flee from home in the famine year, worked for two seasons as a coal hauler in a Taiyuan steel mill. Chou Cheng-lo, a Communist recruited from among the village militiamen, had worked as a shepherd from the age of six, but he too spent two years as a steel worker when drought destroyed Long Bow's crops. Cheng-k'uan, the ex-Catholic chairman of the Peasants' Association, was employed for years as a teamster by the Cathedral in Changchih where he came into contact with iron workers and railroad men. Li Hung-er, who became captain of the militia when Chang Chiang-tzu, the organizer of the corps, joined the army, served as an apprentice in a spinning and weaving factory starting when he was 11 years old. Fu-yuan worked in a carpentry shop in Taiyuan that employed 90 men.

All of these men knew what it was to work for wages. They had travelled on trains, seen modern mines and mills, and heard something of unionism. When the Party leaders spoke of the working class, its unity and discipline, these men recognized what they were talking about, admired it and tried to emulate it.

What then of the "idiocy of village life" and the shortsightedness and lack of social experience of its victims which were stressed in an earlier chapter? The answer is that the isolation of thousands of out-of-the-way rural villages such as Long Bow was modified to some extent by the crisis of the 1920's, 1930's, and 1940's. The setting up of large-scale industries along the coast and the Yangtze River and even in hinterland capitals like Taiyuan, the penetration of internal markets by manufactured goods, the ten-year Civil War in South and Central

China, and above all the Anti-Japanese War, imposed an unwanted, a violent, and often a tragic mobility on a basically stagnant society, but a mobility that was nevertheless invigorating. The great famine of 1942–1943 also played a major role. This famine probably did more to lay the groundwork for a revolution in the Taihang Mountain region than any other single event or influence—first, because the terrible toll of lives it took reinforced widespread doubts as to the viability of the old way of life, and second, because it drove so many of the poor and dispossessed onto the roads. It forced them to travel to distant places, there to meet and talk with other disaster victims and persons of entirely different backgrounds. It forced them to hear new ideas, to open their eyes and ears, and eventually to return home remolded to a degree by their own experiences. When county leaders talked of Marxism, these returnees recognized that their words touched reality. They welcomed what seemed to them good sense and were eager to hear more.

Those who had traveled and worked in industry greatly influenced those who never left home. At least some of the broader outlook they brought back rubbed off on friends and neighbors. In this sense they acted as the yeast that causes the dough to rise.

Regardless of whatever motive or motives loomed largest in the decision of any given individual to become a Communist, all of the Long Bow recruits were influenced, at least to some extent, by the extraordinary prestige of the Eighth Route Army, which they identified with the Communist Party, and the even more extraordinary prestige of the Party's national leader, Mao Tse-tung, who appeared to them as nothing less than the savior of the nation. They wanted to be Communists because they admired Mao Tse-tung and trusted his leadership. If they won victories they attributed them to Chairman Mao. They said, "Chairman Mao gave us land," even though they themselves had built the Peasants' Association, manned the militia, and actively dispossessed the gentry. Failures and injustices they also attributed to Chairman Mao. "Chairman Mao should not be like this," said a man who had been beaten because he continued to go to church after the local priest had fled. In either case, it was taken for granted that Chairman Mao, whose name was synonymous with that of the Revolution, was responsible for every facet of the government, great or small. It was an enormous compliment and an equally enormous responsibility.

****

The small-producer social origin and outlook of the new Party members, their subjective, shortsighted, often selfish, and certainly

mixed motives for joining the core of the revolutionary movement
did not discourage the Party leaders. "That certain people come to
rely upon the Communist Party, come to the Party to seek a way
out, and give support to the Party's policies—all this cannot be regarded as wrong. They are not mistaken in having sought out the
Party. We welcome such people," said Liu Shao-ch'i.* He made it
quite clear that the non-proletarian social origin of so many of its
members and their subjective, one-sided motivation did not determine the class character of the Party as a whole. The Party remained
a working class Party which transformed its non-working class recruits rather than allowing them to transform it. "The determining factors are our Party's political struggles and political life, its
ideological education, and its ideological and political leadership. . . .
Through Marxist-Leninist education, Party members of petty-bourgeois (peasant) origin have undergone a thorough-going ideological reform, which changes their former petty-bourgeois (peasant)
nature and imparts to them the qualities of the advanced fighters
of the proletariat."**

The principal problem in building the Party in the village was thus
frankly recognized as a problem of "ideological remolding"—the education and reformation of revolutionary-minded peasants. The first
duty of every Party member, as laid down in the Constitution of the
Party adopted in May 1945, was therefore to "endeavor to raise the
level of his consciousness and to understand the fundamentals of
Marxism-Leninism and Mao Tse-tung's theory of the Chinese Revolution." The other three duties were:

(1) To observe Party discipline strictly, to participate actively in inner-
Party political life and in the revolutionary movement in China, to carry
out in practice the policy and decisions of the Party, and to fight against
everything inside and outside the Party which is detrimental to the Party's
interest.
(2) To serve the mass of the people, to consolidate the Party's connection with them, to learn their needs and report them in good time,
and to explain the policy of the Party to them.
(3) To set an example in observing the discipline of the revolutionary
government and the revolutionary organizations, to master his own line of
work and to set an example in various fields of revolutionary work.†

In the long run, the educational program of the Communist Party
—the patient, reiterated efforts to reform, remold, and inspire the

* Liu Shao-ch'i, *How to Be a Good Communist,* pp. 37–38.
** Liu Shao-ch'i, *On The Party,* Peking: Foreign Languages Press, 1954.
p. 18.
† *Ibid.,* pp. 159–160.

peasant recruits—was effective. Regardless of their social origin, regardless of their original motives for joining, the overwhelming majority of Long Bow's Party members ended up wanting to be and trying to be good Communists.

It was a long, hard road.

To want to be a good Communist and actually to become a good Communist were two different things. Chairman Mao wrote that it took ten years to remold an intellectual of peasant, small business, or professional origin, ten years to rid him of conceit, personal selfishness, individualism, and contempt for manual labor. Peasants, according to this view, had less to overcome than intellectuals—at least they were not strangers to manual labor—but even peasants found that it took years to remold themselves.

To master Marxism-Leninism, to expand each individual's political consciousness, to overcome subjectivism, reduce unprincipled vindictiveness, uproot that small producers' tendency to take advantage of others for personal profit, and unite to build a new world—this was the struggle that began in April 1946 in Long Bow with the founding of the Communist Party branch there. The struggle continued year after year, with varying intensity and success; no doubt it still goes on.

The vitality of this effort was due to the fact that at all times the transformation of the Party members' outlook was linked to the actual struggle going on in the village to transform the peasants' miserable way of life and forge something better. From the very first day that the branch was set up its members undertook to lead the village to *fanshen;* and lead they did, for better or worse, therafter—not in isolation, of course, but as a basic unit in a nationwide Party of over a million members. The District Committee, the County Committee, the Border Region Committee, and the Central Committee with Chairman Mao at its head, all gave them guidance, but in the last analysis they had to do the work and they were responsible for its success or failure.

The leadership exercised by the Communist Party in Long Bow was not of the kind that most people in the West imagine. The Party could not and did not simply issue orders that the peasants had to obey, even though at certain times and on certain issues a strong tendency toward this type of "commandism," as it was so aptly called, arose among the leading cadres, Communist and non-Communist alike. The Party led the village by virtue of the fact that its members held leading posts (but by no means a monopoly of them) in all the village organizations, won considerable prestige by the example they set, seriously studied problems collectively, and spoke and acted together once they decided on a solution. All this, it should be made clear, must be taken as having been accomplished in a relative sense, for not all the members of the Party were able to win prestige; some won notoriety instead. Also, the decisions of the Party branch were not always taken collectively, the whole membership did not always carry out the decisions when made, and sometimes the decisions that were made were quite wrong—as will be seen. Nevertheless, the Party branch was the best organized, the most active, the most serious and dedicated group in the village, and it tried to lead by example and persuasion, not by force.

The branch itself was divided into five groups, each with its own leader. Before any decisions were taken, before any campaign was launched, these groups first met, discussed the matter at issue, and formulated their estimate of the situation in the village and the temper of the people. The five group leaders, who made up the executive committee of the branch, then met to work out policy. When they agreed on a course of action they took their decision back to their small groups. In case of need the whole branch could be called together for a general membership meeting, but since this was likely to arouse the curiosity of the whole village and expose the existence of the Party, membership meetings were not lightly undertaken. Most of the work was done by the small groups and the executive committee.

From the day of its founding in April, 1946 the whole branch operated in the strictest secrecy. The danger of the possible reconquest of the area by the Central armies and the certain reprisal that would have been visited upon all Communists if this had taken place, made this absolutely necessary. Because of this enforced secrecy many elaborate excuses had to be made at home to account for the frequent absence of branch members from family chores and family gatherings. This was particularly true of the women whether or not their husbands were also in the Party, for women were traditionally not supposed to go anywhere, speak to anyone, or have any business outside the home. All self-respecting families enforced these bans quite strictly. Fortunately for the Party, among the very poor who had no property to protect or to pass on, families were not so well established. The poor peasant women who had to fend for themselves in order to eat came and went of their own volition.

Strict secrecy in regard to the Party also meant that whatever prestige individual Party members earned by their good work and whatever notoriety they won by their mistakes was reflected not on the Party as such but on the administration, the whole group of active cadres, Party and non-Party alike, who served as responsible leaders in the village office, the militia, the Peasants' Association, and the Women's Association. There was no question but that the Party members were the backbone of this whole structure, but since the average peasant did not know this, it was the whole structure that took the credit or the blame and not just its guiding core.

How important a role the Party played can be seen by an examination of the activity of the Party members in the main village organizations. All of the branch members belonged to the Peasants' Association. Cheng-k'uan, one of the first recruits to the branch, was its chairman. (The vice-chairman, Wang Yu-lai, was not a Communist.) All the women Party members belonged to the Women's Association. A woman comrade, Hu Hsueh-chen, was its secretary. Three other Party members were group leaders among the women. All the male Communists were enrolled in the militia. Li Hung-er, a Party member, was its captain. Hsin-fa, whose recruitment into the Party was described in the preceding chapter, served as educational director of the militia. As for the village government, its cadres were divided about equally, half of them Party members, the other half not. A Communist, Fu-yuan, was village head. Another Communist, Kuei-ts'ai, was assistant village head. (The secretary, San-ch'ing, was not a Party member.) T'ien-ming, secretary of the Party branch, was in charge of all police work. The rest of the Party members—more than half the branch membership—held no leading posts at all. They were simply rank-and-file peasants who were expected to take the lead in any work they were asked to do, inspire others to greater effort, and study and make known the needs of their colleagues and neighbors.

20

Contradictions, Internal and External

Comrades! If the masses were all conscious, united, and free from the influences of the exploiting classes and from backward phenomena as some people imagine, then what difficulties would still remain in the Revolution? Such influences of the exploiting classes not only existed long before the Revolution but will continue to exist for a very long time after the victory of the Revolution and after the exploiters have been kicked out of their position of political power by the exploited classes.

Liu Shao-ch'i

TO LEAD successfully the struggle against the gentry, the Communist Party in Long Bow had to combat not only the splitting tactics of the enemy, but also the centrifugal tendencies constantly generated among the people, the landless, the land-poor, and the middle peasants. Combating enemy disruption proved to be the easier of the two tasks. Once the Party members realized just what the gentry was doing and why, they were usually able to neutralize its effects by education among the people or by a change in policy.

When the question of "air raid shelters" became serious, District Leader Liang, who was in touch with the work in 18 villages, soon realized that attacking poor families who had been persuaded to hide property only played into the gentry's hands. As soon as he convinced the Communists in Long Bow of this, they persuaded the Peasants' Association to change its tactics. Thereafter, instead of suffering attacks, the "air raid shelters" were rewarded for turning over hidden property with a share of the property itself. Those who had already been punished were given compensation for the damages. As soon as this was done, quantities of clothing, jewelry, and other goods that had once belonged to landlords were brought to the Peasants' Association headquarters without a struggle and the ranks of the peasants were strengthened rather than split.

In those incidents where rank-and-file peasants had been seduced or bribed into a lenient attitude toward some exploiting family, the Party also advised education and persuasion rather than punishment and ostracism. Chang Ch'un-hsi, the hired laborer who was so infatuated with his former employer's daughter-in-law that he would not join in any attack on the landlords of Long Bow, was chosen to attend a district-operated training class for just such "backward elements." There the students studied the feudal system by recalling their own past lives. Listening to classmates whose situations had been so close to his brought all the bitterness of Ch'un-hsi's past before his eyes. He remembered how he had been forced to drive his own mother away from the gate in the famine year, and wept. Seeing this emotion the other students focused their attention on him. They ridiculed his love for the landlord's daughter-in-law. They pointed out what a shame it was to fall for a girl who had treated him like dirt in the past and now used him only as a shield for her family. In the end he resolved to give her up. When he returned to the village he joined actively in all the campaigns that followed and before long was himself enrolled into the Party branch.

Toward Party members and village cadres who wavered in their stand, the attitude of the Party was more strict than it was toward the rank-and-file peasants. Inside the branch much time was spent analyzing the class position of those who, out of lust for material gain, or just plain lust, gave protection to their class enemy. They were asked to change their ways. Seeing how despicable their actions appeared to others, some members voluntarily confessed to illicit affairs with gentry women and broke off such relationships. Others continued these affairs in spite of this education, the most notorious being Hsin-fa, who could not bring himself to break completely with Pu-ch'ao, the rich widow's daughter. He rationalized this on the grounds that she was herself a poor peasant by marriage, even though it was obvious to others that by the favors she granted him she helped protect her mother from attack and expropriation. Since Hsin-fa was by that time a leading member of the branch, he went his own way in spite of sharp criticism.

Finding superstition still a powerful weapon in the hands of the landlord class, the Communist Party organized a special campaign throughout the district to free the minds of the people from bondage to geomancy, astrology, spirit talking, and mud idols, and to convince them that they themselves could remold the world according to their own desires. An important breakthrough in this campaign came in Sand Bank, a village several miles northwest of Long Bow. There stood a shrine to the god Ch'i-t'ien, a very powerful Buddhist deity who, when displeased, could curse one and all with dysentery. Since people only too often died of this disease, Ch'i-t'ien was greatly to be feared. Many a stick of incense was burned before his image and many an offering of food was left for his spirit to eat. The Party

members of Sand Bank decided to attack Ch'i-t'ien just like any landlord. They figured up just how much money they had spent humoring
him over the years and discovered that it was enough to have saved
many lives in the famine year. When they took these calculations
to their Peasants' Association, many young men and women got very
angry. They went to the temple, pulled the god out of his shelter and
carried him to the village office. Before a mass meeting they "settled
accounts" with him by proving that he had squandered their wealth
without giving any protection in return. Then they smashed his mud
image with sticks and stones. Some of the older people tried to stop
them. They prophesied that everyone involved would die of dysentery
within a few days. But the young men and women went right ahead.
When no one fell ill that night nor throughout the whole of the
next day, the hold of Ch'i-t'ien on the village collapsed. Only a handful of old women ever burned incense before his ruined shrine again.

News of this victory quickly spread to other villages. When the
Party members in Long Bow heard of it they decided to deal with a
similar god of their own—a god who was supposed to have the power
to cure sickness. His image sat in a little temple on the southern edge
of the settlement. Sick people traditionally burned incense before him,
made obeisance by touching their foreheads to the ground, and then
scraped up a little dust from around his feet, mixed it with water,
and swallowed it. His devotees were lucky if they did not add dysentery to their other ailments after this "cure."

The Communists first freed their own minds of dependence on
this god by a long discussion in the branch and then led a similar
discussion in the Peasants' Association. Before long everyone was
laughing at the "muddy water cures" of the discredited god. When
a militiaman knocked the god's mud head off, only a minority of
old people were dismayed.

By such means the bonds of specific superstitions were broken
down.

The success of the Settling Accounts Movement had a general
effect that reinforced these intensive efforts. Once the gentry had
been overthrown, it became obvious even to the slow-witted that
the configuration of the "eight ideographs" at birth or the position
of one's ancestral graves no longer determined one's fate. People
took less and less stock in ancestral spirits who prophesied the immediate return of Chiang Kai-shek or in rumors that red sunsets
symbolized the decline of the Communist Party. As their faith in
superstition declined, their trust in the Peasants' Association, the
Eighth Route Army, and the Communist Party increased.

Since Long Bow was not a Border Village, the local Party branch did not have to mobilize people physically against those murderous forays of the Home Return Corps that in many places lent substance to the dire prophesies of the gentry. The Long Bow Communists, however, did combat the fear of a "change of sky" by reporting the victories of the armed working groups organized by the Party in Border Counties where the Revolution had no recourse but to meet the white terror of the gentry with a red terror of its own. Dressed in civilian clothes, the bravest and most skillful guerrilla fighters on the borders raided Kuomintang-held villages at night. Notorious counter-revolutionaries and landlords who had been responsible for the assassination of underground workers were kidnapped from their homes, tried in the fields for their crimes, and executed on the spot. This irregular war on the borders grew in bitterness and scale as time went on in spite of the fitful peace that prevailed on most of the battlefronts under the auspices of the Marshall mission. The situation resembled very closely the border war in Kansas in the days of John Brown, and the peasants of Long Bow took as much heart from reports of small successes as did certain abolitionists of New England when they heard the news of Ossawatomie.

Everyone realized that the real test would come if and when the truce ended without an agreement on peace. Then the future of China would be decided by the armies in the field. Thus the strengthening of the Eighth Route Army, renamed the People's Liberation Army in mid-1946, became a major concern of the Communist Party in Long Bow. A second area-wide recruiting drive was launched in the spring, and Party members were urged to lead the way by volunteering themselves or getting other members of their families to volunteer. Three Party members went in the second drive. Kuo Cheng-k'uan got his brother to go. T'ien-ming did the same. Li Hung-er saw both his brothers off. Ch'eng Ai-lien, who had stopped her husband's blows by going to the Women's Association and who was now a Communist, persuaded her new husband Chin-sui to enlist. Altogether another 25 young men signed up. Again several were sent back because of ill health, but more than 20 were accepted and went on to become fighters in a rapidly growing army of peasant volunteers who had won land at home and meant to hold onto it.

This time, not only did the village government give the volunteers a grand banquet and a musical send-off, but each man was also given a brand new shirt and a brand new quilt, and a laquered plaque was hung beside his front door with the words "Glorious Army Family" written large upon it in ideographs of bright red. Many poems com-

posed on the spot and recorded with free-flowing grass characters on
large sheets of rice paper were pasted to the adobe walls beside these
plaques. A typical one read:

> Glorious are those who volunteer
> To throw down tyrants.
> March to the borders when the millet sprouts.
> Fight for the people!
> Defend our homes and lands!
> Most glorious are the volunteers!

The biggest problem in recruiting for the army was not to overcome fear of enemy bullets or the hardships of campaigning, but
to convince the men that their families would be well cared for and
their livestock and crops well tended. The village government undertook to see that this problem was solved by organizing a "Preferential
Treatment Committee" which set up a system of *taikung* or "substitute tillage." Under this system every able-bodied man in the village
was asked to do his share of work for the more than 40 men who
had left for the front. Here again the Party branch played a big role.
It was the Communists, with individual exceptions, who guaranteed
the success of the system by doing their share, or more than their
share, and inspiring others to do the same. On the "Preferential
Treatment Committee" they led the way in establishing a system of
inspection to make sure that all substitute tillage was well done and
that all complaints by wives and mothers were promptly looked into.
It was preferential treatment for soldiers' families that really made
possible a volunteer army in the first place and gave such a solid
base to morale in the field.

One young woman wrote to her husband, "Since you joined up
the neighbors often come to visit me. The three Wangs have all
volunteered to do some work on the land. I suppose what worries you
most is my pregnancy and you are afraid that there will be no one
here to take care of me. But it is already arranged that beside my
mother, our neighbor's wife who is a member of the Women's Association committee, is to live here with me. And if we haven't enough
millet to get through the year, the village office will supply us. So
don't be downhearted about home."

****

Checkmating each new move of the gentry was not enough to
guarantee victory. The Party branch in Long Bow had to make sure
that the ranks of the people did not break down due to conflicts of

interest and quarrels between the various groups and cliques that made them up. Since the main strength of the peasants lay in their numbers, it was important that their ranks be as broad and solid as possible. Where analysis showed an objective community of interest the Party tried to bring people together regardless of the subjective animosities and suspicions that divided them. Here the main criterion was class interest. The basic principle taught by the Party was that the class interests of all the poor and middle peasants, while not completely identical, were certainly mutually dependent and that this must, in the long run, override all other considerations. It followed that all poor and middle peasants could be united in a movement for *fanshen* in spite of splits and divisions arising out of family and clan ties, religious affiliations, erstwhile collaboration, past criminal activity, present illicit love affairs, or any other factor.

A most serious cleavage was that which existed between the minority of the peasants who had been attacked for collaboration and the majority who had attacked them. Once branded as traitors, the minority earned universal contempt, were often taken advantage of by their neighbors, and treated as second class citizens by the village government. If such treatment were to continue indefinitely, the collaborators would have no choice but to join forces with the gentry. At the suggestion of the district secretary, the Party branch studied this problem and decided to remove the stigma of collaborator from all those whose role in the puppet regime was minor. This included all the *lu* and *chia* leaders, the rank-and-file members of the puppet Self-Defense Corps, and the members of the counter-revolutionary Love the Village Corps who had taken refuge in the fort during the liberation battle.

T'ien-ming mobilized every Party member to take part in solving this problem. Communists visited each collaborator personally, discussed the past with them, and offered a constructive role in the future to all those who realized their mistakes and sincerely indicated a desire to join the revolutionary ranks.

"We are all poor brothers," the Communists said. "The only difference between us is that you were deceived by the puppet officials. Think it over. For whom did you carry the guns? Was it not for the landlords? How come they sat comfortably at home and enjoyed life while you faced the bullets? They feared the Eighth Route Army. They knew that when the Eighth Route Army came the rich had entered upon their last day of rule. So they tricked you and deceived you and sent you to the fort to defend their power. Think it over. Who died when the bullets spattered the fort? Was it the rich or the poor?"

This was just what most of these young collaborators had been waiting for. They were not at all proud of the role they had played and wanted very much to be forgiven and invited to join the Peasants' Association. Each was asked to go before the executive committee, speak frankly about his past errors, and explain what was in his mind when he went to the fort. All those whom the committee felt to be sincere in their repentance were admitted to membership in the Association and included thereafter in the "grades" when confiscated property was distributed. In the end no one was rejected.

The Party branch had no cause to regret this action. Not only did all of these young men actively join the Peasants' Association, but many of them also became members of the militia, and several eventually joined the Party as well; among them were Shen T'ien-hsi who had served in the puppet Self-Defense Corps and Hsiao Wen-hsu who had been a soldier in the Fourth Column.

The split between the Catholic clique and the rest of the community was far more difficult to overcome. For one thing, the quarrels and mutual suspicions were deeply rooted, tracing back to the years before and immediately after the Boxer Rebellion, when the Catholic hierarchy lorded it over the people and imported converts from as far away as Hopei to settle in Long Bow on Church lands. This historical division was greatly aggravated by the Anti-Traitor Movement because of the predominantly Catholic nature of the puppet regime. By making peace with all rank-and-file collaborators, some of these wounds were healed, but the struggle against the Church itself opened new and deeper ones, particularly among the older believers. For one thing, charges of disloyalty arising out of the escape of Father Sun continued to be pressed with vigor. The three who had originally been arrested for aiding him—Lu Hsien-pao, Wang Hu-sheng, and Fan Ming-hsi—were released from the county jail after eight months, but since they themselves confessed that they had helped the father escape under orders from the Kuomintang leader, Wang En-pao, they were kept under surveillance.

Fan Ming-hsi, the landlord's son, decided that his life was not safe. He met with Hsien-pao and Hu-sheng and suggested that the three of them join forces, assassinate one or two leading cadres, and flee to Hungtung. When he went to Horse Square to raise money for this flight, T'ien-ming became suspicious and ordered his arrest. Before a large public meeting, Fan Ming-hsi admitted his plans and was beaten to death by the militia. Hu-sheng and Hsien-pao lived on in Long Bow under a heavy cloud of suspicion thereafter.

A small group of believers who continued to attend mass also aroused suspicion. By that time the only services held in the district

were held in Horse Square. There, one mile to the north of Long
Bow, a Catholic priest still lived. The cadres wondered, often out
loud, if those who walked the long mile every Sunday morning really
did so only to worship God.

On Easter Sunday in the spring of 1946, an incident occurred that
fanned all the latent suspicion and hostility into flame. Because of
the religious importance of the day, more than the usual number
of Catholic peasants went to Horse Square that Sunday. After the
services some of the Long Bow contingent gathered in a Catholic
leader's courtyard. A man whom everyone said had led Father Sun
to Hungtung was also there that day. A rumor started that he met
in secret with the peasants. When those who had come from Long
Bow returned home, every one of them was arrested and questioned
and, in the course of the questioning, beaten. Not only were they
believers in an "agent" religion, not only did they support a Church
tainted with collaboration, not only were they present at a meeting
with a notorious agent, they also went to Horse Square without
applying for travel passes.*

Because they went to Horse Square without passes, T'ien-ming
crowned all the Easter Sunday worshippers with "agents' caps"—
i.e., he charged them with being Chiang Kai-shek's agents and enemies of the Liberated Areas.

After that, those who still wanted to go to Church were afraid to
ask for passes. When they went secretly without passes, they aroused
even sharper suspicion than before and were beaten whenever they
got caught. Among those who, in spite of all this, continued to go to
Horse Square whenever they found a way to leave the village unde-
tected were three whom the village cadres especially distrusted. These
were Li T'ung-jen, former assistant village head under the puppet
regime, his brother, Li Ho-jen, also a minor puppet official, and
their close friend and neighbor, Shen Ch'uan-te. Each time they were
detained and questioned they insisted that they only went to attend the
mass, but rumors of meetings that had nothing to do with religion
persisted and kept the issue very much alive.

The suspicion under which these practicing Catholics lived deepened
the traditional rift in the community. A clique grew up, with Li Ho-jen
at its center and Shen Ch'uan-te as its mouthpiece, that hated the
revolutionary cadres, opposed the work they were trying to do, and

---

* In all the Liberated Areas a pass system had been in effect from the
beginning. During the Anti-Japanese War it served to prevent communication
between collaborators within the area and especially any liaison between them
and the Japanese or puppet forces on the outside. When the Civil War became imminent it served the same purpose in regard to the Nationalist
sympathizers. To be caught without a pass was a serious offense.

developed in time into a potential center for counter-revolutionary activity. That this potential never flowered was not due to the efforts of the Party branch at the time. On this question they were unable to rise above the prejudices of the past and the fears of the moment and consequently took no effective remedial action.

In the meantime, among the majority of the non-Catholic peasants in Long Bow, the Easter affair and the continued illegal travel to Horse Square only confirmed the already deeply rooted suspicion that the Catholics were in fact agents who were not to be trusted. The popular reaction to the emergence of the Li Ho-jen clique was to spread rumors that isolated its members even further.

This widespread suspicion did not touch, or touched only slightly, the many ex-Catholics or nominal believers like Cheng-k'uan, who joined wholeheartedly in the struggle against landlord domination and against the Catholic Church as one of its aspects. Wang Yu-lai, vice chairman of the Peasants' Association, and his son, Wen-te, both of whom were ex-Catholics, actually took the lead in denouncing other Catholics as agents and traitors, an activity which won them the confidence of the other cadres and the intense hatred of the Catholic community.

The most serious rift in the ranks of the peasants was that which began to show up in the course of the Settling Accounts Movement between the land poor on the one hand, and the independent small holders or middle peasants on the other. It was serious because of the numbers involved. Even if the Catholic community as a whole had been alienated by the attack on the Church, which it was not, this would have involved, at most, one fifth of the village. The small holders made up two fifths of the village. Since the poor peasants were in no position to "go it alone," a split between them and the small holders could doom the revolution.

The Anti-Traitor Movement made a solid alliance of all peasants difficult because there were small holders among the collaborators who were dispossessed. The attack on the Catholics as agents greatly aggravated the difficulty because among them there were also small holders.

The Settling Accounts Movement threatened the very basis of cooperation between the two groups because no clear line was drawn between friends and enemies, between the peasants and their exploiters. Many prosperous peasants who owned their own land did not see much difference between their economic status and that of certain "objects of struggle." They remembered loans given out to neighbors in the past and the hiring of help during the harvest season and broke into a cold sweat. "Maybe we are exploiters too?" they said to one another. They quietly withdrew from active participation in village affairs, could be brought to meetings only if the militia went knocking on doors and ordered them out, and were often overheard making sarcastic remarks about *fanshen*.

The leaders of the Party branch saw this change in the attitude of many families, heard the warnings issued constantly by higher Party and government bodies against damage to "middle-peasant" interests, and decided to do something about it. Through the Peasants' Association, special meetings were held to talk things over with the independent tillers. They were urged to speak their minds. One who had been attacked as a puppet block leader said, "I have already been punished. If things go on this way I'm afraid the same thing will happen all over again." Another asked, "What is going to happen when you equalizers run out of oil (landlord and rich peasant property)? Who will be next?" Others asked why they had not been in the "grades." Even though they had many difficulties, lacked implements, stock and tools, they received nothing from the "fruits." "Why," they asked, "should we be active in the struggle?"

All welcomed the cancellation of debts and the new progressive tax system designed to reward hard labor. But they feared that if they took advantage of it by laboring hard, they would eventually be cut back like chives whose flat green leaves were cut off for food each time they pushed their way above the soil. Was this to be the ultimate reward of thrift and hard labor?

In order to dispel "the chive cutting outlook," branch members urged the Peasants' Association to "open the grades" to all families who lacked anything vital to everyday welfare, and even to those who really had everything they needed, as a demonstration of solidarity. Furniture, grain, and clothing were then handed out much more widely than before. Two hundred and ten out of 252 families in the village received at least something in the later distribution. This relieved the fears of the more prosperous to some extent, but it did not solve the problem because there were still tremendous pressures from below for further expropriation. Since all the really wealthy people, the well-known "money bags," had already been cleaned out, the moderately prosperous could hardly feel safe.

In the summer and fall of 1946 the worst fears of this group were realized, for during these months a new wave of struggle was launched.

21

All Out War—Retreat

Those who advocate "halting the enemy beyond the gate" oppose strategic retreat on the ground that retreat means losing territory, endangering the people ("breaking up the pots and pans," so to speak), and creating an unfavorable impression on the outside world. If we will not let the pots and pans of a section of the inhabitants be broken for once, then the pots and pans of the whole population will go on being broken for a long time.

Mao Tse-tung

IN THE SUMMER of 1946, the fragile truce between the Communist Party of China and the Nationalist Government of Chiang Kai-shek broke down completely. The Truce agreed upon on January 13th was for six months only. It officially expired June 30th. Although both sides acted to extend it pending further talks, spreading battles in July made this impossible.. Civil War began in earnest during that month.

Both sides blamed the other for the breakdown of the truce. General Marshall, in his report to President Truman, tried to apportion the blame equally between the two Chinese parties and thus absolve himself and his government completely, but it soon became obvious from the trend of the war, if from nothing else, that the truce came to an end because Chiang Kai-shek and his American advisers thought they had accumulated enough strength in North China and Manchuria to wipe out the Liberated Areas.. During the entire six months of the truce, military supplies poured into Nationalist-held ports for allocation to armies being trained by American officers and transported to strategic positions in North, Northeast, and Central China by American ships and planes. This was done under the innocent cover of delivering lend-lease supplies already "in the pipeline" and completing the 39-division program inaugurated while the Anti-Japanese War was still in progress. Between V-J Day and the end of July, over $600 million worth of lend-lease supplies reached China—more than had come in throughout eight years of international war. In addition to this, hundreds of millions of dollars worth of surplus property, abandoned in the Pacific theater by the American Army, Navy and Marine Corps, were turned over to Chiang Kai-shek. This included over $17.5 million worth of guns, ammunition, communications equipment, and miscellaneous supplies owned by SACO (Sino-American Co-operative Organization), a joint espionage and sabotage operation carried on by the American Navy and Chiang's security police under the notorious Tai Li, China's Himmler.*

By the time the truce expired, most of the 39 American-equipped and trained divisions, plus 167 re-armed regular divisions of Chiang's army, were ready for battle and strategically placed throughout the North. They moved confidently for a showdown. In the campaigns of that summer and fall it was Chiang's armies that took the offensive and Mao's armies that were on the defensive.

The White Paper issued by the American State Department in 1949 makes this quite clear:

> During the period of General Marshall's mission in China, the govern-
> ment considerably improved its military holdings. Government armies in
> mid-1946 comprised approximately 3,000,000 men, opposed by something
> over 1,000,000 Communists of whom an estimated 400,000 were not
> regular troops. During the latter part of 1946, the Nationalists made
> impressive gains, clearing most of Shensi, Kansu, north Shansi, south
> Chahar, part of northern Hopei and Jehol, and nearly all of Kiangsu. The
> government seized Kalgan, Tatung, Chengte, and gained control of the
> Ping-sui Railroad.
> In Shantung the Nationalists achieved a major advance, clearing much of
> the Tsin-pu Railway (Tientsin-Pukow). Communist gains during this
> period were limited to minor advances into Honan and Hupeh, and in-
> filtration around government positions in Manchuria. By the close of
> 1946, the superiority of the Government's forces was in most areas as
> yet unchallenged.**

The pressure exerted by Chiang Kai-shek's American-backed offensive increased tension throughout the Liberated Areas. No attempt
was made to conceal the gravity of the situation as important cities
and railroad lines on all sides of the Taihang region fell to the enemy.
The reaction of the peasants in Long Bow was mixed. Some were badly
frightened and wondered if they ever should have begun the struggle.
Others strengthened their determination to win in the end, come what
might. The national leaders of the Communist Party took the forced

---

* *United States Relations with China,* Washington, D. C.: Department
of State, 1949, p. 940.
** *Ibid.,* p. 313.

withdrawals calmly. This was but another encirclement similiar to
the five that Chiang Kai-shek had mounted in the 1930's and to
countless others carried out by the Japanese during eight long years
of occupation. With many years of experience to draw on and a
vastly stronger position than they had ever held before, the members
of the Central Committee were confident that the encirclement could
and would be smashed.

Such an outcome depended, in the last analysis, on the kind of
support which millions of peasants were willing to give to the Revolution. The crux of the matter lay in the land question. With land in
their own hands the peasants could be counted on to volunteer for
service in the regular armed forces by the hundreds of thousands,
to support the front with transport columns and stretcher brigades,
and to organize irregular fighting units in every corner of the Liberated Areas. Land ownership was capable of inspiring both at the
front and in the rear the kind of determination among the rank and
file that no terror could shake and no reverses deter. Land ownership could also release among the people that infinite capacity for
concealment, harassment, ambush, and surprise attack that is the
despair of enemy commanders. It could serve as the foundation for
a wall of silence capable of sealing the ears and stopping the eyes
of the enemy's offensive intelligence so that both the regular and
irregular forces of the Revolution could concentrate and disperse,
attack and retreat with relative freedom.

In short, only the satisfaction of the peasant's demand for land
could provide during the coming period of Civil War the kind of
inspiration and cohesion that the spirit of resistance to national sub-
jugation had provided during the war against Japan. Furthermore,
"Land to the Tiller" was a necessary step in the transformation of
China, the key to the destruction of the old pattern of society and
its replacement by an independent, modern industrial society. In
the land question both the short- and the long-range interests of the
people coincided.

In order to insure that the full potential of the people for victorious
defense against the impending Nationalist offensive was aroused in
good time, the Central Committee of the Chinese Communist Party
had already issued a directive which reversed the wartime policy of
"Double Reduction" and called once more for "Land to the Tiller"
inside the Liberated Areas. This policy declaration, issued on May
4, 1946, came to be known as the May 4th Directive. It was at one
and the same time both a call for all-out land equalization wherever
such a program had not yet been attempted and a recognition of
the kind of struggle that had already taken place on the initiative of

local Poor-and-Hired Peasants' Leagues and Peasants' Associations in the Taihang Mountains and elsewhere. The directive said, in part:

In the struggles of opposing traitors, settling accounts, reducing rent and interest, the peasants have been acquiring land directly from the hands of the landlords and have thus been carrying out the system of "Land to the Tiller"....

Under these circumstances our Party must of necessity have a consistent policy: we must resolutely support the direct action adopted by the masses to carry out land reform and assume a planned leadership so that in every Liberated Area land reform may be quickly accomplished in accordance with the scale and intensity of the development of the mass movement.

In line with the defensive aim of all policy at this stage, the provisions of the May 4th Directive were relatively mild. Rich peasants were to be subject only to rent-and-interest reduction. Expropriations were to be carried out against landlords but, as David and Isabel Crook have pointed out:

Distinctions were to be made between "tyrants," traitors, and big landlords on the one hand and ordinary small and medium landlords on the other. Wherever possible the latter were to be dealt with by negotiation ... It goes without saying that even the former were to be left with means of livelihood. Commerce and industry, even that belonging to landlords, was to be protected, and in general a policy of magnanimity was to be pursued, with no physical violence and above all no taking of life except by formal legal procedure. All, including people of the landlord class, who had co-operated in the struggle against Japan were to be treated with consideration. Together with the various non-peasant elements, they were, so far as possible, to be drawn into a united front against feudalism and Kuomintang dictatorship and for peace, democracy, and national unity.*

In regard to the status of middle peasants the May 4th Directive was unequivocal. Middle peasants were to be drawn into the movement as allies, encouraged to participate fully in all decisions, and under no circumstances were their lands or their interests to be harmed.

* David and Isabel Crook, *Revolution in a Chinese Village,* London: Routledge and Kegan Paul, 1959, p. 180. It should be stressed again and again that the target of the land reform movement in all its phases was the "feudal" property of the "feudal" classes—i.e., the land, livestock, implements and personal property of the landlords in the countryside. Capitalist forms of property were specifically exempted. Investments in industry and commerce, and even capitalist-type farms, were considered progressive under the conditions then existing in China; hence, stringent bans on the confiscation of industrial and commercial holdings of landlords were written into all land reform laws and regulations.

The May 4th Directive reached Lucheng County after the Civil War had already reached flood tide. In the heat of a defensive campaign, with a large Nationalist army advancing to within 50 miles of the county seat, its moderate proposals were honored more in the breach than in the observance. The struggle that actually developed became even sharper and more violent than that which had gone before. The County Committee of the Communist Party called for *san t'ou, szu yu, wu pu liu,* which meant "three things thorough, four things possessed, and five things resolved." The three basic goals were to accuse thoroughly, to struggle thoroughly, and to *fanshen* thoroughly." "Food to eat, clothes to wear, land to till, and houses to live in" were the four things to be possessed by all landless and land-poor peasants. "Let no poor peasant remain poor, let no backward element remain backward, leave no question between the people be unresolved, leave no feudal remnants in the people's thinking, and leave no landlord in possession of his property," were the five problems to be resolved.

These slogans summed up the whole agrarian revolution in one sentence and inspired the young cadres to complete the transformation of their society within a few weeks.

The campaign that resulted was based on two assumptions: first, that serious feudal exploitation still existed in the county, and second, that large numbers of peasants had not yet *fanshened.*

Since almost every family of wealth and position had already lost most of its open holdings (land, houses, draft animals, and farm implements) and at least some, if not all, of its hidden wealth (buried silver and gold), the first assumption might well have been questioned. On the other hand, since there were thousands of poor peasants in the village who lacked much that was necessary to make them independent producers, it seemed obvious that the confiscations had not been complete enough. In practice, the stubborn persistence of poverty was taken as proof of both assumptions and provided the rationale for a new assault. If the poor were ever to *fanshen*— and who dared say they should not?—more wealth would have to be found.

But where was the "oil" to come from? Who would provide the fruits? On the one hand, all the remaining hidden wealth of the gentry must be dug out; on the other, all those families who tried to pose as ordinary peasants but who were in fact in one capacity or another exploiters must be expropriated. The attack, in other words, had to be deepened and the target had to be broadened.

One way to broaden the target was to examine not only the exploitation of the recent past, but to go back through the generations and seek out all the wealth which had originally been acquired from the blood and sweat of tenants and hired laborers by the fathers or even the grandfathers of the small holders of 1946. This was called seeking out the "feudal tails." Tracing back three generations did indeed unearth many new "objects of struggle" who possessed "feudal tails." So great had been the inherent tendency of Chinese society toward the dissipation of wealth through the practice of equal inheritance that very few persons could claim with confidence that their families were free from the taint of past exploitation, that they possessed nothing that was not earned by hard labor.* Those who had inherited the divided estates of recognized landlords were especially vulnerable. They were automatically designated as landlords themselves. And this was so even though they worked every day in the fields, for these very fields were considered to be "feudal tails."

With such an approach the cadres and poor peasants of Long Bow began a second whirlwind campaign to expropriate for the poor the fruits of exploitation, past and present. The campaign lasted 20 days. Since the heads of most of the well-known gentry families had already either fled the village or been killed, wives, sons, daughters, and relatives were brought before public meetings to answer accusations. Not the leading male representative, but whole families became the object of attack. The militia took advantage of the divisions and hatred within families. By individual cross-questioning, by playing off one against the other, by severe beatings and threats, many more silver dollars, a number of gold boats (an ancient form of money), and large quantities of fine clothes were unearthed.

After dealing thus for the second time with the gentry, the militia moved on to the "feudal tails." One such family, with the surname Wang, was all but wiped out.

Wang Hsiao-nan and Wang Hua-nan were well-to-do peasants who had not divided the six-acre holding which they inherited from their landlord father. They lived in one courtyard with their wives and their aging mother. The elder brother, Hsiao-nan, had a son. Huanan was childless.

When the second wave of confiscation began in Lucheng County, their married sister, who lived in North Market, about a mile to the northeast, came home one day with 2,000 silver dollars which she

---

* A poor peasant in Ten Mile Inn, a village on the eastern slope of the Taihang range, pointedly asked: "How could any man in our village claim that his family had been [bare] poor for three generations? If a man is poor, then his son can't afford to marry; and if his son can't marry, there can't be a third generation." (See David and Isabel Crook, *Revolution in a Chinese Village*, p. 133.

begged her mother to hide for her. This represented a great part of her landlord husband's family savings. At a secret consultation which Hua-nan and his wife knew nothing about, Hsiao-nan and his mother agreed to bury the treasure behind their house. In all of Long Bow only the two of them knew that there was such a sum of money and where it was hidden. Neither of them told. But the sister in North Market, when pressed by her husband's own tenants, confessed to the cache. A greater part of the population of North Market thereupon marched to Long Bow in triumphant procession, dug out the money and carried all of it home with them. So elated were they at finding such a huge sum that they hired a drama corps to stage a Chinese opera and celebrated with food and drink for three whole days and nights.

The young men of Long Bow, taken completely by surprise, and angered by the removal of so much wealth from under their very noses, attacked the whole Wang family as landlords and landlord protectors. They reasoned that if 2,000 silver dollars had been successfully hidden for so long, perhaps thousands more still lay buried in the ground. When Hsiao-nan could not lead them to a second cache, they beat him cruelly. They would have done the same to Hua-nan but for the fact that he was away from home hauling grain. When Hua-nan could not be found, the enraged peasants seized his wife and beat her in his stead. The beatings served no purpose other than punishment, for no further wealth was ever found; but both Hsiao-nan and Hua-nan's wife died of the injuries they received. Five of the family's acres were confiscated as were most of the sections of their house, and all of their personal property from clothes to the round bottomed pot they used for cooking.

When Hua-nan returned, a few days later, the excitement had died down. The peasants let him live, but with no property left in the family he had to work out as a hired laborer in order to feed himself, his sister-in-law, her son, and his old mother.

****

By the time the millet ripened in the fall of 1946 the military situation had become more critical than at any time since the Japanese surrender. Not only were the Central Armies taking back strategic positions on the fringes of the Liberated Areas, but a strong detachment of Yen Hsi-shan's Provincial Army was simultaneously driving across the heart of Southwest Shansi in an effort to seize as much of the autumn harvest as could be carried away before the peasants had a chance to hide it. This detachment had already reached

Hsincheng, only 45 miles to the south, and was expected to attack Changchih within a matter of days.

The People's Liberation Army, heavily engaged on other fronts, let Yen's troops come. This was one of the successful tactics for breaking encirclement worked out by Mao Tse-tung in the 1930's. Armies that could not easily be smashed by frontal attack were allowed to drive deep into a Liberated Area, tempted to overextend themselves, and then, under constant and clever harassment, forced to withdraw or face piecemeal annihilation under the combined attacks of local and regular forces quickly concentrated for the counterattack. Villages in the path of such a drive prepared for temporary occupation by hiding all grain and valuable property, by sending their women and children deeper into the mountains, and by mobilizing their young men for harassing action. Experienced leaders had seen this work out time and time again, but peasants, facing reoccupation for the first time, could hardly help but feel nervous. The gentry, on the other hand, assuming that the advance of their armies signified a turn in their fortunes, openly threatened people with reprisal, arranged to fire "black shots" in the night, and joyously looked forward to a "change of sky."

Strange happenings set the whole village on edge.

A militiaman left a meeting early one night because he was not feeling well. As he stepped out onto the main street he found the village lying quiet under a crescent moon. Only the lone sentries, out of sight at the edge of the fields still moved about. Looking south the sick man saw, or thought he saw, a figure squatting in a dark corner where a side alley ran off from the street. He walked toward the place. Nothing moved. He shouted. There was no answer. Then he took his gun from his shoulder, cocked it with a loud click, pointed it at the man, or the shadow, he wasn't sure which, and called out, "I'll shoot." The shadow suddenly came to life. Before the militiaman could move a muscle the sound of running feet in the alley made clear that a hostile intruder had escaped.

A few days later the majority of the militia went to Li Village Gulch for a training session. Seven men stayed behind. Four of them kept watch in the north, south, east and west, while three who were sick slept in the temple that was their headquarters. These were Kuei-ts'ai, vice-head of the village, who had syphilis, and two rank-and-file corpsmen who suffered from itching sores of the skin. In the middle of the night Kuei-ts'ai heard loud knocking on the street side of the wall. He moved quietly to the compound wall, slid along it, and peered through the crack between the two halves of the wooden gate. There stood a man carrying at his waist a bright object that looked like a pistol. Kuei-ts'ai asked the man why he knocked. The reply came in a dialect that was unintelligible. Kuei-ts'ai repeated the question twice but received no further answer. Then he ordered the man to leave. The stranger made no move to go. Finally Kuei-ts'ai pulled the pin on a grenade and threw it over the wall. The nocturnal visitor left in a hurry and was never seen again.

Unable to explain these incidents and fearful lest the gentry, with the help of enemy infiltrators, might actually be preparing a conspiracy in the village, T'ien-ming ordered a nightly check-up of the homes of all rich peasants and landlords, all important ex-collaborators and all Catholics implicated in the escape of Father Sun. In the middle of the night militiamen made their rounds in pairs, knocked on the doors of all suspects, ordered the occupants to let them in, and searched the premises for unregistered guests, leaflets, weapons, or other signs of counter-revolutionary activity.

At the same time the village government, under instructions from the Party and government leaders of Lucheng County, launched a "Hide the Grain Movement" to prevent seizure of the autumn harvest should the enemy troops advance that far. Thousands of families dug pits in the ground or found caves in the hills where they could store their crops and possessions. They also arranged with more isolated villages for temporary shelter for their women and children. Some peasants went even further. They were so frightened that they secretly sent back to landlord families the property and clothing they had received in the distribution, or they began to pay a little rent for the use of expropriated land. The wife of one village chairman even hired herself out as an unpaid servant in an ex-landlord's household in return for a promise of protection when the gentry again took power. All this was known as *ming fen an pu fen or* "take the fruits in the light, return them in the dark."

In the face of this spreading panic the Communist Party took steps to strengthen morale and prevent the return of "fruits" in the dark. Through the Peasants' Association they extended the Hide the Grain Movement into a movement to "examine *fanshen*." The situation of every family in regard to land and property was again reviewed. Those who had secretly returned property were urged to take it back. The method of breaking an encirclement by temporarily yielding territory while mobilizing all the forces of the people to combat the enemy was clearly explained to all. "Unity will certainly defeat the counter-offensive" became the slogan of the day.

What began in the fall of 1946 as a defensive move was soon transformed by the village cadres and more active poor peasants into a third great offensive against the gentry. Under the slogan *pu ta lo shui kou, p'ao ch'i lai yao liao shou* (if you don't beat down the drowning dog, he'll jump out and bite your hand), all the remaining members of the families already under attack were again brought before public meetings. Their last remaining wealth was demanded. With the enemy troops so close at hand and the threat of counter-revolution growing day by day, the campaign was more than ever charged with emotion and marred by excessive violence. Since, by this time, there was no more land, housing, or ordinary property left that could be confiscated, buried silver and gold became the main objective of the active peasants. This time the ancestral tombs of all the prominent families were dug open and searched for valuables. The tireless treasure seekers left the yellow subsoil piled in scattered heaps around the gaping holes where underground vaults had been found. Carved obelisks of granite and marble lay like scattered dominoes where they fell. So numerous were the rifled tombs that the whole countryside seemed to have been bombarded at random by huge shells. These scars inflicted on the land itself in bold defiance of all superstition demonstrated to all who passed that the poor had indeed turned over. To the gentry, this earthly resurrection of their ancestors was an affront which in their wildest nightmares they had never dreamed possible.

But it was the living, not the dead, who really felt the bite of the poor peasants' angry blows. In many cases the living, at least those among the living who still remained in the village, were women. Hence it was they who bore the brunt of this final attack.

The gentry wives astonished the peasants by their fierce resistance and contempt for pain. "All you had to do to make a man talk was to heat an iron bar in the fire," a militiaman told me years later, "but the women were tougher. They would rather die than tell us where their gold was hidden. Burning flesh held no terror for them. If they weakened at all, it was in the face of threats to their children."

In the long run, however, even the gentry women were no match for the aroused peasants. One after another they were forced to confess where they had hidden the last of their family wealth. Cache after cache of money, silk, embroidered clothes, and jewels was discovered. Each new discovery so angered and excited the people that the campaign mounted in intensity with each passing day. In January the wealthy landlord Sheng Ching-ho had himself turned over to the peasants over $500 in coins. Then he ran away. In July his wife surrendered another $400 and a golden boat. Then she fled with her children. Only the sister-in-law remained in the village. During this third campaign she yielded up another $1,000. Nobody believed that this was the full extent of Ching-ho's buried wealth, but the sister-in-law, even when tortured, would reveal no more. Two hundred dollars were confiscated from Chou Mei-sheng, the chief of staff of the puppet government before he too ran away. No gold, but quantities of fine silk and woolen clothes were found in the vaults that belonged to Hsu Chen-p'eng, the absentee general. His sister led the peasants to them to save her own life.

The enemy advance that created the extraordinary tension of this third wave of assault did not get beyond Hsincheng after all. As the military crisis eased, the Peasants' Association in Long Bow, frustrated by the fact that no major new sources of wealth could be found and unable to single out any more families that could legitimately be called exploiters even under the three generation rule, gradually dropped the campaign altogether. This brought an end to the expropriations inspired by the May 4th Directive.

****

The land equalization campaigns of the summer and fall of 1946 were disappointing to the poor peasant activists who had manned them. When all the "fruits" were divided there were still many families who felt that they had not truly *fanshened*. Nevertheless the shared wealth did strengthen to a certain extent the ability of the community to produce. The land-poor gained approximately 80 acres of tillable soil and scores of sections of housing. More important than real estate, however, was the treasure unearthed. The silver, the gold, and the jewelry extracted from the once affluent gentry amounted to over $4,000 in value. When distributed among 200 families, each got approximately $20, or a year's earnings for a hired man.

Most of this money was immediately converted into means of production by the peasants who received it. An indication of this was the sharp rise in the number of draft animals in the village. Within a few months large livestock increased from 71 to 103 head, a 45 percent jump that was the result of cash-in-hand expeditions to other regions to buy stock. Carts, plows, seeders, and other implements also increased.

Checking on the accomplishments of the land reform movement at this time, the Communist Party Committee of Lucheng County found that feudal landholding and feudal political power had been effectively destroyed throughout the five districts under its supervision. It also found that the means of production had been broadly redistributed and was consequently satisfied that the goals of the May 4th Directive had been achieved. The County Committee therefore turned its attention to the next big problem on the agenda—

how best to put the liberated wealth and resources of the county to work, how best to stimulate production. The general welfare of the people, the ability to provide sufficient support for the armies defending the Revolution at the front, and the ability of the economy to survive the strains of the blockade imposed by Chiang Kai-shek —all this depended on the success of the production movement.

CHANGES IN LANDHOLDING BY CLASSES (1944-1947)*

I. *Before Liberation*

	No. of families	% of families	No of persons	% of population	Land held (mou)	% of land held	Mou per capita
Landlord	7	2.8	39	4	680	12.2	17.4
Rich Peasant	5	2.0	27	2.7	303	5.4	11.2
Middle Peasant	81	32.2	395	40	2532.6	45.3	6.4
Poor Peasant	138	55	462	46.8	1386.7	24.8	3.0
Hired Laborer	19	7.6	59	6	—	—	—
Tenant	1	.4	5	.5	—	—	—
Institutional	—	—	—	—	686.2	12.3	—
Totals	251	100	987	100	5588.2	100	

II. *Between Liberation and May 4th, 1946*

	No. of families	% of families	No of persons	% of population	Land held (mou)	% of land held	Mou per capita	Change (in mou)
Landlord	2	.8	6	.6	18	.3	3	−662
Rich Peasant	4	1.6	20	2.1	138.8	2.5	6.9	−164.2
Middle Peasant	76	31.2	349	37.4	2157	38.6	6.2	−375.6
Poor Peasant	162	66.4	559	59.9	2841.4	50.8	5	+1455
Institutional	—	—	—	—	433	7.8	—	−253.2
Totals	244	100	934	100	5588.2	100		

III. *After Completion of May 4th Movement*

	No. of families	% of families	No of persons	% of population	Land held (mou)	% of land held	Mou per capita	Change (in mou)
Landlord	1	.4	2	.2	18	.3	9	0
Rich Peasant	4	1.6	12	1.3	82.6	1.5	6.9	−56.2
Middle Peasant	76	30.4	338	35.5	2095	37.5	6.2	−62
Poor Peasant	169	67.6	599	63.0	3309.6	59.2	5.5	+468.2
Institutional	—	—	—		83	1.5		−350
Totals	250	100	951	100	5588.2	100		

* Six *mou* = one acre.

22

Organizing Production

For thousands of years a system of individual production has prevailed among the peasant masses, under which a family or household makes a productive unit; this scattered individual form of production was the economic foundation of feudal rule and has plunged the peasants into perpetual poverty. The only way to change this state of affairs is gradual collectivization, and the only way to bring about collectivization is, according to Lenin, through co-operatives.

Mao Tse-tung

SPLASHED on a Long Bow wall in whitewashed ideographs larger than a man was the slogan, "The Battle for Production Is As Vital As The Battle at the Front."

In a courtyard behind these words four women wound the warp on a loom. From a nearby doorway came the peristent hum of spinning wheels in motion. The sound was created by a mother, two daughters and a small son sitting cross-legged on grass mats and spinning as if their very lives depended on it. An older woman in the same room threw a shuttle back and forth over a clacking wooden loom. She caught the tapered block as it emerged and tossed it back again almost faster than the eye could register.

Out on the street numerous small children wound thread on shuttles as they ran about. In their wandering they had to duck between clusters of donkeys and mules that almost blocked all traffic through the village center. These animals, equipped with pack saddles, were about to be led off to the mines at Yellow Mill. There they would pick up coal and haul it to Changchih. In charge were two peasants of a mutual-aid production group whose members made the animals available for transport work while they themselves were preoccupied with other tasks.

Keeping a watchful eye on the pack animals were several boys with small iron forks and wide wicker baskets shaped like clam shells. Into these baskets they deftly gathered any manure dropped by the animals and carried it off to their father's cistern where it supplemented the family store of night soil and promised an increase in next year's crop.

Peddlers pushed with difficulty down the crowded street. Here a man with a heavy load of pottery balanced on a high-wheeled barrow sold the produce of a mutual-aid group in Licheng, a county town more than 40 miles to the east. There a lean hawker shouldered a carrying pole laden with slabs of ink individually wrapped in coarse yellow paper. He too represented a mutual-aid group made up of ten poor peasants in Wuan County who made writing materials in the slack season.

In the village square, carts from the mountain counties laden with coal, ore, hemp, dried persimmons, walnuts, live pigs, wool, and other highland products on their way to southern markets locked hubs with similar carts from the Yellow River Valley laden with reed mats, bamboo chairs, raw bamboo poles, and other lowland produce bound for the mountains. Every table in the village inn was jammed with carters. They consumed great bowls of broth in which floated strips of mutton and fat cracklings obtained from the fat-tailed sheep that were the property of still another mutual-aid group. By marketing their meat locally the group members earned far more than they would have by taking it to the county town. The men eating the broth carried with them tales of production achievements from widely scattered villages and unconsciously stimulated further mutual-aid efforts in the communities through which they passed.

Such variety and intensity of productive effort had never before been experienced, certainly not within living memory. The boom could be attributed to two main sources.

On the one hand, it was the natural result of the fact that every peasant had, at last, some land to till, some equipment with which to work, and the prospect of a good crop. The fact that the crop would go into his own jars and bins and not into the storerooms of some landlord or usurer greatly enhanced the incentive to produce. The increased yields that resulted expanded per capita income and with it purchasing power. This in turn stimulated the rebirth of hundreds of slack-season handicraft products which again in their turn increased both income and purchasing power.

On the other hand, the boom was stimulated by the planned policies and determined organizing effort of Communist Party committees, government administrators, financial institutions, and the leaders of mass organizations at all levels.

Mutual-aid groups for labor exchange on the land and the pooling of resources for subsidiary occupations did not simply appear. They were organized and promoted on a vast scale. The whole purpose of the land distribution, as envisioned by the Communist Party, was to remove the fetters that bound production, to release the energy and enthusiasm of the peasants, and to lay the basis for a transition from "individual labor based on an individual economy to collective labor based on a collective economy." Once the question of land ownership was settled the mutual-aid movement—the embryonic form of co-operation in production—was considered to be the key to progress in the rural areas.

Mao spoke many times of the two great "organizings"—organize to overthrow feudalism and organize to increase production. One without the other was futile. Mutual aid, labor exchange, and co-operation in production were impossible on any large scale as long as landlord-tenant relations predominated. Where one man owned all the means of production—the land, the implements and the draft animals—and the other man owned only his own two hands, there were no grounds for getting together. There was no basis for exchange. The rich man simply hired the poor man. Once the sharp attack on the landlords and rich peasants had created a community in which all families held approximately equal amounts of land, implements, and livestock—mutual aid, labor exchange, and co-operation began to sprout up on every side.

In the Taihang Mountains in 1946 and 1947, mutual aid was not only relatively easy to initiate, it was absolutely necessary if the peasants were to produce at all. There simply were not enough carts, donkeys, oxen, seeders, or even iron hoes to go around. In order to produce, people had to share. Mutual aid was necessary for still another reason. Primitive as the means of production were, no family could afford to have a complete set of the implements and draft animals necessary for production. One good mule could farm 20 acres. But no family owned as much as 20 acres, or even half that much. The largest holding in all of Long Bow was a little more than eight acres for a family of nine people. Even this large family could not use all the productive capacity of one mule. If they had tried to keep a mule and a cart and a plow and a harrow and a seeder, the capital investment would have been grossly out of proportion to the production possible on eight acres of land. Therefore a family that owned a mule was not likely to own the other essential implements, not even a cart, even though the latter was used as much for transport on the roads as it was for agriculture.

Since there were not enough draft animals and implements to go around and since the landholdings were too small to engage efficiently any complete set of equipment, it was essential that people get together, swap and share what they had, and help each other out.

Labor exchange, which had existed in China for thousands of years on a spontaneous but limited basis, suddenly became a great agricultural movement.

Yang Chung-sheng, a landowning Long Bow peasant with a large family to feed, led the best-organized local mutual-aid group. Starting with five families who joined together of their own accord in 1946, it soon grew to include 22 families who owned a total of over 80 acres of land. Among the earlier members were four soldiers' dependants and two families without able-bodied members who had been left out by other groups. But even this dead weight did not dampen enthusiasm. The group produced so well that new families constantly applied for membership. As finally constituted the 22-family constellation mustered 12 able-bodied men, two "half-labor-power" children, and two "half-labor-power" old people for field work. In spite of the fact that they had a very large area to till per man, they were always the first to finish any work, whether planting, plowing, hoeing, or harvesting. This was because they got along well and helped each other out, not only in the fields but also in solving all problems of livelihood. For example, Li P'an-ming, the peasant who was director of public affairs for the whole village, fell sick just at planting time. He was not able to get up off his *k'ang*. The group met to discuss what to do and decided that they would tend his land without asking anything in return as long as he was sick. They agreed that they would not even accept meals in his home. At the same time, because Li P'an-ming was short of grain, the group loaned him enough to tide him over until the summer harvest. Before Li got well the first hoeing had been completed. The group told him that he could pay them back another year if he wanted to, but in fact they never recorded the work done and never demanded payment. Thus all of Li P'an-ming's problems were solved. This greatly encouraged the other members of the group, for they realized that if they were ever in trouble they too could get help. Their morale rose. They all worked harder than before and at the end of the year were chosen as the model team in the village.

Aside from the fact that the members of Yang Chung-sheng's team were good friends to begin with, they attributed their success to the fact that they organized well, met often, discussed every problem thoroughly and worked out a good system of keeping records so that the exchange of labor time balanced out in the long run. Yang never tried to tell the group what to do. When they met they talked things over and only when they agreed did they act. They always tilled the land of soldiers' dependents first, asking only their meals in return. Families without manpower paid wages for all work done, but the group did not demand that these wages be paid at once. Those who had no grain could wait until after the harvest to settle up. A committee of four was elected to report on all hours put in and on all exchanges of implements and draft power. One member who could write and figure on the abacus was appointed to tally up the accounts. At the end of every period—that is, planting, hoeing, harvesting, etc. —a balance sheet was drawn up and a settlement made. Everyone paid up what he owed except those who were in difficult circumstances and needed more time. This satisfied all participants and helped to maintain morale at a high level.

The group met briefly every evening to plan the next day's work. When the cocks began to crow before dawn, no time was wasted in consultation. Everyone went straight to the field without having to be called. When the six animals possessed by the group members were not needed in the fields, they were taken by their owners on transport work that was individually planned and executed. In other words, the group did not try to pool all the activities of its members. They worked together where the advantage was greatest and went their separate ways where that was more suitable. To add to their winter production they pooled their resources to set up a beancurd plant. They hired an old peasant, Ch'un-ching, who had just come from the old people's home in the Catholic compound at Kao Settlement, to work there full time.

In the fall of 1947, elections were held throughout the Taihang for model peasants and workers. Among the six chosen to go from Long Bow to the district elimination meeting was Yang Chung-sheng. None of the Long Bow contingent was chosen to represent the district at the county or Border Region level. Nevertheless, the meeting did inspire them to organize further production groups.

When Yang returned he and the Long Bow blacksmith, Huan-ch'ao, helped to set up a co-operative carpentry shop. The village still held a sizable quantity of wood that had been confiscated from the gentry but had not been distributed. It also had available more than a hundred pounds of iron. This wood and iron, plus some tens of thousands of Border Region dollars (1,000=$1, U. S. currency) were loaned by the village office to Chung-sheng and Huan-ch'ao as operating capital. All the carpenters in the village were invited to join them. Eleven of the 14 agreed to come in. Together with Huan-ch'ao the blacksmith, and Li Lao-szu the stone mason, this constituted a membership of 13.

Whenever work was slack on the land these 13 gathered in one of the big empty rooms of the "foreign house," as the big brick compound formerly owned by absentee general Hsu was known, and fashioned things of wood—shovels for use in winnowing grain, hubs for cart wheels, cart bodies, chairs, tables. At first they were not able to make whole wheels because Huan-ch'ao did not know how to fashion or shrink on the iron hoops that held the wheel together. But a request for help was sent to the county Workers' Union and two experts were immediately assigned to Long Bow to teach Huan-ch'ao all that he needed to know. They stayed for a month, made sure that the blacksmith learned the whole process from beginning to end, and then returned to Lucheng.

The co-owners of the carpentry shop were paid on a point system according to their skill. The blacksmith got the most points—98. The seasoned carpenters got 80 points. Li Lao-szu who was really a stone mason got 79 points (they were lenient with him because he was poor), and one young apprentice got 48. From the total gross income of the shop, expenses were first subtracted. These included the wood, the iron, and the other materials used to make implements and carts, plus the food and fuel used to make the meals which the men shared while at work. Twenty percent of the net income was then turned over to the village in payment for the capital put in from public funds. The remaining money was divided according to the points allotted each man. When the accounts were settled, the members found that they made only about three *sheng* of millet a day as against the seven that could usually be earned by a good carpenter working on his own.* This did not make them very happy but they reasoned that anyway they had steady work. Many a carpenter, though he got seven *sheng* a day, could not find work each day, and so in the long run came out no better. Granting credit also lowered their earnings. Since the purpose of the carpentry shop and of the whole production movement was to help poor peasants *fanshen,* these poor carpenters undertook to build carts and implements for many families that could not afford to pay cash. As a result they had many accounts outstanding in both Long Bow and other nearby villages. If they could collect all these funds, their earnings would almost double. There were even a number of prosperous peasants who had bought things that they could afford to pay cash for but hadn't because, they said, "Others don't pay; why should we?"

In spite of all these problems, the carpentry shop flourished, technique improved, orders grew, and more and more products were turned out each month. Wood supplies soon ran low. Then the co-operators had to make a journey to Fu Village in the distant Western Mountains, where they bought standing trees, cut them down

---

* A *sheng* is .028 bushels, or a little less than a quart.

with hand tools, and hauled them home by cart. Later, the logs were cut into boards and billets with bucksaws, one man standing high in the air on top of the braced log while another man stood on the ground below him. Each day spent on such work earned the worker three *sheng* of millet.

Mutual-aid type organization was not confined to work on the land or to the labor of male craftsmen. Women also organized mutual-aid groups, most of which concentrated on textile production. Because of the inroads of machine-made textiles in the previous decades, many wives and mothers no longer knew how or had never learned to make cloth from raw cotton in the home. The Women's Association therefore had to start from the beginning with a spinning and weaving class whose students, coming from dozens of families, lived together in the "Foreign House" of General Hsu, and learned by doing. Once the students became proficient they transformed their class into a spinning and weaving group rather than return to their homes for individual production. This was because the women, young and old, found it much more congenial to work together in a large group than to sit isolated in their homes endlessly spinning or pushing a shuttle. Also, when one worked alone at home, it was easy to fall asleep early in the evening and thus shorten the hours of work. By meeting together, exchanging gossip, studying, and singing, the long evenings passed quickly and productively. Some husbands and fathers soon complained over the absence of their women from home for such extended periods. When complaints could no longer be ignored, the women compromised by working at home during the day and with the group in the "Foreign House" in the evening.

I have no record of the amount or value of the cotton cloth which this one large Long Bow group created, but a similar group of 70 women in another Taihang village won region-wide recognition by producing enough textiles in one season to buy 55 sheep, 35 pigs, two draft animals, and farm implements worth $335 in U. S. currency.

Almost as important as mutual aid in stimulating production was the new tax system introduced on the heels of land reform by the Border Region Government. The new regulations as they finally crystallized out of a very confused situation constituted what was known as "The Proportionate Single-Tax System with Exemptions."* The old tax system, when it did not simply take everything that police and troops could find, penalized the conscientious producer by demanding a

---

* The system, which gradually emerged out of post-war chaos, was completed in September 1948. In 1946 and 1947, the features outlined here were applied one by one.

fixed proportion of the actual crop harvested. The bigger the crop, the bigger the tax. The new tax system reversed this and rewarded the conscientious producer by basing its demands not on the actual crop harvested in the current year, but on the average amount harvested in previous seasons. What was taxed was not the land as such or the crop as such but standard *mou*. A standard *mou* was defined as any amount of land that yielded 10 *tou* (one *tou*=0.285 bushels) of millet. To determine how many standard *mou* a man possessed one only had to calculate his annual average yield in *tou* and divide by ten. The tax that he paid was set as a proportion of this standard. Anyone who worked hard, applied new methods and increased his yields, paid no tax on that part of the crop exceeding the fixed standard no matter how large it was, and this was true for a definite number of years. If, for instance, a peasant dug a well, irrigated his fields, and thereby doubled his crops, this made no difference at all to his tax base until three years had passed. Similiar provisions rewarded other forms of effort such as reclamation.

All crops grown on virgin land (land uncropped for more than six years) were tax free for three years. Crops grown on reclaimed land (land uncropped for any period up to six years) were tax free for two years.

To guarantee that all families retained enough grain after taxes to survive (a matter with which the old regime had never concerned itself), the yield from one standard *mou*, or 2.85 bushels of millet per capita was entirely exempted from all taxation. These exemption provisions were similar to the $600 exemptions of the United States federal income tax law. However, the Border Region tax regulations went the United States one better in this respect. Oxen and donkeys were granted an exemption equal to 40 percent of a standard *mou*, or 1.14 bushels of millet, while horses and mules were granted 70 percent, or 1.9 bushels, thus guaranteeing a minimum of food for livestock as well as for their masters.

The proportional features of the law also paralleled the United States income tax provisions. Families harvesting an average amount of land per capita paid 25 catties of millet, or approximately 20 percent of the yield on all taxable standard *mou*, but families who held more than the average amount of land and hence harvested more than the average paid a proportionately higher tax.* Those who harvested twice the per capita average of the community paid as high as 40 percent of their income in taxes. Above this the rate did not go. A higher rate was hardly needed. After land reform there were

* These were wartime rates. After 1950, rates were cut to between 12 and 15 percent.

very few households that harvested more than twice the per capita average.

All of these features together—the exemptions, the standard *mou* method of calculating the tax base, the deferred taxation of improvements and the proportionate increases for higher incomes—combined to develop a tax system reasonable in the eyes of the peasants. It was clearly designed to guarantee subsistence, reward effort, and discourage laziness and neglect; and it definitely helped to stimulate a tremendous movement to improve and reclaim land and raise production.

Before mutual aid and the new tax regulations could stimulate a truly mass movement, other important subjective and objective problems had to be overcome.

Some people had to be convinced of the need for winter work. Having harvested from their own land more grain than they had ever seen before, they tended to be complacent. One peasant said, "In the past when I earned two bushels of millet and three of corn I thought I was well off. This year I harvested between 15 and 20 bushels and I said to myself that I would relax for a few months and enjoy myself and stop worrying about food and clothes." But a group of neighbors meeting to figure up family accounts soon stripped him of any illusions of prosperity. They found, after careful calculation, that in order to live until spring he would need at least five bushels more than he had. A second peasant said, "There's no use figuring for me. There's no question but that in one year I have harvested enough food for two." Skeptical neighbors added his totals and found that he hardly had enough grain to last the winter, not to mention salt, cooking oil, and other essential staples which still had to be bought.

Other families, fully convinced of the need to produce, were discouraged by lack of capital. Here mutual aid, by pooling the meager resources of several poor families, solved part of the problem. But credit from the local co-op or the newly organized People's Credit Bank of Lucheng County was also important. The bank didn't wait for the peasants to come to it. Bank managers and clerks travelled through the villages of their neighborhoods and made first-hand surveys of the people's needs. The limited funds which they had to lend were thus channelled into the hands of those who needed them most. Traditional banking practices, such as loaning money only to good risks who could guarantee collateral, were sharply condemned by the revolutionary press which gave wide coverage to the experience of Comrade Ts'ao of the Pinghsun Credit Bank. This energetic man personally visited every village served by his bank. In one hamlet he found eight families who, although they had received some land and housing in the distribution, had no surplus whatever that they could use for winter production. Four of them were soldiers' dependents and two were widows with children. He loaned each family 100,000 Border Region dollars ($35). They immediately invested these funds in a hemp shop and a transport brigade that provided work for all. They told Ts'ao, "Our government is really concerned with people. Now bankers bring money right to our homes and see to it that our problems are solved. We will do our best to produce."

Just as the provision of credit was not left to the profit calculations of private entrepreneurs, so the supply of raw materials for spinning and weaving was not left to the vagaries of local weather and its influence on the cotton crop or to the ability of women and children with scant resources to purchase fibre. Ginned cotton from the plains of Hopei was advanced to mountain communities through their Women's Associations, thus guaranteeing a large spinning and weaving movement wherever hands lay idle.

At the same time the dampening influence of middlemen's high profits and speculatory manipulations was mitigated by the creation of a vast network of village-controlled and financed consumer co-operatives. These popular institutions provided staples at low prices and an outlet for rural produce at a fair return.

An expanding market was also greatly aided by the growth of transportation facilities. Easy credit stimulated transport by carrying-pole, wheelbarrow, bicycle, pack animal, and two-wheel cart. So did the improvement of roads and highways. Most striking of all was the construction of a narrow gauge railroad which, under the direction of the embryonic Railroad Bureau of the Shansi-Hopei-Honan-Shantung Border Region Government, pushed halfway through the Taihang Mountains from the east.

The new railroad was not the only form of public enterprise that grew up alongside the extensive private and co-operative forms already mentioned. The government also went heavily into mining, smelting, and munitions manufacture, to mention but a few important areas of public production. Even in Long Bow a munitions plant was established that soon rivalled the community's two distilleries in size and volume of output. This produced nitrates from organic ash. The nitrates were used to arm the explosive shells that the People's Liberation Army was demanding in ever increasing numbers. Changing tides at the front had brought massive windfalls of captured American equipment. Gradually the peasant-style rifle-and-hand-grenade army was being transformed into a modern force that boasted both tanks and artillery.

Twice a year, by government decree, every peasant in the Fifth District was required to bring five catties of ash to the new plant housed in an empty building on Long Bow's eastern rim. For this ash the peasants were paid a standard price. The demand for organic ash soon mushroomed far beyond anything that could be satisfied by the embers of the peasants' cooking fires and stimulated an endless search for waste material. Over the hills and valleys of the district arose wisps of smoke that were visible for miles, as young and old burned the leaves, weeds, roots, and trash that would make it possible to blast Chiang Kai-shek, "The Old Root of Reaction," right out of Nanking.

****

Whether or not Chiang Kai-shek could ever actually be blasted out of Nanking depended in large measure on the uninterrupted progress of this production movement and the solid basis which it alone could provide for a new politics and a new culture. Yet, as the months passed, many signs indicated that all was not entirely well on the home front. The full potential of the economy was being undercut by several negative trends, all of which arose from the same source —the very thoroughness with which the drive of the poor to *fanshen* had smashed down all feudal barriers and then gone on to "level the tops and fill the holes."

One of these trends involved a clear violation of policy. In spite of repeated warnings by the Central Committee, in spite of the clear language of the May 4th Directive, the expropriation proceedings against the gentry had not stopped with feudal property. To the young activists in the villages a landlord was a landlord, a rich peasant was a rich peasant, and an exploiter was an exploiter. They did not recognize any such phenomenon as a dual personality—a landlord capitalist, or a capitalist landlord. When they attacked they took everything—land, housing, stock, tools, buried treasure—and also business ventures. As a consequence, in the whole of Lucheng County, very few enterprises of a private nature survived the 1946 campaigns. Most of them had either been destroyed by a division of their assets or had been taken over by various mutual-aid groups to be run as co-operatives. The over-all effect of such expropriations was to stifle private initiative, a drag on production which the underdeveloped state of the economy could ill afford. While co-operative efforts filled a great need, they could not, on their own, provide all the capital and incentive necessary to an all-around development of production. For this, private enterprise was considered essential.

An even more serious drag on expansion was the growing reluctance of those families who had been attacked as exploiters and those of their more prosperous brethren who feared such an attack, to produce with zest. While the poor who had *fanshened* went at production with unprecedented enthusiasm, those who had helped to make their *fanshen* possible, or feared that they would be called upon to contribute to it later, hung back. The "chive-cutting thought" that had sprouted in the spring of 1946 spread with accelerated speed in the following fall and winter. At a time when the majority were doing their best to create wealth and make themselves as rich as Li Hsun-ta, a substantial minority hesitated.* They did only as much as was necessary to feed their families and guarantee another year's crop. In the meantime they waited to see what the shape of the future might be.

Most serious of all was the political friction which the deepening of the expropriation drive and the broadening of its target produced. The excesses of the movement divided the peasants as surely as its over-all objectives had united them. And it was this tragic division which served as seed-bed for the growth of all kinds of abuses of power and arrogant misbehavior on the part of some leading cadres and militiamen when they began to be confronted with apathy and opposition from unexpected quarters.

* Li Hsun-ta was a famous labor hero of the Yenan region.

23

Abuses of Power

Some comrades have committed mistakes of commandism, adventurism and closed-door-ism. . . . They did not believe that it was the masses who were emancipating themselves. Instead they stood above the masses to fight in their stead, to bestow emancipation on the masses, and to issue orders. . . . Especially when doubt and dissatisfaction had arisen among the masses because of slogans that were too advanced or policies that were too "left," they tried all the harder to carry on the work by issuing orders, by coercion or even by punishment.

Liu Shao-ch'i, May 1945

ONE AUTUMN EVENING when the "Beat Down the Drowning Dog" campaign was at its height, the poor peasant Kuo Yuan-lung worked until after sunset on a plot of land in the middle of the fertile flat southwest of Long Bow. This was the first piece of earth the lean young man had ever owned and he spent every spare minute on it. On this particular evening he was busy pulling the stubble left behind from a crop of millet that had already been harvested. After uprooting the stubble clusters from the ground, he shook the dirt from the roots and piled the truncated clusters together so that he could carry them home for fuel. At the end of a row he straightened up to rest his tired back and heard Kuei-Ts'ai's megaphone-magnified voice announcing another meeting. The strange sound came, as always, from the top of the church tower. What the meeting was about, who was to be settled with this time, it was difficult to make out. The only words that came clearly across the open fields at that distance were "Come to the meeting—everybody out—meeting tonight—."

"Your mother's ---," said Yuan-lung. "Another meeting! Will there ever be an end to meetings?" And he hummed a little jingle that he had heard that day from the disgruntled Li Ho-jen: *"Kuomintang shui to, kungch'antang hui to."* (Under the Nationalists too many taxes; under the Communists too many meetings.)

"They can meet without me tonight," he muttered. "What's to come of all this anyway? There's nothing left to dig up, no oil left to find. We shake the trees again and again, but the fruits and nuts have already been knocked down and the branches are bare. Now that I have land I'd rather work it. Besides, I'm tired," he added as he leaned down to pick up the last pile of stubble and roots. He carried it across the field and added it to the huge bundle he had been collecting all afternoon. Swinging this enormous burden onto his back he headed down the path toward the village. In the semi-darkness, with only a faint glow in the sky behind him, Yuan-lung and his load looked like a haystack that had suddenly grown legs and started to walk. When he reached his own house, a low mud hovel on the very edge of the settlement, he dropped the roots and sat down for a moment to rest. He took a deep breath and shut his eyes.

When he opened them, Wang Man-hsi, the militiaman, was standing in front of him.

"Didn't you hear the call to meeting?" asked Man-hsi in a menacing tone.

"I heard it but I couldn't leave the stubble," said Yuan-lung, standing up and moving warily back a step.

"If you heard it, why aren't you there? Come along now, we want everybody," growled Man-hsi, moving toward Yuan-lung as Yuan-lung moved back.

"But I haven't eaten."

"Eat your mother's ---. A struggle meeting has already begun and you talk of eating. I'll teach you to eat!" and with that Man-hsi hit him across the chest with the flat of his hand. "Come on, get going."

Man-hsi, though shorter than Yuan-lung, was far stronger. Over his shoulder he carried a rifle. Yuan-lung had no choice but to obey. He started out the gate. As he did so Man-hsi gave him a kick and fell in behind him swearing loudly.

"You donkey's penis! As if we didn't have trouble enough without rounding up slackers like you. Where do you think your *fanshen* came from? The Lord of Heaven?"

They had not gone far when Man-hsi told him to stop. The militiaman ducked into another courtyard and soon came out with a second poor peasant, old Pao, who had obviously been asleep. Under Man-hsi's orders the two proceeded down the alley. By the time they reached the main street Man-hsi had collected seven peasants. As they turned the corner and headed toward the square they met another militiaman, K'uan-hsin, who came from the other side of the village with five more. In this manner a large crowd was brought together that night.

****

What had happened? Why did the militiamen have to go out and round up a crowd? If the struggle was in the interest of the poor peasants, surely they would have been in the very front ranks of the gathering. A year earlier one could have attributed their reluctance to "change of sky" fears, but to say now that they were afraid would have been only a part of the story. Almost all these people had been very active during the winter and throughout the spring and summer. Why did they hang back in the fall?

The reluctance of a growing number of landowning peasants and even many poor peasants to continue the struggle grew out of uncertainty in regard to the future. The tremendous gains brought by the Anti-Traitor Movement in 1945 and the Settling Accounts Movement in early 1946 had not been matched by the campaigns of the following summer and fall. The expenditure of a vast amount of time and energy had pried loose a few much-needed dollars, but these dollars had by no means solved the problem of poverty or made any radical change in the over-all *fanshen* situation.

Many felt that the effort expended in mass meetings, interrogations, tearing down *k'angs,* and opening up tombs could more fruitfully have been spent weeding and hoeing, digging privies, and sinking wells. At a time when the Communist Party members and cadres of the village government might have been leading a production movement they had been absorbed in a treasure hunt. Though the rewards of this hunt were not negligible, still the cost seemcd far out of proportion. The damage inflicted in terms of people killed, households disrupted, buildings demolished and graves uprooted could not be shrugged off. Meanwhile the tendency to lop off "feudal tails" raised specters that refused to be laid to rest. Where would it all end? Was anybody really safe?

The peasants supported violence in smashing the old regime. But violence for loot alone, violence that was basically punitive, violence that turned on those who practiced it, turned out to be stark, senseless, repellent. Though no one in the village put it thus in so many words, such thoughts undoubtedly lurked in the recesses of their minds and made them draw back. Yet as more people drew back from active participation in new campaigns, the leaders began to push harder; and so a crack appeared between the dedicated revolutionaries and many rank-and-file peasants who had supported them wholeheartedly up until that time.

The style of work that developed out of the cadres' attempt to "keep things moving" in spite of this growing rift was called "commandism." Without realizing what was actually happening, many leading cadres in Long Bow began to issue orders instead of educating and persuading people, and because most people obeyed these orders —some because they too thought the redundant attacks necessary, some because they always followed orders, and some because they dared not do otherwise—the leaders did not realize how much support they had lost. Those peasants who did not obey they condemned as backward—*suan liu liu te,* or "sour and slippery" trouble-makers who needed to be taught a lesson. Some of these were arrested, beaten, and punished with extra work for soldiers' families, or extra terms of rear service such as stretcher bearing or transporting supplies to the front. Some were even sent off to join the army, but since they went unwillingly the army wisely rejected them.

The towering war tension of those months coupled with this emerging commandism created an atmosphere in which all the other weaknesses of the peasant cadres as revolutionary leaders took root and grew apace. The individualism, the lack of vision, the impetuosity which characterized these men and women as small producers began to manifest themselves in many of the ways Mao Tse-tung had outlined 20 years earlier.* That strange dichotomy—slack discipline within the revolutionary ranks coupled with harsh measures to enforce obedience among the people as a whole—mushroomed to alarming proportions, and with it, vindictiveness, cliquism, loyalty to persons rather than to revolutionary principles, and ultimately hedonism leading to petty theft, evasion of public duty, wide-spread philandering, and even rape at the point of a gun. Abuses of power characteristic of the political machine of the old regime re-emerged, albeit still in pale reflection. But without that patina of wealth, leisure, culture, and tradition which had long served to obscure the basic violence of gentry rule, these new abuses paraded in stark relief against the background of the people's utopian dreams.

The militia, on whom the main burden of each campaign fell, were quick to slide into certain habits well known to traditional upholders of "law and order." They developed among themselves a battlefront psychology that served as justification for everything they were tempted to do. Since they spearheaded every drive, led in beating the "struggle objects," poured out their sweat to dig up the *k'angs,* courtyards and tombs of the "old money bags," and above all, risked their lives through the long cold nights as they stood guard against counter-attack, they felt entitled to special privileges. Many of them thought it unfair to receive no return for service to the people beyond the *fanshen* in which all shared. Among them were some who also thought it unfair to be judged by ordinary standards of morality. As heroes of the hour, these began in small ways to help themselves. When

* For Mao's catalog of peasant weaknesses, see pages 56–57.

some article among the hundreds confiscated from the gentry caught their fancy, they took it when nobody was looking. If some comely woman aroused their passion, they seduced her if she was willing. If she were a "struggle object," they took her whether she was willing or not. When asked to do their share of labor service, these men began by thinking up all kinds of excuses and ended up with outright refusals. They even shirked work for soldiers' families and prevailed upon their neighbors to go in their stead.

Perhaps the most notorious practitioner of this type of abuse was Wang Man-hsi, the rank-and-file militiaman and Communist Party member who was known as "The King of the Devils" for his readiness to beat up the people's enemies. He had played a very important part in the Anti-Traitor Movement and the campaign against the gentry. Now, like the cop in the city market place who helps himself to the fruit in the stalls, Man-hsi took it for granted that the people owed him a few extras. The nighttime check-ups of the campaign against counter-revolution gave him ample opportunity to tip the scales in his own favor. Since the homes which he entered were almost all homes of "struggle objects," he had no qualms about carrying off whatever suited him. He took two catties of hemp seed from Li Pao-chin's house. From a widow's garden he helped himself to garlic and chives. He liked the fruit on Yu-hsien's trees so well that he came back several times for more. In Shao Lao-chang's yard he not only picked ripe plums, but broke off a whole branch and carried it with him on his rounds. From Kuo Fu-kuei, ex-puppet police chief, he took a beautiful dry gourd because "it was so pretty." From another ex-puppet he took a ripe watermelon. When the man protested, he shut him overnight in the village lockup.

When Man-hsi found a woman of gentry origin alone he took full advantage of his good fortune. Saying, "Bastard landlords, they took our women, why shouldn't we take theirs?" he raped one landlord's daughter, a visitor from another village, in the back court of his newly acquired home. Later he and another militiaman ordered the daughter-in-law of a local "money-bags" out of her neighbor's house on the grounds that no one was allowed to sleep away from home. Then they took her to an empty yard and forced themselves upon her. Man-hsi, on his own, approached the wife of the fugitive Chinming several times, threw stones over her wall, questioned her about her husband, and ordered her out to village meetings. He only failed in his plan to possess her because her neighbors lived so close to her back wall that they could hear every noise in her house.

From being the scourge of the gentry it was an easy transition for Man-hsi to become the scourge of the average man. By rapid stages he developed many of the habits of the traditional village bully. When Li P'an-ming, the peasant in charge of public affairs, asked him to do rear service, Man-hsi swore at him, claimed that his ox was sick and sent him to see the poor peasant Lao-ts'un instead. When Lao-ts'un, for his part, also refused to transport grain, Man-hsi beat him up as a shirker. Another time, when asked to transport grain, Man-hsi went grudgingly, took the straw and beans another man had set aside for the trip and, by depriving the other man's animal of feed, caused it to founder on the road. On that same trip he beat an honest poor peasant and threw his quilt on the floor because the fellow had the nerve to take for himself the only empty spot on an otherwise crowded *k'ang* in the only inn in the village.

Man-hsi refused to do his own share of work for soldiers' families, but became very angry when others were slack in this respect. He beat them and brought them to the village office for questioning. When it was his turn to stand guard over the "fruits," Man-hsi also took a few items from the public warehouse. He stole a small mirror, a sickle, an umbrella and a pack basket suitable for hauling grain on the back of a donkey. Later, when others wanted to borrow this basket from him, he refused to lend it, saying to himself, "Easy come, easy go."

A militiaman who rivalled Man-hsi for stubborn misbehavior was Shen Yu-hsing. He was a tall, raw-boned man with a dour disposition and a sad face already deeply lined before the age of 30. Although his father was a life-long hired laborer, Yu-hsing had somehow managed to study six years in the village school, had learned to read and write, and had then peddled sugar for a living through several mountain counties. During the famine year, without any money with which to buy sugar, he worked in an industrial plant in Taiyuan. When Long Bow was liberated he was far from home. He returned empty-handed with nothing but rags on his back and not even a single quilt for a cover. Everything that he later acquired he owed to the Revolution. From the Peasants' Association he first borrowed a pair of pants and a jacket. In the redistribution of collaborators' property he was given a quilt. When he went to the front as a stretcher bearer, a women's sewing group made him the first pair of shoes he had worn in over a year. As the Settling Accounts Movement gathered momentum he did well. He added an acre and a half to the original half acre inherited from his father and received four sections of housing. He very early joined the militia. In the spring of 1946 he also joined the Communist Party. He did this because some of his closest friends were already members.

Sudden prosperity, membership in a powerful party, and a rifle in his hand went to Yu-hsing's head. Like Man-hsi, he craved women. A prostitute who had slept with him for money in the old days refused him when he came to her empty-handed. He twisted her arm and took her anyway. When a landlord's daughter rejected him, he arrested her and took her to the village office on charges of spreading false rumors. One night he broke into a poor peasant's home by prying open the lock with his knife and seduced the mistress of the house, who was sleeping there alone.

The object of his attentions was Chin-chu's wife, an earthy woman of loose morals who had had many lovers over the years. Her husband was strong but cowardly, very slow-witted, dirty, and quarrelsome. It became almost a game in Long Bow Village to cuckold the heavy-browed, unhappy laborer and then taunt him about it afterward. In his rage all he dared do was beat his wife, a routine duty which he performed with gusto. For this harsh treatment she repaid him with never-ending nagging, quarrels over trifles, and continued unfaithfulness.

Yu-hsing, who was still a bachelor, took a liking to Chin-chu's wife after that first night. He tried to persuade her to leave Chin-chu and marry him, a very serious crime in the eyes of the villagers who were willing to overlook much licentious behavior, but never the break-up of a marriage. In order to have time alone with Chin-chu's wife, Yu-hsing ordered Chin-chu out to all public meetings and then slipped back to the house himself. When there were no meetings, he brazenly carried on his flirtation in Chin-chu's presence. One winter night he broke the door open, complained that his hands were cold and put them under Chin-chu's quilt to warm them. There he kept them for more time than it takes to eat a meal. When Yu-hsing left that night Chin-chu beat his wife so cruelly that she woke all the neighbors with her cries.

Although Shen Yu-hsing was himself head of the production committee of the Peasants' Association, the more important he became, the lazier he got. He swore at others when they worked badly on co-operative projects, but did as little as possible himself. Once he was asked by Fu-yuan, the village head, to organize a group to work on the land of a soldier's family. The soldier's mother sent hot food to the field early in the morning so that the men would have something to eat when they arrived, but nobody came to eat all day. Yu-hsing had simply ignored the request. When the peasant Chao-ch'un refused to loan Yu-hsing his cart the latter attacked him and took it anyway. Whenever Yu-hsing saw Ch'un-ching, manager of the beancurd plant set up through mutual aid, peddling beancurd on the street, he popped a piece of the curd in his mouth to try out the flavor, but he never bought any and never paid for what he ate. When Ch'un-ching finally lost patience and refused to give him any more free samples, Yu-hsing felt insulted. He broke into Ch'un-ching's home at night and stole several pounds of the newly-made curd. The other members of the mutual-aid group thought Ch'un-ching himself had stolen it and questioned him sharply. The quarrel that ensued almost broke up the group.

Both Yu-hsing and Man-hsi were rank-and-file militiamen. Though they were the worst behaved, they were not the only ones who did as they pleased. The question arises—why didn't the corps keep its members in line? Why didn't the militia captain call them on the carpet and discipline them? If Chang Chiang-tzu, the founder and first captain of the corps had remained in the village, he might well have done so, for he was a dedicated and conscientious man. But this very dedication caused him to volunteer for the army in the very first recruiting drive. When he left for the front, Li Hung-er took his place as captain. Li Hung-er was young, active, and eager. He was a brave leader of men in action, but like many in his command felt entitled to special privileges after having faced danger. This weakness was aggravated by a liking for high living and beautiful women that was stronger even than that of his most susceptible subordinate. Since he himself spent his evenings courting other men's wives, it was unrealistic to expect that he would hold his colleagues in check or maintain high personal standards before the corps in other respects.

Hung-er, with a German Luger on his hip, a white sash around his waist, and a sparkling white towel on his closely shaven head, cut a dashing figure. He knew well how to charm young women and also how to bully them when necessary. He courted five or six mistresses at a time and kept them in line by making them jealous of one another. One of his first affairs was with Chao Ch'uan-e, the young wife who feared that her family would be attacked as rich peasants. Since her husband was away most of the time working the family holdings on the Western Mountains, she had plenty of opportunity for casual flirtation. Later Hung-er took a liking to Ts'ui-ying, the very attractive bride of a recent recruit to the People's Liberation Army. Since it was an arranged match between two young people who had never set eyes on each other, the bride had no particular attachment to her soldier husband and was much flattered by Hung-er's attentions. Hung-er arranged for her to move out of her in-laws' one-room house into the quarters of a second soldier's bride who had a room of her own. There he visited her night after night. For variety he seduced the hostess too. The latter was afraid to protest because, as Ts'ui-ying said, "Hung-er is a king in this village. If you displease him he might mobilize the whole of Horse Square against your father's family since they are so prosperous."

Later, still another young woman caught Hung-er's eye. Her name was Fu-e and her husband was a member of the militia under Hung-er's command. Hung-er arranged for him to depart on a long trip and then went to Fu-e with the announcement that "now everything is convenient for us." When the girl's aunt came to stay, Hung-er sent her home. When Fu-e remonstrated that this open flaunting of convention might arouse the village against her, Hung-er ordered her to be happy. When she wept instead, he beat her. When Fu-e's husband returned, Hung-er arranged for her to join the weaving class sponsored by the Women's Association. Since the students all lived and worked together in the "Foreign House" at the south end of the village, Hung-er was able to visit his mistress there every night. When the girl expressed fear that Hu Hsueh-chen, the head of the Women's Association, might discover their liaison, the militia captain said, "She dare not oppose me. She's in the palm of my hand."

In order to cut a more dashing figure, Hung-er was not above taking a few items from the public warehouse. Chief among these was a pair of spectacles which he thought made him look cultured (an attribute he most certainly lacked at the time). He also took a fountain pen and a pair of brightly colored socks. Gifts for his favorites of the moment cost money, and since in the winter he had little produce that he could sell for cash, he took what he needed from the village stores. Once he took a large jar of salt. Salt, in that saltless region, was as good as silver dollars. The salt taken by Hung-er had been confiscated from Chief-of-Staff Chou Mei-sheng, who had himself grafted it from the public supplies when he was a puppet official. When the keeper of the warehouse found the salt missing and raised a hue and cry, Hung-er lined up the whole militia and demanded to know who had stolen the salt.

Since Man-hsi had stood guard that day, the weight of suspicion fell most heavily on him and no denial on his part did much good because of his already established reputation for carrying away property.

Thus did Hung-er, to cover up his own misdeeds, reward Man-hsi, his most active corpsman, faithful follower, and partner in many an amorous escapade. Hung-er and Man-hsi were so close, in fact, that they had swapped sisters in marriage. With such close personal and family ties one could hardly expect that Hung-er would supervise or correct Man-hsi's behavior or vice-versa.

Hung-er, Man-hsi, and Yu-hsing were not only militiamen; they were also Communists. Why didn't the Party branch criticize them, make them correct their behavior, or expel them? As a matter of fact, Fu-yuan and T'ien-ming did make efforts to reform all the the wayward and especially to reform Hung-er, who was setting a bad example for the whole militia. Several times he was brought before the branch executive committee and criticized for his "rascal affairs." When confronted with his transgressions in open meeting Hung-er was very contrite, apologized for bringing disgrace to the Party, swore that he would correct his behavior and promised to hold the militia in check in the future. But within a few days he seemed to forget his promises and returned to his old ways. When T'ien-ming criticized him privately, Hung-er became angry and swore at him for a meddler. Both T'ien-ming and Fu-yuan found it hard to make a big issue of loose morals because they themseleves were also involved in illicit affairs. Until they found the strength to give up their own liaisons and learned to lead by example, they could not hope to have too much influence along such lines.

Yu-lai, the deputy leader of the Peasants' Association, made this point clear. This very selfish and quarrelsome man took over a privy that had already been allocated to another peasant, An-feng. When Fu-yuan criticized Yu-lai for occupying An-Feng's privy, Yu-lai retaliated with direct action. He came to Shih Hsiu-mei's home at night with several of the militia and arrested Fu-yuan as he slept with her on the *k'ang*. Thus was Fu-yuan ridiculed before the whole village. He found it difficult to criticize others after that.

24

The Blackmail of Wang Yu-lai

Certain persons, when solving all kinds of concrete problems, place their personal interests above the Party's interests; or they are always worrying about their personal gains and losses, weighing their personal interests; or they engage in jobbery, taking advantage of Party work to achieve certain personal aims; or they attempt to pay off their personal grudges against other comrades on the pretext of a question of principle, or of Party interests.

Liu Shao-ch'i, 1942

IRONICALLY, it was Wang Yu-lai, vice-chairman of the Peasants' Association, who was responsible for the worst abuses of power—abuses which were of a very different order from the petty transgressions and excesses of a Man-hsi or a Yu-hsing, however crude these might be. The ex-bandit, ex-Catholic Yu-lai developed a system all his own for gradually extending his power and influence until he became the most hated man in liberated Long Bow. His method was as old as politics—the witch hunt. Even though T'ien-ming, chairman of the Party branch and director of public security, was responsible for all anti-agent work and asked no help from Yu-lai, the latter, who was neither a Communist nor a policeman, set himself up as a one-man investigation committee, security guard, and arbiter of political loyalty. He prowled around alone at night checking on the state of law and order and accused all those with whom he quarrelled of having secret liaison with the Kuomintang. It was he, more than any other cadre, who put the "agents' caps" on Catholics' heads and then used these "caps" and the threat of punishment that went with them to buttress his own position.

By such activity Yu-lai impressed the district leader, a worried man who was glad to see such zeal, especially from an ex-Catholic. At the district leader's suggestion, Yu-lai's son, Wen-te, was transferred from the militia to public security work. In the fall of 1946, Wen-te became T'ien-ming's assistant. Thus, through the back door, Yu-lai gained a foothold that he had been unable to establish through the front door—an official connection with police work. Since his

son, Wen-te, was very much under his influence it was as if Yu-lai
himself had been appointed to assist T'ien-ming.

Like most self-appointed guardians of political purity, Yu-lai apparently believed that he was really saving the community from
counter-revolution. When he went to the county seat on an animal-
buying expedition, he boasted that he had single-handedly turned
Long Bow upside down. "I can discover enemy agents without even
putting on my spectacles," he declaimed before a skeptical audience
at a street-corner mutton-soup stand. "My beard is a high official's
beard and whoever is ordered by me to die must die." So saying he
scowled the fierce, eyebrow-clashing scowl for which he was famous
and looked intently at the faces in the crowd in front of him as if
about to pick out an enemy agent right then and there.

During those fateful months of late 1946, when Nationalist troops
were driving on Changchih and many persons truly expected a
"change of sky," there was some truth to Yu-lai's boast that he had
turned the village upside down. More than 20 peasants came under
suspicion through his efforts alone and though none of them was
officially investigated, charged with any crime, or sentenced to punishment, they were subject to constant harassment, detentions, questioning, and discrimination in day-to-day affairs.

If Yu-lai had any doubts about his self-proclaimed mission, they
were easily stilled by the gains that accrued to him personally while
his anti-agent campaign lasted and his colleagues still believed his
accusations. He silenced all critics and solved all personal problems
in the same monotonous manner. When he was criticized for refusing to do rear service, he attacked his critic as an agent. When
one of his neighbors questioned some joint production accounts, that
neighbor was declared an agent. When the parents of his son's "bought
and paid for" fiancee tried to delay the wedding because their daughter was under age, he called them agents too.

This latter accusation and the forced marriage that resulted became a famous case in Long Bow and led eventually to Yu-lai's
own removal as a cadre. The girl, Shen Hsien-e, was without question the most beautiful teenager in the village. She had perfectly
proportioned features, lips like twin cherries, jet-black almond eyes
under thin arched brows, a glowing olive complexion set off by a
delicate cascade of bangs that reached halfway down her forehead
and a long black braid that hung to the middle of her back. Her
feet, though unbound, were small, as small as many bound feet, and
her hands, delicate and slim-fingered, moved with the grace of a
butterfly in flight. Animating this outward beauty was an irrepressibly
saucy spirit, full of song, laughter, temperament and mischief. Hsien-e

was like some mountain flower, exquisite in shape and bright in
color, that had somehow blown in and managed to blossom amid the
dirt and squalor of the dilapidated, war-wrecked community. There
was no man so old, so sick, or so busy that he did not turn his
head when she went by.

Yu-lai did not need his glasses to spot feminine beauty any more
than he needed them to unearth alleged subversion. He had picked
out Hsien-e for his son during the famine year when she was still
a little girl and had offered her father, Shen Hsi-le, $90 and 40
catties of millet in return for a promise that she would become
Wen-te's bride when she came of age. On that money and grain Hsi-
le kept his family alive through the terrible winter of 1942. In 1946,
although the girl was still only 14, Yu-lai demanded that she marry
his son without delay. Hsi-le refused to let her go. Yu-lai demanded
his money back with interest. Hsi-le set out to raise the money. Afraid
of losing the girl, Yu-lai changed his tactics and accused Hsi-le of
being an enemy agent. Since the poor man had actually helped
Father Sun escape and was among those Catholics who returned to
the church at Horse Square for mass on that famous Easter Sunday,
it was not hard to make this accusation stick. Yu-lai arrested Hsi-le,
strung him up and beat him with a mule whip until he himself confessed that he was in fact an agent. To make doubly sure, Yu-lai also
arrested Hsi-le's nephew, Hei-hsiao, a boy from Hukuan, where
Hsi-le had orginally lived and where his daughter, Hsien-e, was born.
Hei-hsiao was beaten by Wen-te until he confirmed the story told by
his uncle. Then Yu-lai put it up to Hsi-le—either give up his daughter
or face investigation by the county police. Hsi-le agreed to the match.

When Wen-te took his fiancee to the district office for a marriage
license he told her to lie about her age if she valued her father's life.
She said she was 16. The license was issued and the marriage duly
consummated by carrying the bride to her husband's home in a red
sedan chair. Once they had her there, her husband and father-in-law
never let the captive beauty out of the house. They worked her like
a slave in the traditional manner and beat her frequently. Because
Yu-lai had such power in the village, even the Women's Association
dared not intervene.

Yu-lai's closest neighbor, Ch'ou-har, had reason to believe that
the father and son beat the young bride most severely when she rejected her father-in-law's advances. Ch'ou-har told some of his cronies
what he suspected. When wind of this got back to Yu-lai, he sent
his son, Wen-te, to thrash Ch'ou-har. The son did his job well. He beat
the old man with a plow handle until he fell unconscious, and when
Ch'ou-har came to on the ground, Wen-te beat and kicked him some

more. From that day onward Ch'ou-har also wore an agent's cap.

Seeing just how ruthless Yu-lai could be, the cadres all gave him a wide berth. Since nobody could positively prove that his charges were false, and since it was common knowledge that counter-revolutionary conspiracies did exist, Yu-lai's growing blackmail went unchallenged for a long time. When the vice-chairman of the Peasants' Association issued orders, people thought twice before refusing them.

****

Early in 1947, Chang T'ien-ming, Shih Fu-yuan and Chang Kuei-ts'ai, the three most able and experienced cadres in the village left Long Bow to help organize land reform and winter production in other communities. The promotion of these three to full-time district work no doubt strengthened the administration of the Fifth District as a whole, but it was a severe blow to progress in Long Bow itself.

The men who replaced the three all lacked prestige, experience, and political understanding. Either they were wanting in strength of character or else they were very self-interested. Not only did they prove unable to reform the political climate, but under their novice leadership all the excesses, transgressions, and abuses of power characteristic of the militia under Hung-er, and the political blackmail carried on by Yu-lai and his son grew to even more alarming proportions.

The tall, handsome Hsin-fa, who had for some time been educational director of the militia without achieving any remarkable results, replaced T'ien-ming as secretary of the Party branch. Unlike T'ien-ming, however, he did not have the prestige of an underground anti-Japanese fighter to draw upon in leading the people. Nor was he strong-willed enough to make a fight for the principles in which he believed. He preferred rather to keep on good terms with everyone and become known as a *lao hao jen* or "old good fellow."

Ch'un-hsi, the hired laborer, who had refused for a long time to join the attack on the gentry because of his love for his former employer's daughter-in-law, was chosen to take Fu-yuan's place as village head. He not only lacked prestige; he lacked confidence in his own ability, wanted above all the good opinion of others, and therefore, although he worked hard, was unable to criticize, correct, or lead others.

An older man, Wang Hsi-yu, a close friend of Wang Yu-lai, replaced Kuei-ts'ai as deputy village head. Hsi-yu had been active in all the campaigns of the Settling Accounts Movement but at heart was a self-seeker. His father had exploited the whole village in the old days as a licensed middleman—a person officially designated to act as a go-between in business transactions, extracting a commission whether or not he performed any service. Perhaps because of this background Hsi-yu still exhibited a strong tinge of middleman's opportunism on which he relied to advance his personal fortunes at the expense of the rest of the community.

Yu-lai's son, Wen-te, by a natural promotion, took T'ien-ming's place as head of public security. He was very young, very strongwilled, very interested in women—he outdid even Hung-er with his liaisons—and very much under the influence of his father. With Wen-te's promotion, Yu-lai's foothold in police work soon became a stranglehold upon it.

Hung-er, with all the faults previously mentioned, remained captain of the militia.

This left Wang Yu-lai, still deputy chairman of the Peasants' Association, as the oldest, most experienced, and strongest-willed of the cadres. Even though he was not a Communist, he easily dominated the others and set the tone of public life. The chairman of the Peasants' Association, the ex-Catholic Cheng-k'uan, the one man who by his rank and position could and should have kept Yu-lai in check, was no match for him. Cheng-k'uan was sincere, good natured, hardworking, but he had no conception of the evil Yu-lai intended and was easily misled. He was the type of man known to the peasants as *lao shih* or honest. Wang Yu-lai well knew how to impose upon such "honest" peasants as Cheng-k'uan.

With such a constellation of leaders it was hardly a coincidence that the Chinese New Year, which fell in February in 1947, began with a shocking incident. A large group of militiamen, who for convenience were still quartered in the North Temple, decided to celebrate the coming of the long-awaited holidays in the manner of oldtime rural guards. They chose Man-hsi to go to the puppet Chief-of-Staff Chou Mei-sheng's home, seize his daughter-in-law and bring her to headquarters for their collective enjoyment. There in the temple they stripped her and possessed her, one after the other.

It was likewise hardly a coincidence that after the promotions of January the spring recruiting drive degenerated into a farce which brought political life in Long Bow to its post-liberation nadir. When the Border Region Government issued its third call for an enlarged army, Party members and militiamen were asked to take the lead as before. Hung-er, whose two brothers were already in the army, went to Ch'un-hsi, the new village head, with a frown on his face. "Look here," he said, "You'll have to decide whether I should go or not."

"Wait a minute," replied Ch'un-hsi. "Don't get excited. Maybe there is some other way."

Egged on by Yu-lai, who had old scores to settle and did not fancy sending his own son off to fight, they decided to fill the village quota with some of those "sour and slippery" characters who had given the new administration the most trouble from the very beginning. With Man-hsi's muscular help, the outstanding puppet leaders and the disaffected Catholics who wore invisible "agent's caps" were hauled to the village office and told to prepare for a trip to the recruiting office.

Li Ho-jen, the leader of one dissident clique, had himself just returned from a term as stretcher bearer at the front. He brought back with him a discharge paper stating that he had been sent home early because of illness. Despite this paper Yu-lai charged him with deserting the stretcher corps and ordered him to enlist at once in the army. Shen Ch'uan-te, Ho-jen's mouthpiece and chief admirer, although well over 40 years old, was likewise instructed to report for duty. So was Chin-chu, the slow-witted peasant whom Yu-hsing, for one, wanted out of the way, the better to court his free and easy wife. Chin-hung, a middle peasant whose career as a member of the puppet Self-Defense Corps had been especially notorious, "volunteered" when Yu-lai said to him, "You were eager enough to serve the foreign devils; how come you are afraid of battle now?"

Altogether a dozen or so "sour and slippery" characters were collected. Along with a few genuine volunteers, they were packed off to the recruiting office in Lucheng. Old Shen, whose hair was already turning grey, looked around him as they marched off and said, "This is indeed a father and son army"—a play on words which the local cadres did not find funny. (The People's Liberation Army was commonly called by the affectionate title of "Brother and Son Army.")

When the Long Bow contingent arrived at the county seat, the recruiting officers were shocked by the advanced age and bedraggled appearance of the majority. They questioned the recruits closely and soon discovered that they were not volunteers at all. They thereupon sent them home together with an investigator whose task it was to find out how such a motley crew had ever been assembled in the first place.

A second drive was organized with great difficulty. In the end another dozen young men were found who really wanted to go or were persuaded to do so. Among these was at least one who had little choice. This was Li K'ao-lur, a young immigrant from a Nationalist-held village in Hopei province. He had eloped only a few weeks before with a girl of the same surname who was a resident of his home village and a distant cousin. He had fallen in love with her, and she with him, but according to local custom the match was out of the question. Not only was a match between cousins considered incestuous, but both the young people had long since been promised to others. When they defied the whole community and ran away, they were sentenced to death in absentia. They fled to the Liberated Area of the Taihang Mountains and finally arrived in Long Bow where young Li had an uncle to whom he appealed for help. This uncle let the young couple live in his house temporarily, but word of their refuge somehow reached their home village. A representative was sent by the Li clan to bring them home for trial and punishment. When the representative arrived in Long Bow, he went straight to the village office and demanded that the runaways be turned over to him. Ch'un-hsi stalled for time by pretending that he had never heard of the two lovers. Then, hard up for recruits, he made a bargain with Li K'ao-lur. If Li would join the army, Ch'un-hsi would deny all knowledge of his whereabouts, send the clan representative home empty-handed, and recommend to the Peasants' Association that the pair be given land and housing in Long Bow. With his life, his marriage, and his future assured, Li K'ao-lur agreed. The army got a fine recruit.

This recruiting drive only pointed up what had become increasingly obvious for a long time—that the revolutionary cadres and militiamen of Long Bow were gradually alienating themselves from the people by arbitrary orders, indiscriminate beatings, the assumption of special privileges, and "rascal behavior." Nor was Long Bow the only community in the district where a relatively small number of active young men had "mounted the horse," as the peasants so aptly put it, and were riding around to suit their own fancy. By the same token the Fifth District was not the only district where such things were occurring in Lucheng County, nor was Lucheng County itself an exception among the counties of the Taihang Region. In the spring of 1947, the government and the Party organization of the Taihang Region took note of the critical situation and launched a "Wash Your Face" campaign designed to put a stop to all such tendencies, and to overcome the opportunist and hedonist attitudes that fostered them.

The method adopted in this campaign was to set up a *gate* or council of delegates, elected by the peasants at large, before which all the cadres had to answer for their motives and their actions. The phrase "Wash Your Face" came from Chairman Mao himself who had many times explained that the thoughts of revolutionary leaders inevitably became spotted and stained by the corrupt habits of the past and the rotten social environment that surrounded them on every side, just as their faces became spotted and stained by the dust and dirt of the natural environment. These spots and stains had to be washed off frequently just as people daily washed their faces to make them clean again. And just as one could not see the dirt on one's own face without consulting a mirror, so one could not clearly see one's own bad thinking and bad behavior without consulting the people who suffered as a consequence of both and could therefore reflect a truer image.

Delegates were duly chosen by the peasants of Long Bow, and the village cadres went before them to review their records and examine their errors, but the movement was not successful. As soon as the district leaders called for criticism, not only the honest majority but also the "sour and slippery" minority came forward with opinions. The opinions of this latter group were destructive, designed to overthrow rather than reform the revolutionary cadres. Those who raised them spoke without thought as to who might be found to replace the objects of their wrath. From such an overthrow only the landlords stood to gain.

Instead of allowing this storm of criticism to rage and using it to educate the peasants to distinguish honest from dishonest opinions so that the cadres could reform and all the people profit from a living political lesson, the district leaders lost their nerve and retreated. They intervened on behalf of the cadres and in effect suppressed criticism, both honest and dishonest. As a result, although some cadres, getting a scent of things to come, changed their outlook to a certain extent and corrected some of their faults, others, such as Yu-lai, only became more arrogant than before and retaliated against those who had dared to criticize them. Clearly something more drastic was needed if the tendencies which were already alienating the leaders from the people and undermining not only the village administration and the Peasants' Association, but the Communist Party branch as well were not seriously to undermine and compromise the Revolution.

****

In January 1948, the future of the whole movement, in spite of its extraordinary successes, was far from certain. In Long Bow the upheaval had swept like a whirlwind through the village, had broken up the old landlord-tenant system, and smashed it beyond repair. It was mourned, if at all, by only a small minority. But only bits and pieces of that which was to replace it had as yet been created. Exploitation and privilege, some of it new in form, still existed. Very little had been permanently settled. The oligarchy of the gentry based on centuries of tradition and buttressed with all the sanctions of custom, religion, Confucian ethics, and the naked force of hired guns, had been replaced by an interregnum of young, formerly landless or land-poor peasants. They were bitter, creative, passionate, selfish, full of energy, full of hatred, full of yearning for something new and better, yet easily diverted down paths of pleasure and privilege. Suddenly thrust onto the stage, backed by the rifles of a 100-man militia and supported by the overwhelming majority of the people who had divided the "fruits," what would they do with their new power?

Did these leaders, who had climbed from the mud and slime and still carried with them the stains of their origin, possess the vision and the skill to correct the excesses that marred the movement? Could they abolish petty advantages won through the lever of leadership, lead all the poor to stand up, and unite the whole population around that vast program of private, mutual, and public production which alone could lift Long Bow out of the miasma of the past? And if they did not possess such vision and skill, who did?

PART III

The Search for the Poor and Hired

Since powerful imperialism and its allies, the reactionary forces in China, have occupied China's key cities for a long time, if the revolutionary forces do not wish to compromise with them but want to carry on the struggle staunchly, and if they intend to accumulate strength and steel themselves and avoid decisive battles with their powerful enemy before they have mustered enough strength, then they must build the backward villages into advanced, consolidated base areas, into great military, political, economic and cultural revolutionary bastions, so that they can fight the fierce enemy who utilizes the cities to attack the rural districts and, through a protracted struggle, gradually win over-all victory for the revolution.

Mao Tse-tung

25

Cosmic Wei Ch'i

O wait for the pure sky!
See how charming is the earth
Like a red-faced girl clothed in white!
Such is the charm of these mountains and rivers
Calling innumerable heroes to vie with each other
                                    in pursuing her.

                                    Mao Tse-tung

WINTER IN North China is a radiant season. Clear skies often follow one another in unbroken succession for weeks at a time. Day after day the sun, no bigger than a ten-dollar gold piece, slides across a translucent sky and bedazzles all the visible world with light so bright that one has the feeling of living at a great height, of existing on a high plateau from the edge of which one can well look down on all the less-favored, nether regions of the universe. Adding substance to this feeling is the barrenness of the landscape. Surely, only on the moon are such vast expanses of hill and mountain so desolately bare of trees, so stripped of brush, so plucked of thorn or scraggly heather.

In the loess regions of the Yellow River bend this other-worldliness is accentuated by the contouring and terracing by means of which men, through countless generations, have transformed the dome-shaped heights. Like the drooping petals of many-petalled flowers, the fields of loess overhang each other. And though, in reality, they are all made up of the same ochre-brown, wind-blown soil, the play of light and shadow on the many-surfaced knolls and ridges brings to the countryside an ever-changing pageant of color.

A stranger travelling here is startled to see smoke rising from the ground. Is it possible that the blanket of loess on the earth's crust also serves as cover for volcanic furnaces? No. The smoke comes from the kitchen fires which the peasants have built in their cave homes. The cavernous native dwellings burrow horizontally into the perpendicular walls of earth that drop from the edges of the terraced fields and line the sides of water-gouged ravines. From the innermost

243

recesses of these caves, flues rise to the slopes above, emitting smoke that bears witness to domestic life in places seemingly devoid of human habitation.

From such a cave as this, lost in the badlands of North Shensi, Mao Tse-tung, Chairman of the Communist Party of China, surveyed the continent that surrounded him in the last weeks of December 1947, and discussed what he saw with those colleagues of the Central Committee who had remained with him on the western side of the Yellow River.

Superficially, their position seemed perilous indeed. In March the Nationalist General Hu Ts'ung-nan, famous for his celibacy and his concentration camps, had invaded the Yenan region with 300,000 men, all crack troops that had never been risked in battle against the Japanese. These forces quickly occupied Yenan itself and then moved north to take Yenchuan and Suiteh. By autumn General Hu held most of the county towns and all of the main highways of North Shensi. Mao, with a small headquarters group, played hide and seek with the enemy's scouts while the 25,000-man Northeast People's Army enticed the main body of the invading forces into a hare-and-hounds trek through the hinterland. To observers in Shanghai and Washington, this looked like the last of the annihilation campaigns of the 1930's with the revolutionary forces completely encircled and the Communist leaders in danger of capture.

The balance of forces was assessed quite differently by the Communist Party. Mao summed up the Party's estimate in an address entitled "The Present Situation and Our Tasks" which was delivered on Christmas Day, 1947. Mao later called it "a programmatic document in the political, military, and economic fields for the entire period of the overthrow of the Chiang Kai-shek ruling clique and the founding of a new democratic China."* It was a speech so extraordinarily calm and confident in tone that it is hard to believe, even now, that it could have been delivered from hidden heaquarters by a leader with a price on his head.

In the preceding decades, Mao had covered most of China's 18 original provinces on foot. As he prepared this speech he must have recreated, in his mind's eye, the whole sweep of his vast country and tried to envision entire, in all its variety, in all its contradictory and dialectical motion, the ebb and flow of the great struggle then in progress in China. In the context of such a panorama, the predicament of his headquarters group came into focus as only one facet of a many-sided nation-wide campaign, the outcome of which could

* Mao Tse-tung, *Selected Works,* Peking: Foreign Languages Press, 1961, Vol. IV, pp. 157–176.

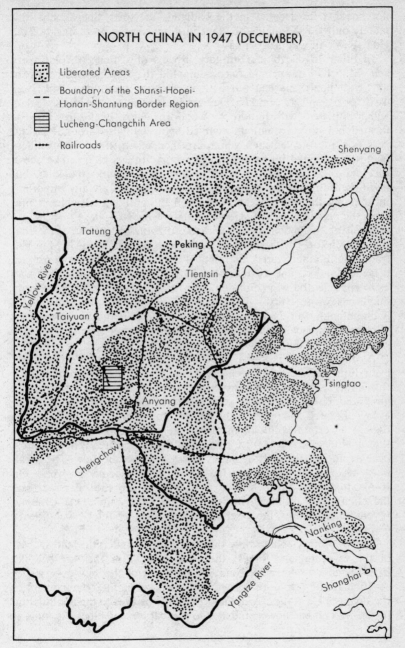

NORTH CHINA IN 1947 (DECEMBER)

Liberated Areas

Boundary of the Shansi-Hopei-
Honan-Shantung Border Region

Lucheng-Changchih Area

Railroads

Shenyang

Yellow River

Tatung

Peking

Tientsin

Taiyuan

Tsingtao

Anyang

Chengchow

Nanking

Yangtze River

Shanghai

not possibly be decided in the badlands of North Shensi, but ultimately only on the plains of Manchuria and in the great basin of the
Huai River in Central China.

In order to clarify the military aspects of China's revolutionary
war, Mao had more than once compared the Chinese sub-continent
to a vast board marked out with intersecting mountains and rivers
as if for a game of *wei ch'i* (known in Japan as *go*). In this game,
which is played with hundreds of uniform chips, enclosures may be
formed not only around unoccupied spots but also around the adversary's unprotected men which are then taken, their empty places
being transformed into conquered territory. In *wei ch'i*, unlike chess,
the interest is not concentrated in one spot, around the king, but
is diffused all over the board. Every single spot is equally important
in affecting the outcome and counts in the grand total which represents the position of each side at the end of the struggle.

Refusing to "match pearls with the dragon god of the sea" (that
is to match force with superior force in head-on collision), Mao had
traditionally maneuvered his relatively scarce red chips—the armies,
brigades, and regiments under his Party's command—in such a way
as to encircle and wipe out, one after the other, the enemy's far more
numerous white chips—the armies, brigades, and regiments under
Kuomintang, later Japanese, and then again Kuomintang command.
"Preserve ourselves, annihilate the enemy"—such was the primary
requirement of the struggle.

As the Civil War of the late 1940's spread across North China,
even little children soon learned to grasp the lethal arithmetic of
this strategy. Lists of enemy soldiers killed, prisoners taken, and
guns and bullets captured were tabulated on conspicuous walls in
every liberated village. As the tallies mounted, it became obvious
that at a certain point all the terms of reference must change and
that qualities must be transformed into their opposites. The few must
become the many and the many must become the few. The weak
must become the strong and the strong must become the weak. On
front after front the defensive must evolve into the offensive, and
the offensive must decay into the defensive. Eventually a dynamic
revolutionary China must replace a stagnant, counter-revolutionary
China.

In the military sphere only one thing could undermine the success
of the revolutionary forces: the abandonment of the *wei ch'i*-like
fighting tactics refined by Mao Tse-tung out of the raw experiences
of 20 years of revolutionary warfare. As long as the commanders of
the People's Liberation Army addressed themselves to the annihilation
of enemy combat power and not to the capture of cities, as long as

they avoided battles of attrition and obtained quick decisions by concentrating three, four, even five or six times the forces arrayed against them in any given battle, as long as they replenished their units with most of the manpower and all of the arms captured in such battles and thus made the front, as well as the rear, their recruiting ground and supply base, the People's Liberation Army was bound to win every major campaign and ultimately victory in the Civil War. Thus did Mao project the military future in his Christmas Day speech.

But war is only an instrument of policy, a continuation of politics by violent means. Without a valid political line no volunteer army could long hold together, no military strategy long succeed. To the problem of over-all policy, therefore, China's revolutionary leaders had always devoted the bulk of their attention. Applying *wei ch'i*-like tactics to this sphere as well, the revolutionary forces aspired to occupy as much political space as possible, to win as large a section of the social fabric as could be won, to neutralize those sections that could not be won over, and so isolate the genuinely hostile sections that they could be overwhelmed. As Mao put it, the political line of his Party was one of "developing the progressive forces, winning over the middle forces, and isolating the die-hard forces."

By "progressive forces" Mao meant the workers and poor peasants. By "middle forces" Mao meant the middle peasants, small independent craftsmen and traders, students, teachers, professors, and free professionals. He also meant all those capitalists who had not yet been swallowed up by the four big families of the Chiang clique and the foreign business interests to whom they were linked. These two latter groups, plus the landlords, made up the "die-hard forces."

The "middle forces" could not be won over if the "progressive forces" insisted on socialism as the immediate goal. More basic still, the objective conditions required for a transition to socialism, for the abolition of private ownership in the means of production in all fields, did not exist in China. Mao therefore proposed as the goal of the Civil War an intervening stage of society to be characterized by a mixed economy and a multi-class government. He outlined in three sentences how such an economy should be created: "Confiscate the land of the feudal classes and turn it over to the peasants. Confiscate monopoly capital, headed by Chiang Kai-shek, T. V. Soong, H. H. Kung, and Chen Li-fu and turn it over to the new democratic state. Protect the commerce and industry of the national bourgeoisie."

Upon the three-fold foundation of this proposed public, co-operative, and private-enterprise economy, Mao called on the Chinese people to erect a coalition government in which many groups and parties would share power with the Communists. Such was the basic program of the Chinese Revolution put forth by Mao Tse-tung on the eve of 1948.

"Develop the progressive forces, win over the middle forces, isolate the die-hard forces"—the whole of this political line, and not some single aspect, was vital to success. Yet warping pressures constantly arose. Reports from widely scattered areas indicated that tendencies toward Left extremism in land reform and commandism in leadership were all too common. From below came the impulse for an all-out struggle which would ignore the "middle forces," destroy private commerce and industry, expropriate middle peasants and re-order the world in the interest of the poor peasants and workers alone. At the same time the reports showed a strong Right tendency on the part of certain middle-level cadres and some key leaders in the villages. They were thwarting the just demands of the poor peasants and workers and advocating compromise with the gentry because they feared the Kuomintang offensive and hesitated before the prospect of massive U.S. aid to Chiang Kai-shek. Mao and the Central Committee of the Chinese Communist Party waged an unending battle against both these impulses, either of which could lead to disaster. The emphasis, however, at least at the beginning, was against rightism, for rightism undermined the very will to fight.

In the countryside the "middle forces" were predominantly the middle peasants. These independent small holders numbered close to 100 million in the nation as a whole and comprised 20 to 40 percent of the peasants in any given community. Their support was absolutely essential to any realistic program of social change.

In his Christmas speech, Mao outlined a balanced peasant policy very concisely: "First, the demands of the poor peasants and farm laborers must be satisfied; this is the most fundamental task in the land reform. Second, there must be firm unity with the middle peasants and their interest must not be damaged. As long as we grasp these two basic principles, we can certainly carry out our task in the land reform successfully."

To make sure that these policies were not only understood but also faithfully carried out, Mao further called for a drastic overhaul of the whole Communist Party organization:

In the Party's local organizations, especially the organizations at the primary level in the countryside, the problem of impurities in the class composition in our ranks and in the style of work is still unsolved. During the 11 years, 1937–1947, the membership of our Party has grown from several tens of thousands to 2,700,000, and this is a very big leap forward.

This has made our Party a more powerful party than any in Chinese history. It has enabled us to defeat Japanese imperialism, beat back Chiang Kai-shek's offensives, lead the Liberated Areas with a population of more than 100 million, and lead a People's Liberation Army two million strong. But shortcomings have also cropped up. Many landlords, rich peasants, and riffraff have seized the opportunity to sneak into our Party. In the rural areas, they control a number of Party, government and people's organizations, tyrannically abuse their power, ride roughshod over the people, distort the Party's policies and alienate these organizations from the masses and prevent the land reform from being thorough. This grave situation sets us the task of educating and re-organizing the ranks of our Party.

Three days after this speech the Draft Agrarian Law which clearly defined the content of the Communist Party's new agrarian policy was announced to the whole nation. The road ahead was as precisely marked as law and verbal declaration could make it.

But to define a policy and to carry it out in practice in tens of thousands of isolated villages are two different things. This is especially so when that policy contains within itself some elements of conflict. Mao's two basic principles on the peasant question seemed clear enough; yet they were difficult to carry out in practice because, to a certain extent, they embodied a contradiction. As has been demonstrated in the case of Long Bow Village, poverty in North China was so all-embracing that the demands of the poor peasants and farm laborers could hardly be satisfied by distributing the property of the gentry alone. The expropriation of at least a part of the property of the less onerous exploiters was necessary if the poor peasants were to gain the minimum worldly goods they needed. In many communities even major inroads into the possessions of such middle families could not guarantee *fanshen* to all the poor. Yet even the slightest inroads invariably threatened the middle peasants if it did not, in fact, actually dispossess them. To protect the interests of the middle peasants and not harm them in any way apparently meant to disappoint many poor peasants and leave them without such essentials as a share in a donkey, a cart, or a plow.

Here was the hard kernel of the problem, the issue around which, once the landlords had been overpowered and stripped, the storm of the land revolution continued to swirl. On the antagonisms thus engendered, commandism, hedonism, and opportunism fed. If this contradiction was not properly resolved, democracy could hardly be expected to flourish. A major clash between poor and middle peasants might well do away with peasant self-rule before it had a chance to establish itself. From such a denouement only the Kuomintang and its American backers stood to gain.

That is why, in the winter of 1948, the Communist Party organized work teams in all the old Liberated Areas and sent them to
representative villages to check on the status of the land reform
movement. By concentrating strong forces in a few places the Communist Party and the Border Region Government hoped to obtain
an accurate estimate of differing conditions and to work out a program of action suited to the peculiar problems of each area. The
guiding strategy here was the point-and-area method by which China's
revolutionary leaders approached all serious problems, investigating
and solving them first on a small scale in individual communities,
then applying the lessons learned on a large scale to whole districts
and counties.

In Lucheng County the Communist Party picked 11 communities. Long Bow Village was chosen as one of these not because it
was typical but because it had so many special problems; and these
problems had created an extremely complicated, difficult, and potentially dangerous political situation. If the knot in Long Bow could
be untied, there were few tangles in the whole region that could not
be unravelled.

All this, of course, my interpreter Ch'i Yun and I were quite unaware of when we went to Long Bow to see what the land reform
movement was all about. We chose Long Bow simply because it was
the village closest to the university where we were teaching, a village
to which we could easily walk each day and return before dark.

26

To the Village

The only way to know conditions is to make an investigation of society, to investigate the life and activities of each social class. . . . To do this, we should first cast our eyes down and not hold our heads high and gaze skywards. If a person does not care, or does not make up his mind, to cast his eyes down, he can never really learn anything about China.

Mao Tse-tung

ON THE March day in 1948 that Ch'i Yun and I first set off for Long Bow, the weather was far from auspicious. Two inches of snow had fallen in the night, completely obliterating the promise of spring which had so stirred me during the New Year celebrations of the previous week. Instead of puffs of white in an azure sky, an unbroken overcast pressed down on all the visible world. So dark was the underlining of this cloud mass that the new snow seemed to have lost all its whiteness and to have absorbed the dark, near-black of the sky. A cold wind gathered chill as it swept the frozen land. Even the heavy wool-lined greatcoat that was my most valuable possession failed to keep me warm, while Ch'i Yun, who wore only a single woolen scarf about her neck to supplement her worn padded suit, actually shivered as she walked.

Ch'i Yun was not quite five feet tall. In order to see her face I had to stoop. Even then I couldn't see much of it as her head was bent forward to avoid the wind and she had pulled her soft visor cap so far down over her forehead that only her lips, now drawn and grey, were still exposed. She warmed her hands by shoving each of them into the ample sleeve opposite so that her arms formed an unbroken roll against her chest. Head down, elbows pressed against her ribs, body thrust forward into the wind, she was a lumpy bundle of faded blue that might have been woman, child, or walking panda. I almost laughed, but the cold was no laughing matter. It had, however, one advantage. It kept the snow dry so that our feet, clad in cloth-soled shoes, were not immediately soaked through.

In such weather one expected the countryside to be deserted, but that day it seemed abnormally desolate. Not one human being, nor for that matter any other living thing, stirred on the surface of the land. The village we were approaching seemed like some ruin long abandoned to the rats, the field mice, and the wolves.

Nor was our first encounter in the village any more reassuring than the weather. We found no one on the main street. Quick glances through the gates we passed revealed courtyards just as empty. Then suddenly, from a side alley, stepped a young man clad in a dark blue cadre's jacket. In his hand he held a revolver, cocked and ready to fire.

"Comrade," said Ch'i Yun calmly, "We are looking for the district magistrate." As she spoke she handed the armed man a letter stamped with the great seal of Northern University. Her black eyes, under heavy lashes, liberated from under the visor of her cap at last, looked boldly at him.

"I'll take you to him," said the man, holding his revolver in his right hand while he turned the letter awkwardly around with his left. Then, seeing us both staring at the gun, he added "Pardon the armament. We had some trouble here yesterday."

He turned and led us down the street, glancing into each courtyard and alley as he went, obviously on edge, ready for anything. We passed a high brick wall that cut the large grounds of the former Catholic mission off from the street and turned into one of the outer courts of this extensive compound. This court turned out to be the seat of the district government. In a low-ceilinged, earth-floored room two more blue-clad cadres were seated at a low table. As they stood up to greet us, we could see their breath on the air. Both were armed, as was our guide, with German Lugers.

One of the men who rose from the table was District Magistrate Li. He took our letter of introduction, read it, welcomed us, and then he too apologized for the guns.

"We don't usually carry them," he said. "But conditions here are exceptional. Someone tried to kill one of us yesterday."

"Don't you know who it was?" asked Ch'i Yun.

"We've arrested four suspects, all of them leading cadres in this village. But who knows? The attacker may still be at large. We can't take any chances."

This Li was a short man with a friendly smile and a gift for lively talk. The second man, taller by a head than Li, was Comrade Hou Pao-pei, leader of the land reform work team. Magistrate Li turned over to him our letter with the suggestion that he arrange for us to visit one or two poor peasant families as an introduction to the village.

"That is what we are doing now," said Hou, speaking slowly, as if his every word were weighted. "We have been in the village a week and we have done nothing but visit the homes of poor peasants. We have already found a number of basic elements. If you'd like to talk to some of them, I can arrange it."

By "basic element" Hou meant an honest-to-goodness poor peasant.

Ch'i Yun and I were as anxious to meet some real poor peasants as Comrade Hou was to introduce us to them, even though under the circumstances I felt very much like a visitor at a gallery being led to a hall of living exhibits.

Team leader Hou strode ahead of us out the door and through the compound gate to the street. He did not bother to draw his gun as he went, nor did he glance nervously around as had our first guide. Although apparently aware of great danger, he faced it stoically. He was obviously not a man to panic easily.

We turned southward down the main street and then eastward up a narrow lane. It lay so deep in shadow that I wondered for a moment if night had fallen.

Comrade Hou led us directly to a mud hut that was miserable, dark, almost bare of possessions. Its furnishings consisted of one tall wooden cabinet set against the wall, a low *k'ang,* and a mud-brick stove. The only utensils in sight were one large earthen jar, three cracked bowls, and one round-bottomed iron pot. This was the dwelling place and these the worldly goods of the poor peasant, Wang Wen-ping.

Inside the hut the still air was as cold as the north wind that blew down the open alley outside. Wang's iron pot sat on the stove, but there was no fire burning there, nor was there anywhere in sight any fuel from which a fire could be made. That fire was not a complete stranger to this dwelling was indicated by the paper on the single window. This had not been renewed for many years and had been stained dark brown by smoke. In two or three places the paper was badly torn, but these breaks did not add chill to the interior because there was no door across the entrance in any case. Once our eyes got used to the darkness we saw also that all four walls and the wattled ceiling overhead were black with layered creosote.

On entering this hut our nostrils were assailed by an indescribable odor—organic, sharp, yet not foul. This was an odor that we were to become familiar with as time went on, the odor of raw garlic from the throats of the occupants of the house. When one came close enough to catch the air that one of the garlic eaters had just exhaled, the stench was overwhelming, stinging, rank, but diffused as it was in this cold room, it hung like some memory of decay and puzzled us both.

We sat down on the edge of the *k'ang.* Wang's wife huddled into a corner and covered herself with the only ragged quilt that the family possessed. Wang himself squatted by the doorway, his back to the wall opposite us, and used the sill as a convenient obstacle against which to knock his pipe to remove the ashes. This pipe he constantly filled, lit, puffed, and filled again, thus infusing into the garlic-tainted air an acrid tinge of tobacco smoke.

Wang's broad face was heavily accented by two full eyebrows and a ragged mustache. His skin was rendered abnormally dark by a patina of grime that nothing short of an afternoon in the bathhouse at Changchih could remove. His clothes, hanging loose as a lizard's skin over his gaunt frame, were patched at the arms and worn through in many places so that they revealed, as through a lattice, the soiled cotton padding beneath. This padding had been so mauled and compacted by years of wear that it hardly seemed capable of insulating him any longer from the cold. Yet he appeared to be quite comfortable as he squatted in front of us.

The room was so gloomy that it was hard even to make out the features of Mother Wang. I recall only a few wisps of greying hair, a toothless grin, heavy lines on a leathery face, and a black tunic spotted with grease.

Slowly, haltingly, in response to persistent questioning, Old Wang began to tell Ch'i Yun about his life, and she relayed everything he told her to me.

Wang and his wife had once owned land in Long Bow but lost it to a landlord through default on a small debt. Famine drove them from the village and they wandered many years as beggars. When they finally came home after the war, they brought with them enough money to buy half an acre and received two and a half more as their share of the "fruits," but since they owned no draft animal and since Wang could no longer work hard, life was still very difficult for them.

"I belong to a mutual-aid team," the old peasant said dolefully. "But it seems as if I am always working for others and they never work for me. There are four poor families in the group, and all the work for soldiers' dependents is done by the four of us. We get no return for that.

"As for the distribution, I didn't get much. The cadres said I was an obstinate old man and didn't give me any part of an ox or a donkey. Others got them all right. I didn't even get a cart. They didn't even let me buy a chest that I liked. It was given to someone else. But the cadres got what they wanted."

"Didn't you get anything useful?" Ch'i Yun asked.

"I did get a long table, a little wooden box, an old pair of trousers, the felt mat on the *k'ang,* and two ragged suits for the boy."

"What about the wooden cabinet?" asked Ch'i Yun, pointing to the tall chest.

"Oh no, that is not mine. That belongs to the neighbors. They needed room for their loom and had to get it out of the way."

"Didn't you get a house? What about this house?"

"This is the house I used to live in. It was mine years ago. I lost it when I lost the land. Now I have it back again," said Wang without the slightest trace of enthusiasm.

"What do you think about your class? Do you think you are still a poor peasant?"

"I think I have really *fanshened*," said Wang, "because now I have three and a half acres, a house, food to eat, no debts. But still I am a poor peasant. Everybody says I am poor because I have no draft animal. I have to pay for plowing and when I grind grain I have to push the stone around by myself. My land is poor. None of the land around here is any good. Also I am old. I have no capital for handicraft production though the old lady does do some spinning. But she can only spin two ounces a day. If she does any more her arms ache. For a catty of thread she can get a catty and a half of cotton at the co-op. But that's a poor rate."

Old Wang blamed many of these difficulties on the bad cadres and suggested that all the poor peasants should organize strongly together to protect themselves, "because there may still be some bad elements in the village."

Just as we were about to take our leave a second peasant pushed his way through the door. He was in a loquacious mood and extremely anxious to contact the foreigner. A sprightly man of 54, well-muscled and energetic, he sported a combed and clipped grey beard that gave his face the distinguished look of some gentleman in a London club. To add to this effect, his padded pants were made of white undyed homespun in a village where most men wore dark blue or black. This was actually a sign of poverty, an indication that he could not afford dye, but to me the white recalled the cricket club affluence of the colonialists in Shanghai and Hong Kong. His jacket was light blue and very clean. On his head he wore a felt skull cap. Instead of the usual wood and brass tobacco pipe, he carried in his hand a pipe made of silver.

This peasant introduced himself. His name, he said, was Shen Ch'uan-te and he was a "basic element." Then he launched into a rambling story that seemed to have no end. There was no need to ask him questions, for the words poured from his lips in a torrent.

The hardships of his early life closely paralleled those suffered by Old Wang but he did not dwell on them. What he wanted to tell us had to do with events that followed the liberation of the village after the Japanese occupation. The new cadres, he swore, were worse than the old. He listed them all in order of merit, beginning with Hsin-fa, the secretary of the branch, who was tolerable, and ending with Wen-te, the captain of the police, and Hung-er, the captain of the militia, who were both tyrants.

Exactly what the cadres had done to our informant was not clear. He spoke up, he said, and they called him an agent. Then they denied him his share of the "fruits of struggle." Almost in the same breath he boasted that he had received three acres of land, some grain, and some clothes. All he had ever done to arouse the cadre's wrath was to go to Horse Square to pray in the Church there. For that they clapped an agent's cap on his head. Though he still went to meetings, he did not dare say anything and only sat in a dark corner afraid.

"Mao Tse-tung," said Shen, "should not be like this!"

This poor peasant with the silver pipe and the white cotton pants would have kept us the rest of the day and half the night as well if we had been able to sit and hear him out. Unfortunately, we could not do so. We had to get back to Kao Settlement before dark and so broke off the interview and took our leave of Wang and Shen while the latter was still detailing the grievances so long pent up in his breast.

As we walked back across the flat at nightfall I asked Ch'i Yun what she thought of the men we had met.

"Old Wang seemed honest enough to me," Ch'i said. "But he doesn't understand much. As for that Shen, he likes to blow the cow [boast]. I don't believe half of what he said."

"One thing is certain," she added after taking a few quick steps in silence. "There are plenty of problems in that village."

****

One immediate problem overshadowed all others. This was the need to investigate the attempt to murder a work team member which had occurred the day before.

Undisputed facts about the attempt were few. They had been summarized for us by the Team Leader Hou as follows:

Chang Ch'uer, the youngest member of the team, was returning to the District Office from Shen Ch'uan-te's home after dark when an unknown assailant leaped on his back, pulled him to the ground, choked him into unconsciousness, and dragged him toward a nearby well. Hu Hsueh-chen, the leader of the Women's Association, heard Ch'uer cry out. She jumped up from her k'ang and ran out into the street, but by the time she got there Ch'uer's assailant was gone. She found the young cadre lying gagged and senseless a few feet from the deep well. Hu barely had time to take a close look at what she assumed to be a corpse before her Catholic neighbors, Shen Ch'uan-te and Li Ho-jen, came out of their homes. These two immediately ran for help in the direction of the District Office. They returned with several work team cadres, put Ch'uer's limp body on a stretcher, and carried him off to the hospital in Lucheng. There the county's sole doctor found him badly bruised and suffering from shock due to partial suffocation but not seriously hurt. He was expected to live, perhaps even to return to work within a few days.

Who could have made this attack? Both Shen and Li, the peasants who had arrived so promptly on the scene, insisted that Yu-lai and his son Wen-te must be responsible. Were they not former bandits? Had they not made threats against the whole village? Surely none but these two could have attempted a deed so foul. Of course, it was admitted, these two might not have done it themselves. They might have persuaded Vice-Chairman Hsi-yu or Militia Captain Hung-er to carry out their plans. They were all in the same clique, after all, but whether or not they had done it with their own hands, they were surely behind the crime.

This opinion was shared by a large number of people. Wherever the cadres of the work team asked, they got the same answer—Yu-lai. And so, on that same night Yu-lai, his son Wen-te, and the two village leaders most closely associated with the father-and-son pair were arrested and taken to jail.

Faced with what appeared to be a flagrant counter-revolutionary act, Team Leader Hou made some rapid-fire decisions. He distributed side arms to all his team. He asked them to sleep and eat together in the District Office, and he arranged for them to drop all other work until they succeeded in tracking down enough evidence to convict the arrested men.

Hou followed these steps with a drastic reorganization of the village administration. All village cadres, both Party and non-Party, were suspended. All mass organizations such as the Peasants' Association and the Women's Association were dissolved. All members of the Communist Party branch were called into secret session for a critical review of their past work. This effectively removed them from all normal activity and responsibility.

These moves left the village without a government, without any village-wide organizations, and without any guidance from the Party branch which, for better or worse, had decided upon and led every action since midwinter of 1946.

The only group in a position to fill the vacuum thus created was

the work team itself. Of necessity, Team Leader Hou and his assistants had to assume the powers of the village government and take
responsibility for all day-to-day affairs; all this, of course, in addition
to the investigation and reorganization of the *fanshen* situation for
which they had originally come and the detective work required
by a serious crime.

The latter task continued to absorb the attention of the entire
village. Morning, noon, and night the peasants met in gatherings
large and small to assemble concrete evidence, to review the circumstances surrounding the mysterious assault, and to reassure one
another that counter-revolution could never challenge their new
power. Many bits and pieces of circumstantial evidence supported the
prevailing opinion that Yu-lai and Wen-te must be responsible for
the crime. Li Ho-jen carefully examined the towel that he had removed from Ch'uer's mouth and found that it was exactly the same
as six other towels found in Yu-lai's home. Wen-te's wife, Hsien-e,
confirmed the identity of the towels. Shen Ch'uan-te said that Yu-lai
and his notorious son had been seen plotting together near the scene
of the crime only a few hours before it took place. He even claimed
that he had heard one of them say, "Never mind, as long as I am
cadre, we can always take revenge." None of this information, however, could be called conclusive. Most of it was offered by people
who had reason to hate the men they implicated. It would not make
very convincing evidence in the County Court. Everyone knew, for
instance, that almost all the towels in the village came from the
same supplier, a Hantan cooperative that embroidered "Good Morning" in English on its wares.

On March 11, the Party Bureau of the Taihang Subregion ordered
Team Leader Hou to turn the investigation over to the police department of Lucheng County, where it belonged, and put his team
back to work on the land reform problems which they had come to
solve. This Hou did, but with a heavy heart. He felt that he had failed
in a very important job and that the days spent on the abortive investigation had been days completely wasted. The other team members shared Hou's frustration, but Ch'i Yun and I, who walked the
long mile to Long Bow each day as observers, felt differently. For
us, each visit had widened our acquaintance with the village, had introduced us to new and colorful inhabitants, and most important of
all, had familiarized us with the work team in whose hands the destiny of the community now lay.

27

The Work Team

The Chinese Revolution at the present stage is in its character a revolution against imperialism, feudalism and bureaucratic-capitalism waged by the broad masses of the people under the leadership of the proletariat. By broad masses of people is meant all those who are oppressed, injured or fettered by imperialism, feudalism and bureaucratic-capitalism, namely, workers, peasants, soldiers, intellectuals, businessmen and other patriots.

Mao Tse-tung, 1948

THERE WERE no higher cadres, no leading Communists, no persons with long revolutionary experience as organizers and propagandists among the people sent to Long Bow to help put the Draft Agrarian Law into effect. The team consisted in part of peasant leaders from Lucheng County who had only recently been promoted to full-time work outside their own villages; the other part of the team was composed of students and teachers from Northern University, many of whom were getting their first experience of village life. Altogether some 15 people joined in the work. However, the number actively engaged on the team varied from time to time due to the fact that some of those originally assigned to the task were later transferred to urgent work elsewhere, while others occasionally took leave to straighten out personal affairs at home, recuperate from illness, or harvest their crops.

The local cadres who were assigned to Long Bow were the equivalent of such peasant activists as T'ien-ming, Kuei-Ts'ai and Fu-yuan. After leaving Long Bow to become district cadres, those three were assigned to just such work teams in other "basic villages." It was their counterparts from other districts of the county who were appointed to the Long Bow team. In the interest of objectivity, people who grew up and became leaders in one village went to another village to help reorganize and vice versa. Such nuclei of local cadres on every team were then leavened and strengthened by the addition of intellectuals and students from distant places, many of them city bred.

The team which Ch'i Yun and I found in Long Bow reflected in microcosm the Chinese society from which it was formed. Almost every one of the social classes in the country was represented on it, including the gentry. Although the landlords as a class were a main target of attack, the coalition had always found room in its ranks for what were known as "enlightened gentry." As individuals, therefore, even landlords, or to be more accurate, sons and daughters of landlords, found their way to the Revolution and onto the team. This heterogeneous make-up of the land reform team was neither an accident nor a coincidence. It was the result of policy, the policy of the Communist Party of China, which viewed the Revolution as one vast action of many classes and strata against imperialism and feudalism and tried, even on the lowest level, to give life to that coalition.

Hou Pao-pei, the leader of the Long Bow team, came from Sand Market, a village in the Fifth District of Lucheng County only a few miles northwest of Long Bow. He was 29 years old, tall, strong, and dour. What one noticed first about Hou were his hands. They were large, powerful, calloused, more suited to grasping the handle of a hoe than to wielding a writing brush. These hands were attached to a pair of solid arms and these in turn to a raw-boned, rugged frame that rested on two ample feet always firmly planted on the ground. Despite his size and solidity, Hou moved gracefully and with vigor, though never quickly. Every move he made was careful and deliberate. He thought slowly and talked slowly, but he was no fool. He was absolutely honest, painfully shy, very much weighed down by his responsibility for the work of the team, and not at all sure about how to proceed. Though he felt himself poorly qualified to lead, it was easy to see why the county leaders had made him team captain. Hou was so thoroughly steeped in peasant ways and peasant culture that he hardly needed to ask what other peasants were thinking. He knew it already, as if by instinct. His speech was down to earth and full of popular proverbs, trite, pedestrian; yet when he opened his mouth people listened because what he said made sense.

"From childhood I was always very steady and firm," he told us when we asked him about his life. "Our relatives despised my family because we had nothing, but I would not humiliate myself before them. From the beginning I had the idea that if you fall on the ground you should get up by yourself. As the saying goes, 'Judge one's youth at three, judge one's manhood at seven.' When I was still a little child all my relatives and the villagers decided that I would either be a very able man or a very bad fellow. Though my family was poor we always said, 'We are poor but our will is not poor,' so I always tried my best to work and never asked help from anybody."

Hou, like so many of the active young men already described, had labored many years as a wage worker. At an early age he left home for a job as a room boy, later clerk, in a large, market-town inn. He returned to his village as a hired laborer, went into the hills as a coal miner, picked up seasonal jobs at harvest time, was conscripted into the labor gang that built the railroad to Changchih, escaped from this gang to become a rickshaw puller in the county seat, and ended up working in a large flour mill as a mechanic. He had thus seen a good deal of the country, had travelled to cities large and small, and worked with men from many places. Though the sophistication of the towns had not rubbed off on him, a lot of worldly knowledge had.

Throughout his wanderings Hou maintained close ties with the anti-Japanese resistance movement. His elder brother led the underground organization in Sand Market and was killed shortly before V-J Day by soldiers of the puppet Fourth Column. When the village was freed from Japanese control, Hou returned home immediately and joined the drive against the puppets and collaborators. He showed such courage and ability in this campaign that his neighbors elected him village head, chairman of the Peasants' Association and director of military affairs.

By the time the Settling of Accounts Movement began, Hou had become the leading figure in his home community. He led it so well that he was elected *"Fanshen* Hero" not only for Sand Market but also for the whole Fifth District. In the county-wide elections that followed he won the fourth highest number of votes as a model land reform worker. "For the prize I won a new plow," Hou said. "After the election we heroes were invited to a grand festival in the county seat. We saw plays and operas, both old style and new. Flowers were pinned to our tunics and we rode on horseback through the city. When we returned home we were welcomed by every village along the route. The people met us with parades and music and marched us through the fields to the border of the next village."

Hou was obviously not a man completely unknown to the people of Long Bow.

Hou's assistant on the work team was Li Sung-lin, known to all as "Little Li" because of his short stature. He was a plump jolly man of 26 who came from a middle peasant family of Bone Village, a community far back in the mountains that had never been occupied by the Japanese but had been repeatedly raided in an effort to destroy the guerrilla forces based there. In the course of the raids the Japanese killed the Li family ox and seized the Li family donkey, but all the people of the village escaped harm by hiding in mountain caves which the Japanese never found.

Li went to school until he was 15. Then he worked for two years on his father's land. When the war began he joined the guerrilla government of the county as an orderly, but because he was literate soon won promotion to the post of stencil cutter, then to the position of secretary to the Third District, and finally to the post of assistant judge of the County Court. All of this work was carried out under conditions of guerrilla war, with the government constantly on the move and its personnel never knowing from which direction the next attack might come. Three times Little Li was surrounded by Japanese squads and each time he barely escaped with his life. Once the whole county staff climbed over the back wall of a compound as the Japanese broke down the front gate. The enemy caught and killed the county clerk and shot the magistrate's personal guard. Li had time enough only to pull on his pants and run. He lost his coat, his bedroll, and his precious fountain pen.

When the war ended Li was appointed to various important jobs such as editor of the local gazette, cadre in the organization department of the Communist Party, and vice magistrate of the Fourth District.

The other four local members of the team who stayed in Long Bow until the work was completed were Han Chin-ming, 30; Chang Ch'uer, 23; Li Wen-chung, 25; and Liang Chi-hu, 26. All of them had impressive records as guerrilla fighters and peasant organizers in their home villages. The background of Li Wen-chung, a good-looking man with enough energy and spirit for two, who had started life with no hope at all, was typical.

Li began his story by saying: "I was born in the village of West Snake River. My own family owned neither land nor house nor anything else. When I was two years old I was bought by a poor peasant who had no children of his own and was brought to Horse Square. This man—you could call him a stepfather—worked as a hired laborer, but because he smoked opium he never had any money. As for me, as far back as I can remember I worked for others or begged for food. Thus I lived until I was 14."

At 14 Li ran away from home and joined the Shangtang Guerrilla Corps, a detachment of Yen Hsi-shan's Provincial Army. Soon after he joined this force it was surrounded by the Eighth Route Army and went over to the revolutionary side. The young recruit found a place as a bugler with the famous Eighth Routers, but a few months later he was left behind because the detachment moved on to Shantung and he was considered too young to serve as a soldier.

Li then worked two years in a factory, served six months in a conscript labor corps, farmed at home, saw his stepfather die of starvation after trying to live too long on beancake, and barely crawled away alive himself to find work as a rickshaw coolie in

Taiyuan. There he was shanghaied onto a construction gang, escaped, worked as a coal coolie, and finally returned home a few months before his native Horse Square was liberated by the same massed attack of militia and regulars that reduced the Long Bow fort.

The former beggar immediately plunged into the anti-traitor and land division movements. He won a post of leadership in the community by helping to solve an inter-village fight over who should divide the property of one very rich landlord who had hoarded more than 37,000 silver dollars. Soon thereafter he was elected secretary of his local Party branch and then called to the Fifth District Office for full-time work. When the work in Long Bow began, Li Wen-chung was still single, a rare thing for a male over 18 years of age in Lucheng County.

Such were the local men who came to Long Bow to carry out the Draft Agrarian Law—all native sons, blood of the blood, flesh of the flesh of Lucheng County's people. They had all been through the searing catastrophes of war and famine, and all had taken a leading part in transforming village life after the liberation. To carry on this work came as naturally to them as breathing.

But to succeed in this work was something else again. Success depended on many factors: on one's grasp of a complex situation, on one's ability to analyze and organize, on the validity of the policies to be carried out. The key to all but the last of these was training.

Training for land reform work had started at the very highest levels of the Communist Party and the Border Region Government as early as October 1947. Long before the Draft Agrarian Law was made public it had been circulated to all leading personnel in the vast Shansi-Hopei-Honan-Shantung Border Region and had then been formally considered at a gigantic marathon conference. This conference, held at Yehtao, in the heart of the Taihang range, was attended by 1,700 leaders of county magistrate or regimental commander rank. The deliberations, which centered on the ideological examination of every participant, lasted 85 days.

Out of the Yehtao Conference had come an estimate that the land reform in the Border Region as a whole was still far from adequate. At Yehtao the idea that the revolution might have gone too far in some places tended to be overlooked. Plain warnings that middle peasants must never be made the "objects of struggle," that landlords and rich peasants must not be left without means of livelihood, and that commercial and industrial holdings must not be touched, though often repeated, in the main went unheeded. Emphasis was placed on the first of Mao's two principles: "Satisfy the demands of the poor peasants and hired laborers."

"We must start from the class outlook, the method, the stand of the poor-and-hired peasants. We must stand firmly at their side; we must refer all things to them and do everything starting from their interest." These words of Regional Party Secretary Po Yi-po, words which represented only a part of his position, were raised aloft as the banner under which the Revolution should march.

As a result, when the members of the Lucheng Party Committee returned home from the Border Region Conference, they came intent on a shake-up. They immediately set about to study anew all pertinent data concerning the *fanshen* in Lucheng County. When statistics showed that thousands of poor peasants had not yet truly stood up, they assumed that this was because landlordism had not yet been thoroughly uprooted. And if, after three years of "thunder and lightning, drum and cymbal" campaigning, landlordism had not yet been uprooted in Lucheng County, could anyone but the Communist Party be blamed?

A quick and superficial check on the background of the comrades in the village branches convinced the County Committee that at least 40 percent of the local Communists were of landlord or rich peasant origin. The failure of the poor to *fanshen,* the commandism, the hedonism, the nepotism, and the favoritism so common everywhere they attributed to the counter-revolutionary class origin and disruptive activity of this large group.

As a result of this survey, the optimistic estimate that had been made by the county leaders in 1946 was reversed. In 1948, the Communist Party Committee of Lucheng County declared that land reform in the area under its jurisdiction had been seriously compromised, if not aborted.

A conference of all full-time political workers in Lucheng was immediately called. It convened at a village called Lu Family Settlement and lasted the entire month of February. Secretary Ch'en presented the County Committee's new estimate of the situation to the assembled cadres in great detail. He blamed himself and the Party members before him for the sorry picture and demanded and received from each participant a statement of class origin and a searching self-criticism of past behavior. Those who admitted serious errors received discipline in the form of warnings and suspensions. A few who subbornly refused to criticize themselves or justified their past wrong-doing were expelled from the Party. At the conclusion of the meeting, the majority went back to their work in the field prepared to lead a drastic redistribution of the land and wealth of their county and a drastic reorganization of village administrations, Party branches, and mass organizations.

In the minds of these men and women as they took up their new tasks there lingered a vivid phrase from Secretary Ch'en's final report: "'He who cannot find poor peasants in the villages doesn't deserve to eat!'"

****

The students and young teachers from Northern University who joined this nucleus of peasant cadres were from an entirely different world. Either directly or indirectly they were tied to the landlord class whose overthrow was the object of all their work. There was, for instance, the lean, sharp-nosed Professor Hsu, an intellectual from Peking. He had never known physical labor in any form, not to mention hunger or hardship. His experience of the actual life of the Chinese people was thus one-sided, to say the least. His academic qualifications, on the other hand, were impressive. As an economist he had read a large number of books, was an enthusiastic student of Marxism, and could debate the fine points of value theory with anyone. He looked upon his assignment in Long Bow as an opportunity for research, as a chance to collect first-hand material about Chinese rural life which would add to the theoretical insight which he had already stored up. He came to the village well supplied with books and writing materials, but was at a loss when face to face with the peasants. He found their accent hard to understand, their motives strange, and their manners uncouth. Professor Hsu, for all his good intentions, was like a fish out of water in the countryside. He made one mistake after the other.

Much better adapted to work in the village was my assistant and interpreter, Ch'i Yun. She was typical of the three women who came from the University. Although officially assigned only to help me, she soon became an important and lively addition to the team and was allocated as much work as any other member. Unfortunately, we were so busy attending meetings, interviewing peasants, taking down verbatim notes, and translating charts and papers that I never formally requested her life story, and she, on her part, volunteered very little about herself. Even her name was an assumed one that she had adopted in order to protect those members of her family who still lived in Nationalist-controlled regions.

About Ch'i Yun I learned only that she was a college graduate from a large coastal city who, very soon after the Japanese invasion of North China, went to Yenan. There she married a revolutionary of similiar background and bore two children. She rarely mentioned her husband but I gained the impression that he and she were separated, not only temporarily by their work but permanently by choice.

Because Ch'i Yun's own work took her away on long trips through the Liberated Areas, her two children were brought up in the nursery school for cadres' children in Yenan.

After the Japanese surrender in 1945, trained people were urgently needed all over North China. A great exodus by foot, donkey, and ox cart took place from Yenan. Ch'i Yun joined this exodus, worked as an interpreter for the truce negotiation teams set up by General Marshall's mission, and then was transferred to the Liberated Areas Relief Administration for similar duties. Her children, left behind in Yenan, moved eastward with their school when the Kuomintang attack on the Northwest began. In 1948 they were located somewhere in the mountains to the east of Changchih—close enough so that she was able to see them occasionally, make clothes for them, and tend their other special wants, but not close enough so that she could visit them every day or every week.

Ch'i Yun's round friendly face was not beautiful in any particular detail but, taken together, her features were attractive and feminine. By dress and coiffure she did nothing to enhance them, however. Her fine long hair was rolled up each morning and tucked under a visor cap in such a way that only a few wisps ever strayed to lend a touch of charm to an otherwise austere appearance. Her bulky padded suit completely concealed her figure. Only from the small size of her feet, encased in dainty, self-made cotton slippers, could one guess that her limbs might be graceful and well-proportioned.

I often thought what a hardship it must be for such a woman to live the life of a spartan revolutionary cadre in the bleak North China countryside after a childhood of relative luxury and comfort in the city. Yet she seemed to pay no attention whatsoever to cold, fatigue, lice, fleas, coarse food, or the hard wooden planks that served as her bed. For her this was all a part of "going to the people" who alone, once they were mobilized, could build the new China of which she dreamed.

Ch'i Yun's high spirits in the face of extreme physical hardship pointed up a curious fact which we discovered on our very first day in the village. This was that the morale of the intellectuals, for whom land reform represented a complete change in way of life, was far higher than that of the local cadres.

The local cadres worked steadily but without enthusiasm. When they met in the evening to discuss what had been done or to make plans for the future, they often sat for minutes at a time without saying a word. It was as if some heavy burden weighed upon their thoughts and inhibited their tongues.

Not so the students and teachers from Northern University. They plunged into the heart of village affairs with eagerness and enthusiasm, made discovery after discovery about the life of their own country-men, developed new and interesting friendships with people whom they would never have met in a lifetime of academic pursuits, and looked on the hardships involved partly as adventure and partly as steeling for future revolutionary activity, a test they hoped to pass without flinching. That is not to say that village life was much harder than life at the guerrilla University. In some ways it was less spartan. In Long Bow the food, at least, had some variety and ocsionally a peasant's *k'ang* was warmed by fire. The same could never be said of the University, where neither wheat nor corn ever broke the monotony of boiled millet in the students' mess and fire never warmed the clammy stone corridors, the high-ceilinged rooms, or the backyard adobe sheds that served as dormitories for staff and students alike.

What made village life a challenge was the dirt and the squalor which surrounded the poorest peasants and the unbearable suffering that was the lot of so many victims of disease. While the itch of lice and the welts left by bedbugs were passed off jokingly as "the revolutionary heat," the suppurating headsores, malarial fevers, slow deaths from tuberculosis and venereal disease were not joking matters. Land reform workers slept on the same *k'angs,* ate from the same bowls, and shared lice and fleas with people diseased beyond hope of recovery. Yet I never saw anyone complain. They came prepared for this and for much worse.

Their training had no more been left to chance, to spontaneous revolutionary enthusiasm, than had that of the local cadres. The outlook of the intellectuals had been consciously developed during an extended period of education and discussion, criticism and self-criticism, that preceded the departure of all team members for the countryside. During the weeks of small meetings which occupied the time of all teachers and students after the promulgation of the new Draft Law, every person in the University, regardless of status, made a survey of his or her own past and examined his or her own class origin. In the freezing quarters where the students lived, they met day after day in small groups of 15 to 20 to study the class nature of Chinese society and to discuss where each one fit as landlord, peasant, bourgeois merchant, or free professional. In order to "join the revolution," persons with upper-class backgrounds had to give up all attachment to their pasts and take a firm stand with the workers and peasants. They had to resolve to apply in life the revolutionary principles which had so easily caught their imaginations in theoretical form and to bring their everyday behavior into line with their professed opinions.

For many individuals, taking a new stand was no abstract question to be decided by cool reasoning simply on its economic or political merit. Their own families had been or soon would be under attack. Some of their parents had already been beaten to death by angry peasants. Some of them were apt to end up in charge of land division in areas where their own property lay. They had to face the possibility of accusations and actions leading to the destruction of their homes and families. The new Draft Law opposed all beating and torture, opposed any treasure hunt for buried wealth, opposed all "sweep-the-floor-out-the-door" solutions. Nevertheless, peasants and cadres had been carried beyond policy in the past and, if the battle became heated, might well be carried beyond it again. It would be naive to think that everything would be peaceful in the future.

Many participants found that they could not sleep at night. They lost their appetites and burst into tears when they faced this choice, or confronted past mistakes. Even the students from less privileged families found this educational process painful. They had to rethink their lives from the very beginning, re-examine all their values, and rededicate themselves to a cause that gave them no personal advantage whatsoever.

Yet those intellectuals who were changed by the process seemed to be grateful. The spartan life, the intellectual ferment, the group companionship, and the physical and mental well-being that developed as a result of remolding their ideology moved most of them deeply. They were exhilarated by the knowledge that they were drawing closer to the heart of the Revolution and were themselves undergoing an awakening, a metamorphosis from "I and my wants" to "we and our needs." They could feel the great thrust of this awakening both subjectively and objectively. When the call came to go to the villages they went eagerly to do battle with all of the past that was rotten, corrupt, and painful.

28

Those With Merit Will Get Some
Those Without Merit Will Get Some

Why should the poor and hired peasants lead? The poor and hired peasants should lead because they make up from 50 to 70 percent of the population, are the most numerous, and work the hardest all year long. They plant the land, they build the buildings, they weave the cloth, but they never have enough food to eat, a roof to sleep under, or clothes to wear. Their life is most bitter, they are oppressed and exploited and pushed around. Hence they are the most revolutionary. From birth they are a revolutionary class. Inevitably they are the leaders of the fanshen movement. This is determined by life itself.

Proclamation to the Peasants, March 1948
Shansi-Hopei-Honan-Shantung
Border Region Government

A NEW starting point for the work of the team was provided by an announcement explaining the meaning of the Draft Agrarian Law which was sent out by the Party Bureau of the Shansi-Hopei-Honan-Shantung Border Region and printed simultaneously in all the newspapers of that vast area. The announcement was couched in simple terms and outlined, in a few short paragraphs, just what the new law meant for peasants who, in spite of years of effort, had not yet *fanshened*.

Little Li, vice leader of the work team and a surprisingly accomplished orator, introduced the document to Long Bow Village by reading it aloud. As he read he stood at the end of a long loft that made up the second story of the foreign-style house that had once belonged to the absentee landlord and militarist, Chief-of-Staff Hsu. The building was now held as "surplus property" by the village office. Scattered about the loft, seated on bricks, chunks of wood, and an occasional folding stool, all of which had been carried up the steep ladder on the outside wall, sat about 50 or 60 peasants especially selected by the work team as the poorest in the whole community. The men sat in clusters, lit their pipes, smoked, or simply listened with rapt attention; the women, grouped in their own coteries, worked busily at domestic chores. Some sewed shoe soles, some spun hemp, others wound cotton thread from large reels into balls. The mothers among them kept a watchful eye on their young children, ragged urchins with smudged faces and bare bottoms exposed from behind, who tumbled about among the assembled people, laughed, chased each other, and cried. Small babies, not yet able to walk, sucked at deliciously exposed, milk-swollen breasts or fell asleep in maternal arms blissfully unaware of the historic words that rang through the loft, claiming the power to change their whole lives.

"Brothers and sisters, peasants of the Border Region," read Little Li with genuine theatrical flourish. "In the course of the past two years our Border Region has carried on a powerful, enthusiastic land reform movement. Already over ten million people have thoroughly *fanshened* but there are still areas with a population of 20 million who have only partially *fanshened* or not *fanshened* at all."

From the nodding heads, the whispered asides, it was obvious that the peasants in the loft counted themselves among the 20 million whose *fanshen* was still incomplete.

"Now everyone must *fanshen*.

"There were some mistakes in the past. Some of our village cadres were landlords; others, even though they weren't landlords, listened to the landlords. Some soldiers' and cadres' relatives were landlords. These were not thoroughly settled with."

Without stopping to analyze whether this was actually true in Long Bow, the peasants accepted the statement with enthusiasm. It implied that there would be further struggles and further "fruits" and that they, as the organized poor peasants, would get these "fruits." They nodded and waited for more.

"Some families got more in the distribution because they were soldiers' relatives, or cadres' relatives. The fruits were distributed according to many systems, according to need, according to membership in the Peasants' Association, according to one's activities in the struggle. This was not fair. Because of this some got a lot, and others got very little."

Here indeed was something to savor. The peasants remembered the early struggles well. Politics rather than class had decided the outcome then. It was traitors and collaborators who had been attacked and those who beat them down who received the wealth. Later movements corrected but never entirely overcame these inequities. Religious prejudice, political suspicion, and a measure of favoritism continued to distort the results.

"That's exactly right," said an old woman who sat close to Ch'i

Yun, never for an instant ceasing to wind thread. "You had to be on the inside to get anything."

"The Draft Agrarian Law is designed to correct all such mistakes," declared Little Li, still reading from the document. "Articles One and Three call for destruction of the feudal system and the creation of a system of 'land to the tiller.'

"What does this mean? It means that no matter who you are, whether you are a county magistrate, a commander-in-chief, or an official of whatever level, if you are a feudal exploiter your property will be confiscated. Nothing will or can protect you."

"Hear that now!"

"That's the way it should be!"

"Nobody can escape this time."

These comments and many others in the same vein emerged at random, like corn popping in a pan.

"Article Six says that property will be distributed according to the number of people in the family. It is very simple—those who are politically suspect will get some, and those who are not politically suspect will get some. Those with merit will get some and those without merit will get some. Landlords will get a share and rich peasants will get a share also. Some middle peasants will give up a little, some will get a little, most will not be touched at all. That which was not equally divided in the past is to be divided. Those who got too little in the past will get more. Those who got too much will give it up. The surplus will be used to fill the holes. Everything will be divided so that everyone will have a fair share."

If the previous paragraphs had aroused enthusiasm, this paragraph sent it bubbling and rippling through the loft. The peasants were beside themselves with delight. Among them were at least a dozen who had been called agents, had received less than equal treatment because of it, and lived in the shadow of further attacks. For them the announcement cleared the sky. Politics, religion, furtive trips to Horse Square, collaboration, past mistakes, quarrels, personal vendettas, the weighing and balancing of thoughts and activities, merits and demerits—all these were declared irrelevant. The only thing that mattered was poverty. If you were poor you would get property— land, tools, livestock, houses.

"Do you understand what I have read?" asked Little Li over the hubbub engendered by his words.

"We understand it very well," said the old woman next to Ch'i Yun. "We only wish we could remember every word of it."

"It couldn't be better," said a man in a ragged jacket. "I myself never *fanshened*."

"Understand it? Of course we do!" declared many voices from all over the loft.

Little Li went on to declare that the poor peasants themselves must right the wrongs and unite with the middle peasants to elect a democratic Village Congress which could then supervise the work of all cadres and recall all those who abused their power. But the main point, the point that impressed the people most, had already been made: *Those with merit will get some and those without merit will get some. Everything will be divided so that everyone will get an equal share.*

****

The statement read by Comrade Li, which outlined the coming campaign for the mass of the peasantry, was supplemented by a far more detailed directive which explained to the cadres of the work team just how they were to go about accomplishing their major objectives.

According to this directive, which was issued by the Central Committee of the Chinese Communist Party on February 22, 1948, the villages of the Liberated Areas fell into three basic types. Included in the first type were those in which land reform had been successfully carried out and only minor readjustments and corrections were needed to complete the movement. The second type comprised the villages where equal distribution was more ragged, landlords and rich peasants still owned more and better land than the average and many cadres had received more than their fair share of the "fruits." In the third type were those villages where, in spite of certain efforts at equal distribution, land reform had not been effectively carried out and feudal relations of production still remained dominant.

The first task of the work team was to determine which of these types best characterized the village of Long Bow. In case of doubt, a complete class analysis of the community had to be made and the holdings of the various classes compared. Villages of the first type had to contain not only a majority of *fanshened* peasants (50 to 80 percent of the population) but the per capita holdings of the remaining poor had to be at least equal to two thirds of the per capita holdings of the middle peasants.

To determine the type of any village meant to determine the course of action which must subsequently follow. If the village were of the first or second type, the necessary economic adjustments were to be made as quickly as possible so as not to disrupt the year's production work, and the work team must then concentrate on the democratic reforms which were to usher in a new political life for the whole community.

If the village proved to be of the third type, then the whole Draft Agrarian Law had to be applied from the beginning. A Poor Peasants' League had to be organized, a campaign against the remaining gentry mounted, confiscation of gentry holdings completed, and equal distribution of all confiscated property effected. Only after all this was finished could the democratic reforms be undertaken.

Whether the situation in the village was good or bad, whether the land reform had been carried out well or poorly, future progress depended upon the quality of the political leadership inside the village and consequently on the quality of the members of the Communist Party branch. It was necessary therefore not only to classify the villages as outlined above but also to classify them according to the kind of Communist Party branch that existed in each. If a nucleus of Communists with reasonably good records existed, then the branch was called Kind I. Such a branch need only be re-educated by means of criticism and self-criticism meetings and encouraged to take a leading role in all future work. If the branch was dominated by landlord or opportunist elements then it was declared Kind II or III. Such a branch must certainly be reorganized, perhaps even dissolved. Political direction of the village must temporarily be turned over to the Committee of the Poor Peasants' League or the Peasants' Association and a new branch constituted only during the course of the reforms.*

The democratic reforms which were to accompany or follow the completion of the land reform program were to consist of:

(1) A re-examination of and reorganization of the Communist Party branch and a critical re-evaluation of the records of all village officials, whether Party or non-Party.

(2) The establishment of a sound Peasants' Association made up of the vast majority of poor and middle peasant families and led by democratically elected officers.

(3) The eventual establishment of a new village government composed of an elected Village Congress, representative of all social strata, and the appointment by this Congress of all village officers, such as the village chairman, the village clerk, the militia captain, the police captain, and the man in charge of public service.

Such in brief was the task that faced the work team in Long Bow. The members had to decide which type the village fell into and what kind of Communist Party branch it contained. On the basis of these estimates suitable organizational steps had to be taken and suitable reforms carried out.

---

* A Poor Peasants' League was an organization composed only of poor peasants and hired laborers. A Peasants' Association was a much broader organization composed of poor peasants, hired laborers and middle peasants.

Simply to make an accurate estimate of the true state of affairs was a major project. No outsider could hope to possess enough detailed information to decide who were middle peasants, who were poor peasants, and how much each actually held. To gather such information required the active support of all the peasants. First it was necessary that they acquire standards of judgment, and then they must collectively undertake the work of classification and evaluation.

In their haste to get started on more fundamental problems, the work team cadres in Long Bow did not wait until they had completed this arduous task of investigation before they made up their minds about the basic situation in the village. Without consultation among themselves, without taking any formal decision, they assumed that land reform in Long Bow had been stillborn. It followed that the village must be Type III and its Party branch Kind III. All mass organizations remained dissolved, all village cadres remained suspended, all Communist Party members continued to meet in secret session. Long Bow was treated as a village where the whole slate had to be wiped clean and the peasant movement had to be reorganized from the ground up.

The first step in any such reorganization had to be the creation of a new Poor and Hired Peasants' League. But before such a League could even be started, some determination had to be made concerning who were the poor and who the hired. A detailed classification of the whole community therefore became mandatory and the thoroughgoing investigation which the cadres had earlier bypassed crowded all other matters off the agenda after all.

29

Self Report, Public Appraisal

For those whose duty it is to give guidance and direction, the most essential method of knowing conditions is that they should, proceeding according to plan, devote their attention to a number of cities and villages and make a comprehensive survey of each of them from the basic viewpoint of Marxism, i.e., by means of class analysis.

Mao Tse-tung, 1941

"THERE ARE seven in my family. Last year, before the marriage of my son I had six."

So spoke Wang Kuei-pao. He was a heavy-set man perhaps 40 years old. Crow's-feet spread from the corners of his eyes. On his weathered face grew a ragged stubble of hair that had never matured into a beard.

"Why speak of last year? Speak of the way it is now. Soon you will have a grandson and that will make eight," said a wit from across the room. He was pressed against the side wall of the hut by the crush of people at the meeting and I could not even see who had spoken, as I myself was pressed against the opposite wall.

Wang, the expectant grandfather, continued his report unperturbed. "I have three and a half acres. I reap about ten bushels to the acre. My son is a teacher in another village. I have no draft animal."

"No doubt you are a poor peasant," said a third voice.

"That's easy. He's a poor peasant. He hasn't even *fanshened*."

"Your family has increased but your land remains the same. In the future you'll have even more mouths to feed." The speakers supported one another.

"Well," said Wang, with a bravado based on the security he felt in being poor. "Go ahead and classify me. Call me a rich peasant if you want to. It doesn't bother me at all."

But everyone agreed. There was not the slightest doubt. Wang Kuei-pao had been a poor peasant all his life and a poor peasant he remained.

A man named Ting-fu followed Wang. He reported three and a

275

half acres for three people, no livestock, no implements, a broken-down house of three sections, and a shared privy.

"Ting-fu has toiled his whole life through," said one of his neighbors.

"He is the hardest worker in the whole village," said another.

Ting-fu was classed as a poor peasant without further ado.

Thus classification of the classes began in Long Bow.

****

The handful of peasants who listened to Wang Kuei-pao and Ting-fu were "basic elements" chosen by the work team as the nucleus of the new Poor Peasants' League—a League which was to remain "provisional" until it assumed its final form. Their primary objective was to find others as poor as themselves who could swell the ranks until the new organization became capable of exerting leverage on the whole community. In the process they would also make a preliminary estimate of the potential allies (middle peasants) among their neighbors and of the "objects of struggle" (rich peasants and landlords) who still lived among them.

The classification method used was called *tzu pao kung yi,* or "self report, public appraisal." The "self report" meant that every family head must appear in person and report his sources of income and his economic position prior to the liberation of the village. "Public appraisal" meant that all members of the Provisional League must discuss each report and decide, by sense-of-the-meeting, on the family's class status.

Everyone knew that these classification proceedings could transform the Draft Agrarian Law from a general declaration of purpose into a concrete reality. Decisions concerning class status would eventually determine the future of every family. Those classed as poor peasants could expect to gain prestige as members of the new Poor Peasants' League and to acquire prosperity by coming into enough worldly goods to make them new middle peasants. Those classed as rich peasants could expect expropriation of all their surplus property, leaving them with only enough to earn a living like any other *fanshened* peasant. Anyone classified as a landlord faced complete expropriation and then the return of enough property to live on. The classification, in other words, could not be regarded as an academic matter, as a mere nose count, as a census. It laid the basis for economic and social action that affected every family and every individual in the most fundamental way.

Because this was so the peasants took an extraordinary interest in the classification meetings and gathered without complaint, day after day, to listen, report, discuss, and judge.

It soon became obvious that every family wanted to be classed as far down the scale as possible. To be called a middle peasant meant to receive nothing. Only those classed as poor peasants could expect to gain. Therefore every family wanted to be classed as poor, and every family head, no matter how poor, tried to minimize what his family had possessed prior to liberation and deprecate what the family had received since.

For the minority at the upper end of the scale, downgrading was even more vital. All the prosperous peasants were fearful lest they be shoved over the line into the rich-peasant category and lose out. Even the middle-peasant category included an upper group, the well-to-do, who could legitimately be asked to give up something. Those who feared that they owned enough to be called well-to-do wanted no part of any such condition and fought hard to convince their neighbors that they really had no surplus, that they were simply average middle peasants.

Since everyone wanted to be downgraded, since "poverty was best," I expected the final result of the classification to be a general shift downward. But this was not the case, and the reason for it was quite simple. The preliminary classification was undertaken by a group of families already designated by the work team as poor. It was in their interest to place others in higher brackets for two obvious reasons—in the first place, unless some families were classed as landlords, rich peasants, or well-to-do middle peasants there would be no property to distribute; in the second place, if there were large numbers of families classed as poor, whatever "struggle fruits" materialized would have to be spread thin. Clearly, the fewer families there were on the sharing end, the more each family would be likely to get.

The two contradictory trends, the desire on the part of all those being classed to be downgraded, and the desire on the part of those doing the classing to upgrade everyone else, tended to cancel each other out. In the course of the reports and appraisals the true situation of each family tended to be revealed.

For this happy result, credit must also be given to the method of discussion employed, a method that enabled every individual to talk over each case. This method was known as *ke ts'ao,* a word that literally means "ferment" and finds its American equivalent in the "buzz session." After each family presented its report, the chairman called out, *"Ke ts'ao, ke ts'ao."* Then all those who were sitting together in those natural clusters formed as people came to the meeting fell to discussing the case. They continued to discuss it until they more or less agreed. As agreement was reached in various parts of the room, the hum of voices gradually died down. Then the chairman called out, *"Pao kao, pao kao!"* (report, report).

A spokesman for each group, designated on the spur of the moment by those who sat around him, then expressed the consensus arrived at by his companions in the course of their "ferment." If the opinions of the scattered groups did not coincide, the chairman tried to clarify the differences, review the facts in the case, and ask the family under consideration to report in greater detail. Then he called for another *ke ts'ao* and repeated this process until a real sense-of-the-meeting was reached. No votes were taken. To decide such matters by a vote meant to impose the will of the majority on the will of the minority, with all the hard feeling that such an imposition was sure to cause. Objectively, the work team felt, any family must stand somewhere in the scale. A real understanding of the family's condition should enable the peasant judges to place the family in its proper niche. To vote meant to admit defeat, to make a subjective rather than an objective decision. When no sense-of-the-meeting could be reached, the cadres advised putting off the classification until further study of the standards and further investigation of the facts clarified the whole picture.

The complete lack of facilities for any form of large gathering established ideal conditions for the informal *ke ts'ao* discussions that characterized Long Bow meetings. Instead of coming together in a room equipped with rows of chairs, such as would be found in any Western meeting hall, the peasants had to gather in some empty loft, some abandoned room, some quiet portion of the street, or in the largest of their private homes. Each had of necessity to bring his or her own private seat—usually a brick, a block, or a little stool made of wood and string—and sit down wherever the company proved most congenial. The groups that crystallized in this way formed natural discussion circles that made it possible for any meeting to switch to a "buzz session" without the least rearrangement or disturbance. Thus everyone had a chance to participate and express opinions whether or not he or she actually spoke to the gathering as a whole. This system enabled shy people to speak first in small groups and gradually build up confidence to the point where they were willing to stand up and talk before the multitude. Truth was well served by such an arrangement because what one person forgot another was sure to remember. The collective proved wiser than any individual, and in the end a consensus of the participants emerged.

For Ch'i Yun and myself these meetings served as a window opening on the inner life of the village. The peasants, who had seemed on first acquaintance to constitute a fairly homogeneous mass—poverty-stricken yet energetic, ignorant yet shrewd, quarrelsome yet good humored, suspicious yet hospitable—turned out to be a most varied collection of individuals. Each possessed marked originality, and each faced problems peculiar to his or her situation that often obscured the general problem of livelihood, the overriding necessity to *fanshen*.

With a "well bottom" view of the world still limiting their vision, most peasants found it hard to separate their personal problems from the basic economic situation that was the root of their misery. They tended to concentrate on traits of character, unresolved feuds, past insults, and other peripheral issues to the neglect of the true criterion for determining class status—their own relation to the means of production.

The audience, also made up of peasants, was equally subjective. Time and again, Little Li, Ch'i Yun, and the other work team cadres who sat in on the meetings had to bring the discussion around to objective economic facts and warn against classifying some family in the upper brackets because the family head had collaborated with the Japanese, habitually beat his wife, or sided with his wife against his mother.

Yet so strong ran the feeling against exploitation, collaboration, and criminal behavior that sometimes the team cadres themselves were carried away. When this happened, their prestige and eloquence were such that they easily swayed the whole meeting.

30

Rich Man, Poor Man, Beggarman, Thief

The class status of most of the population in the rural areas is clear and can be easily differentiated without much divergence of view. Their class status should first be ascertained. In the case of a small proportion of the people whose class status is unclear and difficult to ascertain and where there is a divergence of view, they should be dealt with later and classified after thorough study and after obtaining instruction from the higher authorities. Impatience in determining the class status of these people must be avoided lest errors should be made which lead to their dissatisfaction. If any mistake is made, it must be corrected.

Liu Shao-ch'i

CHANG CH'I-TS'AI, one of the poorest individuals in the whole village, provided the first stumbling block to that nucleus of poor peasants who set out to classify the whole village in March.

The group had little trouble just so long as they dealt with typical cases. Heads of families had only to make the briefest kind of report before they were unanimously declared to be poor peasants or middle peasants. Consequently, during the first two or three days of the proceedings some 40 families were classed without controversy and most of those who were declared to be poor were invited to participate in classifying those who followed them.

When they got to Ch'i-ts'ai, however, the peasants disagreed sharply. The difficulty stemmed from the fact that he had never owned even a fraction of an acre of land. Furthermore, he had never worked on the land for others. All his life he had labored as a builder of houses. On the wages thus earned he had raised two sons and a daughter. A second daughter he had given away as a child bride during the famine year. After the birth of his fourth child his wife had died.

In the distributions of 1945–1946, Ch'i-ts'ai had received almost five acres of land, a donkey, one third of a cart, and many hundredweight of grain. This was enough to make him a middle peasant in 1948. His neighbors all agreed on that. What they found hard to decide was, what had been his class before liberation?

"His class was bare poor," volunteered several peasants after hearing Chang's report.

"But there is no such class as 'bare poor,' " protested Little Li, the work team cadre sitting in on the meeting. "There are hired laborers who own no land and work for wages on the land of others; there are village workers who also own no land but have skills such as carpentry, masonry, blacksmithing, and weaving; but there is no such thing as a class of 'bare poor.' "

The peasants, however, could not conceive of a way of life without land. To live without land was to live in a state of perpetual disaster. Anyone who had no land was "bare poor" and the sooner he acquired land the better. To set up a separate class of people who owned nothing and call them workers did not make sense.

The specific skill possessed by Ch'i-ts'ai also confused the issue. The peasants found it difficult to separate the man from his trade and arrive at the common category "worker." If he was not simply "bare poor," he was a housebuilder. But housebuilders could hardly constitute a class. Could his wife be called a housebuilder too? Could his children be called housebuilders? It seemed that only the person who practiced the trade could be classed according to that trade and hence be called a worker, if worker he had to be. The rest of his family should be something else.

When Little Li repeated his argument the peasants "gave up the gun" and agreed to call Ch'i-ts'ai a village worker, but it was quite clear that very few understood what this meant.

Another worker, Chang Huan-ch'ao, the blacksmith, posed an even greater puzzle. Some peasants wanted to call this hot-tempered, swarthy-complexioned man an exploiter because he did such poor work and charged so much for it.

"He's a middle peasant," said one neatly dressed woman with a reputation as an amorous widow. She spat out the words "middle peasant" as if they bore some sort of stigma. "He's a middle peasant because he earns good money as a blacksmith, and besides his work is no good. Last year he cheated me. He charged me an awful price but the work was no good and even the iron was poor. He exploited me."

"He's not skillful; we all know that," said a grey-bearded elder. "But if you don't want to be exploited by him you can always call in others to do the work. It's different with the landlords. With them you have no choice. You pay rent or you starve. But with Huan-ch'ao, if you don't like his work you can always take your job elsewhere."

"Go ahead, say what you think," said Chang himself, scowling darkly. "Your opinions are very good and I would be the last to get angry."

"Truth is," said a second widow, "the tools you make are no good. You really should improve your workmanship."

"I accept your criticism," said Huan-ch'ao, desperately trying to hold back his rising temper. He knew that to explode now would land him in the middle-peasant category for sure.

"He's never been a skillful blacksmith," the grey-bearded man said again. "But if you say that for this reason he exploits you, then all blacksmiths must become very gloomy indeed."

Finally Yuan-lung, a young neighbor of Huan-ch'ao's, proposed a solution. "He's a poor peasant," he said with an air of finality. Several pipe-smoking cronies of the speaker hastened to back up this idea, but the women still looked doubtful.

"If you can't decide now, we'll discuss it later," suggested Little Li, but this suggestion won no more support than the other.

The League members finally agreed that since Huan-ch'ao had always owned a little land he should be called a poor peasant. This solution had one added advantage. It avoided the mysterious category of "worker."

In the case posed by Huan-ch'ao the peasants confronted a basic problem of economic theory. Their dispute arose from the obvious fact that the work done by different individuals, whether judged by the quantity or by the quality of the output, is not equal. In spite of this, wages and prices tend to standardize, a reflection of the socially necessary labor time required to turn out any given piece of goods. But to arrive at the concept of socially necessary labor time required a breadth of experience and a level of abstract reasoning that could hardly be expected of the peasants of Long Bow at this time. What they saw was a poor craftsman asking for the same return on his labor as a good craftsman, and this smacked to them of exploitation.

Ch'i Yun could hardly restrain her chuckles as she explained to me the give and take over Huan-ch'ao, the blacksmith. That a skilled worker could exploit the people who hired him was a startling idea to anyone with a Marxist outlook, and she marveled at the ingenuity of those peasants who had thought it up. She grossly underestimated their inventiveness, however, for on the very next day they found exploitation in an even more unlikely place—in the relation between a widow and her lover.

There lived in the village a lean old peasant named Wang who had long been in love with, or at least was wont to make love to, a rich peasant's widow named Yu Pu-ho. What little of value he possessed or produced, Wang sooner or later brought to his prosperous and beloved mistress. While his own son and daughter-in-law hired out in order to eat, he skimmed everything edible from his homestead and sacrificed it on the altar of love. If his hen laid an egg, he offered it up. If the eggplant in his dooryard garden produced a firm purple fruit, he brought it around. He even neglected his own land to work long hours on that of the passionate widow.

When Wang's paramour came before the Provisional League, the spokesman for one group of women took the floor at once. "We think she is a double landlord. She exploits hired labor and she exploits her lover. She exploits everything he has, even the eggs from his hens."

At this everyone laughed except the prim black-clad widow herself and Old Wang. The latter, expecting the worst, looked anxiously around the room for some sign of disagreement.

Wang need not have been so concerned. The men did not agree with the women.

"If he's exploited, that's his lookout," shouted a well-groomed youngster from the warmest spot on the *k'ang*. "He wants it that way. What can we do about it?"

The "double landlord" classification was withdrawn.

Some peasants found still a third form of exploitation in the behavior of certain scoundrels or lumpen elements. Just as every Western city has its declassed people, its professional beggars, its small-time racketeers, and skid row derelicts, so every Chinese village once had its *yu min* or rascals, men and women without legitimate means of support, gamblers, "broken shoes" (prostitutes), narcotics peddlers, and drifters. In political tracts and mobilization speeches they rated only occasional mention, but in real life they were very much a part of every village scene.

In Long Bow the most notorious of these *yu min* was Wang T'ao-yuan. Of him people said, *"Hsiang yen pu li k'ou, shou tien pu li shou."* (The cigarette never leaves his lips, the flashlight never leaves his hand.) He had survived the lean years of the occupation on profits from heroin peddling, on brokerage fees earned selling other people's wives, and on the proceeds of the sale of his own wife, a record unsavory enough to have made him an object of universal scorn and hate.

Wang had reformed somewhat after receiving land in the distribution but he still shrank from hard work. Only a few weeks before he appeared to be classified he sent his nephew on a coal-hauling expedition instead of going himself. The temperature that week hovered around zero. The nephew did not know how to care for an animal in such a frost. As a result, the one donkey owned by the family caught a chill, fell ill, and died.

In spite of all this, the peasants were curiously lenient with Wang T'ao-yuan. His broad comic face and genial disposition seemed to charm them. If nothing else he had always been a good companion. Because he knew how to laugh at himself and to make others laugh too, people found it difficult to stay angry at him for long.

But Cadre Liang, who passionately hated dope and purveyors of dope, was not willing to see T'ao-yuan get off so easily. Ignoring the economic criteria for judging the man's class, he slashed at the criminal nature of his past.

"Perhaps there are some who want to save face for T'ao-yuan," suggested Liang. "They had better think it over. Who led the entire family in smoking poison? If Long Bow had not been liberated they would all have died of starvation. And why did he sell the stuff? Why, in this whole village did no one else sell heroin but he? Let's ask why many an honest laborer among you has not yet *fanshened*. Then compare your condition with his. In the past, there were those who stood higher than the poor peasants. Now, after liberation they still have the upper hand. Why are such people always able to take advantage of every situation? Why? T'ao-yuan should be forced to explain his past."

Responding with alacrity to Liang's suggestion, T'ao-yuan said, "I began smoking heroin in the famine year and everything I had went to pay for it." There was a suggestion of languid sensuality in his stance and a puckish grin came and went on his face as he revealed his amoral past. "When I had nothing left I took my wife to Taiyuan. We were half dead from hunger before I finally found a buyer for her. He gave me six bags of millet. That sealed the deal."

Even to T'ao-yuan this sounded a little brutal so he added a twist to the tale that put the blame where it obviously belonged—on his wife.

"While I was out looking for work I had to leave my wife alone at the inn. She took up with another man. The master of the inn tipped me off and suggested that I get rid of her. He also found the buyer.

"I helped Wang Hsi-nan sell his wife too," continued T'ao-yuan, but once again he cleverly absolved himself. "Hsi-nan suggested it and even sought me out; he came over and over again. His wife was 'white, bright, and lovely,' but she was an idiot. She couldn't cook or sew. She couldn't even wipe her own behind. He got stuck with her and he wanted to get rid of her. He wouldn't stop pestering me so finally I undertook to sell her. I got nothing for my pains. Even after she was delivered I didn't have enough left over to buy heroin. I was in terrible shape. But Hsi-nan played square. He at least found me some heroin.

"I know it is a bad thing to sell heroin. I exploited others. I preyed on the addicts. But now I have *fanshened*. I received land and property but I do not deserve any such thing. I know my *fanshen* was due to my poor brothers and I must thank them. I wish you would criticize me more."

"How do you feel about the death of your donkey?" asked a neighbor.

"I borrowed BRC 200,000* to buy the little bastard. Now it is dead. You can imagine yourself how I feel," said Wang, and he began to weep right there in front of the whole group.

"How do you feel about selling your wife?" asked several women.

Wang T'ao-yuan made no answer. He only wept more despondently.

"Well, you sold her, and now you weep about it!"

"No," said Wang. "I am not weeping for my bartered wife. I am weeping for my dead donkey."

To punish him they classed him as a middle peasant, but even this did not satisfy the women. "He ought to be classed as a landlord's running dog," said several. But they said it in a whisper because the men, on the whole, sympathized with Wang.

****

Disagreements over the class status of various Long Bow residents pointed up the need for accurate standards of comparison. In preparatory conferences the work team cadres had studied such standards. Now, as the problems of differentiation grew more and more complicated, they introduced them to the peasants of the Provisional League.

The standards they introduced were roughly the same as those adopted by the Communist Party of China in 1933 when the first "Land to the Tiller" policy was carried out in the old revolutionary base at Juichin, Kiangsi.** Most of the poor peasants, after two years of campaigning, understood the standards fairly well, but as they applied them the deficiencies of the relatively simple concepts of 1933 became more and more apparent.

The Juichin standards, it turned out, were strong in defining the center of gravity of each rural class, that pole which determined the special nature of its typical members and their special relationship

---

* BRC (Border Region Currency): 1000 BRC = U.S. $1.00

** These standards are given in full in the basic definitions of Appendix C.

to the means of production. The standards were weak, however, in defining exact boundary lines between the classes. They lacked the precision necessary to distinguish between the many borderline, atypical cases that showed up so frequently in real life.

By far the most important dividing line was that between the middle peasants and the rich peasants. The Draft Agrarian Law of 1947 had made this the great divide between friend and enemy, between the people and their oppressors, between revolution and counter-revolution. It was absolutely essential that this line be clear and unequivocal. Yet here the Juichin documents were most ambiguous. In describing middle peasants the document said, "Some of the middle peasants practice a *small* amount of exploitation, but such exploitation is not of a *constant* character and the income therefrom does not constitute their *main* means of livelihood."

Anyone using these standards would have to know exactly what *small, constant,* and *main* meant in order to carry out the intent of the law.

In regard to the difference between poor peasants and middle peasants the same kind of difficulty arose. On this dividing line the Juichin document stated, "In general middle peasants need not sell their labor power but poor peasants have to sell their labor power for limited periods." Another sentence indicated that even middle peasants sometimes did sell their labor power. In order to make a precise determination, one would have to know what was meant by *in general* and *limited periods*.

As classification progressed, both the cadres and the peasants in Long Bow keenly felt the need for something more precise. This need was met, in part at least, by a set of supplementary regulations issued by the Central Committee in the fall of 1947. On the dividing line between middle and rich peasants these regulations stated that an income received from exploitation that was less than 15 percent of the gross was *small* and hence permissible for a middle peasant. Anything over that was considered *large* and enough to put the family over the line into the rich peasant category.

On the dividing line between middle and poor peasants, the regulations made clear that the labor power sold by middle peasants was mainly surplus labor power or the labor power of the children and old folks. Any family that consistently sold the labor power of its able-bodied adult members must ordinarily be classed as poor.

Another keenly felt need was for some definite base period. Was one to consider the present status of the family, the status several years back, or the status in the light of several generations? When left to themselves, the peasants of Long Bow tended to go back two and even three generations. This was in accord with habits deeply ingrained in the Chinese people, habits which had much precedent in the culture of the past. Under the old imperial examination system, for example, candidates had to prove not only that they themselves were not representatives of some barred category (boatman, actor, prostitute, or other "wandering" type) but also that their parents and grandparents were free of any such taint. Settlers in Shantung whose parents or grandparents had migrated from Hopei still regarded themselves as Hopei people.

This concept of hereditary social status helped to explain the wide support given to the campaign against "feudal tails" which had so sharpened the struggle and broadened the revolutionary target in 1946. Yet such a concept could hardly be said to conform to conditions of modern life. The disintegration of traditional Chinese society under the impact of foreign conquest, commercial dumping, dynastic decline, civil war and famine had introduced such a mobility into social relations (most of it downward) that it was no longer realistic to think of tracing back even five years, not to mention a few generations.

In view of these facts, the Central Committee of the Chinese Communist Party added to the supplementary regulations a section which strictly defined the base period to be used in making a determination of class status. In areas liberated after 1945 it was to be the three years prior to the liberation of the village. For the Fifth District of Lucheng County this meant the years 1943-1945. Each family was to be judged according to its economic position during those three years alone. The fact that a family had once been very wealthy, rented out land, or hired many laborers, made no difference to its class status if, during the three years of the base period, its able-bodied members earned their own living or a major portion of it by their own labor. Likewise, the fact that a man had once been a poor peasant made no difference at all if, during the base period, he had collected rents, hired laborers, or loaned out money at usurious interest rates.

By the same token, inherited wealth possessed by families who labored for a living during the base period could not be touched. It mattered not in the least what the source of any family's wealth might be. If the able-bodied members of that family earned their living by the sweat of their brow during the three years prior to the liberation of their village, they themselves were not rich peasants or landlords and could not legally be attacked or deprived of any property.

In brief, the reforms called for in the Draft Agrarian Law were to be based on class status, not class origin, on current means of livelihood, not on past privilege or past penury.

31

The Revolutionary Heat

I began as a student and acquired at school the habits of a student; in the presence of a crowd of students who could neither fetch nor carry for themselves, I used to feel it undignified to do any manual labor, such as shouldering my own luggage. At that time it seemed to me that the intellectuals were the only clean persons in the world, and the workers and peasants seemed rather dirty beside them. I could put on the clothes of other intellectuals because I thought they were clean, but I would not put on clothes belonging to a worker or peasant because I felt they were dirty. Having become a revolutionary I found myself in the same ranks as the workers, peasants, and soldiers of the revolutionary army, and gradually I became familiar with them and they with me too. It was then and only then that a fundamental change occurred in the bourgeois and petty-bourgeois feelings implanted in me by the bourgeois schools. I came to feel that it was those unremolded intellectuals who were unclean as compared to the workers and peasants, while the workers and peasants are after all the cleanest persons—even though their hands are soiled and their feet are smeared with cow dung. This is what is meant by having one's feelings transformed, changed from those of one class to those of another.

Mao Tse-tung

THE CLASSIFICATION meetings continued for days. Hour after hour we sat in the ice-cold adobe dwellings of the poor and listened as discussion followed report and report followed discussion. We were glad when the press of people was such that padded limbs and torsos leaned against us from all sides. In such close quarters the heat generated by each participant helped to keep his neighbor warm. When the crush was great enough, body heat even took the chill off the air in the room. Unknown to me this close contact made inevitable a form of heat that continued to warm all participants long after the meeting was over.

One cold night as Ch'i Yun and I walked homeward across the flat toward Kao Settlement, I began to notice an uncomfortable burning sensation on the skin of my shoulders and up both sides of my neck. This soon spread to the small of my back and to those areas of my stomach where a worn leather belt held my padded trousers tight against my flesh.

As soon as I got home I took off my jacket, turned it inside out, held it close to the burning wick of the single, bean-oil lamp allotted to me, and took a close look. The lining was alive with flat, crawling mites, some of them transparently white, others already dark with engorged blood. Lice!

So that was it. The ubiquitous vermin had found me already!

Having examined my jacket, I took off my pants. They were as alive with lice as the jacket.

My padded outfit could not be washed, nor could I in good conscience ask for another. There was only one thing to do—pick off the lice, crush them, and start over. I knew well enough how lice were hunted. How many times had I watched peasants sitting in the warm sun with their jackets over their knees pursuing the slow-crawling vermin, catching them between their thumb-nails and squeezing them until they burst? But that night, holding my jacket close to the flame, I could not bring myself to begin. I pictured to myself how the lice would snap and crumble, how the blood would spurt. I had no stomach for it. Finally I laid the jacket on the floor, found a pair of chopsticks, and picked the lice out of the lining as if I were picking delicacies off a banquet table. One by one I dropped them on a smooth brick and crushed them with a stone. By this aseptic but laborious method I gradually cut down the voracious army in my garments.

While I was in the midst of the hunt one of my English students came to the door. Shamefaced, I dropped the chopsticks and threw the jacket over a chair. It was too late. The student had seen what I was up to and began to laugh. Through him word soon spread to the whole University and into the village beyond that Old Han, the American, was catching lice with chopsticks and crushing them with bricks and stones.

Such was my baptism of fire, such my introduction to the notorious "revolutionary heat" that several generations of Chinese students and intellectuals had learned to bear without complaint because they felt that their country needed them among the people.

When the time came to search my clothes the second time I found that I was far less squeamish than at first. Soon I was hunting lice like a veteran and exhibiting the bloodstains on my thumbnails to anyone rash enough to tease me about chopsticks and bricks.

Just as I became accustomed to the lice I also became accustomed to other aspects of village life that had at first upset me: shaves from an itinerant barber whose hot but far from sterile towel made no

distinction between eyes half closed with trachoma and eyes as yet
unharmed; once-a-month baths in the public bathhouse at Changchih
where the flotsam washed from countless earlier patrons floated in
an oily film on the steaming pools, where men relieved their bladders
in one corner of the room and spat wherever they found it convenient; meals taken in the hovels of the poor where one shared
chopsticks with people suffering from incurable disease and swallowed down, day after day, the dreary boiled corn dumplings called
ke ta; daily encounters with privies in which night soil accumulated
the year round and gave off such fumes of ammonia that tears started
in one's eyes and the stomach churned.

Eating out was the real test. When we first arrived in the village
the attack on Little Ch'uer had caused a general retreat. Team Leader
Hou, fearing for our safety, had asked us to take our meals with
the rest of the cadres in the District Office. But as the days went by,
tension abated. After a couple of weeks Hou decided that we could
eat out as the rest of the team members had already begun to do.
Each day we took millet tickets issued to us by the University and
gave them to a poor peasant's wife in return for our noon meal. In
this way we gradually became acquainted not only with the most
active poor peasants in the village, but with their homes, their wives,
their children, and their less active relatives as well.

Some of these homes were as spotlessly clean as a dirt-floored,
earthen-walled, paper-windowed North China hut could be made. The
floors were swept, the *k'angs* dusted, the bright-colored quilts neatly
folded back against the wall of the sleeping quarters, and the round-
bottomed cooking pot, the bowls, and the chopsticks scoured until
they shone.

In other homes we found the opposite condition. The dwelling of
Tseng Chung-hsi, former puppet policeman and a peasant who had
lost both house and land in the Anti-Traitor Movement, may serve
as an example. Tseng was the informer who had betrayed So-tzu,
Lai-pao, and Fu-yuan to the puppet captain in the Long Bow fort
and so was blamed by the entire village for the deaths of the two
resistance heroes. That he was still alive seemed incongruous,
especially when one recalled the violence of the post-liberation reaction against puppets and collaborators. However, we found him not
only alive but in possession of land and housing handed out to make
up for that which he had lost. That the new equalled the old was
doubtful. Tseng's whole family lived in a cramped shed that was
divided into two equal parts. On one side were housed the farming
implements and carpenter's tools that enabled him to make a living.
Several chickens roosted on these implements and spread their drop-

pings at random on the floor. On the other side six people ate and slept—Tseng, his wife, two daughters (aged one and 13), and two sons (aged three and seven). The room was a shambles, smoke-blackened and cluttered with scraps, wheat roots, broken tools, crocks, and rags. On the narrow *k'ang* that filled the south end of the living space lay the eldest daughter. She lay under a grime-covered quilt; through its holes portions of her emaciated limbs protruded. She coughed, spat blood, and coughed interminably. For a year she had been immobilized there, near death from turberculosis. The rest of the family slept beside her, shared food and utensils with her, and breathed the same air she breathed in that stagnant, smoke-filled hell.

The odor of decay all but overpowered us as we came through the door. In addition to the strong aroma of baby urine that rose from the floor, the pungent scent of chicken dung wafting in from the adjacent room, and the swirling smoke from the wheat-root fire, the air was saturated with the rotten smell of the girl's lacerated lungs. Tseng's 30-year-old wife, thin, careworn, her face already wrinkled like that of a woman twice her age, served us lukewarm corn dumplings in bowls caked with the dried leavings of many a previous meal. For lack of any other resting place, we sat on the *k'ang* beside the dying girl and ate.

I knew that the bowls, the chopsticks, the very air that we were breathing was infected with tuberculousis, but I had to carry on as if nothing were amiss. This was a test of stamina such as every land reform worker went through. Unless one were willing to share the trials of other people, one did not deserve their trust. I thought to myself, "If Ch'i Yun can take this, I can too." One glance in her direction indicated that she was completely oblivious to her surroundings. She was eating her dumpling as if it were a sugar bun, and talking to Tseng's wife. She soon learned the woman's maiden name, where she came from, how much Tseng had paid for her, whether she had ever been to a village meeting, and what she thought of the Women's Association.

Ch'i Yun was magnificent. She was doing her job. The least I could do was to eat the corn in front of me.

Eating out brought us into touch with people in a way that a thousand meetings never could, and soon we became fast friends with a score of peasants who looked forward to our coming and vied with each other in issuing invitations.

Prominent among these was the old woman whom we had noticed winding cotton so intently as Little Li read the Announcement to the Peasants in Chief-of-Staff Hsu's loft. At every subsequent meeting she sought us out, filled us in on the background of the people who appeared before the Provisional League for classification, and related to us all the latest gossip from the southwest sector of the village. At the same time she took an active part in the meetings herself. Ch'i-Yun decided that this woman was a genuine "active element" who could play an important role in the events to come and asked the District Office to arrange a meal in her home.

This old lady's married named was Wang. She was known to most of the villagers as Old Lady Wang, but because her husband was very old and no longer able to work, some ignored him altogether and called her Jen-pao's mother, as if she were already a widow. Jen-pao was the 18-year-old son whom she was sending through high school at the county seat on the proceeds of her spinning and weaving.

When we showed up for our first meal, Old Lady Wang never stopped working and never stopped talking.

"Every day that I work," she said, "I can earn ten catties of millet. Why should I waste time at all these meetings? Well, I want to know more and I think all poor peasants must *fanshen*. One can't just worry about oneself any more. If we don't unite none of us is safe."

That she wasted time at meetings was something of an exaggeration. We knew that she never came to a meeting without some work in hand and spent her time furiously reeling, stitching, or spinning. But we did not challenge her statement. No doubt at home she accomplished twice as much.

She proudly showed us her loom which she was threading in preparation for a new bolt of homespun cloth and boasted of all the skills she possessed such as spinning, weaving, fluffing cotton with a taut-stringed bow, and making shoes. She was one of the few women in the village who still knew how to weave at a time when that ancient art had suffered almost total extinction due to the cheap imported and coastal manufactured textiles.

The old lady told us how she had come from Shantung Province more than 20 years before, after her first husband had died. She, her mother, her brother, and her daughter ran out of money on the road. They tried to sell the little girl for enough cash to continue. A buyer was found, but when the time came to leave the child behind, both the grandmother and the child cried so bitterly that the man thought better of the deal. He returned the child and gave the family enough wheat flour to last them a few more days. But tragedy trod the heels of luck. Even before the wheat had been consumed, the little girl fell ill and died.

The surviving wanderers from Shantung finally arrived in the mountains of Shansi as outright beggars. A distant relative arranged for Old Lady Wang to marry the laborer, Wang-shen, a man 20 years her senior. It was either marry or starve to death, so the handsome young widow consented. The match was ill-starred from the beginning. She was so badly treated by Wang's brother that her own mother and brother walked out one day in protest and were never heard from again.

"I did not hate him," Old Lady Wang said of the brother, who had long since died. "It was the old society that made him cruel. In the old society everyone oppressed others.

"During the famine year I peddled beancake. My pants wore so thin that people could see my *p'i ku* (buttocks) through the holes and made fun of me," she said. "Now things are much better. We got an acre and a half at the time of the distribution and 30 bushels of corn and millet. We also bought half a donkey, and I got an old felt mat for the *k'ang* for five ounces of grain. The cadres didn't want me to have it, but I got it anyway."

In spite of her improved condition, Old Lady Wang thought that she had not really *fanshened*. With only two sections of house, how could she take in a daughter-in-law when her son married in the fall? There would be no place for the girl and the land would hardly yield enough to support them. And what would happen when she had grandchildren? "The only other thing that worries me is the fate of my mother and brother," she said, wiping away involuntary tears. "They left so long ago! I often weep when I think of them."

But the tears soon dried on her cheeks as she got out her bow and began to prepare some raw cotton for the lining of a padded suit.

****

Old Lady Wang's home, though small, was often used for meetings. It was centrally located. It contained no small children underfoot who might disrupt the proceedings, and it was always neat and clean.

It was in this house that the poor peasant Chang Lao-pao clashed with his estranged wife over his class status and exposed another of those domestic tragedies left over from the old society, tragedies that corroded the very roots of Long Bow's social life and made a mockery of the vaunted Chinese family system so celebrated in the West.

One might suppose that the relations between a man and his wife should have very little to do with his class status, but in this case the relationship became central because the per capita holdings of Chang's family varied greatly depending on whether one included his wife and daughter or not.

On March 20th, Lao-pao came before the Provisional League to make his "self report." He was a tall man with a leathery face and deeply wrinkled skin. It was hard to judge how old he was because the wrinkles made him look 50, whereas the vigor of his movements and the fullness of his muscles indicated that he might be still in his thirties.

Lao-pao said that in 1942 he owned three acres and supported four people. They got along well enough until the famine year. Then he took his family to Taiyuan. He brought them back in 1946. He had never owned livestock or farming implements. He said he was a poor peasant.

"But his wife always earned her own living," protested Old Lady Wang, well aware of what that meant in terms of sweat and pain. "Before 1942 she worked in another village as a servant. After that she hired out as a seasonal laborer and supported herself and her daughter. We can't count them in the family."

"Can you get along with your wife?" they asked Lao-pao. "If not, you are a middle peasant."

At this Lao-pao lost his temper.

"Call me any class you like. Call me a landlord if you want to."

"Let's call his wife and ask her," suggested Old Lady Wang.

"She's nothing but an old bitch," said Lao-pao. "Why should you ask her? You're here to class me. Why not do it according to my condition? If you don't believe what I say, do as you like."

He was just like a stone. Everyone agreed on that.

"The fact is, he can't get on with anyone but his mother. She's the root of the whole trouble," said several of his neighbors.

In spite of Lao-pao's objections, they called in his wife.

She turned out to be a thin browned woman, prematurely aged and clad in garments that were dirty, ragged, and many years old. They barely concealed two breasts which hung down like flaps of old leather over her stomach. Her hair tumbled in tangled knots before her face, some strands of it already grey. She talked rapidly, bitterly, but with spirit. She brought with her a wan little girl, about seven years old, but so small she might have been four. The youngster was also clad in rags. She stared silently at the crowd of peasants with her large black eyes and kept her mouth tightly shut.

"I have no opinion about his class myself," said Lao-pao's "old lady." "I've always been walked over by him and his mother. He's not such a bad man himself, but his temper is short. As for my mother-in-law, I can say nothing good for her. She never spoke rudely to my face, but only clawed me when my back was turned and ran me down to her son so that we quarrelled. As for me, I worked as a servant in Horse Square, Yellow Mill, and many other places. Though they never gave me any cloth, still I made clothes for him and supported myself with my own hands. All my neighbors know that. I only speak true words."

"What about your class? Do you want to be classed as one family or separately?"

"It's all the same to me," she said, shrugging her lean shoulders. "I have no opinion." A sharp edge of bitterness was clearly discernible in her voice.

When they asked Lao-pao, he said the same thing. "I have no opinion."

His wife disputed this. "He doesn't want me to return home. We separated the year before last. I was out working. When I got back they had already moved into a new house and locked the door. I wanted to pack up and move there but my big box was too heavy for me to lift, so I went to his mother to ask for help. She said, 'If you want you can move it yourself. Otherwise stay where you are. We have no place for your big box or you either.' I knew what she meant. But since the *k'ang* was so big, big enough for ten boxes of mine, I asked her why she said that. Two people can hardly use one end of that *k'ang*. This started a quarrel. The neighbors came then. They tried to get Lao-pao to carry my box over but he refused. Since then I have lived in the old place by myself. He doesn't speak to me when we meet in the street."

"Lao-pao is always in a squeeze," said one peasant. "He dares not say anything to offend his mother, nor can he make peace with his wife. He's just like a hand towel, always in the middle and both sides lay the blame on him. But really, he only cares for his mother and abuses and beats his wife."

"Don't waste your time on this case," said Lao-pao to the meeting in general. "I know I'm just the dirty towel."

"Don't force him into anything," countered his wife. "I can live on by myself."

A reprimand from Cadre Liang and a sympathtic suggestion from Ch'i Yun that Lao-pao at least try to reunite his family had no effect

"If I had such a good wife, I would kneel down before God," said an old bachelor. He was the same man who had tried to smooth the way for the blacksmith, Huan-ch'ao. "You, you don't know how painful is the life of a single man. You had better look at it from all sides. How will you get on after your mother's death? You'd better take this chance to get off the stage."

But Lao-pao only shrugged at this too. They finally classed him as a poor peasant anyway, but as one who had now *fanshened*. He strode off cursing.

His wife stayed on and, as the meeting broke up, talked to the group of women that formed sympathetically around her.

"You can do nothing to help my family," she said. "My neighbors have already tried many times. It is no use. It's better this way. I live by my own work and my life is better than before. Then it was one quarrel after another. Once I asked him to get some water from the well. But he was too lazy to go. Later he got out some beans and started building a fire. I said, 'You're too lazy to get any water. How do you think you will cook those beans?' He hit me so hard I fell to the floor but I pulled him down with me and only the neighbors finally separated us. If they hadn't, one of us would be dead. Another time he cut my left arm with a spade. Once we cut wheat in the field. His mother brought food and we quarrelled. When she left he cut me across the forehead with his sickle."

After listening to these stories the women all said it was better for Lao-pao's wife to live alone. Then she could bring up her daughter in peace. "If you return, you will only suffer oppression. Only after your mother-in-law dies can you be reconciled."

That there was another side to this story we heard only later. Some of the young women, less sympathetic to Lao-pao's wife, told Ch'i Yun that the sharp-tongued woman earned money in other ways than labor, that she had conceived a child by another man, and that she had killed it with a needle after it was born. If this was true, the tragedy was only compounded.

32

Brothers

And the Lord said unto Cain, "Where is Abel thy brother?"
And he said, "I know not: am I my brother's keeper?"

Genesis

To THRESH the wheat from the chaff, to separate the kernel of truth from the husk of falsehood sometimes taxed the collective wisdom of the whole Provisional League. This was particularly so when families prosperous enough to hire labor came up for review. From below came tremendous pressure to push them over the line into the rich peasant category. From the more prosperous came intense counter-pressure. The cadres of the work team, whose role it was to guard the objectivity of the proceedings and to see to it that the law was followed both in letter and spirit, were pushed now one way, now another. More often than was wise they allowed their weight to fall on the side of extremism among the poor.

This was exactly what happened in the case of Li Pao-yu, a man who owned six acres of land, five sections of housing, and a court-yard with 27 fruit trees. On these better than average holdings lived a family of four: Li, his wife, an adopted son, and a daughter-in-law. On the surface there seemed nothing out of the ordinary about the family, but once the work team cadres began to probe more deeply, all manner of curious facts came to light. Li Pao-yu, some said, was not a peasant at all, but a merchant who had made enough buying and selling in distant parts to purchase land in Long Bow. So unac-customed was he to hard work on the land that six acres were more than he could handle, even with the help of a teen-aged son. He hired as much as 50 days' seasonal labor each year to plant and gather his crops. While the hired laborers sweated in the fields, Li and his wife ran a gambling table in their home. Sometimes they joined the game; sometimes they simply acted as bankers or croupiers. And this was not all. Another rumor had it that Li's wife had been mistress to the landlord Sheng Ching-ho. It was the many gifts which the latter bestowed upon his favorite, not peddling profits, that made

297

it possible for the Li family to purchase land. Evidently, all of land-lord Sheng's gifts had not bought the loyalty of his mistress. It was well known that she had carried on an affair with the lusty peasant Hsiao-tseng for years. Everyone remembered with amusement how she had ended up hanging by her wrists from the gable of the village office when Pao-yu complained to the puppet authorities.

Li himself came before the Provisional League clad in garments faded and frayed from much washing. He said he thought he was a middle peasant. He might have convinced the majority of this, but someone asked him about his brother. Was it not true that his brother had lived with him and worked for two years as an unpaid hand on his land and that his brother's wife had done all the work in their home?

Li did not deny that his brother, Li Lao-szu, had lived with him, but his view of the relationship between him and Lao-szu was just the opposite of that suggested by his questioner.

"I saved Lao-szu from starvation," he said. "I gave him and his whole family a home when they had no place to go. Many times I suggested that they leave, but they were dependent upon me and were afraid to move out. Of course," he added with an embarrassed laugh, "It was nothing. Who wouldn't help a brother?"

Lao-szu, when called, had a very different story to relate. His long sorrowful face well suited the tale he had to tell. "When I came from Linhsien with my family, I gave my brother everything I had. I even gave him one of my sons, for he had none of his own. But he treated us like slaves. We worked day and night in the fields and in his house but we got nothing, absolutely nothing for it. When I tried to leave, Pao-yu swore at me. Told me I was ungrateful. I finally ran away without telling him. I reclaimed some land on the Western Mountain and came back for my family afterwards."

After hearing this side of the story some of the poor peasants called Pao-yu a rich peasant; others said he was certainly a landlord. Pao-yu went home pale and shaking with fear. He was afraid to tell his wife what had happened. When she nagged him he lost his temper. "It's your fault," he shouted. "You couldn't even treat my own brother decently and now look at the mess you've landed us in!"

"What mess?"

"They're calling us landlords," he screamed. "That's the mess."

But Pao-yu's wife did not panic. She remembered that Lao-szu had left their home the year after their adopted son was married. The base period had not even begun at the time. Lao-szu's labor, whether exploited or not, could hardly count.

The next day Pao-yu appeared before the Provisional League

again. Confident and cocky he announced the discrepancy in dates. But the announcement did not have the effect foreseen. Most of the peasants were ready to accept his argument, but Little Li, the work team cadre, suddenly arose and passionately denounced him as an exploiter so mean that he lived off his own brother's labor and then tried to wriggle out of it on a technicality.

"Not only did they labor for you, they even gave you a son! Where is your conscience? Are you so afraid of your wife that you forget the feelings of a brother?" Little Li trembled as he spoke.

"Why did you give your brother a whole acre after liberation? Was that not a crumb to stop his mouth? If I were you I would weep for shame!"

Li's appeal put Pao-yu in a worse position than before. Clutching at any straw that might relieve the pressure, Pao-yu pleaded with them concerning his fruit trees.

"They're really worthless," he said. "Last year I got only BRC 10,000 from the lot."

"Perhaps we had better ask the man who planted them about that," said Shen Ch'uan-te, the Catholic.

This was no problem. Old Hou, the man who had sold the court-yard to Pao-yu, was sitting with the group. "When you shake those trees the money falls down," he said. "What fine trees they are! I planted them myself, but I had nothing to live on. When my son died of starvation, I sold the court to Pao-yu."

"What can I say if no one believes me?" Pao-yu protested, more to the walls than to his audience. Tears were already starting in his eyes.

The next day Ch'i Yun and I ate in Pao-yu's home. The courtyard did not look very prosperous. The ex-merchant and his notorious wife lived in a low adobe shed built along the north wall. The west wall had crumbled in the middle and a neighbor's pig had scaled it. The pig was rooting among the controversial trees. They were thorn dates. Some of them were already dead. Others carried as many dead branches as live ones. It seemed to me that if anyone shook them, dry twigs instead of money would fall down.

In order to impress us with her poverty, Pao-yu's wife fed us the leanest corn dumplings we had ever eaten. Her son, the boy given her by Lao-szu, looked as if he had never had anything else to eat. He was stunted, almost dwarfed, with a head that seemed to sit on his chest. At 12 he had been married to a girl of 20 so that Pao-yu's wife might have a servant to replace the sister-in-law who had run away. Early marriage had certainly done him no good.

The lady of the house was dressed in the plainest of tunics. Her black hair was drawn straight back from her forehead and tied in a severe knot behind. Wrinkles showed around her eyes and mouth. It was hard to imagine that she had once been a successful courtesan. With tears in her eyes she told us of the sacrifices she had made to keep her brother-in-law happy, to give him the best of everything.

"Now I can't think it through. In my family there are only two. This child is theirs. After we die who will inherit the property? We save and work, not for our own sakes, but for the son of another. But he says we have ill-treated him! It is so painful."

That afternoon Pao-yu came once more before the meeting. Cadre Li, having thought better of his outburst of the day before, apologized for having intervened. He read from the book that passage which told how to differentiate a well-to-do middle peasant from a rich peasant. The main point was not the existence of exploitation but the extent of it. In the gross income of a rich peasant, at least 15 percent had to come from rent, interest, or profit on hired labor. On that basis, Pao-yu was clearly no rich peasant.

"Yesterday," said Old Lady Wang, "you got angry and interrupted us. Then we got angry and called you a landlord. But really you are not."

"I was so frightened," said Pao-yu. "How could I suddenly have become a landlord? When I went home I dared not tell my wife. I did not sleep all night. Even well-to-do middle peasant seemed too high. But now I think that is right. Everyone else seems to think so. What can I do? I have thought it through."

Since his words carried no ring of conviction, Cadre Li tried to reassure him. "We don't mind spending time. If you still disagree you can wait until after the mass meeting. Even after that you can appeal to the higher authorities."

But Li had apparently decided that he could not do better.

"I'm a well-to-do middle peasant," he said.

As the meeting broke up someone whispered, "His wife ought to be called to the meeting. Maybe she could learn something."

"She! Never!" came the whispered reply.

* * * * * * * * * * *

Between classification meetings Ch'i Yun and I often went out to visit individual peasants, especially those whom Ch'i Yun thought should be admitted to the Provisional League.

One day we were talking to Old Kao, a demobilized army veteran who lived in the foreign-style house expropriated from Chief-of-Staff Hsu. Suddenly, Li Hsin-ai, the girl who had eloped with her cousin from central Hopei, burst into the room.

"Oh!" she said when she saw Ch'i Yun and myself. "I thought Comrade Liang was here."

"Why Comrade Liang?"

"I need help. My chimney just fell down. All my pots and bowls are smashed to powder. The roof is ready to follow the chimney down. What will happen to my child? When I asked the carpenters to repair it for me they said, 'Where will you get all that money? It will take several days' work.' With my husband off in the army I have to do everything myself. This morning I went out to find fuel; then I had to carry water. Now I have left my baby on the *k'ang*, but I am afraid. The mutual aid group gives me some help, but I have to do so many things by myself and the baby takes so much time that I can only spin an ounce a day in exchange for the help."

Here she broke down weeping, but wiped away her tears and went on between sobs, "I don't want to move. I have many friends in my courtyard, but I don't know what to do."

She was a very beautiful girl, not the delicate willow-wand type, but full-bodied, almost voluptuous, especially with her breasts distended and ready to nurse. Concealment of the upper body was not a part of modesty in Long Bow, and the girl stood before us now with her tunic unfastened so that both her breasts and her soft stomach were exposed to view.

Kao, overcome by her presence, gallantly offered her the pick of the rooms in his "foreign house."

"You can have this section. I'll move on down a few doors if you like."

When the young mother hestitated, Ch'i Yun told her not to worry. Something would surely be done to resettle her. After all, her man was in the army. Li Hsin-ai left us smiling. Only two streaks of dirt down her cheeks indicated that she had been weeping desolately a few moments before.

When we took leave of Kao we decided to have a look at the house where the chimney had fallen down. Ch'i Yun wanted to get better acquainted with its occupant, the unusual young woman who had defied convention and threats of death to marry the man she loved. In Long Bow men made fun of Li Hsin-ai. The middle peasant Chin-hung, a former puppet soldier himself, was fond of telling the story of her "rascal affair" to anyone who would listen. Then he laughed as if it would kill him. Young women took a different attitude. None of them said it aloud, but in their hearts they admired and even envied the girl for her courage. The older women, on the other hand, tended to side with the men. It was their veto that blocked Li Hsin-ai from membership in the Provisional Poor Peasants' League.

We found Li sitting on her *k'ang* nursing her handsome baby. One whole corner of the adobe building had collapsed to form a heap of rubble at her feet. As she had already made up her mind to move, the house no longer weighed on her mind. What she wanted to talk about was Chin-hung and his ridicule.

"He should not laugh at me like that," she said, pouting. "My parents would not agree to our marriage so we had to run away. But as for the child, it is my husband's. Chin-hung laughs as if his pot were clean, but everyone knows about his doings. He ought to speak out in the village meeting if he has so many opinions. Let's hear what the others have to say. Just because my husband is away in the army he oppresses me." With that she broke down and began to weep again.

Ch'i-Yun asked about her husband and his life in the army. Immediately she brightened up once more. She had recently been invited to stay at the army camp where her husband was stationed. She had lived with him there nine days. "The life of the soldiers is very good," she said. "They live much better than we do here in the village. They eat noodles and meat. Now he has gone across the Yellow River and I don't know where he is. I want to make a pair of shoes for him but I don't know where to send them. When the reactionaries are beaten down, then he will return and we can lead a peaceful life together."

Remembering the bargain which Fu-yuan, the former village head, had struck with her husband when the latter's Hopei relatives came to take him away, we asked her if he really wanted to join the army and if she herself really wanted him to go.

She said, "Sure I wanted him to go. If no one went, how could the reactionaries be defeated?"

But later she complained that the cadres gave him no choice. He left her with nothing to live on, no house, no tools, nothing. The cadres promised to help her with everything so she did not object, but her husband worried about her and their child. How could he help it?

Thus she vacillated between pride in her soldier husband and pity for herself, a mother still in her teens, left behind in a community that mocked her, in a home where she had no family or childhood friends.

33

A Curved Road

The purity of the leadership of the peasants' associations at all levels should be safeguarded. The masses should be mobilized to re-elect the leadership where there is impurity. Here, the term 'purity' does not mean the adoption of a closed-door attitude toward such farm laborers, poor peasants or middle peasants who have committed certain errors. Nor does it mean their exclusion from the peasants' associations. On the contrary, they should be welcomed into the associations, educated and brought into unity. The term 'purity' here means to prevent landlords, rich peasants, and their agents from joining the peasants' associations and, still more important, from holding leading positions in the peasants' associations.

Liu Shao-ch'i

BY THE END of March all the families in the village had been classified. Many difficult cases had come up, and with each case a story—a traitor who had been expropriated even though he was bare poor; a nine-year-old orphan who held twice the average landholding in the village but had nothing else to his name, not even a bowl or a pair of chopsticks; a spendthrift who had sold all his land before the liberation to buy food, had squandered his share of the fruits since, and then contracted a debt that already amounted to three hundredweight of millet and several silver dollars; a cook who made so much money that he bought up land in the famine year and married a landlord's widow; a professional castrator of pigs who had so prospered on high fees that he was able to hire others to work his land; a Long Bow-born laborer who, returning home penniless after 30 years employment in another county, arrived after everything had been divided and received nothing; an old man who had given his share of the family land to a brother and then gone to live with and work for a neighboring widow. Now his brother wanted him to demand back wages from the widow and share the bonanza with him, but the old man refused to break with his benefactress.

An almost endless succession of tragedies, incidents full of pathos, greed, rollicking humor, cruelty, and kindness unfolded as the people reported their condition. But what the peasants were really looking for didn't turn up. There just did not seem to be any landlords or rich peasants left in the village and that meant that there would be very little to distribute when all was said and done. As the peasants themselves admitted, they could find no more "oil."

The only family still in possession of any surplus property which might make them rich peasants was that of the lusty old widow, Yu Pu-ho, mistress to poor peasant Wang and mother of the exquisite Pu-ch'ao. Because her status was still obscure, she was called before the Provisional League several times.

Everybody had to admit that the widow was clever. She had always carefully observed which way the wind was blowing and tacked accordingly. When the puppet troops held power in the county, she married her daughter off to a squad leader in the headquarters battalion. Although a poor peasant by birth, this soldier's rank was exalted enough to provide his relatives with some protection against looting and rape. The widow also persuaded her son to enlist. Later, when the puppet troops surrendered to the Eighth Route Army, she persuaded both men to volunteer for service with the revolutionary forces and brought her daughter home to Long Bow as "cadre bait." Thus she shifted course without getting hurt, won the right to aid as a soldier's dependent, and even received her share of the "fruits." So intimate did her daughter become with the village cadres that she bore one of them a son. No one knew who the father was, but he apparently had influence, for the fact remained that no attack was ever launched against the widow.

The publication of the Draft Agrarian Law and the arrival of the work team plunged Pu-ho into renewed danger. This time it looked as if she would not be able to find a way out. Nevertheless she was determined not to give up without a fight. When she appeared to answer questions she wore several layers of thickly padded clothing.

"Up to her old tricks again," confided Old Lady Wang to Ch'i Yun in a loud whisper. "When the struggle movement first began she put on all the padding she could find. She thought she wouldn't feel so much pain when we beat her. But she was never even attacked. Her daughter saw to that."

The widow reviewed her sources of income with a slight nervous stutter. She listed five people, eight acres, eight sections of house, a donkey, a cart, all necessary implements. She said that her husband had died long ago. Since then, because her son was young, she had employed hired labor. What she forgot to mention was the fact that while her husband lived he never worked, and after her sons grew up they never worked either. They had always employed hired hands while they themselves followed the "Five Don't Go Policy":

don't go to work if it rains, don't go if it is cold; don't go if the wind blows; don't go if the sun is hot; don't go if you are tired. After Liberation the widow held onto all her land but sold her donkey and her cart.

"How come you no longer have the cart and donkey?" she was asked.

"One day my son took a trip and sold them."

"But why?"

"How should I know? He sold them without asking me."

This seemed very unlikely. The peasants did not believe a word of it. They felt sure the donkey had been sold to avoid confiscation.

"In any case, she later bought another donkey," said one.

"Yes, when she thought she was safe."

"But this new donkey is old and torn," protested Wang, her lover, rushing to her defense.

At this all the women burst out laughing.

"How can a donkey be torn?" they asked.

This upset Old Wang very much.

"Of course a donkey can be torn," he said. "Why do you want to make out that the donkey is sound when he is really falling apart?"

His words fell on deaf ears. The peasants knew that Old Wang would defend his beloved to the end. They did not deign to argue the case. Instead they held a *ke ts'ao* and there decided that the widow was a rich peasant.

****

The discovery of one rich peasant still in possession of some wealth was small solace to the members of the Provisional League. In the course of their investigations they had unearthed a total of 174 families who had been poor peasants during the base period, only 72 of whom had as yet *fanshened*. This meant that there were over 100 families in the village who still faced great difficulty in making a living. The problem was not primarily a shortage of land, for there was enough land to give every man, woman, and child almost a full acre. The problem was the shortage of livestock, carts, implements, housing, and manpower. For even though most of the draft animals had already been shared among four or more families each, there were still dozens of households that did not even own one leg of a donkey, not to mention a spoke in the wheel of a cart. There were also large numbers of widows and old people who had no one to help them in the fields. How to make middle peasants of all these people was the problem that faced the Provisional Poor and Hired

Peasants' League. On the face of it, the problem seemed insoluble.

The work team had no more idea than the peasants of what to do about this discrepancy, but proposed, as a first step, that the Provisional League be enlarged to include all honest poor peasants. At the same time the work team launched an examination of the village accounts in order to determine where all the "fruits" had gone. This idea came from a newspaper story that described just such an "accounts examination" in another village. Perhaps in that way enough property could be unearthed to fill some of the gaping holes. In the absence of landlords and rich peasants this examination tended to focus attention on the cadres as possible "objects of struggle."

The enlargement of the Provisional League proved to be a slow process. The standards used for classing a family were, by their nature, objective. One had only to look at the per capita holdings and measure the proportion of the family income derived from exploitation to arrive at a decision. But the standards for deciding who should or should not be members of the League included the words "honest" and "hardworking." About such concepts there was plenty of room for argument.

Some of the women, and especially Old Lady Wang, were sticklers for moral purity.* They had vetoed Li Hsin-ai because she had eloped and they had vetoed Hsiao Lao-chang, a life-long laborer, because he lived with a widow as if she were his wife. Now in the interest of expanded membership the women finally decided to offer Hsiao a big concession. If he would only break with the widow, he could join the Provisional League. A message was sent to him to that effect.

Old Hsiao turned the tables on them. He was too honest to promise to do better, which was the attitude that many others took. He said instead, "Unless I can marry the woman, I'll never join the League. What's the use of your old League if it can't help me get what is good for me?"

For this alone they might not have rejected Hsiao, but he went on to attack all the rest of the membership.

"Everyone's face has a smudge on it," he said. "All pots are black; in and out of the League it makes no difference. Help me marry the widow and I'll join up with you."

"How can we possibly do that?" they asked one another.

---

* She was a remarried widow herself, but she was also a famine refugee, far from home and already separated from any in-laws who could object to remarriage. Under these circumstances she apparently saw no parallel between her position and that of others.

They took it for granted that Hsiao Lao-chang must remain a widower and his paramour, Tzu-ming, a widow. The fact that the lovers were fond of each other, faithful to each other, and wanted to marry had nothing to do with the case. By tradition a wife was supposed to remain loyal to her dead husband until her own demise. That this was impossible for most people made no difference. A widow who married brought disgrace on her husband's whole family and lost all claim to her children into the bargain. All children were considered to be the heirs of the male parent alone. On them devolved the duty of caring for ancestral tablets and maintaining the family line. Their mother was only a convenience, a chattel, a servant brought in to provide male heirs. If she chose to leave, she left alone and in disgrace. That is why, instead of second marriages, there were so many illicit liaisons between widows and bachelors in Long Bow.

Only if the male partner agreed to take the woman's married name did the situation change. Such a couple were allowed to marry because the alliance constituted no threat to the in-laws, gave the husband no right to the children, and posed no threat to the ancestral tablets. There were several such matches in Long Bow. One of them was the alliance entered into by Chin-chu, the irascible, oft-cuckolded shepherd whose difficulties with Militiaman Shen Yu-hsing have already been described.

But poor Chin-chu was long denied membership in the Provisional Poor Peasants' League even though legally wed. Men regarded the surrender of his family name as a crack in the solid front of male supremacy, a crack that threatened the status of all males. Women looked down on him for "dancing to his wife's tune." "If she says a few sweet words to him, he forgets his own birthday," they gossiped. They also disliked his wife. Rumor had it that she frequented market-day fairs in order to solicit business as a prostitute. And she not only slept with strangers for money, she regaled them with stories. Anything that happened in Long Bow would sooner or later be relayed by her to villages far and wide.

Men like Lao-pao, who mistreated their wives, men like T'ao-yuan, who had a reputation as rascals, all notorious former puppets and their relatives were also barred from the League. The only people about whom questions formerly had been raised but who were now admitted with alacrity were those dissident Catholics who had once been called agents. Most of them lived in the southwest corner. A few had been included in the League from the very beginning. They saw to it that the rest were invited.

As a result of exclusion for the above-mentioned reasons, almost

half of the poor peasants in the village were not invited to join the
Provisional Poor and Hired Peasants' League. A full month after
the work team arrived, nothing lasting could be said to have been
accomplished in this direction.

The meetings set up to examine the village accounts also bogged
down. Comrade Hsu, the intellectual from the University, undertook
to head up this work because he had a good head for figures. He
selected a committee of poor peasants to help him. Among them was
Shen Ch'uan-te, the talkative Catholic whom Ch'i Yun and I had
interviewed on our first day in Long Bow. Shen and the others
selected by Hsu were convinced that the village cadres had misappropriated vast quantities of "fruits," but all their efforts to gather
facts bogged down in confusion. They went at the problem like a
board of judges. They called one cadre after another and bombarded
each with questions. When the answers led to contradictions or indicated that someone else was responsible they threatened their witnesses with dire punishment, swore at them, and put them under
house arrest. Cheng-k'uan, former head of the Peasants' Association,
became so distraught by this treatment and by his inability to provide
the committee with satisfactory answers that he tried to commit
suicide by jumping in the well behind his house. Fortunately, he was
discovered before he took the plunge.

When it became clear that the local cadres could not answer all
questions concerning the *fanshen* accounts, the committee decided
to interrogate those who had already left for work in the district and
the county. Kuei-ts'ai, former revolutionary vice-head of the village,
came home to visit his wife and was detained. T'ien-ming, former
public security officer and founder of the Party Branch, returned to
Long Bow for a production meeting of the Fifth District and was
also detained. Fu-yuan, former village head, who was working on
a land reform team in another village, was ordered home by mail.
All were asked to stay in one courtyard until their interrogation
was completed.

But neither Kuei-ts'ai nor Fu-yuan nor T'ien-ming helped clear
up the accounts. Although they were able to answer many questions,
they would admit to no large amount of graft and gave reasonable
explanations for the disappearance of such valuables as the church
candlesticks. Old Shen took the lead in suggesting that they go to
the ex-landlords for information concerning the wealth that had been
taken from their homes. Comrade Hsu supported him but Team
Leader Hou recognized the move for what it was—an attempt to
convict revolutionary cadres with information solicited from their
class enemies. Hou called in both Hsu and Shen and sharply repri-

manded them. Such a move could only open wide the door to chaos. It would give the landlords a heaven-sent opportunity to split the peasants' ranks with false charges.

Old Shen was stunned by the criticism. He insisted that his only aim had been to get at the facts and that he had completely forgotten how the landlords had falsely fingered people in the past. But the more he denied it, the more the suspicion took root and grew that he was not entirely innocent in the affair. Crestfallen, he took a back seat on the committee.

With the impasse at the accounts examination, the work of the Long Bow team reached a stalemate on all fronts. The morale of the team members, including that of the intellectuals from the University, dropped sharply and so did that of the villagers.

Many people began to suspect, though no one said it openly, that there simply was no "oil," either in the form of surplus property remaining in the hands of the prosperous or in the form of misappropriated "fruits" in the hands of the leading cadres. Continued *fanshen* on any significant scale was therefore out of the question. Meetings were still held to enlarge the Provisional League and to survey cases of extreme hardship resulting from the depletion of grain stocks as spring approached, but they were poorly attended and indifferently conducted. Nobody seemed to know what was wrong or what to do.

The Party Secretary of the Third Administrative District of the Taihang Subregion arrived unexpectedly in the midst of this stalemate. I was favorably impressed by the man who wore that exalted title. Secretary Wang was obviously well educated, yet he had none of the arrogance so typical of many Chinese intellectuals and so amply demonstrated by Comrade Hsu. Nor did he put on any of the airs of the old-style Chinese bureaucrats. He projected instead the warm extroversion of a hard-working peasant. He wore a faded blue-grey cotton jacket, arrived in the village on foot, and departed on foot when his work was done. He made it easy for the team cadres to tell him their problems because he listened patiently and questioned calmly. As he listened his broad face took on a serious but never severe demeanor; he nodded often but did not interrupt. He smiled often, spoke slowly, and emphasized his meaning with expressive motions of his hands.

All morning and most of the afternoon he listened. In the evening he suggested what amounted to a completely new approach. He advised the team to drop the accounts examination meeting immediately. It was not going well, he said, because it was premature. The Poor and Hired Peasants' League had not been consolidated, there was no mass base,. no democratic platform from which to examine the past work of the cadres. To set up an accounts examination off in one corner could never bring good results. Only the active participation of the whole village could ever straighten out the record of the past. This could become possible only when the people became well organized and themselves took the work in hand as a major task. Nor were the accounts the heart of the problem; they were only one aspect of the old cadres' life and work. At the proper time the whole of the cadres' existence, their "style of work," their willingness to serve, their outlook, their honesty, everything—not just how many items of property they received—must be examined.

Secretary Wang also advised greatly intensified efforts to enlarge the Provisional League. He estimated that not more than 20 poor peasant families would be found unfit to join. All the rest should be in—former collaborators, cadres' relatives, immoral widows and all. He pointed out that it was the conditions of the past, the buy-and-sell marriages, the ban on divorce, the restriction against the remarriage of widows that made illicit sex relations common throughout rural China. To set high standards in this regard would not be realistic. Those peasants who continued to object to others on moral grounds should be convinced that the strength of the whole poor peasant community was needed to carry through reform and that in most cases the behavior that shocked them was not an individual matter but the inevitable result of the society in which they were all born.

"What must be stressed is class," said Secretary Wang. "The class origin of people and nothing else. Only on the basis of the growth of class consciousness can any of the problems be solved. This includes the religious problem. By uniting on a class basis the most diverse religious elements can be brought together."

This brought Secretary Wang to the question of the counter-revolutionary suspects, most of whom were Catholics. Here also he advised leniency. As long as the people involved were poor peasants they could be won over, he said. But they could never be won over if they were isolated and discriminated against; they had to be drawn into full participation politically, economically, and socially. In order to make a dramatic progress on this question he suggested that the work team send for Chin-ming, the young man who had fled in 1946 when charged with aiding Father Sun. If Chin-ming agreed to return home, he should be given a full complement of land, housing, and implements. This would dispel the fears that still lingered in the minds of so many other Catholics and would immensely strengthen the League.

Finally, Secretary Wang suggested that the dissolution of all the old organizations and the suspension of all the old cadres as if they were all bad, corrupt, or even class enemies, was a mistake. He felt certain that Long Bow Village would turn out to be, not a Type III but a Type II community, a place where much good work had been done and most of the cadres were basically sound politically. If this proved to be so then the work team was on the wrong track entirely. The whole course of its work would have to be re-examined.

Comrade Hou immediately carried into practice Secretary Wang's three main suggestions. Hsu's Accounts Examination Committee was dissolved. The cadres held under house arrest were released and allowed to return to work, but only after each had appeared before the Provisional League and promised to heed any call for future questioning. The new lenient standards for League membership were explained to the existing League groups and within a few days more than 100 families were admitted. The new members included Li Hsin-ai, the girl who had eloped; Lao-pao, the wife beater; and Wang T'ao-yuan, the former dope peddler. Even Kuo Fu-kuei, village head under the puppet regime and the most hated collaborator in Long Bow, was accepted. In addition one of Hou Chin-ming's cousins was dispatched on foot to Hungtung to explain the new situation to that involuntary exile.

It was obvious to everyone that a new wind was blowing.

As if to emphasize the change a whole platoon of students from Kao Settlement suddenly appeared the next day and replaced all the slogans on the village walls. The new slogans, which they painted in huge white characters, dealt more directly with land reform and mentioned the Civil War less. A random sampling translated for me by Ch'i Yun read:

"All Power to the Peasant Congress"
"The Communist Party Is the People's Hired Laborer"
"Level the Tops, Fill the Holes, Equalize Good Land and Bad"
"Criticize and Correct the Cadres' Mistakes"
"Elect Good Cadres, Remove Bad Ones"
"Protect and Develop Commerce and Industry"
"Establish a Democratic, Free, Peaceful and Prosperous New China"
"Graft and Corruption Is Forbidden. Seized Fruits Must be Returned"

On one wing of the village school the slogan writers painted a line of characters which said, "Raise Our Cultural Level, Strengthen Our Political Consciousness." On the other was blazoned, "Combine Teaching, Learning, and Labor."

34

Drama in the Fields

Since our art and literature are basically intended for the workers, peasants, and soldiers, popularization means extending art and literature among these people, while elevation means raising their level of artistic and literary appreciation. What should we popularize among them? The stuff that is needed and can readily be accepted by the feudal landlord class? Or that which is needed and can readily be accepted by the bourgeoisie? Or that which is needed and can readily be accepted by the petty-bourgeois intelligentsia? No, none of these will do. We must popularize what is needed and can readily be accepted by the workers, peasants, and soldiers themselves.

Mao Tse-tung

TOWARD THE END of March, Ch'i Yun and I received permission to move to the village to live. Thereafter, instead of staying at the University to teach and visiting Long Bow daily, we stayed in Long Bow and visited the University two or three times a week for classes.

The move to the village made us a more integral part of its life. By spending our leisure as well as our working hours there, we soon became much more widely acquainted and genuinely accepted than before. Although for our own safety we were not allowed to board out in peasant homes, the quarters assigned to us were in no way barred to the public. We each had a room in the old rectory behind the Church. Peasants came and went there as freely as they did in their own courtyards. Ch'i Yun soon became the trusted confidante of many poor peasant women, and I established a reputation as "King of the Children."

This reputation came about because, besides roughhousing with the youngsters, an activity which most Chinese never indulged in, I fixed all their school slates so that the wooden frames did not come apart at the corners. The trick was to cut strips of metal from old tin cans and tack them across the corners of each frame. Someone else might have done this long before if there had been any tin cans lying about, but tin cans were about as scarce in those mountains as river bottom land. I had some old ones left over from my UNRRA rations

312

and so set up shop. As a result, the children came to me to solve all kinds of problems, to play games, and to relay exciting news.

One morning three ragged little girls, black eyes shining, long braids dancing in the wind behind them, ran up to take me by the hand. They half dragged, half pushed me to the eastern edge of the village shouting, "The play has come." Sure enough, there in the middle of a large field a stage was rising, a stage of long pine poles bound together with rice straw rope and overlaid with boards.

This mushroom-like apparition turned out to be the creation of the Lucheng County Drama Corps, now on tour. The corps was composed of 50 members, most of whom had been poor professional actors until they received land in the great distribution of 1946. Now they worked their land half the year and gave plays the other half —from harvest time in the fall until spring planting came around again. They received no pay for their work but did get millet tickets from the county government for room and board. They carried on because they enjoyed acting and wanted to tell the story of the Revolution to as many peasants as possible. They moved to a new village each day and performed every afternoon and evening. They ate in village homes, as we did, and lodged with their mealtime hosts. Props, travel expenses, and incidentals were all paid for by the county government. Performances were free.

In contrast to the traditional Chinese opera, which was performed on a bare stage, this traveling troupe went in for realism. They provided a curtain, props, colorful scenery, and sound effects that included singing birds, croaking frogs, chirping crickets, pattering rain, and howling wind. These radical innovations, even though they sometimes shattered the illusion of reality which it was their purpose to create, were extremely popular. So was the modern content of the plays. People travelled for miles to see the performances and often followed the company through two or three villages.

With this exciting attraction in town for the day, all other activities ceased. Three one-act presentations in the afternoon followed by a full-length modern opera in the evening kept both cadres and people from whatever work had been planned.

The afternoon plays were comedies. In the first one a young Liberation Army soldier, home on leave, pretended to be a deserter. This so upset his wife that she tried to commit suicide. Only after the neighbors arrived to honor her husband's battlefront heroism with a large red carnation did she realize that he had been fooling her in order to test her revolutionary ardor. The second play portrayed an army cook who overslept and did not have time to steam the bread which was his unit's staple fare. Calamity was averted by an old peasant woman who stayed up all night to prepare the much-needed rations.

In the interval between plays a troupe of brightly-costumed boys and girls performed lively *k'uai bar* or singing rhymes spoken to the accompaniment of bamboo claques. These rhymes dramatized themes of current interest such as the Draft Agrarian Law, the production drive, and the impending Party purification. All this was only a build-up however, for the evening's *pièce de résistance*—a four-hour-long modern opera entitled "Red Leaf River."

As night fell thousands of peasants moved onto the level ground before the stage, each one carrying a brick or a stool to sit on. By the time the curtain rose, the whole area was solidly packed with people sitting knee to back and shoulder to shoulder in animated yet orderly expectation.

"Red Leaf River," the name of a village as well as a stream, told the story of Old Wang and his neighbors, poor peasants who had gone to the mountains to reclaim waste land just as Li Lao-szu of Long Bow had done. After years of root grubbing and terrace building, they created a habitable settlement only to learn that their wild mountain was now claimed by a landlord. He demanded heavy rents and feudal exactions but very cleverly allowed his agent to pressure the tenants for payment while he himself played the charitable gentle-man. This landlord wore a long, fleece-lined gown, smoked a water pipe, washed his mouth out with boiled water which he spat on the floor to settle the dust. Whenever anyone offered him a cup of tea he carefully wiped off the rim that his lips were about to touch. After eating his fill of delicacies he picked his teeth with grotesque dis-regard for the sensibilities of others and belched contentedly. Each of these gestures created a commotion in the audience, for the peasants recognized in this man an uncanny likeness to Long Bow's own Li Tung-sheng.

Old Wang, desperately in debt, thought if he could only get past the agent and speak to the landlord, he might win some relief. He shed these illusions quickly enough when the landlord raped his daughter-in-law, outlawed his son for throwing a rock through the mansion window, and destroyed Wang's hut. The grief-stricken daughter-in-law committed suicide. Wang's son ran further into the mountains to join the Red partisans. Old Wang himself, now a land-less beggar, stoically waited for the wheel of fortune to turn.

As the tragedy of this poor peasant's family unfolded, the women around me wept openly and unashamedly. On every side, as I turned to look, tears were coursing down their faces. No one sobbed, no one cried out, but all wept together in silence. The agony on the stage seemed to have unlocked a thousand painful memories, a bottomless reservoir of suffering that no one could control. It was a scene not easily forgotten—a makeshift stage of pine poles set under an enormous vaulted sky, a night so dark that even the brightest stars seemed faint and far away, and below the stars nothing but utter blackness, not a flicker of flame visible anywhere except on the stage. There a single kerosene lamp cast a pale yellow glow on actors and scenery alike. It was as if the attention of the whole universe were focused on that small space. And, in the very center, a young girl, her song more a wail, more a sob than a song, spread her arms wide in despair and asked, "Why? Why? Why?"

As that cry carried out across the field, the women, huddled one against the other in their dark padded jackets, shuddered as if stirred by a gust of wind, and something like a sigh moved in a wave from the front to the back of the multitude.

The girl flung herself into Red Leaf River. Abruptly the music stopped. The silence on the stage was broken only by the chirping of a cricket. At that moment I became aware of a new quality in the reaction of the audience. Men were weeping, and I along with them.

The second act brought a complete change of mood and a theme so up to date that one wondered how the company had found the time to write and stage it. Three years had passed since the suicide. The Liberation Army had come to Red Leaf River. An attempt at land reform had already been made, but the landlord was still alive, still belching contentedly, and still in control of the village. He talked now in a very progressive vein, praised Mao Tse-tung, offered to give up four acres, and fraternized openly with the village head, an opportunist who considered the landlord to be a very enlightened man.

Into the plot at this point walked a county cadre of poor peasant origin. His mission was to organize a Poor and Hired Peasants' League. When he asked the landless people if they had any problems, they all said, "No."

This negative response caused uproarious laughter in the audience. "That's the way we treated you when you first arrived," said the peasants sitting around us.

In time the county cadre gained the people's confidence, organized a strong League, exposed the landlord's machinations, and took the lead in expropriating his holdings. The second act reached its climax at a rousing mass meeting where a group of angry peasants led by Old Wang's son, rushed forward to beat the landlord. He would have been killed on the spot but for the cadre who stopped the attack and suggested that the tyrant be turned over to the People's Court. A grand, hope-filled finale, in which the entire cast burst into a song of joy for the future, ended the performance.

As the crowd broke up, I listened to the excited comment of the people. They were unanimous in proclaiming the second part of the play more to their liking than the first, although, from a dramatic point of view, the first part seemed to me undoubtedly superior. In fact we had seen two plays, with the second and positive one falling far behind the earlier tragedy in emotional appeal. But the people did not enjoy the tragedy. The pain it recreated was too acute, too close to their own bitter lives of such a short time ago. They preferred the optimistic final half, the battle and the victory. The only fault they found with the final part was that no one beat the landlord. He was turned over to the People's Court instead of punished on the spot as the "son-of-a-turtle" deserved.

PART IV

Who Will Educate the Educators?

Why are there such bad things in the splendid organization of our Party? The reason, I think, is very simple. It is that our Party is not a Party that has fallen from the heavens; it is a Party that has grown out of the existing Chinese society. Although in general our Party members are relatively the best Chinese men and women, the vanguard of the Chinese proletariat, they come, however, from every stratum of Chinese society and are still living in this society which is replete with the influences of the exploiters —selfishness, intrigues, bureaucracy and every kind of filthy thing. . . . Is it anything strange that there are muddy stains on a person who crawls out of the mud and who constantly dabbles in the mud?

Liu Shao-ch'i

35

Confrontation at the *Gate*

In areas of the first and second category feudal forces have in general been eliminated and the dissatisfaction of the peasants is focused on a group of Party members and cadres who utilize their political position to commit evil deeds and usurp the fruits of agrarian reform. Hence the work of adjusting land ownership in such areas must be combined with the work of reorganizing and purifying the ranks of the Party. At times it is even necessary to begin the reorganization and purification of the ranks of the Party before the initiative of the masses can be aroused.

*Directive of the Central Committee
of the Chinese Communist Party,
February 22, 1948*

ON APRIL 10, 1948, under a morning sky that stretched grey and unbroken from horizon to horizon, a group of delegates elected by the poor and hired peasants gathered in Long Bow's gully-like main street. They had come together to launch the campaign for the reorganization and purification of the ranks of the Communist Party that had so long been promised by the work team.

Sensing the importance of this campaign, a large part of the population of the village turned out to give moral support. As the crowd milled about, a conclave of middle peasants, hastily called together, elected three of their number to join the delegation. Later, amidst a welter of excited talk, laughter, and cheers, the representatives of both classes formed loose ranks and began to march to the meeting place.

Chou Cheng-fu, having been rejected as a delegate, now characteristically sought the limelight. He fell in beside the marching delegates and began to shout slogans. "Support our representatives!" "Work hard for the Poor and Hired Peasants!" "Let the Party members become good hired hands!" These words, chosen by Chou in the enthusiasm of the moment, were taken up not only by the marchers themselves but by many in the crowd that still filled the street.

The delegates, some 30 in number, and carrying along in their wake an equal number of laughing, shouting people, not all of whom were children, passed through the outer court which housed the

319

district office, circled the brick rectory that extended eastward from
the massive rear wall of the church itself, and went on to a third
courtyard where a long barracks-like building that had once housed
the mission school provided an austere meeting place. This was a
narrow room some 40 feet in length, paved in undulating grey brick
and completely open to the outside air since all five of the windows,
frames and all, had long since been removed for firewood. In this
room rows of benches had been placed. Some of these were already
occupied by the 26 Party members whose fate was now to be decided.*
They all stood up at their places and warmly welcomed the new arrivals. As the delegates, with much bustle and confusion, settled on
the remaining seats, that variegated crowd of curious children and
adults which had followed them through the gate crowded the open
apertures in the south wall. Throughout the proceedings which followed, these onlookers engaged in a continuous tumult as they shoved
and pushed one another for a better view and added their own
gratuitous comments to those of the official participants.

Ch'i Yun and I, along with several members of the work team who
had been on the street to watch the procession, squeezed into the
room behind the peasant delegates and managed to sandwich our
bodies into the meager spaces still available.

We had no sooner settled into place than all the people in the
room rose to their feet and bowed their heads three times before a
large poster-style portrait of Chairman Mao. This traditional *chu kung*
which once served to honor the Emperor, later the memory of Sun
Yat-sen, and now at Party meetings the ideas of the Revolution itself
as exemplified by the Party Chairman, was followed by a very
unexpected event. Suddenly the Communists began to sing. Standing
erect in their places they launched, without warning, into what seemed
to be some poorly remembered Christian hymn. One or two of the
comrades sang loudly, a dozen more somewhat hesitantly, while the
remainder added a note only now and then. The various sounds produced in this fashion did not fall into any one key nor did they con-
geal into any easily recognizable tune. Nevertheless, after a few bars
of this strange and halting disharmony, I realized that they were singing the *Internationale* and that only Ts'ai-yuan, who had spent eight
years in the Eighth Route Army, and Hou Pao-pei, leader of the work
team, knew both the words and the tune. The rest of the members
of the branch chimed in as best they could, now singing a few words,
now waiting for Hou and Ts'ai to give them the lead, until at last
they came to the finale, which, because it was more familiar to all,

* There were 28 Party members in Long Bow in 1948, but at the time
of the *gate* two of them were in jail.

rang out loud and clear. Those last words, "The International Party shall be the human race," might well have shaken the windows in their frames had there been windows or frames left in the wall.

The song, despite the grave defects of rendition, made a powerful impression upon us all. It revealed in an unexpected and dramatic way the existence, hitherto only conjectured, of a strong, organized center at the heart of village life, a center which followed a well-established tradition—however new or strange that tradition might be—and obviously commanded great loyalty from its adherents. Certainly no coercion could have caused these stolid peasants to attempt in public a song only half learned. With this revelation any tendency that one might have to view the village as "a pile of loose sand" could hardly help but crumble. Here stood in solid if somewhat ragged phalanx the vertebrae of the community's backbone.

The drama of this confrontation between the assembled members of the Communist Party branch and the people of Long Bow jarred me into acute awareness of the boldness of the method chosen for the reorganization of the Party. The method was simple enough. The Party had declared *open* its own traditional self-and-mutual criticism meetings. But to declare these meetings open meant to make public figures of all the village Communists, to break with decades of war-enforced security measures, to take a step that could never be undone.

With Kuomintang assassins still roaming the countryside, with the Civil War battlefront still only a hundred miles away, with a massive counter-attack still under preparation by Nationalist generals, who could guarantee the life of a Communist? If Governor Yen's troops ever returned, every active revolutionary in the village would most certainly be hunted down and killed. Fathers and mothers, sisters and brothers, sons and daughters, would also become objects for extermination. Yet here stood 26 peasants, raised in this valley, tied by a thousand threads to its people and its culture, who dared proclaim before the world their militant revolutionary purpose.

True, this was not the first moment that their identity had become known. Team Leader Hou had read off their names several days before. But at the time the names, to me at least, were abstractions. Here stood in flesh and blood the people whose lives were placed in jeopardy by the reading of the list. Just as I suddenly became aware of them as living human beings, so the jeopardy in which they were placed emerged as agonizing fact.

The decision to make grass-roots Party membership lists public in the Base Areas came directly from the Central Committee, now in hiding somewhere in the loess hills of North Shensi. It was a measure of the Party leaders' confidence in the success of the Revolutionary

War. It was also a measure of the seriousness with which they regarded
the weaknesses so apparent in the rural Party branches, weaknesses
which, if not overcome, could themselves undermine the Revolution
more thoroughly than defeat in battle. By declaring in favor of open
membership, they had assumed a great risk in order to take a giant
step forward.

The timing was crucial. Such a decision could not have been made
a year earlier because at that time the People's Liberation Army was
fighting a war of strategic defense in which it was often necessary
to trade space for time. The victories of the second half of 1947 had
made a fundamental change in the military situation. The revolutionary forces were now on the strategic offensive. The necessity to trade
space for time had shifted onto the shoulders of the counter-revolution.
The relative security thus won made it possible for the Communist
Party to operate publicly throughout the Base Areas, to place its
personnel under the supervision of the people and thus to strengthen
the strategic offensive itself, by making these old Base Areas more
unified, more democratic, and hence much stronger than before.

Having discounted the risks and staked the future of the Party
and the Revolution on the gains, the Central Committee now boldly
declared, "All meetings of all Party branches to discuss problems
concerning the interests of the masses, including Party meetings for
criticism and review, should be participated in by the non-Party
masses. Secret meetings are not allowed so that feelings of mystery
toward the Party organization and Party activities can be removed
and all the good and bad phenomena within the Party can thus be
exposed before the people for supervision and criticism or for support."

But what if the strategic estimate of the situation turned out
to be wrong? I found it hard to suppress a shiver of apprehension for
the future of the village Communists and in this I was by no means
alone.

When the last strains of the song had died away and everyone had
once again found a place to sit, Comrade Hou, dour and serious as
always, briefly outlined the purpose of the meeting. He then called
on Hsin-fa, secretary of the branch, to speak for the local members.
As we had not seen Hsin-fa or any other leading Party member before, Ch'i Yun and I looked at him with intense interest. The secretary was tall, lean, graceful, a man in the very prime of life. His well-
proportioned face was burned a deep bronze by the spring sun. It
contrasted sharply with his scalp, which, because it was ordinarily
covered by a hand towel, remained light, almost white. The skin of his
scalp was so closely shaven that it shone like the pate of a bald man

and added a touch of military severity to an otherwise genial countenance. As Hsin-fa spoke, a prominent Adam's apple moved up and down in his throat. His hands, long and supple, inscribed wide arcs in the air to emphasize his words. He obviously had some skill as a public speaker, but at this moment his words did not come easily.

"Comrades, honorable delegates . . . ," he began, then stopped, uncertain as to how to proceed. He swallowed and his Adam's apple jumped above the tight collar of his padded tunic.

Hsin-fa was nervous, we realized, because he did not know how this day was going to turn out. For weeks the Party had been meeting to prepare for the ordeal at the *gate;* yet now that the proceedings were about to begin it seemed as if all the preparations had been inadequate. Comrade Hou had assured them all that the spirit of the reorganization was one of "kill the disease and save the patient," but how well was this understood by the peasants?

Had not Comrade Hou himself, the Border Region Press, the drama "Red Leaf River," and certain angry poor peasants, not only in Long Bow but in the market towns as well, all said that large numbers of the poor and hired had not *fanshened,* and that this was the fault of the local Communist Party members? Did not the peasants now believe that most Communists were actually landlords and rich peasants who only posed as revolutionaries or were opportunists who had sold out to such impostors? Was it not repeated a hundred times a day that these unscrupulous people had seized property and land that by rights belonged to the peasants? And had all this not long since moved from the realm of talk to the realm of action? Had not all cadres been removed from their posts, ostracized completely, and denied admission to the Poor Peasants' League or any other organization of the people? Had not this discrimination already reached their relatives and those neighbors who still remained friendly to them? Had not loose talk of beatings—"an eye for an eye, a tooth for a tooth"—run through the village and helped to fan an atmosphere of struggle against the Party members, a struggle in which they could be as harshly attacked as collaborators and gentry had earlier been? Faced with such a prospect it was easy to let fear take over.

Doubts and fears Hsin-fa had certainly known in the last few weeks. When T'ien-hsi, a leading militiaman, had lamented, "If we had never joined the Party, we could now be members of the Poor Peasants' League and basic members at that," Hsin-fa had agreed with him. When Cheng-k'uan, suspended chairman of the Peasants' Association, threatened to throw himself into his well, Hsin-fa had not tried to dissuade him but had returned home to survey his own well. When Hsiu-mei lost her appetite, vomited everything she tried to swallow, and became so weak that she could not rise unaided from her *k'ang*, Hsin-fa had expressed his sympathy. He knew that it was no common dysentry that had brought her low, but fear, fear of this *gate* manned by the people which each Communist had to pass. "Even if I die the very next day I must pass this *gate*," said Hsiu-mei as she was carried to one of the preparatory meetings. Inadvertently she expressed the feelings of all the members of the branch.

The attack on the young work team cadre, Chang-ch'uer, had only heightened the Communists' fears. While many peasants blamed dishonest cadres for the attack, the Party members felt certain that it was meant as a blow against the Party and had been organized by the Catholic minority. They were afraid that once their names were read aloud, dissident villagers would take whatever means for revenge came to hand. Those who had committed serious crimes dared not walk out on the street alone.

Such had been the situation inside the Party when Cadre Hou first met with its members. He blamed them for the inadequate *fanshen*. He then outlined for them the basic principles of the coming movement—to examine impurities in class composition, impurities in ideology, and impurities in working style within the Communist Party. He impressed upon them the fact that they must objectively review their class background, their motives, and their past acts. They must listen to the people's delegates, accept all valid criticism, and overcome weaknesses. Those who did not could be punished, even expelled from the Party. Those with a record of serious crime who refused to reform could be sent to the People's Court for trial. Hou stressed again and again the glorious future that lay before those who spoke out frankly, corrected their mistakes, and resolved to serve the people well. But though Comrade Hou stressed both aspects of the *gate*, the main thing that registered in the minds of the Party members was the demand that they accept responsibility for the *fanshen* situation, receive criticism, and bow their heads. Most of them felt even if they spoke frankly, they could never expect to pass. The people so clearly wanted revenge, and what was more important, were demanding "oil" to fill the numerous gaps in the peasants' inventory of necessities. Since the landlords had long since been dispossessed, some new source of fruits had to be found. Now it looked as if the revolutionary cadres would be that source. Under the circumstances how could mere recognition of past mistakes ward off the blow?

Here was the root of the problem, and Hsin-fa, as he stood before the delegates that morning looking anxiously into their faces, had quite obviously found no solution. In conversations with Team Leader Hou he had already admitted that many poor peasants had not *fan-*

shened. But, he had asked himself again and again, was that his fault? Was it the fault of his comrades in the Party or of the non-Party cadres? Had they really seized large amounts of property? Had any of them become rich? As for himself he had one wooden bowl and one basket that could still be said to be public property since no committee had ever allocated them to him. But could any peasant complete his *fanshen* with a wooden bowl and a basket? And what about all the work the Party members and cadres had done? The endless meetings, the guard duty at night, the searches, the arrests, the interrogations? Could anyone in the village have *faned* half a *shen* without all that effort so freely given? The very thought of the traitors and puppets now flocking into the Poor Peasants' League to sit in judgment on the Party had made him flush with anger.

But when Hsin-fa looked out over the crowd in the room in front of him that day he saw not one collaborator's face. Hou Chin-ming's wife was there, but whatever her husband might have done to help the priest escape, she herself was but a young girl, sold right out of the Catholic orphanage. How could she be held responsible for her husband's politics? Having no object on which to fasten, anger was out of the question. Hsin-fa stood alone, face to face with that hard necessity—the Party's demand that all its members publicly examine their records, expose their own mistakes, and accept the correct opinions of the people.

"Comrades," said Hsin-fa, starting over again, "on behalf of the Party I welcome you, the delegates of the people, and I hope you will all speak out clearly and fearlessly what you think. Certainly you need not fear any reprisal. As for me, in the past you made me a cadre, but I forgot my poor friends after I myself had *fanshened.*"

This was short and to the point. The delegates were impressed and showed it by halting most of their private conversations to listen.

As Hsin-fa sat down, the middle-aged poor peasant from the northwest group, Yang Yu-so, rose to speak for the delegates. Yang, looking neither to the right nor to the left, spoke out loudly but much too rapidly. Like a small boy running through the Confucian classics in shouting school, he gave every syllable of his memorized talk the same emphasis.

"I am a poor peasant chosen as a delegate to help purify the Party," recited Yang. "I hope every Party member will examine his past honestly. I cannot speak much. We are here because the poor peasants want us to help the Party so that we can all *fanshen* thoroughly."

As he sat down, his forehead was covered with bright beads of sweat. He turned to a friend in the row behind him and said, "I was so worried I couldn't sleep last night. I felt as if I had bought something I couldn't sell. I wanted someone else to be spokesman, but it was too late."

"You did fine." "You said what was on our minds." "If you sweat that's only because you aren't used to speaking." These and other remarks came from the peasants on the benches all around him. They seemed to spring from a genial, confident mood that belied all of Hsin-fa's fears. There was certainly no hint of revenge, no current of violence lurking beneath the surface of the emotions that swayed the delegates that day.

****

The reasonable tone that prevailed was the result of many days of detailed preparation. If the Party members had practiced for this confrontation, so too had the poor peasants of the League. Mass meetings of the whole organization, meetings of the three sectional groups, and meetings of activists especially chosen by the work team for intensive education had all preceded the final election of the delegates. Night after night, dozens of people had crowded into meeting places that were often too small for a single family to live in with comfort. *K'angs,* benches, stools, doorsills, and the earth floors of these peasant dwellings had been packed with men and women made bulky by extra layers of heavily-padded winter clothing. The air they breathed was soon saturated with the now familiar odor of garlic and tobacco smoke. The smoke added its own peculiar haze to the atmosphere and so subdued the flame of the single, wick-in-oil lamp that only those faces nearest the light could be seen at all. Voices from other parts of the room came disembodied out of the darkness.

Under conditions such as these, four major questions had been discussed. What is the Communist Party? Is the Communist Party good or bad? If it is good, how can it contain bad members? What should be done with the bad members?

As for the Communist Party itself, most of the peasants had come to understand that the Party was not Chairman Mao in Yenan, but hundreds of thousands of peasants and workers in every village and town in the Liberated Areas. More difficult to grasp was the fact that not every village, district, or county cadre was a Communist Party member. Everyone said that the Communist Party led. If it led, its members must be the leaders and the leaders must be its members—such was the logic of the peasants. It was very hard to clear up this question as long as the names of the Party members remained secret. That there were women members in the Party also had to be stated again and again. Women did not find this strange, but men shook their heads and said, "Ah." They obviously did not believe that women could lead anyone to *fanshen*.

Nobody had argued that the Communist Party was bad. The fact that so many people had *fanshened* very little or had *fanshened* only half way could not erase what was obvious—that the general conditions of life had improved for everybody and that this would not have been possible without the Communist Party.

But if nobody had attacked the Party as such, some people had attacked all of its members, which amounted to almost the same thing. The Catholics, still smarting under the agents' caps imposed by Yu-lai, made up the core of this group. Old Shen, in his artless way, was their most vocal spokesman. Every time he opened his mouth he condemned the village Communists. He said, "The Party ordered its members to serve the people and lead them to *fanshen*. But only the members really *fanshened*. They became officials just like the feudal ones. They climbed onto our heads and did everything they wished. So we must throw them down. We are the masters now."

Old Lady Wang, who was no Catholic, had adopted a different, but equally severe approach. She worried tenaciously about the "fruits." As far as she was concerned, the Communists had them all. "During the struggle we fought together," she complained. "But after the victory they got the 'fruits' and some of them just stayed home and did nothing and lived a luxurious life. And some smoked cigarettes and just wandered about. They sold the grain from the struggle and bought delicious things to eat."

Objectively her position reinforced that of Old Shen, and when it came to what must be done about it the two saw eye to eye. "All the grafters must be put in prison," declaimed Shen with the mien of a judge. "All the 'fruits' which they grafted must be immediately given up," said Old Lady Wang. "If they die of starvation that's not our problem. When they took everything to their own homes, did they care one little bit for us?"

This *chih shemme huan shemme* or return-as-good-as-you-got attitude had found considerable support. Remembering the "Wash-the-Face Movement" of 1947, many peasants had little faith in the possibility of human reform and still less faith in public self-criticism as a means to that end. Bad practices soon became habitual, they said, and quoted the old proverb, "Can one stop one's mouth from eating or one's two legs from running?" Their conclusion was, "We must beat the bad ones."

This had been one pole of opinion—the tough pole. At the other pole were peasants like Yuan-lung, who took a moderate position

despite the fact that he too was a Catholic and had suffered severe
beatings at the hands of Man-hsi. Fluent of speech and at least partly
literate, he had constantly defended the Party and the majority of its
membership. He liked to use the poetic images popularized by Mao
Tse-tung. Comparing the Party members to swimming fish, he said,
"The people are the water. Without water the fish immediately die.
Now some of the fish have left the pool and we must help them to
return home." Comparing the Communist Party to a pine tree, he
said, "We want the tree to grow high and straight, so whenever we
find an ugly branch we must find a way to straighten it or prune it in
order to help the tree. Of course there are bad elements in the Party,
but we must distinguish between the good and the bad, and in my
opinion the majority of them are good. Otherwise, how could they
lead us to *fanshen?* Though we have not *fanshened* thoroughly, still
everyone of us can live with enough food and clothes."

Yuan-lung had been supported in this by T'ai-shan's mother, a prematurely aged, work-worn widow whose unkempt hair kept falling
in front of her face as she sewed. "Shall we force the cadres to jump
in the well?" she asked, pushing an offending strand of hair from in
front of her eyes. "Then we ourselves would be feudal. We want the
'fruits' but not the cadres' lives. What good would that do?"

Ch'ung-lai's wife, whose flesh had been cut with scissors when the
peasants suspected her of aiding a landlord, felt the same way. "After
all," she said, "we shall find out the truth in the end. As for beating
and swearing, that is the feudal method. We must not use it. Haven't
we all suffered from feudal blows in the past? How can we think of
treating others that way?"

This had been the other pole of opinion—the reasonable pole. In between were many peasants who wavered or were inconsistent, first
speaking of punishment, then of reform.

The public announcement on April 8 of the names of the Party
members had strengthened the reasonable trend. This was because
the list contained two surprises. The first of these was that several of
the most feared and hated cadres were not Communists at all. Neither
Yu-lai nor Hsi-yu nor San-ch'ing had ever been members of the
branch.

The second surprise was that many rank-and-file peasants, people
who had never been cadres, were Communists. The stolid hard-working An-k'u found it hard to believe that his rosy-cheeked bride, 18-
year-old Hsiao-mer, could be a comrade. Others felt the same way
about Meng Fu-lu and Chou Cheng-lo. To be sure these two
had been active members of the militia, but so had 50 or 60 other men,
certainly no less devoted to the corps and no less able than they. Then

there were the young wives such as Wang Man-ying and Jen Ho-chueh, women who almost never left their own courtyards. Where did they fit in?

The publication of the list had thus quite destroyed the common assumption that cadres and Communists were one and the same. Much popular thunder was diverted when it was recognized that several of the worst cadres were not members of the Party. The peasants began to think of the Communists as individuals, and certain leaders whose very real prestige had been smothered in the general condemnation began to gather support. Among these were the Eighth Route Army veteran who owned the store on the square, Ts'ai-yuan; the suspended head of the Peasants' Association, Cheng-k'uan; and the suspended head of the Women's Association, Hu Hsueh-chen.

Reading the list had accomplished another important service. It had stripped away that veil of mystery that obscured the Party. The people of Long Bow came face to face with a group of their own kind —peasants so typical of the village that they seemed almost a caricature of it. This caused a sharp readjustment in attitudes. People who had for so long associated the word Communist with Chairman Mao, a god-like figure in distant Yenan, now found it hard to apply the same designation to Little Mer, quarrelsome old Meng Fu-lu, or the muscular but slow-witted Man-hsi. Here certainly were no deities. Yet neither were they devils and none of them could by any stretch of the imagination be called rich. The very poverty and humanity of the Party had undercut vindictiveness.

****

In the North China countryside poverty had for so long been so universal and so chronic that a glazed china bowl counted as an important possession. Many peasants ate out of the same bowl from cradle to grave and passed it on to their offspring. If a bowl broke, the pieces were taken to one of the itinerant bowl menders who followed the market day fairs around the county. These craftsmen cleverly drilled pottery fragments and stapled them together with bits of brass. Like the proverbial cat, these oft-resurrected bowls came to have nine lives and through long-continued usage became closely identified with their possessors.

This close personal relationship between each peasant and his bowl had made possible the electoral procedure by which the largely illiterate members of the Provisional Poor Peasants' League finally elected their delegates to the *gate*. These were the first formal elections to take place after the arrival of the work team in the village and probably only the third or fourth elections ever to be held there. As such they aroused great interest.

In each Poor Peasants' League group 12 men had first been nominated from the floor for the seven male delegate seats. Each of these nominees then set his bowl on a long bench that had been placed in the center of one of the larger courtyards. One at a time left the area. The voters, each of whom held seven black beans and five white ones in hand, then filed past the bowls and dropped a bean, black or white, in the bowl of whichever candidate was absent. A black bean meant a vote for the man, a white bean a vote against him. After this process had been repeated 12 times, the beans in the bowls were counted by a committee of three.

In order to insure that the women won more than token representation among the delegates, six women had been separately nominated, and three voted in by the same method.

The work team cadres, who had found in the village more resentment than they had expected and had underestimated the results of two weeks of education, had been surprised when the elections produced a clearcut defeat for the tough line, and especially for the dissidents of the Catholic clique. In the southwest group of the League, Li Ho-jen, the real leader of the dissidents, got but one vote. Old Shen, with his goatee and his silver pipe, was not even nominated. Kuo Yuan-lung, helped no doubt by the fact that Li had opposed him, won by far the largest vote. Five of the six men elected with him turned out to be like-minded reasonable young peasants, known, if at all, for their reticence. The sixth, Old Pao, whose quarrel with his wife has already been described, could be called a maverick who transformed every issue into a personal challenge and was therefore unpredictable. In the election, for example, he cast a lone bean for Li Ho-jen out of spite simply because Li Ho-jen had opposed his own nomination. In the elaborate code of face to which he adhered, this return of good for evil meant a loss of face for Li and a gain in face for Pao. Thereafter, the latter lost no opporunity to inform all and sundry just whose vote Li got and why.

Among the women the tough line had fared a little better. Although the very open-minded widow, T'ai-shan's mother, got the most votes, Old Lady Wang came in second, and Chin-ming's wife third. The northern and eastern groups did not follow suit however. All their women delegates, like their men, adhered to the reasonable position. Outstanding among them were Ch'ung-lai's wife and Wu-kuei's wife, two women who intuitively identified their interests as poor peasants with the interest and vitality of the Communist Party.

After the delegates had been provisionally elected in the village's three sections, the League groups met together in a great mass meeting to pass on one another's selections. At this meeting the proponents of the tough line made one last effort to change the composition of the delegation. Li Ho-jen himself challenged the right of Party members' relatives to act as "gatekeepers," a challenge aimed at the northern group which had elected both the wife and the cousin of Chou Cheng-lo, a Communist member of the militia corps, and the brother of Hsiao Wen-hsu, another Communist militiaman.

The northern group countered this challenge by pointing out that the poor peasants of the southwest corner had themselves elected a Communist's husband to serve at the *gate*. This was An-k'u, husband of Little Mer, whose Party membership still seemed so incongruous as to be disregarded by her neighbors.

The question of Party members' relatives was finally settled by majority vote. Cheng-lo's wife and cousin were voted down. An-k'u, a very diffident but honest peasant, was approved 81 to 31, as was Hsiao Ch'ing-hsu, a teenager.

The northern group members, for their part, were not too pleased with the election of Old Lady Wang and Old Pao. "Old Lady Wang is too selfish," they said. "Her temper is so short, if you cross her she jumps three feet in the air. And as for Old Pao, he can't even get on with his wife! How can he represent the rest of us?"

These two controversial figures were asked to stand up and speak before the meeting. Old Lady Wang outdid her critics. "I am so selfish," she said, "that when I am paid a quart of grain I want a quart and a half." Old Pao merely agreed with his. "I can't solve my family affairs, how can I solve the problems of this village?"

This was equivalent to saying, "We don't want to run." But the peasants decided to put them in office anyway and passed them both by a big majority vote.

That same evening the sectional groups had met singly once again to gather opinions and grievances against those Communists who were to come before them the next day.

Now, with the meeting already underway, they appeared confident and ready.

When the stir occasioned by Delegate Spokesman Yang's asides subsided, Comrade Hou asked if anyone else wanted to speak. Nobody volunteered. Hou waited a long interval to make sure, then called on Chang Ch'un-hsi, suspended village head and one of the best known village cadres in the whole Fifth District, to begin his self-examination.

36

The Village Leader Bows His Head

*The adoption of the [open meeting] method for reorganizing and purifying
the ranks of the Party . . . will, on one hand, enable participating non-
Party masses unreservedly to criticize and examine the Party members
and cadres whom they oppose or approve, and enable them to feel that
they have linked up with the Party of Mao Tse-tung. On the other hand,
the leaders of the Party can, according to the opinions of the masses and
the situation within the Party, consider questions from all sides and
distinguish right from wrong, the degrees of seriousness, and mete out
justly due punishment and reward so that both Party and non-Party masses
will feel satisfied.*

> *Directive of the Central Committee of
> the Chinese Communist Party,
> February 22, 1948*

As CHANG CH'UN-HSI stood up, a hush settled over the room and
soon spread even to the rowdy crowd outside. The formalities, the
speeches, the explanations were now over. The actual struggle to
purify the Party had begun. Nobody wanted to miss a single word.

Ch'un-hsi helped to extend the silence by speaking very softly,
so softly that we had to strain to hear him. As he spoke, wrinkles
furrowed his forehead and he looked somewhere over our heads
toward a spot on the wall behind us. I was struck by his youth and
his good looks. Like Hsin-fa, the secretary of the Party branch, he
was tall and lean and moved with a grace that belied his rustic origin.
Like Hsin-fa also, his head was closely shaven, but here the resemblance ended, for this did not lend him an air of severity but on the
contrary seemed to accentuate the gentle features of his face and to
exaggerate the pallor of his complexion. If Hsin-fa looked like a man
of action, Ch'un-hsi struck one as more of an intellectual, a student,
perhaps even a poet. The manner in which he spoke heightened this
impression, for he took his past seriously, examined his motives as
well as his actions, and judged himself very harshly, much more
harshly, in fact, than his record warranted.

His very first words set the tone. "I hope the delegates will help me to correct my bad behavior," he said. He then began a brief review of his life history that was suffused with diffident self-criticism. "My family are natives of Chih-chou, but I was born here. My grand-father was a middle peasant, but my own father was a poor peasant. I studied two years in primary school. Then I became a hired laborer and worked for others until Liberation. Under the leadership of the Party my whole family *fanshened,* but I took advantage of the people's struggle, and I will say later how much I got from the movement. At the time of Liberation I was working as a hired laborer in Kao Settlement. The landlord there offered me money and tried to buy me off. I was tempted. I took the money and stayed with him. Afterwards many friends talked with me. They persuaded me to leave the old money-bags.

"Then I got almost an acre of land. Later I was offered land in Long Bow and came home. But my thought was still wrong. I was afraid the Kuomintang would come back. I was not active. Later I learned more about the politics of the Communist Party and joined the militia. Because I could read a little the cadres asked me to take charge of financial work in the village. Then I became proud. During the first distribution I was selfish. I chose the best piece of land for myself. The year before last, when the government ordered tax grain, we cadres did not talk it over with the masses or discuss with them how to collect it. We just consulted among ourselves and then ordered the people to hand out the grain. It was very unfair."

The delegates, impressed by the speaker's manner, remained silent. Ch'un-hsi, on his part, gained confidence with practice, and as his confidence grew, his voice became louder. His audience was able to relax a little.

"After I took charge of the financial work I became proud," continued Ch'un-hsi. "I looked down on others. I made false reports. I behaved badly, grafted money, and beat people."

It was hard to imagine this slender quiet man doing all these things, but nobody contradicted him.

"Last May I was chosen as leader of this village. Everyone wanted me to serve the masses, but I only became more arrogant. I thought I had become an official, just like a leader in the old society. I could order anyone in the village about. Because Yu-hsing was a struggle object, I ordered him out of his house and occupied it myself. I borrowed BRC 10,000 from the co-op and paid back BRC 5,000 with grain tickets that weren't mine. I grafted five pairs of shoes that the women made for the soldiers at the front. Last year three cadres went with me to the storehouse. We wanted cloth to make flags for the village school. But while we were there, we each took a pair of pants. I struck Old Pao when I found some of the grain in the storehouse missing. He was supposed to be in charge. During the Enlarge the Army Movement last year I helped send older people, all former puppets, to the recruiting station. This was worse than the Kuomintang. Of course they were sent back. The Army had no use for them."

At this point one of the Party members who was sitting in the front row interrupted. "Don't give us every little detail. Just review the high points, the important things."

"Yes," chimed in Old Lady Wang, to whom the forced recruitment of over-aged men was obviously a minor matter. "Tell us how you yourself *fanshened*. Tell us what you grafted!"

"In the *fanshen* I got more than the masses," said Ch'un-hsi, glad of some hint as to what the delegates regarded as important. "I got ten hundredweight plus one peck of millet. Also some wheat. As for clothes, I got ten pieces of good quality and two short bolts of silk. Last year when I went to Hukuan on village business, I spent BRC 600 for cigarettes and collected this money from the District Office as expenses."

"What were you thinking of when you grafted it?" asked a Party member, trying to bring to light the motive behind the deed.

'My thought was very bad. Because my family was a soldier's family and I a full-time cadre, I didn't want to labor but only to sit down, eat delicious food, and have others work for me. Because there was a meeting every night, I got up late every morning. That was my excuse. Once someone called me early in the morning and I swore at him . . ."

As Ch'un-hsi told one incident after another, I began to think that he must be one of the worst cadres in Long Bow and leaned over to ask Ch'i Yun if this were so.

"No," she whispered in reply. "He is one of the best. He is very well liked. That's why Hou chose him to go first."

I tried to keep this in mind as the village head continued his catalogue of transgressions but found it hard to balance such an estimate against the unrelieved picture of wrongdoing which he painted.

"After I joined the Party last February, my thought became even worse," said Ch'un-hsi. "I thought I had found a place that could protect me and lead to higher positions, and I thought I could do anything. No one dared punish me, I thought. Every day I work hard. What for? If I don't spend money and live a little better, what is the use of working so hard?"

With this frank admission Ch'un-hsi ended his presentation. There remained only the question as to what he proposed to do about it.

"I will give up all the fruits and land and housing that I got extra.

As for the grain, I really want to give it up but I have no surplus grain because I bought half a donkey this spring. I want to pay back the grain after the harvest is in . . ." Here he paused, thought hard, then added, "I have done so many bad things, I can't remember them all now. Please give me criticism."

The critical moment had arrived. I saw Comrade Hou glance anxiously at Little Li. The meaning behind that glance was clear. Numerous discussions held by the work team had made clear that unless a very delicate balance was maintained, this campaign could easily fail. In work review meetings during the past week Comrade Hou had stressed the need to keep the movement from developing into a "struggle" against the Party and cadres as individuals. The work team must keep in mind the real virtues of those whose records were under review. It must sustain their morale, preserve their sanity, and keep alive in them that spark of courage, energy, and ability which had made them leaders in the past and had made possible the transformation of the village up to this point. On the other hand, Hou had stressed the need to expose the real abuses of the local administration. The work team must make the village Communists aware of the real dangers of commandism, loose morals, self-indulgence, dishonesty, and petty corruption. It must help them root out these dangers completely, irrevocably.

That was one side, the side of the Communists and the cadres. The other side was the side of the people. This the work team had also discussed again and again. Could the people actually overcome their fear of reprisal? Could they be led to speak out without any reservations? To speak out even if their sentiments were wrong, even if their attacks were completely misguided? Could the mistakes of the Wash-the-Face Movement, when the people took a step forward only to be pushed back again, be avoided? Hou knew that the Communist Party must show that it intended to carry through, must show that the movement really meant what the Party said it meant, and that no favoritism would be shown to anyone just because he or she was a Party member. The history of other political movements in China certainly provided scant precedent for such a thing. Was it any wonder then that many peasants still hesitated and talked of beatings? What was required here was a leap to a new way of handling problems. The trouble was that those who leapt couldn't always be sure they would land on their feet.

Hou's problem was made even more difficult by the fact that the work team was not united in its outlook. There was, at least to a certain extent, a split between the cadres from the University and the peasant cadres from Lucheng County. From the beginning the intellectuals had tended to downgrade the past contributions of the village leaders and exaggerate their mistakes. They had tended to regard the village Communists essentially as opportunists, corrupt and wrong-headed. Thus they had lent an especially sympathetic ear to the dissidents who were full of vindictive criticism and eager for revenge.

The work team cadres of peasant origin tended to be much more sympathetic to the village leaders. They themselves were, after all, but recently promoted village cadres. They could not downgrade the achievements of the Long Bow men without at the same time slighting their own past. Having lived in this area throughout the Japanese occupation, they were also much more involved emotionally than were the University personnel when it came to former puppets, collaborators, and dissident Catholics, all of whom seethed with resentment against the repressions which they had later suffered.

Now two months of effort on the part of this variegated team, which Hou captained but had not yet been able to unite, hung in the balance.

Action began in an unexpected quarter. Thin-faced Li Lao-szu, one of the most timid peasants, a man who had never found the courage to stand up to his own sister-in-law, stood up and urged each delegate to voice the opinions that he or she had collected from the people the night before. He himself led off with a question about the public money and grain that Ch'un-hsi had spent while on his trip to deliver tax grain more than a year earlier.

Ch'un-hsi, contrite as before, tried to explain this matter. "I transported grain together with An-ho and we stayed away more than ten days because it rained without stopping all that time. We spent a lot of money but really only BRC 2,600 of this was public money."

This explanation did not satisfy Old Lady Wang, who went right on sewing as she fired questions, like mortar shells, one after another. "You spent a hundredweight and a half of grain just for traveling expenses. When ordinary people transport grain they dare not spend a cent. What were you thinking of?"

"Fu-yuan said I could take out my expenses."

"Why blame it on Fu-yuan? Speak for yourself," jibed the old lady, punching her awl through the shoe sole on which she was working as if it were graft and corruption personified.

"This grain belonged to everyone, but you spent it for yourself," added Chin-ming's wife, anxious to give Old Lady Wang some support.

"I have thought it over for days," said Ch'un-hsi, badly shaken by the sharp attack. "The only thing to do is to give up an equal amount of millet."

"Say everything definitely and clearly. How much, what, when, how will you pay?" This advice came from Team Leader Hou who interrupted now for the first time.

But Ch'un-hsi was unable to think in concrete terms.

"Surely I will repay the millet, and I beg your pardon," he said in a voice choked with distress.

"What about the money then?"

"I spent the villagers' blood so I must give it up."

This well-intentioned offer turned out to be a mistake.

"You say that two of you spent the money. Why promise to pay all of it back by yourself. You aren't sincere."

This time the speaker was a woman from the Party members' ranks. She sat very straight on the bench in front of us. The black hair that showed beneath the white towel on her head was bobbed, a very unusual style in Long Bow.

Ch'i Yun nudged me. "That's Hu Hsueh-chen, leader of the Women's Association."

Ch'un-hsi, taken by surprise by the reverse twist in Hsueh-chen's question, admitted, "Four of us spent the money."

"Well then, say so. We only want the truth from you. We don't want you to take the blame for what four people did."

Having led himself into a corner by his eagerness to admit all charges and make good all wrongs, Ch'un-hsi had only himself to blame when the pressure against him increased. Once Hsueh-chen had exposed the fact that he "bowed with the wind" and did not always answer questions objectively, new questions came thick and fast. They ranged from the disposal of the tax grain to the accounts of the village consumer co-op, from a grindstone which Ch'un-hsi jointly owned with the co-op to the management of the Western Inn, that Mecca where cadres were wont to get a free meal. From the Western Inn, the barrage shifted to the Enlarge the Army Movement, in the course of which several "sour and slippery" dissidents were sent off to war and twice as much grain was collected for the send-off banquet as was spent on the affair. From the Enlarge the Army Movement the questioning jumped to the distribution of Church property and especially the disposal of such valuable things as candlesticks, white robes, and one enormous wool blanket that no one could ever forget.

When the sun reached its zenith, the meeting finally adjourned for lunch, but it reconvened as soon as everyone had eaten and continued as intensely as before.

"Why did you beat me?" "Why did you collect seven percent on the government seed loan?" "Did the Party tell you to oppress us?"

"Do you know anything about Fu-kuei's donkey?" "Why was Li Ho-jen sent off to join the Army?" "Are you speaking fine words now only to take revenge on us in the future?"

These and a score of other questions cascaded down upon the helpless Ch'un-hsi, who, because he was the first to come before the *gate* and because he had been village head, was expected to know everything and clear up everything, even matters in which he was not directly involved. He patiently answered every question, apologetically assumed responsibility, and methodically promised to make amends. The more the delegates pressed him the more he admitted and the more he promised.

Late in the afternoon the emphasis finally swung back to Ch'un-hsi's personal record. The delegates asked him to tally up the total amount of the goods and property he had illegally taken. The list that he then ran through was pitifully small.

"Altogether I took BRC 9,000, eight pecks of millet, some shoes, a few clothes, four feet of cloth . . ."

Nobody questioned the amount or disputed the items.

"Will you be happy to give all this up?" asked Lao-szu.

"Yes," said Ch'un-hsi. "Because in the past I had nothing to eat, and now since Liberation I have everything. In the past I was a bad laborer for the people. In the future, if you still want me, I will double my effort and become a good servant of the people."

Because the sun was already bumping the rim of the hills in the West, Team Leader Hou intervened to conclude the session. "It is late," he said. "Let us consider what we should do about this man."

The delegates filed outdoors in order to be able to discuss their conclusions freely and immediately entered into hot debate among themselves.

"Two or three pieces of clothing! That's not enough," snorted Old Lady Wang, all primed for further battle.

But Old Tui-chin, the bachelor peasant, who was more and more emerging, by virtue of his extreme objectivity, as spokesman for the northern group, disagreed. "We don't want the things. Our aim is to get him to admit his mistakes and speak the truth."

At this, Old Lady Wang spat furiously on the ground. "Who can eat self-criticism?" she asked.

Delegate Spokesman Yang skillfully sidetracked a quarrel by proposing that they set a date on which Ch'un-hsi must give back all that he had illegally taken, and ask him to name what article of the Agrarian Reform Law he should be punished under.

The delegates quickly assented to this, more perhaps as a way to get home to supper than as a just solution to the problem, and filed noisily back into the room. There, with a hint of newly-acquired pomposity, Yang announced the collective decision.

"As for the *gate,* we must report back to the people and ask their opinion before it can be decided, but now we want you to say something about your future. You yourself can decide your punishment."

Ch'un-hsi's eyebrows almost met over his nose as he considered his sentence. "According to the rules inside the Communist Party I should be suspended for five months. If I should fail to correct my mistakes I should be thrown out by the Party and sent to the People's Court for punishment. If the masses pardon me for my past crimes I shall do my best to turn over a new leaf. I am ready to receive your criticism. I wait patiently for the decision of the masses."

With that the sesssion ended but not the day's work.

****

"He himself suggested five months' suspension."

"That's no concern of ours, that's inside the Party."

"He should be punished according to law and sent to build the highway."

"Send him to the People's Court. Make him give back everything he grafted."

So argued members of the southwest group of the Poor Peasants' League as they gathered after dark in T'ai-shan's mother's sagging hut. Elated by their delegates' report on the confrontation with Ch'un-hsi and dizzy with their new-found power, they had already persuaded each other to impose a vindictive punishment on the village head. They only disagreed as to the precise nature of that punishment.

Work team cadre Liang was disturbed by the rising spirit of revenge. He decided to temper enthusiasm with reason. In his quiet, persuasive way he took the floor. "The People's Court is for serious cases that we cannot solve ourselves. As for Ch'un-hsi, his case is big, but not, in my opinion, big enough for that. Suppose you punish him severely? Are his crimes as big as those of others? Then what will you do with the others? Their punishment must be even more severe. I think it would be better to compare records. Let's balance his crimes against those of others. Let's consider his attitude. Did he speak frankly?"

Part of the problem was the assumption by most of the peasants that punishment within the Party had no meaning. In order to clear this up, Liang summarized the four grades of discipline inside the Party. These were (1) personal warning; (2) warning before the masses; (3) suspension; (4) expulsion. "To be expelled is the most serious punishment the Party can impose," Liang explained. "It is just as serious as execution, for every Party member leads two lives, his social life and his political life. To kick him out of the Party is to kill one life."

Liang's explanation swayed the group. A more realistic discussion of Ch'un-hsi's role followed. The peasants finally agreed that suspension from the Party would be a serious blow to the village head and recommended five months. They also decided that outside the Party he must pay back what he owed the public after the autumn harvest. His future—whether he would ever again be eligible to hold public office—would be determined by the way in which he behaved in the next few weeks.

This last point was most bitterly argued. Old Lady Wang joined the Catholic dissidents in the conviction that Ch'un-hsi should never again be allowed to be a cadre, but there were at least a dozen peasants who thought he had a good record on the whole and should be allowed to continue.

The very idea that the Poor Peasants' League might actually allow Ch'un-hsi to serve as village head once more caused several Catholic peasants to lapse into moody silence. Liang sensed what was on their minds and tried to bring it out. "In the past many members of our group wanted to beat the bad cadres. But now it seems they have changed their minds and lean too far the other way. They think even to criticize is no use at all."

"I have just such a thought now," said Ch'ou-har's wife, a white-haired woman who lived next door to Yu-lai. Her husband had been beaten by him, and she was both bitter and fearful.

"The reason you feel that way is because you have been beaten," said Liang. "Now we oppose beatings and this makes people gloomy. They think it is no use. They think, 'It will be just like last year; the men will speak out but everything will continue as before.' That is quite natural. He beat you. You want to beat him. But that is feudal behavior. We are now in a new society. We must investigate facts and examine behavior. If the crimes are big enough, people will be sent to the court."

But some were still not convinced.

"Only those who have been stung know the pain," said a voice from the back of the room.

37

"I Dare Not Say I Have Finished"

It is inevitable in the course of inner-Party struggle for everyone to meet with correct or incorrect criticisms, attacks or even injustice and humiliation. This must be undergone by every comrade. It is not because our Party is merciless but because this is an inevitable phenomenon of the Party in the course of the class struggle. However, [some] comrades fail to take this into account; therefore, the moment they come across such phenomena they are surprised and feel exceptionally miserable and disheartened.

Liu Shao-ch'i

"TRAVEL PASSES ABOLISHED" "LOYANG LIBERATED AGAIN" read the headlines in the People's Daily of April 11th. Before the second day's proceedings began, Comrade Hou read both announcements and postponed his opening remarks long enough to give everyone a chance to discuss them.

The first news item concerned a step as important to the development of democracy in the villages of this area as was open Party membership. It was living proof, if proof were still needed, that the Communist Party and the Border Region Government really meant business. The right to withhold or grant permission to travel had put enormous social leverage into the hands of local cadres. Although security in wartime could not have been maintained without this leverage and without the cooperation of hundreds of thousands of children who enforced the pass system on the highways and byways, there was no question but that the regulations had often been abused. If the incursions of counter-revolutionary agents had been restricted, so too had the legitimate movements of normal dissidents and many honest peasants who, for one reason or another, had fallen out with the leaders of their village. To deny a travel permit had meant *de facto* denial of the right to appeal decisions made in the village. This was because all appeals had to be carried to the district or county seat and if the injured party was prevented from going there, there was no assurance that his appeal would ever see the light of day. Now if any person felt that he had been wronged he could himself take his case to the county Party secretary or the county magistrate or the People's Court. He need not ask anyone's permission, and nobody could stop him on the road. This was a great gain.

Like other gains it entailed a risk, the risk of uncontrolled counter-revolutionary activity. Many peasants immediately asked, "What's to stop agents and disrupters now that everybody can come and go as he pleases?"

Hou told them that suspicious persons could still be legally detained and interrogated. The whole people must now be on the alert to help maintain security. They could not simply depend on the pass system, as before.

The second news item also stirred discussion. Loyang city—a former capital of ancient China—had been taken once in 1947 when Liu Po-ch'eng's armies crossed the Yellow River on their way to the Yangtze Valley, but it was relinquished a few days later because the People's Liberation Army did not have sufficient forces to hold it. Now it had been liberated once more, and for good. Chiang's armies had retreated westward in disorder and would hardly be able to launch a successful offensive in the same area again. Since Loyang was only a few days' journey to the south, its liberation heartened the people of the whole area.

The good news in the paper, coupled with the successful confrontation at the *gate* the day before, had raised morale noticeably in the village. People talked more, moved faster, ate more quickly, and got more done than they had a few days earlier.

****

The rising morale was a lucky break for Man-hsi, who faced the delegates as soon as the discussion ceased. He was a very different type of man from the suspended village head, Ch'un-hsi. He had none of the natural poise or sophistication possessed by that leading cadre. On the contrary, he was a stolid, one might almost say dull-witted, peasant but strong as a Taihang Mountain ox. Even the thick cotton quilting of his black jacket could not conceal the bulging muscles in his arms or the enormous expansion of his chest. The padded winter clothes of North China made people look chunky whether they had any flesh on their bones or not. But Man-hsi's powerful physique shaped his clothes and threatened to burst them. One look at him confirmed his reputation as the strongest man in the village. Yet he was by no means a giant. He stood a good three inches shorter than Ch'un-hsi and just reached my shoulder.

"They say he was very brave in the struggle!" Ch'i-yun said to me as we both made the most of our first real chance to study this

"King of the Devils." " 'Change of Sky' thought never bothered him. He always took the lead in every attack!"

But this confrontation at the *gate* was something different. Now Man-hsi was called upon for introspection, and he was perplexed. A man of action, unaccustomed to speaking even at home, he looked at the rows of Party comrades in front of him and at the delegates in solid ranks behind and found it hard to begin. He stepped back, as if to sit down, glanced around for a word or sign of encouragment, but met only several score of eyes, most of them hostile, all of them stern, waiting for him to say something. This was surely the most difficult trial of his life. What he revealed at that moment was youthfulness. He was, after all, only 23.

"My grandfather had six acres, eight sections of house," he said, beginning on neutral ground. "My father had two and a half acres and four sections of house. He was a hired laborer and a poor peasant. He had to sell one acre in the famine year. After the Liberation I got land, and now we have five acres and five sections. Since that time I have been a new upper middle peasant . . ."

The delegates stirred uneasily. They knew his history as well, if not better, than he did himself. Why waste time with that? But no one spoke out, and Man-hsi went on, fumbling for words.

"When I was nine I studied two years in school. When I was young I stole a quilt from Kuei-hsing's shop. After the Liberation . . ."

He was already lost, rambling from one thing to another.

"When you speak out wrongs you must also criticize your behavior," said one of the Party members in an effort to encourage him.

"At that time I had no quilt and took one," said Man-hsi, grasping at this early straw which really had very little to do with the case. "Later I was afraid I would be caught so I returned it. Now I know it was wrong to take the quilt. The village leader fined me."

"You must confess honestly the behavior of your whole life, all the things you stole. You often stole things," suggested another Party member.

"You can't hope to conceal anything before the masses. We know what you did," added a delegate in a tone designed more to intimidate than to encourage.

"Today is not your day. We are the masters now."

"I'll tell you everything I stole," said Man-hsi.

His large black eyes set wide apart in a round, surprisingly honest face, cast desperately around the room for help.

"Even if you want to conceal something you can't. You must admit all your crimes, not only the stealing."

"I stole a pair of pants," said Man-hsi. "And I stole more than two packs of hemp seed from Li Pao-chin's house. Pao-chin's wife found it out and went to Fu-yuan. I had to own up then and I returned the hemp."

"I saw you steal that," said Lao-pao. "If it hadn't been for that, you would never have given it up."

"Let him talk, let him say it himself," admonished several other delegates, impatient with all the interruptions.

"I stole fruit from Fan Hsi-le at night, four or five times. I stole the fruit because I had no money. I ate Pao-chin's mother's fruit also. I said I would pay for it but I never gave her any money. I also stole garlic from Huai Lao-p'o's mother's garden."

"Was it garlic or leeks you took?"

"I took both. That's because I was a militiaman. I thought I could take anything I wanted. I took fruit from Yu-hsien many times. Once I went to Chang's home to make a night-time check-up. I climbed a tree to pick some fruit and broke off a whole branch."

"He's always eating other people's things," said a delegate.

"That's right, he's just like a bear," responded another.

"I must pay for all that now . . . Once, I can't remember when, I went with Hu-le to open the door of the storehouse. As soon as we went in someone came. We ran out and each of us took a mirror. Whoever it was told Fu-yuan we had been there, and he accused us of stealing 80 catties of salt. Hung-er backed him up, but we didn't know anything about the salt. Once I kept watch on the storehouse while K'uan-hsin went to take a letter to the County Office. Someone came and took a small box. I didn't know about it, but later it was found under K'uan-hsin's quilt."

At this a number of delegates swore out loud.

"What in your mother's ——— do you talk like that for. This is your self-criticism. Don't drag others into it."

Much taken aback, Man-hsi started on something else. "I took some corn from Tung-le's field . . . I can't remember any more . . ."

By this time the whole audience was angry.

"You're just wasting our time."

"Go on."

"Own up."

"And I took Liu's corn. More than two basketsful. The corn was not fit to eat." He said this as if the rottenness of the corn made the theft reasonable.

This loosed a storm of comment.

"Maybe the corn was bad," remonstrated Hu Hsueh-chen. "But the owner paid taxes on it. That's no excuse for you to take it."

"Now I'll talk about other things," said Man-hsi mechanically.

Having started down his list of crimes he would follow it to the end, throwing in big things and small without any sense of proportion. It was this aspect of his self-examination that alienated the delegates more than anything else. Man-hsi had some concept of what was wrong, but he made no distinction between big wrongs and little wrongs.

"After the Liberation I beat many people."

When they heard this, his audience quieted down and began to pay more attention. It was the beatings for which Man-hsi was notorious, and it was the beatings for which he was hated by so many.

"The first time I beat someone, it was my uncle. He tried to protect Ching-ho, the landlord, so I beat him up. Others began to beat him so I joined in. My uncle was a poor hired laborer. Another poor peasant, Chang, also tried to help Ching-ho, so I joined in beating him too. I myself felt sorry for the landlords, but I forgot my poor brothers of my own class."

"This is nonsense," said a voice from the back benches.

"In the third case I beat Lien-yu," continued Man-hsi, ignoring the voice. "I beat him twice because they said he was a rascal. He and his wife were both fined. Yu-lai and Wen-te hated Hsi-le [the father of Wen-te's bride, Hsien-e] and wanted to call him an agent. They consulted with T'ien-ming and decided to arrest him. I was ordered to bring him in, and it was I that beat him. I intended to win support from Yu-lai."

"This is also nonsense," said Old Tui-chin. "What has Yu-lai got to do with your confession?"

Man-hsi ignored Tui-chin just as he had the others. He was afraid that he would forget what came next. "At that time it was very hard to get people to come to meetings. I was worried. I decided to pick out some leaders among the rank and file and teach them a lesson with a stick if need be. After that they came promptly to meetings. Chao-chun was a landlord. He gave a new quilt to his hired laborer, An-ho, because he feared the man would accuse him. When I heard about it, I whipped An-ho for taking the quilt.

"Hu-sheng, Chin-ming, and Hsien-pao were all called agents. They themselves confessed. But I don't know whether it was out of fear or not. I helped beat them seriously several times."

"Have you proof that they were agents?" asked Chin-ming's wife, for whom this was the most crucial question of all.

"It was Fan Ming-hsi, the leader of the agents, who spoke out their names. T'ien-ming was responsible for such cases because he was in charge of security during the Anti-Traitor Movement. I did what he asked.

"Ch'ih-hsuan's wife hid some valuable things for a landlord and I tied her up. I struck Hsiao-tseng because he carried on with Pao-yu's wife and I thrashed Yuan-lung because Yu-lai told me to. I went to call Chin-ming's wife to a meeting. She said 'I just got back from the mill.' I asked, 'Where is your husband?' and I threatened her with my gun."

"You should speak out all your bad behavior, not just the beatings. Let's hear about beatings, corruption, and seized fruits," scolded Delegate Spokesman Yang, expressing the sentiments of the whole audience.

Man-hsi quickly changed the subject.

"I grafted a foreign lock and a rope. Once when the militia divided some things I got a belt. And I asked Fu-yuan to choose a pair of red trousers and a green coat for my bride. And I have been a tyrant and a rascal. When a woman doesn't obey me, I beat her and force her. One night I went with other militiamen on a search, and we threw stones to frighten people. It was all in fun. When I went to Li Village Gulch to attend meetings, I spent a lot of money that belonged to the village office. Once I went to Tunliu to catch a landlord who had run away. I spent more than BRC 10,000.

"When I went to Lucheng I took BRC 200. I will give it all back now. Once I knocked a person down and took away his shirt."

"You're only telling trifles now," complained Hu Hsueh-chen.

"Let him finish. Then we can begin our criticism," said Team Leader Hou, anticipating trouble ahead.

But Man-hsi's self-criticism was not soon finished. The delegates were just as hostile after an hour as they had been at the beginning and the Party comrades, who had been tolerant at first, were now thoroughly disgusted with him. Man-hsi was afraid he would forget something and so continued down his list, a list that he had committed to memory since he could neither read nor write. The trouble was that like any memorized list it had been badly mauled by interruptions. Man-hsi was not quite sure where he was.

"People call me *Shan Ch'iao Kuan* [the King of the Hill, a figure from Hell]. It is a good name. For really I have been a tyrant up to now. As for my working style I have been a tyrant and a rascal.

"Once the village office asked me to transport grain. I didn't want to go. I said my ox was sick. They had to find somebody to go in my place. They asked Lao-ts'un and I went and swore at him because he didn't want to go either."

With this Man-hsi's memory seemed to have exhausted itself. He turned to what he would do to make amends.

"I offer to give up an acre and a half and three sections of house.

I got 21 hundredweight in the distribution, and I will give up one hundredweight immediately after the harvest. As for the three acres of wheat that the militia divided, I got two pecks. I will give it up. There are two things from the public stores that are still in my house, a fodder-chopping knife and an embroidered singlet for an official gown. There is also a big sack of grain."

"Are you finished? Have you said everything?"

The delegates were anxious to start in with their own questions.

"Year before last during the Hide the Grain Movement I intended to leave for the old Liberated Area because I was afraid to stay home when the enemy came. I can't remember . . ."

"Have you finished or not?"

But Man-hsi dared not say that he had finished. He knew that the treatment meted out to him would depend on the quality of this review of his past, whether or not it was thoroughgoing, and though he could not think of anything more to say, he still did not dare to stop for fear that he had forgotten something. With the delegates so hostile and so eager to begin, it was obvious that they had remembered many things even though his own mind was empty. Large beads of sweat broke out on his forehead.

"I dare not say I have finished," he said.

"We want you to take time to say everything. We aren't going to hurt you, even though you hurt us. You must know you cannot conceal anything from the people," said Delegate Spokesman Yang, reassuringly.

"Another thing," said Man-hsi. "Ch'eng-wei had a landlord's wife working at his house because his own wife was pregnant. Another militia man and I took the woman to a nearby courtyard and had her there. One night the militia were hungry. We broke into the Western Inn and took some wheat. Another time I took some mutton from the inn without paying for it. This was the poor peasants' inn but I took things just the same. Once I took a rabbit from Ch'un-hsi's court and killed and cooked it . . ."

"You're talking trifles again!"

"Please criticize me one by one. Otherwise I can't remember . . . Once I passed through Hsi-t'ai's gate. His daughter-in-law was there, the mad one. She sat naked in the yard, and I shot at her with blank cartridges. She screamed and ran."

"You prolong your story just to waste our time," said Old Lady Wang, shaking her fist at him.

"What about the salt in the storehouse?" asked Lao-szu, returning to a point that was most important to the delegates because of the value of the salt and the fact that he denied all knowledge of it.

"I didn't take any."

"Do you know who took it?"

"I heard Fu-yuan say that Hung-er and his father went to Yellow Mill to sell sulfur and they also took salt. When I broke in I intended to take something, but someone came and really I got nothing."

"How many times did you enter the storehouse?"

"Only once."

"That's only because you were seen once. If you wish to pass the *gate,* you had better say everything frankly. Otherwise do as you like."

The delegates had the impression that on this matter Man-hsi was lying, but try as they would, they could not get him to change his story.

It was already late. People were hungry. The meeting was adjourned until afternoon.

During the lunch period Team Leader Hou talked to several of the delegates and advised them to investigate the case of Fu-hsu's wife. This woman, who lived in the southwest corner, claimed that Man-hsi had raped her, but he had never admitted it in the Party meetings and had not mentioned it in his public self-criticism.

Since the delegates had made clear that they were not going to beat him, Man-hsi was not as frightened in the afternoon as he had been in the morning, but he was still very much in the position of an animal at bay who dares not advance and can find no path down which to retreat. He began with an apology that sounded as if it had been borrowed from Ch'un-hsi's final speech.

"My behavior is just like that of a landlord. I *fanshened* myself and forgot my poor brothers. In the future I will do my best to correct it."

"How will you correct it?"

"In the future I will throw out all the bad thoughts from my brain. If I still do anything wrong you can all beat me to death."

"We aren't going to kill anyone, you know that!"

"Well, you can send me to the People's Court," suggested Man-hsi, countering with next most fearful thing in his ken.

"What about the rape cases?" asked Yuan-lung, acting on Team Leader Hou's advice.

"Of course I forced myself on them. If anyone raped my wife I couldn't stand it," said Man-hsi.

But when they asked him about Fu-hsu's wife, he denied over and over again that he had had any intimate relations with her.

"I threatened her. ' If you don't submit I'll arrest you!' I said. But she refused and started to go to headquarters so I was afraid."

"Why did you come back later? What did you say to her the second time? None of this *ma ma hu hu* (horse horse tiger tiger, i.e., confusion of one who can't tell a horse from a tiger)."

"I did not return," stated Man-hsi flatly.

The delegates did not believe him.

"Every night you went to a different house so you can't keep them all straight?"

"Can you so easily forget your masterpiece? If a woman promised to sleep with you, she was all right. Otherwise she was an agent. We know everything, so let's hear it."

"I did not return," said Man-hsi again.

No amount of abuse, heckling, questioning, or prodding could budge him from that position. This angered the whole audience. Even the onlookers outside the window were shouting at him. But Man-hsi stood his ground, defiant.

"Let's drop Man-hsi for the time being," said Team Leader Hou. "Let him think it over. We'll go on to another case."

The delegates agreed.

Man-hsi sat down, his head unbowed.

He was still outside the *gate*.

38

Days and Nights

If they [comrades who adopt an absolute attitude towards the mistakes of others]. . . understand that even mankind, with all its weaknesses, can in the long course of struggle, be steeled, educated, and converted into highly civilized Communists, why can they not educate and reform the Party members who have joined the Party but who still retain to some degree or other the remnants of the ideology of the old society?

Liu Shao-ch'i

MORE DRAMATIC than any stage play, the Party consolidation meetings inevitably became the center of all village activity. All day long the 33 delegates stood guard at the *gate*. In the evening they met with their respective sectional groups and reported what had happened. The hundreds of rank-and-file peasants who came to these meetings evaluated each day's events and recommended appropriate action in regard to those Communists who had been heard. Then they went on to make accusations and register complaints against those who would be heard on the morrow.

All the grievances of three tumultuous years came to light. So eager were the peasants to make known their opinions and to hear what happened that dozens continued to gather outside the windows of the meeting hall each day while that vast majority who, because of the pressure of work, could not be there in person hour after hour, impatiently awaited the delegates' reports each evening. Whereas a few days earlier the work team cadres had to wait for a quorum to show up in the Poor Peasants' League groups, and even had to send runners to round up the laggards, now the people were already waiting for them when they arrived to open the meetings. The composition of the groups themselves had also changed. The designation "Poor Peasants' League" was no longer correct because the middle peasants who had been invited to participate in all proceedings were turning up in increasing numbers. From a campaign which began by involving only a few activists among the people this Party purification took on the proportions of a truly mass movement, an evolution which bore out the realism of the Central Committee's prediction:

350

"At times it is even necessary to begin the reorganization of the Party before the initiative of the masses can be aroused."

The Party members also met every evening after a full day at the *gate*. They took up the manner in which each comrade had reviewed his or her past and the reaction of the delegates. In an effort to encourage sincere self-criticism, they went over each person's record point by point and demonstrated that the truth, no matter how terrible or embarrassing, met with better response than evasion. Those who were to appear the next day received special attention, as did those who, like Man-hsi, had failed to pass.

A campaign as intense, as all-pervading as this could hardly have taken place in any but an agrarian community, restricted to grain culture and therefore burdened with a long slack season. In no other private-enterprise society could a whole village have taken the time out to carry through such prolonged meetings. The results promised to repay the effort many-fold.

The village would never be the same again!

****

If all confrontations at the *gate* were not as tense as that between the delegates and Man-hsi, still each added its own peculiar element of conflict to the developing movement. The change in pace and tone thus generated kept all participants alert and sometimes brought them to their feet.

After the notorious militiaman had been rejected and dismissed, the teen-aged Little Mer was asked to take the stand. As the lamb follows the lion, she stood up and trembled from head to foot. Her shaking hands were clearly visible even to those sitting at the back of the hall. When she finally opened her mouth to speak, her voice quavered.

"I can't remember my grandfather," she began, evidently quite worried because she could not match Man-hsi in this respect. "My father was a hired laborer. I was married at 13. I became a leader of the women's small group in the southwest corner, but my attitude was not good. When I remade clothes for the school children, I grafted a collar lining. I must give it up. Hsiao Lao-chang's wife was a foolish woman who sold corn. She stole the corn from her husband. I swore at her and slapped her."

That was all. There was a silence in the room.

"Please, you criticize her first," pleaded An-k'u, her husband, beside himself with embarrassment. His face flushed red from the collar of his tunic to the roots of his hair.

Old Tui-chin struck flint to steel in an effort to light his pipe. "We haven't any criticism for her," he said.

Other members of the northwest contingent nodded in agreement.

"How can we make false criticisms?" asked Old Lady Wang with surprising affability. "Whenever we say anything to her, she always smiles and says, 'I am wrong.' So really we can't find fault with her."

This in itself seemed like a rather grave fault for a Communist, as Ch'i-Yun remarked for my benefit, but the delegates did not seem to find it so and fell silent once again.

"During the Hide the Grain Movement my thoughts were like this," volunteered Little Mer, remembering the discussion in the branch meeting. "I will follow the Eighth Route Army wherever it goes. I dared not beat the landlords in the struggle because I was afraid that when their forces returned I would be beaten."

"You are a good but useless cadre," said Hu Hsueh-chen, under whose guidance Little Mer had worked in the Women's Association.

"Ask her what punishment she should receive," suggested a peasant delegate.

"Advice," said Little Mer.

"From now on you must do your best to serve the masses," said Tui-chin blowing on the glowing tinder that he had at last managed to set on fire. Before he could light his pipe with it, Little Mer's ordeal was over.

"It's all done," "You pass the *gate*." "We approve you."

Many delegates spoke at once, each trying to demonstrate good will.

Everybody in the room heard An-k'u's sigh of relief as his gentle, teenaged wife stepped down.

* * * * * * * * * *

If Little Mer passed with ease, the same could not be said for militiaman Chou Cheng-lo. This 25-year-old man, cousin to Chou Cheng-fu, was neither an ox in strength, like Man-hsi, nor one of the tall finely-featured sophisticates like Chun-hsi, but a plain, ener- getic man of the soil who was also skilled as a carpenter and mason. He wore a sparkling white towel on his closely-shaven head, and his patch-free tunic and trousers were neatly sewn and clean. These were all signs of the affectionate care which he received from a wife and a mother, engaged in a contest for his favor. That the compe- tition between them also had its drawbacks was soon made evident.

Cheng-lo's difficulties before the *gate* were not due to the fact that his record was particularly bad or his self-criticism poor. He freely admitted having beaten several people, having taken several items from public stores—a knife, an umbrella, a pair of foreign scissors —and having been involved in several illicit affairs of the heart. But no one questioned him about these transgressions. What upset the delegates was a matter that he did not even mention, the way in which he treated his mother.

It turned out that his wife had quarrelled with and then come to blows with his mother, and that he had sided with his wife.

"Why did you take your wife's part?" asked Old Lady Wang.

"My wife fought with my mother because she did not want to share the fine clothes I gave her from the distribution. I gave them all to my wife and forgot my mother who brought me up. I thought, my mother is old. What if she does wear ragged clothes?"

"You had better think it over," Old Lady Wang warned. "You don't care if your mother has to sleep on straw. Everything you have you give to your wife. Your mother wept all day in the field. If your wife went out and wept like that, what would you do? I know how you feel. You think your mother is old and useless. You wish she would soon die."

"I got all my land and house from my uncle," Cheng-lo replied. "And my uncle found a wife for me. So I cared little for my mother. In the future I will be a filial son."

"Who brought you up anyway?" demanded several voices at once.

"If your wife told you to throw your mother in the well, you'd do it," said T'ai-shan's mother. "You say you will correct your conduct. But what about your wife? Will she go tearing up silk clothes rather than give your mother a share?"

"I always obeyed my wife before, but I am a man. Why should I bow down before a woman? In the future I will consider what my wife says, but I will not follow her blindly. I'll treat my mother better than my wife, for it was she who brought me up."

"We will watch your filial behavior in the future," declared Delegate Spokesman Yang. Then, mindful that this hardly seemed a matter for official concern, added, "We are only helping you to solve your family affairs. This is quite a different thing from corruption. Do you accept our criticism?"

"I am very glad for it," said Cheng-lo, but there was certainly no trace of gladness on his face.

It was not easy for me to understand at first why the peasants made such an issue of this. When I thought it over, I realized that it was the older women who had "mounted the horse," and with millenniums of tradition on their side, no one dared contradict them. They saw in the new equality which gave a daughter-in-law the right to challenge her mother-in-law a threat to the only security they had ever known: filial obedience from their sons and absolute command over their son's wives. Bought, sold, beaten, and oppressed as they had always been, they traditionally had but one chance for power, one opportunity for revenge, one possibility for prestige, and that was as a mother to a grown son, as mistress to a daughter-in-law. Now, it would appear, even this was threatened. Young women no longer obeyed. Sons sided with their wives. Old women might well pass out of life as girl babies came into it, unwanted, neglected, and quickly forgotten when gone. Unable to comprehend the many-sided security which the land reform and the new property laws were bringing in their wake, many older women were fearful lest reforms destroy the one traditional prop, the one long-awaited support of their old age.

Old Lady Wang felt this keenly because her only son was soon to marry. She herself had handpicked the girl and had tried to choose a compliant one. But she still feared that new ideas might transform even this young bride. What would happen then?

****

That the Party members and village cadres had made many mistakes and committed a number of serious crimes was confirmed by the meetings at the *gate*. But that these people took all the good things for themselves and let the poor peasants *fan* an empty *shen*, as we had been hearing ever since we arrived in the village, proved to be an exaggeration. Another six Communists passed the *gate* in the next few days, and none of them had misappropriated anything worth worrying about.

One of these was Hu Hsueh-chen, suspended head of the Women's Association. We had heard, mostly from Old Lady Wang, that Hu was a tyrant, that she oppressed everyone and that she took piles of valuable clothes and ornaments while others got only rags. But when it came time for the women's leader to go before the *gate*, people had no important grievances against her.

In the preparatory meeting held the night before, only Pao-ch'uan's mother spoke up. "She forced our small group to make shoes. Twelve of us had to make six pairs. It wasn't fair."

The handsome widow was quickly silenced.

"To make shoes was our duty. If she forced you to make more, it was only because she wished to fulfill the quota. It had nothing to do with her private interest."

"As soon as I open my mouth, you cover it," complained Pao-ch'uan's mother. "I'll not criticize others again."

But no one sympathized with her.

"Hu Hsueh-chen's attitude is very good. She is gentle and modest," said T'ai-shan's mother. The others agreed.

The secretary of the branch, Hsin-fa, certainly the most important Communist in the village, also passed easily. The fact that he had never been a leading cadre in the village administration helped. Everyone seemed to like him and only criticized the fact that he was too easy-going. They called him a *lao hao jen*, or "old good fellow," meaning someone who wanted to get along with everyone and have pleasant relations all around. This was a serious fault for a Communist and particularly for the leader of the local branch, but at that moment the peasants had their eyes on more concrete matters and so were lenient with him.

How strict the delegates could be where property was concerned was revealed when they got around to Ts'ai-yuan, the village storekeeper, a man whose popularity was legendary. They forgave him a fairly notorious record as a ladies' man when he said, "I didn't force anybody, they were all willing." Considering his good looks, his charm, and his prestige as a local man with the longest Eighth Route Army record, no one had any reason to doubt his word. They criticized him sharply, however, for smashing the big mirror that his brother Fu-yuan lent him for his wedding but would not let him have as part of his share of the "fruits." They criticized him even more sharply for bringing home from the front eight rounds of captured ammunition and then selling them for cash. They made him promise to turn over the proceeds to the government.

As a wounded soldier, Ts'ai-yuan was entitled to free help in the fields, a privilege which he had taken full advantage of in the past. But by now his wound had healed. He was able to do a man's work. He was, therefore, asked to pay for whatever help he might need in the future. This he also agreed to.

The strictness shown by the delegates in the above matters was balanced by their generosity when it came to an expensive quilt which Ts'ai-yuan offered to give up because it had not been allocated to him by any committee. They told him to keep the quilt as a token of their gratitude for the services he had rendered in the war.

* * * * * * * * * * *

Of those who had so far come before them, only Man-hsi was still barred by the delegates from passing the *gate*. He appeared the second time on April 15th, and for the second time he was held over. The intervening period had helped him but little if at all. He continued to deny ever having returned to Fu-hsu's house, insisted that he had not taken the by-now-famous salt, and also claimed that he knew nothing about a finely woven flour-sifting screen made of copper which had also disappeared from the warehouse.

No matter how angry the examiners became, no matter how many people shouted at him, he held to his original story. There was something admirable about his stubbornness. I got the impression, this time, that he was telling the truth. Whereas Ch'un-hsi, who had a comparatively good record, had exaggerated his transgressions to please his hearers, Man-hsi, whose crimes had really been serious, stuck to the facts and would not bow his head. The only difference between his second hearing and his first was a slight change in the manner with which he denied the accusations. Defiance had given way to dogged insistence, but this made little difference to the delegates.

****

The only man whose record rivaled Man-hsi's was Shen Yu-hsing. Like Man-hsi, he failed to pass. The incident which barred his way involved a ridiculously small thing—one piece of steamed bread. The story behind it, however, was complex.

One day the mutual aid group to which Yu-hsing belonged was working on the land of a soldier's family. Yu-hsing volunteered to go back to the village and bring out lunch for the whole group. The lunch, prepared by the family that owned the land, consisted of steamed bread, not a luxurious food, but still something of a treat since it was made of wheat flour in an area where the staple diet consisted of millet and ground corn. The head of the family, a widow, carefully counted out three buns apiece, or 36 in all.

When Yu-hsing returned to the field the bread was soon devoured, but one member of the group got only two pieces. He accused his hoeing partner of having taken his third bun. The latter blamed someone else. The quarrel that ensued so embittered relations among the members of the group that they split up. Since that time these particular peasants had been working as individuals rather than together.

As part of his self-criticism, Yu-hsing made a surprising admission. "Halfway to the field I got hungry. I ate one bun. I delivered 35 instead of 36. I will pay for it."

Instead of welcoming his frankness, the delgates were exasperated by his obtuseness. What good would it do to pay for one bun? The damage could not be measured in money. The whole aid group had fallen apart.

"You must examine your thoughts," said Old Pao. "Look at the harm you did. This trifling bun created such hard feeling. What were you thinking of?"

"I stole the bread," repeated Yu-hsing. "I had no purpose in mind. I was just hungry."

This was probably the truth, but the delegates refused to believe it. They began to shout at him.

"Plenty of people get hungry." "Tell the truth." "Speak what was in your mind."

"If you don't want to talk, we'll leave your case and go on to someone else," threatened Team Leader Hou in anger.

"I ate it, I ate it, I will pay," Yu-hsing yelled back, quite angry himself now.

"Why are you so stupid now, but so cunning when you stole the bread?" asked Delegate Spokesman Yang.

"He only began to recognize one piece of money from another last year," exclaimed Old Lady Wang in disgust. "Now he wants to resist us by keeping silent just like a dead pig who is not afraid of scalding water."

They decided to hold him over until the next day.

****

With the examination of so many persons already successfully completed, the peasant delegates began to feel more and more confident, and so did the Party members. The atmosphere in the meeting hall relaxed. There was a growing tendency to laugh when something funny was said, and to enjoy sharp repartee when it was clever. The gulf which existed between the Party members and the delegates at the beginning of the campaign gradually disappeared and was replaced by a growing camaraderie between those who had passed the *gate* and had consequently been restored to full citizenship and the delegates who had allowed them to pass.

There was far more humor than anger when Meng Fu-lu came before the meeting. He was almost twice as old as any other Party member and looked it. His broad face was weathered and wrinkled like the skin of a dried persimmon. This man, who had been in charge of education in the branch, said he joined the militia because he thought his brother was going to be attacked as a landlord.

"My attitude toward the masses was bad, wasn't it?"

He asked the question in such a quizzical way, as if he needed the assurance of the delegates that he was bad, that everyone burst out laughing.

A little later he was asked, "Why did you quarrel with your wife?"

"Because I have another woman—only one though," he added, as if this meager number made the affair reasonable.

This produced a second wave of laughter.

"Ch'un-fu's mother's grave is in your field. Whenever you plow you make it smaller," said Old Tui-chin.

"I wanted more land," admitted Fu-lu. "Since I am a militiaman I thought I could get away with it. I thought, 'A grave is not so important.' "

"What did you say when Ch'un-fu complained to you?"

"I said, 'Ah,' " said Fu-lu.

"What was your thought?"

"I was a militiaman; I had a gun. I thought I could cheat the grave."

"How will you settle this matter?"

"I will pay it," said Fu-lu slowly and deliberately.

"What? The grave?" asked Yuan Lung.

Everyone laughed once more.

Later, as Fu-lu walked back to his seat a woman delegate asked him, "Is your heart jumping?"

****

After eight days of hearings, four Communists, Man-hsi, Yu-hsing, K'uan-hsin, and the rich peasant's daughter, Ch'uan-e, were still outside the *gate*. They all had not only a second but also a third chance to speak, but the delegates either did not like what they said or the way they said it.

Actually Man-hsi's attitude had continued to improve, but nobody was sure that he really had reformed, and so they thought it better to keep him waiting for a few weeks.

As for Yu-hsing, he proved unable to understand that eating one piece of steamed bread was more than a piece of petty thievery.

Chao Ch'uan-e, who admitted that she had joined the Party and had become intimate with several important cadres in order to protect her father's property, wept before the meeting. The delegates understood her tears as an attempt at coercion. They therefore treated her more roughly each time she appeared. What really barred her path was her insistence that she had sold two silver bracelets and a fur-lined overcoat during the Settling Accounts Movement only because her husband was sick and the family needed money to buy medicine. In the opinion of the peasants she was afraid of expropriation at the time and had tried to liquidate her assets.

The fourth Communist barred by the delegates, the handsome, slightly built K'uan-hsin, vice-captain of the militia, made the last session lively by admitting that he had tried to rival Police Captain Wen-te in the number of his mistresses and by denying that he had ever kicked K'ao-lur's wife, Li Hsin-ai. Old Lady Wang, who had been asked to present this latter grievance, went in person to summon the young mother to the hall. When Li Hsin-ai came, she held her pretty head high and told in a quiet but firm voice how K'uan-hsin had come to her house and had asked her to call his sweetheart-of-the-moment over.

"When I refused, he kicked me."

"No, I didn't," interrupted K'uan-hsin. "If that were true, I'd go to the People's Court myself."

"Yes, you did," retorted Hsin-ai, her voice already choked and her eyes filling with tears.

"Her husband joined the army, and she is all alone at home. But you, you want her to be your servant and help you out with your rascal affairs," said Team Leader Hou with all the scorn he could muster.

"I went there, but I didn't kick her," replied K'uan-hsin, weeping now himself.

The two young people, rendered speechless by sobs, ended up pointing accusing fingers at each other, as they stood before us.

"Even the People's Court can't take in the likes of you," declared Old Lady Wang, shaking her fist at K'uan-hsin.

39

A Summing Up

Party branches in general have some good Party members as a rule. The responsibility of the higher Party leadership lies in being versed in discovering such good Party members and relying on them as the backbone to absorb fresh strength into reorganized Party branches, and not discarding or ignoring them. . . . While seriously paying attention to phenomena of impurities within the Party, we should at the same time not forget that the total general condition of our Party is one of having undergone long term testing, one of possessing great prestige among the masses and one of victorious advance.

Central Committee Directive
February, 1948

THE FIRST PHASE of the campaign to reorganize and purify the Communist Party branch in Long Bow Village concluded with the tearful confrontation between K'uan-hsin and Li Hsin-ai on April 17, 1948. In the course of the unprecedented hearings 26 persons had come before the *gate*. Twenty-two of them had been accepted by the delegates and four rejected. On the afternoon of the last day Comrade Hou Pao-pei gave a brief report in which he summed up the immediate results of the movement. In the process he cleared up a number of important misconceptions about the local Party branch.

Hou first took up the question of the class origin of the members as revealed by their life stories. Of the 28 Communists in the village branch (including the two who were in jail in Lucheng) only one, Chao Ch'uan-e, was considered to be of rich peasant origin. There were seven middle peasants. The other 20 were either poor peasants or village workers. It was, therefore, not true, as had been charged, that the Communist Party branch in Long Bow was dominated by landlords or ever had been their tool.

He next took up the question of the motives which caused people to join the Party. He listed the information brought to light at the *gate* as follows:

Wanted to win equal rights, freedom to speak   10
Supported the Party because they had *fanshened*   3

360

Wanted to serve the people	2
Wanted to beat down the landlords	1
Wanted to become cadres	4
Wanted to cover up shortcomings	4
Wanted to avoid confiscation under Party protection	1
Didn't know what it was all about	1
Unknown because still in jail in county seat	2
Total	28

While not all of these motives could be classed as admirable, still none of them bespoke an intent to wreck the Party or to use it for counter-revolutionary purposes.

The third question examined in Hou's report was that of self-enrichment. Detailed information on the economic position of each Communist household showed that the Party members, with one or two exceptions, were originally very poor. Before Liberation they and their families had owned, on the average, less than a third of an acre per capita. Several had never owned any land at all. In the course of the Settling Accounts Movement they *fanshened* pretty thoroughly and received altogether a total of 60 acres of land, 134 sections of housing, large quantities of grain, and many implements, clothes, articles of furniture, and other items. As a group they had received slightly more per capita than the rest of the villagers. Ts'ai-yuan and his brother Fu-yuan were allocated the most grain—more than 30 hundredweight. Man-hsi came next with 26 hundredweight. As to the other articles, they got about the same number as the rest of the poor peasants, but often received goods of slightly better quality because as cadres or militiamen they had a chance to pick out what they wanted before the crowd got there.

Even if the Communists had benefited slightly from this practice, it was not true to say that they grossly misappropriated the fruits of the struggle against the landlord class. They certainly could not serve as a source for the *fanshen* of those who were still poor.

The crimes and mistakes committed by the Party members constituted the fourth question examined by Hou. He classified them under four headings: (1) bad working style; (2) personal selfishness and corrupt practices; (3) "rascal behavior," loose morals, philandering; (4) forgetting one's class.

The beating cases came under the first heading, but the beatings which had occurred were quite clearly of two kinds—those administered in an effort to carry out official assignments and these administered for purely personal reasons. Although no beatings could be condoned, the latter were considered far more reprehensible than

the former. Altogether 55 grievances concerning physical assault
and corporal punishment were brought up by the delegates. Of these
20 fell in the first category and constituted the cases of bad working
style. The other 35 fell in the second category, had nothing to do
with work at all, and were therefore considered much more serious.
Man-hsi, of course, was the outstanding example of a rough fellow,
but almost all the cases in which he was involved had to do with
the performance of his duties as a militiaman—a fact which, to a
certain extent, mitigated his guilt.

When it came to personal selfishness and corrupt practices more
than 100 grievances were presented, and almost all of them were
accepted as true. They included squeeze, illegal seizure, outright theft,
and favoritism in the distribution of the "fruits." In order to square
accounts with the people, the Party members promised to swap one
good acre of land for one of poorer quality and to return to the village office for subsequent distribution the following items:

Land	6	acres
Grain	10	hundredweight
Housing	6	sections
Clothes	50	sets
Implements	34	
Livestock	1	old chicken
Bricks	400	
Roof poles	13	
Money	23,600	BRC

Seventeen cases of illicit sex relations or "rascal behavior" were
charged. Almost all the men and women comrades had been involved
in some sort of extra-marital relations, but since buy-and-sell marriages
had been the norm, this type of behavior was almost universal in the
village, and only those cases where men forced their attention on
women were listed as grievances. Some of these involved out-and-out
rape. In regard to others the situation was not clear, but there appeared to be at least some measure of coercion involved. Because
the victims were almost invariably the wives and daughters-in-law
of dispossessed landlords and rich peasants, the peasants tended to be
lenient in regard to punishment but strict in their demand for reform.
Since no form of restitution was possible, apologies and promises of
better behavior in the future had to suffice.

The fourth heading, forgetting one's class, meant collaboration
with landlords, trying to protect landlords, or not attacking landlords
during the land reform movement. Eleven cases of this nature were
brought up during the hearings. These included six instances of con-

cealing landlord property, one instance of informing a landlord as to what to expect next, one instance of harboring a landlord in the home, one instance of doing a landlord a favor, one instance of sending a landlord a gift, and one instance of inactivity when a certain landlord was under attack. From the point of view of the Communist Party these were considered to be very serious errors, certainly as serious as any of the others. Communists were expected to draw a firm line between themselves and the gentry whom they had vowed to expropriate. Any weakness in this key area was ground for discipline, even severe discipline; but education rather than punishment was favored in most cases. In this respect the *gate* proved to be a very effective school.

In regard to punishments, Hou announced that the recommendations of the delegates, the Party branch, and the work team would all be forwarded to the higher authorities as soon as possible. He promised that action would be taken by these authorities right away.

****

Hou's report covered what might be called the statistical and the tangible results of the Party purification. All the members of the team felt that the intangible results were far more important. They saw the *gate* as a turning point in the political *fanshen* of the people. It had already created a new climate of opinion, a new political atmosphere, a new relationship between the Communist Party and the people, and a new relationship between the people and the Border Region government.

These changes were profoundly democratic. They transformed "supervision by the people" from a slogan into a reality and effectively drew people, whom the land distribution had made equal economically, into activity that enabled them to project this equality into the political sphere.

The most important result of the whole campaign was certainly this drawing into meaningful action of hundreds of peasants who, because of various inhibitions and fears, had remained passive throughout the revolutionary years, or had lapsed back into passivity once the big struggle against the landlords had been victoriously concluded. The campaign to purify the party made clear to all participants that the people were sovereign, that they were responsible, and that they could and must decide their own future.

Almost equal in importance to the changes wrought by the campaign in the conciousness of the peasants were the changes it wrought in the consciousness of the Communists. In the agony of public self-examination, they were forced to face up to their weaknesses, to ask themselves fundamental questions concerning their character and their intentions, and to make important decisions about the future. Under fire for every lapse, every weakness, they began to catch a glimpse of the Revolution as "the hundred-year great task" that Chairman Mao had so often called it, rather than a great upheaval impetuously entered into and soon completed. "Service to the people" assumed new and demanding dimensions.

The enthusiasm engendered by the success of the *gate* was tempered by the realization that not all had gone well. The obvious disproportion between the fanfare of the build-up and the actual findings of the delegates was disturbing. One could hardly help wonder whether truth had been served as impartially as it should have been. Concentration on the weaknesses, errors, and crimes of the Party members had completely obscured any merits they might have had, any contribution they might have made to the *fanshen* movement. This followed inevitably from the thesis that the movement itself had been abortive. Yet if this were actually the case, what accounted for the great progressive change that had, in fact, taken place in the village? To insure the reality of supervision by the people, an atmosphere had been created in which only those who bowed their heads won approval. Those who had the courage to stand up for themselves and deny charges which they believed to be false had not been able to pass the *gate*. Yet possibly they had served truth better than those who had accepted all accusations, admitted full responsibility for crimes that they shared with others and agreed to give up property that was perhaps as rightfully theirs as anything that any family held. The disproportion between allegation and fact showed up sharply in this area.

Even the new sovereign power felt by many people could hardly be said to be solidly grounded by this one *gate*. Yu-lai, Wen-te, Hunger, and Hsi-yu were still in jail. These were the four cadres whom the people feared most. Without them the *gate* could hardly be viewed as anything more than a rehearsal. The real test of public criticism as a method of supervision and reform was yet to come.

In spite of all these reservations, the members of the work team felt that the *gate* had, on the whole, been a triumphant success, and so apparently did the people of Long Bow.

*   *   *   *   *   *   *   *   *   *   *

The confrontation at the *gate* concluded at an opportune time. Two days later, on April 20, 1948, a conference of all the work teams in the 11 basic villages of Lucheng County convened at the county seat. On April 19, Comrade Hou turned the administration of the village over to the delegates who had so successfully manned the *gate* and departed for Lucheng with all the local members of the team. The University contingent, which included Ch'i Yun and myself, also departed on that day but did not go directly to the site of the conference. We returned instead to Kao Settlement to be measured for our summer clothes, pick up our monthly millet allowances, and visit old friends.

That night, back in my own high-ceilinged room in the mission compound, I lay awake for a long time thinking over the events of the last few days. The power of the Revolution to inspire and remold people had stirred me. It seemed to me then that no decent person could fail to be touched by the challenge of the new society and that this was what gave the movement such confidence and momentum. Sometime after midnight I fell asleep only to be awakened by wild singing, incoherent shouting, and rapid talk. The sounds came from the next room. I thought at first that a party was going on. Then I realized that the uproar was the achievement of one person, probably a drunkard. When he failed to quiet down, I became very angry. I went out into the hall and spoke through the door that adjoined mine.

"There are people trying to sleep," I said.

The occupant of the room, completely disregarding my words, called out loudly in English, "Come in, come in."

I pushed the door open. The room was unlit, but enough moonlight flooded in through the paper on the windows to enable me to distinguish one object from another. On a board bed set against the far wall sat a young student dressed only in a pair of shorts and an undershirt. He never stopped talking, even when I addressed him. Sensing that I was cross, he ignored the fact that he had invited me in and protested what had suddenly become, for him, an unwelcome intrusion.

"Do what I like in my own room," he shouted. "If you shut your door, you won't hear me—American police coming in here!"

I slapped him lightly on the side of the face thinking that the shock might jar him to his senses, but he went right on shouting as if nothing had happened. Then I realized that he was sick, that he was suffering from some sort of breakdown, and that I had made a mistake. Not knowing how to mend matters, I retreated quietly to my own room. That proved to be a second mistake.

The distraught student began to shout at the top of his voice, "American, American, where are you? American, come back here!

Funny, I have forgotten his name, but I know him well. Say, American, if you are not my enemy, come back, come back."

Finally he got up and came to my room.

"I met you in Shihlitien. We came on the same truck. I want to be friends," he said. He held out his hand. It was cold as ice. Then he launched into a rambling discourse that began with the startling statement, "You long for your home. That's why you come here. This Catholic mission reminds you of home" and ended with "I plan to go to medical college, move to Hsingtai."

I suggested that he had better go to sleep first.

He went back to his own room, but he didn't go to sleep. He talked steadily to the four walls until morning.

When, at ten o'clock, Ch'i Yun came to tell me that she was ready to go to Lucheng, the student was still talking wildly, striding up and down, and pulling at his undershirt. All the "little devils" attached to the University staff had gathered outside his window and were peering shamelessly at him through holes which they had made in the paper with their thumbs. From them, I learned that the object of their curiosity had joined a work team, had struck a peasant in the village, had been arrested, tied up, and taken to the county seat for questioning. There he had run away. Caught for the second time, he had been brought back to the University where he had friends.

As Ch'i Yun and I set out over the fields, I asked her for further details about the young man. She said that he was a student from Tsinghua, the National College of Engineering in Peking. He had come to the Liberated Areas without any real understanding of what the Revolution was all about. In the study sessions he met rebuff after rebuff when he refused to face the implications of his landlord origin. On the land reform work team he was sharply criticized by his colleagues for arrogance. Frustrated, lonely, unable to understand or sympathize with the peasants, a nuisance to his comrades and himself, he finally broke down completely. Then he tried to run back to the Kuomintang side.

Here was one young cadre whom the land reform had failed to remold. Temporarily, at least, it had crushed him.

40

The Lucheng Road

Swiftly the years, beyond recall.
Solemn the stillness of this fair morning.
I will clothe myself in spring-clothing
And visit the slopes of the Eastern Hill.
By the mountain stream a mist hovers,
Hovers a moment, then scatters.
There comes a wind blowing from the south
That brushes the fields of new corn.

T'ao Ch'ien

BRIGHT SUNSHINE flooded the whole valley. A cool breeze caressed the earth. It rippled the winter wheat that shone emerald green on plot after plot. It stirred the young leaves that made feathery wands out of the village aspens. It scattered the blossoms that emblazoned the fruit trees. Everywhere peasants moved on the land spreading manure, sowing millet, planting peas, and hoeing wheat.

I hardly noticed these signs of burgeoning spring. The encounter with the mad student still engaged my mind and made me feel depressed. Had his colleagues been too hard on him? Had they tried to remake him too swiftly? Mao said it took ten years for an intellectual to achieve a truly revolutionary outlook. It could not be done in a few months. So ran my thoughts, but I found it impossible to concentrate on this or to remain depressed for long. The mood of the season would not allow it. The air was too pregnant with new life; the joy of spring after a bitter winter was too exuberant. With every step forward, the countryside around me absorbed more of my attention.

Ch'i Yun, Professor Hsu, and I were on our way to the land reform conference in Lucheng. The shortest route to our destination ran over two round ridges of land, fingers of bedrock covered with loess, that thrust out into the flat from the high ground to the west. From the tops of these ridges we looked down on the valleys below, the roofs and courtyards of the hill villages, the threshing floors and straw stacks that ringed them, the rifled grave mounds that scarred the fields, the checkered land broken as it had been for ages past into a thousand strips and patches. The endless brown of all the land harkened strangely back to winter. Even the scattered plots of wheat, when seen from above, carried only a thin sheen of green. Between the rows of lusty shoots the bare ground stood out sharply, almost menacingly, as if to demonstrate the fact that life had but a tenuous grip on earth and could hardly aspire to clothe her nakedness for long.

From the tops of these ridges we could also see the Taihang Mountains standing stark and naked in the east like a forbidding fortress wall. Absolutely treeless, monotonously bare they were, and yet not barren, for they were clothed with grass right to the top, and now, in the spring of the year, that grass too was turning green. It was as if some giant with a watercolor brush had washed the whole scene with light pigment that shone yellow-green in the sunlight, blue-green in the shadows. Because the young blades of grass did not have to push through heavy layers of last year's growth, but on the contrary showed themselves on slopes winter-grazed by thousands of small flocks of sheep, the green shoots changed the tint of the skyline as soon as they burst the ground and thereby demonstrated the overgrazing to which the mountains, in spite of their vastness, were subject.

Grazed and overgrazed the mountains were, to the point of serious erosion. At that very moment one could make out the scattered sheep and goats on the flanks and buttresses of the range. With patience, one could even spot the minute figure of an occasional shepherd. The highlands, wild and forbidding as they appeared, were in fact populated with men and animals. In all that great expanse of ravines, cliffs, and saw-tooth summits there was hardly any place where the bleating of one stray would not fix at attention 'the restlessly moving ears of another, hardly any place where a shout from a human throat would not bring an answering shout.

What was true in the highlands was multiplied many times over in the lowlands. There, as we walked, we could at all times hear voices —the abrupt commands of peasants guiding donkeys to the proper spot in the fields for unloading their baskets of compost, the cries of shepherds warning their flocks away from the young wheat, the conversations of men hoeing their way down the parallel rows of fields cultivated by mutual aid, the laughter of women out hunting greens for their supper pot.

That is what one remembers most vividly about the Chinese countryside—the fact that one is never beyond the radius of human voices, that one is surrounded by people laboring and talking to their animals and to one another. Every square foot of ground shows the mark of labor, even if it be only the herding of sheep. Centuries of human effort have transformed, molded, built up and also to some extent torn down the landscape, and yet, so natural has been this process, so gradual its sculpture, that the works of man appear to be a part of nature. The two are united, bound together, inseparably intertwined. The land without the people cannot be imagined, nor the people without land.

On that April day the road to Lucheng was no less populated than the land around it. We met and joined forces with other cadres bound for the County Conference. A peasant hurrying to deliver a government message overtook us on a steep grade. We in turn passed a young woman clad in a striped tunic. She carried a full basket on one arm, cradled a week-old baby in the crook of the other, and all the while balanced herself precariously on the back of a minute donkey whose every step was supervised by her proud young husband. No doubt these two were on their way to show their first-born to his maternal grandmother. On one slope so steep that we had to maintain our balance with our hands, an old man sped upward past us in a cloud of dust, his miraculous ascent facilitated by the fact that he had seized the tail of his heavily-laden mule and forced the animal to pull him along by shouting terrible oaths at him from behind.

As we approached the county seat, other paths converged on ours until at last they made a road. Peasants driving carts, pushing wheelbarrows, shouldering carrying poles, or simply strolling along as if out for air became too numerous to take special note of. Many of them were engaged in transporting towering stacks of new straw hats. Lucheng County, I learned that day, was famous all over China and even in certain cities of Europe for its straw wares. International conflict and Civil War had cut off markets in the last seven years, but now, with the expansion of the Liberated Areas, business was picking up again. Young and old alike were returning to the traditional craft, a craft based on the tough long straw of Taihang Mountain wheat and on the nimble fingers of Taihang Mountain people.

Our road gradually broadened into a highway that cut straight through the long, strung-out village of Nan Kuan (South Portal) and then stopped abruptly at the edge of the moat in front of Lucheng's ancient wall. There, what must once have been a massive and forbidding entrance to a strongly fortified town was now reduced to rubble and ruin. The town dwellers were tearing down not only the gate towers but the walls themselves. Though they had only half accomplished this task it was obvious that a few months would see the bastions levelled. The salvaged bricks, each of which rivalled a

western concrete block in size, were already reappearing in the
scattered new housing that ringed the outskirts of the town.

Once inside the dwindling battlements, we found an almost empty
plain. One main street lined with a few dozen restaurants and shops,
several village-like clusters of adobe walls and courtyards interspersed
with lanes and alleys, an extensive *Yamen* compound—that was all.
The rest of the huge quadrangle consisted of land that had never
been built upon or land that had long since been abandoned. Ruined
dwellings showed more clearly in some sections than in others. These
were the areas looted by the Japanese during the last years of the
Second World War. Desperately short of fuel, the "sun devils" had
torn the timbers from whole blocks of houses. The adobe walls thus
exposed had rapidly disintegrated under the erosion of wind and rain.

The condition of the town did not surprise me. It was typical of
hundreds of county towns in North China in the 1930's and 1940's.
Their emptiness was the result of a process that had begun long
before the Japanese invaders arrived. County towns had been fort-
resses against rural unrest for so long that the very life had been
choked out of them. Unable to enter or leave the walled enclosures
freely, the people had come to depend on the sprawling communities
outside the gates for trade and handicraft services. They had left the
decaying inner cities to officialdom, to the grain warehouses of the
gentry, and to the barracks of their mercenary rural guards.

We proceeded past rows of dilapidated dwellings and acres of
debris to the *Yamen* compound at the center of the area. Much of
this also lay in ruins. Not content with despoiling the outlying sections
of the town, the Japanese troops had finally gutted even their own
headquarters. But while the destruction had been great, the portions
of the compound that remained untouched were still extensive. A
series of courts within courts, which bespoke past splendor of imperial
proportions, still contained many a standing wall, many a tight roof,
and many an idol-filled temple. There, amidst piles of rubble and
brick-strewn yards, we found the offices of the new county government.

All the southernmost courts of the compound had been turned
over to the civil administration. To indicate this a long wooden
plank hung beside the front gate. On it were inscribed the characters
Lu Ch'eng Hsien Jen Min Cheng Fu (People's Government of Lucheng County). The northernmost courts had been set aside for the
use of the Communist Party. To indicate this a second plank hung
beside a side-street entrance. On it were painted the characters *Lu
Ch'eng Hsien Tang Wei Hui* (Lucheng County Party Committee).
The courts in between housed the county police, the County Court,

and the chambers of the county judges. Of the many public organizations in Lucheng County, only the People's Liberation Army had its headquarters in another part of town.

It would be difficult to say which part of this rambling headquarters, the civil administration or the Party center, was the busiest. Scores of peasants, merchants, cadres, policemen, soldiers, and townspeople of all descriptions streamed in and out of both gates. If any difference could be noted in these two streams, it was that ordinary citizens in homespun clothes predominated at the front gate while land reform workers and district Party functionaries in cadres' uniforms of machine-made cloth predominated at the side gate.

When we arrived at the Party headquarters, the whole area was alive with more than its usual quota of bustle and confusion. The county-wide meeting of land reform workers had brought more than 100 cadres in from the countryside. Most of the male participants had found living quarters on the straw-covered floors of a series of small temples that faced each other across a small courtyard. They hung their dispatch cases, towels, and jackets on the colorful clay idols that lined the walls and made themselves at home amidst the gods. The female participants, far fewer in number and most of them students from Northern University, had taken over a large *k'ang* in a temple that faced a separate court. I, as a foreign guest, was given a room to myself. It was in a structure that was removed from the center of activity but was still a part of the same building complex.

Each division of the temple row was supposed to house the cadres from one village, but because the team members came from all over the county and many of them knew each other well from guerrilla warfare days, they by no means remained in their assigned quarters. They wandered freely around seeking old friends, greeting them with hearty shouts, and forming constantly shifting groups for discussion and gossip. The meeting had all the atmosphere, excitement, spirit, and warmth of an alumni day, veterans' reunion, and political convention all rolled into one.

The conference, however, was really a school—a school for the study of the strategy and tactics of the New Democratic Revolution, a school of class consciousness and of socialist morality. It was a school in which cadres exchanged experiences, extended their knowledge, unified their outlook, and wrestled with their weaknesses, so that they might return to the villages better prepared to guide and teach the Communists of the village branches and the people.

Although the destiny of the "basic" villages lay in their hands, although the majority of the peasants looked up to them as seers, the full-time district cadres and the staff members and students from

Northern University who made up the work teams were not political geniuses, but only ordinary human beings, products of the old society only partially remolded by their experience with the new. Considering the vast needs of the time, their knowledge was woefully inadequate, their political consciousness limited, and their character development deficient. These educators needed educating certainly as much as did those local Communists who had so recently come before the *gate*. And so a form of *gate* had been organized for them—the county land reform conference. It differed from the village *gate* in that there were no direct representatives of the people to give opinions from below; nevertheless, the cadres heard and judged one another and were guided in an agonizing appraisal of their work by a group of men more advanced and more experienced than themselves.

This higher level of educators was made up of the leaders of the county government and of the county organization of the Communist Party. The key figure at this level was Secretary Ch'en, chairman of the county Party Committee and chief organizer, leader, and teacher of Lucheng's 2,500 Communists. All the myriad problems engendered by land reform found their way to his door. If the movement went well, he deserved much of the credit. If it went awry he had to assume a large part of the blame.

Secretary Ch'en kept in touch with current developments and exercised leadership over the land reform movement in various ways—by frequent, unannounced visits to the "basic villages," by weekly written reports sent in by the work team leaders, and by directives issued from time to time as guide lines for the teams. More important than any of these, however, were the county-wide conferences of full-time cadres such as the one we now had joined. At such a conference time was unimportant. Discussion could last a week, ten days, two weeks. The cadres met for as long as was needed to examine all work, study policy, and solve problems of individual attitude and morale. No group could go through such an experience without being shaken down and strengthened. Few individuals could attend such a session without being changed by it.

41

In the Dragon Hall

Now the mallet is lifted to smite the lips of the metal monster. . . . Hear the great bell responding! How mighty her voice, though tongueless! KO NGAI! All the little dragons on the high-tilted eaves of the green roofs shiver to the tips of their gilded tails under that deep wave of sound; all the porcelain gargoyles tremble on their carven perches; all the hundred little bells of the pagodas quiver with desire to speak. KO NGAI! All the green-and-gold tiles of the temple are vibrating! The wooden goldfish above them are writhing against the sky; . . . KO NGAI! What a thunder was that!

Lafcadio Hearn

IN THE HEART of the *Yamen* area a large temple, unharmed by vandalism, stood solid and imposing amidst the ruins. It had been converted into a hall by emptying it of all trappings and idols. Thus stripped down the building displayed an awe-inspiring symmetry. Two great beams 25 feet in length and three feet thick supported the center of a heavy tiled roof. This roof swept up and out at the four corners as if poised for flight, while across its ridge pole four enormous dragons in colored tile battled each other for supremacy in the sky.

The deep tones of the temple bell summoned the cadres from far and near. Under the fiery dragons, under the spreading roof, under the ancient beams where countless worshippers had once bowed their heads in a grey swirl of incense, the County Conference met in plenary session. Two tables and a brick rostrum constituted the only furnishings in the vast hall. The tables were used by note-taking secretaries, the rostrum by various speakers as they made their reports. On the wall behind the rostrum hung a large portrait of Mao Tse-tung. Above this, painted in gold on a large red board were four characters in Mao's distinctive calligraphy. They said, "Serve the people."

Small group discussions followed the mass meetings. They were held wherever the participants found it convenient. Some teams met in their sleeping quarters. The hubbub created by the first two or three teams to begin a session inevitably drove the others away. Each

373

of the others had to find a quiet spot in the shadow of the big temple
or in one of the abandoned ruins behind it, and carry on as best it
could, using 1,000-year-old bricks for seats. After dark the Long
Bow team often met in my room, but during the daylight hours we
chose as our special preserve a pile of rubble at the base of an old
bell tower.

On this tower, a ruined brick structure that overlooked the whole
temple area, four ghostly characters, each one taller than a man,
proclaimed a slogan out of the past. It was a slogan so encumbered
with irony that it engraved itself on my memory. From top to bottom
the characters read *Jih Chun Yung Tsai*—The Japanese Army Forever Remains.

****

It took three full days for the leaders of the various work teams to
report to the whole conference on the six weeks they had spent in the
villages. Their reports lasted one hour, two hours, even three hours.
They were rambling, confused, repetitive; yet the assembled cadres
listened in absolute silence, intent on catching every word. Those
who could write—perhaps 50 percent of the total—held their copy
books on their knees and took notes without pause. All found themselves listening to experiences that, while differing in detail from their
own, reflected as if in a mirror the essence of what had happened to
them. As one team leader followed another, each person present experienced a sense of having his own past reviewed.

Ch'i Yun and I arrived at the first session a few minutes late. An
old man was already speaking from the rostrum. He was the leader
of the East Portal team. For 40 years he had worked as a hired
laborer before receiving land and a donkey as a result of the "Settling
of Accounts." Those years of toil had put a stamp on him that no
subsequent experience could erase. He had only to don a new govern-
ment-issue suit to transform it into a peasant-style outfit. A wide sash
wound round his waist and trouser cuffs bound tight to his ankles
with strips of cloth gave his modern garb an unmistakably rustic
flavor. On his head he wore, not a visor cap, but a towel.

"When we first set out to find the poor peasants, we made mistakes
because our standards were too rigid," the old man said. "We thought
that the people who lived near the county town would be canny and
dishonest, so we trusted very few and opened the door only a crack.
That's why the ranks of our League remained lean. When we visited
them the peasants didn't want to talk to us. They still remembered
the Wash-the-Face Movement of last year. We had to change our
methods. Each of us began to talk about his own past. Soon one of

our cadres who had worked in the mines found an old miner among the poor peasants. When we started to talk about the hardships of underground work the old peasant began to speak of his own sorrows. Soon his friends also opened up."

Since the speaker had never been to school, he found reading difficult. He had to pause frequently in order to decipher the notes which had been prepared for him by the efforts of his whole team. Finally he pulled an old pair of spectacles from his pocket and fixed them on his nose by means of a string which he tied around the back of his head. That these antique spectacles with their square lenses of ordinary window glass could help him to see more clearly was doubtful, but they did seem to give him confidence and that was reason enough to wear them.

"In front of the poor peasant delegates the Party members were very afraid," he continued. "They dared not reject any opinion or speak their minds at all. They just accepted every criticism no matter what, but in their minds they couldn't think it through. We had to explain to them that they had the right to speak their own opinions, that this was an education for them. Later we discovered that some of the delegates were not quite honest themselves. One was there only to take revenge on a Party member whom he hated."

As he progressed through his report, this old peasant-turned-cadre launched into stories that required no notes and soon found that he could hold the audience spellbound. Then he took his glasses off. One of the stories which he told concerned an illiterate like himself, an East Portal Party member who had taken more than 60 objects from the public stores. Faced with the necessity of admitting his misappropriations before a *gate* manned by poor peasants, the man became panicky. What if he couldn't remember everything? He stayed up five nights in a row, took out one article after another and drew a picture of it. To these primary reminders he added sketches that would help him recall the motive for the theft. On one piece of paper he first drew a pair of leather shoes. Next to the shoes he drew the outline of a woman. The woman represented his wife. She had always despised him, threatened to leave him, and never made shoes or clothes for him. This, he decided, was because he was "bare poor." As soon as he received land and house he tried to relieve domestic tension by bringing home to his wife things which might impress her. All this he easily recalled when he looked at his sketch of her. The confession which he finally made with the aid of such pictures was so detailed and comprehensive that the delegates allowed him to pass the *gate* without further delay. There was one stipulation, of course. He must return all 60 of the misappropriated items.

The captain of the East Portal team told this story to illustrate the sincerity with which many Party members approached their self-examination, but the story simultaneously illustrated another facet of the campaign, a facet that emerged more and more clearly as the team reports followed one another. This was the tremendous pressure which had been brought to bear on the Party members to make them acknowledge the failure of the *fanshen* movement and concede their part in it. The pressure was so great and carried with it such overtones of revenge that many honest Communists felt they had no way out. Attempts at suicide had occurred in village after village.

Reports like these demonstrated to the members of the Long Bow team that they were not the only ones who had made mistakes, lost their way, travelled a curved road, or failed to find the conditions which they had gone to the village to seek. But this was scant solace in the face of the very sharp criticism which Party Secretary Ch'en directed at all the land reform cadres and the Long Bow team in particular.

County Secretary Ch'en was not the sort of warm-hearted friendly man we expected to meet after our experience with Regional Secretary Wang. He was a lean fellow with a stern jaw and penetrating eyes that looked out from behind dark-rimmed spectacles. An intellectual through and through, he did not easily unbend. Surrounded by that crowd of boisterous, talkative rural cadres, he seemed ill at ease. When anyone wandered in his presentation or talked of trifles, Ch'en had a way of looking very bored. In the midst of one report he snapped, "Let's stick to the point." He later stopped a speaker in the middle of a sentence with, "Let's hear your own faults, not someone else's." The respect which the cadres nevertheless felt for him stemmed from the intellectual brilliance which he demonstrated every time he rose to speak. His speeches were well-ordered, disciplined, and clear, although they could not be called concise. He presented every idea in several complementary ways so that all might understand it and patiently went over ground he had covered twice before so that there would be no doubt as to his meaning. His speeches even demonstrated a flash of humor now and then, but it was a humor that was incidental to what he had to say. He was not one to be funny just to amuse his listeners. For all this the cadres respected him, even admired him, but they found it difficult to get to know him. He was too much the typical commissar of the novel—reserved, iron-willed, hard-working, and self-sacrificing. And what he demanded of himself he also demanded of others.

Within an hour after our team arrived in Lucheng, Secretary Ch'en had called Comrade Hou and Little Li into his headquarters and questioned them about the arrest of Yu-lai, Wen-te, Hsi-yu, and Hung-er. He pronounced the arrests a mistake. He pointed out the bad influence which the action had had on the whole region. Somehow a rumor had started that the four arrested cadres had been tried before a mass meeting and shot on the spot. More than 100 li (30 miles) away, peasants were repeating "eyewitness" accounts of the execution. The effect of these rumors was to confirm the guilt of the four men in the popular mind and divert any effort to look more deeply into the case. Yet no firm evidence had come to light that the arrested men were actually responsible, and thus the county police had already decided to release them.

Secretary Ch'en did not stop there. He went on to criticize Hou and Li for holding the district cadres under house arrest at the accounts examination meeting, for disarming T'ien-ming, and for unreasonably attacking and harassing the whole Party branch. All of these actions added up to extremism, Left extremism, he said.

A document that amplified this criticism was assigned as required reading for all the teams. It had been prepared by the Third Administrative District of Taihang Subregion. It pointed out that radical Left tendencies had caused many teams to seek support only among the poor peasants, to neglect the middle peasants, to ignore and suppress all old cadres, to treat Party members as if they were class enemies, and to underestimate the extent of the poor peasants' *fanshen*. Here was a poor peasant point of view elevated to the status of a "line," a "line" that was in opposition to the Party's expressed policy.

Secretary Ch'en's broad censure and the critical tone of the subregional pamphlet all but destroyed the élan of a team that had maintained morale only with difficulty. What hurt the cadres from Long Bow most was the charge that they had unreasonably oppressed the members of the village branch. Up to this point they had felt that their *gate*, for all its shortcomings, had been a success. They might have been misled by Old Shen concerning who were the honest poor peasants, wasted time in an accounts examination meeting, falsely arrested four innocent men, wrongly detained three others, failed to establish a solid Poor Peasants' League, and mistakenly treated the village as Type III; but all this had to be balanced against the fact that they had succeeded in mobilizing the Party members and the people for the purification campaign, that the Party members' self-criticism had uncovered real problems and had paved the way for real reforms, and that morale in the village, both inside and outside the branch, had picked up sharply thereafter. Now even these achievements were called into question.

42

When Poverty Outranked Heaven

Men are products of circumstances and upbringing and . . . therefore changed men are products of other circumstances and changed upbringing, [but] circumstances are changed precisely by men and . . . the educator himself must be educated.

Karl Marx

WHEN THE Long Bow cadres gathered on the bricks under the bell tower to review their work, the local men, Hou and Little Li, Han, Liang, Li Wen-chung, and Chang-ch'uer were in an angry, bitter mood. If it was wrong to arrest the four cadres, then Secretary Ch'en must share the blame, they thought. After all, the Secretary himself had approved the arrests at the time and the county police had ordered Team Leader Hou to drop everything for an investigation into the crime. As for the district cadres who had been held for questioning about the village accounts, they had not really been arrested. They had only been asked to eat and sleep together for convenience's sake, so that they would be available when needed. Nobody had stood guard over them. They were free to come and go in the village.

As these opinions were expressed and debated, the mood of the cadres gradually changed. They began to understand how deeply they had been influenced by an exaggerated reliance on the poor. They laughed as they remembered the first few days in the village, how they had dropped their bedrolls and gone looking for poor peasants while not daring to speak to anyone who looked at all prosperous, and completely ignoring the Party that had led the village for three years. The image they had in mind of the poor peasant they were looking for was of a man dressed in rags with a torn towel around his head, scratching lice and flea bites. If any peasant said he had *fanshened* they thought he was dishonest. If he had no grievances against the village cadres, they dropped him. Many peasants had obviously seen through this right away. They hid their quilts, their pillows, and their better-looking clothes and dropped wild herbs and

378

chaff into their cooking pots while they waited to see which way the wind would blow.

"When I arrived in Long Bow," said Little Ch'uer, still pale from the effects of the assault upon him, "the only thing I had in mind was the poor-and-hired-peasant line. I thought that poor peasants were everything. I looked only for poverty. Poverty outranked heaven. As soon as I had some idea of who the poor peasants were, I ordered the old cadres to arrange for me to eat in their homes and especially in the homes of those who had been called agents or were suspected of dishonesty. Right away I met Shen Ch'uan-te and I believed everything he told me. Now I realize that I was wrong. I looked only at a man's living conditions. I paid no attention to his character. That was mechanical."

As they talked, the cadres also began to see how concentration on the poor and avoidance of the Communists in the village Party branch had been linked.

"My attitude toward the Communists was very severe," said Li Wen-chung. "I criticized them relentlessly and tried to force them to admit crimes. Otherwise, I thought, they will think I am afraid. But the result was not so good. Many Party members were gloomy and their self-criticism was not all honest. As for the accident, I thought, 'The landlords and rich peasants have all been beaten down. No feudal element would dare commit this crime. It must be the Party branch.' So I said to the Communists, 'We must uncover this matter and find which one of you is guilty.' I thought they were worse than the puppet troops. I attacked Chao Ch'uan-e over and over again. I made her review all her rascal behavior and insisted that she had slipped into the Party and seduced important cadres only to protect her family. The other Party members joined in the attack. That night Chao Ch'uan-e refused to come to the meeting. She lay on her *k'ang* and wept. Then she tried to hang herself. Fortunately, someone saw her and stopped her; otherwise I would be responsible for her death. This was certainly leftism."

Comrade Hou agreed and went even further than the others in his analysis of what had happened. "We kept telling them that they were still poor because the cadres had taken all the 'fruits,' " he said. "But really, how much did they take? And if it were all divided up, what difference would it make? It could still never fill all the holes that remain. Surely the problem must be solved in the future by production. But we kept saying, 'You have not *fanshened,* you have not *fanshened,* the cadres are bad!' So of course the peasants are ready to go after the cadres for whatever can be taken from them, and they are ready to call middle peasants rich peasants so that their property too can be taken. Meanwhile, everyone wants to be a poor peasant so that he can get something. But where is it all going to come from?"

* * * * * * * * * * *

When the conference convened again in the big temple, the teams all reported on the sectarianism that marred their work. Once again the men and women from Long Bow realized that they were not alone.

Here, for instance, are a few passages from the report of Chia Village:

At first we found some poor peasants who could speak well and had many grievances against the cadres. They opposed the cadres blindly, and we relied on them because we thought all the old organizations bad. . . . We were in a big hurry and thought we could understand the whole village within three days. We avoided the Communist Party members. We accepted the poor peasants' request and ordered the Party members to live and eat together—*ch'ih ta kuo fan* (eat out of one big pot). . . . But the Party members were very upset, and many of them wept. The village chairman's wife swore at her husband. "You stupid ass, wasn't being head of the whole village enough? Why did you have to go and join the Communist Party as well?". . . . We repeated our work several times over. We visited, explained, and visited again. Many poor peasants got tired of it. So did we. We couldn't find much to do and thought we ought to go and find another village, but when Secretary Chang came and asked for material, facts and figures, we had very little to give him!

From these reports, two questions emerged. Where did the poor-peasant line originate? Why had they all adopted such extreme measures? At a small group meeting the following day, the local members of the Long Bow team all agreed that they got their poor-peasant line at the Lu Family Settlement meeting, the big month-long education conference that preceded the departure of the Lucheng County teams to the "basic" villages. At the meeting, Secretary Ch'en himself had set the tone. He had declared that the poor of Lucheng County had not *fanshened*. He had said that any cadres who could not find poor peasants in the villages didn't deserve to eat. He had held the cadres before him responsible for the abortive *fanshen* movement and insisted that they all examine their shortcomings and make public statements of their conclusions.

Liang Chi-hu recalled his own reaction to that meeting. Here was a cadre whose service to the Revolution could not be ignored. He had faced the Japanese Army as a militiaman at the age of 18. He had led his militia detachment in the battle for Long Bow and then had helped liberate Changchih. As head of the police department of the Second District, he had ridden herd on the reactionaries and helped to guarantee the *fanshen* of thousands. "Yet," said he, "when I learned what was expected of us I was very afraid. I worried all the time and wondered if I could pass the *gate*.* I even lost my appetite and grew very pale. I had to look back over the years. Was I active or not. What was my attitude during the land reform? What mistakes had I committed? I finally admitted four mistakes. I had protected two rich peasants who were neighbors of mine. I had kept in my home property that belonged to a family that everyone believed to be gentry. I had helped to expel from the Peasants' Association a man who criticized us all for taking more than our fair share of the 'fruits.' I had received an acre of land that was not allotted to me by any distribution committee. That was because I was away when the land was parcelled out. When I came back there was very little left. I protested and was given an acre by the other cadres.

"In my heart I thought, 'All these mistakes are not mine alone. Others were also involved.' But it was a sorry business to blame others. I took full responsibility. I asked for punishment and received a warning from the Party Committee. This warning went on my record. After that I was troubled. I thought, 'All these things were not done by me alone, but I have taken punishment for all of them.' Whenever I fill out a form in the future I must write 'Received Punishment.' I was very upset."**

The pressure at the Lu Family Settlement meeting had been such that many cadres did as Liang had done. And because the record was thus distorted beyond reasonable resemblance to reality, they felt oppressed and despondent. While, on the positive side, the meeting had burned into every heart the seriousness of graft, corruption, influence peddling, nepotism, and maneuvering for personal advantage no matter how small, on the negative side it placed a burden of guilt on the shoulders of the district cadres which they were not able to bear. It now became clear that when these cadres came from the Lu Family Settlement meeting to the "basic" villages, they came prepared to examine the village Communists as severely as they themselves had been examined. In Long Bow, the attack on Little Ch'uer only gave further impetus to this determination. The Party members were blamed for the crime as a matter of course.

Open discussion of these problems at the County Conference did

* In this case the *gate* consisted of his fellow delegates at the meeting.
** After the Lu Family Settlement meeting, the County Committee reviewed Liang's record again and withdrew the warning. The damage to his morale was not repaired at one stroke, however.

not automatically lead the Long Bow team to any solution. In fact, the more they talked about it, the more dejected the cadres became. Comrade Hou, always dour and serious, looked beaten. He held his head in his hands and stared off into space. Little Li, who before had always been ready with a joke and a laugh, adopted the dour mien so characteristic of Team Leader Hou, while Han, Liang, Little Ch'uer, and Li Wen-chung fell silent altogether. They contemplated the rubble around them as if the whole world had collapsed and they themselves were derelicts lost in the ruins. With the peasant members of the group in such a mood, the intellectuals also lapsed into unusual silence.

****

A brilliant four-hour report by Secretary Ch'en on the right way to organize work in the villages and in the village Party branches only deepened the gloom that hung over the conference. At one point in his report Secretary Ch'en charged that in six weeks of work the Long Bow team had done only two things, both of them wrong. They had examined the village accounts without result, and they had oppressed the village Party branch.

When they met that evening in my room, the Long Bow cadres quarrelled openly for the first time. Little Li blamed Hou for the Secretary's unfair criticism. "I had all the material," protested Little Li, "but when the Secretary asked you for facts and figures about the village you told him you didn't have any! You were so busy with the Party branch that you didn't even know what we were doing. Yet you tried to answer for everything yourself."

"Why didn't you speak up then?" snapped Hou.

"Because you always do what you want, no matter what we say," replied Little Li, glaring at his partner.

If Han had not spoken at that moment they might have come to blows.

"The trouble with our group," said Han, "is that we have a beginning but no end. We have a leader but no follow-up. We have a tiger's head but a snake's tail. And so our work doesn't go well."

The team had reached an impasse. The low morale of the local cadres had reached a nadir.

The time had come for an evaluation on a different level. Up to this point the cadres had been talking about a general line—their relations with the peasants, the mistakes made in estimating the situation in the village, whether or not they had treated the branch members too harshly. The question of their internal relations, the question of personal problems and grievances that might stand in the way of their working together had not been touched upon. Yet these questions could become a greater obstacle to effective work than any other. Unless the inner contradictions that plagued the team and its individual members were exposed, there was little chance that the larger contradictions in the world outside them could ever be successfully tackled. Perhaps an extended period of self-examination could clear the air. If each individual could be granted ample time to think through his own problems, make clear his own thoughts and attitudes, his own reservations, his own gripes, he might then be able to formulate, isolate, and finally lay aside the burdens that distracted him and wore down his energies.

Secretary Ch'en and his assistant, Secretary Chang, were aware of this problem, On the very next morning, April 26, 1948, they called all the cadres to a meeting in the temple and announced a Party Day. "We call this a Party Day," said Secretary Chang, then added for my benefit and that of several of the University students, "but everyone can join whether they are Party members or not. What we want to do is to speak out what we have in our minds honestly and sincerely. Even if you try to suppress what is bothering you, it will burst out sooner or later and perhaps influence your work badly. For example, on the Long Bow team many workers didn't agree with the leader, but they didn't speak out in the meetings and their morale was low. What started as a problem for two or three soon influenced others, and very soon the work of the whole team suffered. So now, while we have the opportunity, we will examine ourselves and try to wipe out the gloomy atmosphere that has taken hold of some comrades and some teams."

Secretary Chang, a plump man whose cheerful temperament contrasted sharply with that of the austere Ch'en, went on to analyze some of the hidden problems which the cadres had not yet discussed in public. He knew these problems well, for the morale of the Party was his special sphere of responsibility.

"Part of this gloom is due to the influence of the purification meetings on the cadres. Many of you fear examination in your own villages. You are afraid you cannot pass the *gate* at home. At the same time, the mutual-aid teams have refused to help your families. You worry lest your children have nothing to eat. But you ought to know by now that if you make up your minds to be honest, serve the masses sincerely, and acknowledge your mistakes, you can pass the *gate*. As for problems at home, we can also take steps to solve them. Nobody should worry unduly. Let each speak out frankly now and not complain and gripe in the corners later."

The mass meeting broke up. The teams spent the rest of the day in self-and-mutual criticism. The Long Bow cadres once more sought out their favorite place, the rubble at the base of the bell tower.

Thus began a strange, halting meeting that lasted until twilight, broke briefly for a meal of boiled millet and cabbage, and then continued in my room until well after midnight. To dig beneath the surface, to expose what one truly thought about oneself and about others was always difficult, often extremely painful; yet it had become as necessary as breathing. The cadres talked in subdued tones, approached problems, dropped them, and took them up again, each time probing deeper. Sometimes they succeeded in laying bare the heart of the matter. More often they fell short, but even when they failed they struck closer to the truth than before.

The meeting plunged first into a problem that was, in the main, objective and easy to define—the problem of the team members' own livelihood. Secretary Chang's statement about the situation in the cadres' home villages was confirmed in a most concrete way by Han Chin-ming. His moon-round face assumed the solemnity of a stone Buddha as he revealed the problems that beset him. To begin with, he was sick, had been sick for several months, with chronic dysentery. Though this sickness did not prevent him from working, it tired him, worried him, and made him far less effective than he aspired to be. Far harder to bear than any sickness, however, was the political attack which had been launched against him by self-appointed "poor peasants" in his home village. When he took leave for a week in order to overcome his dysentery by resting at home, these peasants immediately started a rumor that he had been fired from his job as a county cadre. They said he had been sent home in disgrace. When a neighbor, a man with whom he had long shared a cow, called on him, the members of this clique took the visitor aside and asked, "Why do you help Han? Are you still trying to flatter the cadres?" After that his neighbor dared not return to Han's courtyard, sold his share of the cow, and tried to pull out of the mutual-aid group to which they both belonged. When Han's mother went to the mutual-aid group for help with the spring sowing, a former Japanese puppet reprimanded her. "From now on nobody will help you. If you want anything, you must employ hired labor." The old lady returned home in tears. A few days later Han opened an underground pit to get out the last millet that his family had stored as insurance against the "spring hunger." He was accused of digging out grain in order to sell it and thereby avoid confiscation. It was just as if he were a landlord. On top of all this, his taxes went up ten points. The harassment was so great that Han could not face it. He returned to work in Long

Bow before he had fully regained his health. As a result he suffered frequent relapses and often had to stop work in the middle of the day.

"I don't understand all this," Han said. "I don't understand why my taxes went up. I know that during the distribution I exchanged one acre of poor land for less than an acre of fertile land, and that last year although I got ten days help with the crops, I wasn't able to return the labor. Yet when I offered to give back the land and pay off the debt with money, the new cadres wouldn't listen to me. Since then I have carried a great weight on my shoulders. I don't think that my debt to the village and my land exchange are such great crimes. Under the guns of the puppet forces I worked hard and risked my life countless times. But now I am treated worse than a landlord. When my mother wept, I felt as if a great knife were turning in my heart. What I want to do is to return to the village, speak out everything, and settle this problem. If it goes on like this, I cannot work."

With that Han heaved a deep sigh.

At first nobody said anything in reply. What answer could there be? I, for one, was appalled by his story. A wife, a child, and a mother at home, very little left to eat, and nobody willing to plant his crops. Yet he was supposed to work full time away from home. He was supposed to help other peasants solve their problems. He was supposed to lead them in reforming their own officials. No wonder the morale of the cadres was low.

Team Leader Hou finally spoke. "It is no use being so depressed," he said, himself the very picture of depression. "Such a mood can only hurt your body. It can certainly never solve any problems. I myself have had such thoughts as yours. I too have been attacked at home. I don't know how my land will be planted. I thought to myself, 'If I cannot pass the *gate* at home, still I am better than a landlord. If the masses don't want me as a year-round hired laborer, still I can be a seasonal laborer for my family.' But later I realized that this was a pretty sorry attitude for a Communist. A distant journey tests the strength of a horse, and a long task proves the character of a man. The only way out is to work hard and serve the people. When I thought about that, the wind drove away the clouds."

Those who spoke after Hou had finished all took the same view. They agreed that dishonest peasants in many communities were making things hard for the old cadres. But this was not the policy of the Communist Party. In time all this would be corrected. In the meantime, Communists must not waver. They must go on with their work, maintain their faith in the Party and the people, and not worry too much about rumors and unjust criticism.

But Han was not so easily cheered. It was all very well to counsel steadfastness, but would that put grain in the pot or seeds in the ground?

"During the first week here I thought of nothing but my family," he said. "Later I decided—anyhow, I am better than a landlord. But even a landlord can get his share; why not I? They are our enemies. Yet we pardon them. Why should I be punished so severely for a small debt owed to the people?"

One colleague who offered no advice to Han was Little Ch'uer. When he finally did speak up it was not to criticize or encourage; it was to tell of his own plight. It turned out that Little Ch'uer was no better off than Han or Hou. The attempt on his life had so damaged him that he lay for two weeks in the Lucheng County Hospital. After he recovered sufficiently to walk, he returned home; but his convalescence in the village was far from peaceful. He found that the mutual-aid group had thrown his family out. "Better wait and see if he can pass the *gate*," said his neighbors. The refusal of the mutual-aid group to help meant that the family had to hire labor to get its work done. Several dispossessed landlords were available for hire, but the village ordered the family to pay high wages to the village office for the landlords' labor.*

"Now I am puzzled," said Little Ch'uer. "How will the government treat the cadres? After the beating I found that my lungs were damaged. The medicine the doctor gave me is very expensive. Who will pay for it? When I asked help from the mutual-aid group they said, 'Cadres must serve the masses like good oxen. Why do you ask help from us?' My sister-in-law had nothing left to eat. She decided to sell her cart and donkey. But the leader of the poor peasants' group said, 'Why are you selling your animal? Do you want to oppose the land reform program?' Whenever I go home my aunt and uncle weep and complain to me. I don't know how to console them. Also all our taxes have been raised ten points. But I haven't grafted anything or tried any rascal tricks. My neighbors are sympathetic. They say, 'We ought to help him but *unfortunately* he is a cadre, so what can we do?' "

What could anyone tell Ch'uer? Simply to have faith, to report his problems to the county leaders, to keep working? This seemed pitifully inadequate.

---

* This practice was discontinued after the Draft Law was put into effect country-wide. It was an aftermath of the "sweep-the-floor-out-the-door" tactics of the Settlement of Accounts Movement, which deprived gentry families of all property and wrongly refused them the land and buildings necessary for maintaining life.

Only in regard to taxes did the discussion answer any of the questions posed by these men. It turned out that their taxes had increased in 1948 because land received the year before had been taxed lightly in order to help the recipients establish themselves as producers. Now all the land, both original holdings and newly acquired plots, were taxed at the same rate.

"Then why did my taxes go up?" asked Liang. He was an old middle peasant. He had received no land in 1947. Yet his taxes had also been raised in 1948. No one had an answer to that. Perhaps, suggested Ch'i Yun, it was part of an attack on him as an old cadre. If that were so, it was the only form the attack took. Through an old acquaintance from his home village who was also attending the County Conference, Liang had learned that day that all was going well with his family. His father and his wife were both in good health. His wife had borne him a son and the mutual-aid group had agreed to prepare his land for spring sowing.

Here at least was one cadre who had no serious domestic problems to worry about. His relative peace of mind had shown up in the quality of his work. From the beginning he had been conscientious and steady. The only fault anyone could find with Liang was that he did not speak out enough. He did not make suggestions or criticize his colleagues, but concentrated on his own work and did it well.

A second member of the team whose morale had held up through the six weeks of work in Long Bow was Li Wen-chung. The reason for this was not hard to find. Assignment to the Long Bow Team had brought Li the greatest boon of his life—a wife. In the village he had met, been properly introduced to, and then married the daughter of a *fanshened* widow. His head had been in the clouds ever since. For ten years he had sought a bride in vain. Now within a few weeks he had his heart's desire. But all this had not helped his work.

"Ever since you found this girl it has been very hard to find you," said Hou, gently but firmly. "You never ask leave. You just disappear. Often, during meetings, your bride can be seen wandering around outside the building trying to catch a glimpse of you. And you, you seem to be very absent-minded. Now that you have solved the wife problem I think it is time for you to get down to business. All this has influenced your work too much."

43

Unity Through Struggle

I sent out invitations to summon guests.
I collected together all my friends.
Loud talk and simple feasting:
Discussion of philosophy, investigation of subtleties.
Tongues loosened, and minds at one.
Hearts refreshed by discharge of emotion!

Sui Ch'eng-kung
(died, 273 A.D.)

THE HUMAN consciousness may be compared to an artichoke. Its tender core is enclosed in layer upon layer of defenses, excuses, rationalizations, approximations. These must be peeled off if one is to discover the true complex of motives driving any individual. Such a process would hardly be possible if an individual's acts, as distinct from his words, did not reveal in a multitude of unconscious ways something of the core of his thought. Even then, with acts serving as guides to motivation, no progress can be made unless the individual is willing to co-operate. What made self-revelation possible for the work team members that day was the deep commitment every one of them had to the success of the land reform movement. They freely examined themselves and their comrades, not for partisan advantage, not for the sake of exposure, not as an exercise in *mea culpa,* but in order to remove obstacles in the way of more effective work. This was the objective framework around which the unfolding of the subjective attitudes revolved. And this, not coercion, not curiosity, not some narcissistic self-torture made self-and-mutual criticism viable and grounded it in necessity.

By first taking up some of the objective problems that weighed on the cadres' minds and slowly moving from there to subjective reactions, the Party Day meeting began to pull the group together. I could feel that this was happening but could not find any decisive reason for it. No major problem had been solved. It seemed as if the mere exposure of trouble had brought about a changed relationship between these people. As they gained insight into the background of each others' weaknesses, they felt a growth of mutual sympathy, of common ground. Still, the most important barrier to trust and cooperation had not been touched. This was the question of the relationship between Team Leader Hou and the rest of the group. It was not until Hou began to criticize his own outlook and examine his own motives that the incipient change of atmosphere that had begun to penetrate the consciousness of the group crystallized into something new.

The discussion came around to Hou obliquely, by way of Li Wen-chung's wife. Everyone knew that Li's new-found happiness had distracted him from his work, but only Little Li knew that shortly before Team Leader Hou came to Long Bow, his wife had left for her home village alone. According to local custom, a bride that went back to her mother's home unescorted rarely returned. Hence, those who knew Hou best thought his marriage had come to an end. Little Li, as was his wont, brought up the subject in the form of a joke. He asked Hou how he liked being a bachelor.

This brought a response far too vigorous to be taken at face value. "We married of our own free will," said Hou. "I told her when she left for home to do as she liked. If she doesn't want to come back that is all right with me. That doesn't worry me at all."

Did this self-assurance cover up hurt pride, perhaps even a broken heart? It was hard to tell. Hou did not discuss the matter further. He launched instead into an over-all appraisal of his own work. Looking intently at his large feet clad in outsized cotton shoes and now propped against a broken brick, he spoke in the slow deliberate manner that had become his trademark. Clearly it was not easy for so proud a man to reveal what he proposed to talk about.

"When I arrived in Long Bow I put everything aside. I was very proud and confident at that time and made light of the job we had to do. I thought that with so many members we would easily fulfill our task. But as soon as we began to work I ran up against many difficulties. I began to hesitate and worry. I began to realize that this work was more difficult than anything I had ever tried before. Then I went to the other extreme. I feared the dragon in front and the tiger behind. I got timid and dared not fix a plan. I depended on the other members of the group and sometimes followed the people blindly, but the other members of the group kept silent a good deal of the time, and everyone worked on his own. This upset me and made me even more timid. I found I could not draw a proper conclusion at a meeting or make clear and definite decisions to help guide the others. I found I was very green and I felt the other cadres were much better qualified than myself, since many of them had worked as cadres for eight years or more. I dared not criticize them even when I found fault. I was unable to sift our good experiences from our bad ones, and before each meeting I found I didn't know where we were going or what to say. We began the meetings blindly and closed them blindly.

"All this made me sensitive. I thought the vice leader (Little Li) was just standing aside and waiting for me to lose face. I thought he was cracking jokes to show me up. But later I understood his character better. I know now that he was only joking and making fun with everyone. At night I couldn't sleep. I tried to estimate the comrades one by one. Finally I concluded that I myself must be the one to be blamed because I had no ability. So I wanted the authorities to relieve me of my position. I wanted to join the army, or at least ask that another leader be chosen and let me become just an ordinary member. Ever since I heard Secretary Ch'en's report I have felt this even more strongly. I have been very depressed.

"I hope you will all give me a lot of help in the future, but still I wish you would choose another leader. I am very reserved. I don't know how to relax and fool around with others. I was once given the nickname *Ta Kung Niu* (The Great Ox) because I carry such a long face, such a serious face, and this long face is easily misunderstood. People thought I was angry with them. Of course I am crude and impatient. I wish you would give me more opinions."

I was impressed by the frankness of Hou's statement and with the humility which he projected. Hou seemed to take on stature as he made this first attempt at self-analysis. But it was just this humility that the others criticized most sharply. They told Hou that he should not underestimate his own ability. In fact, from the way he worked, it was obvious that he made all important decisions himself and didn't sufficiently trust the rest of the group.

"You are too sensitive," said Little Li. "You lack confidence in others. Instead of criticizing them to their face you criticize them to the Party Secretary. I am thinking of that time when you told Ch'en that we didn't have any material on the village. It made us all so angry. Why didn't you consult with us? Actually you have a streak of individual heroism. You want to be a hero; therefore any failure is your personal failure. I remember once when we went to the County Office to report. The Secretary did not take any notes of what we said. You were very unhappy. You said, 'It seems as if we had done nothing, for our report made no impression.' Your criticism was correct. They should have taken notes of our report, but in the back of your mind what you were really thinking was that the authorities would know nothing about our merits.

"As for your relations with me," Li continued, "I was afraid you would think I wished to take the spotlight from you, so I always hesitated when I thought we ought to work in some new way. But you thought I was just standing aside to wait for you to lose face."

This opinion broke the ice. In its wake other team members began to say the things they had long suppressed.

"You always emphasize your lack of ability," said Ch'i Yun. "But in fact you don't trust the rest of us, so you always think of trifling things; you are sensitive beyond reason and don't pay sufficient attention to basic principles."

"Lying awake at night, thinking things over, that is a very subjective way to make decisions," said another. "It is much better to talk with others and judge from reality. Take the accounts meetings, for instance. Many comrades told you they ought to be stopped. But you neglected their opinions. You were so busy with the branch that you didn't have time to think it over. Your working style is not democratic enough. You are timid about criticizing others but at the same time you don't like to be criticized either. You think the investigation of our work from above, by the county leaders, is sufficient. But because you work blindly you were always busy, even worn out, but still the results were not so good."

Hou's offer to step down and find someone else to lead aroused even more opposition than his self-deprecation.

"Such a thought is quite wrong," said Little Li. "You just want to escape in the face of trouble. A Communist should never think like that. Mistakes are unavoidable. The thing to do is to examine and correct them, not run away."

"If everyone were to talk like you do, who would be the leader?" asked Ch'uer. "That is quite wrong. When we return to the village and begin work again we shall be quite frank with each other, exchange reports frequently and help one another. In that way we can surely overcome our mistakes."

Hou did not reject these opinions. Although the criticism was sharp, the other cadres were speaking out, showing concern for his problems and taking on a share of the burden. He felt a sense of relief that at last some communication, some real give and take was developing between him and the rest of the team. He even raised his head a little as he spoke in reply.

"Why have I been so sensitive?" he asked. "I think it is because before I came here I was leader of all work in 13 villages and everything went smoothly, but as soon as I came here everything became very hard. I thought, 'Little Li has more experience than I.' We divided the work. I took the Party branch, and he took the village as a whole. When I asked him about the detention of the cadres he said, 'Don't worry about it. If it is wrong, I am responsible.' And he always laughed as if caring for nothing at all, while I was always earnest and worried all the time. Whenever I brought up a problem, he turned it into a joke. At night when I talked to him he fell asleep. So I thought to myself, 'If we have made such errors he must also take some blame. If I am to be kicked out of the Party, he must be too.' So I turned against him, and I thought, 'If you despise me, I shall never ask you for help.'

"Now I understand how wrong that is. That is a subjective, individual point of view. It has nothing to do with the needs of our work. In the future I shall study problems with the rest of you and read carefully all the reports."

Hou paused here, as if he had finished, but then he thought of something else, of the accusation that he had spoken to the Party Secretary behind their backs, and he went on. "I have a very stubborn character. When I disagree with someone I just keep silent—seven or eight days—and never say a word. That's the way it was when I quarrelled with my wife. I never said a word to her afterwards. So when I came to Comrade Ch'en he pried it out of me. It wasn't that I wanted to talk to him, but I came to him for advice and he dug to the root of the matter. It was because I met trouble that I thought of many unreasonable things in the middle of the night. In the future, whenever I have some opinion, I shall speak it out and consult with other comrades."

Having said what they thought about Hou, the other cadres found themselves suddenly free of the bitterness they had felt toward him, and Hou, having heard their opinions and found them reasonable, suddenly felt warm and friendly toward them all. The "Great Ox" turned out to be a far more likeable human being than anyone had suspected. Right then and there they decided never to hold back their ideas again but to speak out frankly and help each other in the future.

****

If one crucial drag on the work of the team was the friction between the team members and their leader, a second and almost equal drag was the friction between the intellectuals from the University and the uneducated cadres of local origin. The Party meeting did not remove this friction in one session, but some progress was made in the direction of mutual understanding. Before the meeting ended each of the intellectuals critically examined his or her own work and listened to suggestions from the whole collective.

Of the five University people on the team, Comrade Hsu had made the worst impression and established the worst relationships. Ever since the failure of the accounts examination meeting which he led, he had been morose. He sat through meeting after meeting looking bored. He never took part in any debate unless it touched on his own abortive project. He more often than not ignored the proceedings altogether, sat off in a corner by himself, and read some newspaper or pamphlet. At the Lucheng Conference he found the straw in "Temple Row" distasteful. He was afraid he would catch some disease from the other cadres and was openly distressed about the lice that invariably sought him out no matter how clean he kept his clothes and his person. No one ever picked lice from his garments with more fastidious repugnance than did Comrade Hsu.

This professor's real problem was one germane to intellectuals everywhere—how to translate theory into practice. He was like the revolutionary described by Mao Tse-tung, who held the arrow of Marxism-Leninism in his hand, caressed it and exclaimed ecstatically, "What a fine arrow! What a fine arrow!" but never let it fly.

Hsu himself said, "I have been criticized for swinging first to the Right and then to the Left. That is true. I had never been in a village before I came to the Liberated Area. I had some grand ideas. I thought I would collect material for future study. So I brought along many books. But my plan failed. So I became unhappy. My aim in joining this work was to learn something, but suddenly along came the accounts meeting and I was made responsible. I had to do something. Then I became very hesitant about speaking out. I found I couldn't speak the peasants' language at all and I didn't really understand the village. At the same time I was afraid I would be thought proud. While in Chiang's area, I always stayed in a small room and studied. Now I want to break that habit but I can't break it very quickly."

The reaction of the local cadres to this speech was polite. They praised Hsu's skill with figures and his familiarity with the writing brush and added that since his background was so different from their own it was hard for them to understand him. Remembering how he had questioned landlords for material against cadres, several suggested that his class stand was not firm. He should look into it, they said.

Little Li, who as clerk, editor, and judge had some pretensions to intellectuality himself, spoke more sharply. "You started out with a great deal of enthusiasm, but ever since the accounts meeting failed you have been in low spirits. That's because you think you made a bad mistake. The trouble at those meetings was that you did not try to educate the delegates and help them see things clearly. You tried to do everything yourself. When you sensed the least bit of injustice, you became very angry and tried to crush it all by yourself. That's why you were persuaded to go to the landlords for help. The main trouble is that you don't think before you start working. But now if you are timid, and dare not work at all, it will be hard for you to correct anything."

Ch'i Yun, whose background closely paralleled Hsu's and hence was more aware of what was going on in his mind than the others, spoke even more critically. She was of the opinion that he had not revealed his true thoughts.

"You say you wish to study and learn from village life. But what? We all have to combine concrete work with theoretical study—only that way can we gain real knowledge. But it has been very difficult even to make a suggestion to you. Sometimes you do not even listen, but turn and walk off. I think you have problems that you yourself have not thought through. You don't want to speak them out here. You'd rather avoid criticism. But the right way to learn is to speak frankly and to listen to others. You only work at what interests you. If you continue with such a style and such an attitude you will only isolate yourself."

Cadre Hsu listened carefully to all this and took the opinions down in his notebook. Perhaps even he could change if he faced himself honestly. The mere fact that he had made a beginning at self-analysis removed some of the barrier between him and the rest of the cadres.

It was an hour after midnight when discussion ended. We had been sitting and talking since eight in the morning with only a short break for meals. The meeting broke up in silence as all moved off toward their respective sleeping quarters.

****

My own reaction to the Party Day meeting was one of wonder —wonder at the perseverance of these people, especially the stubborn perseverance of the local men. What kept them working under such conditions? Why didn't they give up and go home? Certainly it had nothing to do with money. Right there in the middle of the meeting the county clerk had come round to ask them to sign their monthly vouchers. I knew exactly what each received for his work. This was a bundle of millet tickets sufficient to provide 30 days' food and the cash equivalent of eight catties of millet for spending money (50¢ U. S.). In addition to this, they got two summer suits and one winter suit a year. That was all. At home on the land they could easily earn more.

No, they had no material incentive to be cadres. Nor was their chosen road a path of glory. Only a stubborn devotion to the cause of *fanshen* made sense as a motive. I had never known men who consistently put principle above self-interest as these men appeared to do.

I wondered also at the new level of tolerance and understanding attained by the whole group through the method of self-and-mutual criticism. The method, I began to realize, was something that had to be learned. It did not flow naturally out of the extremely individualistic, face-conscious culture in which the majority of the team members had been reared.

To practice self-and-mutual criticism well one had to cultivate objectivity in several ways. First, one had to be willing to be objective about oneself. One had to be willing to seek out that kernel of truth in any criticism regardless of the manner in which it was presented. Second, one had to be objective about others; one had to evaluate others from a principled point of view with the object of helping them to overcome their faults and work more effectively. One had to raise others up, not knock them down. In practice these two considerations meant that one had to pay great attention to one's own motives and methods when criticizing others, while disregarding in the main the motives and methods used by others towards oneself.

Above and beyond this, one had to cultivate the courage to voice sincerely-held opinions regardless of the views held by others, while at the same time showing a willingness to listen to others and to change one's own opinion when honestly convinced of error. To bow with the wind, to go along with the crowd was an irresponsible attitude that could never lead to anything but trouble for oneself, for the revolutionary movement, and for China. The reverse of this, to be arrogant and unbending was just as bad.

The work team members practiced all these things much more effectively than the Communists of Long Bow or the rank-and-file delegates who faced them had done before the *gate*. As I listened I began to think that the distortions which had marred the *gate*—the pressures which had caused people to attack the cadres as if they had been enemies, and the pressures which had caused many cadres to respond by admitting more than was objectively true—were not something inherent in the method but a consequence of its unskilled application. They were a consequence of the low level of political understanding of most of the participants. As their understanding and experience increased their objectivity could well increase, and the method thus serve more effectively to unite the whole village for the future.

44

When I Get My Share

In the women of China the Communists possessed, almost ready made, one of the greatest masses of disinherited human beings the world has ever seen. And because they found the key to the heart of these women, they also found one of the keys to victory over Chiang Kai-shek.

Jack Belden

A CONFERENCE, like a drama, a party, a lecture, or a love affair is greatly enhanced by a change of pace. Ebb and flow, introversion and extroversion serve to keep the participants alert. Such a change was provided on April 29th by a special discussion on the problems of women. Switching attention sharply away from internal Party affairs, Secretary Ch'en asked every team to report on the mobilization of the peasant women in their respective villages.

"Even if you haven't done anything, tell us about that and state the reason why," he said. It was his way of keeping the issue alive. The cadres knew that they would be asked about women the next time as well; and the chances were, even if they had done very little in the past, they would have more to report in the future.

As a matter of fact, most of the team leaders made very good reports. Little Li's account of the work in Long Bow did not match up. But that may have been because Li did not give the matter enough thought. Much had actually been done, especially by Ch'i Yun and Comrade Kao, the other woman cadre from the University.

The right to own land and property in their own name was the key to the liberation of women, according to all the cadres who reported. On many other questions the women were divided. While the younger women were very concerned about free choice in marriage, older women saw this as a threat to their control over daughters and daughters-in-law. While younger women opposed all family beatings, older women tended to countenance beatings just so long as mothers-in-law administered them. On one issue they all agreed, however. Women should be able to get and keep a share in the land.

In Chao Chen Village, many women said, "When I get my share I'll separate from my husband. Then he won't oppress me any more."

In Chingtsun the work team found a women whose husband thought her ugly and wanted to divorce her. She was very depressed until she learned that under the Draft Law she could have her own share of land. Then she cheered up immediately. "If he divorces me, never mind," she said. "I'll get my share and the children will get theirs. We can live a good life without him." Another woman in the same village had already been deserted once. Her second husband was a local cadre, but he oppressed her. When a member of the team visited her, she wept. "Chairman Mao is all right, but women are still in trouble," she said. "We have no equality. We have to obey our husbands because our life depends on them." After the new law was explained to her, she said, "This is really fine. I can have my own share now."

In Yellow Mill, many women had no confidence in their powers. They said, "Our husbands regard us as some sort of dogs who keep the house. We even despise ourselves. But that is because for a thousand years it has been, 'The men go to the *hsien* (county) and the women go to the *yuan* (courtyard).' We were criticized if we even stepped out the door. After we get our share we will be masters of our own fate."

Some were afraid that they could not do the field work necessary, but others said, "What difference does that make? Women depend on men, but so do men depend on women. What the women do around the home is also labor, and they can swap that for work in the fields." One woman said, "Always before when we quarrelled my husband said, 'Get out of my house.' Now I can give it right back to him. I can say, 'Get out of my house yourself.' "

The more oppressed the woman, the more urgently did she demand her share. The women of Ke Shih said, "Child brides but no child husbands." "If you even speak to another man, you would be suspected." One child bride, sold at the age of seven, told how much she had suffered from her mother-in-law and concluded, "When I get my share I'll never look for a husband again. A husband is a terrible thing."

In Chingtsun one old woman said, "I sold four daughters because I had to pay back a landlord debt. I wept the whole night, and the tears burned my eyes. Now I am blind. Poverty forced me to sell my own daughters. Every mother loves her child." Others said, "In the old society no one loved a daughter because you brought them up and they left the house. Many parents drowned their little daughters. In the old society feet were bound with cloth. Small feet were thought to be one of the best qualities of women. But to bind a woman's feet is to tie her body and soul. Small feet are a symbol of the old society."

Many stories revealed that Liberation had not yet guaranteed free marriage or even the property rights upon which free marriage must be based. In East Portal one woman had been forced to marry a veteran. The cadres said, "This man has fought for us many years. How could we live a peaceful life if it hadn't been for his efforts? We must reward him with a wife." When the woman refused, she was ordered to explain herself at a mass meeting.

A second woman there wanted to marry a man from another village, but the local cadres would not give her a permit. Why make things difficult for themselves by further reducing the number of unmarried women?

Obviously, a lot of work still had to be done before women could call themselves really free. But from the reports we learned that in every village there were a few women who were starting to play an active role in public affairs. Large numbers had joined the Party purification meetings and almost all of them had learned to speak.

****

At the county conference itself the women seemed to me to be far less bashful than the men. It was they who sought me out and asked questions about the world outside China. The women who did this were not, as might have been expected, the intellectuals from the University, but that small handful of local women who had distinguished themselves as district cadres in a movement still overwhelmingly staffed by men.

Meal breaks provided the only time available for such spontaneous discussion. Meals were served outdoors in the courtyard where the male cadres were quartered. The southern entrance to this yard consisted of an imposing central gate topped by a heavy tiled roof and flanked by two gate-houses, one of which had been temporarily converted into a kitchen. There a vast cauldron of millet was boiled up twice a day over a fire that looked like a blacksmith's furnace. When the millet was ready (about eight o'clock in the morning and four o'clock in the afternoon), the cauldron was carried out into the yard by two stout men with a carrying pole. The cadres then lined up, each with his own bowl and chopsticks in hand, and proceeded to help themselves. So big was the circumference of the cauldron that five or six people could easily stand around it and fill their bowls without crowding one another.

A second, smaller fire in the gate-house produced a pot of cabbage.

This was placed on the ground some distance away from the millet. After each cadre had filled his bowl with steaming grain he walked over and topped it with cabbage. Then he sought some place to sit or squat and eat. Small knots of friends formed at such times, and discussion flourished until the temple bell sounded the call to return to the conference sessions once again.

On the afternoon of the second day of the conference, I found myself the center of one of these meal-time discussion groups. A lively trio of village-born female cadres boldly approached me as I ate. Their spokesman, a young woman with bobbed hair and natural feet, asked me such a stream of questions that the millet in my bowl grew cold before I could get it into my mouth.

"Do you eat with chopsticks in America?" "What crops do you raise?" "Do American women wear pants?" "Why don't Americans treat all races equally?" Such were the questions she asked.

The women no sooner began their "interview" than a number of men, most of whom had been too shy to approach me, also gathered round and added queries of their own.

"Why does Tu-lu-men (Truman) support old Chiang?" "What does a tractor look like?" "How big is the American Communist Party?" "Does it have an army like ours?"

The temple gong rang long before I had a chance to answer all of these questions. On the next day the discussion continued, and on the next as well, and always it was the women who took the initiative.

45

Unite Real Friends, Attack Real Enemies

Who are our enemies, and who are our friends? This question is one of primary importance to the Revolution. All past revolutionary struggles in China achieved very little, basically because the revolutionaries were unable to unite their real friends to attack their real enemies. A revolutionary party is the guide of the masses, and no revolution ever succeeds when the revolutionary party leads it astray. To make sure that we will not lead our Revolution astray but will achieve positive success, we must pay attention to uniting our real friends to attack our real enemies.

Mao Tse-tung, 1946

As THE CONFERENCE progressed toward a conclusion, two questions emerged with increasing frequency: What constituted adequate *fanshen?* And what constituted a correct policy toward middle peasants? The questions were, of course, linked. As long as *fanshen* was taken to mean the achievement of middle peasant status for all the remaining poor, the more prosperous middle peasants sensed a threat to their position. Since the worldly goods required for more *fanshen* could only come from those who still possessed a little surplus, no amount of reassurance concerning the middle peasants' status as allies could allay this group's gnawing fear that its members would be victimized in the future.

In his long report of April 24, Secretary Ch'en flayed all tendencies to ignore and alienate the middle peasants.

"When Chairman Mao read the Suiteh report and learned that in one village 27 middle peasants' families had been wrongly expropriated, he said, 'This is a most terrible thing! This is more dangerous by far than American imperialism. American imperalism is only a paper tiger but if 27 middle peasants can be expropriated in one village, what would happen if this spread to the whole nation? This is forcing our friends to join our enemies.'

"Some of our team members even brushed aside the middle peasants when the latter sought them out," continued Secretary Ch'en. "The policy of our Party is to depend on the poor peasants, but that doesn't mean that we neglect the middle peasants or that we fail to unite with them. On the contrary, we must make clear to them that they have their political, organizational, and economic rights. The middle peasants can join the Peasants' Association, and their land and property cannot be touched. We even distinguish upper middle peasants from others. Why? In order to protect them, to make sure that nothing is taken from them to fill the poor peasants' needs. If we do get something from them it can only be with their agreement. Middle peasants are entitled to at least a third of the seats in the village congresses which already exist in many villages and will soon be established in all. They are an important factor in the coalition governments of the counties and the regions."

Secretary Ch'en summed up policy thus: "With the poor peasants as a core, we form the Poor and Hired Peasants' League. Then with the middle peasants as allies, we form the Peasants' Association. Then with all the other anti-feudal elements in the community as additional allies, we form the Village Congress. Thus we unite our friends and isolate our enemies.

"This policy is fixed by the character of our Revolution at its present stage. The more the enemy is isolated the quicker can victory be won. If we say that poverty is all and work along a narrow poor-peasant line and neglect all our friends, we will only isolate ourselves. Whoever commits the error of isolating himself is guilty of Leftism. Whoever does not isolate those who should be isolated is guilty of Rightism."

This was well put. The cadres understood it. But exposition was no longer enough. What was urgently needed was not another review of the theory but a more adequate definition of "middle peasant," a yardstick for determining when a poor peasant had *fanshened*, and a practical method for reconciling the legitimate demands of the poor peasants for more property with the legitimate concern of the middle peasants lest they be attacked.

To meet this need Secretary Ch'en on April 28, 1948, distributed a new set of class definitions and proposed the addition of a new category to the class standards.

The new category was that of "new-middle-peasant." Into this group all those poor peasants who had *fanshened* were henceforth to be placed. By comparing the size of the new-middle-peasant group with that of the remaining poor-peasant group it would be possible to obtain an accurate picture of what land reform had done for any village. As to the yardstick to be used, this was still vague. The general idea was that a new-middle-peasant family had to have enough land and other means of production to be self-supporting (i.e., enough to bring it up to the level of the established middle peasants). But there was room for considerable argument over the question of just what level of self-support was meant, for everyone knew that there had always been upper, middle and lower middle peasants in the villages. All of these were henceforth often called old-middle-peasants to distinguish them from their newly *fanshened* brothers, the new-middle-peasants.

As for the revised class standards distributed by Secretary Ch'en, they had been issued by the Central Committee of the Chinese Communist Party only a few weeks before. They replaced all previous declarations on the subject. The main innovation which they introduced was a shift in the line drawn between middle peasants and rich peasants, a shift toward the rich peasant side to the advantage of the middle peasants. Instead of allowing middle peasants only 15 percent of gross income from exploitation, the new line allowed them up to 25 percent.

The effect of this shift was to enlarge the united front of the people and to isolate as popular enemies only those diehard elements who could not possibly be mobilized to support a "land-to-the-tiller" policy.

In proposing any basic social change, Secretary Ch'en explained, revolutionaries had to decide who should be brought together and who isolated, who should be called a friend and who an enemy.

The theoretical basis for such a determination rested on a proposition propounded by Marx long ago: "It is not the consciousness of men that determines their being, but on the contrary, their social being that determines their consciousness." This could be restated, although not without danger of oversimplification, as "It is not what you think that determines how you make your living, but how you make your living that determines how you think" When applied to any Chinese village, this meant in practice that poor peasants who owned very little and were consequently heavily exploited could be expected to think one way about land reform, while landlords who owned a lot and consequently were able to live by exploiting others could be expected to think another way about the same question. The poor wanted to transform the system. The landlords wanted to maintain it inviolate. Here were two clear-cut extremes. One could predict with relative ease how representatives of these two classes would react to a revolutionary program of land equalization. In practice, however, as the movement developed, not only the extremes but all the groups in the middle were drawn into the struggle on one side or the other. Since the landlords, few as they were, controlled the economy, dominated the state, and had the support of powerful imperialist forces, they could easily buy off certain sections of the population and many individuals in every stratum. Hence, the poor peasants, numerous as they were, must find allies if they were to challenge the system. On whom could they count for support? Basically on all those who worked for a living, suffered from the system, and also wanted a change. Such allies included most of the self-supporting middle peasants who owned their own land, the peddlers who owned their own stocks, the shopkeepers who owned their own shops, the free professionals (doctors, lawyers, teachers, who provided services for fees), even the plain poor people and vagabonds who, unable to find gainful employment, were forced to beg, gamble, or steal for a living.

So far the question remained relatively simple. All the above-mentioned people depended on their own labor to live or welcomed the opportunity to do so. They were natural allies in the fight against the landlords. What complicated matters was the existence of large numbers of people with mixed incomes, families that lived partly by labor expended and partly by exploitation, families who planted, hoed, and harvested themselves, but also hired labor, rented out land, or loaned out money. Where did these people fit in?

If any and all income from exploitation was to be opposed and all families receiving any income at all from exploitation were to be regarded as enemies of change, then millions of families who earned most of their livelihood by means of hard labor and wanted to transform society must artificially be forced into the enemy camp.

If, on the other hand, all people who labored for any portion, however small, of their income were to be regarded as friends, then many heavy exploiters who hated the Revolution and feared change must be called allies.

No such simple method of differentiation was therefore practical.

Obviously neither exploitation alone nor labor alone could determine this question. The line could not be drawn at either end of these overlapping phenomena. It had to be drawn somewhere in between. The question was where? *Not exploitation but the proportion of exploitation income in the total income of a family, not labor as such but the proportion of labor income in the total income of a family became the crux of the matter.*

The principle, "How you make your living determines how you think," was held by Ch'en to be as applicable to mixed incomes as it was to incomes from one source. One could expect the major source of income to play a more important role than the minor source in determining the attitude and behavior of an individual.

Countless experiences from everyday life showed that such expectations were indeed borne out by the actual behavior of the people.

Those who derived more than half of their income from their own labor tended to identify themselves with working people and consequently to support the revolution. Those who derived more than half of their income from the exploitation of other people's labor tended to identify their interests with those of the exploiters and consequently to ally themselves with the counter-revolution.

It therefore made sense to divide that large group of families who had mixed incomes, who both labored and exploited, by drawing a line right down the middle. Those who earned more than half of their income by exploitation were classed as rich peasants and treated as enemies.* On the other hand, those who earned half or more of their income by their own labor were classed as middle peasants and treated as friends.

It should be stressed here that these standards applied only to rural conditions and only to families engaged in or living off agricultural production. The only kind of unearned or exploitative income that could cause a family to be classed as a landlord or rich peasant was income of a feudal or semi-feudal nature—that is, land rents, interest from usurious loans, or the surplus value extracted from direct labor on the land. All forms of strictly capitalist profit were excluded from this category as were the capitalists themselves. The object of the land reform was not to destroy what few capitalist sprouts had managed to grow up in the shambles of the feudal economy but rather to encourage them. Therefore, income derived from the employment of labor in commercial shops, agricultural processing plants, manufacturing enterprises, or even modern factories owned and controlled by Chinese was not included when judging whether or not a person was to be classed as a feudal exploiter or as one of the people. If a rich peasant or a landlord derived part of his income from a cotton gin, a bean-pressing plant or a commercial shop, this part was excluded when classifying him. And if it was decided that he was in fact a landlord or rich peasant because of other income, only his agricultural holdings were confiscated, not his commercial or industrial holdings. As a feudal exploiter he was considered to be a backward force, but as a capitalist exploiter he was considered to be a progressive one. His feudal holdings were divided up among

* This was true, however, only at this stage of the Revolution when the Civil War was being fiercely contended and the outcome of the battle was not clear to most people. At that time the rich peasants sided with the landlords. After 1949 the policy of the Communist Party towards rich peasants changed. Instead of attacking them, the Revolution tried to neutralize them. Their surplus property was not confiscated and their profits were guaranteed. This was a major and very significant shift in land reform policy.

the people but his capitalist holdings were held intact as his private property.

Could the political attitude and role of every individual in fact be determined by an analysis of the main source of his or her income?

Of course not. There were too many well-known cases of poor peasants who were counter-revolutionary and of landlords who were revolutionary for anyone to expect such a thing. No line, however accurate, could hope to separate people according to their subjective position with 100 percent accuracy. All that was claimed for the dividing line was that it was the most rational and practical basis for dividing the people from their enemies and it would prove valid for the vast majority. As for the exceptions, those above the line who were sincere revolutionaries would remain revolutionaries.even though they lost their holdings, while those below the line who opposed basic change might well be won for the Revolution once they received property and land and saw how life had been improved for all.

Having determined precisely *where* to draw the line, Secretary Ch'en proceeded to explain *how* to draw it in the actual process of differentiating the classes. Concrete methods to determine gross income, net income, percentages of exploitation, etc., were demonstrated.

To divide middle peasants from rich peasants on the basis of a one-half-of-net-income rule was simple enough in certain cases. It was clear, for instance, that if two men worked together to produce a crop and they shared the labor equally, half the crop would be due to the efforts of one and the other half would be due to the efforts of the other. Therefore, a man who employed labor equal to his own derived no more than half his net income from that labor and was clearly a middle peasant.

A man who employed more labor than he himself put in must obviously derive more than half his net income from other men's labor and must therefore clearly be a rich peasant.

The quickest way, then, to judge the class status of a peasant family was to look at how many men were hired and compare this with the amount of labor put in by the family. If the two forces were equal, the family was, by definition, a middle peasant family. But if the hired labor exceeded the family labor, the family was, by definition, a rich peasant family.

This simple rule of thumb was recommended for use whenever possible in judging the class status of the rural population.

If the hiring of labor had been the only form of exploitation that existed, nothing more would have been needed than this first rule of thumb. All families could have been judged on the basis of labor hired versus labor expended. But the more affluent families in any Chinese village also derived income from other sources, such as rent and interest. Some method for equating these sums with the profits derived from hiring labor had to be found in order to make comparisons, figure totals, and determine whether more or less than half of any family's net income derived from exploitation.

Of course, in those many cases where the labor hired equalled the labor expended by the family, any additional income from rents or loans must be enough to place the family in the rich peasant group. But in the numerous cases where the family contributed more labor to production than it hired from outside, it was necessary to know the actual amount of the net income received from all sources in order to compare the net income derived from exploitation with the net income derived from family labor.

The same problem arose in analyzing the income of families who hired no labor at all but received substantial amounts of rent or interest in addition to the crops harvested by their own efforts.

Before classifying such families it was necessary to arrive at actual net income figures. This was very difficult to do. Net income was defined as the amount of money or goods which remained each year after all expenses for seed, fertilizer, land, and labor had been deducted. For the middle peasant working on his own land, this was the gross amount of goods or money which he received for his year's labor minus all costs, including his own living expenses. But few peasant families kept accounts accurate enough to figure net income. The one figure they usually had but were exceedingly reluctant to reveal to anyone, was a figure for gross income—i.e., the total crop harvested. To arrive at a figure for net income it was necessary to develop another rule of thumb based on average experience.

The results of many studies made over the years had shown that under village conditions in China, net income was usually equal to about one third of gross income. That is to say, out of three parts of gross income one part represented surplus value, or profit, and two parts represented capital outlay for wages and fixed expenses such as seed.

Using this second rule of thumb, one could easily figure net income once the figure for gross income was known. Take, for example, a family with a gross income from the land of 30 hundredweight of grain. The net income amounted to ten hundredweight. If in addition to this crop, the family also received up to ten hundredweight of grain as income from loans, they were still middle peasants. Their net income from exploitation did not exceed their earned net income and therefore amounted to only half of their total net income.

Since the net income rule was, at best, an approximation, it was a more common practice to judge directly from gross income. In the example given, the gross income from all sources equalled 40 hundredweight. The most that this family could receive in exploitative income and still be classed as middle peasants was ten hundredweight. Ten divided by 40 equals one quarter of the gross. By such figuring, a third rule of thumb was arrived at. This could be called the one-quarter-of-gross-income rule. Any family whose exploitative income did not exceed one quarter of its gross income was a middle peasant family. If exploitative income exceeded one quarter of gross income, the family must be classed as rich peasants.

Careful study of this last rule of thumb showed that when it was applied to the exploitative income from hired labor it did not work very well. It has already been stated that two thirds of gross income represented capital expenses and one third represented surplus value, profit or net income. Imagine now the hypothetical case of a peasant who hires labor equal to his own and together the two producers create 30 hundredweight of grain. Together they produce a net income equal to one third of the gross. Each of them is responsible for half of this or five hundredweight. The net income from exploitation thus turns out to be one sixth, rather than one fourth of the gross income. Yet on the basis of labor hired and on the basis of one-half-of-net income, this peasant has already reached the top limit allowed for any middle peasant.

To resolve this problem it was the practice, when figuring net income from hired labor, to leave out of the equation the fixed capital expenses and figure only the wages. According to figures from the numerous studies mentioned above, constant capital or fixed expenses in agricultural production in China amounted to one quarter of the annual outlay, and variable capital, or wage expenses, amounted to three quarters. The variable capital was therefore the main item in the cost of production. By leaving out the constant or fixed capital costs entirely, total expenses could be reduced from two thirds to only one half of gross income.

By this method of figuring, the net income resulting from each of two equal laborers on the land amounted to one quarter of the gross. Returning to our original example, the net income produced by the two men can now be estimated as equal to 15 hundredweight. Each of them is responsible for half of this or 7½ hundredweight. This is equal to one quarter of the gross. Thus we arrive at a figure comparable to the one arrived at when all exploitative income is received in the form of rents or interest payments. By this method, net income, whether derived from hired labor, rent, or interest, could be equated across the board and the one-quarter-of-gross-income rule could be used in every case as the criterion for determining whether any given family was to be classed with the people or with their oppressors.

****

The shift in the line dividing the middle from the rich peasants was made even more emphatic in the new regulations by other supplementary measures that also tended to enlarge the united front. One of these was a modification of the base period rule. The three years prior to the Liberation of the village (1942-1945 for Long Bow) were taken as the base years, as before, but any family had to have status as an exploiter for the full three years in order to be classed as a rich peasant or a landlord. Those who lived the life of a poor peasant or a middle peasant for as little as 12 months prior to Liberation were classed as poor peasants or middle peasants even if they had previously been landlords.

A third innovation had to do with labor power. The new regulations stipulated that families possessing land and property equal to that of rich peasants but who were lacking in labor power and therefore unable to maintain living standards superior to those of middle peasants, should not be classed as rich peasants if they lived under such conditions for three years or more, but as middle peasants, or even as poor peasants, depending on the actual conditions of their life. This rule took the pressure off those rich peasant widows who, because they lacked able-bodied men in the family, were not able to make use of the capital they owned.

A fourth innovation had just the opposite effect. It narrowed down the united front by penalizing families with above-average holdings, regardless of whether they rented them out, tilled them with hired labor, or tilled them with family labor. The decision to penalize families with above-average holdings was based on the Marxist theory of rent. As stated in Paragraph Eight, Chapter Six of a publication entitled *Decisions Concerning the Differentiation of Class Status in the Countryside, 1948:*

The rent received by the landlord is neither a return for his own labor nor a return on his own investment. It is an entirely feudal exploitation based on land ownership alone. It is created by the whole of the peasant's surplus labor (labor expended beyond that necessary for a minimum standard of living) and a part of the peasant's necessary labor (labor necessary to maintain a minimum standard of living). The landlord is thus a parasite on society who takes no part in production. By his feudal possession, at least in part, of the peasant's own person (this special power of the landlord is reflected in politics by the Kuomintang reactionary clique's denial of civil liberties to the people of the whole nation), he has been the fundamental obstruction to the growth of China's agricultural and industrial productive forces for a long time.

That part of the rent referred to as having been created by "the whole of the peasants' surplus labor" is that part generally known as "differential rent"—rent which represents the difference between the crop harvested on any given piece of land and the crop harvested on the poorest land currently under cultivation. That part of the rent referred to as having been created by "a part of the peasant's necessary labor" is that part known as "absolute rent"—rent extracted from those who labor by virtue of the fact that land is limited. Those who claimed ownership of the land were in fact monopolists able to levy tribute for the use of it simply because the landless had no alternative.

It followed from this that the mere fact of land ownership enabled any owner to extract a certain amount of unearned income from his land—the absolute rent. This income, whether extracted by a poor peasant, a middle peasant, or a rich peasant was no different in nature from the income of a landlord who did no work at all, and was therefore classed as feudal in character.

The regulations issued by the Central Committee of the Chinese Communist Party considered only surplus land (land held in excess of the per capita average in the community) significant as a source of absolute rent. Thus in Chapter Seven of the above-quoted *Decisions,* we find the following: "Some peasants occupy more land than the average of the village; hence their gross income derives in part from land ownership which is feudal in character and can be said to be the same as the rent taken by a landlord. The more land they occupy the more rent income they get."

In order to take into account this special form of exploitation, families with above-average holdings were subject to supplementary regulations as follows: "(1) Any family which holds more than twice the average land held by the middle peasants of the area shall have its rate of exploitation doubled. (2) Any family which holds more than three times the amount of land held by the middle peasants shall have its rate of exploitation quadrupled."

To double the exploitation rate meant to multiply by two the net income received from exploitative sources before calculating whether or not such income exceeded one quarter of gross income. For example: a family in Long Bow with two acres per capita, or twice the average land holding, even if it received only four out of 30 hundredweight from rent, interest, or the hiring of labor, must be classed as a rich peasant family because that four hundredweight had now to be doubled when figuring the rate of exploitation and the resulting figure (eight) amounted to more than one quarter of the gross income (30).

To make matters even more complex, other regulations regarding above-average holdings had an effect just the reverse of those quoted above. Single people living alone and old couples without labor power were allowed up to twice as much land as others without incurring any penalty in the determination of their class status.

For old couples this provided a form of social security. The produce from extra land enabled them to hire whatever work was necessary for crop production and still have enough left over to live themselves. For single people, the extra land filled a similar need. It enabled a man to hire the kind of services—like cooking, sewing, and housekeeping—ordinarily supplied by a wife; it enabled a woman to hire the labor in the fields ordinarily supplied by a husband.

The distinction between middle peasants and rich peasants was by no means the only social division defined with precision in the class standards issued in 1948. There were many paragraphs on landlords, on the difference between landlords and rich peasants, on the difference between managing landlords and ordinary landlords, and on the difference between new-type managing landlords and old-type managing landlords, on the question of tenants who were also exploiters of labor, on the distinction between new rich peasants and old rich peasants, and many others. But since the most important thing in the spring of that year was to gather into the popular alliance all forces that could legitimately be gathered in and to leave out as objects of attack those forces that could not possibly be drawn in, most of the time at the County Land Reform Conference was spent in studying the regulations on the dividing line between middle and rich peasants, and the proper way in which to determine it.

This question has been gone into in some detail both because of its intrinsic importance and because such an exposition may give some idea of the extraordinary thoroughness with which the work team cadres at the County Conference studied these questions. They not only examined the theoretical propositions, but they also practiced with hypothetical cases and tested each other until they understood all facets of this aspect of the classification standards and their application.

****

The appearance of new class standards meant that every family in the 11 basic villages had to be classified all over again and, in order to insure that no mistakes were made, must be classified not only once more, but three times, each time at a different level.

The County Secretary outlined the work to be done as follows:

(1) Establish a solid Poor Peasants' League.
(2) Have the League membership classify the village.
(3) Establish a strong Provisional Peasants' Association.
(4) Have the Provisional Peasants' Association membership classify the village again.
(5) Elect a Village Congress.
(6) Have the Congress classify the village for the third and final time.

To the *tzu pao kung i* (self report, public appraisal) slogan of the earlier stage a new phrase was added: *san pang ting an* (three times and then decide).

After each separate classification all those families who did not agree to the class in which they were placed had the right of appeal. From the decision of the League they could appeal to the Association (once that had been established), and from the decision of the Association they could appeal to the Village Congress (once that had been elected). If the decision of the Congress was still not acceptable, the family had the right of appeal to the County Government. There all problems of class status were finally to be decided. The decision of the County Government was declared to be irreversible.

"This means," said Secretary Ch'en, "that we must explain, discuss, report, evaluate, classify, post results; explain, discuss, and report— again and again. This is very troublesome, very difficult, very time consuming. But the people do not find it troublesome because it fixes their fate. This is the most important work of the whole movement. He who leads the classification holds the knife in his hand. If you class a middle peasant as a rich peasant, it is as serious as killing him. You push the family into the enemy camp. You violate the policy of uniting with the middle peasants to isolate the enemy. If, on the other hand, you classify a landlord as a middle peasant, you protect a landlord. You clasp a viper to your bosom. You violate the policy of destroying feudalism."

The line drawn according to the new standards and delineated with so much care was bound to have disturbing results. It was a foregone conclusion that many families once called rich peasants, perhaps even landlords, would turn out to be nothing more than middle peasants after all. Many *tou cheng tui hsiang* (objects of struggle) who had been expropriated must inevitably be transformed into *ts'o tou te chung nung* (wrongly-struggled middle peasants).

Secretary Ch'en pointed this out as clearly and emphatically as he could and stated that when such families were found they must not only be reclassed and returned to the big family of the people *in the records;* they must also be repaid, re-established on the land and converted to their former middle peasant status *in fact*. The excesses of the past must be corrected. If the original property taken from them could not be gathered together and returned, then property of equivalent value must be given them. This was a must. It was an obligation that could neither be avoided nor evaded.

"If anyone in our group thinks that this is too much trouble," Secretary Ch'en warned, "if he doesn't work correctly and patiently, he is working for Chiang Kai-shek. He is isolating himself. He is helping American imperialism."

As the necessity to repay the "wrongly-struggled middle peasants" pushed its way into the consciousness of the land reform cadres their morale was shaken more deeply than ever before. In the first place, it was clear that they themselves and their colleagues were responsible for all such excesses. Had they not been village leaders during the period when the land was divided? In the second place, they did not see where all the land and property was going to come from. Were there not hundreds of families of poor peasants in the basic villages who still had not *fanshened?* To this number must now be added a dozen, perhaps two dozen families per village that required repayment. Where was all the "patching material" to come from?

This question, which was in fact a key one, did not emerge as clearly from the ten-day-old conference as its importance warranted. In spite of the emphasis placed by Secretary Ch'en on the middle peasant question, restitution tended, in the context of the whole conference, to be equated with many other tasks: plowing, planting, and hoeing must not be neglected; a permanent Poor Peasants' League must be organized; the village Communists must be helped to assume a leading role once again; those who had not yet passed the *gate* must be given another chance to do so; apologies must be offered to cadres who had been arrested; poor peasants who had not yet *fanshened* must take the lead; women must be encouraged. Alongside all these tasks that of reclassifying and repaying "wrongly-struggled middle peasants" emerged as one single facet of a many-faceted job. To an individual unable to distinguish which tasks were more and which less important, the whole complex of what had to be done appeared confused, even contradictory.

If the earlier emphasis had been on the first of Mao's principles ("satisfy the demands of the poor and hired peasants"), now the second of them ("there must be firm unity with the middle peasants, and their interests must not be damaged") had been brought into

focus. Since, as has already been pointed out, the two principles embodied a contradiction, the job before the cadres appeared much
more difficult than ever before. Few felt confident that they could
carry their work to a successful conclusion.

In his final speech Secretary Ch'en made one last effort to overcome the uncertainty and hesitancy of the cadres.

On the crucial question of their own day-to-day livelihood and the
livelihood of their families he first assured them that concrete steps
would be taken to guarantee all necessary aid at home to full-time
political workers. He blamed the "Leftist" attitude of the cadres leading production work for the hardships thus far encountered. "They
have absorbed the sectarian spirit of the poor peasant line and despise
old cadres, even hate them. This is quite wrong. The county administration has decided to help you, so don't worry. As for those who
are sick, don't worry either. Just find the doctor, buy the medicine,
and the county office will pay the bills."

Secretary Ch'en then launched into a head-on attack against the
lack of Communist spirit among the conference participants. "Some
cadres say, 'We are treated worse than the landlord struggle objects.'
But how can landlords and revolutionary cadres be compared? This
outlook is entirely wrong. If you yourself are a landlord and oppose
the revolution, then of course you will become an object of struggle.
If not, then to compare yourself with such a person means you
only look down upon yourself.

"Of course we have shortcomings in our working methods. Leftism
has had a bad influence, but this is only temporary, a shortcoming of
our method. This is not our policy. Why should we be discouraged
by temporary phenomena?"

He swept the room with a long glance and looked straight into the
eyes of one man after another. "I want to ask you a question," he
said, warming up for battle. "Why do we live in this world? Is it
just to eat and sleep and lead a worthless life? That is the landlord
and rich peasant point of view. They want to enjoy life, waste food
and clothes, and beget children. But a Communist works not only
for his own life. He has offered everything to the service of his class.
If he finds one poor brother still suffering from hunger and cold,
he has not done his duty. Anyone who is concerned only with himself lacks the fundamental standards necessary for a Party member.
Right now several comrades are thinking, 'Life is easier at home. Why
not leave this work and go home?' But think it over. Who led your
fanshen? From where did the 'fruits' come? Such thinking is typical
of those who have forgotten their class. A good Communist, whenever he meets personal difficulties, thinks of others' difficulties. If you

haven't understood that during the purification meetings, you should understand it now. If you want to go home, you can go home. But give some thought to your future. Where is the man so benighted he no longer has any political needs? Anyone who has no political demands cannot be said to be fully alive. Even the most abject villager is upset when he cannot join the Poor Peasants' League. But you Communist Party members, have you no political demands? If you give up your duty now and return home, will the people want you back in the League or Association? Wouldn't it be reasonable for them to say that you have no desire to serve the masses, hence no reason to join their League?

"And there is another reason," said Ch'en, again looking directly from man to man—across the whole group. "There are those who prefer to work outside in other villages because they fear they cannot pass the *gate*. But the spirit of the policy is to educate and help you, not to beat you down. Really, even though you work outside, you cannot escape the *gate* because in the end you must return to your own village. Anyone who would do otherwise is just an opportunist, even worse than the landlord who slips into our ranks to disrupt them. If a Communist cannot stand the examination of his own Party, how can he stand firm under the blows of the enemy? The purification is a sort of revolution within our own Party. It is inevitable that some will be left behind. There are always some who cannot keep up. That cannot be helped.

"Suppose I buy a ticket and get on the train without giving a thought to my destination, but the train is on its way to Moscow, and when we pass Shanhaikuan and reach Siberia, I suddenly find I don't want to go there. Of course I will try to jump off. It's just the same with someone who joins the Party without any desire to serve the masses. When things get tough, he wavers. So you had better examine your aim now and decide whether you want to go to Moscow or New York. So do not complain if the Party examines you. It is just for this reason that the Party must be purified."

If the land reform cadres were Communists, they had to go forward and face the difficulties. I could sense, sitting in the midst of the audience in the temple, that his words had made an impression, that his challenge had been taken up. At the same time it was very clear that the basic frustration and confusion remained. The cadres were still unhappy. They did not intend to give up, but neither were they moved to sing as they worked. They were ready to put their heads down and plod like oxen. They were not ready to gallop forward like spirited horses.

In the Secretary's speech I found part of the answer to the question: Why didn't the cadres give up and go home?

They didn't give up because the Communist Party held them to-gether. In spite of mistakes and confusion, these men and women had faith in the Communist Party, they had faith in Mao Tse-tung, and they had faith that Mao and the Party would lead them through this period as they had led them through the Anti-Japanese War. The Party in its turn did not cast them out because they had made mis-takes. It asked them to reform, to correct past errors, and it gave them a huge new job to do. It placed more responsibility on their shoulders, not less. Even though they did not see how the future would work out, even though they did not see how their dependents would live through the year, they resolved to prove their mettle in the face of all difficulties. They resolved to carry on with their work.

****

Even as the work team cadres made their way back to their basic villages in Lucheng County, the County Party Committee met to sum up and think through all the facts that had been brought to light at the Conference. As they laboriously pieced together the informa-tion available, they saw a new pattern emerging which must, if con-firmed, alter still further the over-all estimate of conditions and con-sequently of the work to be done. The figures on land holding and property distribution brought in by the teams indicated that most of the land and property of the feudal classes had already been divided and that the majority of the poor peasants had already *fanshened*. Even in the worst organized villages of the Fifth District most families had enough land. If as many as 30 percent still needed other essen-tials, this high proportion was due to special circumstances. The real task therefore was not to launch a new land reform drive but to "fill holes" here and there, particularly the holes created by illegal ex-propriation, and to fill them moreover with what was available, rather than to seize more property from families as yet unharmed. *An pu ting k'ulung* (patch the holes according to the cloth on hand) was the principle to be followed. If there were not enough goods to make everyone a middle peasant, then there simply were not enough. There was no help for it. Some people would have to be satisfied with less.

As this estimate emerged more clearly, the County Committee made several important decisions. First, they sent out word that all the vil-lages should be reclassified as Type I—communities where the land re-form had been successfully carried out. Second, they appropriated BRC 22,000,000 (U. S. $22,000) to be used to repay middle peasants who had been wrongly attacked, announced the appropriation to the teams, and asked for estimates of how much each "basic" village needed. Third, they reversed the decision concerning aid to full-time cadres' families and ordered all team members to plant, hoe, and harvest their own crops by taking leave, when necessary, from public work.

The first two decisions considerably eased the task of the work teams. The third, however, almost cancelled out any good done by the other two. When the cadres learned that they would not receive help at home after all, their morale was badly shaken and more people asked for immediate leave than could possibly be spared from the work.

PART V

Recapitulation

Only through the people's own struggles and efforts can their emancipation be achieved, maintained, and consolidated. It cannot be bestowed or granted by any outsider. Nor can it be fought for or secured through the efforts of anyone except the people themselves. Hence, an attitude of gratuitously bestowing emancipation on the masses or of fighting in their stead is wrong.

Liu Shao-ch'i

46

The Native's Return

A tiger that has wounded too many men is liable to fall into a mountain ravine.

Old Proverb

THE SHARP-TONGUED old woman, Ch'ou-har's wife, was preparing supper one April evening. The sun had already set, and the light in the sky was fading fast. In the courtyards of Long Bow dusk blurred vision even though, in the open fields, one could still see far into the distance. Ch'ou-har's wife, impetuous by nature, fanned the straw fire in her stove a little too vigorously. Her fanning propelled a cloud of cinders and ashes up into her face. One hot ember found its way to her eye. She jumped to her feet and rushed for the door, rubbing her eyes with both hands as she went. She stumbled as she stepped over the sill and dropped her hands just in time to see a figure distinctly resembling Yu-lai come noiselessly through the courtyard gate. To her moisture-filled eyes it seemed to be floating above the ground. The hair stirred on the back of her head. Cold beads of sweat broke out on the skin up and down her spine. Was she not face to face with a ghost?

The figure moved to Yu-lai's own front door, glided over the sill, and spoke to the girl within. The sound of the voice that boomed across the courtyard convinced Ch'ou-har's wife that this was no ghost, but Yu-lai himself, returned from jail. Better by far a ghost than that terrible man in the flesh, she thought. A new terror gripped her heart. She began to tremble from head to foot. A veritable deluge of sweat dampened her back. She turned and ran into her own house, crying, "Ch'ou-har, Ch'ou-har!"

Ch'ou-har, startled, sat up on the *k'ang.*

"Yu-lai has returned," wailed his wife. "I am sweating all over. Feel it. Do you feel it here on my back."

Ch'ou-har felt his wife's back and true enough, her tunic was wet clean through.

When the white-haired old woman turned again to the stove she found that the millet in the pot was already burned.

419

Ch'ou-har's wife had good reason to be frightened. She had taken advantage of Yu-lai's absence to exact revenge for the beatings his son had administered to Ch'ou-har in the past. In the process, she had not neglected to skim off a few advantages for herself. On the very day that the four men were taken away to jail she had started to assert herself in the courtyard and to strut like a peacock. She announced to Yu-lai's daughter that her father would most certainly be executed. When the girl began to weep, the old woman plunged into further lurid predictions concerning the fate of the arch-criminal's family, then feigned sympathy and announced that she would look after his luckless daughter if only the girl would give her something useful in return.

Yu-lai's daughter was so shaken that she wept for the better part of three days. In the meantime, Ch'ou-har's wife came and went in Yu-lai's house as she pleased. She even went up in the loft and rummaged around. When she came down she demanded potatoes for her supper. When Yu-lai's daughter refused, she swore and spread a rumor that the girl was as vicious as her father. Finally she ordered the bewildered youngster to spin some thread and, when the job was completed, refused to pay for it.

Obviously, Ch'ou-har's wife never expected to see Yu-lai again.

When Yu-lai walked in, the sky fell down. Ch'ou-har's wife decided to go back to her mother's village, thereby putting 30 long *li* between herself and the vengeful ex-bandit. Her husband was of the same mind, but when they announced their decision to their neighbors, they found little support.

"If you go back to Chao Settlement," said the neighbors, "who will prove all the bad things that Yu-lai has done? All the things that you have spoken of in the past will be buried. Why not wait at least until the work team returns from the county seat?"

Since Yu-lai made no move to harm the couple, never even spoke to them, in fact, and since flight had certain obvious disadvantages, they decided to wait.

Ch'ou-har's wife was by no means the only villager to be frightened by the unexpected reappearance of the four cadres. The return of the erstwhile prisoners as free men at a time when the work team was away struck the whole village like a thunderbolt. Many peasants who had spoken up boldly in the investigation meetings, even demanding the death sentence for Yu-lai, now wished that they had remained silent. In conversations over steaming supper bowls they denied that they had ever sought the execution of the four and assured each other that they had really meant something quite different, or had not expressed any opinion at all.

Old Shen Ch'uan-te worried more than most. He lived just around the corner from Yu-lai and met him face to face on the street the day after the ex-vice chairman of the Peasants' Association came home. Yu-lai turned his back on Shen and walked away without saying a word. Shen stood there, trembling so violently that he could not light his silver pipe. "I accused the four," he said to several friends afterwards. "I spoke out everything I knew at several meetings. Unfortunately we have many people who would like to pat the horse's back. Surely the bad ones will soon learn what was said and who said it. I can't help being afraid."

Those who had not spoken out at the investigation meetings congratulated themselves. "I'm not afraid of anything," said Pao-ch'uan's mother. "I never said anything against them publicly. So what if they have returned? Since I have not wronged anyone, why should I be afraid?"

Dozens of people began to follow the handsome widow's prudent example. They decided it was better, after all, not to talk too much in public meetings. One of these was Chin-ming's wife, whose husband had returned from Hungtung about the same time Yu-lai was released. The brother-in-law sent to find Chin-ming had talked with him for several days and had assured him that things had really changed in Long Bow and that he would be safe there. Two things finally convinced Chin-ming to come home—the fact that his wife had been elected delegate to the *gate* and Yu-lai, Wen-te, Hung-er, and Hsi-yu were in prison. When he arrived home and found the four "bad cadres" walking around the village as big as life, his heart skipped a beat. He went straight to his hut and had a long talk with his wife. He persuaded her that her daring activity had been a mistake. From that day onward she never left her courtyard, but busied herself making shoes, sewing clothes, and spinning thread. With her own grievances settled (the work team had not only arranged for her husband to come home but had loaned her an extra acre of land to be used pending the final allocation of plots), she suddenly became a dutiful housewife. She took no interest in meetings, protests, accusations at the *gate*, elections, or any other public activity.

"We have wronged Yu-lai," she said with a voice full of sarcasm when anyone asked her opinion. "He is obviously an innocent man."

* * * * * * * * * * *

Why this man Yu-lai and his son so frightened people was hard to understand. Somehow they had convinced the villagers, or at least the majority of them, that they were absolutely ruthless and sooner or later would take revenge. This revenge seemed to the villagers as certain as fate. Yu-lai had once been a bandit, people said; he had killed in cold blood. With his son's help he would do so again—unless the people settled with him first, and not by criticism or censure but by force. Method, it turned out, was the crux of the matter. Yu-lai, his son, and their henchmen had been able to paralyze the village only because physical assault had been ruled out. Education and persuasion, not beating, was the method indicated by the work team, but the peasants had not yet learned to have faith in this method, especially where "rotten eggs" were concerned. Their principle of operation up until the arrival of the work team—"Don't beat good people, but beat bad people"—was one they all understood and knew to be effective. But now the authorities had come out against all beatings, and in the minds of many a suspicion lurked that this principled stand had unprincipled roots. Wasn't this peaceful method favored only in order to prevent bad Party members from being beaten to death—to prevent, in other words, their receiving their just deserts?

The majority were quite ready to do away with Yu-lai and his son. They had no fear of corpses. They would even have settled for a thrashing so severe that the two would think twice before ever threatening anyone again. But since the Party and the work team insisted that this must be a mental struggle, all militancy collapsed like a goatskin float that has been punctured.

Yu-lai's bearing and manner did nothing to belie these misgivings. After their triumphant return from jail, Hung-er and Hsi-yu kept to their houses, but Yu-lai and Wen-te walked about the village as if nothing had happened. "The county police could do nothing against me," said the latter, frowning ferociously as of old. "They held me for 40 days, but in the end they had to let me go. What makes you think you can beat me down?"

Only a handful of persons opposed the general retreat of the population before Yu-lai's *chih kao ch'i yang* (spur-flashing, fighting-cock strut). Among them were two or three of the more outspoken delegates chosen to man the *gate* and several Party members who had resumed their political activity after winning the approval of the masses. Together they tried to rally the village for some sort of counteroffensive.

Among the communists, the bold ones were Ts'ai-yuan, the Eighth Route Army veteran, and Hsin-fa, the branch secretary. The latter had evidently taken seriously the charges made against him at the *gate* that he was too much of "an old good fellow." He was eager to show his mettle.

Among the delegates the boldest of all was Old Lady Wang. She reminded people that the four released men still had to pass the *gate*. "Even if they are not responsible for the 'accident,' that still doesn't mean they did nothing wrong. We may not have proof that they beat up Little Ch'uer, but we certainly have proof of many other wrong things they did. Since they were under arrest and everyone thought they would never return, many other cadres blamed everything on them. Before the *gate* they said Hung-er did that, Yu-lai did this. I think it is a good thing that they came back. Now we can really clear up the facts. As long as they were stuck in jail, that was impossible."

Another peasant who seemed to fear nothing was Old Tui-chin. He had realized long since that very little in the way of material benefits could result from any re-examination of *fanshen,* but he saw beyond that to the political ferment that was taking place in the village. He summed up the situation in a little rhyme all his own. *"Ts'ung hsien kai hui ch'ih mi, hsien tsai kai hui shuo li."* (For millet alone we spoke before, now it's reason we rally for.) He too assured his friends and neighbors that the four must still face the people. In his opinion they were no match for the Communist Party and the Provisional Poor Peasants' League.

The four militants prevailed upon Ch'un-hsi, the acting village head, to call a mass meeting.* Their purpose was to reassure the people, solve any problems that had emerged since the departure of the work team, and plan an energetic sowing and hoeing campaign for the weeks ahead. But the meeting did not go well. Many people did not show up. Those who did appear soon began to drift away. The Party members who had always worked together to make meetings successful were timid, afraid of criticism, even sorry that they had been so active in the past. They did not try to stop anyone from leaving as they might have done a few months earlier. Thus this first attempt to rally the healthy forces of the community ended in a fiasco.

By the time the work team returned from the County Conference, morale in the village had dropped to a very low level indeed. When the cadres scattered out through the homes and huts of Long Bow's three sections, they heard over and over again: "What's the use of speaking out? The old cadres mount the horse as if nothing had happened." "Yu-lai has returned and he is the same as ever." "It is better to work hard at production and let those meet who want to meet."

"We are gloomy because our opinions are no use at all," said Old

* This was a temporary appointment held by Ch'un-hsi pending the establishment of the Village Congress.

Shen testily when Ch'i Yun and I went to his hut. "We offered such clear proofs, but the police said they were no good. Wen-te went out and in less time than it takes to smoke two pipes we heard Little Ch'uer moaning. Surely he must have done it. I can't think it through. Did a star beat Ch'uer down?"

"Maybe the wind did it," said Li Ho-jen, who had dropped by as soon as he saw Ch'i Yun and me talking to Shen.

Over and over again the cadres of the work team had to stress the fact that the *gate* was still in effect, that those who had not passed it must still go before it, that the four from the county jail had yet to be examined, that punishments for those who had passed had still to be decided, and that the movement for democracy in village life was definitely not yet finished. But the many long personal visits and the heart-to-heart talks barely dented the mood of apathy. For every peasant who took heart and began to move, another dropped back into passivity.

Li Lao-szu, the conscientious delegate who had once been exploited by his own brother, summed up the prevailing outlook in a long soliloquy that was interrupted only by an effort to light his pipe. "What's the use of all this talking? There are four cadres who couldn't pass the *gate* but what difference has it made in their lives? They were dishonest and resisted the masses, but they live on as before. They go every day to work in the fields, and it makes no difference at all. And as for the four who returned from the county jail, they haven't received any punishment either. Of course, they will take revenge in the future. In the struggle movement, at least we got something for our hard work. In those days, whenever an accusation was proved, a call went out from the tower for the accused to report to the village office and bring his millet with him. But now . . . ," he shook his head. "It is very hard to *pao ch'eng yi ke tan* (draw together like an egg). Even though I try to work hard and actively, when I look behind me no one is following me at all. So why shouldn't I be gloomy?"

****

The only encouraging phenomenon in the whole village was the condition of the Communist Party branch itself. The morale of the members was somewhat better than it had been. Most of those who had passed the *gate* were working hard to gain the confidence of the people and had hopes of being able to do so. In the meantime, however, they were far from bold when it came to leading and criticizing. They waited for the rank-and-file peasants to move first; they dared not speak emphatically about anything for fear it would be said that they were oppressing the people and repeating their errors. Over their heads hung the power of the Poor Peasants' League to refuse them admission, or expel them if they offended anyone. It was a power sufficient to unnerve them.

Both Hsiao Wen-hsu and his wife had been refused admission to the Poor Peasants' League group in their section of the village. Wen-hsu was charged with being lazy, his wife, Ho-ch'ueh, with encouraging a young bride's defiance of her mother-in-law. When the branch met, Ho-ch'ueh wept bitterly. "I am a Party member but I can't join the League. That is too shameful." Others tried to comfort her with the thought that she need only wait a while. "When the people understand that your husband wishes to correct his bad habits and that you are only fighting for equality they will accept you as members, never fear."

"Look at Ch'un-hsi," said Hsin-fa, the branch secretary. "When he spoke at our last mass meeting, the people supported him. That goes to show that if your opinion is correct the masses will support you even if you are a Communist Party member, so everyone should work boldly and bravely. Only by hard work can we regain our prestige and the confidence of the people."

"That's right," added Cheng-k'uan, "we must try to be good hired laborers for the people. If we now hestitate and waver back and forth and do no work because we are afraid to make mistakes, then it will be so much the worse for us."

These brave words served more as a facade to cover up real confusion and despair than to express a deeply-held conviction. As Hsiao Wen-hsu said, "Before the purification we never thought much, but nov' I feel as if I were a person full of scabs, scars, and lumps. In the past others didn't know my faults, but now they are revealed for all to see, and it is hard to go forward."

****

The work team that returned to Long Bow from the County Conference on May 1, 1948, was not the same as the team that had left the village in April. The change was due to the withdrawal of the intellectuals. They were recalled because the University to which they were attached was about to move. Progress on the battlefront was responsible for this. The previous November, the People's Liberation Army had won a great victory at Shihchiachuang, a rail and textile center at the edge of the Hopei plain. The annihilation of 50,000 Nationalist troops in one battle made possible not only the capture of an industrial town but also the linking up of the two great Liberated Areas in North China—the Shansi-Chahar-Hopei Area and the Shansi-Hopei-Honan-Shantung Area. Consolidation after the victory also made possible a merger between the two great universities of the Liberated Areas—Northern University (in the Taihang Mountains) and United University (in the Wutai Mountains). Together they formed North China University and established a campus at Chengting on the plain. In that county town outside Shihchiachuang a mission compound far larger than anything available in the mountains sat abandoned and empty awaiting occupancy. Word of the merger reached Lucheng County late in April. All the personnel of Northern University serving with land reform teams were immediately recalled from the villages. Then, early in May, the entire staff and student body under President Fan's leadership set out on foot for Chengting. The march took several weeks and covered more than 300 miles.

Professor Hsu, Comrade Kao, and the student Wang all left the Long Bow team. In the normal course of events, Ch'i Yun and I would also have had to leave, but I asked special permission to stay on. President Fan not only granted permission for both of us to stay but also left behind a graduate student of the English Department to help us. This decision not only relieved Ch'i Yun of a heavy translating burden, but also replenished, at least in part, the strength of a team which had been cut almost in half by the withdrawal of the University contingent.

The instructor who stayed behind with us was Hsieh Hung, a landlord's son from North Hupeh. Slight of build, sharp featured and brilliant, he was an ardent supporter of the Revolution. Although cursed with a case of tuberculosis so advanced that he coughed blood whenever he became tired, Hsieh plunged into the work in Long Bow Village with enthusiasm and soon became, like Ch'i Yun, an indispensable member of the team. Not only did he help make up for the withdrawal of the other teachers and students, but he also helped to fill the gap left by those local members of the team who had to take leave, one after the other, to plant, hoe, and harvest their crops at home. First Liang, then Han, then Hou and Little Ch'uer absented themselves for this purpose. The absence of each was keenly felt by those who remained. Their work load was made tolerable only by the fact that the Long Bow peasants too were busy with spring planting and could not devote as much time as usual to meetings and discussions.

With the advance of spring the pressure of work on the land became overwhelming. In May the fall-planted crops had to be hoed, the early spring crops thinned and weeded, corn (the main crop) had to be planted and, in preparation, all the accumulated night soil of the previous 12 months had to be carted to the fields and spread. In order to accomplish these tasks it was necessary for the men to depart for the fields before dawn each day and stay there until after sunset. They called this *liang t'ou pu chien t'ai yang* (both ends sun unseen). When they finally returned home they were exhausted

At the height of the corn planting rush all other tasks were dropped. Even the cadres of the work team went to the fields to help out and when they returned after dark they fell into bed like everyone else.

47

Both Ends Sun Unseen

On the hands of the people
Callouses will never go away
For on their hands they depend
To create the new day

        Wang Hsi-chien

ONE MORNING in May I was awakened long before dawn by the sound of iron-clad wheels clattering down the street on the far side of the mission compound wall. In courtyards throughout the village, cocks were crowing. I rolled out of bed in the semi-darkness and groped my way to the gate. In front of Old Lady Wang's privy the middle peasant Li P'an-ming had already parked his donkey-drawn cart. He and his son were busy scooping "black gold" from the street-side cistern where it had been fermenting all winter. By the time they had filled the large barrel-like tank that was lashed to the axle of their vehicle, the rest of P'an-ming's mutual-aid group had emerged from the shadows. They rubbed sleep from half-open eyes and hunched their shoulders against the pre-dawn chill. They had come to help Old Lady Wang plant corn, and so had I. When the old lady came out, vigorous and vocal as ever, we departed for the fields together. Our hostess, tottering along on her bound feet, led the way.

When P'an-ming's cart reached the end of Old Lady Wang's best plot, Li pulled a sliding board from the tail end of the tank and allowed its liquid burden to pour into a reservoir that had been fashioned for this purpose on the previous day. Two of us then dipped the nauseating soup from this reservoir with the aid of wooden buckets slung on carrying poles and carried it to the far end of the field. There two others hurriedly scooped out small hollows in the ground. These hollows, each of which was formed with one blow of the hoe, were spaced some three feet apart in rows that were likewise separated by three feet. Into each hollow a generous portion of night soil was poured. The hoe-wielders then flung some dirt back over it to form a bed for the seed, and Old Lady Wang herself dropped three seeds—no more, no less—on top of the dirt. To complete the job the seeds were covered with loose earth and lightly tamped in with foot pressure. The important thing was to surround the seeds with a rich pool of manure without allowing any of it to come into direct contact with the tender shoots and root hairs which these seeds would soon produce.

According to local custom, one bucket of liquid night soil was enough for only two or three hills of corn. This meant countless trips back to the reservoir at the end of the plot and required Li P'an-ming to make at least a dozen trips to the village with his cart. It was hard work, made doubly so by the stench of the liquid we were distributing.

Old Lady Wang's field lay due west of Long Bow in the center of a wide expanse of flat land. Other groups were planting corn in that area that day, and their voices came clearly across to us on the still hot air. Strips of millet surrounded us on every side. They had been planted some weeks earlier and were already in need of thinning. Wheat, knee-deep and lush, alternated with the millet. Because early spring rains had been ample, the whole countryside seemed to pulse with life. Under the hot noonday sun I even fancied I could see the leaves and stalks grow. Never had the monsoon cycle provided better weather for corn

We worked in almost complete silence for several hours—Li Lao-szu, a former delegate at the *gate,* Old Lady Wang and her son Jen-pao, a genial middle peasant named Kuo Ch'ung-wang and I. We finally caught up with Li P'an-ming by emptying the reservoir before he could return with another load. Then we had a chance to sit down at last. Old Lady Wang opened a bundle of steamed bread and I soon found myself chewing this cold fare with a relish I would not have thought possible. The steamed bread made us all so thirsty that we finished off a large pot of boiled water within a few minutes. Our hostess had to send Jen-pao back to the village for more.

As we sat in the field, stinking from the night soil that had slopped onto our clothes and from the sweat that ran from every pore, I was surprised to see how low the mountains appeared from the middle of the flat on that bright day. I had already noticed that on clear evenings they seemed to tower in the sky, completely enclosing the plain on which Long Bow and Kao Settlement lay. Now the highest peaks appeared to be no more than low hills on the horizon.

All too soon Li P'an-ming's cart came rumbling out, and once more we fell to work. But by this time less than a quarter of our task remained. Before the sun slid halfway down the afternoon sky, we had completed the whole field. That was none too soon for me. I was exhausted. When I got back to the village, I fell asleep on my bed in the parish house before I could take my clothes off. For several days thereafter a certain not-so-delicate reminder of the Wang family lingered on my quilt.

****

As the work load on the land around Long Bow increased so did the load of domestic work in the yards and hovels inside the village. The severe frugality of winter fare no longer sufficed to nourish bodies taxed by heavy labor. Substantial meals of whole grain had to be prepared morning, noon, and night. In order to accomplish this, some women and children scoured the village, the fields, and the hills in the distance for anything that would serve as fuel for their mud stoves, while others pitted themselves against the stone mills scattered throughout various courtyards and corners. All day long they ground out the last remnants of the previous year's crop.

Prosperous families put donkeys to work at this task, but the majority possessed no source of power other than the frail limbs of their women and children. It made one wince just to watch them straining to drive the solid stone cylinders round and round on their stone beds. Most of these women had bound feet so small they could be held in the palm of a man's hand. Yet they toiled on these crippled stumps like any roustabout and thrust them against the hardpacked soil that circled the mills as if they were clubs of wood. More than once I joined some poor woman behind the boom that drove the stone and circled with her until Hou's megaphone, from the top of the church tower, announced the beginning of another important gathering.

During that period, few peasants found the energy to respond to Hou's call. But backbreaking labor at home, at the stone mills, and in the fields was not in itself sufficient to explain the apathy of the peasants, male and female alike, toward the political work the team was trying to carry out. The spring season had not prevented the vigorous land reform drive in 1946. Hundreds of people had participated with enthusiasm then in spite of the need to plant corn. What was holding them back in 1948?

Part of the answer to this question lay in the program proposed by the work team. It was primarily a program of recapitulation—first, the organization of the poor peasants into a league (this time an official rather than provisional league); next, the classification of the whole village (this time according to the new standards); and finally, the establishment of a Provisional Peasants' Association made up of the majority of the poor and middle peasants together (here the wave of recapitulation broke onto higher ground). After all this, the first task of the Peasants' Association turned out to be still further recapitulation—a second *gate*.

To traverse once more this familiar cycle was like leading an expedition over a mountain that had already been explored, a mountain on the far side of which no gold had been discovered but only another mountain. And this under conditions far more trying than had been encountered on the first attempt. Only the most dedicated activists participated of their own accord. To get others to come to any meeting required special pleading. Even then the results were disappointing.

Thus, what really held the peasants back was not exhaustion but *ch'ih mi szu hsiang* (millet eating thought). From the endless meetings of March and April they had realized no concrete gains, no material goods. Now they were asked to repeat these meetings with even less prospect of material reward. To many shrewd tillers this did not appear to be worthwhile. Better to have a good sleep.

Since coercion and beatings were absolutely forbidden, people did just as they pleased. They came out if they wanted to; they stayed home and slept if that suited them better. As Lao-pao, a delegate to the *gate,* said to his friend Lao-szu when the latter dropped by to call him out, "I'm tired. I'm going to bed early. I don't want to go to any meeting. Can anyone arrest me for that?"

The work team called this "extreme democracy."

"Extreme democracy" slowed progress to a walk but never quite stopped work altogether. In spite of poor attendance the neighborhood groups of the Poor Peasants' League reviewed their membership lists for a second time, added 20 families, dropped eight (most of them households thought to be middle peasant), and then on May 11 elected an official Poor Peasants' League Committee. The balloting was done with beans and bowls as before.

At this stage in the development of village institutions, elections were significant mainly as a sort of litmus test to show the trend of popular thought. As such, this election both encouraged and disturbed the work team cadres.

In most sections of the village the poor peasants chose candidates whom the cadres considered to be the most active and reliable leaders. Among them were eight Communists—four men and four women. The large vote which these Communists polled showed that they still enjoyed great prestige. In the southwest section, for instance, bobbed-haired Hu Hsueh-chen won twice as many votes among the women as her nearest competitor, a sign that her popularity was rising day by day. Old Lady Wang, on the other hand, though nominated, failed to be elected. Apparently her neighbors had begun to tire of her single-minded determination to get something out of the movement and her harsh condemnation of all who did not live up to the strict moral standards which she set. These results were encouraging.

What disturbed the work team cadres was the big vote won by Shen Ch'uan-te among the men of the southwest section. As it turned out, Shen had solicited support from every one of the Catholics who still had a grievance against the revolutionary administration. Men and youths who had never attended any previous meetings showed up to put a bean in his bowl.

The women of that section were shocked.

"Shen has already mounted the horse. He struts around the village as if he owned it," said one.

"He doesn't know how high the sky is or how thick the earth," said another.

In a runoff, where both men and women voted together, the women cast their ballots for Li Lao-szu. Since the men split their vote, Shen was defeated, but only by a narrow margin.

As far as the work team was concerned, Shen had already proven himself to be thoroughly unreliable. The big vote which he received did not speak well for the judgment of the men in his neighborhood, nor did it speak well for the educational program carried on there by the team. When they met to discuss their work that night, the team cadres spent several hours reviewing the weaknesses that had shown up in the southwest section. But no one had a convincing answer to the problem posed by the dissident Catholics, who, it was generally agreed, had taken advantage of the spreading political apathy to win a place in the sun.

****

The frustration felt by the team cadres over Shen's near triumph was offset, at least in part, by a letter which arrived that day in the village office. The letter came from Resistance University, the military training school that had once been housed in the Long Bow mission compound. It read as follows:

Lucheng County
Long Bow Village

To All Members of the Peasants' Association
From the Third Group of the Military and Political Training School

Has the land reform been completed? How is the spring sowing coming?

Having parted from you for more than one year, we still clearly remember the help you fellow countrymen gave us even though you were very busy in production work and in the *fanshen* movement. This help, up until the time that we left, we never rewarded. Now we send you this letter to make our apologies and to express our gratitude for your help.

The most shameful thing that we must admit and ask pardon for is that at the time quite a few of our cadres and members of the general department of our school, influenced by landlord and rich peasant thinking, neglected the suffering of the peasants and misappropriated some of your struggle fruits.

Now, in the land reform study, every comrade has made a serious and deep examination of this matter. All feel and recognize that such mistakes are extremely grave, in fact inexcusable. Such acts violate the land reform law and those who are responsible should come in person to apologize to you face to face. Due to the pressure of work we cannot come personally, but we are sending back all the things that we have here that belong to you. As for those that have been damaged, we are sending back money instead. These are all the articles that we have found and that we can remember. Probably there are some omissions. We sincerely hope that you will point out those things that we have forgotten and we shall accept your opinion with all our hearts. From now on with your help and advice we shall strengthen the education of our cadres and try to be good servants to the masses, serve them wholeheartedly, take an active part in the present *fanshen* movement, and never violate the people's welfare.

> With our sincere apologies,
> (Signed with the seal of the Political Department
> of the Third Group of the Military and Political
> Training School, April 13, 1948.)

This letter was read aloud at all the election meetings held that day and made a deep impression on the peasants. It had been delivered by a carter who brought with him all the articles mentioned. These were put in the village warehouse pending the final distribution of property after the establishment of the Village Congress. There was nothing of great value in the shipment—a roll of white cloth from the church linen closet, a landlord's silk gown, several pairs of shoes, a brass candelabra, a length of rope, an iron hammer—but the fact that the staff and students of Resistance University on their own initiative and without any request from the village, had actually taken the trouble to gather these things together and send them back moved everyone deeply. Their action demonstrated that concrete results could be expected from examinations at the *gate,* from self-and-mutual criticism. It also demonstrated that the movement in Long Bow was not some isolated phenomenon but part of the great wave of land reform and Party consolidation that was sweeping the whole of North China.

48

Class Differentiation Repeated

We must explain, discuss, report, evaluate, classify, post results, explain, discuss, and report again and again. This is very troublesome, very difficult, very time consuming. But the people do not find it troublesome because it fixes their fate. This is the most important work of the whole movement. He who leads the classification holds the knife in his hand.

Secretary Ch'en
Lucheng County Party Committee

RAIN!

Rain fell heavily in the middle of May. Each succeeding downpour came as a blessing. Rain blessed the young shoots and the seeds in the ground. It brought moisture enough to insure lusty growth well into the summer season. Rain blessed the toil-exhausted peasants. It gave them time to rest. Rain also blessed the work team. It provided the cadres with a chance to call meetings and push ahead with the program of *fanshen* which had already been delayed far too long.

Nobody went outdoors while the rain was falling because nobody had any protective covering. Very few had even an extra set of clothes to change into should they be caught in a sudden downpour. To get wet in the rain was to court pneumonia, to flirt with death.

When the rain stopped, it was still necessary to linger indoors. All shoes were made of cloth. They soaked up water from the wet ground after only a few steps. Rain also turned the structureless soil of the Shangtang plateau into a quagmire. It was no use trying to hoe, thin, plant, or plow in the mud. Cultivation had to wait until the sun dried everything out. Rain in the morning meant a day of enforced leisure. Rain today meant rest tomorrow, a welcome double holiday.

The first time that it rained, Hou climbed the church tower and called on all the poor and middle peasants to gather for an afternoon of study devoted to the new classification standards. This session continued right through the following day and into the evening. The second time it rained, the Poor Peasants' League groups began to classify the families in their respective sections. Later in the week a tremendous downpour so drenched the land that no one could go out for two or three days in a row. Then these groups had a chance to finish up their work.

The apathy which had all but stalled the village since the team returned from the County Conference seemed to recede as work on classification began. A few protested that it was all a waste of time, but the mounting interest shown by the majority bore out Secretary Ch'en's prediction: "The people do not find class differentiation troublesome because it fixes their fate."

The man-hours spent in study alone were prodigious. Hundreds of people spent dozens of hours in discussion and practice before the actual work of judging their neighbors even began.

On the most crucial of all issues—the division between middle peasants and rich peasants—solid progress was made. Some of the peasants soon mastered not only the definitions but also the methods for calculating net income, gross income, percentages of exploitation, and fixed and variable expenses. Kuo Yu-tzu, a middle peasant who had had enough schooling to enable him to read the classification documents, soon found himself acting as teacher to group after group. As a guide in simple cases, Kuo made up and hammered home a formula of his own: *lao li p'eng lao li* (match labor power against labor power). To make clear the nature of net income he acted out the role of a middle peasant dividing up his harvest. First he scraped a pile of dust together with his hands and called this his harvest or "gross income." He then set a section of the pile aside "for seed and fertilizer" and pushed another section to the other side "for wages and food for the hired man."

"This pile, the one I have left, that's the net income," said Kuo triumphantly.

His listeners, a group of pipe-smoking peasants who squatted round him in a circle, had little trouble understanding such graphic lessons.

****

Careful preparation made the second classification far more precise and scientific than the first, without detracting in any way from the human interest which any review of the people's life was bound to bring to the surface. As a matter of fact, with their newly acquired knowledge of the principles involved in class analysis, both cadres and peasants were able to probe more deeply than before into every aspect of village affairs. Rules which had seemed dry and difficult when studied in the abstract at the county seat suddenly took on lively new dimensions when they were applied to concrete cases.

Since the emphasis was now on repayment, all those families that had ever been attacked as gentry were now studied with particular care. One example will suffice to illustrate the method: the family of Kuo Ch'ung-wang.

During the base period there were nine people in Ch'ung-wang's household. They lived on the produce of 23 acres, five of which were rented out. The family had 40 sections of housing, two draft animals, two carts, and three able-bodied men, two of whom worked full time on the land, while the third worked about half the time.

When Kuo Ch'ung-wang was attacked as a landlord in 1945, he and his wife ran away. His brother Fu-kuei stayed behind only to be beaten to death when he refused to reveal where his buried wealth lay. Six other members of the family lived on in Long Bow with leftover assets approximately equal to the poorest of all the poor peasants. These six now claimed that they had always been middle peasants, not landlords. They demanded that their land and property be restored in accordance with the new regulations.

On the basis of comparative labor power Ch'ung-wang's heirs seemed to have a case. They claimed that the elders of the family had never hired more than 40 days of labor a year, exclusive of harvest help, and that therefore the family income from exploitation was a mere fraction of its earned income.

When they brought their case to the southwest group of the League, stolid Ank'u, husband to the young Party member, Little Mer, recalled that he had worked for three solid months on Ch'ung-wang's land in 1944. When others confirmed this, the peasants decided to take Ank'u's labor, rather than the 40 days claimed by the family, as typical of the base years. Then, with Kuo Yu-tzu's help, the economy of the family was analyzed as follows:

1. Income from five acres of rented land	7	hundredweight
2. Income from eighteen acres of family tilled land	70	hundredweight
3. Total gross income	77	hundredweight
4. Produce created by Ank'u's labor	10	hundredweight
5. Ank'u's wages	.5	hundredweight
6. Ank'u's board (1.5 pints a day)	1.5	hundredweight
7. Surplus created by Ank'u	8	hundredweight
8. Total income from exploitation (line 1 and 7)	15	hundredweight

This was less than one quarter of the gross, but Ch'ung-wang owned more than twice as much land per capita as the average of the village. Therefore, the income from exploitation had to be doubled.

This made it 30 hundredweight or considerably more than the limit allowed.

Kuo Ch'ung-wang was classed as a rich peasant. The expropriation of his property had not been a mistake.

****

A second important objective of this classification was to determine how many new-middle-peasants had been created in Long Bow and how many poor peasants still remained. To accomplish this required a close look at all those previously classed as poor on the basis of their holdings during the base period. Those who had since received enough in the various "struggle movements" to support themselves were henceforth to be called new-middle-peasants.

This was a designation which no family welcomed. To be called new-middle-peasants meant for that family that the Revolution was over, that it had received its due. Most families so designated fought hard to reverse the stand of their neighbors and indignantly denied that they had everything necessary for an independent life. But the reality of "no more oil" intervened against them. Since most of the more prosperous families had already been downgraded, it followed that among the poor there must be some who must be upgraded. With very little property still in the hands of the village administration and little else that could be seized, the definition of *fanshen* itself had to be trimmed. Talk about the need to possess everything necessary for a prosperous middle peasant life gave way to talk about the minimum necessary to support a family on the land. As time went on, even this minimum tended to shrink.

The kind of struggle this trend aroused was illustrated in the case of Old Kao, a veteran from the Taiyueh region who had retired in Long Bow on land allocated by the distribution committee.

Because he was single and a veteran, Old Kao had received four acres of land. This was much more than the average and more than he could till by himself. He always had to have help from his mutual-aid group. But because he had nothing else besides this to his name except one bare room—no animal, no cart, no implements, not even a wife—Kao still considered himself a poor peasant.

"But you have four acres of land. Surely you are a new-middle-peasant," said several.

"I don't even have a pot to cook in. How can I be called a middle peasant?" Kao demanded indignantly. And indeed he did not look very prosperous. His padded clothes were soiled and patched and the towel on his head was almost black from lack of washing.

"When you were mustered out you got nine hundredweight of grain. You could have bought a donkey, a plow, and a dozen pots. And the four acres of land were heavy with standing wheat when you got them. From that harvest alone you could have saved enough to buy all that you needed. But no, you spent it all on fancy living. If you aren't a new-middle-peasant, it's your own fault," said acting Village Head Ch'un-hsi.

Old Kao was so upset that he couldn't say anything more. He grew red in the face, placed a tobacco-stained thumb against one nostril and blew the contents of the other onto the floor. Then he coughed and mumbled something unintelligible. Obviously, "new-middle-peasant" didn't suit him at all. He regarded the term as an insult.

"Well, what is your opinion?" asked Yuan-lung.

"If the masses think I am a new-middle-peasant, then. . ."

"It's not what the masses think. What do you think?"

"I think I have no wife. No one makes clothes for me. I have to buy them. I have nothing but land. I think I am a poor peasant."

"Well, we don't want you to bear any burden," said Hsieh, the interpreter who was representing the work team at the meeting. "But after all, what is wrong with calling you a new-middle-peasant? That's a poor peasant who has *fanshened*. It's no insult. If we call you a new-middle-peasant, will you carry a burden the rest of your life?

"You shouldn't," said Hu Hsueh-chen. She was one of those who had already accepted that designation herself and was learning to live with it.

"What do you say, Old Kao?"

"Well, I haven't any burden. It's all right with me," said the sad-faced veteran.

But as he said it he blew his nose again and averted his eyes from those who had done him such an injury. He was obviously still upset, and so were many others who had been classed in the same way.

Their indignation was only exceeded by those few who had formerly been classed as poor but were now upgraded to old-middle-peasant and consequently considered to have always possessed sufficient property to maintain independent life. However, nothing they said caused their neighbors to relent. There simply was no "oil."

****

When every family in the village had been reclassified a master list was drawn up. It was posted on the brick wall of the church compound so that it could be read by anyone who came along the main street. The list was so long that it was impossible to read while standing in one spot. A poor peasant who started deciphering the names at the southern end, where the landlords and rich peasants were listed, had to walk northward more than 30 paces before he found his own name among the propertyless.

Certain families at the upper end of the scale who had lived in fear of attack or had already been expropriated were overjoyed when they saw how far down on the list they stood.

Li Pao-yu, the nervous merchant with the date orchard and the licentious wife, found himself listed as a plain middle peasant. He strode up and down the main street, chest out, eyes shining, and told everyone who would listen, "They tried to class me as a rich peasant or even a landlord. But now, in spite of all their tricks, I am a middle peasant. Indeed, who cares what class they put me in. They can call me anything they like. The facts are plain."

Wang Shen-nan, the man whose brother had been beaten to death when 2,000 silver dollars were found buried in his yard, looked wide-eyed at his name in the middle-peasant section. Then he returned home as if drunk and immediately went out to plow a piece of land on the hill that he had not set foot on for four long years. "Whether they repay me or not doesn't matter. I'm well enough off as it is. I'm a middle peasant and I don't care what happens," he told his old mother.

Chao Ch'uan-e, the Party member whose in-laws had previously been classed as rich, also found herself listed with the middle peasants. She appeared on the street for the first time since her rejection at the *gate* and walked its full length with her head up.

Other peasants were not so pleased. They were the ones who had been upgraded. Without exception they all objected.

Ch'ung-lai's wife complained bitterly that she had not yet acquired a draft animal or a cart or even one small share in either of these two prerequisites for new-middle-peasant status. Wang Hsueh-shen resented being called an old-middle-peasant because others had received gratis everything that he had received in a lifetime of toil. "My wife and I slaved in the fields for ten years with our backs bared to the sun. If I had known we would end up being called old-middle-peasants I would have stayed home. I would have sat on the *k'ang* and done nothing," he said.

Li Ho-jen, the leader of the Catholic clique, and Chang Huanch'ao, the blacksmith, were among those raised from new to oldmiddle-peasant status. This was not due to any extraordinary holdings of capital or land but to the fact that they were both craftsmen. Ho-jen was a skilled carpenter, and Huan-ch'ao, though he lacked skill, was the only blacksmith in the village. In judging their class the peasants added their earnings from carpentry and blacksmithing to their earnings from the land and came up with old-middle-peasant status for both. When Huan-ch'ao pleaded a shortage of land, they told him, "If you till the land you can't beat the iron, and if you beat the iron you can't till the land."

Both men were incensed by the decision. Ho-jen reacted with sarcasm. "Of course I am happy to be a middle peasant. As I drove my cart over the hill today it seemed as if I were flying," he said.

Huan-ch'ao became sullen. He did not show up for work at the co-operative carpentry shop the next morning. When the carpenters sent one of their members around to find out what was wrong, he growled, "Just because of this iron pounding they call me a middle peasant. Yet my cart, my house, and a third of my land I got only during the distribution. I won't pound iron any more. Anybody who thinks it's so easy better try it himself."

The work team and the Poor Peasants' League Committee had to take into account not only the opinions of those who objected to the class they had landed in but also the opinions of those who disagreed with the way others were classed. Beneath the official list on the wall a suggestion box was placed. In it many notes were found. One of them read:

"Old Lady Wang, Li T'ung-jen, Ch'en Chun-fu, Kuo Feng-tzu, Lu Ken-ti poor peasants? We disagree. Land, tools, draft animals enough!"

This note was from the northern group.

When Old Lady Wang heard about this, her mouth began to twitch. She already felt that her neighbors were ganging up on her. This was the last straw. Not only had they failed to elect her to the Poor Peasants' League Committee, not only had Li P'an-ming asked a heavy price in return for the use of his donkey and cart in the corn field, but also the mother of her son Jen-pao's bride-to-be had suddenly announced that her daughter no longer wanted to marry. Behind this most grievous blow she knew was an effort to extract more money for the match.

The bride's brother, it seemed, had recently died. His family now wanted Old Lady Wang not only to find a dead girl that could be buried alongside him, not only to pay half the expenses of the posthumous wedding ceremony, but also to buy a coffin for the dead girl and pay half the expenses of the dead pair's funeral. Only then would they allow the dead man's sister to marry Jen-pao.

The price was far too high. Old Lady Wang wanted to call the whole thing off. But delay could spell even greater trouble. With only three in her household, people could argue, just as those in the northern group were doing, that Old Lady Wang had property enough.

Old Lady Wang stopped Team Leader Hou in the street and shouted at him so that all her neighbors could not help but hear, "I lack land, tools, housing, and labor power. I received nothing in the whole movement. Yet they want to call me a middle peasant."

"Don't worry," said Hou, trying to calm her. "It has not been decided yet. There are still two rounds of classification to come."

"Do I have a right to say anything?" asked Old Lady Wang, trembling with rage.

"Of course! If you have an idea speak it out," said Hou. "As if anything on earth or beneath it could stop you!"

"Don't worry about it," he added, putting a restraining hand on her shoulder. "Don't worry about it."

"Don't worry about it! How should I not worry about it? Anybody can see that there is no hope of getting anything!"

"We'll solve it some way."

"How? Is anyone going to give me a house? Where are they going to get it from? The holes are many, the patches are few. I don't think I'll go to any more meetings. It's no use."

"But we'll solve it, I tell you. If the masses work together, they can solve anything," said Hou patiently.

Old Lady Wang did not wait to hear him out. She turned abruptly on her crippled feet and hastened back into her courtyard, cursing under her breath.

49

It Is Too Slow!

Certain young cadres . . . often complain that this place is no good and that place is no better; that this kind of work is no good and that kind of work is no good either. All the while they are looking for some kind of ideal place and work so as to enable them to smoothly 'change the world.' However, such places and such work do not exist except in their wishful thinking.

Liu Shao-ch'i

DESPITE real or imagined shortcomings, the class list, as posted, served as a basis for the next step—the formation of a Provisional Peasants' Association. This Provisional Association was finally established on May 28, 1948, after several days of discussion, a review of the qualifications of all poor and middle peasant families, and another round of elections—this time with written ballots. The minority who could write wrote their own. The majority, who could not read or write, went to certain mutually acceptable ballot writers and told them for whom they wanted to vote.

Most of the Poor Peasants' League Committee were elected as officers of the Provisional Peasants' Association. To this core was added a representative complement of middle peasants that included several from each section of the village. The final roster of elected officers represented the poor peasants, the new-middle-peasants, and the old-middle-peasants in almost equal proportions. This was as it should be, people said.

A great mass meeting was held to celebrate the establishment of the Provisional Peasants' Association, but somehow it proved anti-climactic. These organizational steps, since they no longer served as way-stations on the road to an all-out struggle against a still dominant gentry with wealth to hand over, were transformed into a shadow play, a form of rehearsal-in-reverse, a demonstration of the way in which things should have been organized long before. Consequently, they lacked vitality.

The response of the people was more apathetic than ever. Morale continued to drop and every day brought more problems. Wherever

Ch'i Yun, Hsieh Hung, and I went, people came with their woes great and small and asked for help.

On June 2, we went to eat at the home of a peasant named Lai-tzu. The family was weeping. Lai-tzu's newborn child was dying, and Lai-tzu's mother could not get off the *k'ang*. The child had been born into a washbasin on the floor three days before. Because the child's mother was dumb, she could not describe her condition to anyone. When she felt the baby coming in the middle of the night, she climbed from the *k'ang* alone. Her mother-in-law awoke just as the baby dropped into the basin used by Lai-tzu to wash his feet. The old woman jumped up, retrieved the thrashing infant, and held it all bloody to her naked body, As she did so, she ordered her son to fetch the midwife.

It took more time than is needed to eat a meal for Lai-tzu to return with the midwife. Throughout that long wait his mother, shivering with cold, clutched the baby to her stomach and tried to keep it warm without ripping the umbilical cord that still bound it to the placenta inside its mother. To relieve tension on the cord she had to stoop far forward.

The midwife, when she finally arrived, cut the child's cord with a pair of rusty scissors. By that time the distraught old woman was locked in a jacknife position and could not straighten her back. Her son had to lift her bodily onto the *k'ang*. There she lay immobile with her eyes staring at her bloodstained knees.

They did not wash the baby for three days. They carefully buried the placenta vertically in the ground outside the door in such a way that the end of the cord protruded as far out of the earth as the matching end of it protruded from the baby's navel. But in spite of these precautions against the "six day wind" (navel ill), the child fell ill.

When Ch'i Yun and I came to the house the baby was gasping for breath and wailing piteously. Lai-tzu's mother told us between sobs that he had not slept since the sun set the night before. She begged Ch'i Yun to save him, but Ch'i Yun knew that it was already too late. The rusty scissors, gruesome symbol of the old society, had doomed the newborn infant as soon as they touched the cord.

Lai-tzu himself had recently quarreled with a neighbor named Hsi-yu. The two families had dissolved a bean curd manufacturing co-operative without settling all their accounts. Now Hsi-yu threatened to hang himself in front of Lai-tzu's door unless the latter paid what he owed, and Lai-tzu's mother begged Ch'i Yun to intervene. Until tempers cooled there was little that Ch'i could do about this either. We left the household stunned.

On the same day, Pao-ch'uan's mother accused the stubborn cuckold, Chin-chu of outrageous wage demands for planting her corn. Criticized for quarrelling over so minute a matter, Chin-chu took out his frustration on his wife and started beating her again. Meanwhile, Pao-ch'uan's mother fell ill. Since she didn't have enough millet to buy herbs at the medicine shop, she walked out to the long-abandoned temple of the god of health, scraped up some dust and ate it. When Team Leader Hou criticized this superstitious act from the top of the church tower through his megaphone, a "god board" appeared in front of the temple.* The following words were scratched on it:

> Heaven fear not, earth fear not,
> Hou Pao-pei also fear not.

The "god board" set tongues wagging and families quarreling throughout the village.

When the Committee of the Peasants' Association met a few days later to consider which families needed relief grain, its members were shocked by the length of the list they finally drew up. As if this were not problem enough, the southwest section reported four babies born in as many days and four more on the way.

"That means we need eight additional acres," said a spokesman. "Where can they all be found?' '

"Speaking of lacks, Old Kao lacks a wife," said Little Mer.

"And Hung-chou lacks a finger," said Huan Ch'ao, the black-smith. "There are some lacks we just can't do anything about."

Frustration in the face of needs everywhere without the where-withal to satisfy them caused even the most steadfast members of the work team to lose heart. One day Little Li came to Hsieh with an inflamed eye. Hsieh told him he should see a doctor. Little Li said doctors in China were no good. In fact, he said, nothing in China was any good. He wanted to leave China and go to the South Seas; he wanted to leave Asia and go to the Soviet Union. If not that, then he wanted to leave the countryside and go to the city, leave Lucheng and go to Taiyuan.

"I am discouraged," said Little Li. "Ten years ago when I began to work as a cadre people said, 'When the Japanese are defeated, then the Revolution will succeed.' But the Japanese surrendered and war continued. Now ten years have passed. It is too slow. Where is the industry we dreamed about?"

---

* A "god board" was a piece of wood bearing a written message sup-posedly left there by the god of the temple.

All these incidents were straws in the wind. They indicated a social squall arising. Some problems, like the tetanus that was killing Lai-tzu's baby, flowed naturally out of the terrible poverty of the past and tended to strengthen in the peasants a burning desire for change, a categorical demand for another way of life. But the problems that sprang from the new life itself were more elusive, more subjective. In a period of discouragment such as this they tended to raise doubts as to goals, direction, and method. They eroded the optimistic spirit and mutual trust that had accomplished such miracles in the past; and in the wounds opened up by this erosion, ugly sprouts of individualism continued to sink roots and grow.

This was an atmosphere that played into the hands of the four who had returned from jail. Individualism was a phenomenon which they well knew how to exploit. Nursing a grudge at having been falsely arrested, very much aware that the whole village wished them ill, and actually frightened by it, they concentrated on enhancing as much as possible their reputation for audacity and ruthlessness.

Yu-lai did this by a particularly outrageous act. He went to a village warehouse that had formerly been under his supervision and removed from it a valuable log. The log had been confiscated from a peasant hitherto regarded as rich. Its owner had fled the village under attack and all his property had been turned over to the Peasants' Association for safekeeping. Now Yu-lai claimed that the log was his in lieu of wages still owed him by the refugee. Without asking anyone's permission, he took it. By this act he served notice on the whole community that he considered himself more than a match for the lot of them.

"A man capable of doing that is capable of doing anything," people said.

It was not a very auspicious reaction for a village that must soon man a *gate* to examine Yu-lai's record and the record of each member of his clique.

50

Who Dares Man the Second *Gate?*

Every comrade . . . should help the masses to organize themselves step by step and on a voluntary basis to unfold gradually struggles that are necessary and permissible under the external and internal conditions obtaining at a particular time and place. Whatever we do, authoritarianism is always erroneous because, as a result of our impetuosity, it makes us go beyond the degree of the masses' awakening and violates the principle of voluntary action on the part of the masses.

Mao Tse-tung, 1945

DEAR SECRETARY CHANG

We have met with great difficulty in carrying out the second round of Party purification in our village. Now we send you this report to let you know of the situation and our discussion and wait for your instructions.

After Wang Yu-lai, Wang Wen-te, Li Hung-er and Wang Hsi-yu returned from the county jail their attitude was very bad. The *ch'i yen* (air and smoke) atmosphere they created made the villagers afraid. They threatened the masses, saying, "We were arrested by the county for more than 40 days, but the county police could do nothing to us. What can you do?" They said this on the street, and at the same time they asked who had criticized them and who had accused them. At the meeting of the branch their attitude was also bad. They resisted all criticism from others. All this, together with their past record, has made the masses afraid. The members of the work team have done their best to explain to the people, but no one dares say anything. The people remain silent and say nothing. Some of the villagers say, "We have opinions; we hate them, but we dare not speak out." Some say, "I would rather die than criticize them." Most serious of all is the fact that most of the Party members in the branch have the same feeling and dare not criticize them. Though the work team members visited the people and backed them up and gave them strength and called meetings of the active leaders, still the villagers did not believe us. They thought all that the work team could do was to speak beautiful words. In our opinion, after a study of the real situation we think this is not just a common anti-cadre opinion. The real fact is that the behavior of these men has been too bad, especially the air and smoke they breathed after their return from the county jail and the threats they made. This is not blind opposition to cadres on the part of the masses, so we must solve this problem. If we cannot solve this problem, not only the purification work will fail, but also the masses will misunder-

446

stand the whole policy of purification and the future consolidation of the Party will be undermined. So we suggest the following action.

(1) Announce to the people that these men are officially removed from their posts right now. Why? Because of their present action and their words since their return and their intention to harm the work of purification.

(2) According to the request of the people, the Peasants' Association wants to receive a part of the fruits which the Communist Party members promised to give up, these fruits to be kept by the Association until the future "filling holes movement" takes place.·

We wait your answer.

Chopped*
Hou Pao-pei, Leader
Li Sung-lin, Assistant Leader
Long Bow Work Team

This letter, which was carried to Lucheng by Comrade Hou Pao-pei, was a painful admission of failure on the part of the work team cadres.

Inability to arouse the peasants to challenge Yu-lai and his clique had already caused a split among them. Hsieh Hung and Ch'i Yun, responsible now for the whole southwest section of the village where most of the clique's victims lived, were demanding some sort of decisive action. Though feeling against the four was strongest in this section, so was fear of retaliation. It effectively checkmated all the "education and persuasion" that the two cadres from the University had been able to apply. Hsieh and Ch'i felt that a breakthrough must be made from above, preferably by some tangible evidence of support for the rank and file. The handing over of goods illegally acquired by the cadres and the dismissal rather than the suspension of Yu-lai, Wen-te, Hung-er, and Hsi-yu would constitute such evidence.

Team Leader Hou disagreed strongly. He was not as worried as Hsieh and Ch'i about the lack of public opposition to the four bad cadres. He felt that more routine mobilization work would eventually move the people to speak out. At the same time he was reluctant to put excessive pressure on former activists and Communists. He felt that the unwarranted arrest of the four had only added fuel to their defiance. Heavy blows such as summary dismissal and the surrender of property on order, at a time when nothing had been settled according to the due process outlined in the Draft Agrarian Law, could only fan the flames and lead to worse difficulties later. The

---

* In China, documents are "chopped," not signed. A chop is a small block of wood or stone with the individual's name carved into one face. Since the ideographs making up the name are hand carved, a chop cannot easily be duplicated and consequently has the validity of a personal signature.

problem was to correct past mistakes and save all the cadres for future work.

The team members argued bitterly over this question. Hsieh and Ch'i accused Hou of shielding the bad cadres. They thought he had a pedestrian, mechanical approach to what was rapidly becoming a very serious crisis. Between themselves they even called him a "right opportunist." Hou, on his part, accused Hsieh and Ch'i of "anxious heart sickness" (impetuosity). He felt that they wanted to oppress the four cadres unreasonably. Privately, he considered them to be "leftists."

The other members of the work team were undecided at first. Little Li, the assistant team leader, finally tipped the balance. He sided with Hsieh and Ch'i, took the lead in attacking Hou's position, and carried the rest of the local men with him. As a result, on June 3rd, Comrade Hou carried the letter, the contents of which he opposed, ten long miles over ridge and plain to the county seat and personally delivered it to Secretary Chang.

Hou came back in the afternoon more depressed in spirit than when he left. Secretary Chang had agreed to let some of the "fruits" be handed over, but he had called the proposal to remove the cadres from their posts "adventurist." If the work team in Long Bow could not deal with the four men, then the two who were Party members must be sent to Lucheng with a letter detailing their crimes. Secretary Chang would talk with them himself. "It's not enough to say that the people are afraid. You have to find out why," said the Secretary to Hou.

This reply angered everyone.

"Adventurist," snorted Little Li. "I knew he'd say that before you told us! And what's the use of sending the two Party members to Lucheng? If the Secretary fails to solve the problem and, in the end, sends the two men back, we will be in a much worse state than ever before."

"Well," said Hou, "let us really search out the people's opinions. Let us ask them why they are afraid. And as for the Party members, let us tell them that Communists are not afraid of death itself. For the sake of the Party we have risked our lives many times. Why should we be afraid of a few individuals?"

These bold words upset the other team members further.

"You can't use empty rhetoric on Party members," said the interpreter Hsieh Hung. "Just telling them they must not fear is no good. They must be helped to understand and think it through."

"Everyone knows the phrases," said Little Li, so exasperated that he pulled off his cap and threw it on the floor. "That can solve nothing. If we beat them over the head with the glorious spirit of Party members, the result will be very bad. We've got to discuss according to the real facts and find a method."

In the end Hou made a concrete suggestion. "Let's call a meeting of the Provisional Peasants' Association groups, a branch meeting, and a meeting of those who have not passed the *gate*. Let's see if we can't get some opinions from people and find some way out. If we get nowhere, tomorrow morning I'll go back to Lucheng. But I can't go back without another try, because if Secretary Chang asks me again what is the matter and I say the people are afraid, it will be no use at all."

****

The three meetings held that evening produced some positive results, and a good night's sleep calmed frayed nerves. In the morning Team Leader Hou had another good suggestion.

"Tackling these men is like eating a bowl of hot soup," he said. "Whoever tries to swallow such a bowl down in one mouthful will surely scald himself to death. But if you sip it bit by bit from around the edge you can swallow it all in the end. Therefore I say we should set up the second *gate* right away, but we should leave Yu-lai, Wen-te, Hung-er, and Hsi-yu to the last. We'll start with the easy ones, first those who have already passed, then those who have not yet passed, and finally those who have never been faced."

Since no one had a better idea, the whole team agreed with this plan. That very afternoon the second *gate* began. This time there were no delegates. Instead, all the members of the Peasants' Association, some 90 percent of the population, met outdoors behind the Church on the grounds of the old orphanage. There only a zigzag slit trench, left over from the days when the compound had been the headquarters of Resistance University and its administration feared bombings, prevented the huge crowd from filling the space from wall to wall.

Cheng-k'uan, chairman of the old Peasants' Association and Ch'un-hsi, acting village head, led off with very short statements about their work since the last *gate*. Vigorous discussion then arose among the numerous *ke ts'ao* groups that had formed spontaneously among the crowd. When the voices died down, group after group reported that they had no opinions and were in favor of passing the two a second time. Ts'ai-yuan, the storekeeper, T'ien-hsi, the militiaman, and Hu Hsueh-chen, suspended leader of the Women's Association, all passed in the same manner. After that, instead of asking each

Communist to make a statement, Little Li simply read off the names, and the people voted to pass or not to pass as they saw fit.

What began as orderly voting soon broke down into mass shouting. When Li read off a name, the people shouted, *"T'ung yi, t'ung yi"* (agree, agree).

"This is no good at all," said Little Li, raising his voice to a roar in order to be heard above the noise of the gathering. "If anyone disagrees, they have no chance to speak. We had better vote in a more orderly way."

But just at this moment Ch'un-hsi's mother stepped backward and fell into the slit trench. Everyone rushed forward to see what had happened. As two men pulled the unfortunate woman out, several by-standers broke into uproarious uncontrolled laughter which soon spread to the whole crowd. Even Ch'un-hsi's mother, once she got over the shock of her fall, began to laugh.

After that it was hard to take anything seriously. The reading of the names continued and so did the voting, but confusion grew apace. Many people could not even hear what was being voted on. When those whose record was about to be considered raised their hands to say something, only those people standing next to them heard even a syllable. This so amused those who could not hear that they laughed again, and everyone looked around to see who else might have fallen into the gaping trench that divided the crowd.

The whole procedure was a formality. Unprepared to tackle the real problem at hand, the whole village was backtracking through well-known territory and no one took the maneuver seriously. The meeting inevitably degenerated into a farce; yet farcical as it was, it had great positive value. The laughter eased the tension in the public mind and brought the divergent groups closer together. The poor and middle peasants had not often met as a body, and in the past there had been fear and friction between them. This afternoon they rubbed shoulders with an ease and familiarity that could only arise between people who were learning to trust one another. The informality of the proceedings, in its own ridiculous way, united people more than a whole series of more earnest gatherings. In spite of themselves, the peasants became more conscious of their strength than ever before. To fear the revenge of several discredited cadres seemed a little preposterous to anyone who stood out in that warm afternoon sun and watched his fellow villagers milling about, laughing, and shouting for all the world as if they believed themselves to be the true masters of their fate.

In the afternoon the crowd had time to consider only those who had already passed the *gate* in April. By the time the last of these had been approved, the women were already drifting off to make supper. The meeting had to be adjourned until evening. At that time a much reduced gathering took up the four men who had failed to pass the first *gate*. This was a more serious matter and the peasants acted accordingly.

Man-hsi, K'uan-hsin, Yu-hsing, and Ch'uan-e had all prepared many days for this second chance. They were determined to win approval. Man-hsi considered it a matter of life and death. Rejection at the first *gate* had shaken them deeply and all but destroyed Man-hsi. He had lain on his *k'ang* and wept for several days, and when he finally stopped crying, he was still too ashamed to walk about on the street.

"Why did you weep so much after the first *gate?*" other Party members had asked as they helped him to prepare for the second round.

"Because I could find no way out. I prepared in the branch for so many days, but when I got before the delegates they were like a brick wall."

"And why did you stay at home after that and never go out in the daytime?"

"Because when I spoke to people, they did not answer me. They despised me because I could not pass the *gate*. Whenever they saw me coming they just turned away. So I just stayed home."

"You had better speak about your future. Have you made up your mind to pass? How will you correct your bad attitude?"

"I can correct every habit of mine except eating," replied the muscle-bound militiaman in despair. He was ready for any sacrifice, but he was not at all sure that a change on his part would solve the problem. To his listeners, however, his sincere words sounded facetious.

"If you give such an answer to the masses, you will not pass this time either," said Hsin-fa. "We must analyze the opinions of others. Those things that we cannot accept, we must explain. We must reform our attitude and let people see it clearly."

When, after this sort of preparation, Man-hsi finally came before the members of the Provisional Peasants' Association, he detailed every past transgression patiently, but still denied having raped Fu-hsu's wife and disclaimed any knowledge of the missing salt. This time the people believed him. A few tried to harass him about beatings that he frankly admitted, but one after another their opinions were rejected by the majority as indecisive. In every case Man-hsi had gone wrong trying to carry out orders. That his methods were crude they all agreed, but that his intent was evil they would not allow. Man-hsi promised that he would never act brutally again. "I know I have hurt many people," he said. "But if you decide to pass me, I will be grateful. And if you want me to work for you in the future, I will do my best. The only thing I cannot stop is eating."

The peasants did not consider this remark facetious at all—quite the opposite. "That's very well spoken," said Yang Yu-so. "If you had had such an attitude before you could have passed easily."

They approved him.

Man-hsi's face lit up with joy. As he walked back through the crowd, many people slapped him on the back and wished him well. "Do your best in the future," they called out.

It was clear that Man-hsi was regarded with warmth and affection by most of his neighbors. Strong as he was, brave as he was, and terrible as he could be in action, he was no tyrant but only a simple fellow who wanted very much to do the right thing, to win the approval of his peers, and to enjoy the friendship and support of all his fellow countrymen. Ideas of avenging the criticism he had received never entered his head.

The woman Communist Chao Ch'uan-e passed even more quickly. Now that she had been classed as a middle peasant, all the grievances against her seemed to appear less venal. She was not a class enemy boring from within, but a self-centered ally trying to shield her family from an unjustified attack. Viewed in this new light her actions appeared quite ordinary. There was no reason not to pass her.

K'uan-hsin and Yu-hsing were not so lucky. K'uan-hsin could not explain the loss of the sifter screen that had disappeared while he was on guard duty and lost his temper when they pressed him about it. Yu-hsing still misunderstood the damage he had done by eating one piece of steamed bread.

The Provisional Peasants' Association membership unanimously decided to hold both these Party members over until after the establishment of the Village Congress. Then a final *gate* could dispose of the whole question. No one disagreed with Old Tui-chin when he said, "It is not proper for us to be in any hurry. If there are difficulties we can leave them to the Congress. With the *gate*, as with the classification, we have three rounds. Our policy is not to wrong anyone but to let each speak all his opinions. Perhaps there are some who think that we spend too much time on this, but since it is such hard work we should expect to spend a lot of time." Then he repeated his favorite proverb:

> For millet alone we spoke before.
> Now it's reason we rally for.

****

These apparently inconclusive events, though not decisive in themselves, changed the whole trend of village affairs. Passing the *gate* for the second time made the Communists realize that in spite of all gripes and grumbles, the people really did support them. It gave them new heart. As a result, the branch meeting that was held the next day got under way with vigor and spirit. Before it was over, many Party members had followed the lead of Ts'ai-yuan and Hsin-fa in daring to voice grievances before the new *gate*. It did not take long for the changed situation inside the Party branch to influence the whole Provisional Peasants' Association. When the Association groups were later called together to register complaints against the four, ideas came as thick and fast as the chaff that falls from a winnowing fan.

The stalemate had at last been broken, but only insofar as evidence was concerned. No rank-and-file peasant had yet agreed to take the lead in voicing charges in public. Since a few bold Party members could not possibly substitute for the action of the people themselves, it was necessary to mobilize still further among the sectional groups of the Association.

51

A Young Bride Leads the Way

In all sections of the masses there are generally to be found the relatively active elements, the intermediate elements, and the backward elements. In the initial stages the active elements are usually in the minority, while the intermediate elements and the backward elements make up the broad masses. In accordance with the mass line, attention must be paid to the majority, that is, the intermediate and backward elements; otherwise the advanced section will become isolated, and nothing can be done satisfactorily.

Liu Shao-ch'i, 1945

JUNE 5TH dawned hot and humid. A haze that blurred but by no means obscured the sun hung over the village and veiled the gaunt hills on both its flanks. This haze was a product of the approaching summer solstice. Over the Shangtang plateau the concentrated summer sunlight heated up a land surface sodden with rain and converted the air into an invisible blotter that sucked up water in superb defiance of the law of gravity. Suck as it would, the air could not dry out the land in a few hours. A thousand puddles still lay on the roads, and countless particles of clay still clung together as gumbo in the fields. In spite of this, the able-bodied men of Long Bow were out hoeing. They had to be. If they waited any longer the weeds would smother the young corn.

Just before the sun reached its scorching zenith Comrade Hou's voice boomed out from the top of the church tower: "Women's meeting today! As soon as you finish eating, come to the churchyard. Women of the Peasants' Association, come to the meeting!"

When I heard Hou's call I jumped up from the bed where I lay dozing, delighted at the prospect of any action that could divert attention from the insufferable heat.

By the time I reached the street the women were already streaming out of their homes in all the lanes, yards, and back alleys of the settlement. They converged on the Church grounds by way of the main street and the gate of the District Office. It was the biggest turnout of women the village had ever seen. The older ones minced

along on their bound feet as if on stilts. Girls with single braids down
their backs to signify that they were not yet married, chased each
other through the crowd. Young brides whose hair had only been
bound up in a bun for a year or two, sought each other out and
held hands as they walked along. They obviously longed to skip and
dance as their little sisters were doing, but a strong sense of propriety
caused them to maintain instead a demure and dignified gait and
content themselves with mischievous side-glances at the few male
bystanders who loitered in the open gates along the route.

Inside the mission grounds Hu Hsueh-chen stood on the stone
steps of a small outbuilding, welcomed the women, and explained
why she had summoned them. "Hsien-e has agreed to accuse her
husband and her father-in-law before the *gate*," said the leader of
the Women's Association, "but she is afraid to return to their house
to live. She will speak if she is granted a divorce. For this she wants
our backing."

With that Hsueh-chen beckoned Hsien-e to join her on the steps.
Standing side by side the two women posed a striking contrast. Hsueh-
chen was clad in a frayed black tunic that had suffered many fierce
poundings at the edge of the village pond. The bobbed hair that
hung straight down on both sides of her face accentuated the mas-
culinity of her features. The long nose, the square jaw, the jutting
chin were all set in an expression of the utmost seriousness, as if
their possessor bore on her shoulders all the cares of a sorely troubled
people and had long since forgotten, if indeed she had ever known,
frivolity, joy, or even laughter.

Hsien-e, on her part, exhibited the quintessence of youthful femi-
ninity—slight of build, breathtakingly beautiful, she wore a new
tunic of bright-colored flowered cloth. It fitted very tightly at the
shoulders and then belled out toward the waist but not so abruptly
as to obscure the firm figure underneath. A pair of baggy slacks concealed her legs but her feet, which were so small it was hard to believe they had never been bound, were set off in a pair of red embroidered slippers, perfect for a lady's boudoir but out of place on the
street. Hsien-e's lovely face, radiant as a snow apple in high bloom,
revealed not the slightest sign of suffering but only a childlike fresh-
ness, an innocence of spirit that seemed to belie all that she had
gone through.

Without any urging, Hsien-e began to relate the story of her life.
Her voice was high-pitched but steady and clear. "Even before the
famine year my parents could not maintain the family. I don't know
how much they got from Yu-lai, but three different people acted as
go-betweens and we received grain and money in return for my en-

gagement to Wen-te. During the famine year my father had to go to
Taiyuan. There was nothing to eat at home and mother was afraid
that I would die of starvation. So she sent me to Yu-lai's home though
I was only ten. I lived a hard life there. I went to the fields every day
to find herbs in order to stay alive. They ate millet while I drank
the water. They beat me often. Later, when the famine was over, my
father came and I went back to live with my parents. But when I
was 14 Yu-lai demanded that I return and get married. I wanted
to wait until I was 16, but they threatened us. They said our lives
were in their hands and accused us of being agents for Chiang Kai-
shek. I was afraid and did as they wished. After the marriage I was
not allowed out of the house. I never dared join a meeting although
I often wished to go. Once Yu-lai locked the gate and Wen-te locked
the door so that no one could come in. Then they whipped me, both
of them, with a mule whip. Hu-Hsueh-chen heard me screaming and
went to the District Office for help. If it hadn't been for her, I would
have died that night.

"A few months ago my mother fell sick, but I didn't dare return
home to see her. My husband said, 'If you return home, I will divorce
you.' But my uncle came many times to call me. Finally I took a
quilt and escaped to my father's home, and now I dare not return
to my husband's family. I have made up my mind to divorce him
because if I return, then I shall be killed surely. If I cannot divorce
him, then I shall commit suicide."

She said this firmly, coldly, as one would announce a business
decision. Yet there was not the slightest doubt that she meant it. Her
poise before the group, her self-assurance, struck me as extraordinary.
She was only 17, but she spoke and acted like a mature woman twice
her age—no smiles, no coquetry, no hesitation, not even any visible
emotion. What came across to the crowd was a hard, all but desperate
determination.

In the village Ch'ou-har's story that Hsien-e had been beaten so
cruelly because she refused to submit to her father-in-law's advances
was widely believed. Whatever the truth, the events that took place
behind those locked doors had burned such hatred into Hsien-e's heart
that she no longer cared what happened.

All the men of the work team who heard her speak were deeply
moved by Hsien-e that day. If Yu-lai and Wen-te were men of iron,
here surely was a girl of steel. It was obvious that in this slip of a
girl the pair had met their match. Hsien-e was fighting for her life,
for her right to live as a free person. One look at her clear black
eyes was enough to suggest that when the battle was truly joined
she would give no quarter.

If the work team cadres could have granted Hsien-e a divorce, they would have done so without any public spectacle. But the question was not that simple. The attitude of all the villagers had to be taken into account. Divorce had never before been sanctioned in Long Bow. In all the centuries that the land had been settled no woman had ever had the approval of the community in leaving her husband. It could be taken for granted that the overwhelming majority of the men would oppose such a step. Many of the older women, especially those in conflict with their daughters-in-law, could also be expected to oppose it. Hsien-e could count only on that small core of progressive young women who rallied around Hu Hsueh-chen in the Women's Association. If a divorce was to be granted, a much wider section of the female population had to be mobilized, and so the women of the whole village had been called together.

When Hsien-e finished speaking, Hu Hsueh-chen asked the women a question. "How shall we solve this great problem? The oppression which she suffered is the oppression of us all."

In their small groups the women discussed the problem, quietly at first and then with mounting vigor. Finally they began to report, group by group, to the whole meeting. Most of them favored divorce. A few suggested separation. Hsien-e, they thought, should remain in her father's home. Unexpectedly, the wife of a peasant named Feng-le took a contrary position. She declared that as far as she could see the young husband and his reluctant bride got along well.

"I can't accept that," said Hsien-e, stepping forward to interrupt before the woman could finish speaking. "If we got on so well, why did he beat me? Does this show that we got on so well?"

But Feng-le's wife was not so easily deterred. "Beatings!" she said. "What husband doesn't beat his wife? That proves nothing. The fact is that they *fanshened* very well and they helped her family *fanshen* too. Both households benefited as anyone can see. I have often seen her smiling."

This statement met with protest.

"You are trying to shield Yu-lai," shouted several women.

"They both benefited. I'd change places with her any day," said Feng-le's wife, defiant.

"Just because your husband beats you . . ."

Hu Hsueh-chen quieted the storm by raising her hand. "Let me say a few words. The girl knows her own condition. I live in the same courtyard. According to what I have seen, she is oppressed and suffers a great deal. Of course she does not weep all day long. If it were so, they'd beat her for it. She must pretend to be happy and go about with a smiling face, but the tears are rolling down her heart just the same. Staying with her parents is no solution. She wants a divorce. Two or three groups agree to this. What do the rest of you say?"

A great chorus of women shouted their agreement. Feng-le's wife, clearly outvoted, said no more.

"Then we will write a letter to the county government and present our advice," said Hu Hsueh-chen.

Before she had a chance to formulate what this advice would be, a commotion broke out at the back of the court. Old Lady Wang had arrived. She was breathing hard. Sweat dripped from her forehead and long wisps of hair which had broken loose from the knot at the back of her neck blew about her face. But she was grinning broadly. She held by the hand an attractive young woman, Kuei-pao's daughter-in-law. On her own initiative, Old Lady Wang had walked all the way to Horse Square to find her. If Hsien-e could accuse Wen-te, then Kuei-pao's daughter-in-law could accuse Hung-er.

"Let her up front. Let her through," shouted the women at the back. They opened a passage for the pair across the packed church grounds to the speaker's stand. As the middle peasant's daughter-in-law mounted the steps Old Lady Wang jumped up beside her, as pleased and proud as if the new witness had been the issue of her own womb.

With a voice that was barely audible, the shy young woman told how Militia Captain Hung-er had arranged for his mistress to sleep in her home. Then, by threatening to launch an attack against her parents in Horse Square, he had prevailed upon her also to accept him as a lover.

This tale temporarily diverted attention from Yu-lai and Wen-te to Hung-er. It aroused a flood of memories concerning the militia captain's "rascal affairs." Incident followed incident as the women vied with each other in recalling salacious tidbits of past history. As they talked they forgot their fear of the "bad cadres" altogether and began to accuse them of many kinds of injustice. Enough charges were recorded in Little Li's book to last the Provisional Peasants' Association several days before the *gate*.

As the meeting closed, Ch'ou-har's wife made one last accusation. "Wen-te, when he heard the megaphone calling us to this meeting, said to his father, 'Oh ho! Listen to that. They're calling the dogs!'"

When they heard this many woman spat on the ground. Dozens called Wen-te a turtle's egg and worse. There was no doubt that the women were ready to do battle. If the *gate* had started then and there the four "bad cadres" would not have had a chance.

This mass meeting, the result of mobilization work done by Ch'i Yun, inspired Hsieh Hung to do some ground work of his own among the men.

On that same day Hsieh learned that Hsien-e's cousin, Hei-hsiao, was visiting in Long Bow. Hei-hsiao was the youth who had accused Hsien-e's father, Hsi-le, of being a Kuomintang agent. It was well known, however, that he had done so only after having been severely beaten by Wen-te, then a village policeman. Under the circumstances, the accusation could hardly be considered voluntary. If the boy could be persuaded to tell the truth, neither Wen-te nor Yu-lai could "escape from the corner."

Hsien-e took Hsieh Hung to the house where her cousin was staying. They found him hiding on the *k'ang*. As soon as the door was clear he tried to run away, but Hsieh caught him by the collar of his new machine-made tunic and began to question him. Since Hei-hsiao was small for his age, Hsieh had no trouble holding him, but no amount of questioning brought results. Hei-hsiao denied that he had ever been beaten by anyone in Long Bow. Finally Hsieh let go of his collar and tried a new approach. He asked the boy what kind of a man his uncle was.

"Hsi-le is a good man," said Hei-hsiao. "An honest man. He treats everybody well, so of course he treated me quite well too."

"Too bad his good deeds are only on the surface," said Hsieh, holding his face expressionless. "Perhaps he makes a very good impression, but after all he is an agent, so he must be a very bad man."

"Who said he is an agent?" exclaimed the boy, stepping back as if in recoil from a slap on the face.

"A few people in this village say so," said Hsieh Hung coolly, "and Wen-te says so too."

At this the boy began to swear. "Wen-te's mother's cunt stinks. His words are drivel."

"Why swear at Wen-te? He never harmed you!"

"Now you are lying," said Hei-hsiao. "You know very well that Wen-te beat me and just a few minutes ago you wanted me to accuse him of it. But now you are saying he did nothing to me."

"But it was you who said nobody in Long Bow ever beat you."

Hei-hsiao recoiled again as he realized the box he was in. He sat down and remained sitting in stunned silence.

"Since he really beat you," said Hsieh, taking full advantage of the break, "why should you deny it?"

"Because I am afraid he will beat me again."

"Why be afraid?" asked Hsieh. "Many people are going to accuse Wen-te tomorrow. It is time to reckon accounts with the bad cadres.

And so it is time for you too. Since you are not native here, you have nothing to fear anyway. You can go back to Hukuan and they can't do anything to you. Look at Hsien-e. She is not afraid. Why not stand up and fight beside her? Who is stronger? You are much stronger; yet you are afraid and she is not. That means she is brave. But it also means that the people here are on top, and the bad cadres no longer ride the crest of the wave."

Hsieh saw that Hei-hsiao was weakening. He continued his offensive. He stressed the obligation which the nephew had to clear his uncle's name. Soon the boy broke down and began to weep. In the end he cursed Wen-te and vowed to take revenge.

"If I don't stand up and accuse him tomorrow, I cannot be called a human being," said the teen-aged visitor between sobs.

By such efforts as this Hsieh Hung managed to mobilize several men, all of whom promised to back up Hsien-e if she once began the struggle. The most militant among them was Old Ch'ou-har, who swore he had never forgiven Wen-te for the beating received at his hands. Behind Ch'ou-har stood Yuan-lung, Shen Ch'uan-te, and the village treasurer, Chin-hung. All of them vowed to speak out the next day.

52

The *Gate* in the Church

In exposing errors and criticizing defects, our whole purpose is the same as the doctor's in treating a case: namely, to cure the patient but not to kill him. . . . Any person who has committed errors is welcome to treatment until he is cured and becomes a good comrade, so long as he does not conceal his malady for fear of taking medicine or persist in his errors until he becomes incorrigible but honestly and sincerely wishes to be cured and made better. You cannot cure him by subjecting him to hearty abuse or giving him a sound thrashing. In treating cases of ideological or political illness, we should never resort to violence, but should adopt the attitude of 'treating the illness in order to save the man,' which alone is the correct and effective method.

Mao Tse-tung, 1942

I DID NOT sleep well that night. Ch'i Yun and Hsieh Hung had both worried so much about the impending confrontation that they had succeeded in communicating to me their deep anxiety. I was half afraid to see the morning come lest the work team and the villagers prove to be unprepared for the crisis it was sure to bring.

Though I woke at the first cock crow, Hsieh-Hung was already up. He had gone to see his "big guns"—Hsien-e, Hei-hsiao, Ch'ou-har, and Old Lady Wang. If they dared speak out, others must surely follow and the meeting would be a success. If they faltered at the last minute there would be no one to step into the breach, and Wen-te would face down a cowed and silent crowd.

I was sipping a bowl of hot millet porridge in the cook house behind the District Office when Hsieh Hung came back. He had made his rounds and seemed well pleased. Old Lady Wang was in the best of spirits. The coming conflict filled her with energy and anticipation. Hsien-e had not backed down one inch. Hei-hsiao was morose but said he would speak if Hsieh stood behind him. Ch'ou-har was rambling around like a sleep-walker and repeating an old saying that Hsieh himself had taught him: "Those who are loyal are not afraid to die."

Because showers were anticipated, the meeting had to be held indoors. The only building in Long Bow large enough for such a gathering was the great hall of the Church. This hall was usually locked. It was used as a storage bin for the public grain. Now all that remained of last year's grain had been piled around the altar at the east end of the building. This left the nave free for a popular assembly.

Inside the Church, the huge pile of millet, reaching 10 or 12 feet in height, lapped half way up the windows behind the cross. It made an impressive backdrop for the events to come. The people, as they streamed indoors, were dwarfed by this mountain of their own creation. Lying there in golden majesty, the millet expressed, perhaps better than any other symbol could, the power of the Revolution. Only collective action could possibly have produced that incredible mountain of yellow seed, and only collective action could possibly straighten out the men who were to come before the people that day.

By the time the meeting got underway, the nave of the Church was filled to capacity. The villagers had apparently realized how important to their future lives the decisions of that gathering would be. Almost the entire population, old and young, had come.

One of the last to enter the huge doors was Hsien-e. The pallor caused by a sleepless night only enhanced her beauty. Gracefully, she seated herself near the aisle that had been left between the door and the chairman's table at the center of the hall. But Yu-lai was brazen enough, even then, to try to frighten her. As soon as he saw his daughter-in-law, he walked back and sat down in front of her. Hsien-e immediately jumped up and moved through the crowd to the side wall. She had not been there long when Yu-lai's daughter sidled close to her. Was this part of a plan of harassment worked out by her in-laws? Hsien-e evidently thought it was. She got up again and pushed her way to the center of the crowd. There she was at last completely surrounded by other people, and neither Yu-lai nor any other member of his family made any move to follow her.

The proceedings began with the placing of the non-Party cadre San-ch'ing, suspended clerk of the village office, on the stand. As the people warmed to the task of questioning him, Hou switched them to Hung-er, suspended captain of the militia. Hung-er soon found himself in trouble. He had to adimit that it was he who took the now-famous salt and that it was he who had blamed the theft on Man-hsi. When Man-hsi heard this, he jumped to his feet and denounced Hung-er so boldly that he inspired a dozen others to speak out. Thereafter the denunciations came so fast that Hung-er found it impossible to handle them. He was asked to wait until all the people had spoken before making his reply.

The members of the work team exchanged triumphant glances. The meeting was going better than they had hoped.

I could see Yu-lai well from where I sat. He had not expected anything like this. The mounting spirit of the people brought sweat to his partly bald head and his glance shifted nervously from one section of the crowd to the other.

Intrigued by Yu-lai's obvious dismay, I turned to scrutinize Wen-te, the son. He sat near the chairman's table waiting his turn. Apparently unmoved, he surveyed the crowd with a confident air and smiled at the various friends he spotted as if this were some sort of celebration. Nothing in his pleasant face or relaxed manner suggested that he could possibly share any responsibility for all the fear and agitation that had stirred the village for so many weeks, or that he himself would soon face the ordeal that Hung-er was at the moment undergoing.

"The man has nerve," I thought. "I wonder if he knows something that no one else knows?"

Events proved that Wen-te had no such knowledge. By the time the meeting got around to him a subtle change in the crowd's attitude had produced a more sober response from the day's star witness. The peasants had refused to pass Hung-er. Then they had adjourned for lunch and assembled once again. For this second session their numbers had not thinned out as might have been expected. On the contrary, peasants packed the Church in greater numbers than before, a sign that the afternoon could well be tougher than the morning. When Wen-te stood up to talk, his right hand played nervously with the cloth fasteners of his homespun tunic and all the color in his cheeks drained away. Instead of staring calmly at the crowd as he had done all morning, he looked at the floor and found it hard to choose his words. Even Man-hsi had made a better speech before the *gate* than Wen-te made now.

"I don't want to tell my whole history . . . I will begin with my work . . . When I was public security officer I beat Hsi-le and called him an agent. This was because he talked sour grapes with Fan-liu . . . Now I understand that I was wrong. I should have made an explanation . . ."

Wen-te spoke a few sentences, stopped, looked around, cast a hurried glance at the floor, spoke a few more words, and hesitated. He was quite tall and very lean, leaner than any of the other cadres who now faced him. The cords on his neck stood out like ropes.

"I lost my temper and beat Chin-chu because he bothered me so

much about his wife. Once in the middle of the night he got me up
to scold his wife. I hit him . . . and I gave Ch'ou-har a thrashing because of some trifling gossip. Now I know that that was wrong. I beat
other old men. Why didn't I beat my own father?"

Ch'ou-har stood up when Wen-te spoke his name. He was trembling
with rage and shouted at the top of his cracked voice, "What did you
beat me for? What evil haven't you done?"

But the people standing around the old man stopped him. "Let
Wen-te talk," they said. "Let him finish."

"I beat Hsi-a because he protected Chao-ch'eng in the struggle.
Once Hung-er called me to transport public grain, and I took several
boards from the warehouse. Nothing more . . . That's all I can remember. As for the rascal affairs, I am guilty. I thought, if others can
get away with it, I can too."

That ended his self-report. He sat down.

As soon as Wen-te finished, old Ch'ou-har stood up again and
started walking through the tangled mass of people toward the table.
As he walked he pulled up his sleeves and cursed the man he hated:
"Turtle's egg, donkey's penis, your mother's foul cunt!"

Before anyone could stop him, he strode to the spot where Wen-te
sat on the floor, pointed a long quivering finger straight into the
young man's face, and shouted with all the fury that was in him, "You
beat me! You almost killed me! I lay sick for weeks. And when you
beat me you said, 'If I beat you to death I don't care!' "

Ch'ou-har took another half step forward, raised his fist and
made ready to strike. A score of men in the back of the Church rose
to their feet. They began to move forward as if by command. Across
the floor other men stood. Every person in the crowd strained to see
the action in the center. An ominous silence pervaded the whole vast
space as a thousand eyes concentrated on Ch'ou-har's long hands.
Wen-te, crouched and ready to spring, stared up at them also. If
Ch'ou-har hit out, as he certainly intended to do, Wen-te would die
in the next few minutes, for such was the feeling of hatred for him
and his father that no power on earth could stop those peasants once
Ch-ou-har galvanized them into action. The members of the work
team stood as if hypnotized.

It was one of those moments when time stands still and every
word and gesture is reduced to slow motion. A catastrophe was
spontaneously being generated. I felt it, and the members of the
work team felt it too. But no one moved.

"Tell me, who are the dogs? Who are the dogs?" said Ch'ou-har in
a hoarse whisper.

At this Wen-te sprang erect.

"I never said that. I never called anyone a dog!"

His face was chalk white.

With a quick jerking movement Ch'ou-har reached out both hands toward Wen-te's throat.

A cry rang out.

"Make him stand back!"

It was Ch'i Yun. She ran forward and flung her arms down between the two men. Some one else—was it Hsieh Hung?—pulled Ch'ou-har back a foot or two. Then Little Li and Chang-ch'uer pushed him on into the crowd. He stood there looking helplessly at his cheated hands. They were still moving as if to throttle the wind in a human throat. He raised his eyes to meet Comrade Hou's and his eyes asked, "Why? Why have you stopped me?"

Those men in the crowd who had stepped forward drew back a little.

With a shudder Ch'ou-har recovered control of himself. His arms dropped to his sides. He began to speak and suddenly felt the weight of his years crushing him. All his joints began to loosen, the muscles of his careworn face sagged, and the words came stumbling from his toothless mouth.

"I risk my life to accuse this man," he said. "If I should be murdered in some nameless place I only want to warn you beforehand. I put myself under your protection. All my life I have never beaten others or . . ."

He could say no more. Slowly he went back to his seat.

Even before Ch'ou-har sat down, Hsien-e rose to her feet. As she walked to the center of the hall Wen-te looked at her with disbelief. It was as if he were observing a spirit risen from the dead.

Hsien-e told her story very bravely; Hei-hsiao made his accusations just as he had promised; and many other peasants, following the lead of these two young people, spoke out without equivocation. But Wen-te did not bow his head. Quite the opposite. As the meeting progressed and he realized that he was not going to be beaten, he regained his composure and finally his arrogance. He ended up not only rejecting all the criticisms made against him but also turning the charges against those who had made them. When Shen Ch'uan-te asked him who beat Little Ch'uer, Wen-te said that Shen ought to know the answer himself. When Hu Hsueh-chen asked him if he had beaten his wife, Wen-te answered proudly, "Yes, I beat her. I beat her once because she stayed out so late that we got no supper. I beat her a second time because she flirted with another man in the cornfield. Of course, for a man to beat his wife is wrong, but I had good reason."

This last reply was more than Little Li could stand. He climbed up on the table where everybody could see him and denounced Wen-te bitterly, passionately, as a man who could not possibly continue to be a Communist.

But the object of his scorn did not even seem to hear him.

****

When the work team members got back to the District Office they found Hung-er waiting for them. The suspended militia captain had a hang-dog look on his face. All the defiance was drained out of him. He asked for a copy of the opinions that had been spoken against him, saying that he wanted to study them and answer each one in detail at the next meeting.

Hung-er had reached that critical point in his own education where defiance gave way to despair. It was a point at which most people had to arrive before they could begin the painful process of reform. The task before the work team was to bring Wen-te to this same threshold, to break down his defenses, and to make him see himself as others saw him. Only then could the difficult process of remolding his outlook begin.

The public meeting, successful though it had been in overcoming the people's fears, had not yet conquered the suspended police captain. The only effective method for putting further pressure on him was to mobilize the people of Long Bow more thoroughly. Up to that point, of the scores who had suffered at the hands of the father-and-son pair, only 20 or 30 had spoken out. This was not enough. With a man as proud and determined as Wen-te, only a united community could prevail. By calling a mass meeting from which Wen-te and Yu-lai were barred, the work team encouraged several dozen others to find their voices. When on the evening of June 9th, Wen-te again appeared before the *gate,* the sheet of paper recording the charges against him was five feet long.

The most damaging of these charges had to do with the "agent's caps" that he and his father had fastened on all who opposed their will. As these were presented, one after the other, Wen-te did not have time to regain his composure.

Old Tui-chin, the bachelor peasant from the northern group, interrogated him like a district attorney before a court of law.

"How old was your wife when you married her?"

"Fifteen."

"How then did you get a license at the District Office?"

"I ordered her to say that she was 16."

"You demanded the immediate return of all the money and grain your father paid for her?"

"No, I didn't do that, but I did force her to say she was 16."

"How?"

Wen-te hesitated.

"He threatened her parents. That's what she says. What do you say?" cried Old Lady Wang.

Wen-te said, "I don't know what to say. I am afraid. I have forgotten what happened." His composure was draining fast.

"We won't beat you. Why should your heart jump?" asked Yuan-lung.

"You are so brave at doing things, why be so afraid to talk about them?" asked Hu Hsueh-chen derisively, her lips curled in a sneer.

"I forget everything. Please, you criticize me," muttered Wen-te.

"The opinions of the masses pile up like a mountain," said Old Tui-chin. "He says he has forgotten, but how can he forget the affairs of his own family? We have tried our best to win him from the wrong path, but he doesn't understand at all, so we ought to kick him out of the Party and send him to the County Court for further action."

"Wen-te, what do you think of those suggestions?" asked Little Li.

"I agree," said Wen-te. "I think it is right. I have nothing to say."

Then Hsien-e spoke up. Both Tui-chin and Little Li had ignored the most important point.

"Do you grant me a divorce right away?"

"I'll never agree to that to the last day of my life," said Wen-te. The very idea seemed to send him into a sort of frenzy. He threw himself down and began to hit his head against the floor so hard that the sound of his skull knocking brick could be heard throughout the Church.

"Never!" he cried with each blow. "Never, never!"

"Why not? Tell me the reason why not," demanded Hsien-e.

"Though I beat you before, still I can correct that. I'll never do it again. I can correct that," said Wen-te from the floor. He had stopped beating his head, but he did not get up.

"How can I believe you?" asked Hsien-e. "What if you beat me to death?"

"If I do that, then I should be punished with death," replied Wen-te.

"But even if you paid for her life with yours, that would be no bargain for her," said Old Lady Wang.

"Let the girl state why she wants a divorce," demanded Yuan-lung.

"No, let Wen-te state why he wants to keep her," said T'ai-shan's mother.

But Wen-te could give no reason. He only made the statement,

"I'll take an oath before the people. If you return home, I will never beat you."

"That's enough," said Cheng-k'uan, who, as head of the Provisional Peasants' Association, had chaired the whole meeting. "I think we should decide what to do with him. He forced an under-aged girl to marry him; he oppressed and beat many people for trifling reasons; he falsely called many people reactionary agents. I say send him to the People's Court. Is that right or not?"

"Right, right," shouted the crowd. "That's the best thing that could happen."

This time, after the meeting was over, Wen-te sought out the cadres in the District Office as Hung-er had a few days before. He was on the verge of tears.

"I prepared thoroughly for two whole days, but as soon as I stood up I got completely confused. I want to be honest. I want to speak it all out, but I can't. I am afraid the masses will jump on me in the street and then turn around and say that I attacked them. What shall I do."

"The masses are kind," said Ch'i Yun. "They wouldn't do anything of the kind. Only a twisted brain like yours would think of such a thing."

Yu-lai, who had followed Wen-te in, shook his head in disgust at his son. "I coached him for several days, but this son-of-a-bitch is so stupid he forgot everything when he got before the people."

"But it has nothing to do with coaching," said Little Li, throwing up his hands. "He need only speak out his behavior. According to him he is not skillful at self-criticism. But the question arises, how come he is so skillful at oppressing people? If he insists on defying the people he will only punish himself."

"My style and my attitude were too bad in the past," admitted Wen-te. "But I beat the landlords bravely."

"Are they the only ones you beat?"

"Well, no, I beat others too."

"Yes, you beat your wife and your father-in-law, who is like a second father to you. Can you call him a landlord?"

"No," said Wen-te, mournfully.

Since the meeting had voted to send Wen-te to the People's Court, and neither Little Li nor Ch'i Yun showed the least inclination to sympathize with Wen-te, Yu-lai thought his son was already under arrest. He assumed that the youth would immediately be led off to Lucheng to await trial. Not wanting to be caught unprepared, Yu-lai asked if he should go home and find a quilt for the prisoner to take along with him to jail. He was surprised when Little Li dismissed both of them and told them to go home.

The worried father and distraught son had no sooner stepped outside the door than Yu-lai returned alone. He took Little Li aside and, in a low tone, engaged him in a very serious conversation. It turned out that what concerned him most was the divorce. Both he and Wen-te considered a divorce to be out of the question. "In the last few days, whenever the subject came up, we both stopped thinking. For us it is too awful to think about," said Yu-lai, pulling nervously at Little Li's tunic.

Little Li listened attentively but promised nothing.

Yu-lai, uneasy but by no means repentant, departed once again.

****

The next day, June 10th, brought Yu-lai before the *gate*. If ever a man strode the political stage with a tiger's head only to depart like a snake's tail, Yu-lai was that man. His final performance, his "day in court," proved to be less than an anti-climax; it was a farce. In facing down Wen-te, the son, the people had lost their fear of Yu-lai, the father, and Yu-lai in turn, when confronted by a united community, lost all his bluster. His threats and boasts evaporated like a puddle on a sun-scorched field. What remained was an evasive man with watery eyes whose every tactical twist and turn was anticipated by his accusers.

The people responded with contempt, locked the *gate,* and told him he would have to wait for the People's Congress.

That afternoon, when the *gate* adjourned for the third time, Wen-te and Yu-lai came together to the work team. This time Wen-te wept in earnest. Clearly, he no longer knew what to do or which way to turn. His father, as stubborn in defeat as he had been in victory, still hoped that clever words and demagogy could pull them both through the crisis. He cursed his son for a stupid ass as he had done before. But it was obvious to the latter that wit and maneuver had outlived their usefulness. Only sincerity counted now. Both men must face up to their past. What made Wen-te weep was his fear that it was already too late. Would he not be punished anyway? Was not the divorce a foregone conclusion? Could any words or acts on his part head off catastrophe now?

As Wen-te wept and Yu-lai cursed, Secretary Liu, a subregional leader whom none of us had met before, walked in. He had come to check on progress in Long Bow's land reform just as Secretary Wang had done several weeks earlier. When he saw Wen-te in tears he asked him, with great kindness, to sit down and tell his side of the story.

"I know I am doomed," sobbed Wen-te. "If I go to the People's Court, I will be shot. And if I am kicked out of the Party, it will be as

bad as if I were shot. Whether I confess or not, there is no way out
for me. So I had better be silent and await my fate."

Gently but firmly Secretary Liu disagreed. "You can still decide
your own fate," he said. "It is up to you."

The Party Secretary then told Wen-te about many cadres whom
he personally knew who had done worse deeds than Long Bow's
police officer but who had determined to face them honestly, had
turned over a new leaf, and had then been accepted once again as
leaders by the people. "As for your marriage, if the girl insists on
leaving you, she has that right. We can't do much about that. But,
if you reform, in a year or so you can certainly find another wife,"
said Liu.

The tears gradually dried on Wen-te's cheeks as he listened. He
promised Secretary Liu that he would speak with a different attitude
before the next *gate* and went home calm and thoughtful.

As soon as he had gone, Secretary Liu called the members of the
work team together and warned them, as they had so often been
warned before, against "leftism" in the treatment of cadres. "In a
number of places Party members have been so oppressed they have
committed suicide," he said. "This is a great loss to the Party and to
the people. We have to show everyone a way out. It is not enough
to cure the disease. We must save the patient. And besides, many of
these men, especially the younger ones who are in the deepest kind
of trouble, are often the most brilliant, fearless, and creative sons of
the people. Reformed, they are a most valuable asset. They often
prove to be stronger and wiser than those who have not made
mistakes."

A long discussion followed. The cadres decided that Wen-te could
be re-educated, but that his father's attitude stood in his way. If only
the young man could be separated from his father for awhile, he
might well straighten out his own life and even win back his wife.
But where could he go and what could he do away from home?

Secretary Liu suggested a solution. A school had been established by
the Communist Party for just such cadres as Wen-te. It had already
opened its doors in Changchih and was taking in students from all
over the Taihang Mountain area who could not pass the *gate* in their
home communities. Removed from the temptations and tensions of
their native environment, given plenty of time to think and study,
encouraged by sympathetic teachers who tried to widen mental hori-
zons, and aided by association with other men whose problems were
similar to their own, many hard-core delinquents had found it possible to assess themselves objectively and to choose a new path.

Secretary Liu suggested that both Wen-te and Hung-er be sent to this school and that all other decisions affecting their lives—what punishment they should receive, whether or not a divorce should be granted—should await the outcome of the education they received there.

Liu's suggestion challenged the work team's whole approach to the problem of the bad cadres. Belatedly, Ch'i Yun and Hsieh Hung realized that in their anxiety to arouse the people and overcome the awe in which Yu-lai and his son were held, they had ignored the possibility of reforming the men. They had attempted to crush the people's new oppressors, not remake them. In working thus they had distorted the essence of the "Purification Movement," and had followed in the wake of those impetuous poor peasants who demanded only revenge for past injuries and who had no vision of the potential of leaders who had temporarily gone astray.

Now, for the first time, Ch'i Yun and Hsieh were asked to look at Wen-te in the light of his future worth. As soon as they did, they both became enthusiastic about helping him. An important factor in making this shift possible was, of course, the fact that the battle had already been won. Wen-te had met his match in the aroused peasants of Long Bow. The myth of the man of iron whose revenge must be forever feared was difficult to maintain in the face of this badly frightened young penitent—distraught, weeping, and begging for help.

Team Leader Hou, who had all along opposed crushing the spirit of the men, who had all along wanted to give them a fair chance and who had been attacked by the rest of the team as one who had leaned over backwards to aid them, did not say, "I told you so." He simply used whatever time he had available to talk with Wen-te and prepare him for the problems he would meet at the training school.

Little Li alone remained unconvinced that such bad cadres should be treated so leniently. Even if they reformed, he thought, they should be severely punished for their past crimes. At the very least, Wen-te should be expelled from the Party. If such men as he could remain Communists, what was the campaign all about?

****

The final result of the second *gate,* organized and manned by the Peasants' Association, was to pass all four of the Party members who had failed earlier and to approve five of the seven non-Party cadres who had come up for criticism for the first time. Only Yu-lai, Wen-te, and Hung-er remained beyond the pale. Further action on these cases could only be taken by the People's Congress, a governing body which had yet to be elected. In the meantime, application was made to the higher authorities to enroll Wen-te and Hung-er in the special school for rejected cadres.

But no matter what happened, some villagers were always ready to misinterpret the decisions of the Party and the government. As soon as word of this school got out, a rumor began that the two Party members had been promoted. Repeated explanations by the work team cadres failed to lay this "small broadcast" low. Apparently only time and the return of the re-educated men could clear the matter up once and for all.

Ironically, Wen-te did not believe what he was told about the school either. He thought he was being sent to some sort of a prison and said that he would not fill out the application to go there until a satisfactory explanation was given for the fact that Hsien-e had identified the towel used in gagging Little Ch'uer as one belonging to his household. Thus he mounted the offensive again and only much patient explanation finally persuaded him to yield.

53

Upgrading

There is just one criterion for determining class standing. It is based on the different relationships of the people to the means of production, for this determines every kind of class difference. The possession or lack of the means of production, the quantity of the means of production owned, how these are utilized, and, moreover, all the various kinds of different productive relationships between the exploiter and the exploited—these, then, constitute the only criteria for determining class standing.

Jen Pi-shih

ON JUNE 12TH, the sectional groups of the Peasants' Association met to classify the village once more. This time there was no need to review the status of every family. Only those families about whom some question had been raised were placed on the list for consideration. By the evening of June 14, all such cases had been considered by the small groups. A mass meeting was therefore called for the purpose of making a final review. It was held outdoors on the grounds of the mission compound.

All the peasants were tired after long hours spent hoeing corn and weeding millet. As a result, only a minority of the Association members showed up. Under the brilliant light of a waning moon, those who did come were very active, however. They finished off all remaining problems with gusto—a little too much gusto, it seemed, for they dispatched some very difficult cases rather quickly and left those concerned with an impression that inadequate attention had been paid to their complaints.

Old Lady Wang, who had for days resisted all attempts made by the southwest group to call her a new-middle-peasant, was immediately classed in just that category by the northern and eastern groups. To be thus classed meant the collapse of all her plans—plans for some good land close to the village, and for a few additional sections of housing for her son and his bride.

She strode to the center of the meeting and protested vigorously. Her argument was that she had inherited all the land she had received since Liberation from her brother-in-law and that she had

bought the donkey she now owned with borrowed money. None of
her wealth was due to the land reform. Could this be called a *fanshen?*

To prove that she had not *fanshened,* she talked louder, faster,
and more sarcastically than she had ever talked before, but the people listened unmoved. When she finally realized that no word of
hers could turn the tide she lapsed into silence, moved back to the
center of her own group, and finally, with an oath, picked up her
stool and stomped off homeward in a very surly mood indeed.

If Old Lady Wang had only stayed long enough to witness what
happened to others like herself, she might well have taken a more
philosophical view of her defeat. As it turned out, the upgrading of
this old woman was only the beginning of a run on the poor peasant
status of dozens of her neighbors in the southwest section. Because
the other sectional groups of the Association had used strict standards
of poverty in their preliminary work, they were quite perturbed when
they saw who had been classed as poor in the southwest. They made
Yuan-lung read the list through twice and then slashed it without
mercy. Shen Ch'uan-te, Yuan-lung himself, Kuo Wang-yueh, and
many others were forthwith promoted to the rank of new-middle-
peasant.

The leaders of the upgrading movement were Hsin-fa, Party branch
secretary, and Yang Yu-so, the man who had served as spokesman for
the delegates at the first *gate*. These two squatted beside a kerosene
lantern set at one edge of the crowd and by its light perused the lists.
Having been classed as new-middle-peasants themselves they didn't
want to see any other family get by with a poor peasant designation
if its material condition in any way matched their own. Since draft
animals, carts, and farm implements were obviously in short supply,
they ignored these things as *fanshen* requirements and based their
arguments on the possession of land and housing alone.

Two single men with an acre and a half apiece were summarily
upgraded. A peasant named Chang-lan was not only plucked from
the poor peasant group, but was pushed all the way up into the old-
middle-peasant level on the grounds that he had for years possessed
enough land for self-support.

A ripple of humor enlivened the meeting when the southwest
group turned the tables on the upgraders by finding a man in the
northern section who should have been called a new-middle-peasant.
They based their argument on the half-donkey which he owned but
which his neighbors had ignored. Caught in an oversight, Hsin-fa and
Yang Yu-so apologized for having forgotten the donkey and promptly
reclassified the family in a higher bracket. Someone remarked that
the man now owned two half donkeys (the original donkey, a female,

had foaled a few days earlier, and half the foal belonged to each owner). Whether two half-donkeys equalled a whole donkey became the subject of some comic debate.

Not all the changes made that night were upward ones. Li Ho-jen, the carpenter, and Huan-ch'ao, the blacksmith, won a determined fight to be called new rather than old-middle-peasants. T'ien-hsi, the militiaman, who had also been called an old-middle-peasant, disagreed so violently and won such support in his section of the village that the meeting finally voted to accept his view.

As the evening wore on, the proceedings grew more and more boisterous. Although the peasants from each of the three sectional groups had started their discussions sitting separately, as the moon sailed higher into the sky they somehow intermingled until it was hard to tell exactly what was being discussed by which group. Many people on the fringes of the crowd, unable to follow the trend at all, gradually lapsed into inactivity or fell to gossiping about personal problems. Toward midnight everyone became so eager to go home to bed that a number of decisions on very complicated cases carried almost without debate. Little wonder that some of those whose class was fixed that night felt bruised. But, as Little Li pointed out, it didn't matter very much. There was still a third classification coming up and all those who disagreed could still ask for a review.

PART VI

Drastic Reappraisal

Because of the distinctive peculiarities in China's social and historical development and her backwardness in science, it is a unique and difficult task to apply Marxism systematically to China and to transform it from its European form into Chinese form; in other words, to solve the various problems of the contemporary Chinese Revolution from the standpoint of Marxism and with the Marxist method. Many of these problems have never been solved or raised by the world's Marxists, for here in China the main section of the masses are not workers but peasants, and the fight is directed against foreign imperialist oppression and medieval survivals, and not against domestic capitalism.

Liu Shao-ch'i, 1945

54

On the Eve of Victory

All comrades in the Party should understand that the enemy is now completely isolated. But his isolation is not tantamount to our victory. If we make mistakes in policy, we shall still be unable to win victory. To put it concretely, we shall fail if we make, or do not correct, mistakes of principle with regard to any of the five policies—on the war, Party consolidation, land reform, industry and commerce, and the suppression of counter-revolution.

Mao Tse-tung

SEVERAL TIMES in the late spring of 1948 the peasants of Long Bow awoke to find the main thoroughfare of their village clogged with soldiers. The soldiers filed in so quietly that few people even heard them arrive. They rested awhile, refreshed themselves with boiled water and then moved on, walking, not marching, toward their destination.

These troops bore no outward sign of formidable fighting prowess. Their uniforms, made of homespun cotton and colored with a yellow-brown dye that bleached quickly under the sun, seemed more like the costumes hastily issued to a company of stage warriors than the garb of a victorious army. The same makeshift quality character-ized the hand grenade slings that hung at the men's hips, the long sleeves stuffed with millet that crossed their shoulders, the ammunition belts that circled their waists, the packs on their backs, and the puttees that bound their trousers to their legs. All these accouterments were of faded, handwoven cloth. The People's Liber-ation Army, it appeared, was a "cotton cloth" army. Even the soldiers' feet shuffled across the mountains in cloth shoes.

The only non-cotton items of equipment which these troops pos-sessed were the rifles in their hands, the millet bowls that dangled from their belts, and the straw hats on their heads. The latter, with their wide, floppy brims, lent a touch of holiday gaiety to outfits that, even without them, seemed incompatible with serious fighting. When the soldiers moved off, the hats hanging over their packs made them look from behind like a bevy of poker chips bobbing across the landscape.

If, at first sight, this equipment seemed simple, even shoddy, a moment's reflection indicated that it was nevertheless practical. By such means a soldier could carry on his back everything he needed for daily living or prolonged fighting whether he stayed with his comrades or found himself cut off and alone. With the exception of his rifle, which often came from the other side of the world and weighed almost as much as everything else he carried put together, he could be re-equipped in every detail in any county town in China's vast hinterland. The same could never be said for the American-supplied legions of Chiang Kai-shek. Even the fatigue caps issued to certain Nationalist units came from the mills of New England and the lofts of New York.

But equipment alone never created a fighter. One had to look more closely in order to discover the qualities that made these men so much more than a match for the well-armed Nationalist forces whom they were advancing to engage. These soldiers of the People's Liberation Army came from the same stock as the conscripts herded to the front by Chiang. Many of them actually were former Nationalist troops captured in battle and recruited at subsequent "speak bitterness meetings." But instead of the morose stares and scowls so common in the ranks of the counter-revolution, these men—many of them hardly more than boys—were cheerful and full of spirit. At the same time they were quiet and well disciplined. This discipline did not show itself in the form of obeisance to rank or position, but rather in the mature way the soldiers behaved. They treated the village people with respect. They did not block traffic; they refused to accept anything but water. Those few who played games to while the time away enjoyed themselves without disturbing the serenity of the life around them. The soldiers were carefree yet dignified, fun-loving but not raucous, friendly but not condescending. These attitudes reflected something inside them, an inner integrity, a sense of collective pride, a confident and purposeful spirit. All this could never be imposed by command but was the result of revolutionary commitment strengthened by education.

That spring the Army had gone through an intensified educational campaign that paralleled in many ways the movement for Party consolidation and democracy in the villages. The campaign included mass meetings for airing grievances against the old society and the *san ch'a* or "three checks." In the course of the latter, all soldiers and all officers had mutually examined themselves in regard to class origin, performance of duty, and will to fight. They had also studied land reform policies, policies in regard to commerce and industry, and the over-all goals of the New Democratic Revolution. Officers had taught soldiers, soldiers had taught officers, and soldiers had taught one another. The campaign had resulted in unprecedented unity throughout the Army, a high level of political consciousness, and surging morale. We were witnessing the results.

What struck me about the troops that I saw in Long Bow was their confidence. They were, after all, moving up to the front. Another two days on the road would bring them to the Taiyuan plain where a long and bitter battle to liberate the provincial capital was already under way. In less than a week they would be under fire, perhaps even engaged in a frontal assault on fixed positions. Soon some of them would surely be dead. But they showed no trace of anxiety, hesitation, or doubt. They seemed to take for granted the justice of their cause and its ultimate triumph. They were approaching the front with eagerness!

These boys in uniform, resting by the village pond and polishing their rifles until the barrels reflected the full brilliance of the morning sun, revealed in their eager faces something of the excitement of impending victory, an excitement which served as an antidote to those other faces of the war which Long Bow knew so well—the pain in the eyes of a wounded man as he waited in front of Ts'ai-yuan's store for stretcher bearers to carry him further along the road toward home; the tears coursing down the cheeks of Lai-hao's widowed mother as Ch'i Yun read her the letter that announced the death of her only son at the front; the eerie all-night keening of two women prostrate beside a coffin that had been brought home by mule cart from a battle fought more than 12 months before . . .

****

June 1948 marked the end of two full years of all-out civil conflict. No military analyst in the Liberated Areas doubted that Chiang Kai-shek was already doomed. Throughout the region, in articles and speeches, cadre after cadre emphasized the same basic idea: "Our 20-year war for the future of China has reached its final stage. The last few months have seen a qualitative change. Not only can Chiang Kai-shek no longer expand the territory under his control, but he can-not even defend what he now holds. Any place that we really want to take we can now take."

The basis for this optimism was to be found in the figures for men killed and captured and arms taken in the 24 months that had elapsed since July 1946 when Chiang tore up the truce agreement negotiated under the direction of General Marshall and launched his all-out attack on the revolutionary bases in the northern half of China. In these months Chiang had lost a total of 2,640,000 men who were killed, wounded, or captured. In the same period the People's Liberation Army had added 1,600,000 regular and irregular troops to its forces. By means of frantic conscription Chiang had maintained his total strength at more than 3,500,000 men, but the enormous and growing casualty list coupled with massive defections cut the very heart out of his effective armies at a time when the Communist-led forces, by mustering volunteers at home and absorbing huge blocks of prisoners at the front, were approaching numerical parity.

Many a minor battle in many an obscure place made this fact clear. There was, for instance, the siege of Linfeng. This ancient fortified town lying due west of Long Bow was less than three days' foot journey away. It was one of the key outposts in the defense of Taiyuan. Units of the People's Liberation Army laid siege to Linfeng in April. The tough old warrior Yen Hsi-shan, still in control of a formidable Nationalist army in the heart of Shansi, made a decision to defend the town to the end. Over and over again he called on Chiang Kai-shek for reinforcements. "If Linfeng falls," General Yen wailed, "Taiyuan cannot but be next." But Chiang could not spare any reinforcements. No armies came to Yen's rescue. The siege of Linfeng continued. In desperation the Nationalist radio called on the Linfeng garrison to come out fighting even if it meant death for all. The officers in charge of the defense ordered their troops to use poison gas. But try as they would, they could not break out. Linfeng fell early in May, and every man in the garrison was captured.

In distant Manchuria, the Kuomintang forces holding the key rail junction of Szepingkai surrendered early in March. The city of Changchun was thus cut off. The Nationalist radio, despairing of the future, suddenly announced that Changchun had no strategic importance and that its loss would make no difference to the government in Nanking. Thus they laid the groundwork for retreating from a city that had once been the capital of puppet Manchukuo, and was still the Kuomintang administrative center for the whole Northeast.

In Shantung the revolutionary armies under General Ch'en Yi kept the Tientsin-Pukow railway closed and prepared to surround the capital, Tsinan. Wang Yao-wu, leading Chiang commander in the province and governor of one of China's most populous and wealthy areas, complained, "I have only 50,000 men. How can I hope to stand against a Liberation Army 250,000 strong?"

"It is typical of the Nationalists, in the defense of an area or a city, to dig in or retire within the city walls, and there fight to the end, hoping for relief which never comes because it cannot be spared from elsewhere," wrote General David Barr of the United States advisory group. But all his efforts to impose other tactics failed miserably. In the face of a universally hostile population, the Nationalist forces had no choice but to dig in and await their fate.

Generalissimo Chiang talked publicly of one thing and one thing only, and that was American aid. The only argument he could think of to encourage his hard pressed forces was, "More arms are coming." Each time one of his generals lost a battle, Chiang turned on his American advisors and complained that their succor had been too little and too late. The American officers, he remonstrated, trained his men too slowly.

But the soldiers of the People's Liberation Army understood the truth embodied in Mao Tse-tung's famous phrase, "Imperialism and all reactionaries are paper tigers." They laughed about the American supplies that poured in day after day to shore up Chiang's rotting front. They knew that sooner or later all that hardware would fall into their own hands. To sum up the situation they even coined a cocky new slogan: "America is our arsenal and Chiang Kai-shek is our quartermaster." In every major engagement they captured thousands of rounds of ammunition, mountain guns, machine guns, trucks, bazookas, and even tanks. Every bullet, every rifle, every gun captured was tabulated as before on village walls in the rear areas. And, as the running record of weapons taken and armies annihilated mounted swiftly, so too did confidence mount.

The Chinese Communist Party estimated three possible forms of aid to Chiang and discounted them all. American leaders could dispatch their own armies directly against the Liberated Areas in a desperate effort to save the situation. But to do this they would need at least 2,000,000 men. Even then they could not hope to wrest permanent control of the area from the Chinese people, for there was no reason to suppose that Americans could succeed where the Japanese had failed. In addition, American leaders had to consider the protest that open intervention was sure to engender from their own people and from other countries and the many domestic and international problems it would inevitably create.

In the absence of direct intervention, America could send more advisory personnel. But there were already thousands of military advisors with Chiang Kai-shek's troops. Their efforts had availed them nothing in the past. Sending more people could hardly change the situation.

The third way to help Chiang was to redouble his supplies. But if the supplies already sent had not enabled him to win, how could more supplies change the situation? The weapons and materials available to him already outstripped the manpower he could tap and train.

So, as the leaders of the Liberated Areas and the People's Liberation Army saw it, militarily Chiang was already finished. It was only a matter of time.

Chiang was bankrupt militarily, they said, because he had isolated himself politically. His dictatorial rule, his reliance on military means to subdue the country, and his surrender of basic Chinese rights to American business in return for massive military assistance made it impossible for the moderates to support him. Unable to win to his side the only important "third force" group in the country, the Democratic League, he ordered it dissolved on October 27, 1947. But no sooner did he slay this liberal dragon than it sprang up hydra-headed. On January 1, 1948, many democratic elements within the Kuomintang met in Hong Kong to establish the Kuomintang Revolutionary Committee. On January 5, several Democratic League leaders re-established the leading body of their outlawed League. At about the same time the China Democratic National Construction Association, an organization of liberal business and commercial people, announcing a more radical program than it had ever previously supported, stepped up its activities.

In 1948 Chiang Kai-shek's policies also brought him into increasingly fierce conflict with the students and professors of China's colleges and universities. As the students expanded their agitation for peace and against American intervention, Chiang opposed them with increasingly oppressive measures. Hundreds of agents invaded classrooms and dormitories across the nation. They posed as students but actually devoted their energies to spying and informing.

"During the night," wrote one student of North China College, "gestapo students inspect dormitories with pistols in their pockets. Anyone can be arrested for being impolite or hated by these students. If we hold a debating meeting to discuss technical problems, we are closely watched by the gestapo students. If we speak one word of criticism, we are reported and our names put on the blacklist."

Several thousand students and 230 professors and lecturers were dismissed from various colleges in 1947. In numerous instances armed squads raided campuses, beat up male and female students alike, wounded hundreds and arrested thousands. In May, 1947, a co-ed was killed in an attack on the Shanghai Law College. In October, the murder of Yu Tse-san, a student at Chekiang University, became a *cause celebre* that led to nationwide demonstrations. By May 1948, when it became clear that Chiang had acquiesced in the American plan to rearm Japan, student protests reached an all-time high. Across the nation several hundred thousand college and middle-school students demonstrated in the streets, and everywhere they met hoses, clubs, and rifles in the hands of Chiang's troops and police.

Chiang crushed the mounting protests of industrial workers with the same brand of extreme violence. One of the worst incidents occurred in Shanghai on February 2, 1948. On that day, three workers were killed and 60 wounded in an open clash between the strikers of the Shen Hsin Textile Mill No. 9 and Kuomintang troops and police. This came to be known far and wide as the Shen Hsin massacre.

Chiang's legal response to the nationwide unrest caused by his own betrayal of national interests was to set up "special criminal courts" in which democrats, liberals, and persons merely suspected of harboring "unpatriotic thoughts" were prosecuted wholesale. But the assemby-line convictions handed down by these courts, like the shooting down of strikers, the police raids on campuses, and the banning of all "middle-of-the-road" political parties only aroused more determined resistance and isolated Chiang and the Kuomintang more than ever.

There was only one possible development that could save Chiang from complete rout. That was the dissolution of the Revolution from within. Historically the status quo in China had been saved from revolutionary overthrow time and time again by excesses, sectarian blunders, naiveté, and disunity in the ranks of her rebels. Popular forces on the verge of victory had isolated themselves in 1864, in 1900, in 1911, and again in 1927. Chiang hoped and prayed that history would repeat itself. While he talked publicly of more dollars and bullets from Washington, privately he based his plans on the internal disruption of the Liberation Areas. His secret service, financed and trained by the American Navy under the SACO (Sino-American Cooperative Organization) agreement, worked hard to organize a revolt of 100,000 people in the Communist-led rear.* The political basis for this revolt was to be the dissatisfaction among the middle groups in the countryside, resulting from adventurist and "leftist" mistakes made by the Communists and the poor peasant activists whom they inspired and led.

At this crucial moment, when the pace of the war was accelerating hour by hour, when a victory great or small was reported from one front or another almost daily, when the confidence of the People's Liberation Army commanders, of the rank-and-file troops, and of the

* Evidence of such a plot was given by the secretary of the Lucheng County Party Committee in a report made at the second County Conference.

cadres in the rear was approaching its zenith—at just such a moment mistakes were easy to make, very easy to ignore, and therefore capable of being aggravated to lethal proportions. The danger was great that revolutionary cadres, flushed with victory, would waive fine points of policy, ride roughshod, because they had the power to do so, over the interests of this or that small sector of the people, and thus erode the very cement of the new social order before it had a chance to set. This road to disaster was paved with temptation.

But if Chiang had learned something from history, so too had China's revolutionaries. Mao and his colleagues at the helm of the Chinese Communist Party had diligently studied the failures of the past. They had gone as far back as Li Tzu-ch'eng (1630) and even beyond. They recognized full well the pitfalls that followed on the heels of victory, and therefore in the spring of 1948 made a careful check on all revolutionary policies and the manner in which they were being carried out in every Border Region. Particular importance was attached to the land reform; and Mao himself, while en route with his Central Committee headquarters to a new base in Hopei, stopped long enough in Northeast Shansi to make a personal investigation of the peasant situation there.

Mao summed up his findings on April 1, 1948. He did so in a speech that was delivered to a conference of rural cadres gathered from various part of Northwest Shansi and Suiyuan where land reform work had advanced further than in the Taihang. Mao characterized the land reform efforts in the Shansi-Suiyuan Border Region as successful, but pointed out that success became possible only after the correction of serious errors. These errors were: (1) Erroneously placing in the landlord or rich peasant category many laboring people who did not engage, or engaged only slightly, in exploitation; (2) the indiscriminate use of violence against landlord and rich peasant families, "sweep-the-floor-out-the-door" confiscations, and a one-sided emphasis on unearthing landlords' hidden wealth; (3) serious encroachments on commerce and industry, particularly the commerce and industry owned by landlords and rich peasants.

All of these errors together constituted a "Left deviation" of dangerous proportions. Behind this Left deviation, Mao said, lay notions of "absolute equalitarianism"—the demand on the part of the landless and land-poor peasants for absolutely equal division of all land and property.

"We support the peasant's demand for equal distribution of land," said Mao, "in order to help arouse the broad masses of peasants speedily to abolish the system of land ownership by the feudal landlord class, but we do not advocate absolute equalitarianism. Whoever advocates absolute equalitarianism is wrong. . . . Such thinking is reactionary, backward, and retrogressive in nature. We must criticize it."

Explaining why absolute equalitarianism was a mistaken concept, Mao restated the basic content of the Chinese Revolution at that stage of its history as being a "revolution against imperialism, feudalism, and bureaucratic capitalism waged by the broad masses of the people under the leadership of the proletariat." He also restated the general line of the Communist Party in regard to the work of agrarian reform: "To rely on the poor peasants, unite with the middle peasants, abolish the system of feudal exploitation step by step and in a discriminating way, and develop agricultural production."

"The target of the land reform," Mao stressed, "is only and must be the system of feudal exploitation by the landlord class and by the old-type rich peasants, and there should be no encroachment either upon the national bourgeoisie or upon the industrial and commercial enterprises run by landlords and rich peasants. In particular, care must be taken not to encroach upon the interests of the middle peasants, independent craftsmen, professionals, and new rich peasants, all of whom engage in little or no exploitation."

And then he came to the crux of the question:

The development of agricultural production is the immediate aim of the land reform. Only by wiping out the feudal system can the conditions for such development be created. In every area, as soon as feudalism is wiped out and the land reform is completed, the Party and the democratic government *must put forward the task of restoring and developing agricultural production,* transfer all available forces in the countryside to this task, organize cooperation and mutual aid, improve agricultural technique, promote seed selection, and build irrigation works—*all to ensure increased production.* . . . The abolition of the feudal system and the development of agricultural production *will lay the foundation for the development of industrial production and the transformation of an agricultural country into an industrial one.* This is the ultimate goal of the new democratic revolution.*

Not abstract justice, not absolute equality, but the development of production, the industrial transformation of the country—this was the goal of the Revolution, for only thus could real problems of livelihood be solved.

* All quotes from Mao's speech are taken from Mao Tse-tung, *Selected Works,* vol. V, pp. 227-239. (Emphasis added.)

55

We Tried to Be God!

Policy is the starting-point of all the practical actions of a revolutionary party and manifests itself in the process and the end-result of that party's actions. A revolutionary party is carrying out a policy whenever it takes any action. If it is not carrying out a correct policy, it is carrying out a wrong policy; if it is not carrying out a given policy consciously, it is doing so blindly.

Mao Tse-tung
February, 1948

MAO'S SHANSI-SUIYUAN speech, as it came to be called, was published in the People's Daily early in June 1948. It had a decisive effect on the whole land reform movement in North China. During the previous fall and winter the extensive ideological preparations made for carrying out the Draft Agrarian Law had all emphasized the harm done by "Right opportunist" tendencies, by half-hearted measures, by compromise with the gentry, by fear of head-on conflict and all-out war. They were based on estimates that the land reform had been less than thoroughgoing. They called on all cadres to take a clear stand on the side of the poor-and-hired peasants and urged a complete rooting out of the feudal system on the assumption that this had not yet been accomplished. All through the spring season, partial corrections had been made in these early estimates. On the basis of careful reclassification whole villages once thought to be Class III had been upgraded, Party branches suspected of infiltration by class enemies had been declared sound, and expropriated middle peasants had been promised repayment; but still the emphasis had remained on the *fanshen* of the poor-and-hired. Here at last was a major speech warning of the opposite extreme, warning against leftism as a dominant trend, a general line, a whole system of thought.

As soon as these ideas appeared in print, high-level conferences were called in every Border Region to consider their implications. The Party leaders of Lucheng County, Secretaries Ch'en and Chang, went eastward to attend a gathering of cadres at the subregional level where evaluation and discussion lasted for several days. As soon as the local men returned home they made a spot survey of actual conditions in Lucheng County, called in the team leaders from all the "basic villages" for individual talks, listened to the parallel problems that these men faced in village after village, and decided that there was indeed something radically wrong with the way in which they were leading the county. They immediately sent out a call for a second County Conference.

On June 17th, Ch'i Yun and I joined the rest of the Long Bow work team as they trekked for the second time to Lucheng County town. Only Team Leader Hou was missing from the group. He had taken home leave to tend his crops. The second conference was almost twice the size of its predecessor. Not only had all cadres from the "basic villages" been called, but also all full-time cadres from the ordinary, or "production villages."

Once the cadres were seated before him in the great temple at Party headquarters, Secretary Ch'en wasted no time in preliminary remarks. He adjusted his spectacles, picked up his notes, waited a few seconds for his audience to quiet down, and then plunged right to the heart of the matter. "We have called this meeting as a turning point in our work. I want you to pay close attention because many wrong ideas have been shared by all of us and many wrong actions have been taken."

All those who were literate sat with pens poised, ready to record what was to come, while the illiterate majority looked straight at Secretary Ch'en, intent on catching his every word and noting his every gesture.

"Actual conditions in this county are quite different from the estimate that we made at the Lu Family Settlement meeting last February," announced Ch'en. "Then we thought the land reform in our county was far from complete. After intensive surveys in 11 basic villages, we now know that this estimate was wrong. The feudal system in our county has already been fundamentally abolished. The poor peasants have, in the main, *fanshened*."

These words created a stir in the room. People spoke to each other in excited whispers. "I told you that three weeks ago." "The peasants all say there is no 'oil.' " "Well, why didn't we see it before?"

The commotion was so great that Secretary Ch'en had to interrupt his speech. When the cadres finally noticed his disapproving glance, they held their tongues and he continued, quoting facts and figures.

"In the whole of Lucheng County there are 120,000 people farming 100,000 acres of land. The average holding is approximately four fifths of an acre per person. The *fanshened* poor peasants already hold just under an acre per person, the middle peasants slightly less, while the landlords and rich peasants, having been expropriated, hold only one sixth of an acre apiece.*

"In Tungwu Village, after the third classification, it was found that only four families lacked land. In Chia Village the whole population was short only three acres. Three families of landlords and rich peasants have not been completely expropriated, but these three families between them hold but two acres of surplus land. Such figures prove that the land reform work in Lucheng County has already been all but completely fulfilled.

"That is not to say that there is no problem of land," Secretary Ch'en continued. "On the contrary, there are still many problems in regard to land holding, but most of them are just the opposite in nature from what we estimated in the past."

Many heads bent forward as ears strained to catch exactly what he meant by this.

"The attack has been overdone! Many middle peasants have been injured economically and many commercial and business establishments have been harmed. When it comes to rich peasants and landlords, 'sweep-the-floor-out-the-door' tactics have been used. But families cannot be driven from house and home forever. Neither can commerce and industry thrive when private business is attacked. Yet in Lucheng and in South Portal, outside the gate, there remain only three or four private businesses. A shop owner in Yellow Mill has been forced to surrender his house. This case is not exceptional.

"We have neglected Article 16 of the Draft Agrarian Law. And what does Article 16 say? It says: 'In places where the land has already been distributed before the promulgation of the law, and provided that the peasants do not demand redistribution, the land need not be redistributed.'

"Is not our county exactly such a place?" asked the Secretary, looking from cadre to cadre in the audience. Everywhere he looked, heads nodded in agreement.

Having summarized the situation in regard to the land, Secretary Ch'en turned his attention to the condition within the village Party branches. In the past the County Committee had estimated that the class composition of the Party branches was not pure. At the Lu Family Settlement meeting, Ch'en himself had reported that 40 percent of the Communists in the county were landlords or rich peasants. Now, with the results of the Party purification movement in 11 "basic

---

* From this it can be seen that the middle peasants, rich peasants, and landlords in Long Bow were better off than the average.

villages" available, it was obvious that although the branches had many shortcomings, poor class composition was not one of them.

To support this conclusion Secretary Ch'en pointed out that in the Party branches of the basic villages not one landlord or rich peasant had been found. The Long Bow team thought they had found one rich peasant, the woman Comrade Chao Ch'uan-e, but according to the new class standards she was only a middle peasant. On the basis of class origin the Party branches had proven to be sound and solid. Consolidation, not the wholesale reorganization that had been envisioned in February, was what the Party needed, said Ch'en. The teams should cure the disease and save the patient with a policy of criticism and education. Love, protect, educate, remold and unite —these should be the five basic principles used in dealing with Communists and cadres.

Judging by the pattern of land distribution and by the class composition of the village Party branches, it was obvious that previous estimates of the situation in Lucheng County had been wrong, and these estimates had led to much trouble and confusion. Why had such erroneous estimates been made? What made such big mistakes possible?

Secretary Ch'en suggested that the judgment of the cadres had been colored by a faulty outlook that expressed itself in two main ways—as an "ultra-poor-peasant line" and as "absolute equalitarianism."

The ultra-poor-peasant line said, in effect, that the poor peasants and hired laborers should conquer the country and rule the country. "Base everything on the interests of the poor peasants; carry out the demands of the poor peasants." Such notions had penetrated every field of work. "Yet," said Secretary Ch'en, "even to speak of such a 'line' is wrong, unreal. A Communist can have none but a proletarian line, the class line of the working class, and that class line is: depend on the poor peasants; unite with the middle peasants; and join up with all anti-feudal elements to eradicate the feudal system. That is the whole of it. No one part can be omitted. This statement determines the line, the policy, and the tactics of the land reform movement. Wherever the land reform movement has been completed and the majority of the peasants have already become middle peasants, then the main task becomes production, and it is absurd to rely in the main on the poor peasants, for by that time the majority of the peasants are no longer poor peasants but have become new-middle-peasants. *Land reform policy cannot be applied mechanically to post-land reform conditions.*"

Ch'i Yun nudged me. "That's just what we have been doing," she said.

Now that Ch'en spelled it out, it seemed obvious to me too.

"Absolute equalitarianism is also basically wrong," said the Secretary. "It is because the cadres judge their work from an equalitarian point of view that they end up thinking the land reform has not been completed. As soon as this point of view is disregarded it is easy to see that the work of land division has not only been completed, but that it has been carried too far. With the same objective conditions, with the same set of facts, two different conclusions can be arrived at because we start with two different points of view. The hills that loom so high in the evening appear to be low mounds at noon. Because many of us had the wrong point of view in the past, many middle peasants and many new-middle-peasants became uneasy, and unhealthy tendencies appeared. In Long Bow poor peasants knelt in the dust to find medicine and prayed to mud gods for cures.

"Marx, Engels, Lenin, Stalin, and Chairman Mao Tse-tung all oppose absolute equalitarianism," said Secretary Ch'en emphatically. "At Yehtao in December Secretary Po said, 'Under present conditions we can never have such a thing.' Even if we were to push it through today, in the future a thousand happenings in the village would reverse the situation. What if today we gave every peasant an exactly equal share? This peasant gets sick and spends his money, that man neglects his crops, this peasant's wife gives birth to a baby, that man is lazy, this man works hard. Can equality continue? Only under Communism, when the land belongs to the country as a whole, and abundance is the order of the day, can equality be realized. The best we can do now is to use what patching material we have for holes. We cannot go out looking for material to fill all the holes that exist, for to do that would mean to injure the middle peasants and destroy their prosperity.

"In the light of these facts," said Secretary Ch'en, "our point of view toward *fanshen* and the abolition of feudalism has not been correct. Our goal is to abolish the *system,* to do away with the landlords as a class. We oppose the feudal system primarily because it hinders production. But, under the influence of wrong ideas, we have taken as our standard for successful struggle the wrong thing, namely 'sweep-the-floor-out-the-door' and we have applied it to individuals, not to the class. Our standard for judging *fanshen* was also wrong. We took absolute equality as our banner. We did not look to the further interests of the people and of the Revolution. We tried only to be charitable. We wanted to give everyone what they needed. *We tried to be God.*"

The last phrase initiated a second great commotion in the room. Sitting in the midst of the audience Ch'i Yun and I could hear remarks coming from all sides. "We tried to do the impossible." "No wonder it was hard to get the peasants to meet!" "The people saw through it right away."

Some of the comments indicated relief. "So that's what's the matter!" "I knew something was wrong but I couldn't figure it out."

Others showed a measure of disgust, even annoyance. "Well, who led the way, I'd like to know?" "Our policy changes every few days. Who knows where we are going? We are like a mouse in a box."

"As a result of these movements," Ch'en said, "the landlords and rich peasants were treated much too harshly. Many prosperous families were wiped out altogether or driven away. Worst of all, the middle peasants were badly frightened. Some offered to give up land because they were afraid. Others made contact with counter-revolutionaries. The Left tendency has been with us so long that many peasants and cadres sincerely believe that Left is better than Right. They resent doing things according to policy and believe that this limits them, clips their wings, so to speak. And even though we have suffered this serious tendency for a long time we have not examined it thoroughly, not to mention wiping it out. Instead we have created a theory to justify it and have built a whole system of thought—the poor peasant line—around it. It is time to correct this and do away with it altogether."

The Secretary then attacked the idea that Left was better than Right. "In reality, both Left and Right are wrong. To carry on work based on the real situation is neither Left nor Right and is the only correct way. History has proved to us that whenever victory draws near it is easy to commit leftist, adventurist mistakes. And now victory is drawing near. We no longer treat Chiang Kai-shek by washing his face to expose him. Our slogan is to kick him down. Now everyone knows that victory will be ours within three to five years. Now is exactly the time to be made dizzy by success and to commit the mistake of Left adventurism.

"Once we get over the idea that Left is better than Right, what practical steps should be taken to correct past errors?" asked Ch'en. "That is relatively easy. Our work during the next period must be to repay all middle peasants wrongly expropriated, to return all commercial and industrial property to its original owners, to resettle landlord and rich peasant families wrongly driven from their homes. Only in this way can the people of every village be set at ease and the foundation laid for high morale in production. The revival and development of production—that is our main work from now on."

Having covered the main question before the conference, Secretary Ch'en wound up his morning-long talk with a survey of some minor problems. He discussed the recruiting drive, the problem of aid to soldiers' families, the question of rear service, and finally what was closest to the hearts of the district cadres themselves, the problem of community aid to full-time political workers. Whereas only a few weeks earlier word had come down that the cadres would have to solve their own home production problems, now Secretary Ch'en announced a new policy that completely reversed this. "From now on, aid to cadres' families is to be the same as aid to soldiers' families," he said. "The directive has already been sent to the villages. All administrative units have been asked to put it into effect immediately."

This last announcement was greeted with excited cheers. Secretary Ch'en could not have said anything better calculated to set the cadres at ease and raise their morale. By itself, however, this promise of aid was not enough to overcome the shock of the political analysis which had been presented that day.

56

Who Is to Blame?

Within the revolutionary ranks, it is necessary to make a clear distinction between right and wrong, between achievements and shortcomings, and to make clear which of the two is primary and which is secondary. For instance, do the achievements amount to 30 percent or 70 percent of the whole? It will not do either to understate or to overstate. . . . It would be entirely wrong to describe work in which the achievements are primary as work in which the mistakes are primary.

Mao Tse-tung

SECRETARY CH'EN'S speech jarred all the cadres loose from their familiar ideological moorings and set them to examining and questioning on a scale hitherto unknown. Never had these rubble-strewn yards and temples-turned-dormitory seen such dedicated, concerted debate and argument. The work teams first met where they would; then they met together with the other teams and production cadres from their respective districts in assigned courtyards. Finally they met *en masse* in the great central hall where the dragons fighting each other across the ridgepole aptly symbolized the mental struggle going on below. Such meetings, alternating in the order described, continued for several days.

None questioned the basic conclusions stated by Secretary Ch'en. As soon as he reported that the feudal land system had basically been abolished and that the *fanshen* of the poor-and-hired peasants had virtually been completed, everyone recognized the fact. The cadres' months of investigation, study and mass mobilization in the 11 "basic villages" left no room for doubt on that score. There simply were no great accumulations of wealth left, whether in the hands of landlords, rich peasants, corrupt cadres, or public institutions; nor was there any significant treasure stashed away in secret *k'angs,* grave mounds, or any other place. All of these prospective sources had been pursued to the end and each had proved a mirage. Team after team reported that most local gentry had been expropriated and that landholdings had already been distributed among the former landless and land poor.

Secretary Ch'en's second conclusion that expropriation had gone too far was not questioned either. The painstaking classification proceedings had demonstrated that many families of landlord and rich peasant status had been cleaned out completely. In too many cases family heads had been killed. Dependents had either run away or else stayed on to face extreme poverty and discrimination. Worse still, the classification revealed that many middle peasants had been similarly treated. No one who had taken part in the investigation of the preceding months could doubt that serious excesses marred the land reform movement in Lucheng County and that they must be rectified.

As for the Party branches, not only did they not contain a single member of landlord or rich peasant origin, but they also turned out to be composed primarily of the least selfish and the most forward-looking people in the villages. This had been demonstrated by the day-to-day work. A report on this question by the team leader from Chin Village was typical: "When I first got there, I treated the five big cadres as oppressors. But they turned out to be the most honest and active people. Though they had made serious mistakes, they were willing to examine their pasts and have now corrected their outlook and behavior. The more I work with them, the more respect I have for them."

These conclusions might well have lifted a heavy burden from the minds and hearts of all those who attended the conference. They demonstrated, after all, that the main problem of the agrarian revolution had been solved. But at first this tremendous news was overshadowed in the cadres' consciousness by the fact that they had all gone so far astray in attacking nonexistent problems and imaginary enemies. The argument and soul-searching that went on in the county seat after Secretary Ch'en's speech flowed from a sense of shock at having lost the way, astonishment at the harm that had been done, and confusion as to where the blame lay.

How could it have happened?

In the face of mountains of evidence, how could the Party have so misjudged the true situation? How could it have set off on the wrong road to begin with and then continued to march down it for so long? That such a serious mistake was possible, that it had been made by county leaders, and even Border Region leaders, that the newspaper of the Central Committee had backed it up, had itself promoted the "poor-peasant line"—this shook the confidence of the district cadres. Up to that point, from all that they had seen and learned in the course of years of hard fighting and organizing, the Communist Party under Mao's leadership seemed infallible, or nearly so. Out of the disaster of the Anti-Japanese War and throughout the early postwar years, the Party had led them from victory to victory. They had come to depend upon it like children on their mother. The sudden realization that their approach had been misdirected left them temporarily helpless. If the Party itself could get lost, as it seemed to have done, what was there to cling to?

Ch'en's report unleashed a veritable river of pent-up grievances and complaints. At first the cadres tended to blame everyone but themselves. Many participants attacked the peasants. They were backward, they were selfish, they asked only how much millet was in it for them. Even those who had already *fanshened* hid their quilts and pretended to be poor. After the suspension of the old cadres they put on their "democracy caps." They did exactly as they pleased. They refused to come to meetings; they even refused rear service, and neither the work team cadres nor anybody else had the power to discipline them. It was this, they argued, that had led the cadres into Left policies.

"If you aren't Left there is no way out," said Little Ch'uer with an air of gloomy certainty. "In order to complete our work we have to violate policy."

Others blamed all the trouble on the county leaders and on the Lu Family Settlement meeting where these leaders had prepared the district men ideologically for the campaign. At Lu Family Settlement the county secretaries had made a wrong estimate and then developed it into a system of thought.

"It is true," said a team worker from Yellow Mill, "that we learned many valuable lessons at Lu Family Settlement. One of them was that graft and corruption cannot be tolerated. None of us will ever misappropriate anything again. That lesson we learned very well; but the spirit of oppression against Party members we also learned there. Whenever anyone said anything in self-defense, the rest stood up and said, 'What is your thought, what is your thought?' Was this our fault? I say we cannot bear the whole burden on our backs."

"The higher cadres must take responsibility for such mistakes," said the team leader from Ke Shu. "They must be brave enough to listen to criticism from below."

****

Little Li, now the acting leader of the Long Bow team, exchanged sharp words with the genial Assistant County Secretary Chang when the latter came to discuss Long Bow in detail with Li's group.

Chang tried to demonstrate the sectarian trend of the cadres' work by bringing up the way in which they had handled the *gate*. The extremism that had driven certain comrades to the verge of suicide before the first *gate* had only been compounded at the second, he said.

Little Li disagreed emphatically.

"Why couldn't Wen-te pass the *gate* then?" asked Chang.

"He wouldn't talk," said Little Li with feeling.

"Why wouldn't he talk?"

"Because he was arrested and held in the county jail and felt he had been wronged."

"That was our mistake, not his," said Secretary Chang. "We should not treat him harshly on that account."

"How can you say that?" interrupted Ch'i Yun, chiming in on Li's side. "He did many bad things. He himself had a wrong attitude."

"Just as Secretary Ch'en said, the Communist Party is not pure, particularly in working style, and this must be corrected. If we deny the need to correct and educate Wen-te, then we deny that the Party makes mistakes."

"We were very patient with him," exclaimed Little Li. "The masses met all day to help him, but he didn't want to speak frankly. After the meeting we talked to him for hours and asked the people to be patient and meet with him again. But it was all no good, no good at all."

"You must remember that Wen-te did not get all the education that the others received," said Chang. "They had a whole month of preparation while he was in jail. Also, we here in the county were not clear when we set him free. At that time we still thought that the attack on Little Ch'uer was inspired by the Communist Party in Long Bow, and so Wen-te was afraid. He thought responsibility might still be placed on his shoulders."

"But you don't understand the way in which Wen-te and Yu-lai threatened people," replied Little Li, so agitated he could sit still no longer. He stood up and strode back and forth across the temple yard. As he walked he described in detail the situation as it had been in the village in the weeks before the second *gate*. He pointed out that unless Wen-te had been harshly ostracized the people would never have dared to speak. But Secretary Chang still did not seem to understand. Again he criticized the way in which the whole matter had been handled.

"We did our best," said Little Li, turning toward the Secretary with both hands flung wide in a gesture of despair. "We went without food and sleep. We visited the peasants day and night. We went to no end of trouble. And now we are all wrong." He was at a loss for words.

"I'll tell you one thing," he said finally in a voice choked with feeling. "If Wen-te and Hung-er are not kicked out of the Party, I myself will lead the people of Long Bow to petition the Subregional Bureau for redress."

****

That night the Long Bow team members sat in their favorite spot amidst the rubble. The bell tower, with its ghostly slogan, "The Japanese Army Forever Remains," loomed above them. The air was warm and moisture laden. A full moon was so bright that the bricks strewn on the ground cut shadows as sharp as any made under the noonday sun. The shrill cantata that poured from the countless dark hiding places of the cicadas merged with the surging hum of voices rising from discussion groups in neighboring courtyards and served as treble to the latter's base.

After 16 solid hours I found it hard to concentrate. My eyes wandered to the moon, to the wispy clouds that crossed it at irregular intervals, then back to the rubble-pocked yard. Sitting in the ruins of a building that had collapsed, I could not help but notice the grotesque symbolism of our surroundings. Like the bricks on every side, the old society had been knocked apart. The new edifice which was to take its place seemed still more plan than fact, more dream than solid substance.

Little Li was in no mood to build. To him it seemed that all roads were blocked. He had thrown himself heart and soul into the work only to be accused of leftism. So be it. If Left he was, then Left he would remain. He agreed with Little Ch'uer—in order to get anything done one had to go Left; one had to violate policy.

"Anyhow," said Little Li, "no one can punish us for it. The worst that can happen to us is love, protect, educate, remold, and unite." He paused to let the irony of his remark sink in, then added, "There, I have said everything now."

"Ai," exclaimed Ch'i Yun. "This is a regular 'speak bitterness' meeting."

Extreme though Little Li's response to the sudden shift in course was, it was not different in kind to the reaction of many others. Hurt by censure, beset by self-doubt, their confidence in the Party shaken, many cadres saw only wrong and no right, only bad and no good in the past. As a consequence, the future also looked black. Viewed from the vale where they now sat, the myriad small obstacles yet to be tackled loomed up as insurmountable barriers.

How, for instance, would they introduce the about-face in land reform policy to the villages? How explain the absolute necessity of paying back middle peasants and resettling landlords to poor peasants who had heard nothing for months but, "We are here to help you *fanshen*"? And suppose they succeeded in convincing the peasants that these steps were necessary—where were all the worldly goods to come from? Where would any village find the wherewithal to pay all injured parties? What about those people who were sure to demand not only goods equal in value to those they had lost, but the actual goods themselves? And what about those who had lost their lives?

"You can give the struggle objects back their things, but what about their sons? Will you give them a doll? A doll can't walk," said Ch'uer.

"The difficulties are tremendous. Our discussion is no use," said Little Li, sighing as he tried to imagine how fair restitution could ever be carried through in Long Bow.

Actually, neither the embarrassment which a reversal of policy entailed nor the scarcity of worldly goods which made that reversal so difficult, nor even the total inadequacy of restitution where lives had been erased were problems so immense as to overwhelm the cadres under ordinary circumstances. In the last analysis it was not these objective difficulties but subjective disorientation that dissolved their morale and nourished their despair. Inevitably therefore, the discussion veered in the direction of introspection, but introspection only deepened the gloom.

"In the past we followed the leaders much too blindly," said Han Chin-ming, breaking the silence that had settled upon the whole group. "Perhaps they said something about shielding landlords. We rushed around to collect material on it. No one wanted to come up with a different opinion. If anyone did speak out he met only ironic words such as 'What a hero!' 'Such good ideas!' It was better to lie down and sleep."

What then gave a person the courage to speak out? What caused any individual to keep on working when others became disillusioned, turned against him, or spoke sarcastic words? What upheld him when policies went awry and the way was lost?

In the absence of any deeper understanding the group fell back, as they had before, on greater dedication, deeper faith in the ultimate rightness of their cause.

"Because our difficulties are great, we have all the more reason to study them," said Cadre Han in reply to Little Li. "How can you say it's no use discussing them?"

"We must find a way out," said Liang, as if talking to himself.

"Though it is difficult there is a way. The leaders do not order a cock to lay eggs."

"A sense of responsibility to the people, that's what we lack," said Ch'i Yun. "And our problem is not simply to explain the mistakes of the past, but to inspire the people with a vision of the future worth fighting for. Orders can never do it. We have to make our dreams clear to the village cadres. How can we make them see that they are the builders, not simply the cogs of the new society? That the future depends on them? How can we tap their revolutionary heroism?"

No one answered her. It was clear that they must first see a way out themselves. They must first tap their own revolutionary heroism. Perhaps that was why Ch'i Yun, in her quiet way, had asked the question.

****

The meeting in Lucheng County was important enough to bring Secretary Wang, of the Third Administrative District of the Taihang Subregion, to the county for a few days. He spent one long afternoon with the cadres of the Fifth District. This included those from Long Bow and Chia Village. I remembered him well from the visit he had made to the Long Bow team many weeks before. Looking back, it was clear that he, more than most, had long been aware of a strong Left bias in the work and had already rescued the team from some of its worst errors. Now he concentrated his remarks on an evaluation of basic policy. Was it true, as some were saying, that policy changed every few days and that the Party leaders did not know where they were going?

As he discussed this problem, Secretary Wang sat on a brick in the middle of the group. His faded blue tunic was unbuttoned at the top and his soft visor cap pushed back on his shaven head. He spoke softly but persuasively, taking first one cadre, then another, into his confidence.

"The land reform policy laid down by Mao Tse-tung has not only been consistent, it has been correct," Wang said. "Is there anything wrong with the formulation, 'Depend on the poor peasants, unite with the middle peasants, join with all anti-feudal forces to destroy the feudal land system and institute the system of land to the tiller'? No. That has always been the policy, is still the policy, and will be the policy wherever the feudal system has not yet been uprooted.

"Our problem is that we have applied this policy to a county and to villages where the feudal system no longer exists. In such places, to promise more material *fanshen* is misleading. To plaster all over our county at the present time such slogans as 'Equally Divide the Land,' and 'Make Sure That All Poor-and-Hired Peasants *Fanshen*' is formalism of the worst kind. In the Fifth District in 1948 such slogans can only raise hopes among the poor and make the middle peasants fear for their land and chattels. They hold a promise of still further expropriation, still further equalization which would only further aggravate the real mistakes of the past.

" 'Throw out all the bad Party members' is another fine sentiment. But in areas where the vast majority of Party members are working peasants loyal to the Revolution and potentially, if not actually, good leaders, organizers, and servants of the people, such a slogan can only give the Communist Party a bad name, confuse people, and undermine morale both inside and outside the Party branches.

"Who then is to blame for the wrong estimate and for the policies which flowed from this estimate?" asked Wang. Without pausing for a reply he answered his own question. "The county and regional leaders are responsible. But the cadres in the field must also be self-critical. Is it not on their reports of conditions that the leaders in the county seat make their estimates? And have not the local cadres sometimes interpreted policy carelessly? Have they not been prone to seize on a single aspect that suited their prejudices and thus neglect the whole? 'Depend on the Poor Peasants' is part of our agrarian policy, but it is certainly not the whole of it. Yet the cadres in the villages have emphasized it out of all proportion."

Wang's listeners were willing to grant that the slogan had been unduly emphasized, but many of them rejected the idea that they themselves were responsible for this emphasis. A cadre from Chia Village complained that he had done nothing in the course of his work that had not been written up in the *People's Daily* or suggested in that paper as the valuable experience of some other place.

This seemed to confirm the point that Secretary Wang was trying to make. "The daily paper," he explained, "reports conditions and experiences from all over North China. But an experience that is valid in some distant village that has just been liberated does not necessarily apply to Long Bow or Chia Village or the Fifth District of Lucheng County.

"In any case," he continued, "the newspaper is not the body directing our work. Why then do so many of you read it as if it were exactly that? Why are you so prone to pick out something you find interesting from the paper and use it as a model even when conditions in your area are not the same?"

That this had indeed happened nobody could deny. But why? That was another question.

In order to make the assumption of responsibility easier to bear, Secretary Wang went on to analyze the roots of "leftism." He explained how naturally it flowed out of the conditions of the past. In the course of the revolution, whenever and wherever the enemy had been especially strong and the battle bitter, sentiment in the countryside had swung to the Left. He reminded his listeners that during the Anti-Japanese War the Taihang Mountains had been one of the most ferociously contested regions in all China. The villages in these mountains had suffered a whole series of "Burn all, Kill all, Loot all" campaigns. These, in turn, had been superimposed upon two terrible famine years. The strength of the Japanese and consequently of the landlord forces who collaborated with them had thus been enormous. Lucheng, on the edge of the Taihang Range, had always been a storm center, and of all the districts of Lucheng, the Fifth had always been the most turbulent. Why was this? Because in the Fifth District the Japanese had built their largest base and set up their strongest puppet apparatus. Because in the Fifth District also, there had always been a large Catholic minority of doubtful loyalty. Was it any wonder then that the class struggle in the Fifth District had been sharp and sometimes Left? Was it any wonder then that they had all been carried along with the tide?

To make this point still clearer, Secretary Wang reviewed the various slogans so well known to every peasant in the county. Had they not been plainly written on a thousand village walls? "He who has taken half a catty must pay back eight ounces!" and "The masses can do anything they want." These had been adopted by a tenants' rally held in 1944. But were they not slogans of Left anarchy? During the Anti-Traitor Movement of 1945, the Party had called on the peasants to "Beat the dog's leg to find the head." Had this not led directly to attacks on middle and even poor peasants? Later the Party adopted the slogan "Do everything bravely," and began the "Three Things Thorough Movement." Was not the standard for "thoroughness" in this movement one of absolute equality? Leftism finally reached a climax at the time of the "Reinspection of the Land Movement" when propagandists wrote in bold strokes, "Beat down the drowning dog" and "The landlords won't lower their heads because their stomachs are full of oil." All of these slogans reflected the one-sided demands of the poor peasants, and all of them were Left.

"If, after considering all this, you still are not satisfied," said

Secretary Wang, "if you think that the self-criticism made by the county secretaries is not thorough-going enough, you certainly have the right to say so and to ask for deeper criticism on their part. But at the same time, you should think over your own work and consider whether or not you too have made mistakes."

****

Wang's patient explanations failed to satisfy the majority. Most of his listeners felt that there was something lacking in his analysis, something unfair. He was putting too much responsibility on shoulders unable to carry it. After all, it was not they who had formulated those slogans. What they believed in their hearts was that the county leaders should accept the lion's share of responsibility. Few were sanguine that this would be done, however. They had all heard Secretary Ch'en curtly reject a criticism made of him by the team leader from Ke Shu Village.

Before a mass meeting in the temple the Ke Shu leader had said, "When we departed for our work in the village, Secretary Ch'en told us, 'The cadres are the oxen of the people. If they work hard, they will be well treated. If not, they will be sent to the slaughter house.'"

As soon as he heard this the Secretary's face flushed red. He jumped to his feet and interrupted the man.

"I never said that," he protested.

"Well anyway," said the speaker from Ke Shu, still calm, "I feared the 'slaughter house' and you did say, 'If you can't find any poor peasants you had better not eat.'"

"Yes," said Secretary Ch'en. "I did say that. It was wrong. I criticize myself for making such a statement. But about the slaughter house? No. I never said that. I have notes. I want to set the record straight on that."

Ch'en's denial was so abrupt and so heated that many wondered whether he was telling the truth or not.

"If that's the way he is going to react, what's the use of criticizing him," said Little Li in disgust.

But Secretary Ch'en confounded the skeptics. The next day he delivered a long report which dwelt on the basic policies of the Chinese Revolution and on the successful foundation which had been laid as the result of these policies. Each change in policy, he said reflected a change in the total situation and each, in its turn, helped to advance the Revolution. Not these policies, but the distortion of them locally, was the root of the problem in Lucheng County. "And who should be criticized for these distortions? Of course, both the upper and the lower cadres. But the upper cadres must bear the greater part of the responsibility because the mistakes of the leaders carry much greater weight than the mistakes of a few comrades in the villages. *Primary responsibility rests with us here at county head-quarters.*"

Secretary Ch'en's admission of primary responsibility cracked the atmosphere of gloom that had dominated the proceedings. As the mass meeting adjourned, many cadres said, "He lifted the stone from our backs." Men who up until that point had only complained, men who had blamed everyone but themselves, suddenly began to examine their past thoughts and acts. No longer afraid of bearing the sole blame for leftism they found themselves able to assume a measure of responsibility for this serious mistake. That afternoon the team leader from East Portal expressed the thinking of many when he said:

"Just as we receive and carry out policy from the county and sub-region in a slightly different way than it is presented to us, so they in turn receive and carry it out in a way that differs from the policy as it is presented to them. Thus, even though Chairman Mao and the Central Committee lay down a proper policy, it is or can be distorted and misapplied on every level until it reaches the bottom. Hence we cannot lay aside all responsibility and blame only those above. What if they did the same thing and those above them the same? It would fall back on Chairman Mao. On him alone would rest the entire burden of the Revolution. No, each locality, each level of leaders must do its best to understand basic policy, apply what is useful locally, correct mistakes as they come up, and help to shape new policies. No one can expect the leaders to tell them exactly what to do."

From this statement it was evident that the conference was establishing among the cadres a new concept of the relationship between leaders and led, a new concept of the role of each individual in the ranks of the Party. Face to face with widespread mistakes, all the participants were forced to leave the safe haven of implicit faith, of automatic instructions coming from above. They were forced to think for themselves, to broaden their knowledge, to investigate and study carefully, and to assume individual responsibility for their acts.

As soon as the acceptance of a degree of responsibility became palatable to the cadres, it became possible to evaluate the past in more realistic terms and to understand on a new level everything that had happened, not only in recent months but in the whole period since the Japanese surrender. This evaluation softened that first involuntary cry of pain, "We are all wrong!" and gradually replaced it with a realization that what had been done was fundamentally right. If the feudal land system had been destroyed, if the *fanshen* of the landless and the land poor had been basically completed, if the Party branches were in truth sound—then the first great battle of the revolution had been won, at least locally. That which they had striven to realize so long and so arduously—"Land to the tiller"—was already a fact. That which they had feared so much—a peasantry betrayed by an infiltrated Party—turned out to be nothing but fantasy, a nightmare of the mind. This was the tremendous, satisfying conclusion that had emerged from months of investigation and mobilization in the 11 "basic villages." This then must be the starting point for any examination of progress on the home front, just as it was obviously the starting point for that long series of military successes won on the battlefront since mid-1947.

Not infringement of the rights of middle peasants, not indiscriminate violence, not confiscation of private commercial and industrial holdings, not "sweep-the-floor-out-the-door" excesses, not commandism, favoritism, and hedonism, but a basic decision to remake the world, the actual *fanshen* of the poor peasants, and the uprooting of feudalism constituted the *main* content of local history since 1945.

As for the actions of the work teams since their arrival in the villages in March 1948, this could not be negated either. In spite of the faulty evaluation which the teams brought with them to their work, in spite of unrealistic promises made to the peasants, in spite of the exaggerated emphasis on the poor, in spite of the unwarranted harshness of the effort to remold the village Communists and cadres, a more realistic picture of the true condition in the villages had been fashioned. The population in the villages had been painstakingly classified, hundreds of people had been mobilized and educated, the worst abuses of the cadres had been exposed, those responsible had begun the process of reform, and the tide of democracy had swept into every sphere of village life. These were solid achievements. They constituted the main aspect of the work.

Once "basically right" replaced "all wrong" as the cadres' estimate of the past, their own mistakes and the mistakes of the Party fell into place as part of a dynamic process. This way of looking at things had already been summed up by Mao Tse-tung in a talk delivered to the staff of the *Shansi-Suiyuan Daily* on April 2nd. Among the editors and writers on that paper were several who had openly espoused the poor-peasant line. When they realized their error, they were as demoralized as the majority of the full-time cadres at Lucheng had been after hearing Secretary Ch'en's report.

To these newspapermen Mao spoke as follows:

When we are correcting deviations, some people look on the work of the past as utterly fruitless and wrong. That is not right. These people fail to see that the Party has led a huge number of peasants to obtain land, has overthrown feudalism, consolidated the Party organizations, and improved the cadres' style of work, and that now it has also corrected the Left deviations and educated the cadres and the masses. Are all these not great achievements? We should be analytical with regard to our work and the undertakings of the masses and should not negate everything. In the past Left deviations arose because people had no experience. Without experience it is difficult to avoid mistakes. From inexperience, one must go through a process. Through the struggles against the Right and Left deviations in the short period since June of last year, people have come to understand what struggle against Right deviations means and what struggle against Left deviations means. Without this process people would not understand.

These words provided a realistic and convincing framework for evaluating the past in Lucheng County. Not a restatement of faith in the future, but a detailed and concrete analysis of the mistakes and detours of the past against the background of the victories won provided the foundation for a true revival of morale.

It would be wrong to give the impression that this revival took place in one great leap. The level of understanding expressed by these words of Mao was not attained by all the Lucheng cadres in the course of this one conference. What did take place was uneven progress towards such understanding. Some men and women grasped the essential point immediately. Others, only partly convinced, remained more or less doubtful. An unconvinced minority continued to express bitterness and bewilderment at the very real injury they had suffered from criticism at work and retaliation at home during the period when the poor-peasant line prevailed.

In the long run, however, neither the bitterness of this latter group nor the wavering of those who still had doubts could suppress the surge of optimism which the final evaluation unleashed. During the last days of the conference the old mood of gloom gave way step by step to a new mood of buoyancy, and the vast majority of the cadres prepared themselves to tackle with confidence and enthusiasm the *fanshen* tasks that still remained.

****

Secretary Ch'en and Assistant Secretary Chang outlined the tasks of the future in a series of long reports.

First, the excesses of the past had to be corrected by resettling all landlord and rich peasant families who had been "swept out the door," by repaying all middle peasant families who had been expropriated, and by returning to the original owners all commercial and industrial property that had been taken from them.

Next, after a final evaluation of all village cadres before the *gate,* a government responsible to the electorate had to be chosen in each village.

Finally, a large-scale production movement had to be initiated and carried, by detailed organization and encouragement, to new heights.

This last was the central task. Everything else must be subordinated to it. The correction of past errors and the establishment of democratic rule were seen as essentials to the primary goal—an unprecedented upsurge of production. The foundation for such an upsurge had been created by the destruction of the feudal land system and the *fanshen* of the poor and hired peasants. It could only reach its full potential, however, when the grievances of all classes were settled and a democratic atmosphere of free give and take prevailed.

In the 11 "basic villages" all of this work was to be carried out as rapidly as possible by the work teams. On the other hand, in the remaining villages in the county, the so-called "production villages," only the correction of past errors was to be handled right away, and this by a short cut. Instead of classifying the whole village according to the latest standards, only those families who had been attacked were to be classified. All those who turned out to be middle peasants must then be repaid. All those who turned out to be landlords or rich peasants must be resettled. In this straightforward manner the land reform was to be completed. Only later on, during the slack winter months, would those many villages attempt to consolidate their Party branches by setting up *gates,* or form new village governments by holding popular elections.

PART VII

Untying the Knot

Victory will go to the exploited, for with them is life, the strength of numbers, the strength of the masses, the strength of inexhaustible resources of all that is unselfish, high-principled, honest, forward straining, and awakening for the task of building the new, all the gigantic store of energy and talent of the so-called "common folk," the workers and peasants. Victory lies with them.

V. I. Lenin

57

Disaster

*And the Lord rained hail upon the land of Egypt; there was hail, and
fire flashing continually in the midst of the hail, very heavy hail, such as
had never been in all the land of Egypt since it became a nation. The hail
struck down everything that was in the field throughout the land of Egypt,
both man and beast; and the hail struck down every plant of the field,
and shattered every tree of the field.*

Exodus

A STRANGE thing happened in the sky. It was several days before
the end of the county conference. The cadres of the various work
teams were scattered throughout the courtyards discussing one of
Ch'en's reports. I was sitting, as usual, with the team from Long Bow.
Suddenly the afternoon sun faded. We looked up to see an enormous
dark thunderhead rushing toward us from the west. Lightning flashed
inside it. Great cauldrons of vapor rose and turned as thunder rum-
bled from its dark center. As we watched this drama in the sky, a
furious wind tore at the courtyard, whirled madly through the temple
gates, and whipped the ubiquitous North China dust high into the
air above the roofs that encircled us. Then, as quickly as it had come,
the wind receded. The air became absolutely still. This, I thought,
must be the eye of the storm. Surely now, at any moment a most
terrible hurricane would break upon us. But instead the unexpected
happened again. A cool and gentle rain began to fall. It dropped
quietly for half an hour. Then the sky cleared. The sun shone forth
again as if nothing had ever threatened the peace of the afternoon.
The participants at the conference dismissed the strange wind and
cloud from their minds and turned back to their discussion. I did
the same. It never occurred to any of us that we had witnessed the
enactment of a terrible disaster.

We remained in blissful ignorance until the middle of the supper
break when Village Head Ch'un-hsi of Long Bow strode into the
temple yard mud-flecked and panting. He had run the whole ten miles
of valley and mountain that separated Long Bow from Lucheng.
Tears coursed down his cheeks as he stood before the county magis-

trate and described how a terrible hail storm followed by a flash
flood had ravaged his village. Twenty sections of housing had already
collapsed. More than half the crops on the surrounding land had been
laid waste. The water in the center of the village had risen so high
it poured over the door sill of the District Office. Hailstones as big
as walnuts had smashed the wheat beyond recovery. The people were
weeping openly in the streets.

The Long Bow team sat in stunned silence as they listened to the
news. Of all the villages in the county, Long Bow had the poorest
land, had enjoyed the least favorable growing conditions that year
and had raised the worst crops. Now even those poor seedlings had
been destroyed. How could the people recover from such a blow?
How could morale ever be restored? The whole team wanted to rush
back immediately to help organize relief and lead in the reconstruction
of the village but Secretary Ch'en would not let anyone go. He asked
the team to wait a day or two until the conference adjourned. In the
meantime he promised that he would do what was necessary to start
relief grain moving and render such assistance as might be necessary.

****

When the Long Bow team members finally did return from the
county seat, it was already the last day of June. As I walked along
with them I found it hard to believe that any calamity had taken
place. Everywhere the crops looked fine. On the flat north of Long
Bow the wheat was ripening to a golden yellow. The vigorous young
millet was already beginning to obscure the brown soil from which
it sprang and cornstalks brushed the knees of any passerby who
walked near the edge of the road. It was not until we passed the
halfway mark south of the village of North Market and approached
the fields of Long Bow itself that we began to see marks left behind
by receding flood waters. Here a rapid current had run through the
crops and rippled the surface of the soil; there odd bits of leaves and
trash lay piled up against the corn stalks. Further on we found the
leaves of the corn plants shredded as though they had been attacked
with a fork. Wheat stems bent way over as if to pay their respects
to the Earth God while the young millet lay flat, half buried in still
moist mud. The closer we came to the village, the greater was the
desolation. Now the corn leaves looked as if they had been fed
through a cotton gin, the road was lined with flood trash, and in
some fields only a stalk or two of wheat still stood. All else had been
flattened and drowned. This, it turned out, was the worst hit section
of the whole village. Some of the fields on the far side of the com-

munity had not been so badly mangled. In many places the wheat still stood upright but the health of the stalks and leaves was no indication of the damage the crop had suffered. The hail had threshed the wheat where it stood. Fields that should have yielded 12 or 15 bushels to the acre would thrash out only three or four. The rest of the crop lay scattered in the dirt, impossible to salvage. Beans that had been interplanted in the corn and the millet had been completely destroyed.

The storm had stunned the whole population. Although a week had already passed since the disaster occurred, we found group after group of people wandering listlessly about. Many were not yet emotionally capable of setting to work to save something from the wreckage. As soon as we put down our bedrolls, we scattered to the four corners of the settlement to visit old friends and catch up with all that had happened while we were gone. I went with Ch'i Yun to see certain of the activists among the women.

Many and varied were the stories of the storm that we heard that day. Hu Hsueh-chen, chairman of the Women's Association, told how she had sat in her home spinning cotton. She took little notice when it began to rain, but soon the water started to pour over the threshold of her house. She grabbed a washbasin and tried to bail it out, but it poured in faster than she could remove it and soon flooded the room to a depth of two feet. She then ran to the neighbors in alarm. They helped her carry out her child and her few belongings, and she abandoned the house. Then, almost as suddenly as it had begun, the storm ended. The sky cleared. Hu Hsueh-chen went to the fields to see what had happened to her crops. One glance was enough to tell her that everything had been destroyed. The wheat, the millet, the beans, and the corn, all gone! She fell to the ground and wept. When at last she recovered enough strength to walk back to the village she found many others groping their way along the streets, their eyes, like her own, blinded by tears.

Li T'ung-jen's wife told us a different sort of tale. When the storm cloud first appeared, Li T'ung-jen was a mile from the village on his way home from Lucheng. He had with him his donkey and cart. Soon hail began to pelt him. He looked for shelter but found none. Then, as the hailstones grew bigger and more dangerous, he put his straw hat on the donkey's head and crawled under the cart. Ch'un-hsi, the village head, found him there as he came over the hill. In spite of the disaster he could not help laughing at the spectacle of the driverless donkey standing in the middle of nowhere with a straw hat on his head.

Man-hsi's wife said the storm came up so suddenly that the chicks in her yard almost drowned. The old hen cried out in terror like a human child. Man-hsi ran out to gather in the hen and chicks. A large hailstone almost knocked him down. He put the poultry on the *k'ang* under a warm blanket but even so, two of the little chicks died.

Lai-so's mother, one of the oldest inhabitants of Long Bow, kept shaking her head as she talked. Over and over again she said that in all her 70 years she had never seen hailstones to match the ones that fell that day. They were as big as eggs, they were as big as ripe persimmons. Never had anything so large fallen from the sky before. She thought it was some sort of portent.

It soon became obvious that the militant spirit built up in the village during the confrontation with Yu-lai had vanished. A sort of lethargy pervaded the whole population. A rumor had started, no one knew where, that the storm was a punishment to the people of Long Bow for allowing their village to be host to the work team. At the time of the first classification an earlier hailstorm had harassed the village. Now a little rhyme made the rounds:

> Twice classify the classes,
> Hail twice beats the masses!

This time the Party members seemed to be as apathetic as the villagers. In fact, their morale seemed lower than that of the rest of the population. Although at least 50 people showed up on July 1st to celebrate the birthday of the Communist Party, more than a third of the Party members themselves were absent. When a production meeting was called by the work team to rally mutual-aid groups for a program that would overcome the effects of the storm, all 12 mutual-aid group leaders showed up promptly, but only Cheng-k'uan and Hsin-fa appeared to speak for the 30-odd Party members.

While before the County Conference there had been at least six or eight leading Communists who took responsibility and met eagerly to carry on work, now Cheng-k'uan alone seemed to care. Hsin-fa, the secretary, and Ts'ai-yuan, the storekeeper, spent their time grumbling. They had to be summoned several times before they would show up at any meeting.

****

The man whose job it now was to revive morale in the village and to set the population moving again was new to Long Bow. His name was Ts'ai Chin. He had been sent to work in Lucheng County by the Subregional Party Bureau in response to a request from the county secretary for someone to replace Team Leader Hou. The secretary had asked for a man with more experience than Hou, a man with greater education and one with a deeper theoretical understanding. He got what he asked for. Ts'ai Chin was an intellectual, tall, thin, sharp-featured like Hsieh Hung, the interpreter, and brilliant in the same quick, impetuous way.

In almost every respect, appearance as well as temperament, Ts'ai Chin was the very opposite of the man he replaced. Ts'ai was high-strung where Hou was placid, quick where Hou was slow, vocal where Hou was tongue-tied, and sharp where Hou was gentle. Ts'ai's hands were long, thin, and tender. As might have been expected, they were adept at handling a writing brush. Ts'ai let his hair grow. A thick black shock of it hung down over his forehead. One of his characteristic gestures was to brush that forelock back. He rarely stood still, but when he did, he seemed to lean forward from his ankles as if bucking a strong wind.

If Hou was typical of the peasant revolutionaries that came to the fore by the tens of thousands during the land reform movement, Ts'ai was a prototype of the intellectuals who turned revolutionary in the course of the Anti-Japanese War. Both types had a role to play in the great movement for *fanshen,* but whereas the former came to the struggle by a process as natural as breathing, the latter came to it only after rejecting much of their past, after coming through a process of education painful enough to leave a mark in the intensity of their eyes and the stormy turmoil of their souls.

The inner turmoil in Ts'ai came to the surface every now and then in a flash of temper that shocked his colleagues and stunned the peasants. We understood that temper better when we learned that Ts'ai's own brother had been beaten to death and his mother and grandfather driven from their many-sectioned courtyard and 50 acres of land during the Settling Accounts Movement.

How had such a man ever become a revolutionary?

As Ts'ai related his story to me, becoming a revolutionary was easy enough for him; remaining one had been difficult. When the Japanese Army took Peking in 1937, Ts'ai was a middle school student in the capital. With a large group of patriotic classmates he made his way through the battle lines to fight in Central Shansi. He was assigned, through the underground, to an Eighth Route Army unit that operated in his home county of Hohsun, about 100 miles north of Changchih. As a student he had read many revolutionary books. He had been impressed by the Marxian descriptions of the class character of mankind. He had recognized truth in the idea that the attitudes, thoughts, and actions of any individual are a product of the way in which he earns his living. In the landlord-dominated, corrupt, and stagnant China of the 1930's, he had seen no future for himself. He had acquired a contempt for the luxurious, dissolute lives led by the sons and daughters of the big warlords, landlords, and generals with whom he went to shool. At the front he met and worked with Communists who asked nothing for themselves, suffered what the people suffered, and shared whatever food and shelter was available. When they invited him to join the Communist Party, he did so without hesitation or misgivings. At this time there had not been any conflict between what Ts'ai, as a landlord's son, wanted for China, and what the Communist Party wanted. The need to liberate their country from foreign occupation united representatives of all classes, and this unity had brought many landlords to the Party. It was only after the Japanese had been defeated, after renewed Civil War had broken out, after the Communist Party had come into open conflict with the gentry over the land question, that Ts'ai began to suffer agonizing doubts. He was convinced that in order to secure the future of China the landlord class must be overthrown, but every time that he thought of his landlord friends and especially of his own landlord family, he had to beat back a great upsurge of affection and pity.

When the peasants began the attack on his own mother and brother, he thought that they didn't understand the Ts'ai family at all. When they beat his brother to death and drove his mother and grandfather away, Ts'ai almost lost his mind. For weeks his thoughts stood deadlocked. All logic, all reason, all the mature ties of his adult life, his work, his colleagues, and his Party demanded that he stand with the peasants, but all his emotions, all his childhood loyalties, all his love for his parents cried out to him to save his family and his land.

Ts'ai finally resolved this personal conflict in favor of the Revolution. To him it became a question of his family and its way of life or China and her future. The landlords as a class had proven time and again that they were incapable of building anything modern in China. They could not even defend their homeland from conquest at the hands of a paltry 70 million Japanese. Many of them had even betrayed her. What future could there be for any Chinese if China herself lay prostrate?

That the destruction of Ts'ai's family was wrong and unnecessary, the result of a brand of Left extremism that took "sweep-the-floor-out-the door" as the standard for successful expropriation, did not make the tragic consequences any easier to accept. To that which is inevitable a man can reconcile himself. But the shock of the accidental, the excessive, can be withstood only with the aid of profound conviction, only by a commitment which is both rational and total.

Ts'ai Chin could not have resolved this conflict in this way had it not been for the great wartime *cheng feng,* or Party Consolidation Movement initiated by Mao Tse-tung in 1942. The movement was designed to solidify in all Communist cadres the kind of revolutionary outlook and class position necessary to cope with the sudden shift in class relations which a victory over Japan was sure to bring. Ts'ai Chin was delegated to take part in this study movement in March 1945. For a whole year thereafter—a year during which the Japanese Army surrendered and a nationwide Civil War began, was called off, and began again—he sat in school, read, transcribed his thoughts, and talked. During that period he minutely examined every facet of his past, his outlook at various stages of maturity, the decisions he had made, both in his personal life and in the course of his work, and the class stand he had taken. All this was discussed and analyzed with the help of classmates whose background was similar to his own. He discovered that much of what he had done lacked a clear-cut class character, that he had often acted empirically, in accordance with the pressures of the moment and the prejudices of the past. Slowly and painfully he built for himself a new class outlook, a new code of loyalty.

In 1927 Mao had made clear to the revolutionaries of China the choice of roads that lay before them in relation to the peasants:

To march at their head and lead them? Or to follow at their rear, gesticulating at them and criticizing them? Or to face them as opponents? Every Chinese is free to choose among the three alternatives, but circumstances demand that a quick choice be made.

In 1945, Ts'ai made his choice. He would march at the head of the peasant rebellion and help lead it if he could.

58

Revolutionary Steeling

When Heaven is about to confer a great office on any man, it first exercises his mind with suffering, and his sinews and bones with toil. It exposes his body to hunger, and subjects him to extreme poverty. It confounds his undertakings. By all these methods it stimulates his mind, hardens his nature, and remedies his incompetencies.

Mencius

Ts'AI CHIN began work in Long Bow with an effort to find out what really lay behind the collapse of Party morale. He took it for granted that the Party was the key to the situation. As long as the Communists themselves remained passive and sullen, little could be accomplished. If he could get the Party moving again, its members would swing the rest of the village into action.

Ts'ai's colleagues on the work team soon traced part of the trouble to the status of the three Long Bow men who had been working as full-time district cadres. Fu-yuan, T'ien-ming, and Kuei-ts'ai were all at home, and rumor had it that this was no coincidence. They had all quit as full-time political organizers, so the gossips said, because they saw no future in it. It was also whispered that the former team leader, Hou Pao-pei, and Li Wen-chung of the Long Bow team had quit for good. If these men saw no future in full-time work for the Party and the government, what incentive was there for the local Communist Party members to keep working?

The rumors did not coincide with the facts. Hou Pao-pei and Li Wen-chung had returned home to help with the wheat harvest on their own land. Fu-yuan, ex-village head and brother to Ts'ai-yuan, the storekeeper, had come back to Long Bow for the same reason. T'ien-ming, the founder of the Long Bow Party branch, was at home convalescing from an illness. As soon as he recovered he intended to report for work once more. Only Kuei-ts'ai, the man who had once been the most daring and active of all the poor peasants in the village, was sulking at home because he was disillusioned with outside work.

But Kuei-ts'ai, it turned out, had prestige enough to influence many minds. Disgusted with political work himself, he tried his best to discourage others. After every meeting he sought out the active local people and asked what kind of a discussion they had had. When they told him about disagreements and quarrels, he said, "It's no use at all. The policy changes too often. I myself don't want to go out and be a cadre again. It is better to stay at home."

His thoughts had run in such channels ever since the day that he had been detained in the village for the accounts examination meeting and had been disarmed by Cadre Hsu. He thought then that he was under attack for having been so active in the past and he could not think it through. "Was I wrong to struggle against the landlords?" he asked himself. His inability to answer this question served as an excuse for doing what he most wanted to do in any case—raise food for his family. Like Li Wen-chung of the Long Bow team, Kuei-ts'ai had only recently married, and the sudden assumption of responsibility for wife and home pushed all collective demands on his time and energy into the background.

In addition to all this, Kuei-ts'ai had syphilis. The penicillin that was needed for a cure was expensive, and he didn't see where the money was to come from if he did not raise crops at home. Swayed by all these considerations and embittered by the attack on his past record, Kuei-ts'ai convinced himself not only that he should quit and stay home but that everyone else should follow his example.

Kuei-ts'ai's bitter words would not have disrupted the Long Bow Party branch if its members had not been in a receptive frame of mind. Material difficulties and political disillusionment had already prepared a rich seedbed for sprouts of discontent. All the Long Bow Party members had been hit hard by the storm, all of them had accepted opinions before the *gate* that were not really fair, and all of them felt that their past records had been too harshly attacked. Hsinfa, for instance, said to Team Leader Ts'ai, "I have some worries too. During the Purification Movement many opinions were raised against me. Some of them were correct but some were very unfair. I accepted all of them without any differentiation. I agreed to hand over some fruits which I didn't really seize illegally. And now that my wheat has been destroyed, where will I find the grain to pay back all that I promised?"

In addition to these aggravating personal problems, the village cadres had to face mounting difficulties posed by the new atmosphere of freedom that had been growing ever since the work team first came to the village. This new atmosphere had made possible the upsurge of political activity that had produced two *gates*, numerous elections, and many lively classification sessions. That was its positive side. There was also a negative side. The new atmosphere had stimulated the growth of "each-man-for-himself" tendencies, which acquired the name of "extreme democracy." This was an expression in political life of the "extreme equality" which was already disrupting economic life.

By the end of June 1948, "extreme democracy" had grown to such proportions in Long Bow that very few peasants could be found who were willing to undertake public service. As a result, the whole burden of stretcher bearing, message carrying, and grain delivery fell on the Party members, on those 28 peasants who had undertaken to be the active heart of the Revolution, come what may. Ever since the *gate* their sincerity had been on trial, so to speak, before public opinion. Consequently, they alone could not make excuses, shift burdens onto others, avoid responsibility. The burden that they bore thus developed from an ideological and organizational one into one that was overwhelmingly physical. From symbolic "oxen of the people" they had been converted step by step into real ones.

Ch'un-hsi, the acting village head, had seven acres of his own to till but hardly ever got to the fields because of the pressure of public duties of all kinds. In the first week of July he was called to the county seat for a production meeting that lasted several days. On the evening of his return a wounded soldier arrived in the village square on a stretcher. It was the duty of the Long Bow residents to take him ten miles to the north where he would be passed on to another group, and then to another until finally he reached home. When Ch'un-hsi tried to find two men who would carry the stretcher, peasant after peasant refused and every one of them had a good excuse. Finally Ch'un-hsi and the Communist Szu-har had to shoulder the suffering human burden themselves.

Ch'un-hsi's mother was so upset by the fact that her son never had time to work on his own land that she decided not to cook for him any more. She saw no reason to feed a man who did nothing to advance the fortunes of his own family. When he got hungry, he had to boil up millet himself, a chore which cut still further into his working time.

"I can't see any solution to it," Ch'un-hsi said. "In the past anyone who dared refuse would have been arrested. But now if we speak a strong word, they criticize our attitude and register a grievance against us. The only way out is for us to go in their place. But even though we don't mind doing all the work, we can't. I myself have only two hands and two legs."

Hu Hsueh-chen had a different sort of problem with the women. She was responsible for the spring cotton loan which the County Co-operative Society had made available as a form of work relief for destitute families. All those who applied were given several catties of cotton without charge. After 30 days they were expected to return a certain amount of spun thread. The extra thread they kept as payment for their labor. Earnings were ample. But 50 days after the cotton was delivered Hu Hsueh-chen was still unable to collect payment from most of the women. A man from the County Co-operative headquarters visited her to inquire about the thread. She herself made a special trip to Lucheng to ask for an extension. She called on each of the delinquent spinners several times but still was not able to collect. Finally, on July 1st, the Co-op gave her three days more. But when she told the women about the deadline, they said they had to have at least two weeks.

To the women who owed cotton thread, Hsueh-chen spoke with tears in her eyes. "I have to take all the blame. I have to walk all the way to Lucheng to apologize for you, but you who took the loan of your own free will and knew its terms, you do not live up to your promises!"

"Over this cotton loan I have wept twice," Hsueh-chen said later to Ch'i Yun. "Sometimes I think of the famine year and how my children died one after the other, and now I have land and have *fanshened* and must work hard. But then I remember that in the ten years that I lived in Long Bow before I became a cadre nobody ever criticized me. I got along with everyone. But now some of my neighbors even hate me.

"All day I am busy with public affairs but when I return home there is just an empty pot staring me in the face and the children are crying for something to eat. So I have thought more than once, 'Though I have worked hard for the people now I am attacked just like a landlord.' Why should I go on being a cadre?"

The 19-year-old Wang An-feng, Hu Hsueh-chen's closest co-worker and assistant, spoke even more glumly. In a private talk with Ch'i Yun she admitted that the Party members came reluctantly to meetings, kept silent while there, and tried their best to forget what had happened when they got home.

"What about yourself?" asked Ch'i Yun.

"My outlook is the same."

"Why?"

"Because now I think with the others that there is no future for us. In the past, whatever we said, the people obeyed it. If it was right they obeyed it, and if it was wrong they obeyed it. But now they just look at us coolly. In the past the Communist Party had only to announce that there was to be a meeting and everyone came hurrying. But now they have to be asked over and over again. To invite them to a meeting is harder than to invite honorable guests to a feast."

This girl, strong and square as a village gate, and possessed of tremendous vitality, was the wife of a soldier who had already been at the front for two years. She tilled all the land at home by herself. She was a Catholic by upbringing but had little praise for the Church. Her father had worked 20 years as a teamster for the Cathedral in Changchih only to be laid off in the famine year of 1943. He came home penniless and broken in health and died of starvation within three months. From that day on, An-feng had done the work of a man and showed it by the strength of her body. She also showed it in her speech—direct, to the point, fearless, as befitted one who earned her own living and made her own decisions.

Yet when Ch'i Yun said that popular apathy was due to the mistakes of the past and could be overcome as soon as the mistakes were corrected, An-feng said, "Women are no use. Since the men are not active, how can the women do anything? No one pays any attention to women's words."

"If that were so, how is it that you have been elected so often to various posts?" asked Ch'i Yun.

"Oh, that's because I am not afraid to speak in public."

But Ch'i Yun did not let it rest there. She argued that in fact An-feng must have considerable prestige or the people would not vote for her at all. If the men would not do anything, it was up to women to mount the stage and start moving. Then perhaps the men would be ashamed and start following them.

An-feng listened attentively to this argument but quickly brought up another problem that had been bothering her. "Hsiao Wen-hsu says that the work team is always asking us to meet and be active but they themselves get 44 ounces of millet a day for their work, while we get nothing but headaches. No one gives us even one tenth of an ounce, and the masses only heap ill words on our heads."

This was a real challenge. Ch'i Yun thought carefully before replying. "The work that is done in this village is for the benefit of this village. If it is well done, Long Bow's peasants will reap the benefits. But as for the work team, our work is never done. Though we get enough to eat we profit nothing from all these meetings. As soon as Long Bow has been reorganized, we must move on to some other place and help some other peasants. Nor do we always get a welcome or high praise, for often we have to support unpopular decisions such as the decision to give Police Captain Wen-te another chance. Then the masses heap abuse on our heads.

"You here and your children can benefit by all the progress that is made," she went on, "but as for us, we do not even know about the fate of our own families. We cannot help them and some of us must even struggle against them if they are landlords. But we all do our best for the Revolution."

"Yes," said An-feng, thinking it over slowly. "I guess if all you wanted was clothes to wear and a full stomach you would not have to come all the way to Long Bow to organize *fanshen* with us. I guess I am rather childish," she added with a bright smile that spread charm across her rough-hewn face and even produced a dimple in one cheek. "Sometimes I am in high spirits for several days at a time. But as soon as I run into difficulty or overhear some sarcastic words, I become very gloomy."

The work team noticed that Ts'ai-yuan, Long Bow's popular war hero, had changed perhaps more than anyone else. Before the second County Conference he had been the most active member of the branch. Now, when he finally did come to a meeting, he sat by himself in a corner and never said a word. He reacted bitterly to criticism and responded to friendly greetings with only a surly, "Have you eaten?"

The difficulties that he met in his political work, the loss of his wheat crop, and the memory of all the opinions which the people had raised against him, most of which he felt in his heart to be unfair, had put him in a very bad state of mind. To make matters still worse, he had allowed himself to be provoked into a fight with an 18-year-old youth, and the exchange of blows had become the talk of the village.

The fight grew out of a game of chess. Ts'ai-yuan, who was winning, taunted his opponent for a foolish error. The youth lost his temper, swore at Ts'ai-yuan, and knocked all the chessmen onto the ground. This so angered the older man that he slapped his opponent on the cheek. The indignant youngster then attacked Ts'ai-yuan and, before the onlookers could separate them, several blows had been struck on both sides.

The whole village blamed the storekeeper for striking the youth, and several peasants made sarcastic remarks about cadres and Party members who still beat people in spite of promises to reform. As soon as this fight was mentioned in the Party meeting, Ts'ai-yuan got angry.

"Ever since the *gate* if we so much as sigh we are criticized. The people point at us and say, 'Shame on you, you are a Party member. You are a former soldier.' "

"If I had been in front of the store, I would have helped Ts'ai-yuan beat the boy," said T'ien-hsi, the huge militiaman, with a scowl.

The trend indicated by these remarks was already quite strong.

The Party members were lining themselves up in opposition to the
rest of village and blaming all their troubles on the people.

****

Instead of going directly to the heart of the matter and telling the
Long Bow cadres that much of their trouble came from erroneous
policies and that a major shift in policy had been worked out at the
County Conference, the work team, under Team Leader Ts'ai's direction, tried to get everyone back to work by appealing to their
Party spirit. Instead of laying bare the mistakes of the past, Ts'ai Chin
called the comrades together and scolded them for their poor morale
and lack of positive action in the face of near famine. Hot words
were exchanged. Hsiao Wen-hsu was told that he was not fit to be
a Party member. This so angered that dour peasant that he got up
and strode out of the room. For the next few days he sat at home
and spoke to no one.

Official silence concerning the work at the County Conference did
not, however, prevent knowledge of it from spreading. The "small
report" or grapevine had already broadcast throughout the county
bits and pieces of information to the effect that basic policies had
gone astray, that the attack on the Communist Party members had
been excessive, that the "poor-peasant line" was wrong, and that the
fanshen which the Party had led, far from being incomplete, was
really overdone. Carters and muleteers from "production villages,"
wanting to get a straight story from one of the "basic villages," asked
questions when they passed through Long Bow. "Is equal distribution
finished?" asked one man from Li Village Gulch as he sipped hot
water at the Village Inn. "I hear the landlords are to be resettled,"
said another, downing a bowl of fried bread. But the Long Bow
people, having had no more information than anyone else, were unable to enlighten the questioners. They only picked up and embroidered what they heard from others.

These rumors, by exaggerating the errors, engendered doubts and
encouraged "sour words" when the Party members met. If it were
true that past policies had been mistakes, then the leading authorities
were certainly to blame for all the trouble the village cadres had been
through. Because of the faulty directives from above, everyone had
suffered. Now the local Communists dwelt on that suffering, and
many bitter thoughts passed through their heads.

Why didn't the work team cadres work to counteract this trend?
Why didn't they seize the initiative as Secretary Ch'en had done the
very first morning of the County Conference? By meeting the prob-

lem face to face Ch'en had made it something for all the cadres to tackle together. Ts'ai Chin could have done the same, but he was not familiar with local conditions. The other team cadres hesitated for fear that the village leaders would react badly to an exposure. They were afraid that a sudden correction would swing the whole situation completely around, cause mistakes and excesses in some other direction, and destroy the morale of all those poor peasants whose hopes had so long been built up by glowing promises. To a certain extent, the cadres lacked faith in the intelligence and good sense of the people.

Also, it seemed to me, the work team members were a little ashamed. They had arrived so confidently in March with slogans about incomplete *fanshen,* bad cadres, and landlord elements in the Party. Thereafter, all the spare time of the village people had been taken up with meetings from which great changes were expected. And now, suddenly, all this was no longer possible. Instead of the poor getting richer, the middle peasants were to be repaid and the landlords resettled. Instead of fat cadres giving up great quantities of land and illegal fruits, a few paltry acres and some small articles of minor value would be returned. It was not easy to face all this directly. And so, instead of making a complete explanation of the new policy and making clear to all why, from now on, production had to be the key to everything, the work team began to concentrate in practice on production problems.

It was not until ten days had passed that Ts'ai Chin and the work team cadres made up their minds to discuss policy changes publicly. By that time it was obvious that in spite of personal visits, branch meetings, meetings of the activists within the branch, encouragements, and scoldings, the root cause of the low morale had not been touched.

On July 9, 1948, a full meeting of the Communist Party branch was called. There, at last, Ts'ai gave a frank report on the incorrect "poor-peasant line," on the damage done by "absolute equalitarianism," and on the faulty estimate of conditions in Lucheng County which had been made by the higher Party and government authorities.

Since "extreme democracy" was the immediate practical problem which concerned the cadres most, the team leader also hit hard at this. "Some of you think that if only you are given the power to beat people you can solve all the problems of the village. But violence is not the answer to the excesses of individualism that now give us so much trouble. After all, those who won't listen to reason and go on doing just as they like are only a small minority. The majority are reasonable. They co-operate with all sensible proposals. But they oppose commandism and arbitrary power. If, because of the provocations

of a few, we try to revive the old style of work and start beating and
arresting people, the people will certainly lose confidence in us."

Team Leader Ts'ai urged the Party members to stand up bravely
and work hard to lead the people along a proper road. "We can
lead the masses in criticizing 'extreme democracy.' We can educate
and correct their attitude. If, after many attempts, there are still those
who refuse to correct their mistakes and take the law into their own
hands, then stronger measures can be taken. Everyone will understand then, and the people will even offer suggestions as to how to
deal with such persons. After all, the meaning of democracy is to
protect the interests of the majority. Those who use democracy as
an excuse for criminal acts must be punished by law."

Ts'ai's words stirred the lethargy of the village Communists.
Thoughts and feelings long bottled up were uncorked. A lively discussion followed.

"When the work team first came, we were certainly confused,"
said T'ien-hsi. "There were no landlords left here, but there were
still quite a few families who had not *fanshened*. From where would
the patches come? We thought the only possible way out was to expropriate us, the cadres, for everyone said we had *fanshened* in excess."

"That's true," said Hsin-fa. "And the people really put the pressure
on us. When we went before the *gate* they said, 'What do you mean
you didn't graft anything? And you a cadre all those years!' When
they met me in the street they scolded me for buying cigarettes.
'Haven't you given up that wasteful habit yet?' they asked."

"As for the 'poor-peasant line,' from the very beginning we thought
that the reason many poor peasants had not *fanshened* was because
of their ugly past," said Ts'ai-yuan. "Take Kuo Te-yu. He was the
puppet village leader and oppressed us all. As soon as he joined
the Poor Peasants' League, he began to act proud. He refused to
do rear service. No one dared say anything about it then. But now
we can put down our burdens. Ts'ai has explained it all."

"The *gate* was certainly good. It had to take place," said the
women's leader, Hu Hsueh-chen. "But really it came too late. As for
the opinions against me, some were right, others were not. I know
they were all meant to help me, but the unfair opinions bother me
still. I haven't been able to think it through and I have become backward. But now, since Comrade Ts'ai Chin's report, I feel much better.
The upper authorities know how hard we have worked and they
stand behind us."

Ts'ai Chin followed up this talk with the political leaders of the
village by calling a mass meeting of all the adult residents of Long

Bow. Before several hundred men and women standing in the square beside the pond, Ts'ai explained the new emphasis in land reform policy and the rights and duties of citizens under the new electoral system. He warned those who wanted to abuse their new freedom as follows: "Now each person can vote for the men and women he wants to see as cadres. But after the election is over, those who have won a majority must be given the right to do their jobs. Everyone is obliged to carry out the decisions of those whom they have elected. You yourselves will soon elect a village leader. If, after the election, he asks you to go on rear service, you must go. If he is no good, if he does his job poorly, then you can elect someone else to take his place. But as long as he is in office, you must listen to him. That is only fair. Otherwise we can have nothing but anarchy."

These words, clearly spoken with a Taihang Mountain accent, made an impression on the peasants and encouraged the Party members. The former had never heard the ABC's of electoral responsibility spelled out that clearly. The latter were relieved to find that enforcement was part of the new system and that the work team meant to tackle the growing trend toward anarchy.

59

Mutual Aid

No matter what names they have; no matter whether they are each composed of a few, or dozens, or hundreds of people, or whether they are formed entirely of people who can fulfil the standard quota of work or include some people who can fulfil only half the quota; no matter whether their mutual aid is rendered in terms of manpower, animal power, or implements, and whether their members may or may not live and board together during the busy season; and no matter whether they are of a temporary or permanent nature—all are good so long as they are collective mutual-aid organizations in which the masses take part of their own free will.

Mao Tse-tung, 1943

WHEAT, foster child of winter and sparse by-product of an autumn harvest economy, played a role in village life disproportionately large in relation to the tonnage it yielded. For many families the wheat crop alone put an end to "spring hunger" and provided the primary nourishment for the heavy labor demanded by the summer season. Without wheat these families could not hope to survive until the corn and millet ripened in September, nor could they possibly mobilize the energy necessary for the repeated hoeing, side dressings, and thinning that made the major crops grow. Hence, although the wheat never yielded enough to feed the population for more than a month or two, it was the keystone in the arch of northern agriculture.

With the wheat crop badly damaged by hail, the first big job undertaken by the work team in July 1948, was the distribution of relief grain to all those left without food. Certain stocks of grain had already been handed out by the village administration itself. These were now supplemented by county reserves stored in the Long Bow Church and by grain carted in from Lucheng. Thus an immediate crisis was averted, and the peasants were able to survive, take stock, and make plans for recovery.

As the days passed it became clear that the spring-planted crops were not so badly hurt as had first appeared. The corn recovered first. The leaves that had been shredded by hail turned yellow and died, but new growth thrusting up from the center of the stalks soon took over and made the plants as vigorous as ever. Most of the millet revived in the same way, though without the same vigor. Only the beans were completely destroyed, but since, in the agricultural scheme of things, beans were a minor crop, their loss was not irreparable. Even from the wheat fields something was salvaged. The hail had not hit with equal ferocity everywhere. Some fields yielded a fair crop in spite of the lashing they had received. Others were cut, threshed, and winnowed in vain. By the time the wheat harvest had been completed, the work team was able to make an overall estimate of the damage caused by the catastrophe and to draw up the following list:

Wheat—282 acres. All damaged. Expected yield: 11,861.5 pecks (an average yield of 11 bushels per acre). Actual yield: 2,536.75 pecks (2.5 bushels to the acre).
Millet—168 acres. All damaged. Expected yield: half normal.
Corn—350 acres. All damaged but recovering well. Expected yield: 90 percent of normal.
Beans—143 acres interplanted in corn. All damaged. No crop expected.
Families suffering losses: 240 (the entire population).

As the corn and millet recovered, the peasants' spirit revived and so did their energy. Soon they were out in force replanting all open land with turnip seed, buckwheat, and 60-day corn. Seeds for these catch-crops were supplied by the County Agricultural Department which obtained them from villages where no catastrophe had taken place. So ample were the supplies of seed that several bushels of buckwheat were left over. The village office presented the surplus to the people of Horse Square, the community directly to the north where hail had also devastated some fields.

****

The harvest rush, the need to replant, and the heavy supply and stretcher bearing duties brought on by the fighting in Central Shansi all sharpened the need for mutual aid and labor exchange, but the demoralization that followed the hail disaster coupled with the go-it-alone tendencies fostered by the poor-peasant line had brought co-operation among the peasants almost to a standstill. At the very moment when the people most needed mutual aid, the system was on the verge of collapse.

Some peasants were happy to work alone. They said it was better not to organize for production. Instead of attending meetings and working in the fields with the aid groups to which they belonged,

they went about their own business and privately ridiculed all co-
operative effort. They did their best to undermine the initiative of
those who still wanted to work together. Some less individualistic
families still joined forces when there was work to be done for soldiers' dependents, but when it came to their own land, they split up.
Their elected leaders found it hard even to locate them to inform
them of meetings. They were off transporting coal from the mines at
Yellow Mill or hoeing their own fields. No one saw them from dawn
until dark. When it rained for a day so that no one could go out,
aid-group leaders sometimes managed to gather a quorum; but as
soon as the rain stopped, co-operation evaporated along with the
moisture in the fields. Everyone wanted to get to his own fields first
in order to knock down the weeds before they had a chance to put
down roots.

Such practical actions spoke louder than words and indicated that
mutual aid was not popular. But when the question "to organize or
not to organize for production" was placed squarely before the Communists in the Party branch, before the leaders and activists of the
Provisional Peasants' Association, and before the sectional organizations of the Association, the response was far from negative. Almost
all the peasants said that the mutual-aid groups were good in theory.
It was only in practice that they did not work out. People insisted
that they wanted to co-operate but that they didn't like some of the
organizational forms used in the past. Once discussion was officially
launched, a very vigorous "airing of views" followed.

The main criticism voiced by the peasants was that the aid groups
were too big. Some included as many as 20 or 25 families. Group
leaders wasted time calling everyone together in the morning. Then
when they got to the fields, many people sat around because the
plan of work was not clear. Large groups also meant friction because
families that did not get on well with others invariably found themselves thrown together. Cheng-k'uan's group, for instance, contained
the quarrelsome Chin-chu and his wastrel wife. Nine tenths of the
group did not want to work with Chin-chu because he was lazy and
ill-tempered. He argued with all comers. Merely to straighten out
the problems Chin-chu raised, the group had to meet every day. The
time spent in these meetings was not worth it. The members lost
sleep and precious moments of leisure.

People also said that large mutual-aid production groups tended
to be organized arbitrarily. Much more natural were the many small
groups that had arisen spontaneously in 1946, on the basis of mutual
interests recognized by friends and relatives. These successful nuclei
had been suddenly and mechanically enlarged when the Communist

Party of Lucheng County issued a call for organized production in 1947. In response to this call, people had flocked or been directed into one mutual-aid group or another on the basis of neighborhood propinquity alone. All other important criteria bearing on the ability of people to work together had been ignored. Once in a given aid group, families found it hard to get out. If they didn't get on well, no other group wanted them. Yet to go it alone was also impossible. They needed collective help and were willing to give as much as they received. Those who got along well together often discussed kicking out those families who made trouble, but it was difficult to do this without provoking hard feelings and a loss of face all around.

Many widows and old persons without labor power had also been included in the large aid groups. Instead of swapping services they simply paid for the work that was done for them. They could not and did not take an active part in the labor of the group; yet they came to meetings, often complained when operations were not performed to their complete satisfaction, and in general consumed time and made trouble. Those on whom the burden of labor fell resented being tied to such dependent persons unless they were their own close relatives.

A further important criticism of the aid groups as they existed was that they were over-organized. In the first flush of enthusiasm the elected leaders tried to plan everything from planting and harvesting, where collective work was most advantageous, to transport and manure collecting, where the benefits were minor or non-existent. Many peasants resisted such super-organization by not showing up for the assigned tasks.

Also pertinent were the grievances concerning the over-all purpose of mutual-aid and labor-exchange organizations. In the course of two years of operation, the aid groups had gradually assumed functions far beyond those for which they were originally designed. The village administration had fallen into the habit of using the aid groups as adjuncts of the government. Aid-group leaders were asked to administer rear service, take care of soldiers' dependents, give relief to widows and needy persons, and perform other welfare functions as well. When the county government called for men to carry stretchers or transport grain, the village head called in the mutual-aid-group leaders and parcelled out the tasks. What began as a voluntary association of peasants to swap labor in production thus grew into semi-official organs for carrying out government tasks, dispensing aid, and supervising aspects of life only vaguely connected with production. This was asking too much.

In spite of all these criticisms most people wanted to continue mutual-aid production. They envied the results achieved by those few groups that still functioned. Hsin-fa, the branch secretary, belonged to such a group. It consisted of eight able-bodied men who worked together constantly and led the village in crop production. These eight never had to settle wages among themselves because they did an equal amount of work for each other day after day. They exchanged labor, not millet, and boasted that they were the first to finish every seasonal job that came up. Model worker Yang Chung-sheng's group also functioned well. When the work team suggested that the best way to reorganize mutual-aid production in the village as a whole was to break up the larger groups and let every family choose new partners, this collective of 20 families refused to dissolve itself. It was examples such as this that kept the idea of labor exchange alive.

The Communist T'ien-hsi was enthusiastic about mutual aid even though his own group had not functioned well. "When we work together we get more done," he said. "Whenever I stay up late at a meeting I sleep through half the morning if the aid-group leader doesn't come to call me. And I get very discouraged whenever I have to go out all alone and face a big stretch of land. With others there to tackle the job, the work goes fast. We talk and laugh and keep each others spirits up."

T'ai-shan's mother, one of the leaders of the southwest section of the Peasants' Association and a very fast worker herself, agreed emphatically. "When I am alone in the field, I often look up and wonder if it is noon. But when we work together, noon comes and goes, and we don't even notice it. Soon the work is done."

Since the majority definitely wanted to continue mutual aid, the work team called on all the villagers to meet with the aid groups to which they had originally belonged and to reorganize in any way they thought best. During this reorganization they were urged to keep in mind the three basic principles for co-operation among peasant families laid down by Mao Tse-tung: 1) self-willingness; 2) equal exchange of labor and value; 3) democratic functioning. They were also warned against three common weaknesses pointed out by Mao: 1) mutual aid in everything; 2) large scale groups; 3) complicated organization.

Out of the reorganization, ten mutual-aid production groups embracing 65 families (approximately a quarter of the village population) came into being or were consolidated. Some of these groups united the most diverse elements, both politically and socially. The Communist Cheng-k'uan, the activist Yuan-lung, the dissident Hou Ken-ming, and the returned refugee Hou Chin-ming got together to set up a group. About the only thing they had in common, it seemed to me, was the fact that they had all once been Catholics.

Yu-lai, suspended vice-chairman of the old Peasants' Association, Li T'ung-jen, former puppet vice-leader of the village, Tseng Chung-hsi, former puppet village leader, Feng-le, an apolitical middle peasant, and Lai-so, a 15-year-old boy, formed another group. Here indeed was variety—a deposed tyrant, two ex-traitors, an honest independent peasant, and a teen-aged boy. Were they birds of a feather? What drew them together? It was hard to tell. Whatever it was, they seemed pleased to have found one another and met eagerly to draw up production plans for the coming weeks.

The new mutual-aid groups were officially established on July 12th, but when the Party branch met again on the 16th to review progress, it turned out that only seven of the ten were actually tilling land jointly. The others had met, gone to the fields together once or twice, and then ceased to function.

Militiaman Ta-hung said, "My people don't want to work together and help each other out. I can't do anything about it. I called a meeting, but very few came. So really there are only two families in my group."

"How can two be called a group?" asked Team Leader Ts'ai.

"That's the way it is. Chang Han-hsing and I work together, but of course in the last few days he has been hoeing and I have been gathering manure."

"So you really haven't helped each other at all?"

"That's right."

A poll of the Party members brought out the fact that only 11 of the 28 had joined any aid group at all. Obviously the Communists were not yet giving effective leadership, and Ts'ai Chin criticized them for this.

"We Communists must find solutions for every difficulty and lead the way to higher production; otherwise there will only be confusion," he warned.

Ts'ai's criticism only depressed the spirits of the branch members still further. Leading by suggestion and example was proving to be much more difficult than anyone had anticipated.

"Today our work is much more complicated than it used to be," commented the handsome Ch'un-hsi plaintively. "We have to do everything in such detail. Whenever we carry out a directive, we have to ask the people what they think about it. I keep thinking to myself, 'I don't want to work in this village any more.' "

"What do you want to do then?" asked Team Leader Ts'ai.

"I want to join the army and work with a big knife and a sharp axe."

Hsin-fa finally walked out of the meeting in disgust. "I have never taken part in such a tiresome, discouraging get-together," he said. "I don't know why it is. I guess it's because no one wants to be responsible for any kind of work. No one wants to shoulder the carrying pole. Whoever can avoid responsibility just stands to one side. As for me, when I'm tired I don't want to come to meetings. When I do come, I hope they will be over as soon as possible. Therefore, when we meet I always gripe and these gripes increase all the wrong tendencies in others."

At least Hsin-fa was learning to speak his mind. He no longer acted the part of the "hail fellow well met" for which he had been so severely criticized before the *gate.* In view of his past, this had to be interpreted as political progress.

With this meeting the work of the team reached an impasse. No amount of exhortation, discussion, self-and-mutual criticism, or evaluation of past mistakes seemed capable of changing the mood of the Communists. Their mood was, after all, only a concentrated reflection of the mood of the village as a whole. It was, more than anything else, a mood of frustration arising out of the lack of forward motion in village affairs. This in turn could be traced to the postponement of all final decisions concerning distribution, resettlement, and Party consolidation until after the establishment of the new village government.

In July 1948, the future hung strangely suspended. All the elements that must come together to mold it floated like detached ions in amorphous solution. They awaited the coming of that catalyst which alone could cause everything to crystallize—the elections which would determine the composition of the People's Congress.

60

The Village People's Congress

In the rural areas in the present period, we can and should, in accordance with the demands of the peasants, convene village peasant meetings to elect the village governments, and convene district peasant congresses to elect the district governments. Since the governments at or above the county or municipal level represent not only the peasants in the countryside but also people of all strata and occupations in the towns, county seats, provincial capitals, and big industrial and commercial cities, we should convene people's congresses at county, municipal, or border region levels to elect the governments at corresponding levels. In the future after the Revolution triumphs throughout the whole country, the central government and the local governments at all levels should be elected by the people's congresses at corresponding levels.

Mao Tse-tung, 1948

WHAT WAS a village People's Congress? What was the difference between the People's Congress that the work team proposed for Long Bow and the other mass organizations that already existed in the village? These were questions which the people had been asking ever since the idea of a Congress had been suggested. There was no need to speculate about the answers. Village People's Congresses already existed in many communities that had been liberated before 1945. Many full-time district cadres knew about such Congresses either from first-hand experience or from study and discussion. When they told the Long Bow peasants what such a Congress would be like in their village they described a political institution that already flourished in many parts of North China and had flourished in one form or another in various Liberated Areas in China since 1927.

The Chinese word for these Congresses was *jen min tai piao ta hui.* This may be literally translated as "people's representative large meeting" or "people's representative assembly." I use the word "congress" because that is the word that Ch'i Yun and Hsieh Hung used, because it is concise, and because it does, in fact, fit the case. A congress *is* a "people's representative large meeting."

The village People's Congress, as it developed in China in the

535

1940's, was a council of delegates periodically elected by all the enfranchised citizens of a given village. Once established, this Council or Congress assumed full responsibility for local affairs. It was recognized as the supreme organ of government at the village level both by the electorate below and regional administrators above. The Congress had the power to draft all village rules and regulations, to arbitrate all the village disputes, and to appoint all village officers from the village head to captain of the village militia and the village constable.* Once appointed, these officers administered the village in the name of the Congress, carried out all Congress decisions, and periodically reported to that body concerning their respective spheres of responsibility. Should they fail to perform their duties satisfactorily, they could be removed at any time by the Congress.

In theory the village People's Congress was distinguished from all other mass organizations or elected bodies in the village by its all-inclusive character. Membership in the Poor Peasants' League was limited to the landless and land poor, in the Peasants' Association to poor and middle peasants, in the Women's Association to women, in the Communist Party to those approved and accepted into the Party on the basis of very strict standards in regard to character, ability, and dedication to the cause of Communism. The People's Congress, on the other hand, was a body established to represent all the people included in the united front nationally.

In Chinese rural society of the 1940's there were many classes and groups in addition to the various strata of the peasantry. There were teachers, doctors, midwives, veterinarians, and apothecaries. There were such full-time workers as carpenters, masons, blacksmiths, and wheelwrights. There were fine craftsmen such as woodcarvers, straw weavers, tinsmiths, mat makers, and furniture builders. There were businessmen such as peddlers, storekeepers, innkeepers, cotton gin operators, wine makers, and millers. In order to establish stable, representative local governments, it was considered necessary to create a political form in which all these groups could be represented and have a voice.

The village People's Congress was that form. It was the political expression, at the grass-roots level, of the new democratic coalition in the nation as a whole, a coalition of all the allied classes, not just the peasants alone, a coalition that excluded only the enemies of the Revolution as defined by the Communist Party—the rich peasants,

---

* Ninety-nine percent of the disputes in any Chinese village could usually be settled by the village officers, or failing that, by the Village Congress. Only rarely was there a dispute so knotty that it had to be taken to the courts.

the landlords, and the bureaucratic capitalists of the Chiang-Kung-Soong-Ch'en clique.*

Because the congress form of delegated assembly was designed to reflect the new democratic class coalition, its organic structure was necessarily different from that of the various mass organizations, each of which represented only one class or group or at most an alliance between two related classes—i.e., the Peasants' Association which represented both poor and middle peasants. Members of these specialized mass organizations elected their representatives on a geographical basis. Peasants living in each sector of the village chose Peasants' Association committeemen from among their neighbors. A Peasants' Association committee was thus composed of representatives from all the neighborhoods that made up a given community. But geography was not the basis of the People's Congresses. They drew their delegates not primarily from neighborhoods but from interest groups, social strata, or classes. The merchants, regardless of residence, sent merchant delegates, the handicraft workers sent handicraft delegates, and the peasants sent peasant delegates. Wherever any large number of people in any one of these categories lived together in a homogeneous community, they did indeed choose individual delegates on a geographical basis as well, but the primary function of the Congress was to reflect interest groups, not sectional interests.

In such larger centers of population as Changchih and Lucheng and in the big commercial villages like East Portal where significant numbers of merchants and craftsmen congregated, the need for such all-inclusive delegated assemblies or congresses was clear. Only such an institution could draw into active political life the non-farming families who had been more or less passive observers of the land reform struggle or even victims of its excesses. Only such an institution could give them a voice and a vote.

But in villages such as Long Bow where the class structure had never been complex, the need for the congress form of representative assembly was not so clear. Not one family in Long Bow made a living primarily from professional work, trade, or handicraft production. Every carpenter, weaver, innkeeper, and peddler in the community

* Members of the rich peasant, landlord, and bureaucratic capitalist classes were deprived of citizenship rights, such as the right to elect and be elected, for an indefinite period after the completion of the land reform. After five years, if they had engaged in productive labor and proved themselves to be co-operative members of the community, they could apply for equal status and win reinstatement if the people considered them worthy of it. This was decided on an individual, not a mass basis, and it was the responsibility of the local Congress to decide each case on its merits.

owned land, raised crops, and considered himself to belong to one or another class of agricultural producer or peasant. The electoral basis for any People's Congress in Long Bow could not but coincide almost exactly with the membership of the Peasants' Association. Then why set up another organization? Why not just call the elected officers of the Peasants' Association the Long Bow People's Congress and turn the responsibility for local government over to the Peasants' Association Committee?

This was almost the solution proposed by the work team for Long Bow—almost, but not quite. The officers of the Peasants' Association could not call themselves a People's Congress because membership in the Peasants' Association was not universal. The Peasants' Association was a partisan class organization with certain self-determined membership standards. New members had to be approved by old members, and there were still more than a score of families in Long Bow who had not won such approval. These included those suspended cadres who had not yet passed the *gate* and all those individuals who, because of "rascal affairs" or past crimes had not yet been accepted as "honest and hardworking." All of these excluded persons were, nevertheless, citizens of the Border Region in good standing. They were neither landlords nor rich peasants, they had not been expropriated, and they had the right to vote. A government, as distinct from a mass organization, had to represent everybody legally entitled to citizenship rights. Hence even in Long Bow, where the peasants made up the whole population, the Peasants' Association could not, chameleon-like, convert itself into a People's Congress.

To many Long Bow residents this seemed a rather fine point. But the all-inclusive character of the village People's Congress was not, in the last analysis, determined by the needs of any given community but by the fact that these Congresses were part of a much wider scheme of government proposed by the Communist Party and accepted by the regional administrations as the goal of the future.

The village People's Congresses were conceived as part of a comprehensive system, as the base of a pyramid of representative Congresses which would eventually find its apex in a National Congress. County and Regional Congresses would make up the in-between layers. In 1948, this pyramid was only an edifice under construction. It had no apex because the Civil War still raged, the Revolution had not yet unified the country, and no national revolutionary government existed. Many sections of the pyramid's base were also blank because many villages had not completed land reform and had not had time to establish Village Congresses. As late as July 1948, Long Bow was still one of these blanks. County and Regional Congresses, the second and third levels of the pyramid, existed in most counties and in most regions of the Liberated Areas, but since these areas were expanding all the time, there were counties from which the Nationalist armed forces had only been expelled a few months or a few weeks. In such counties only temporary military governments or provisional councils appointed by the military or Communist Party leaders held power.

In order to imagine this situation the reader must imagine a countryside in flux with a vast variety of political situations existing side by side. In 1948, the subcontinent of China was divided roughly into two main parts, the Communist-led Liberated Areas of the North and the Kuomintang-administered areas of the South. But these major parts were not solid blocks of unbroken rule for either side. In South and Central China there were areas of liberated territory. In North, Northeast, and Northwest China there were connecting corridors under Nationalist control and also isolated islands where the Nationalist forces, though beseiged, still held out. For the most part the Liberated Areas were expanding, while the Nationalist-held corridors and islands were contracting or even disappearing. But within this general trend the opposite was also taking place. Areas once liberated by the People's Liberation Army were sometimes recaptured by the Nationalist Army. When this happened, the social revolution taking place there was crushed and all forms of popular rule were destroyed or driven underground. In this maelstrom of war and revolution there was, perhaps, no typical political situation but only a variety of disconnected political processes developing in time toward the same goal—a universal new political system centering around People's Congresses.

When completed, the pyramid would cover the nation with Congresses at four different levels. Since the delegates to each higher level would be chosen by the one below, this system would in form completely reverse China's traditional hierarchical rule. Under the traditional system all power centered formally in the Emperor (later in the dictator Chiang Kai-shek). This exalted personage appointed provincial governors who in turn appointed county magistrates, who in turn appointed village leaders, who in turn exercised powers of life and death over the independent proprietors, tenants, and landless laborers under their jurisdiction. The new system that was coming into being on the heels of land reform was just the opposite. In the new system all power formally resided in the people. They had the right to elect the governing bodies of their villages, the village People's Congresses, which in turn had the right to elect delegates to the Regional (later provincial) Congresses. Once the entire nation attained Liberation, these latter Congresses would join with the Congresses of the larger cities in electing delegates to a National Congress representing the people of all democratic classes, all regions, and all municipalities.*

Viewed from this perspective, the establishment of a People's Congress in Long Bow had double significance. On the one hand it would provide the village with a permanent structure capable of dealing with most problems, and on the other it would fill a gap in the political system of the Liberated Areas as a whole and constitute one more building block in the national political system of the future.

****

In Long Bow the birth of the village People's Congress was eagerly awaited. Under the regulations of the Draft Agrarian Law and the directives issued by the Border Region Government, only the Long Long Bow People's Congress could:

(1) Carry out the third and final classification of the village population.

(2) Take over whatever property the landlords and rich peasants still possessed, receive whatever property was to be returned by cadres who had taken an unfair share, and administer whatever property already belonged to the village as a whole.

(3) Make a final distribution of all such property, give out surplus lands, houses, equipment, furnishings, and livestock, and issue deeds for lands and houses.

(4) Set up a third and final *gate* for the approval or disapproval of all old cadres and Party members.

(5) Determine the allocation of taxes on the summer crop.

(6) Appoint permanent village officers and supervise their work.

(7) Elect delegates to the congress of the county.

Since all these problems were ripe for solution, the people were impatient to get on with the elections. But in this, as in so many other matters, the work team decided on a policy of patient education. Comrade Ts'ai wanted to prepare the ground well. He wanted to be sure that everyone understood the reasons for setting up a Congress, the basic principles of such a democratic government, the powers and responsibilities of its delegates and the officers appointed by them, and the powers and responsibilities of the electorate. He therefore delayed the elections for several days while the majority of the population discussed these questions. All those who were members of the

---

* Nationwide elections to the first National People's Congress were held in September 1954, six years after the events described in this book.

Peasants' Association discussed them in their sectional groups. Those who were not members formed a special group of their own.

I attended the discussions in the southwest corner of the village. There Ch'i Yun guided the deliberations. She explained the powers and functions of the People's Congress by comparing it to the board of a consumer co-operative society. The consumer co-operative societies that existed in so many villages were organized with a board of directors elected by the shareholders and a manager chosen by the board of directors. Every once in a while the directors met to examine how the manager was doing. This board looked into the balance sheet, examined the volume of business, totalled up the profits and the losses, and then gave instructions to the manager about taking better care of the business. Under the over-all supervision of this board, the manager and his staff did the day-to-day work of the co-operative, kept the accounts, ordered new goods, and cleaned up the building.

When the Congress idea was explained in this way, most of the peasants understood it quite well. Even though they had had little experience with democratic forms of government, they had all either participated in the organization of co-operatives or observed how they worked.

The first question which the peasants asked, once they grasped the essence of the idea, was, "What about the Communist Party in the village? Isn't the Communist Party the leader of the whole Revolution? If all village affairs are to be handled by a Congress, what is there for the Party to do?"

At a mass meeting of the full membership of the Peasants' Association Team Leader Ts'ai explained the role of the Communist Party in the reorganized village as follows:

The Long Bow People's Congress will be the highest authority in our community. The Communist Party members must obey the decisions of the Congress and carry them out. But at the same time the Communist Party branch must discuss and make up its own mind on all important issues before the Congress, bring its conclusions before the Congress and put them before the other delegates for approval. If the other delegates support these opinions, they will be carried out. If they oppose them, then the branch must reconsider and discuss the whole thing once more. If the branch still considers its judgments correct and the Congress delegates still disagree, then the branch can take the question to higher Party bodies. But even if the latter agree with the branch, they cannot recommend that the Congress be overridden. They can only advise the local Party branch to persist, make further explanations, carry on education on the issue, and wait for agreement in the future. As for the Congress, it has its own higher body, the People's Congress of Lucheng County. This is made up of delegates from similar village congresses all over the county. In case there are serious disagreements, which, in spite of the procedures outlined, cannot be settled in the village, they can be carried to higher bodies for final disposition by both sides.

Thus, as Comrade Ts'ai explained it, the Communist Party in contrast to the People's Congress, was not in a position to exercise state power in any form. It could only persuade and set an example. There was nothing to prevent people from electing Communists as delegates to the Long Bow Congress, but no Communist could have more power there than any other delegate. Communists could exert leadership only through their own unity and their ability to come up with solutions to difficult problems that won majority support.

The leading role of the Communists, in other words, depended not on coercion, not on special powers, but on education, persuasion, and the active participation of all its members in the daily affairs of the village. In the long run, the ability of local Communists to lead depended first on demonstrably correct policies and second on the prestige based on merit and performance of its individual members, on the extent to which they took an active part in all mass organizations and led by example, educated others day by day and hour by hour, and proved themselves to be more selfless, more devoted, and more principled than ordinary people.

This question of prestige was a complicated one because, although the Party tried to recruit into its ranks only the most active, the most resourceful, and the most devoted peasants, there was always the possibility that the over-all prestige of the Party might rub off on members who did not in fact deserve it and give to their words and their opinions a weight that their personal qualities did not justify.

In fact, of course, this did occur. Whether a local Party branch was good or bad, the national prestige of the Party made its opinions important to all non-Party cadres, the elected delegates of the people, and the people as a whole. Whenever a new problem arose, the first thing the peasants wanted to know was, "What does the Party have to say?" For many, the fact that the Party spoke was enough to win their support. And because this was so, all Party members bore a heavy responsibility. They did in fact carry more weight than they would have as unconnected individuals, and the necessity for thinking things through and being right was therefore all the more urgent.

****

As the peasants in their neighborhood groups of the Association discussed the role of the Party in the village as a whole and its relationship to the coming Congress, they also discussed the question of democracy. What did the word mean? Was democracy the same thing as license?

Some said, "I have democracy now so I don't have to go to any meetings; I can do just as I please." But others criticized them sharply. Such an attitude was wrong, they said. In order to carry out democracy one must have meetings, consult together, and make good plans to protect and promote the interests of the people. It was not democracy to refuse to do what the majority had decided. It was just using the word as an excuse for wrongdoing. Democracy meant to carry out what was of benefit to the majority, not to act in the interest of any single person. Perhaps the good results of democratic decisions could not be seen in a few days, but after several months or several years the benefits would certainly become clear.

In order to guarantee the effectiveness of majority decisions, some peasants wanted to set up a "system"—that is, a set of rules. They wanted to criticize and, if need be, punish those who did not come to meetings in the future. Others said no. They held that this was a matter of conscience and maintained that it was no use punishing people for political apathy. Everyone must be convinced from within. Unless discipline was self-imposed, there could be no democracy at all.

Neither of these views was accepted as the final answer to the question of freedom versus control. While agreeing that on the whole people must act from conscious positive motives, the majority insisted that those few who did not co-operate and refused to carry their share of such common burdens as taxes, rear service, and attendance at meetings, should be criticized. "We should ask them to speak out their thoughts in public and help them to think it through. If they don't want any of the responsibilities, then they shouldn't get any of the benefits. Ask them to go and live by themselves. Let them plant their own corn alone, and if they have problems let them solve them themselves. Don't let them come to us for help, for in their own minds they are not members of this village." So spoke Old Tui-chin, the bachelor who was the recognized spokesman for the northern group.

"After all," added Ch'ung-lai's wife, in behalf of the eastern group, "no one can live in isolation. Everyone lives by co-operation and mutual aid. Husband and wife have to consult together and no one can till the land completely alone."

****

On July 21st, elections to the Village People's Congress finally took place. Thirty-five people were elected—16 women and 19 men. Among them were nine old middle peasants, 25 newly *fanshened*

poor peasants (now called new-middle-peasants), and one poor peasant. Of the 35 delegates, eight, or less than 25 percent, were Communist Party members. These included four men: former Peasants'
Association chairman Cheng-k'uan; branch secretary Hsin-fa; militiaman Ta-hung; and the 39-year-old middle peasant, Meng Fu-lu. The
other four Communists were women: chairman of the Women's Association, Hu Hsueh-chen; vice chairman Wang An-feng; and two
housewives, Shih Hsiu-mei and Jen Ho-chueh, the latter the wife of the
Communist Hsiao Wen-hsu. Another four delegates were wives,
mothers, or brothers of Party members. These were Ta-hung's wife,
Chou Cheng-lo's mother, Kuei Ts'ai's mother, and Ts'ai-yuan's
youngest brother, Pu-yuan.

The other 23 delegates to the People's Congress were rank-and-file
peasants with no direct or indirect ties to the Communist Party. They
were chosen by their neighbors because of the role they had played
in village affairs since the work team arrived in March. Outstanding
among them were Old Tui-chin, a bachelor and a worker in the wine
plant who was still classed as a poor peasant, the ex-hired laborer Shen
Fa-liang, and the ex-beggar, Ch'ung-lai's wife, both new-middle-
peasants whose life stories have been related in Chapter 3. Wu-k'uei's
wife, a woman sold three times under the old regime; Old Lady Wang,
the peppery weaver; Li Lao-szu, the doleful wasteland pioneer; Kuo
Yuan-lung, a young activist and former Catholic from the southwest
section; and the widow, T'ai-shan's mother, the hardest working
woman in the whole village, also won places on the list of outstanding
people elected to the Congress.

Old Shen's Catholic clique won no recognition at all. That gar-
rulous old schemer's following collapsed completely soon after the
ex-bandit Yu-lai and his son Wen-te bowed their heads before the
gate.

Viewed from any perspective, this was a very strong Congress. It
was not exactly a cross-section of the village, but rather a selection
of the best the village had produced. There was no doubt in anyone's
mind that the most active, the most trusted, the most brilliant and
hard-working individuals in the community had been chosen as its
leaders.

When the results of the election were announced and the list of
names posted, the population greeted the news with smiles and enthusiastic comment. A fresh breath of optimism seemed to sweep
through the muddy lanes and back alleys of Long Bow. The delegates
were congratulated at every turn as they went about their business.
The cadres of the work group were as pleased as the villagers. They
made a special point of visiting all the delegates in their homes in order
to welcome them to the Congress.

When the 35 delegates met for the first time, they elected a standing committee of five that was outstanding in character and ability. It was composed of four Party members, Cheng-k'uan and Hsin-fa (male) and Hu Hsueh-chen and An-feng (female), and one non-Party delegate, Old Tui-chin. Cheng-k'uan was elected chairman and Tui-chin vice chairman.

The next order of business was the selection of the village administration. Ch'un-hsi, the incumbent, who had held the post temporarily ever since passing the *gate* in April, was unanimously chosen to continue as village head. A second Party member, Shih Szu-har, was appointed captain of the militia to succeed the discredited Hung-er. The other five positions—assistant village head, education director, treasurer, production officer, and rear service officer—were filled by the appointment of non-Party people, two of whom were Congress delegates. The bull-headed middle peasant, Chang Chin-hung, treasurer of the village since its liberation in 1945, was again chosen for this task. Everyone admired his facility with figures and his hard business sense.

Once the delegates agreed on who should fill these posts, they called in those new appointees not already present, informed each about his or her new job and then asked each to make a statement of attitude. All vowed to work hard and do their best to represent the interests of the village as a whole.

The atmosphere of this Congress meeting was relaxed and friendly. Everyone seemed relieved to have a democratically chosen village administration at last, and they talked over the problems that confronted them as old friends. Tension and antagonism seemed to have vanished, at least for the time being.

On the following day, July 23rd, a mass meeting of the whole village was held in the wine plant. There, safe from summer showers, the new administration was formally inaugurated with appropriate banners, slogans, and speeches. This time the celebration, because it was no empty formality but a genuine turning point in the people's lives, engendered real enthusiasm. Long Bow village had entered a new era in its turbulent life.

****

Perhaps the most notable action taken by the village as it created the People's Congress was the vote that plucked Old Tui-chin from the obscurity which had enveloped him for more than 50 years and placed him in the post of vice chairman, second most important position in the whole village. Submerged, oppressed, and disregarded throughout most of his life, Tui-chin never had a chance to demonstrate anything but a capacity for hard labor until the land division laid the foundation for equality of opportunity. Once this took place, he moved to the fore in village life. In this respect, he was typical of the kind of indigenous leaders that the Chinese peasantry constantly thrust onto the stage in those years. As one mass movement followed another, wider and wider circles of formerly voiceless and passive victims of the system were drawn into active political life and demonstrated talents the existence of which they had never suspected.

Old Tui-chin had an open round face, well tanned by the sun and ever ready to break into a cheerful smile. Wrinkles spread from the corners of his eyes and furrowed his broad forehead. A scraggly beard, never more than a finger's width in length adorned his jaw and chin. It constituted the only disorderly thing about the man. Everything else, from the towel on his shaven head to the cloth straps that bound his trouser cuffs to his ankles, was meticulously arranged. His clothing, even though faded, patched and patched again, was always clean.

When the work team arrived in March, few people knew much more about the old man than his name. Within a few weeks he had been elected vice-leader of the northern group of the Poor Peasants' League. With each mass meeting and each crisis, his prestige grew in his own section of the village, but it was not until the policy change initiated by the County Conference that he became well known to the community as a whole. The policy change made Tui-chin a village figure because he, and he alone among the poor peasants, had all along maintained that most of the village cadres were good leaders, that there was very little property still to be distributed, and that political *fanshen*, elections, meetings, and the establishment of the People's Congress were just as important as millet. He took it for granted that Long Bow's people should solve their problems themselves and that they should do it democratically through mass participation in village affairs.

Old Tui-chin was able to see what others missed because he looked at the world with relative objectivity. Not consumed by self-interest, he was apparently content to go on living just as he had, with a simple clay roof over his head and an acre of land under his feet. He had no personal ambitions, burdens, or problems that he could not solve. He was, therefore, calm, seasoned, and reflective, a person of great equanimity to whom others quite naturally brought their quarrels and difficulties.

Circumstances no doubt helped Tui-chin maintain this objectivity. He had no wife and no children of his own. Although he was responsible for the upbringing of his nephew's daughter, the little six-year-old was not a serious drain on his resources. Her company enlivened his life. Already past 50, a venerable age in rural China, he was not torn by passion for some woman not his wife and hence was free of the scandal and gossip that dogged the steps of many a younger man.

Old Tui-chin's admirable objectivity had survived some rather severe tests in the past. The Liberation had not been an unmixed blessing to him, and if he had wished to make an issue out of personal injury as so many other villagers had done, he had the grounds to do so. In the days when the Eighth Route Army and the Lucheng County Militia overwhelmed the Japanese and puppet garrisons of the Fifth District, Old Tui-chin was living several miles from Long Bow in a village called Changkechuang. Here he shared a house with his nephew, the puppet village leader. When the militia entered the village, they arrested the puppet leader and confiscated all his personal property. Included in the confiscated property were Tui-chin's entire possessions. When the nephew was later released, he ran away, leaving his three-year-old daughter and Old Tui-chin behind. He never came back. He never even sent word as to his whereabouts.

Old Tui-chin returned to Long Bow with absolutely nothing he could call his own except the clothes on his back. In Long Bow he still owned an acre of land, the remainder of his father's holdings after the Japanese built their blockhouse on the property. In the distribution he received three sections of a tumbledown house, a few clothes, and a bag or two of grain. This accounted for the fact that he was the only delegate to the Congress still classed as a poor peasant. Yet he nursed no rancor toward anyone. When asked about his attitude he told Ch'i Yun: "As for me, I received housing, clothes, and grain. No one dares to treat me ill or oppress me as the puppet troops did. My life is much better than before. As for the rest of the peasants, they are all better off. If they lacked land, they got it. If they lacked housing, they got it, and the same went for animals, carts, and tools. But still some cranks are dissatisfied with their condition. What they want is just to sit home and eat. But how can the food go trotting into one's mouth? Everyone must labor. That is our duty."

Perhaps the fact that Old Tui-chin had been a wage laborer most of his life had something to do with his advanced outlook. When he was 16 he began a nine-year job as a year-round hired man for a landlord. Then, after three years selling wine on the road as a peddler, he went to work in the local distillery owned by Fan Pu-tzu. For 23 years he labored as a distillery hand, rising before dawn to stoke the fires and quitting only after dark when the plant shut down for the night. This was a kind of life and a kind of discipline that few peasants knew. Perhaps it had instilled in Old Tui-chin some of the steadfastness, some of the toughness, and some of the selfless objectivity of the true proletarian.

61

A Final Determination

The land problem should be considered solved and the question of land reform should not be raised again in areas where the feudal system has been fundamentally abolished, where the poor peasants and farm laborers have all acquired roughly the average amount of land, and where there is still a difference (which is permissible) between their holdings and those of the middle peasants, but where the difference is not great.

Mao Tse-tung, 1948

ON JULY 23, 1948, the newly elected People's Congress met to make a final determination of the class status of every family in the community. The new appraisal of the *fanshen* situation which the work team brought back from the second County Conference had a very definite influence on the proceedings. The Congress delegates accepted the view that feudal property had, in the main, been expropriated, and that the poor peasants had, in the main, *fanshened*. They were therefore very strict in once again judging every family previously classed as poor. This trend, which first developed during the second classification in June, became the dominant feature of the final classification in July. Any family that possessed an average amount of land to till and a roof over its head was considered to have *fanshened* and was accordingly classed as a family that had achieved new-middle-peasant status.

A summary of the three *bangs,* or stages of classification, clearly showed the trend (see opposite page).

The table shows little if any change in the classification of families in the higher brackets but a marked change in the classification of families in the lower brackets. Whereas 95 families were still considered poor in May, only 28 were so regarded in July. Whereas only 68 poor peasants were thought to have *fanshened* in May, 136, or exactly twice the number, were considered to have done so in July.

When the list was posted, a number of poor peasants who had been upgraded to the status of new-middle-peasants protested, but on the whole the people were well satisfied. The final classification reflected reality. It provided a basis for settling, once and for all, the land question. It enabled everyone to get on with production.

	1st *Bang* (May)	2nd *Bang* (June)	3rd *Bang* (July)
Poor peasant	95	57	28
Handcraft worker	1	1	—
New-middle-peasant	68	105	136
Old-middle-peasant	64	64	65
Rich-middle-peasant	7	8	8
Rich peasant	4	4	4
Landlord	1	1	1
	240	240	242 *

With the final classification the Long Bow Congress not only solved this major *fanshen* problem, but it also solved many minor problems concerning the class status of households with mixed incomes. The most difficult case left over from the past was that of Wang Ch'ang-yi, the professional castrator. Although he had already been dead six months, it was still necessary to classify his household on the basis of its economic status during the base period years 1942–1945. While he lived, Wang Ch'ang-yi went out every day with his veterinary kit and earned money cutting pigs. At the same time, his family at home hired labor to till land holdings that were twice as large as the average in Long Bow.

Was Wang Ch'ang-yi an exploiter, a craftsman, or a free professional? Was he a landlord, a rich peasant, or a middle peasant? What proportion of his income did he earn? How much of it came from exploitation?

The Congress finally solved this problem by dividing the Wang family income into two parts—on one side they placed Wang Ch'ang-yi, the veterinarian, and his personal earnings; on the other side they placed Wang Ch'ang-yi's family, the landowners, and their earnings from exploitation. Wang was given a personal class as a craftsman, and everything relating to his craft, from the instruments to the income, was considered to be legitimate property not subject to confiscation. The family as a whole, however, was classed with the rich peasants. Its surplus land, tools, housing, etc., were made subject to confiscation. Thus a fine line was drawn between the gentry as exploiters and the gentry as professionals. The same line was applicable

* Between the second and third *bang* two families divided and set up new households. The table includes only families with members still living in Long Bow. Of the original seven landlord families, only one had remaining members. Of the original five rich peasant families, four had remaining members.

to all rich peasants or landlords who taught school, practiced medicine, or performed any other kind of service for pay.

This concept of personal classification being distinct from that of the family as a whole helped to solve other vexing problems. Huan-ch'ao, the blacksmith, for instance, was called a handicraft laborer, but his family was put in the new-middle-peasant category on the strength of its landholdings, housing, and implements. The same occurred in the case of the carpenter Li Ho-jen, the weaver Wang Kuei-pao, and several others.

****

Once the class status of every family in the village had been determined, it was possible to look back on the whole process of land reform since 1945, and on its various stages. The table on page 592 may serve as a summary of this process. What was finally revealed with striking clarity by these figures was the extent of the damage done to middle peasants by the leftism of the first post-war years. In the winter of 1946, middle peasants as a class lost 66 acres of land, 12 draft animals, and considerable quantities of grain. By the time the May 4th Directive had been fully implemented they had lost another ten acres of land and several head of livestock. Actual losses were more serious than these figures revealed because in these over-all totals the land and livestock gained by certain middle peasant families cancelled out the losses sustained by other less fortunate families. A breakdown showed that 21 out of 64 middle peasant families lost almost 100 acres of land, even though 16 others gained 23 acres. It was the losses of the 21 that explained the prevalence of "chive cutting thought" in 1946-1947 and the reluctance of so many middle peasants to meet or to become active.

All these difficulties arose because the expropriation movement had gone too far, broadened its target too much, called middle peasants rich peasants and rich peasants landlords, and had stripped them all of their property.

Once this situation was revealed by the final classification, the next step was to correct the errors. Those who had been stripped had to be resettled, those who should never have been attacked had to be repaid. But first, all the property available for resettlement and repayment had to be assembled and put at the disposal of the Congress.

62

The Midnight Raid

The main factor in eliminating the landlord class and in wiping out the feudal system is the confiscation for distribution to the peasantry of the lands, grains, plow animals, agricultural implements, and such properties owned by the landlord class, together with the rich peasants' surplus possessions. The most basic of all is land distribution. We should not consume much time seeking out hidden wealth and should not keep the movable possessions that have been confiscated for long without distributing them.

Jen Pi-shih, 1948

IN RURAL CHINA, night possesses an absolute quality long absent in the industrialized West. This, as least, was the case before the transformation of the Chinese countryside by co-operatives and communes. At night everyone went early indoors. If they lit any lamp at all, it was but a twist of cotton in a cup of vegetable oil. The wavering flame thus created pushed back the darkness only a few feet. The glow could hardly be detected beyond the paper windows; and since all windows opened on courtyards that were in turn surrounded by walls, no light at all was visible from the far side of these walls. This meant that as night fell, complete and utter darkness descended upon the land. All human activity out of doors ceased. To wander in the countryside after dark was to wander in the atmosphere of an enormous universal graveyard in which there was no light at all except that which came from the sky. When clouds covered the sky, the darkness could be overwhelming, frightening, primitive in its totality, like a return to the primeval fen before men discovered fire. Little wonder that people feared the dark, believed in ghosts and conjured up all manner of awesome spirits to rule the earth and air. The ever recurring contrast between darkness and light, light and darkness as the world revolved made real and palpable the ancient, cosmic struggle between the *yin* and the *yang*, the black and the white, the female and the male, the evil and the good.

At the nadir of one of the blackest of all nights, I found myself groping my way through the soft mud that the June flood had deposited in the courtyard of Widow Yu Pu-ho's house. All around me

other figures advanced toward the widow's door. Scarcely visible
though they were in the gloom, they nevertheless made their presence
known by muttered curses. Each time a cloth shoe sank in the ooze
or a shin knocked against one of the scattered obstacles on the ground
its owner involuntarily swore under his breath.

A long shed that had once flanked the west side of the yard had
collapsed during the flood. Timbers and piles of straw-matted adobe
lay in scattered heaps on the ground. The whole area smelled of
dampness and mold, a background odor that seemed to sharpen rather
than deaden the occasional whiff of truly rotten matter from an
overflown cistern that assailed the nostrils of our nocturnal raiding
party.

The group around me was made up of members of the standing
committee of the Long Bow People's Congress, several newly appointed village officials, the cadres of the work team, and several
armed militiamen. They were advancing across that courtyard in
the middle of the night in order to take Yu Pu-ho by surprise.

In the final *bang* the lusty widow had been classed as a rich peasant. The list was to be posted the next morning. By that time it
would certainly be too late to seize the wealth of the only gentry
family in the village that had never been touched. Even a raid such
as this, carried out the night before, might well prove useless, for
neighbors had reported strange doings in the flood-damaged courtyard. Relatives of the widow and her daughter, Pu-ch'ao, had been
coming and going at odd hours for weeks. Boxes had been carted
away in the night. Perhaps the bulk of the family's possessions had
already been dispersed. To wait until the lists were posted would
only insure that the dispersal was complete. The Congress, after making a final differentiation of the widow's class, had voted to register
everything she owned before she had a chance to learn her fate.

No one doubted that Yu Pu-ho, despite her modest dwelling place,
had wealth. The peasants recalled the elaborate wedding she had
arranged for her daughter and the lavish funeral she had given her
departed husband. On the latter occasion, the coffin had been transported inside a glass case that was supported by 16 people instead
of the usual eight. All the members of the family had worn fine things,
gowns of silk and coats of fur. Where were these costly garments
now? And where was the gold that represented the savings of several
generations of exploiters and the accumulated labor of several generations of the exploited? People asked each other such questions because they feared the worst. The old widow was cunning, no doubt
about that, and the most cunning trick of all had been to marry off
her daughter to a poor peasant, a soldier in the People's Liberation

Army. Since Pu-ch'ao had already been wed three years she was classed as poor and a soldier's dependent to boot, even though she lived in her mother's house and ate and dressed like one of the gentry. As a poor peasant she was entitled to attend all village meetings, study classification procedures, and carry back to her mother all the knowledge she picked up. Forewarned was forearmed. Only a fool would sit there month after month waiting for the axe to fall. But until the widow's class was settled, the government and the Communist Party forbade any move against her. The frustrated cadres had no choice but to carry on the step-by-step program called for in the Border Region directives, even though they knew full well that Yu Pu-ho could easily outwit them before her fate was finally decided. No doubt her daughter had told her that beatings were no longer allowed, that force was taboo, and that no time would be wasted looking for buried treasure. Goods once hidden need never be revealed. All this explained why, once Yu Pu-ho was declared to be a rich peasant, the Congress decided on immediate action.

The delegation that moved out in the middle of the night to register and seal the widow's property was divided into three groups. One, made up entirely of women, was designated to find and interrogate Yu Pu-ho's much abused daughter-in-law, the bride of her soldier son, Yu Jen-ho. The women thought that the girl, a poor peasant by origin, might well reveal the family secrets without any urging. A second group, led by Cheng-k'uan, the Congress chairman, was dispatched to the home of Yu Pu-ho's poor peasant lover, Wang-er. It was only logical to suppose that he had already hidden valuable things for his beloved mistress. A third group under the leadership of Hsin-fa, secretary of the village Party branch, undertook to handle the widow herself. Hsieh and I joined the latter.

The tall Hsin-fa reached the widow's door first. He pounded on it with his fist, raising enough thunder to awaken the dead.

"Come in, please come in," said Yu Pu-ho in a loud voice. As she spoke she pulled back the wooden bolt and flung the door wide open.

Obviously the visit came as no surprise. Behind the widow a light was burning. It silhouetted a figure made comically bulky by layer after layer of padded clothing. This was topped off by a patched black smock. Strange outfit for so warm a night! The widow's round, usually smooth face was furrowed with anxiety, but she pretended a hearty welcome as she talked without pause in a tone sweet with assumed geniality.

"Here, sit on the *k'ang*. It's muddy out there, I know," she volunteered as we filed silently past her into the cavernous dark dwelling.

"A terrible thing the waters did. Knocked my shed down. I have nothing to rebuild with. That's right. Make yourselves comfortable. Pu-ch'ao, go fetch some bricks so that they can all sit down. We don't have much furniture. Our home has no luxuries—as you can see. No luxuries."

I found myself wishing that she would stop talking. What did she expect to gain by it, the crafty old schemer? She only revealed her nervousness. Pu-ch'ao, by contrast, was as calm and cool as a river reed growing by the banks of the Ssa Ho. She stood in the shadow by the door and did not say a word.

The widow half leaned, half sat on the edge of the *k'ang*. Her hands, fumbling with the hem of her black smock, twitched. Suddenly she stood up, walked a few steps on her disfigured bound feet, and sat down again.

The great size of the widow's house only emphasized its drab emptiness. From its gloomy depths came the same moldy smell that rose from the courtyard outside. The single oil lamp, set on a wooden chest beside the north wall of the room, cast a flickering glow that showed up by turns the smoke-blackened ceiling overhead, the battered *k'ang* along the east wall, and the spacious chamber to the west. Only a thin reed mat and two faded cotton quilts covered the *k'ang*. In the whole west wing the alert and roving eyes of the widow's many visitors could detect only a large wooden box, some rolls of reed matting, an earthen jar, a few bowls, a mirror, and a brush. In the middle of the floor, in forlorn isolation, stood an old wooden armchair. Its black stain had been polished until it glistened by generations of use.

Hsin-fa's newly shaven head reflected the light from the lamp almost as brightly as did the arm of the chair.

"Yu Pu-ho," he announced in as stern a voice as he could muster, "you have been classed as a rich peasant. You have the right to appeal. If you lose the appeal, your things must be given up. We have come to register them. If you speak honestly, all will go well with you."

He took a brush, an ink plate, and a long piece of paper out of his pocket. As the party secretary rubbed the black ink stick over the plate, Yu Pu-ho said, "I won't appeal. I know I am a rich peasant."

"Very well," said Hsin-fa. "We'll start with the grain."

"There's no corn left. I have one bag of millet and three bags of wheat," said the widow in a tone of finality as if she were bargaining at the market place.

"Only three bags?"

"That's all. I used the corn to pay the hired laborer. As for the wheat, we've eaten a bag and a half already. We have only three bags left."

Hsin-fa recorded this, then spoke to Militiaman Ta-hung: "Now for the furniture and the clothes."

Ta-hung rummaged through the west wing. The butt of his rifle thumped on the brick floor as he called out the various articles that he saw. From a box in the corner he took out a bundle of clothes and untied it.

"A pair of silk pants, a padded coat, several dirty tunics."

He threw them down on top of the chest with a gesture of disgust. Everyone knew the widow owned better things than these.

Hsin-fa wrote each item in large clumsy characters.

"Those clothes belong to Pu-ch'ao," said the widow.

"How about the pants?"

"They belong to Pu-ch'ao also."

"Now see here," said Hsin-fa, putting down his brush and looking straight into the widow's face. "You are a rich peasant. You have lived off the blood and sweat of the people long enough. We know you have a great many things. Where are they? If you are not honest with us, you can imagine what will happen to you."

The widow laughed a nervous little laugh but still maintained her cordial manner. Even at 40 she had an attractive face. It was not wrinkled and worn like the faces of most peasant women once they passed their third decade. Her plump hands spread out in a gesture of helplessness as she explained in a torrent of words how the Japanese had ruined her. "They took everything. That's how the devils were. When they saw something they liked, it went.

"I know I must pay my debt to the masses," she continued after a slight pause for breath. "I should have paid it long ago. Today is my day to ask pardon. But really I have nothing. I would like to give up everything, but since I have nothing I can't help you."

"You'd better be honest."

"I am honest. What I have I have. What I haven't got I haven't got."

"How many things have you hidden away? How many things have you stored in other peoples' homes? You'd better remember and tell us."

"There's nothing. How could I overlook a thing like that?" Tears of sincerity came to her eyes as she said it.

"How many jars have you?"

"Only one. The other broke when the shed fell down."

At this everyone laughed.

"How can that be?" asked Hsin-fa, cutting short his own involuntary guffaw. "No matter how poor, every family has jars for its grain."

"We keep ours in a *tun*" (a container made of fiber that wealthy families sometimes used).

Hsin-fa, having lost a round, said no more. He proceeded with his list.

The door swung open. Hu Hsueh-chen and her group filed in in silence. The daughter-in-law, pale and frightened, followed. She had not been able to tell them anything. She did not know whether or not property had been hidden. She rarely stayed with the widow if she could help it, for she was treated worse than a servant in her husband's house.

Cheng-k'uan's group stomped in next. By the time they had all crowded into the house there was hardly room enough inside for anyone to move around. The new arrivals were angry and showed it. They had searched Wang-er's house and yard in vain. Man-hsi, the man of action, his gun slung rakishly over one shoulder, his great muscles bulging under his coat, strode up and down the floor like a caged tiger. As he walked he muttered to himself, "The bastards! They have hidden everything! They ought to be whipped! The bastards!"

Man-hsi's face was contorted into a black scowl and it was only by an extreme effort that he kept his hands at his sides instead of using them to rough up the widow.

When Yu Pu-ho stood up to uncover a box that Ta-hung had overlooked, Man-hsi's hands betrayed him. He ordered the widow to stand back. When she didn't move quickly enough to suit him he gave her a push that sent her reeling against the *k'ang*. Ch'i Yun looked at him in astonishment. Man-hsi reddened and pulled back. Then, overcome with frustration and unwilling to listen further to the stream of words that poured from the widow's mouth, he suddenly disappeared into the night. He returned a few minutes later with a rope which he waved in front of the plump rich peasant's face.

"Tell the truth now, where is the grain? Don't tell me you have only three bags left!"

"That's all," she said, ignoring the rope. "There isn't anything else."

With a shrug, Man-hsi dropped the rope.

Cheng-k'uan, accepting the inevitable, took the writing brush from Hsin-fa and started listing the farm tools that his crew reported from the fallen shed in the yard—a plow, two hoes, a rake, a broken sifter screen—really, there was nothing worth while in the whole establishment.

Hsin-fa, temporarily relieved of his duties as clerk, led Pu-ch'ao, the daughter, outside. He wanted to question her in private. He had once carried on an affair with this girl. He more than anyone else was responsible for the fact that accounts had never been settled with her mother. Perhaps she would tell him things she would not reveal to others.

The attempt was vain. Pu-ch'ao backed up her mother's every word. Neither of them, she said, had hidden anything that the village could claim.

As Pu-ch'ao reassured Hsin-fa, Militiaman T'ien-hsi strode past them with a bundle of clothes under his arm.

"Old Wang finally broke down. He gave me this. They belong to the old bitch," he said, triumphant.

He kicked the front door open with his foot. It flew back with a loud crash. Hsin-fa and Pu-ch'ao followed him into the house.

The bundle found by T'ien-hsi contained a few fine silk garments and a lot of worn cottons. Not in the least embarrassed by the appearance of articles which she had just sworn did not exist, Pu-ch'ao spoke up.

Defiant in the dim light, she looked more attractive than I had ever seen her. She stood like some mystic creation from a cave painting, but her eyes blazed with hatred and her mouth was tight, like the mouth of a fox spirit in a legend of old.

"The clothes are mine," she said. "If you don't believe me, see if they fit me or not!"

This then was the trick! Mother and daughter had altered all the fine clothes so that Pu-ch'ao alone could claim them. Even the work team cadres were angered. They began to wish, along with Man-hsi and T'ien-hsi, that the no-beating policy could be suspended for at least this one night. Then Pu-ch'ao would never dare to challenge them as she was doing.

"Don't think that because you are classed a poor peasant that you can commit a crime and oppose the Agrarian Law," warned Ch'i Yun. "I think you can well remember what happened to 'air raid shelters' who protected landlords in the past. If the masses get angry with you, no one can guarantee your safety."

But Pu-ch'ao was as impervious to threats as to earnest persuasion. She continued to lie, complain, and remonstrate just as her mother had taught her.

****

One by one the cadres and the members of the Congress Committee drifted out the widow's door. They left behind only one armed man to watch the "struggle objects." The rest of the raiding party gathered by the edge of the village pond. There they consulted, broke up, and consulted once again. Now this one left to investigate some hitherto forgotten cranny; now that one went to rouse a neighbor and seek an answer to some hitherto unthought of query. But always the group reconvened. The frustration that oppressed all spirits was as thick as the damp black night itself.

"They won't talk, that's plain," said Hsin-fa. "And we can't beat them. They know that. That's why they talk back so sharply. It's no use trying to bluff them either."

"That's right," said K'uan-hsin, a militiaman almost as well known for physical prowess as Man-hsi. "But if we hung them both up and gave them a good thrashing we'd find plenty of wealth soon enough."

"It was because we fought so fiercely that we got our nicknames in the past," said Man-hsi. "But if we hadn't been tough, we never would have won."

"That's true," said Hsin-fa. "And the people still expect us to bring out the goods. Where property is at stake Man-hsi suddenly becomes a hero again."

"But we're not allowed to beat people, so what's the use of talking about it?" said Ch'i Yun.

"We aren't allowed to beat her; very well then, tie her up and throw her in the pond," said Man-hsi. "Let her drink some good ditch water. Then everything will spill out. We are just wasting our time this way. If this were the year of Liberation, ten rich peasant bastards would have been beaten to death by this time."

Hu Hsueh-chen backed Man-hsi up. So did An-feng. Neither of these two rough-hewn women could stand the sight of the widow or her daughter.

Thus encouraged, Man-hsi started for the house. Two or three militiamen made ready to follow. Just in time, Hsin-fa took the men aside and told them bluntly that under the new code drowning was no more acceptable than beating.

"Then we're beaten," said Hu Hsueh-chen, and as she said it she choked back tears.

The group leaders finally decided that the widow, her lover, and her daughter must find guarantors to vouch for their behavior until the investigation into the extent of their property had been completed. In spite of the lateness of the hour, neighbors were roused and individuals found who agreed to keep an eye on all three. The women's reluctant guarantor undertook to keep the daughter in the house if the mother went out and vice versa. He also undertook to see that neither of them left the village.

With this matter settled, Hsin-fa and Cheng-k'uan returned to the widow's cavernous home. They sealed everything that had been registered. They pasted strips of paper across every box and jar and wrote in black ink down the middle of the strips, "Sealed, by order of the People's Congress, July 25, 1948." They left open only one bag of millet.

"That ought to keep the family until we decide what else is due them," said Hsin-fa.

The placing of the seals completed the night's work. The raiders slipped quietly off to bed, very much aware that they had met with a resounding defeat.

Only Ch'i Yun seemed happy. As we made our way back to the district compound in the semi-darkness before dawn she said to Hsieh and me:

"That was a good night's work."

"How come?" I asked. "I thought everybody felt cheated."

"They did, but they stuck to the policy."

"What do you mean?"

"Didn't you notice Man-hsi? He was aching to beat them both."

"That's true."

"But he didn't beat anyone, did he?"

"No," I said. "He didn't."

"So," said Ch'i, triumphantly, "our work hasn't been in vain."

63

Hsueh-chen Dissents

A Communist best expresses his spirit of discipline precisely when he is in danger or when there are serious differences between him and the Party over matters of principle or personal matters. It is only when he unconditionally carries out organizational principles even when he is in a minority that he can be considered a highly disciplined and principled Party member who is mindful of the whole situation and understands subordination of partial interests to those of the whole, subordination of a small truth to a big truth and the need to submit differences over secondary principles and personal matters to the principle of Party unity and Party discipline.

Liu Shao-ch'i, 1945

THAT THE first decisive act of the new Congress should have been the expropriation of a rich peasant may seem to be an extraordinary perversion of policy. Had not the County Conference and the final classification made clear that all of Long Bow's most serious current problems stemmed from the excessive attacks and confiscations of the past? Was not the crucial question of 1948 the repayment and resettlement of families who had been wronged?

Yes. All this was certainly true, but just because it was so true, the campaign against Yu Pu-ho took on extra significance, both subjectively and objectively. Subjectively, the discovery of one piece of unfinished business, one genuine rich peasant still in possession of surplus wealth, leant added meaning to the whole classification process and justified, at least to some extent, the travail that they had all been through.

Objectively there were also compelling reasons for settling with Long Bow's untouched rich peasant. Considering all the "holes" that needed "filling," it was clear that the Congress would need all the property that it could legitimately get together. Now every bowl, every basket counted. The surplus goods found in the widow's house and yard, when added to the land and housing that could rightly be taken from her, were enough to set several poor families on their feet, and this in spite of the fact that the canny woman had hidden the greater part of her possessions and altered her garments to fit her daughter.

Necessary as this struggle was both psychologically and economically the expropriation of Yu Pu-ho inevitably developed into a headache for the Congress and caused its Standing Committee no end of trouble. On the morning after the raid, proof that Yu Pu-ho had indeed tried to cheat the people came to light from several sources. Ts'ai-yuan, the storekeeper, first came to the office to report that through intermediaries more than a hundredweight of grain had been placed in his granary for safekeeping. The widow and her daughter had not eaten all their wheat after all. Next Hsueh-chen and An-feng found a sack filled with clothes, cotton cloth, and rags. It had been hidden under an old chest in Wang-er's back shed. While they were displaying the contents of this sack to Hsin-fa, word came that Pu-ch'ao had violated her guarantee and slipped out of the village. When she finally showed up at supper time, she admitted she had been to her sister's home in Yellow Mill to check some clothes she kept there in a box. Everyone suspected she had done more than that.

That night the Congress delegates, in formal meeting assembled, confronted Pu-ch'ao with the evidence and demanded that she choose, once and for all, whether she wanted to stay with her mother and be treated as a rich peasant "struggle object," or divide the family, set up housekeeping on her own, and be treated as a poor peasant, a class status to which she was entitled by marriage.

It was a strange confrontation. Hsin-fa, with loud "ho ho's" and "Ai ya's," questioned Pu-ch'ao like a father interrogating a wayward daughter. Pu-ch'ao herself, having been exposed as a liar, stood meek and diffident before her former lover. It was an attitude that enhanced her beauty more than the defiance of the previous evening. But now all beauty seemed lost on Hsin-fa. He was hard as a cloisonné bowl.

As Hsin-fa talked, K'uan-hsin and T'ien-hsi sat on the rectory steps, dismantling their rifles piece by piece and cleaning them. In this they were aided by the light of a full, round moon. Old Lady Wang and Ch'ung-lai's wife half stood, half leaned on the stout staves they had brought with them to fend off wolves. The news that day was that a wolf had attacked and killed a 12-year-old girl in Li Village Gulch. Hence no one dared leave home unarmed.

In the end the young woman chose to set up a home of her own. The Congress then allocated to her two sections of housing, an acre and three quarters of land and an acre of her mother's corn crop. It also undertook to provide her with all the household necessities possessed by the average middle peasant. Thereafter Pu-ch'ao came several times every day to Village Head Chun-hsi and asked for the cooking pots, fuel, grain, implements, and everything else she needed to live an independent life. Chun-hsi spent hours rummaging through the village stores to find the jars required for storing Pu-ch'ao's grain. He no sooner delivered them to her door than she demanded covers for the jars. Soon other peasants began to complain. Why should the village head take such good care of a rich peasant's daughter? Let her fend for herself like everyone else!

If Pu-ch'ao gave Ch'un-hsi little peace, the widow, her mother, gave him even less. Yu Pu-ho quarrelled bitterly with her son's wife, locked up all her remaining millet, and systematically set out to starve the girl. When the young woman tried to return to her mother's home Yu Pu-ho attacked her at the courtyard gate, tore her jacket from her hands, and threw it onto the roof of the house. To Ch'un-hsi fell the task of climbing onto the roof to get the jacket down. And to Ch'un-hsi also fell the task of admonishing Yu Pu-ho to behave herself or face arrest.

To settle the affairs of Widow Yu Pu-ho it became necessary for the Congress to meet and make final disposition of her property, even though much of it was still missing. On August 1st the following list was officially drawn up and declared confiscated:

1 pair red padded trousers (silk)
1 green padded coat (silk)
1 gray padded coat
1 piece of black cloth
1 pair of worn padded trousers (cotton)
1 pair of red cotton sleeve protectors
2 feet of white cloth
1 hand mirror
1 black coat to go with a long gown
1 shawl (wool)
1 quilt
1 white sheet
1 sweater (wool)
2 small jackets (cotton)
2 pair silver bracelets
1 woman's hat (velveteen)
1 black shirt (cotton)
1 pair of cloth strips for binding trousers at the cuff
1 bag of cloth scraps (good for making shoe soles)
1 piece of pink cloth
1 piece of black cloth
1 set of steam baskets for making steamed bread
1 iron pot for steamed bread
1 set of steam baskets (damaged)
1 plow
1 manure bucket (large)
1 manure bucket (medium)
1 worn padded coat (cotton)
1 wooden spade
1 wooden farm fork
1 winnowing basket (large)
2 purses
1 well rope
2 stone hog troughs
1 fodder knife without base
1 sieve
1 vase
1 bamboo screen
1 rake
1 iron pail
1 flowered bamboo door screen
1 wooden beam
1 seeder (two row)
1 broken iron pan
3 bags of wheat
1 knife

3 manure buckets (small)   2 reed mats for storing grain
1 long sideboard   1 cupboard
1 storm door   1 big chest
                                1 wash stand

****

The list of goods confiscated from the rich peasant widow omitted
any mention of the garments altered to fit Pu-ch'ao. This so upset
Hu Hsueh-chen, the dogged, hardworking leader of the Women's
Association, that she protested vehemently to the Congress when it
next met.

But Hsin-fa, backed by a solid majority, insisted on giving Pu-ch'ao
everything that fitted her. According to the regulations, he saw no
other way to handle the matter. "As long as they agree to divide
the family, Pu-ch'ao must have what is hers," he said. "All we have
to do is to call her in, find out what things are hers, and give them
to her."

"But almost everything is hers now," said Hu Hsueh-chen, holding
back tears with difficulty. "She remade her mother's clothes to fit
herself long ago and her sister's clothes as well. She is so smart. She
made fools of us, and you are going to let her get away with it!"

When the rest of the Congress backed Hsin-fa's view, Hu Hsueh-
chen lost her temper.

"What's the use of the struggle then? Everything will be Pu-ch'ao's.
People like me can't get a thing."

As she said this she looked down at her own frayed, three-year-old
tunic, and passed her hands across it with a gesture of disgust. Then,
realizing how selfish her words sounded, she hastened to add, "Don't
think I'm thinking only of myself. I only want to solve this with
reason. As far as the masses are concerned, no matter how much
they get they'll want more, so there is nothing to be gained by fighting for them. The real thing is the trickery—it's not right. Since
she never did divide with her mother before, it's Pu-ch'ao's fault, not
ours, that her clothes are involved. I say they belong to all of us."

"Well, then, are we to divide her dowry too?" asked Hsin-fa. "When
we call her in we must adopt a severe attitude and warn her that
she will be punished for telling any lies, but still she must be allowed
to say what things are hers. As long as she describes the articles correctly and they fit her, they must be given to her, and the same goes
for the daughter-in-law."

As he spoke Hsueh-chen shook her head.

Team Leader Ts'ai suggested that the matter be immediately
brought to a vote, but Hsin-fa opposed this.

"If we vote on it now and Hsueh-chen is voted down, she will carry a burden and maybe she will never raise another opinion again. Better discuss it further. Let everyone speak what is on their minds."

Every other member of the Congress standing committee including all 15 of the remaining women, supported Hsin-fa.

But Hsueh-chen still objected.

"Do you think we want to give things to Pu-ch'ao because we like her?" asked Hsin-fa, still sensitive about the past.

"Who says you like her?"

"Now look here," exclaimed Ta-hung, the militiaman. "If you two are going to quarrel, the rest of us will go to sleep." But quarrel they did until Team Leader Ts'ai Chin intervened for the second time.

"Hsueh-chen's attitude is not reasonable," he said. "We must abide by democratic methods and obey the majority. There must be some reason why, after you have voiced your opinion several times, the others don't want to follow you. And if you are upset because your idea has gone awry, that is still more serious."

Hu Hsueh-chen fell silent then. A decision was made without her participation. Though she did not oppose it, she was obviously very angry. She remained sullen for a week and hardly contributed at all to the many important discussions that took place in the Congress during the critical period that followed. All the work team cadres and the comrades of the Party branch were dismayed to see the woman who had always been the most forward looking and progressive in the whole village, suddenly draw into herself, relapse into apathy, and nurse a grievance because she had been outvoted in a small matter very close to her heart. It was an individual reaction that might have been anticipated, however. The village had already witnessed a similar phenomenon in the case of Kuei-ts'ai. It was not easy for any peasant, even the most advanced among them, to understand and support a policy based on over-all considerations when it conflicted with a strong personal demand. Here the outlook of the petty producer, ingrained from birth, acted as a screen that blotted out the larger long-term interest in favor of the lesser immediate one.

In Hu Hsueh-chen's case, the very bitterness of her poverty was the genesis of her narrow attitude. She envied Pu-ch'ao her fine clothes, her spoiled life, her beauty, and success with men. When Hsueh-chen contemplated her own plain face, her big-boned frame, her lonely state, the lean years of her childhood, the way in which her first husband had beaten and starved her, the straw she had slept on for lack of a quilt, the rags she had worn and the frayed garments that were still her lot, and when she thought of all the hard work she had done to lead the women in the *fanshen* movement, and contrasted this with the way in which many had turned on her, called her selfish, criticized her leadership, told her she must give up paltry things like one lady's collar and one small strip of cloth, while at the same time they leaned over backward to see that Pu-ch'ao got her silk tunics, her embroidered shoes, her velveteen jacket, the enormity of the injustice overwhelmed her. As far as she was concerned, a policy that brought such results was no policy at all. She could not think it through.

Hu Hsueh-chen's reaction to the settlement made with Pu-ch'ao was an extreme one. In kind, however, it was no different from the negative response of almost all the members of the Communist Party branch when the Congress finally got around to that important matter—the return of "illegal fruits," which was the next item on the agenda.

64

"Illegal Fruits" Returned

So it occurred inside the Party that in the course of struggle certain comrades admitted more mistakes than they had committed. In order to avoid attacks, they thought that they had better accept all accusations. But although they admitted all the mistakes, as a matter of fact they still didn't know what it was all about. Here is proof that such methods of struggle cannot cultivate the firmness of a Communist in sticking to the truth.

Liu Shao-ch'i

THE ONLY other surplus property still left in the village consisted of those items which the village Communists and cadres, when questioned at the *gate,* had promised to give up. Since the Congress was empowered to receive these goods, promises had now to be transformed into deeds. This process proved almost as difficult as the expropriation of Yu Pu-ho.

The nub of the problem lay in the fact that most of the Communists and cadres felt that they had been treated unfairly. Under the influence of an erroneous line that had first characterized the *fanshen* in Long Bow as incomplete and then blamed the local leaders for it, most of them had promised to return things which had in fact been quite openly distributed to them with the approval of the distribution committee and paid for with millet. "Paid for" must be understood to mean that the price of these things was subtracted from the total amount of millet allocated to them. In other words, the goods and chattels they received were a part of their just share, insofar as that had been determined by the committee.

No one objected to returning "illegally seized" property. What they could not agree upon, however, was a definition of "illegal seizure." After one distribution session Hu Hsueh-chen had taken home a small box. There was no record of this box in the lists, and no millet had been deducted for it. On the surface this was a case of "illegal seizure." But the other Communists all backed Hsueh-chen up when she said that every single person at that meeting had taken something home. It was the result of a common decision. If Hu had seized her box, then dozens of people, cadres and common folk alike, had been guilty of seizure that day. If Hu was to be asked to give up her box, then everyone else ought to give up what they had received.

Another case in point was An-feng's shawl. An-feng's husband had been an active militiaman before he joined the People's Liberation Army late in 1946. Day after day the militiamen had been called upon to do guard duty in bitterly cold weather. At a mass meeting the people had voted to give each militiaman a shawl. This was done as a favor to the men and as a token of thanks. But before the *gate* the shawls had been labelled "seized fruits" and An-feng had been asked to return the one given to her husband. Now this request did not seem fair.

As soon as these cases came up, all the Party members began to grumble. They made quick comparisons between the total amount they had received and the amount received by other peasants and concluded that for the most part they had received less. How could it be said that they had *fanshened ke tui* (in excess)? And if by chance they had received something especially valuable or especially useful, was it not because at the time no one else dared to take it? They recalled how Cheng-k'uan and Hsin-fa, at the time of the struggle against Wang Lai-hsun, had led a donkey around the village for a whole day and not found anyone courageous enough to claim it. It was not that people did not want the donkey, but that their eagerness was stayed by fear. They were afraid that Chiang's troops would soon return. Then anyone who had accepted anything would pay for it with his life. Under the circumstances those who finally were persuaded to take things were the bravest and most active people in the village. Should they now be punished for that?

Many Party members also recalled that when other peasants hesitated to voice their grievances at the meetings, it was the Communists who brought up the charges in their name, and that when such grievances won property or millet, it was the Communists who carried the articles or the grain to the beneficiaries' homes. At that time, in the heat of the battle, they had not asked who was getting more and who less; they had simply worked night and day to carry through the people's demands. But what thanks did they get for it? No thanks at all, but only accusations that they had themselves seized all the "fruits" and had *fanshened* in excess.

Discussion revealed that all the vindictive statements and unfair opinions voiced by the delegates before the *gate* had burned themselves into the consciousness of the Party members. They tended to forget about those who had been impartial, delegates like Ch'ung-lai's wife and Old Tui-chin who from the very beginning had stood for an equitable solution and had always spoken out against vindictiveness.

The Communists remembered unfairness and forgot fairness because the atmosphere at the *gate* had been extreme. In the first place, the self-and-mutual criticism practiced there had been something new to both cadres and delegates. They had little or no experience with the kind of limited struggle necessary for solving problems that arose among the people. Uncompromising struggle against class and national enemies they knew well. Close unity with friends and relatives they also knew. But how to struggle and unite simultaneously, how to deepen unity through struggle, how to conquer weaknesses with criticism, how to exorcise the bad in friends and allies while developing the good—all this had to be learned.

In the second place, there was the influence of a wrong line. Proper use of self-and-mutual criticism depended on the full realization that one was in fact dealing with contradictions between friends and allies, not contradictions between oneself and the enemy. Under the impact of the idea that poor peasants should conquer and rule the countryside, however, it was just this concept that had been upset. The *fanshen* of the poor had been called incomplete. Not only had the cadres been blamed for it, but suspicion had spread far and wide that many of them were in fact class enemies, landlords and rich peasants in disguise.

At the first *gate* inexperience in this form of struggle, combined with a wrong line that distorted the very basis of the struggle, had produced an atmosphere which all but precluded the possibility of reconciliation. The heavy pressure which was consequently brought to bear on the cadres caused some of them to accept blame outwardly while rejecting it, or most of it, inwardly. Now that the time had come to settle accounts with concrete goods the bitterness engendered by that acceptance bore prickly fruit in the form of an exaggerated rejection. The fruit had to be harvested and digested before the problem could be solved.

Ts'ai-yuan, for instance, could not forget Old Lady Wang's question: "What did you do during those eight years in the army? Eat the people's millet?" It was as if all he had experienced throughout the Anti-Japanese War, the battles he had fought, the wounds he had received, the times he had risked his life—as if all this was nothing and the bringing home of a few paltry bullets had cancelled everything out. It was so unfair that his heart beat faster and his skin flushed whenever he thought of it. All the big equipment he had helped to capture—the trucks, the machine guns, the uniforms—he had of course turned over to division headquarters, but these few bullets that he had personally taken from a puppet prisoner were but a souvenir of his army life that he felt he had well earned. When the village militia found themselves short of ammunition, he had sold the bullets for enough cash to buy a quilt and several suits of clothes. Now that he was asked to give up the quilt and the clothes, it seemed to him that his whole army career was called into question.

Or take the question of proven thefts. Did the fact that Man-hsi had taken ripe fruit from certain peasants' trees or the fact that Hung-er had stolen some salt, make the whole branch a group of thieves? Who else had stolen anything at all? Some of the comrades, women who themselves had never been in a position to graft or steal anything in any case and so had never been tested, even took the position that there had been no illegal seizures in the village whatsoever. They urged that the matter be dropped. But to this the work team could not agree.

The Communists were asked to review their past once again and themselves speak out what they thought should still be given up. Their response was sarcastic.

"I'll hand out three acres," said Ta-hung.

"Why so much? What's the reason for that?" asked Hsieh Hung.

"Since I am a Communist I should be highly conscious and help all those who have not *fanshened*."

This set T'ien-hsi off. "Really, it's true," he said. "Communists must sacrifice. Whatever the Communists do, even though the masses do the same thing, the Communists must be criticized." He spoke in a tone of indignant injury.

"When the masses do something it is right, but if the Communists do the same thing, it is wrong," said Ts'ai-yuan, echoing the others.

"Really, Communists should not eat or drink," added Ta-hung in disgust.

This last remark was too much for Team Leader Ts'ai Chin. Brusquely he brushed the hair from his forehead and took the men to task. "If the masses take things without paying, of course it is wrong. But it is because we are Party members and highly conscious, just as you say, that we should take a leading part and return the "fruits" or pay back with millet. Then the masses may well follow us. Otherwise, if we just sit and wait for people to hand over and pay out, what is there to show that the Communists are highly conscious? What difference would there be between us and the masses?"

Unable to reply to this, Ta-hung went off into a corner and sat down in silence. He didn't stir for many minutes.

The two militiamen, Ta-hung and T'ien-hsi, were most upset by the idea of surrendering "fruits." This could well have been because they had received very little to start with. This was especially true of T'ien-hsi, who, because he was a middle peasant, never needed very much in order to *fanshen*. Certain other Party members accepted the idea more willingly. With their help a list that seemed fair was finally drawn up. It was not very imposing. Hsin-fa promised a basket, a piece of wood, a stump, and one of the three jars which he had been legally allocated but felt guilty about possessing. T'ien-hsi promised an acre of land, one burlap bag, and a jar. When his comrades reminded him of the chicken he had seized, he got angry. The chicken, he said, had died long ago and the chicks that hatched from the eggs she laid had also long since died. He saw no reason to replace the bird or her ill-starred brood. His argument did not seem very reasonable to me, but his colleagues did not press him further.

Cheng-k'uan promised a well basket, ten pounds of iron, four bags of wheat, one waist band, and two silver dollars. Hu Hsueh-chen agreed to give up a piece of cloth an inch wide and one foot long, two small kit bags, a lamp, and two balls of yarn. As for the box, which had never been listed, she offered to pay for it with millet. Ai-lien promised an iron basin and two ladies' collars. An-feng promised two balls of wool, two collars, a leather belt, and a manure fork.

And so it went. With the exception of the acre of land promised by T'ien-hsi and the half cart promised by Jen-kuei, these offerings represented no great wealth. Their return to the Congress for distribution had significance far beyond the value of the articles, however. This was the first time anyone could remember that any of the spoils of power and privilege had ever been tracked down and returned.

In truth, the strip of cloth promised by Hu Hsueh-chen was nothing but a worthless rag, and the eight rounds of ammunition brought home by Ts'ai-yuan were hardly more than a souvenir of his eight years under fire. Could one not, perhaps, afford to be indulgent? The answer was "No!" The articles were nothing in themselves, but the principle they represented was as wide as the world. Twenty years earlier the Old Workers' and Peasants' Red Army had started out with a few rifles, a few lances, and three rules: (1) Obey orders in all your actions; (2) don't take a single needle or piece of thread from the people; (3) turn in everything captured.

These rules meant what they said. The Communist Party, the People's Liberation Army, and the new democratic government of the Border Region took them seriously. Public servants were expected to serve, not to graft. To overlook the misappropriation of one small rag or a single bullet was incompatible with a sincere revolutionary stand.

****

When the Party members finally completed the list of "fruits" to be returned, the non-party cadres were called before the Congress standing committee to add their bit. From the attitude of such men as San-ch'ing, Yu-lai, and Ch'i-te, one could see, by contrast, how far the Party members had progressed. These three men had not had the advantage of the education and discussion inside the branch. They were loath to speak their minds. On trial, as it were, before the representatives of the village, they were anxious to please, worried lest they forget some item, and eager to accept without question what others proposed. This was an attitude which most of the Communists had long since abandoned.

Only one non-Party cadre spoke out what he really thought. This was Chang-hsun, former secretary of the village government. He offered to give back a padded coat, a mat for a *k'ang*, a few catties of iron, four pecks of wheat, and four bolts, but when it came to his cart, a vehicle that had once belonged to the landlord Wang Lai-hsun and was without question the best cart in the whole village, he declared that he had paid a hundredweight of grain for it and meant to keep it.

The matter of the cart provoked long discussion. Everyone thought that Chang-hsun had taken advantage of his position in the village administration when he bought the vehicle. The fact of the matter was that he already had a cart of his own, sold that one for two and a half hundredweight of grain, and then turned around and bought the superior cart from the "struggle fruits" for one hundredweight. This might have been overlooked by the villagers if carts had been plentiful, but because there was no single item in all the inventory of the village in such short supply and in such great demand, everyone looked at this transaction with suspicion. How was it that family after family had no cart, yet Chang-hsun, who already had one, was able to obtain the best in the village?

By selling his old cart for two and a half hundredweight and buying another for one hundredweight, he had not only ended up with a much better cart, but had made a profit of one and a half hundredweight besides. Chang-hsun was notorious for just such shrewd deals. He was miserly and tight-fisted and had made himself unpopular over the years by consistently getting the better of his neighbors when buying or selling. If he had not been such a covetous man, the peasants would not have made such an issue of the transaction, but the combination of the valuable cart and its crafty owner was too much for the Committee of the Congress to overlook.

Chun-hsi suggested that Chang-hsun return to the village the profit he had made from selling his old cart and then pay several additional hundredweight for the cart he bought from the "fruits."

Chang-hsun offered to give up the profit, no more and no less.

When the Committee objected to this, he asked for his old cart back again.

Angry with Chang-hsun and unable to agree among themselves, the Committee members decided to hold the matter over for presentation to the whole Congress.

****

On the last day of July, the whole list of things to be given up by the cadres was finally brought before the Congress for approval. Introducing the subject to the delegates as they sat in the tree-shaded back yard of the mission compound, Team Leader Ts'ai Chin explained the principles under which the property was being returned:

(1) Only grafted or seized property was to be handed over. All things for which millet had been paid or deducted, even if the purchaser had bought more than other people, were to be kept.

(2) No one, after handing out "fruits," should be brought below the level of the average new-middle-peasant, regardless of whether or not he had seized many things.

(3) If repayment in a lump sum threatened hardship to any family, the Congress should not demand immediate payment in full but should arrange for installments and a gradual liquidation of the debt.

"According to my understanding," Ts'ai said, "the corruption in this village is not serious. I personally know of a cadre in another community who had to return BRC 700,000 [about $700 U. S. currency]. In Long Bow all the goods misappropriated by all the cadres put together will not come to BRC 700,000. The main thing is not the value of the goods but the truth, the attitude of the cadres and the Communists involved. By handing out these things they demonstrate that they recognize their mistakes and prove that they keep their word.

"You Congress delegates are the representatives of the masses, so you must speak the truth and find a proper solution. Do not try to save face for others. Do not give the people cause to say that the new cadres protect the old. At the same time keep the two principles in mind: Only illegal possessions are to be handed back; and no one shall be reduced below the level of a new-middle-peasant by this procedure."

The Congress then moved on to check the whole list. It's 35 members were quite lenient. Even Old Lady Wang tried to save face for everyone. She was in an unusually mellow mood. When the question of Ts'ai-yuan's bullets came up, she said, "He worked hard at the front, and the bullets should belong to him." When others argued that he should pay for the mirror which he smashed, she said, "He got angry. Young people get angry easily." When Szu-har argued that a quilt which he had taken without permission was already worn out, she said, "Why not let him have the quilt?"

It looked as if she understood that the new pattern of power and leadership in the village had been settled and had decided to make amends all around. It behooved her, therefore, to try and undo the effect of all the harsh words she had spoken in the past. This unusual attitude on her part was too much for her colleagues. They were all much stricter than she. "We have no mandate to go easy on Szu-har," they said, and they asked him to pay in full for the quilt he had already worn through. They also demanded that Ts'ai-yuan pay for the mirror he had broken and for the bullets that were sold. They were not vindictive, however. They did not demand the last pound of flesh and the last drop of blood.

Ch'un-hsi, for instance, had run through a whole bag of millet while on a trip to the city for the purpose of delivering tax grains. His expenses were high because he was delayed by rain—20 days of rain on end. It was no fault of his and, since he had gone to the city on public business, the Congress decided that the village should bear the expense.

When Hu Hsueh-chen enumerated the pitiful list of things she proposed to give back, all said, "These are but trifles, hardly worth a peck of millet." They told her to keep them all and pay the Congress two quarts of grain. Hu was much relieved.

Shen Yu-hsing had misappropriated 20 feet of cloth, one pair of shoes, a sweater, and half an acre of land. The sweater came from the body of Shen Chi-mei, the traitor who was shot at the meeting that followed the liberation of Long Bow. Old Lady Wang said that Yu-hsing ought to keep the sweater, for it would have been buried with the body if he had not had the gall to remove it. Others disagreed. "That was also public property," they said. "He had no right to take it." And they asked him to hand it over. The shoes were a different matter. They had been given to him by the village when he was called out for rear service. He had no shoes of his own at the

time and could not go to the front barefooted. They told him to keep
them. "To ask them back would be to box our own ears," they said.
"He wore the shoes on a public mission, nor for his private gain."

Thus a line was drawn between what was fair and reasonable and
what was unfair. The line was drawn so responsibly and with such
precision that everyone appeared satisfied.

Chang-hsun's cart alone aroused prolonged controversy. After two
hours of discussion the Congress finally decided that he should pay
three more hundredweight of wheat and keep the cart.

The final list, as approved by the 35 delegates to the Congress, was
then taken back to the sectional groups of the Peasants' Association
and read off item by item. In the southwest section all the small
items, especially those on the women's list, only bored the peasants.
Each time it was announced that millet would be paid in settlement,
but only after the fall harvest, snickers could be heard from those
who were skeptical that any grain would ever be paid. When the
list of goods offered by San-ch'ing was read out with an explanation
that he had confessed it all himself, someone said, "Who knows,
perhaps he stole more things. How do we know that he spoke out
everything on his conscience?"

"That's right," said another. "Plenty of things were grafted."

"Can you prove that?" demanded Yuan-lung, a Congress member.

"No, I have no proof."

"Then you can't just make it up out of your imagination," said
Yuan-lung. T'ai-shan's mother backed him up.

The meeting in the southwest corner of the village was a poor
one. The people were still excessively concerned with the amount
of millet they stood to gain, and when they saw that there was very
little forthcoming, they fell silent, urged Ch'i Yun to read faster, and
began to drift away. In the north and east sections the attitude of
the peasants was much better. The list engendered a lively discussion,
name by name, and on the whole the decisions of the Congress were
supported. Criticism centered around one thing only—the disposition
of Chang-hsun's cart. From all three sections of the village came the
opinion that three hundredweight was too little for Chang-hsun to
pay. They demanded that he pay four hundredweight and give up
half the cart.

Comrade Ts'ai Chin was disturbed by the lack of unanimity. He
decided that this matter of the cart, though a nuisance, was important
enough to get to the bottom of, even if it took a week. He singled
it out as an issue that could serve as an education for everyone. It
turned out that many delegates to the Congress had not supported
the decision of the Congress when they sat with their Peasants' As-

sociation groups. Back among the people they opposed a plan which they themselves had made in the higher body. They not only opposed it, but they led the people to reject it. Ts'ai felt that there was something radically wrong about this. If any delegate disagreed with the decision of the Congress, he should have had the courage to speak out, argue then and there, and settle the matter instead of keeping silent, only to rise and oppose the decision he himself had voted for when the issue came before the whole. people. What was the use of bringing to the people for approval a decision they could not possibly accept? If it were a reasonable decision, all likely objections to it could have been anticipated and considered and the delegates armed with strong arguments for an overwhelming "yes" vote. Democracy, said Ts'ai Chin, could only work if people were frank with one another.

The matter of the cart was therefore taken up as a main topic by the whole village, and first and foremost by the Party members in their branch meeting. In the branch, because the Communists had already acquired the habit of speaking out, the question of the cart could most easily be examined in its many-sidedness. One by one, the issues involved in the dispute were brought out and settled by unanimous agreement. Below are listed the questions posed by Ts'ai and the answers given by the Party.

Question: Was three hundredweight a cheap price to pay for a cart that was worth ten?

Answer: At the time of the distribution in 1947, all prices were low. They were not a real reflection of market value. The "distribution prices" were never meant to be market-value prices. They were set up simply as a means for comparing one article with another so as to facilitate equitable division, and no attempt had ever been made to equate the Long Bow "fruits" with the prices commanded by similar items elsewhere. Therefore, it was not fair to say that three hundredweight was too low a price.

Question: Why was Chang-hsun, who already had a cart, able to buy another?

Answer: At the time, many people were afraid. They feared "change of sky" and although they were willing to take millet, which was almost as anonymous as money, something big and conspicuous like a cart was too obvious. Should Chiang's troops ever return, they would be marked. At that time Chang-hsun was the only peasant in the whole village who had the courage to buy the cart. As soon as he bought it others became jealous and began to criticize him. He went to the district magistrate and asked if he should give it back. The magistrate said no, to give it back would make it appear that he also was afraid. In order to encourage others to join in the struggle for *fanshen*, he should keep it. So keep it he did. Everyone knew that even Chang-hsun was frightened when he took possession of the cart, but he was so greedy that he could not resist the bargain. His avarice overcame his prudence, and almost against his will he took the lead where others feared to tread. Since that was so, how could Chang-hsun be blamed for having bought the cart?

Question: Why were the people so vindictive when it came to this cart?

Answer: Everyone disliked Chang-hsun's miserly nature and his sharp manner. Since he was no longer a cadre, they thought they could squeeze something out of him. "That's all very easy now," said T'ien-hsi. "I know how the people are thinking. They want to compel him to give up the whole cart. Now everyone wants more things —carts, animals, two-story houses, everything. For they all know that the Eighth Route Army will stay forever. Suddenly the cart is worth 20 hundredweight."

Question: Should Chang-hsun pay anything more at all?

Answer: Yes. For even in 1946 other good carts went for three hundredweight, and he paid only one. And besides, he made a very good profit by selling his old cart. He certainly owed the village something.

Question: Why shouldn't Chang-hsun be asked to give up at least half of his fine cart, since carts were so scarce in the village?

Answer: No one wanted to share a cart with him. He was too hard to get along with. Who wanted to buy quarrels? Who wanted to pay good millet for the privilege of fighting with Chang-hsun over the use of this cart? Besides, the principle of sharing carts hadn't worked out very well in the past. When several people owned one cart, no one took full responsibility for it, and it was apt to be left out in the hot sun after a rain to dry, shrink, and crack. Under such treatment even the best cart in the world would not last long.

Having settled all this in detail, the Party members tried to arrive at what they considered to be a fair value for the cart. Hsin-fa again said he thought three hundredweight was right. No one disagreed.

Team leader Ts'ai Chin immediately remarked that this was strange. He knew that there were at least three opinions on this matter. Why didn't someone else speak up? Under such prodding Chou Cheng-lo suddenly began to talk. He said he supported the opinion of many people in his part of the village which was that Chang-hsun should pay the Congress four and a half hundredweight. This brought the disagreement into the open, and the merits of the two positions were then thoroughly reviewed.

The issue was finally resolved, inside the Party branch, at least, with the recommendation that Village Head Ch'un-hsi had originally made—that is, that Chang-hsun should pay back the hundredweight and a half profit he had made on the deal, plus two more hundredweight for the cart itself.

When this suggestion was again brought before the people, it was accepted. When the branch met later, Ts'ai Chin, on behalf of the work team, went out of his way to congratulate Chou Cheng-lo for having had the courage to start the argument.

"The point is," said Ts'ai, "that only through hot argument can we get at the truth. Real democracy means speaking out one's own opinion. Only when we ourselves understand this can we lead others to understand and use democracy."

From millions of just such small incidents the fabric of political life in revolutionary China was being woven.

65

Arrests and Restitutions

Extreme democracy is almost universal in this county. As for the people, since they have suffered dictatorship without democracy for thousands of years, surely they find it difficult to accustom themselves to democracy. They go to extremes. That is to be expected. We can divide those who go to extremes into two kinds: those who do not understand democratic centralism, those who do not know that the minority must bow to the majority, and those who take advantage of the new situation and defy the majority because they think nobody can do anything about it.

Secretary Wang,
Third Administrative District
Taihang

ONE DAY just as the Congress assembled in the mission yard, an old man ran in. He was smeared with mud from head to foot. The right side of his face was so swollen that he could not open his eye. Panting and weeping simultaneously, he described the terrible beating he had received from his son Po-t'ai. He even got down on his knees, laid his head on the ground, knocked his forehead against the bricks of the court and beat and kicked himself to show that he had been attacked while he lay prostrate and helpless.

The Congress Committee sent for Po-t'ai, locked him up overnight, and asked him to atone for the beating by doing ten days' extra labor on the land of a soldier's family.

Family quarrels such as this were common enough. What made the incident significant was the fact that Po-t'ai's father came to the Congress with his complaint. A few weeks earlier he would have come crying for Team Leader Hou. Now he sought out the Congress and by his action indicated that the people were beginning to recognize the existence of the new government.

This was an important step forward. The position of the new Congress as the supreme ruling body in the village was further consolidated when, a few days later, the District Office turned over to it a serious criminal case.

The crime occurred in broad daylight halfway through a hot, humid

August afternoon. Behind the District Office, Village Head Ch'un-hsi was ladling manure out of a privy. The night soil in this privy had been allocated to a plot of land that still belonged to the village school. Since nobody would volunteer to transport the stinking liquid, the Village Head had to do it himself.

Suddenly he heard an angry voice on the other side of the walled enclosure.

"We struggled against the landlords," said the voice, "but the district cadres live in the Church and oppress the people. Everyday they eat wheat while we eat millet. Who built the Church for them anyway? Who told them to occupy the people's fruits?"

Unwilling to believe his ears, Ch'un-hsi went on loading manure.

The tirade continued.

"Really, the Church belongs to us Catholics. We built it, but they deny it to us. The sons of bitches! I'm not afraid of them. They struggled against Wang Kuei-ching and Shih La-ming (Catholic landlords). That was a mistake. If they get in my way again, someone is going to get killed."

This was too much for Ch'un-hsi. He put down his long-handled ladle and stepped to the gate. There, all alone, stood the peasant Ken-pao, a striking figure at any time of day.

Ken-pao had a rugged frame—stocky and squat like a judo wrestler—calloused hands, a weather-beaten face, eyes that were fixed in a perpetual squint from working under the sun, and the walk of a man who knows hard labor. All this was typical of many Long Bow peasants, but what made Ken-pao unusual was the wild look in his eyes, the fact that the towel on his head was always a bit askew, and a disorder about his dress that indicated a total disregard for convention. It was as if he pulled his clothes off and on while still asleep. These external signs of eccentricity were reinforced by the strange behavior of the man. He habitually talked to himself, broke into violent rages, and beat his wife with a single-mindedness that bordered on madness. Little wonder that the villagers regarded him as slightly queer, if not hopelessly deranged.

"What was that you said?" Ch'un-hsi asked.

Ken-pao, taken by surprise, refused to reply.

"Well, you needn't repeat it, I heard it anyway," said Ch'un-hsi. "What did you mean by those words?"

"Never mind what words I said. I'll swap my life any day for the lives of several cadres."

With that Ken-pao leaped at Ch'un-hsi, grabbed his thumb and tried to break it with one swift, backward jerk. T'ien-hsi and Man-hsi, working the village-owned vegetable garden nearby, were startled by Ch'un-hsi's scream of pain. They came running, threw Ken-pao down, tied him up and took him to the District Office.

Magistrate Li thought it very unlikely that Ken-pao's strange soliloquy was entirely self-generated. Though the man had actively attacked the landlords in 1946 and had received a fair share of the "fruits," as soon as the Draft Agrarian Law was announced he began to curse the cadres and loudly proclaim that the poor had not *fanshened*. "We fought to build this 'kingdom,' " he said, "but only the cadres got the benefit." After the second County Conference in July, 1948, his line of attack suddenly shifted. He openly questioned the expropriation of the landlords, particularly the Catholic landlords, and denounced the "Settling Accounts Movement" of the past as a bad and cruel thing. Every day he quarrelled with his wife. Their pot was empty, but instead of working to fill it, he stole. Only that week he had been released from the district lockup for selling shovel blades that did not belong to him.

Did such a man have the wit to respond to policy changes as quickly as he had lately been doing? The magistrate thought not. It was much more likely that someone had put him up to it.

Two hours of questioning failed to pry anything out of Ken-pao, however. He belied all preconceptions concerning his native wit by answering every question with cunning evasion. When Magistrate Li asked if he had ever threatened to kill anyone, he said:

"If you send me to jail, I will have to risk my life and kill someone."

"Who then will you kill?"

"I can only kill myself. I have lived in Long Bow all my life. How could I kill anyone here?"

When Magistrate Li repeated this question, Ken-pao finally admitted that he had made threats, but he blamed it all on his wife.

"I threatened to kill the village leader and four or five others, but I only said such words because I am crazy. It is my wife that drives me crazy. I can't even stretch out a leg in the house without her permission. Now she wants all my wages from the harvest season, and she threatened to go to the village office for help. That's why I cursed the village head."

Magistrate Li took the problem to the Party branch. The branch, in turn, recommended that the standing committee of the Congress call Ken-pao before a mass meeting. With the whole village assembled, it might be possible to tell who supported him and who opposed him and thus expose those who had added fuel to his hatred. When Magistrate Li took this suggestion to the Congress committee it was accepted, but the mass meeting which followed proved nothing. Nobody came to Ken-pao's defense. His wife, amid uncontrollable sobs, told of the terrible life she led with him ever since his return from the army. She revealed that he wanted to get a divorce by going, not to the civil authorities of the Border Region, but to the Catholic bishop in the Cathedral at Taiyuan. Since the Catholic Church was unalterably opposed to divorce and since Taiyuan was in traitor domain, the people all cursed Ken-pao and sided with his wife. Ken-pao begged their pardon and asked for a chance to reform, but the decision of the meeting was to send him to the village lockup, at least until the motives behind his behavior became clearer.

Ken-pao, rooting like a mole in the dirt, twice escaped from the earthen-walled lockup and was twice recaptured. When the militia got their hands on him for the second time, they tied him up very tightly with rope and wire and put him in the home of their captain, Szu-har. The next day the committee of the Congress met to decide his future. He was released on condition that he do 15 days' extra labor for some soldier's family and find three guarantors who would see to it that he did not beat his wife or curse or swear at anyone.

On the morning of his release I was sitting with the work team cadres beside the village street. We were eating the millet gruel served out at the District Office for breakfast. Ken-pao came plodding along with his son at his side and his hoe over his shoulder, all prepared for work on an absent soldier's field. He grinned self-consciously as he passed our group.

Ch'i Yun called out to him, "Do a good job."

Ken-pao nodded and proceeded on his way.

Extreme democracy was definitely on the way out in Long Bow.

****

Considering the seriousness of the crime, the punishment meted out to Ken-pao was mild indeed. A year earlier he could well have been severely thrashed, driven into exile, even beaten to death. Now his counter-revolutionary talk was treated more as a joke than a problem, and the punishment he received for physically assaulting the village head was no worse than he might have expected for stealing grain. In effect, what the Congress offered him was an opportunity to reform. This magnanimity was a reflection of the confidence which the revolutionary forces felt in their cause and of its support among the people.

That a dissident faction still existed seemed obvious. Ken-pao could hardly have acted on his own. Who was it then that egged him on? There seemed to be only one logical answer: that group of disgruntled Catholics who gathered at carpenter Li Ho-jen's house and rallied politically behind Shen Ch'uan-te. On them surely the blame must be laid for the assault on Ch'un-hsi and also for that earlier, much more serious assault on team cadre Little Ch'uer. Absence of concrete evidence made it difficult to prove any such allegations, however, and the general upsurge of confidence that followed the election of the Congress made it unnecessary to do so. The injustices on which dissidence fed were fast being done away with. In the place of "merciless blows," the Congress had substituted a policy of "love, protect, educate, remold, and unite." Behind this policy was the idea, so often stated and restated, that poor and middle peasants, regardless of their views, their past, and their present, could be won to the Revolution if—and this was the crux of the matter—they were treated as potential allies and given time to change their views.

The leniency shown to Ken-pao was a concrete expression of this outlook.

****

Ken-pao's case delayed but did not sidetrack the main business before the Congress. Having disposed of it, the delegates tackled the next big job at hand, the "filling of the holes."

A rough matching of needs against goods and land available led the delegates to believe that a final settlement would not be too difficult. They tallied up almost enough housing to go around, and although they were short seven acres of land, they knew that they could count on the return of some fields from middle-peasant families who did not have enough labor power to cultivate all they owned.

Since top priority in any settlement had to go to wrongly expropriated peasants, a meeting was called on August 2nd to which were invited all those middle- and poor-peasant families who had been victims of attack. The meeting was held in the old clan temple on the village square. This temple boasted a loft from which one could look down on the village pond and the courtyards all around it.

The middle peasants and their wives or widows came into the building with some trepidation. The former puppet Tseng Chung-hsi even hesitated at the door when he saw that all the people present were relatives of "struggle objects." The thought apparently flashed through his head that the struggle was to begin all over again. But since there was no way to withdraw at that point, he moved cautiously in. I gained the impression that Chung-hsi's reservations were shared by others. All the people present were nervous and silent as the meeting began.

Village Head Ch'un-hsi, who had been asked by the Congress to chair the meeting, carefully explained the policy of repayment. His listeners had heard of it before, but it was one thing to know about it in general and quite another to stand there and be told that it was going to be put into effect immediately. Up until that moment few of the people in the temple believed that they would ever be repaid.

Ch'un-hsi asked each family head in turn to tell how much land and property was needed. The peasants then put forward some very modest requests.

Wang Hua-nan, the middle peasant whose wife and brother had both been killed in the uproar over the discovery of 2,000 silver dollars buried in his back courtyard said:

"I need a few sections of housing, nothing else."

But Ch'un-hsi was skeptical.

"How much land do you have?" he asked.

"An acre and a third for four people."

At this many people laughed out loud.

"That's not possibly enough!"

"But I can work out as a hired laborer and support the family that way," said Hua-nan.

This offer was ignored.

"Better speak out what you want, what you need."

But Hua-nan was still reluctant to ask for anything. It almost seemed as if he feared some trap.

"If I said everything that I wanted it would be too much."

"Never mind."

Hua-nan finally screwed up his courage and said, "I want another acre and a half, five sections of house, and a few things to cook and work with."

This demand was modest enough considering the size of his family. The fact of the matter was that ever since the expropriation of the Wang family, Hua-nan had not even had a pot to cook millet in or a hoe to break ground with. Now he was supposed to be repaid not only enough to make him an average middle peasant but enough to restore his family to its original prosperity.

When Hua-nan realized that his request was not considered excessive, but on the contrary was more meager than the village leaders had expected, he began to smile.

"Ever since the struggle I have been worried," he said. "But after the classification, when I was called a middle peasant and the group leader praised me in the meeting for my hard labor, I felt better. Now if I can get some land and housing, that is fine. I can certainly live a comfortable life, for I am strong and I can work."

Shen-nan's widow, son, and mother constituted the other branch of the family. Village Head Ch'un-hsi suggested that land as well as housing be given to the son and that his mother and grandmother share the house. As for the land, until he was old enough to work it himself, his uncle Hua-nan could till it for him.

Hua-nan agreed to this. "I was thinking the same thing myself," he said.

When they asked the old woman, Shen-nan's mother, if that was all right with her, she could not speak. She broke into tears, tears of relief and tears of sorrow for the tragedy that had occurred.

Shen-nan's widow tried to comfort her. She herself was smiling. "Really, ever since the struggle I have never dared make a plan for the future," she said. "I thought, who can tell? When will they attack us again? So I planned only for the next meal and ate whatever was in the house."

Fortunately for the Congress, not every family wanted land. Several even wanted to give some up. Among these was Shen Shuang-niu. He had seven acres for six people and worked at the village inn full time. He preferred his work at the inn to labor on the land and found seven acres far too much to handle.

The same proved true of Shang Shih-t'ou's widow. Her husband had been killed by the Eighth Route Army because, as puppet village head, he had refused to co-operate with the guerrilla forces and had instead hunted them down. Without any able-bodied men left in the family, she found the land a burden.

Another former puppet leader, Kuo Chao-ch'eng, had land and housing enough but wanted some grain to tide him over the summer. From a whole acre planted to wheat, he had harvested only a peck and a half and was left with nothing to eat. "When I was expropriated," he said, "I was very frightened. But later I realized that if I hadn't worked for the enemy I never would have been attacked. It wasn't because of my wealth. Since then I have worked hard. I bear no grudge, for I deserved the treatment I got. Now all that is past, and all I have to do is to work hard for a good life in the future. Nevertheless, in the last few years I have been very upset, and I worried myself sick."

The ex-puppets Tseng Chung-hsi and Li T'ung-jen were dissatisfied with their houses. Each said he lived in a broken-down dwelling. This was certainly true of Tseng's family. I had eaten there with Ch'i Yun and I could not forget the sick girl coughing on that *k'ang* or the odor of decay that hung everywhere in that narrow room.

Further questioning brought out the fact that what really bothered these two families was not their houses as such, but their neighbors. Chung-hsi did not get on well with the widow across the court, and

T'ung-jen quarreled incessantly with the notorious Chin-chu. "Often," said T'ung-jen, "I have thought of building a wall between us and of opening another gate into the yard, but there is only one well, and it belongs to me. If I put a wall around it, other people will call me selfish. So I haven't carried out my plan."

Chung-hsi suggested, half in jest, half in earnest, that he and T'ung-jen swap houses, but the latter did not respond. The village head promised to look into other alternatives.

The meeting did not last long. It took only a few hours to list all the needs of these people and to listen for a while to their recollections and feelings. Short as it was, however, it had a profound effect. All the statements about uniting with the middle peasants, about coalition of classes, about the need for allies counted for far less than this one meeting where the actual repayment of goods to those families that had been unjustly attacked was begun. People had learned to be skeptical of words, but it was impossible to be skeptical of such deeds.

When the time came to hand out property, Wang Hua-nan was truly given special consideration. The Congress gave him an acre of corn land and an acre of wheat land from the very center of the best land in the village—the rich peasant Yu Pu-ho's holdings. They gave his mother and his nephew together an acre of corn adjacent to his own and thus brought the total land under his care to six acres. Two of these had a full crop of corn on them, the only land under crops that was available in the whole village. Everyone envied Hua-nan this stroke of fortune.

In respect to housing, Hua-nan received seven sections of the "foreign building" (the two-storied structure once owned by Chief of Staff Hsu) for himself and five more for his mother and his nephew, making 12 in all. This was the same amount of housing he had originally possessed. In addition to this, the Congress gave him a well-constructed privy at the end of the "foreign building."

Insofar as restitution could ever make up for the attack he had suffered, it was certainly carried out with these decisions.

* * * * * * * * * * *

"In the past we said that the Communist Party loves the poor," said Team Leader Ts'ai Chin, speaking before a mass meeting of the village. "Was this slogan correct? Well, it was both right and wrong. In the past the Communist Party loved the poor because they were oppressed and exploited by the landlords and the feudal system. But now feudalism has been destroyed, and the land is being divided up. Are we still to love the poor? If we leave aside for the moment the sick and the aged who cannot labor, the only poor in the future will be those who do not want to work, who will not lift a finger to help themselves. Are we to love such people? I think not," said Ts'ai Chin decisively.*

"Suppose there is a small hole in this man's roof. He is too lazy to repair it. Instead he comes running to the village office. He says, 'Look here, Ch'un-hsi, there is a hole in the roof of my house. Soon the whole building will collapse and bury me alive. What are you going to do about it?'

"What is Ch'un-hsi to answer?

"He can only answer, 'We are very sorry; of course we don't want to see you buried alive, but if you don't do anything about it yourself you have only yourself to blame.' No. In the future we shall not love the poor. We want everyone to work hard and to strive to become a new rich peasant. With the land question solved there is nothing to prevent us all from becoming as prosperous as Li Hsun-ta."**

Thus did Ts'ai Chin introduce the final period of work in Long Bow, the general distribution of the land and houses. He made it very clear to his listeners that this was the last time land and houses would be distributed. The decisions made in the next few days had to be final because there was no more property to divide. There were no more landlords, no more rich peasants, and no more cadres with special holdings obtained by special powers. And under no circumstances could middle peasants be asked to give up their holdings against their will. Therefore the land and houses that were to change hands at this time were the last that would ever be redistributed without cost.

"After this, if you want land you will have to buy it. Don't expect anyone to give you any," Ts'ai Chin warned. He urged the Congress

* Ts'ai Chin speaks here as if land reform would produce communities composed entirely of new and old middle peasants. This was the outlook of many cadres at the time. It was not entirely correct because although land reform did so rearrange property holdings that middle peasants, both new and old, became a majority in the countryside, after land reform there were still many families who owned only a fair share of land and little else. They were still poor peasants. Ts'ai Chin assumed that as long as they had land, they could, through hard labor, wrest a living from it and prosper. Things did not turn out that way. The poor and the less well-to-do among both old and new middle peasants had to pool their resources and co-operate before they could win security and prosper.

However, at the time when Ts'ai Chin spoke, a production drive based on individual land ownership and mutual aid was the only immediate way out of any and all difficulties. Therefore it was logical for him to stress hard work and the prospect of prosperity through labor.

** Li Hsun-ta was a famous labor hero in the Yenan Region.

to take great pains and do everything patiently and well. "Only thus can we lay a firm foundation for the future of this village forever. If we are careless and make mistakes we shall plant a seed that can grow and do great harm later on."

Once again *tzu pao kung yi* (self report, public appraisal) was adopted as the basic method for deciding what conditions were—this time, who was in need and how much they should get. The results of these reports in the three sections of the village were brought to the Congress by the delegates. A complete list was then drawn up. This list, read off at last to a mass meeting, was still open for adjustment. Families who felt that they had not received fair treatment could demand reconsideration and could even appeal to the county government if necessary.

With the needs of the wrongly expropriated taken care of, the next in line were those still classed as poor. Land was allocated to each of these according to need. After 29 poor peasants had divided between them some 15 acres of land and had brought their average holdings up to an acre per capita, other special cases were considered. I found these extremely interesting and report a few of them to show the complexity of the problems which a simple land distribution can produce.

There was the case of the soldier, Shih K'ao-tzu. He had come home on leave in order to marry. He had brought with him from his unit a "resettlement paper" requesting the village government to give him land, housing, and implements, and help him get started as a new middle peasant in an independent household. This was not an unusual request. In fact, every village had been asked by the county government to set aside some eight or ten acres of land for just such contingencies. The trouble was that in this case Shih K'ao-tzu already owned land and houses and household goods in Long Bow. He also owned an acre of land in Horse Square. What he planned to do was to turn all his original holdings over to his brother and ask the village to resettle him completely with more fertile land and better housing.

"I have been home more than a month. I turned in my 'resettlement paper' weeks ago. But nothing has been done for me. I would have returned to my unit long ago if you hadn't held up this matter," said Shih, very sharply. He blamed the People's Congress for the fact that he was not already back at the front.

But the Congress delegates and Village Head Ch'un-hsi did not think that he was entitled to any such "resettlement." "We are only illiterate peasants," they told him. "We do not fully understand this 'settlement' policy, but in our opinion any soldier who already has land and housing need not be given more. If, like Old Kao, you come to us barehanded and want to settle here, then we must give you land and everything else. But that is not the case with you. If you think you have been wronged you can take it up with your superiors, and we will take it up with ours. If they order us to give you land, of course we will give it to you. Otherwise we will handle this the way we have always done in the past, and that is to give people what they lack."

Poor peasant Wang Kuei-pao's problem was entirely different. He was a weaver who owned very little land, less than half an acre per head. Everyone said that he was lazy. Although he was forced to weave to supplement the income from his land, he still didn't work very hard at his craft and his living conditions were very poor. Hsin-fa wanted to give him another acre and a half. Ta-hung wanted to give him another three acres. But Kuei-pao was very distressed when he heard about that.

"Your mother's cunt," he said. "I can't handle that much."

"Look here!" they said to him. "This is your last chance. Later on you won't be able to get any land at all. If you should find yourself in difficulty and have nothing to eat, the village won't give you any relief, for you are an able-bodied man and should raise your own food."

Kuei-pao finally agreed to take another acre.

The most extraordinary case of all involved the Party member Ch'eng Ai-lien. She wanted her land held in a dead man's name. Ch'eng Ai-lien was the attractive but rather vain young woman whose husband Man-ts'ang had been so severely beaten by the members of the Women's Association in 1946. He died later of an illness in no way connected with the beating and left his land and other property to his wife. She then married the landless peasant Chin-sui. Chin-sui volunteered for the army and left for the front. His mother moved into Ai-lien's quarters. According to the marriage contract, Chin-sui promised to forego all rights to the land and houses. The first son that his wife bore was to be considered the son of her first husband, Man-ts'ang. This son would inherit all the property. The children that followed were to belong to the living husband, Chin-sui. They would not be entitled to any land or buildings.

As the final settlement approached, the mother-in-law, very upset by the arrangement which her son had made, asked for housing and land enough for two. She found living with Ai-lien impossible. The young woman was very strong-willed and, as the owner of the property, had completely turned the tables on her new mother-in-law. "Now you are living in my house, and eating off my land," she reminded the old lady almost daily. "And so you will do things the way I want them done."

When this case came before the Congress, the delegates first asked, "What if she has no sons at all?"

"Then she will buy one or ask a relative to give her one," said the tearful mother-in-law.

Team Leader Ts'ai was consulted as to the law. He pointed out that according to Border Region custom the land of a dead husband did in fact belong to his wife. As the legal heir she could do with it as she wanted.

But the delegates didn't accept this.

"Man-ts'ang is already dead. How can a ghost be the owner of the land and house? If they had a male child, the property would belong to the child, but now there is no lawful owner," said Ta-hung.

The Congress delegates all agreed. The root of the case, as they saw it, was the unheard-of suppression of the mother-in-law by the daughter-in-law. This arose only because the latter owned the property.

"Chin-sui is no use at all!" said one of the men.

"How could he ever have made such a bargain?" exclaimed another.

"He was a poor peasant, one of the basic masses, yet he was so worried that he would not find a wife that he gave up his most precious rights."

They all considered Chin-sui to be a hopeless case. In order to rescue him from his own mistakes, they declared the property of the dead man, Man-ts'ang, to be the property of the village. Then they turned it over to the landless peasant, Chin-sui, and by that act gave his mother supremacy over his wife, Ch'eng Ai-lien. Ch'eng Ai-lien regarded the decision as a total disaster.

The work team did not agree with this decision of the Congress, but there was no way in which to intervene. Only extended education could change the attitude of Long Bow's leaders towards women's rights, and this would no doubt be a protracted process.

* * * * * * * * * * *

After all decisions had been made, the Congress delegates added up the land and property available and matched them against the promises made and found that they were one acre short. Worse than that, they found that they had no reserve left for future adjustments or for demobilized soldiers who might choose to settle in Long Bow. The eight to ten acres originally set aside for that purpose had already been allocated.

The standing committee of the Congress decided to find out if there were not a few middle peasants who would be willing to give up land. A list was drawn up of all those families that actually had a surplus of land in terms of the labor power available to them. Some had already indicated in the past that they might give up some land if it were needed. The list included such people as Ming Lan's mother, a widow who could not work in the fields herself and often said, "Just because of the land we are poor. For we have to employ hired labor and pay taxes. Too much land is a burden." And there was Kuei-hua, who wanted to give more than an acre to Shen Hua-nan because she thought that he would take good care of the ancestral graves there.

Delegates were sent to talk to all the people on the surplus land list. In the evening they returned to report complete success. All the middle peasants who were visited agreed to co-operate. The land thus given up amounted to more than ten acres. The problem was solved. Not everyone was satisfied in every respect. Nevertheless, the delegates felt that the best and fairest distribution possible had been made. They were all in very high spirits. They made all kinds of jokes as the end of this work approached, and laughed almost as much as they talked. At one point Hu Hsueh-chen, who still had not recovered from her disappointment over Pu-ch'ao's clothes, asked petulantly what she would do for a privy if she accepted the new home that the Congress had offered her.

"Use the one you have always used," said Old Tui-chin.

But the old privy was two courtyards and three walls away.

"She'll have to buy a ticket and take a bus every time she wants to go," said Yuan-lung.

"She could take an airplane," said Ts'ai-yuan.

They finally decided to give Hsueh-chen housing in a courtyard that already possessed a privy in good condition.

At another point in the proceedings, the women, who still sat in a circle by themselves, were by-passed on an important matter.

"I have neglected half of China," said Village Head Ch'un-hsi.

He was warmly applauded.

The only member of the Congress who did not share in all this merriment was Old Lady Wang. She was bitterly disappointed by the whole procedure. In anticipation of her son's marriage, she had intrigued and schemed ever since the arrival of the work team for more land and houses. She had fought against being called a new-middle-peasant and antagonized half the village with her bitter tongue, only to find that in the final settlement they proposed to give her nothing. In despair she asked for at least enough building material to repair her five sections of house. She was turned down.

"But her son will get married soon, and there is no place for the young couple to live," said T'ai-shan's mother, coming to Old Lady Wang's aid at the last minute.

"How can we help that?" asked the others. "Many people are going to be married. Maybe next year she will have a grandson. How can we figure him in?"

"*K'ua le, k'ua le*," (I'm finished, finished) cried Old Lady Wang, and she got up ready to leave the meeting. But this time no one seemed to care, so she sat down again.

With the problem of land and housing out of the way, the Congress next settled the question of the distribution of movable property and livestock. First the wrongly expropriated middle peasants were given everything they needed. Wang Hua-nan, for instance, got a cart, a donkey, and a plow. Then the left-over items were sold to those who wanted them, and the millet was distributed to the poor peasant families who still had not *fanshened*. A committee of eight, appointed by the Congress, carried out this action and the distribution which followed.

CHANGES IN LANDHOLDING BY CLASSES (1944-1948)*

I. *Before Liberation*

	No. of families	% of families	No. of persons	% of population	Land held (*mou*)	% of land held	*Mou* per capita
Landlord	7	2.8	39	4	680	12.1	17.4
Rich Peasant	5	2	27	2.7	303	5.4	11.2
Middle Peasant	81	32.2	395	40	2532.6	45.3	6.4
Poor Peasant	138	55	462	46.8	1386.4	24.8	3
Hired Laborer	19	7.6	59	6	—	—	—
Tenant	1	.4	5	.5	—	—	—
Institutional	—	—	—	—	686.2	12.3	—
Totals	251	100	987	100	5588.2	100	

II. *Between Liberation and May 4th, 1946*

	No. of families	% of families	No. of persons	% of population	Land held (*mou*)	% of land held	*Mou* per capita	Change (in *mou*)
Landlord	2	.8	6	.6	18	.3	3	−662
Rich Peasant	4	1.6	20	2.1	138.8	2.5	6.9	−164.2
Middle Peasant	76	31.2	349	37.4	2157	38.6	6.2	−375.6
Poor Peasant	162	66.4	559	59.9	2841.4	50.8	5	+1455
Institutional	—	—	—	—	433	7.8	—	−253.2
Totals	244	100	934	100	5588.2	100		

III. *After Completion of May 4th Movement*

	No. of families	% of families	No. of persons	% of population	Land held (*mou*)	% of land held	*Mou* per capita	Change (in *mou*)
Landlord	1	.4	2	.2	18	.3	9	0
Rich Peasant	4	1.6	12	1.3	82.6	1.5	6.9	−56.2
Middle Peasant	76	30.4	338	35.5	2095	37.5	6.2	−62
Poor Peasant	169	67.6	599	63	3309.6	59.2	5.5	+468.2
Institutional	—	—	—	—	83	1.5	—	−350
Totals	250	100	951	100	5588.2	100		

IV. *After 1948 Movement*

	No. of families	% of families	No. of persons	% of population	Land held (*mou*)	% of land held	*Mou* per capita	Change (in *mou*)
Landlord	1	.4	2	.2	13.5	.2	6.7	−4.5
Rich Peasant	4	1.6	12	1.3	55.5	1	4.6	−27.1
Old Middle Peasant	76	30.4	341	35.5	2056.6	36.6	6	−38.4
New Middle Peasant	140	56	523	54.5	3048.3	54.2	5.8	+67
Poor Peasant	29	11.6	82	8.5	415.8	7.4	5.1	+87.5
Institutional	—	—	—	—	36	.6	—	−47
Totals	250	100	960	100	5625.7	100		

* Six *mou* = one acre. The amount of land held by villagers increased by 37.5 *mou* after the 1948 movement. Reclaimed land and land transferred from other villages account for the increase.

66

"Self Report, Public Appraisal"

Solves the Tax Question

Just one more
Ear of grain;
Just one more
To equal one more bullet
To stop the enemy.

                    Tien Chien

DURING THE first few days of August the heat was intense. Since
it had rained enough in the latter part of July to soak the ground
thoroughly, the heat worked miracles with the crops. Corn grew
luxuriantly. There were no signs at all that it had ever been damaged
by hail. Other crops also burgeoned with unexpected vigor. When
the mutual-aid teams went out to hoe, they disappeared completely in
the green foliage. One could tell that men were at work only by the
snatches of song and conversation that rose from the matted jungle
on the land.

The hot, sticky August air gave evidence of another kind of labor.
It was tainted with a haze that was the result of diffused smoke. All
around the countryside one could see great columns of smoke rising
to the heavens. They were generated by peasants burning weeds and
trash in order to get ashes for the manufacture of saltpeter. Saltpeter
had become the lifeblood of the People's Liberation Army. As guerrilla warfare gave way to mobile warfare and this in turn developed
ever more frequently into positional warfare, shells played a growing
part in the fighting. Since not enough of these could be captured in
battle to insure sustained barrages on widely scattered fronts, supplementary munitions had to be manufactured in small local arsenals
and packed with domestic explosives. In the battle for Linfeng alone
17 railroad cars full of shells were expended in one pre-dawn bom-
bardment. Before the garrison there was finally routed, more saltpeter
had been used up than all the peasants of Lucheng and Changchih

counties combined could create in a year. No wonder the peasants were out in force scouring the hills, the ravines, and the river beds for anything organic that would burn. Not only were they paid a good price in millet for the ashes, but by such labor they could make a direct contribution to victory at the front and guarantee their own *fanshen*.

The mass gathering of ashes and the backyard manufacture of saltpeter demonstrated that the very backwardness of the economy had certain advantages. The lack of large-scale industrial nitrogen fixation which at first appeared to be a drawback was turned into a source of strength by virtue of the fact that it stimulated the active participation of millions in munitions manufacture and ultimately deepened their commitment to victory.

A people's war cannot be won without the mobilization of all popular energies. In a developed capitalist society, even if the political contradictions standing in the way of such a mobilization could be resolved, its effectiveness would still be hampered by that alienation which separates so many people from meaningful production and substitutes the ubiquitous "cash nexus" for socially valid human relationships. In an agricultural society such alienation is still only rudimentary. How much more direct, how much more personal is the involvement of a people who must burn leaves and trash to make their own nitrates than of a people who need only contribute dollars to a munitions industry they have never seen.

Throughout the Liberated Areas of North China even the collection of ordinary taxes had this same concrete, personal quality. Taxes were paid in kind, and at least part of the grain which each peasant brought, all winnowed and weighed, to the collection point, was eventually eaten by some soldier at the front. Each taxpayer therefore had the palpable experience not only of contributing something to a cause in which he passionately believed, but also of supplying a living defender of that cause with hand-grown food, instead of simply turning over part of his income to some vast impersonal government apparatus. In the course of making their contributions to "rear service," these same taxpayers often carried grain directly to the Army and saw how it bolstered the defense of their land. In May, a score of peasants from Long Bow actually transported 20 cartloads of millet to the seige of Linfeng. They spent enough time there to learn at first hand how the battle was going and to see and be influenced by the dedication of the troops.

During the August heat, cartloads of organic ash and public grain jostled each other in the main street of Long Bow. The former were headed for the saltpeter plant in the eastern section, while the latter were being transported to the collection depot of the Fifth District

Finance Bureau. As tax deadlines drew near, grain predominated over ashes. Dozens of horse-drawn, donkey-drawn, and mule-drawn two-wheelers creaked down the rain-softened lanes each day, laden with sausage-shaped bags of clean, hard wheat. Every man in the village who could read or handle a writing brush was called in to help keep records, check and weigh grain, and store it away. Two large brick warehouses on the east side of the village were soon filled to capacity. The district magistrate then ordered the Chur h opened. Three days later the mountain of wheat stacked there dwarfed the dwindling stocks of millet that had seemed so huge when the Peasants' Association met to confront Yu-lai. In terms of the amount harvested by any one family, it was an extraordinary accumulation. Yet, when one considered the needs of a war continental in scale, it was clear that this was not a great deal of wealth to come from one fifth of a county.

Under the system established when Lucheng County was liberated, taxes were collected twice a year, once in wheat after the summer harvest, and once in millet, corn, and sorghum after the autumn harvest. Because hail had hit Long Bow so hard, the county government had at first considered cancelling Long Bow's summer taxes completely. But the officials soon discovered that if they did so, other villages would register complaints. After all, the hail was not the only scourge to hit Lucheng County that summer and Long Bow was not the only village to suffer a reduction in its wheat crop. In some valleys *huang tan* (yellow smut) had damaged the wheat almost as severely as had the hail in Long Bow. Hou Pao-pei, former leader of the work team, harvested so little wheat on his home farm, not ten miles away, that he had to borrow three pecks of grain to pay his taxes. He enjoyed no cancellation. Judging from conditions in Long Bow alone, a flat cancellation would also create almost as many problems as it solved, for it would not benefit all the peasants equally. There were families whose wheat had not been damaged at all. There was no reason why they should not pay their fair share. If all summer taxes were excused, those who had not been hit would enjoy an undeserved bonanza.

The county government, therefore, estimating that the total damage amounted to two thirds of the crop, set the tax rate at one third of the revenue collected in the previous year and asked the Long Bow People's Congress to allocate the burden fairly among all the peasants according to the crop they had actually harvested. This was an unprecedented move. No one could recall any government in Lucheng that had ever granted a cut in taxes because of crop failure or for any other reason.

The village as a whole was relieved and happy when the decision was announced even though some individuals expressed disappointment that their taxes had not been cancelled altogether. Nobody wasted any time celebrating, however. They were all too busy debating how the unprecedented cut was to be divided. The work team, which made the equitable allocation of the tax burden its last major project, suggested that *tzu pao kung yi* (self report, public appraisal) was the only fair method. That way each family could report its own crop and offer the same proportion in taxes that they had paid the year before. Their neighbors, in the sectional groups of the Peasants' Association, could then discuss the amount, judge whether or not it was fair, and draw up a list for the whole group. The lists thus created could be turned over to the Congress for a final decision.

There were many objections to this procedure. Some people did not believe it would work. They thought any effort at self-report in the tax field must end in chaos. They wanted the village leaders to "cut the knot" by assigning points as they had done the year before when there had been no disaster. If it were left to each person to decide, there would be no standard of judgment. Each person would say what pleased him, and who could gainsay him?

"On our land we harvested four bags," said Cheng-k'uan's mother. "But Shang Shih-t'ou's family, on the next strip of land, claims to have harvested but one bag. I don't believe they got so little. But how can I prove it? Are we going to search their house?"

Others who opposed the idea said that "self report" was useless since it could be overthrown by "public appraisal" anyway. Why not start with "public appraisal" and be done with it?

But the work team stuck to its position. Team Leader Ts'ai Chin pointed out that there was no way that points could be fairly assigned. In previous years points had been set on the basis of the land's capacity. Since the productivity of each plot over the generations was well known, this presented no great difficulty. But this year, because of the hail, actual yields stood in no relation at all to fertility, size of plot, or any other known factor. The only people who knew how much wheat had actually been harvested were those who did the work. As for standards, these were very clear. People were asked to pay the same proportion of their crop as they had the year before. If they thought all this was too much trouble, they should remember, the team cadres said, that every bit of grain was important for the support of the front. The soldiers needed the grain in order to carry on the liberation fight. If the soldiers failed to win at the front, the whole question would almost certainly become academic. Then it would not be a question of deciding how much taxes each family should pay. Chiang Kai-shek would decide that, and his troops would simply come to every door, throw some empty bags on the ground and say "fill them up."

These arguments won the day. Most people agreed that in spite of the scattered pattern of the hail, neighbors had a pretty good idea of each other's crops and, through open discussion, could arrive at a figure. It was obvious that a fair estimate was in the interest of the majority because, regardless of how much any one household paid, the whole village was obligated to collect 20 hundredweight. If anyone got away with less than his fair share, his neighbors would have to foot the bill.

This was without doubt the severest test the "self report, public appraisal" method had experienced. Yields were something that for thousands of years people had tried their best to conceal, for the simple reason that higher yields meant higher rents and higher taxes. The need to conceal actual yields had been burned into the hearts and minds of generation after generation of tenants and small holders. Nobody, if he could possibly help it, had ever been honest about how much grain he actually thrashed out. That is one reason why, in the past, before the establishment of the revolutionary regime, taxes had in fact been collected by the simple method of taking what grain could be found. That was also one of the reasons for the adoption of the standard *mou* system in the new tax regulations. By basing demands on estimated productivity, the revolutionary government by-passed all need to investigate actual yields. Now it was proposed that the peasants themselves volunteer these vital statistics.

In order to lead the way, the Communist Party had first to activate its own membership. The branch leaders quite rightly calculated that if the Communists promptly and accurately reported their harvests and offered a fair proportion in taxes, others would follow suit. But even in the branch, "self report" ran into difficulty. Some said they would give two pecks, some one peck. Old Kao offered five quarts, and Shih Hsiu-mei, who had harvested but one peck, offered three quarts. But when they came round to Hsiao Wen-hsu, there was silence.

"I don't want to say it now," he said. "When the time comes, I'll bring the grain to the warehouse."

"How can you talk like that?" asked Ts'ai Chin. "There can be no secrets among Communists."

"I didn't say I wouldn't offer anything," said Hsiao Wen-hsu. "When the time comes, I'll be there with the grain."

"How much?" ased Ts'ai-yuan, insisting on a figure.

"I got four and a half pecks; I'll bring it all."

When he heard this answer, Ts'ai Chin's face flushed red.

"Is that your answer toward paying taxes? What sort of a Communist are you anyway? You don't want to tell the branch, but you will show the masses. You make me so angry, I could hit you." He half stood up and turned toward Hsiao Wen-hsu. "Nobody wants to force you to do anything, but your motives? Your motives?"

"I never said you were forcing me," replied Wen-hsu growing more stubborn with every word.

"What kind of an attitude is that anyway?" said Ch'un-hsi, joining in the attack. "If you talk this way even in the branch, what would the masses think if they could hear you? They would certainly curse you. We all lose face!"

Wen-hsu's wife tried to break in.

"We'll offer five quarts," she said. But no one heard her above the din. Everyone was talking at once, and all of them were attacking Wen-hsu, who faced them in defiant silence.

Village Head Ch'un-hsi took Ho-ch'ueh aside and asked her why her husband was so stubborn. "Is it because you have great difficulties at home, or what?"

Ho-ch'ueh only shook her head and wept. She begged Ch'un-hsi to talk to Wen-hsu after the meeting and reason with him, but the village head looked doubtful.

"He must be publicly criticized; I can't stand his attitude. How can I reason with him patiently?"

The Communists' problems with their comrade Hsiao Wen-hsu was but a preview of things to come when the people met in the neighborhood groups of the Association. Although the eastern group sailed through its whole list easily, the north and southwest groups found appraisal extremely difficult. Some people really had nothing left to eat in the house; yet they offered substantial amounts. Others, who could afford to pay, made ridiculous token offers in lieu of taxes.

The poor peasant Jen-kuei, for instance, when his name was read out, said:

"I'll give one peck."

"Why you?" asked Ts'ai-yuan. "You harvested very little and everyone knows that you have nothing left."

"That's true," said Jen-kuei, "but the members of my small group here all stare at me, just waiting for my report, so I have to speak out."

"How much did you really harvest?"

"Two hundredweight from an acre and a half. But I had a lot of debts. It's all gone. In order to pay taxes, I'll have to borrow a peck from somewhere."

Four families that had no wheat of their own but only gleaned a little in the fields of others offered several quarts apiece.

"They shouldn't have to pay anything," said Cheng-k'uan's mother.

But several men disagreed with her. "Though they were in great difficulty, they have reported according to their own consciences so of course we must accept the offer."

As village head Ch'un-hsi read on down through the list of names the selfish ones also revealed themselves. One family that harvested six bags offered less than a family that had harvested three. Yet nobody spoke out. Nobody wanted to lose face or undermine another by challenging the figures. Once again it became clear that democracy hinged on the willingness of people to speak and argue.

Ken-ming offered only one peck, even though he himself admitted that he had harvested seven hundredweight. His group wanted him to add another five quarts at least, but he lost his temper.

"I have democracy now, and that's all I will give," he said.

After that rebuff his neighbors just said "all right" to everybody else. "Why should we offend old friends?" they asked. "Even when we give an opinion, they don't accept it, so why should we persist? Better keep silent."

"What is actually in the minds of those who did well this year," explained Fa-liang to Ch'i Yun and me afterward, "is that it was their good luck that the hail didn't hit, and as long as they were so lucky they ought to enjoy it. 'Self report,' they think, is self willingness. They want to give only as much as suits their fancy and ignore the 'public appraisal.'"

Such attitudes prevented a full discussion of the actual situation, and the meetings had to be called off until the following day. In the intervening hours, the cadres, the village leaders, and the Communist Party members spoke to people individually. In the morning the sectional groups of the Association were reassembled for a second try. This time the discussion developed more freely, and a tentative list was drawn up by each group for submission to the Congress.

Whatever reluctance the rank-and-file peasants had to discuss their harvests and their taxes was not shared by the Congress delegates. They took the lists and really studied them. When they had doubts about any family's report, they called the head of that family in and questioned him or her until they had the facts straight. They slashed the amounts offered by some and added to those offered by others with a confident sense of right and wrong. Those who had harvested nothing at all, but had gleaned a few odd quarts, were struck from the lists regardless of their willingness to contribute to the support of the fighting front. The same was true of those who had nothing left to eat. Hsiao Wen-hsu, for instance, was relieved of all obligations, even though his wife protested that her offer was genuine and that people would not respect her word in the future if she did not make good on it. Investigation showed that she and her husband were gathering herbs in the hills in order to eat.

A sharp argument flared up over a rich peasant widow. One delegate wanted her to pay a lot because she had originally been rich. But others said flatly, "No. This has nothing to do with her class origin. This is a matter of how much one harvested. They got almost nothing. Therefore they should pay nothing. The land reform is over. There are no rich peasants anymore."

When the situation justified it, on the other hand, the delegates did not hesitate to add to the tax. Ken-ming, who had been so stubborn in the meeting, admitted to his neighbors afterwards that he had refused to add even a quart to his original offer because he didn't like Chin-hung, who had proposed it. The Congress added a whole peck to his tax.

When the task was completed, all contributions were tallied and totalled. They came to 21 hundredweight, just one hundredweight above the amount required of the village by the county government.

On the following evening, August 13, 1948, the list was read to a mass meeting of the village and was approved as read. A major test of democratic rule had been passed. The way in which the Congress had handled this problem left no doubt as to its ability to run the affairs of the village. The work team decided that its work was done.

67

Long Bow *Tsai Chien**

There is no Jade Emperor in heaven.
There is no Dragon King on earth.
I am the Jade Emperor.
I am the Dragon King.
Make way for me you hills and mountains,
I'm coming!

Peasant Song, 1958

ON AUGUST 24, 1948, Ch'i Yun, Hsieh Hung, and I left Long Bow. The contrast between our departure and our arrival six months before could hardly have been more striking. The day was warm but not excessively so, and a golden sun shone down like an old friend on a village at peace. Not a biting wind but a refreshing morning breeze, not a menacing overcast but a blue eternity, not a frozen lifeless street but the warm salutations of many friends greeted us as we emerged for the last time from the gate of the district compound. Tall Hsin-fa, with the poise and assurance of the community leader which he had in fact become, was there to see us off. Beside him stood Cheng-k'uan, his serious face offset by a brand-new towel on his shaven head, and Ch'un-hsi, with a broad smile that indicated among others things that his mother was cooking for him again. Hu Hsueh-chen and Little Mer stood behind them. The women had abandoned their spinning for the occasion, and Ts'ai-yuan had forsaken his store. The cadres of the work team came out of the gate with us— Han, Li, Ts'ai Chin, and Hou Pao-pei. They had long since given up wearing side-arms for protection, and now the very memory of guns and holsters, tensions and fears, seemed like some fragment out of a nightmare.

The peasants of the southwest corner, among whom we had worked for so long, did not turn out *en masse* to say farewell—we had already visited almost every family in its own courtyard and had taken formal leave—but those who saw us going came down into the street and

---

* *Tsai chien* is the Chinese equivalent of *au revoir*.

walked with us southward to the point where the fields began. Among them were the children who had been my constant companions during those odd moments of leisure that had been left to us between meetings. The first of the rascals to run up held both my hands as we went forward, while those latecomers who could not find a finger or a thumb to grab ran around our procession in circles. Hu Hsueh-chen and Ch'i Yun likewise held hands and talked earnestly to one another, Ch'i urging the women's leader to look joyfully to the future, and Hu, in her turn, promising to spare no effort in service to the people.

As we emerged from the street into the open country, the peasants, with friendly goodbyes, turned back one by one. Finally only the cadres of the work team remained with us. We stood momentarily in the road together not knowing what words to say, not knowing quite how to dispel the poignancy of parting. Then we went our separate ways, we three from the University over the hill to Changchih where Secretary Wang would arrange transportation for us back to the new campus in distant Shihchiachuang; the district cadres back to the village where they still had final reports to write before they could move on to other jobs in Lucheng County.

In the days that followed, Ch'i Yun, Hsieh Hung, and I had ample time to think and talk about the extraordinary experience we had been through, for we walked or rode mule carts all the way to our new home in the plains, a journey that took eight days. On the way we discussed the land reform movement with Secretary Wang in Changchih and again with Secretary Lai Jo-yu, leader of all work in 500 "basic villages." His headquarters were at Yehtao, the black pepper center of North China and the revolutionary administrative center of the Taihang Subregion.

What concerned us most at the time was the "poor-peasant line" and the fact that the whole movement had temporarily gone so far astray. Secretary Lai, after making a concise analysis of the wrong line, tried to put our experience in proper perspective by looking at the sweep of the movement as a whole. "Such mistakes," he said, "must be seen for what they are, ripples on the surface of the broad Yellow River. The most important thing is that feudalism has been thoroughly uprooted throughout the whole of the Taihang."

We felt that Secretary Lai was right. Feudalism had indeed been uprooted, and nothing could ever be the same again in Southeast Shansi. Not only had the land system of imperial times at last been completely done away with, but the political and cultural superstructure, and beyond that the very consciousness of men, had also been remade. Of the fall of 1948, one could hardly write as I had written of 1947, that the process begun by the expropriations of the Settling Accounts Movement might be reversed, that the gains inspired by the May 4th Directive might be lost. The democratic reforms, the consolidation of the Party, and the establishment of new organs of political power now guaranteed the new equalitarian base of rural society and set the stage for a great advance.

In Long Bow, it is true, we left behind a few loose ends. Police Captain Wen-te was still attending the school for unreformed cadres in Changchih; his wife, Hsien-e, was still waiting to hear the outcome of her appeal for a divorce; what punishment Yu-lai would receive had not yet been decided upon by the Village People's Congress; Little Ch'uer's assailants had not been apprehended; and the land certificates which would legalize the distribution of the land had not yet been handed out. But, with the basic questions such as land ownership and political power settled, the people of the village were fully capable of tying up any loose ends.

Problems which had deeply agitated the community in March stirred barely a ripple in August. Whether Yu-lai received punishment or not no longer seemed important once the people ceased to fear him. Who bound and gagged Little Ch'uer and dragged him to the brink of the well did not matter very much either, once it became clear that the power of the landlords had truly been uprooted. No matter how vicious such an act might have been, it could no longer be interpreted as a harbinger of burgeoning counter-revolution but only as an isolated instance, a rearguard retaliation. As such it was not significant.

Such was the measure of the transformation which had occurred.

Could it then be said that all the basic problems facing Long Bow's people had been solved? Far from it. Successful completion of the land reform marked but one step in the 10,000-li "long march" which the Chinese people had embarked upon when they dumped the opium into Canton Harbor in 1840.

Land reform only removed the feudal barriers to production. The latent productive forces still had to be mobilized, a great new rural market established, and a prosperous new China built up step by step.

Land reform, by creating basic equality among rural producers, only presented the producers with a choice of roads: private enterprise on the land leading to capitalism, or collective enterprise on the land leading to socialism. The choice between them still had to be made, and there was as yet no unanimity on the question. Only the most advanced among the peasants had even considered it.

Land reform had broken the patriarchal rigidity of the family by granting property rights to women. With property of their own they were able to struggle effectively for equal rights. But there was still a great gap between the potential and the actual degree of equality which women enjoyed.

One had only to think of such problems as illiteracy, the almost complete absence of medical care, and the primitive methods of cultivation still in use, to realize what a long road lay ahead for the village and its people before they could claim full citizenship in the twentieth century.

If one considered the development of democracy in the village, it was clear that here too much remained to be done. Through Party consolidation and the establishment of a popularly elected Congress, serious tendencies toward commandism, hedonism, and personal privilege had been checked. The vast majority of the people had found a voice and a vote. Political life would never be the same again. But could it therefore be said that the problems of village administration had been solved for all time? Certainly not. New temptations, new abuses, new oppressions were bound to arise. Methods of popular supervision over cadres had to be constantly improved. To get rid of the narrow selfishness of the past and create the open-minded dedicated men and women of the future could not but entail a long struggle.

In learning to use self-and-mutual criticism, the people had arrived at a new stage in the conduct of the struggle. The days of coercion and beatings, of cops and jails as everyday sanctions of law and order were gone forever. But in mastering this new method the people still had a long way to go. The quality of objectivity necessary could only be the end product of a persistent, long-term effort.

But if one step and one step only had been taken toward a truly revolutionized society, still, because this was the first it was perhaps the hardest step of all; and the fact that the people had taken it seemed, in retrospect, nothing short of a miracle.

It was not hard to recall how the countryside had looked to me when I first entered the Liberated Area in the middle of the rainy season one year before—soggy land, bursting crops, adobe villages under their canopies of trees, women spinning in the dooryards, and the naked children splashing in the muddy ditches that served as roads. The isolation, the primitiveness, the timelessness of the scene was what had struck me then. It seemed as if peasant life had never changed, was not changing, and could never change.

Nor was it hard to recall the days of frustration that we had lived through between the two county conferences, when all the organizing and mobilizing effort of the work team, the village Communists, and the village activists seemed to lead nowhere, when the momentum which the people had themselves imparted to the Revolution seemed to stall in a contradictory mass of petty self-interest. At that time one could not help but wonder what the future held in store—if, after all, the creation of a new life was not something beyond the power of these earthbound people.

Yet now, a scant 12 months after crossing the line and only two months after attending the second County Conference, I could not doubt the outcome. I had a notebook full of concrete evidence of change. My head was swimming with facts and figures, words and faces, stories and incidents, all of which added up to a basic trans-formation of Long Bow's rural society. How had it all come about?

Certainly not by any miracle, but only by hard work, by the conscious effort of scores of people who took the situation as it was and, with the human material at hand, struggled to remold themselves and their environment. Multiply this by tens, thousands, hundreds of thousands as layer after layer of people in one area after another became active, and the full extent and depth of the revolutionary storm sweeping China became clear.

But the participation of millions could not by itself explain success. After all, there had been earlier rebellions, other massive efforts to abolish the gentry base of rural life in China and free the nation from foreign oppression. All of them had failed. What made the difference this time?

Ch'i Yun and Hsieh Hung argued convincingly that given the situation as it existed—given a people ready to do battle against progressive impoverishment, corrupt and incompetent rulers, and foreign conquest—it was the "proletarian leadership" provided by the Communist Party that made victory possible. Leaving to future study the prickly question of whether the leadership provided by the Communists was "proletarian" or not, it was obvious to me then that without it the Chinese people might well have struggled in vain. The military potential, the productive capacity, and the political genius of the peasants had to be cultivated, mobilized, and organized, not simply "liberated." Experience in Long Bow had certainly demonstrated this. Without the Communist Party the poor peasants could easily have carried the Revolution so far to the Left as to convert it into its opposite, a restoration from the Right. Without the Communist Party the poor peasants might well have divided everything right down to the last bowls and chopsticks on the farmsteads and the last gears and shafts in the factories and in so doing would have destroyed the only productive base on which they had to build. Without the Communist Party the poor peasants might well have driven all their more prosperous allies into the arms of their enemies and rejected, perhaps even destroyed, the most militant, the most devoted, and the most able leaders they had produced. Such mistakes could only have broken the peasant population into factions based on kinship, religious affiliation, personal influence, and gang loyalty, and could only have led to never-ending feuds between these factions. In the end, the peasants could well have gone down to defeat betrayed by a vision of justice and a program of action that was impossible of fulfilment in an economy of scarcity. The vision: absolute equality; the program: extreme levelling; the result: complete restoration of gentry rule.

What the Communist Party brought to the countryside in opposition to these trends was a concept of justice linked to the possible, a justice that unfolded in different ways at different levels of social development, each level establishing its own distinctive norms of right and wrong. For the Communists, history unfolded as a process, as the resolution of a series of contradictions. To leap from one end of the series to the other, even to by-pass a given stage, was impossible. One had to accept the process and advance step by step, stage by stage through degrees of limited equality based on degrees of scarcity and abundance toward an absolute equality that could only be based on absolute abundance.

All the turmoil in the countryside over the right road to *fanshen* ultimately resolved itself into a contest between these two opposing points of view, the one static, the other dynamic. The first was a form of idealism, a demand for abstract justice in an unchanging world. The second was a form of historical materialism, a demand for justice based on the concrete conditions of human life, a justice which changed as conditions changed. The first was mechanical, focusing on the division of existing wealth and existing means of production. The second was dialectical, focusing on the release of old productive forces and on the creation of entirely new forces in the future. The first considered the demand for equality to be right in itself; the second considered that demand to be right in one context, wrong and harmful in another.

At Yehtao, as we talked late into the night with Subregional Party Secretary, Comrade Lai, he pointed out to us an important difference between these two points of view. Equalitarianism, he said, was revolutionary when applied against the power and the property of the landlords and rich peasants, but it became reactionary as soon as it was applied against the middle peasants. "Many peasants do not understand about this turning point, and so they make mistakes.

Whenever the peasants are mobilized for struggle, they push toward extreme equalitarianism, and the cadres are carried along with them. It is just for this reason that the peasants need proletarian leadership."

Obviously one aspect of "proletarian leadership" was an ability to define and anticipate turning points. The Chinese Communist Party, through a grasp of history as process, through diligent study of all pertinent social phenomena, through never-ending analysis and review of all actions undertaken, had developed this to a remarkable degree. It was therefore able to prepare its adherents in advance for major shifts in the spiral of events or to adjust policies quickly whenever events outran foresight.

But this ability possessed by the Communists was not enough in itself to enable them to lead the peasants to victory in the Revolution. Leadership also involves method and in China method was crucially important. Those dedicated revolutionaries who in 1927 went out into the universe of peasant life were not holders of state power as their Russian counterparts had earlier been, but hunted men with a price on their heads. They went into the countryside without authority, without arms, without money, without goods of any kind. They brought with them only the clothes on their backs, ideas for mass action, and the nucleus of an organization capable of overcoming the major weaknesses generic to peasant revolts. Only if the peasants trusted them, made these ideas their own, and gave unconditional support to the new organization could the long-drawn-out process of changing the face of China ever gather momentum.

Under these circumstances, the example which the Communists set in their everyday lives was as decisive as the words which they spoke or the plans which they suggested. In the last analysis, it was the superior moral character exhibited by the revolutionaries, their integrity, their dedication, their willingness to suffer, their honesty in facing mistakes, their acceptance of criticism, and their capacity for self-criticism that moved the peasants. It was because the Communists set public interests ahead of private interests, long-range interests ahead of short-range interests, and the general good ahead of any partial good, and did so in their own personal lives, that the peasants were willing to follow them.

Patience was also vitally important. The capacity of the Communists to postpone advanced types of action, to educate and persuade until the people themselves were ready and willing to move, spelled the difference between victory and defeat, between the helpless isolation of a small group of radicals and an irrepressible mass movement. The Chinese Communists knew well that their countrymen, and particularly the peasants, could not be told where to go. They could not be driven or dragged into any course of action. They had to see their own self-interest and become aware through their own experience of the many dimensions of their predicament and of the viability of any given plan. Then and only then would they consciously and willingly put it into practice. Then and only then would it have any chance of success.

"With us," Liu Shao-ch'i wrote, "everything is dependent on and determined by the people's consciousness and voluntary action, without which we can accomplish nothing and all our efforts will be in vain. But as long as we rely upon the consciousness and voluntary action of the masses and as long as such consciousness and voluntary action are genuine, then, with the addition of the Party's correct leadership, every aspect of the great cause of the Party will triumph. Therefore, when the masses are not fully conscious, the duty of the Communists—the vanguard of the masses—in carrying out any kind of work is to develop their consciousness by every effective and suitable means. This is the first step in our work, and it must be done well no matter how difficult it is or how much time it may take."*

This all-important development of consciousness could only begin with the state of mind and the level of understanding that already existed. That was why Mao always stressed, "from the masses, to the masses," a two-way process which he described as "summing up (i.e., coordinating and systematizing after careful study) the views of the masses (i.e., views scattered and unsystematic), then taking the resulting ideas back to the masses, explaining and popularizing them until the masses embrace them as their own, stand up for them, and translate them into action by way of testing their correctness. Then it is necessary once more to sum up the views of the masses and once again take the resulting ideas back to the masses so that the masses give them their wholehearted support . . . and so on, over and over again, so that each time these ideas emerge with greater correctness and become more vital and meaningful."**

Was this not a summary of what had happened in the land reform movement between 1945 and 1948? The popular demand for equalization of land ownership that resulted in an explosion against the gentry as soon as the Japanese Army surrendered in 1945 had been studied, formulated as a policy, applied, corrected, reformulated, and applied again until it emerged as something extremely clear, sophisti-

---

* Liu Shao-ch'i, *On the Party,* Peking: Foreign Languages Press, 1954, p. 58.
** Mao Tse-tung, *Selected Works,* New York: International Publishers, 1954, Vol. IV, p. 113.

cated, refined, and effective. The several successive stages of the classification standards accurately reflected this distillation process. We had seen the standards evolve from rough guides to action into extremely precise, many-sided analyses of the true complexity of rural life. In the end, they armed the people with enough knowledge to separate with precision that which was feudal and reactionary from that which was democratic and progressive.

Thus the peasants, under the guidance of the Communist Party, had moved step by step from partial knowledge to general knowledge, from spontaneous action to directed action, from limited success to over-all success. And through this process they had transformed themselves from passive victims of natural and social forces into active builders of a new world.

This, as I understood it, was the essence of *fanshen*.

The more I examined the process of the development of consciousness the more complex it appeared. It worked its leaven on many levels at once—on the individual, on the community, and on the nation—and at each level the process followed its own peculiar patterns.

When one broke *fanshen* down to the microcosm, to what happened inside any given individual, it was obvious that no person could break free of the past all at once. The spectrum of a man's consciousness could not be refocused in one night no matter how earnestly he might desire such a shift. Change had to come first in one area, then spread to others. It had to dissolve old contradictions only to set up new ones. It had to expand the struggle between the new and the old until the entire personality became involved in painful conflict. No one going through such inner strife exhibited a character that was all of one piece. Habits, superstitions, and prejudices left over from the past marred and undermined efforts to act on the enlightened motives of the present. Thus it was not strange to find men who had erased most traces of self-interest from their public lives, but who still treated their wives as chattels in the home, or women who stood together in their battle for equal rights, yet fell to quarrelling over the distribution of relief cotton. People placed their feet on the road to *fanshen* as soon as they began to have faith in others. As they marched along it they gradually learned the central lesson of our times, that only through participation in common struggle can any individual achieve personal emancipation, that the road to *fanshen* for one lies through the *fanshen* of all.

When one examined the process of *fanshen* on a somewhat larger canvas, in terms of the whole community, it became clear that, on this level also, change never occurred across the board at the same rate. No social aggregation could advance as a block. Its individual members possessed varying degrees of awareness and varying capacities for learning and growth. In real life one had to depend on the more advanced to lead the less advanced and on the less advanced to lead the backward. When this was done, each successive mobilization had the power to advance the understanding of all. The backward soon reached the level of their teachers, and so understanding spiralled until the whole concept of what was advanced and what was backward had to be revised. When such a process was consciously and systematically unfolded year after year, decade after decade, in a countryside containing millions of people, the total effect was astonishing. The whole people became politicized, became conscious, became active, and finally did indeed become capable of transforming their world, and, in that process, of still further transforming themselves.

When one applied the concept of *fanshen* to a still wider canvas, it seemed evident that the word could be used to describe the rebirth of a whole country. Just as one could speak of the *fanshen* of the individual and the *fanshen* of the community, one could also speak of the *fanshen* of the nation, that process by which a whole people "turned over," that process by which a whole continent stood up.

Clearly such a process could not develop uniformly over so vast a country as China. It had begun some 20 years earlier at certain key spots where, because of splits and quarrels, past revolutionary uprisings, or foreign intervention, the power of China's traditional rulers had temporarily been weakened. Once the Revolution took root on Chingkang Mountain, around Juichin in Kiangsi, and in the badlands of the Yellow River bend, it reached out to influence other places until whole areas were converted into bases. Destroyed in the main in 1934, these bases sprang up stronger than ever after 1937 when the Japanese invaded China, and spread in the wake of foreign conquest to vast areas of countryside in North, Central, and South China.

The significance of the Taihang Mountain region, which included Long Bow and thousands of similiar villages, lay precisely in this, that it was one of those slowly expanding revolutionary bases from which, in the course of time, the Chinese people would be able to challenge and finally overthrow not only the powerful forces of China's native gentry, but also the network of compradore capital built up in China by the Western powers and the military might which they threw into battle to preserve this network.

"Great military, political, economic, and cultural revolutionary bastions"—this was what Mao Tse-tung had called these bases. Was this not exactly what thoroughgoing *fanshen* had built in Long Bow, in Lucheng County, and in the Taihang Mountains? And now because the Communist Party had built so well, over-all victory for the Revolution was in sight.

****

As Ch'i Yun, Hsieh Hung, and I travelled the tortuous road from Lucheng over the mountains to Licheng, Szuhsien, Wuan, and Hsingt'ai, peasant armies were already gathering on the borders of every revolutionary bastion in the North. They were moving into position for the great autumn offensive of 1948. Across the vast *wei ch'i* board of China the lines were filling up. After 20 years of encirclement and counter-encirclement, the contest between the white chips and the red chips was surging toward final decision.

The People's Liberation Army struck first at Tsinan, Shantung. There, in eight days and nights of fierce September combat, Ch'en Yi's peasant volunteers overpowered 100,000 Kuomintang conscripts and captured the once bold "Tiger of Shantung," Wang Yao-wu.

The contest then shifted temporarily to the Northeast. In quick succession Chinchou, the gateway to the region, Changchun, the administrative capital, and Shenyang, the industrial capital, went down. Chiang Kai-shek personally took charge of the battle but nevertheless lost 400,000 of his best troops in three weeks.

No sooner had the dust settled north of the Great Wall than the battle for the Central Plains began. This battle, known as the Huai-hai campaign because it was fought between the Huai River and the sea (hai), developed into one of the largest conflicts in the history of warfare. More than half a million men took part on each side, and the fighting, which lasted for 65 days, resulted in the complete annihilation of the Kuomintang armies between the Yellow and the Yangtze Rivers.

But even this great victory did not exhaust the energy of the revolutionary forces that winter. While the Huai-hai campaign churned toward its culmination, the People's Army of Northeast China joined the People's Army of North China to take Tientsin, surround Peking, and force the surrender of still a third half-million men—the armies under General Fu T'so-yi that represented the last major hope of the collapsing counter-revolution. For the Nationalists, Fu's surrender meant the loss of everything north of the Yangtze River, at a time when the South had been all but drained of combat-ready troops.

The Armageddon of Chinese feudalism thus reached its climax and its denouement all in the space of a few short months. Between one

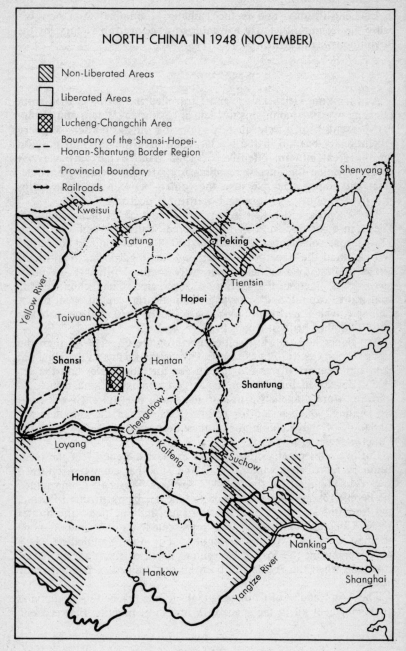

NORTH CHINA IN 1948 (NOVEMBER)

Non-Liberated Areas

Liberated Areas

Lucheng-Changchih Area

— — Boundary of the Shansi-Hopei-Honan-Shantung Border Region

—·— Provincial Boundary

Railroads

monsoon and the next, the main forces of the landlords and the compradores built up over many decades, supplied, trained, and advised in the field by United States officers, were crushed one after the other by the peasant battalions of the Chinese Communist Party.

This triple blow brought about one of those great qualitative transformations that have periodically shaken history and changed the course of world events.

The victories put land reform on the program of a continent, on the agenda of hundreds of millions. It was only a matter of time before the scattered remnants of Chiang's beaten legions were completely wiped out or driven from the mainland. Then, in tens of thousands of villages from the Po-hai Gulf to Hainan Island, peasants who owned nothing but the rags on their backs began to form Poor Peasants' Leagues, to classify the classes, to settle accounts with their landlords, and to march step by step down the road pioneered by their brothers in such obscure northern hamlets as Long Bow—the great road to *fanshen*.

Appendix A

Basic Program on Chinese Agrarian Law Promulgated by the Central Committee of the Chinese Communist Party, 1947.

North Shansi, October 10: The following is the full text of the basic program on Chinese Agrarian Law promulgated on October 10th by the publication of the program.

Resolution:
China's agrarian system is unjust in the extreme. Speaking of general conditions, landlords and rich peasants who make up less than ten percent of the rural population hold approximately 70 to 80 percent of the land, cruelly exploiting the peasantry. Farm laborers, poor peasants, middle peasants, and other people, however, who make up over 90 percent of the rural population hold a total of approximately only 20 to 30 percent of the land, toiling throughout the whole year, knowing neither warmth nor full stomach. These grave conditions are the root of our country's being the victim of aggression, oppression, poverty, backwardness, and the basic obstacles to our country's democratization, industrialization, independence, unity, strength and prosperity.

In order to change these conditions, it is necessary, on the basis of the demands of the peasantry, to wipe out the agrarian system of feudal and semi-feudal exploitation, and realize the system of "land to the tillers." For 20 years, and especially in the last two years, under the leadership of the Chinese Communist Party, Chinese peasants have obtained enormous achievements and rich experiences in carrying out land reform. In September of this year, the Chinese Communist Party convened a nationwide agrarian conference, and at the conference did detailed research into conditions of the Chinese agrarian system and experience of the land reform, and enacted the basic program on Chinese agrarian law to serve as a proposal to the democratic governments of all areas, peasants' meetings, peasants' congresses and their committees. The Central Committee of the Chinese Communist Party is in complete accord with the basic program on agrarian law, and is furthermore publishing it. It is hoped that the democratic governments of all areas, peasants' meetings, peasants' congresses, and their committees will discuss and adopt this proposal, and futhermore will work out concrete methods appropriate to local conditions, to unfold and thoroughly carry through a nationwide land reform movement, completing the basic task of the Chinese revolution.

Central Committee Chinese Communist Party
October 10, 1947

Basic Program:

Article 1: The agrarian system of feudal and semi-feudal exploitation is abolished. The agrarian system of "land to the tillers" is to be realized.

Article 2: Landownership rights of all landlords are abolished.

Article 3: Landownership rights of all ancestral shrines, temples, monasteries, schools, institutions and organizations are abolished.

Article 4: All debts incurred in the countryside prior to the reform of the agrarian system are cancelled.

Article 5: The legal executive organs for the reform of the agrarian system shall be the village peasants' meetings, and the committees elected by them; the assemblies of the Poor Peasants' League and organized and landless and land-poor peasants of villages, and the committees elected by it; *ch'u, hsien,* provincial and other levels of peasants' congresses, and committees elected by them.

Article 6: Except as provided in Article 9 Section B, all land of landlords in the villages, and all public land, shall be taken over by the village peasants' associations, and together with all other village land, in accordance with the total population of the village, irrespective of male or female, young or old, shall be unifiedly and equally distributed; with regard to the quantity of land, surplus shall be taken to relieve dearth, and with regard to the quality of land, fertile land shall be taken to supplement infertile, so that all the village people shall obtain land equally; and it shall be the individual property of each person.

Article 7: The unit for the distribution of the land shall be the *hsiang* or administrative village equivalent to *hsiang.* But *ch'u* or *hsien* peasants' associations may make certain necessary adjustments between various *hsiangs,* or equivalent administrative villages. In areas where the district is extensive and the population sparse, and for the purpose of convenient cultivation, compartivly small units below the level of the *hsiang* may be taken as units for the distribution of the land.

Article 8: Village peasants' associations shall take over the landlords' animals, agricultural implements, houses, grain and other properties, shall further expropriate the surplus animals, agricultural implements, houses, grain and other properties of rich peasants; and these shall be distributed to peasants lacking in these properties, and to other poor people, and furthermore an equal portion shall be distributed to the landlords. The property distributed to each person shall be his personal property, thus enabling all the village people to obtain proper materials for production and for life.

Article 9: Methods for dealing with certain special lands and properties, provided as follows:

Section A: Woods and hills, irrigation and waterworks, land in reeds, orchards, pools, waste land and other distributable land shall be divided in accordance with the ordinary standards for land.

Section B: Great forests, great hydraulic engineering works, large mines, large pasture land, large waste lands and lakes shall be administered by the government.

Section C: Famous sites and historic spots shall be securely protected. Special libraries, antiques, works of art, and so forth, which are of historic or academic value, and which have been taken over shall be inventoried and turned over to the high government of the area.

Section D: Ammunition, arms, and those large quantities of money, valuables, and grain left over after satisfying the needs of the peasants shall be inventoried and turned over to the high government of the area for settlement.

Article 10: Methods for dealing with certain special questions in the distribution of the land, provided as follows:

Section A: Poor peasants with only one or two persons in the family may be given land equivalent to that of two or three people by the village peasants' meetings, in consideration of prevailing conditions.

Section B: Rural laborers, individual professionals, and their families, in general, shall be given land equivalent to that of peasants; but if their profession is sufficient for constant maintenance of all or most of their living expenses, they shall not be given land, or shall be given a partial portion of land, as determined by the village peasants' meetings and their committees in consideration of prevailing conditions.

Section C: For all personnel of the People's Liberation Army, democratic governments, all people's organizations, whose home is in the countryside, they and their families shall be given land and properties equivalent to that of peasants.

Section D: Landlords and their families shall be given land and properties equivalent to that of peasants.

Section E: For KMT army officers and soldiers, KMT government officials and personnel, KMT party members and other enemy personnel, whose homes are in rural areas, their families shall be given land and properties equivalent to that of the peasants.

Section F: For all national traitors, collaborators, and civil war criminals, they themselves shall not be given land or properties. If their families live in the countryside, have not taken part in criminal activities, and are willing to cultivate the land themselves, they shall be given land and properties equivalent to that of the peasants.

Article 11: The government shall issue deeds to the ownership of the land given to the people, and moreover recognize their right to free management, buying and selling, and under specially determined conditions to rent out the land. All land deeds and all notes on debts from prior to the reform of the agrarian system shall be turned in and shall be null and void.

Article 12: The property and legal operations of industrial and commercial elements shall be protected from encroachment.

Article 13: For the sake of making the land reform thorough and complete, people's courts shall be established to try and punish those who resist or violate the provisions of this law. The people's courts shall be organized from personnel elected by peasants' meetings or peasants' congresses and from personnel appointed by the government.

Article 14: During the period of the reform of the agrarian system, for the sake of maintaining the order of the agrarian reform and protecting the wealth of the people, the village peasants' meetings or their committees shall appoint personnel, by definite procedure to take necessary steps for carrying out the responsibilities of taking over, recording, liquidating and holding all transferred lands and properties, to guard against damage, waste, corruption and destruction. The peasants' associations shall forbid anyone from, for the sake of interrupting equitable distribution, deliberately butchering animals, felling trees, destroying agricultural implements, irrigation and waterworks, buildings and construction works, or crops or other materials; and the act of thieving, seizing, secretly giving away to others, concealing, burying, dispersing, or selling their goods. Violations shall be tried and punished by the people's courts.

Article 15: For the sake of guaranteeing that all measures of land reform shall be in accord with the will and interests of the overwhelming majority of the people, the government shall take the responsibility for securing earnest democratic rights for the people; securing full rights for the peasants and their representatives at all meetings freely to criticize and impeach all cadres of all kinds and levels; and full rights at all appropriate meetings freely to remove and change and to elect all cadres of the government and peasants' organizations. Anyone who infringes on the above democratic rights and powers of the people shall be punished by the people's courts.

Article 16: In places where the land has already been equally distributed before the promulgation of this law, and provided that the peasants do not demand redistribution, the land need not be redistributed.

Appendix B

Supplementary Measures for Carrying Out the Basic Program on Agrarian Law

Draft Promulgated by Hopei-Honan-Shansi-Shantung Border Region Government on Dec. 28, 1947

1. "Landownership rights of all ancestral shrines, temples, monasteries, schools, institutions and organizations are abolished," as provided in Article 3. This includes land ownership of churches.

2. "To cancel all debts incurred in the countryside prior to the reform of the agrarian system," as provided in Article 4, does not include debt relations contracted in commercial buying and selling.

3. "In accordance with the total population of the village," as is said in Article 6, denotes the present population at the time of even distribution of land. All even distribution should be made according to the present population with the only exception as provided in Section A of Article 10, i.e., "Poor peasants with only one or two persons in the family may be given land equivalent to that of two or three people by the village peasants' meetings, in consideration of the prevailing conditions."

4. *Supplements to Article 6:*
   (a) All the newly reclaimed land since the 34th year of the Chinese Republic should be owned by the reclaimer, and exempted from even distribution.
   (b) Land of the rich middle peasants may be taken, in consideration of the prevailing conditions, according to the principle of taking surplus to relieve dearth and fertile to supplement infertile; but their houses and properties should not be touched.
   (c) Refugees and migratory persons should settle in one place and receive a share there. No duplicate shares should be extended to them in two places.
   (d) Refugees not at home and no longer heard of should be given land according to law, and not properties. Such shares of land should be put under the charge of the peasants' associations and be tilled for the time being by the poor and hired peasants or other poor people; no rent should be paid but only taxes. But the period for keeping such shares of land is limited to three years (beginning from the date when land is distributed). If they don't come back before the time limit, such shares should be reallocated. If they come back to receive the shares within the

619

time limit they must produce credentials of the peasants' assembly of the village where they come from, if it is in the Liberated Areas.

(e) Land of the mosques should be dealt with by the Moslems themselves according to the principle of even distribution of all land in the respective villages.

5. *Supplement to Article 7:*

In areas where the population is dense and the land is scarce and where the poor and hired peasants cannot have enough means to live on after the distribution, migration may be encouraged on the principle of voluntariness.

6. *Supplements to Article 8:*

(a) In case the landlords also rent out houses in town or townlet, such houses should be confiscated and distributed as well. In general the principle should be to distribute them to the poor people in the said town or townlet. Method of distribution should be decided by the people's assembly (or its committee) of the said town or townlet. In case of some dispute arising with the village, solution may be made in co-ordination with the county peasants' congress (or its committee). If the tenant of such houses is carrying on industrial or merchant business by means of them, the relationship with him should be dealt with in accordance with the accustomed measures on renting houses; the principle is not to influence the carrying on of industry and commerce.

(b) Extra fruits seized by cadres since the Anti-Traitor and Settling Accounts Movement should be recalled.

7. *Supplement to Section A of Article 9:*

Forests, mulberry patches, bamboo patches, irrigation and waterworks, land in reeds, orchards, pools, swamps, and lotus pools should be dealt with through the public discussion of the peasants in the respective places. Those which may be evenly distributed should be so; in case that even distribution is not advantageous for managerial purposes, joint-stock management may be adopted.

8. *Supplements to Section B of Article 9:*

(a) Mines which are being exploited by the government or are going to be exploited should not be distributed; the already discovered mines which government does not work for the time being may be distributed to peasants for management, and should be recalled when it is necessary to work the mine; when recalled, the local government should make adjustment with the land for the peasants by some other means and make proper redemption for the losses in production.

(b) Public land attached to the tracks along the original railroad line, land ready to be used for the railroad which is going to be built, and land belonging to the present agricultural stations, public buildings, parks, mausoleums, and appointed highways and waterways should not be distributed. The usage of such lands should be decided by people's assemblies on different levels together with the governments. Nobody is permitted to retain land at his own will on any pretext whatever.

(c) Land on river banks, sand land, and land for public cemeteries should be dealt with by the peasant assembly (or its committee) of the county or *ch'u* (sub-county).

9. *Supplement to Section B of Article 10:*
Any unemployed worker whose home is in the countryside but who finds no means to make a living may go back to his native place to divide land with proofs given by the government of locality where he now lives

10. "The People's Liberation Army" as mentioned in Section C of Article 10 includes liberated soldiers (defectors from Chiang's forces).

11. *Supplements to Section C of Article 10:*
(a) All martyrs who gave their lives on the battlefront since the beginning of the Anti-Japanese War (including soldiers of the People's Liberation Army, militiamen, civilian cadres, and other personnel) should get a share of land and property equal to that of a peasant for themselves.

(b) Land for placement of honorable soldiers and veterans should be preserved by the Director's Administrative Bureau on a unified plan, and should not be distributed; but the amount of such land should not surpass one thousandth of the total quantity of land in the Director's Administrative Bureau area. Such reserved land should for the time being be handed over to the poor and bitter peasants and other poor people to cultivate through the county peasant assemblies (or their committees) in the counties under the administration of the Director's Bureau. No rent should be paid but only the burden to the government.

12. *Supplement to Article 11:*
The form of title deeds (literally land ownership certificates) should be designed by the Hopei-Honan-Shansi-Shantung Border Region Government in a unified way, should be printed by the Director's Administrative Bureau according to the form, then given to the respective county governments which should be held responsible for the filling out and issuance of the title deeds.

13. *Supplement to Article 13:*
Regulations for the Organization of the People's Court on different levels should be made by the people's assembly of Hopei-Honan-Shansi-Shantung Border Region.

14. *Supplements to Article 16:*
(a) "Areas where land has already been evenly distributed" as mentioned in this article denotes areas where the land distribution has been done in accord with the principle and spirit of the Basic Program

on Chinese Agrarian Law. If illegal holding of extra portions or inequality in fertileness and infertileness still exists, so that the poor peasants have not enough means to make a living, redistribution according to petitions of adjustment should be made.

(b) If, in areas where land has already been evenly distributed before the promulgation of the Basic Program on the Chinese Agrarian Law, the landlords and rich farmers cannot make a living though they have labor power, land may be given to them, in the way of making up, according to law.

15. These measures may be revised at any time when necessary.

16. These measures begin to take effect on the date when they are promulgated.

Appendix C

How to Analyze Class Status in the Countryside
From: The Agrarian Reform Law
of the People's Republic of China

1. Landlord
A person shall be classified as a landlord who owns land, but does not engage in labor or only engages in supplementary labor, and who depends on exploitation for his means of livelihood. Exploitation by the landlords is chiefly in the form of land rent, plus money-lending, hiring of labor, or the simultaneous carrying on of industrial or commercial enterprises. But the major form of exploitation of the peasants by the landlords is the exacting of land rent from the peasants. The management of landholdings owned by public bodies and the collection of rent from school land also belong to the category of exploitation in the form of land rent.

Some bankrupt landlords who, despite their bankruptcy and their ability to work, do not engage in labor, and whose living conditions are better than those of an ordinary middle peasant, shall continue to be classified as landlords.

Warlords, bureaucrats, local despots and villainous gentry are the political representatives of the landlord class, and are exceptionally cruel and wicked elements among the landlords. (Among the rich peasants there are also small local despots and villainous gentry.)

Any person, who collects rent and manages the landed property for landlords and depends on the exploitation of peasants by the landlords as his main means of livelihood, and whose living conditions are better than those of an ordinary middle peasant, shall be treated in the same manner as a landlord.

Supplementary Decisions Adopted by the Government Administration Council

(A) Any person who rents large areas of land from landlords, who does not himself engage in labor, but sub-lets the land to others for rent, and whose living conditions are better than those of an ordinary middle peasant, shall be classified as a sub-landlord. Sub-landlords shall be treated in the same manner as landlords. A sub-landlord who cultivates part of his land should be treated in the same manner as a rich peasant.

(B) Revolutionary army men, dependents of martyrs, workers, staff members, professional workers, peddlers and others who rent out small portions of land because they are engaged in other occupations or because they are unable to work, shall not be classified as landlords. Their class status shall be determined according to their occupations or they shall be referred to as small land lessors, whose landholdings shall be dealt with in accordance with Article 5 of the Agrarian Reform Law.

(C) The class status of any person who receives income from some other occupation and who at the same time owns and rents out a large area of agricultural land the size of which exceeds the average landholdings of each landlord family in the locality, shall be determined according to the major source of his income. He may be referred to either as a person of other class status and concurrently as a landlord, or as a landlord having other class status. The land and property used directly for his other occupations shall not be confiscated.

(D) The average landholding of a landlord family in the various localities shall be computed by taking one or several counties as a unit, and shall be determined only after the people's government of a special administrative district* or of a county has submitted it to a provincial people's government and obtained the latter's approval.

2. Rich Peasant

A rich peasant generally owns land. But there are also rich peasants who own only part of the land they cultivate and rent the rest from others. There are others who own no land but rent all their land from others. Generally speaking, they own better means of production and some floating capital and take part in labor themselves, but are as a rule dependent on exploitation for a part or the major part of their means of livelihood. Exploitation by rich peasants is chiefly in the form of exploiting the wage labor (hiring long-term laborers). In addition, they may also let out part of their land for rent, or lend out money, or carry on industrial or commercial enterprises. Most of the rich peasants also manage the landholdings owned by public bodies. Some own a considerable amount of fertile land, engage in labor themselves and do not hire any laborers. But they exploit the peasants in the form of land rent and loan interest. In such cases, they should be treated in the same manner as rich peasants. Exploitation by the rich peasants is of a constant character, and in many cases the income from such exploitation constitutes their main means of livelihood.

Supplementary Decisions Adopted by the Government Administration Council

(A) If the area of land rented out by a rich peasant exceeds in size the land cultivated jointly by himself and by hired laborers, he shall be referred to as a rich peasant of a semi-landlord type. The land and other properties of rich peasants, or of rich peasants of a semi-landlord type

* A special administrative district is an administrative unit below the provincial level, consisting of a number of counties.

shall be dealt with in accordance with Article 6 of the Agrarian Reform Law.

(B) Where a landlord family has some members who are engaged in major agricultural labor all the year round, or at the same time hires laborers to cultivate part of its land, the said family shall be classified as a landlord family and not as a rich peasant family if the major part of its land is rented out and the rented-out land is three times or more the size of the land cultivated jointly by the family and by hired laborers (for instance, 150 *mou* of land rented out and less than 50 *mou* cultivated by the family and by hired laborers); or in a case where the family possesses large landholdings and the rented-out land is twice or more the size of the land cultivated jointly by the family and hired laborers. (For instance, 200 *mou* rented out and less than 100 *mou* cultivated by the family or hired laborers.)

The land and other properties of such a family shall be dealt with in accordance with Article 2 of the Agrarian Reform Law. However, the part of the land cultivated by the family's own labor shall, after appropriate readjustment, be mainly retained by the family. The status of those members who take part in labor, if their position in the family is not a dominant, but a subordinate one, should be appropriately determined as laboring people in order to distinguish them in status from other family members who do not participate in labor.

3. Middle Peasant

Many middle peasants own land. Some possess only a portion of the land which they cultivate while the remainder is rented. Some of them are landless, and rent all their land from others. The middle peasants own a certain number of farm implements. The middle peasants depend wholly or mainly upon their own labor for their living. In general they do not exploit others. Many of them are themselves exploited on a small scale by others in the form of land rent and loan interest. But generally they do not sell their labor power. Some of the middle peasants (the well-to-do middle peasants) practice a small degree of exploitation, but such exploitation is not of a constant character and the main income therefrom does not constitute their main means of livelihood. These people shall be classified as middle peasants.

4. Poor Peasant

Some poor peasants own inadequate farm implements and a part of the land they cultivate. Some have no land at all and own only some inadequate farm implements. In general they have to rent land for cultivation, and are exploited by others in the form of land rent, loan interest, or hired labor in a limited degree. These people shall be classified as poor peasants.

In general, the middle peasants need not sell their labor power, but the poor peasants have to sell their labor power for limited periods. This is the basic criterion for differentiating middle peasants from poor peasants.

5. Worker

Workers (including farm laborers) generally have neither land nor farm implements. Some of them have a very small amount of land and very few implements. They depend wholly or mainly upon the sale of their labor power for their living. These people shall be classified as workers.

Index

A major function of this index is to help the reader keep track of the multitude of names mentioned in this book. However, no attempt has been made to index the names of all the Long Bow villagers or other local personnel mentioned only incidentally. Also, no attempt has been made to make an exhaustive index of all those names which do appear. The page listings for villagers, work team members, local officials, etc., refer only to certain events or discussions in which they played an outstanding role or which are of particular human interest.

WILLIAM HINTON—who now runs a farm in Pennsylvania, where he lives with his wife and three small children—first visited China in 1937. At that time, after working six months as a newspaper reporter in Japan, he traveled across Manchuria on his way home. He saw much more of the country in 1945, when he worked as a propaganda analyst for the United States Office of War Information in several Chinese cities. In 1947 he returned to China as a tractor technician for the United Nations Relief and Rehabilitation Administration. He stayed on then until 1953, teaching courses in English and mechanized agriculture.

After Mr. Hinton had gathered the material for *Fanshen* in Long Bow Village, another story began to unfold. He says: "I carried the notes on my back over much of North China, dove with them into slit trenches to escape bombing, and marched with them at night to avoid encirclement by Fu Tso-yi's cavalry. When I finally brought them home from China [in 1953, when the United States was in the grip of the fever known as McCarthyism] they were confiscated by the U.S. Customs. Three years of legal maneuvering pried them out of Customs only to have them seized—and impounded—by the Eastland [Senate Internal Security] Committee. A lawsuit against Senator Eastland and his colleagues lasted another two years and swallowed up $6,000. It was 1958 before I finally won possession of my notes and was able to begin to write. By that time I had no resources. I borrowed money, worked overtime to save money, took part-time jobs...What all this adds up to is 15 years of struggle to make this story known."

VINTAGE POLITICAL SCIENCE
AND SOCIAL CRITICISM

VINTAGE CRITICISM,
LITERATURE, MUSIC, AND ART

A free catalogue of VINTAGE BOOKS *will be sent at your request. Write to* Vintage Books, 457 Madison Avenue, New York, New York 10022.